ANTISEMITISM AND ITS OPPONENTS IN MODERN POLAND

ANTISEMITISM AND ITS OPPONENTS IN MODERN POLAND

EDITED BY

ROBERT BLOBAUM

CORNELL UNIVERSITY PRESS
ITHACA AND LONDON

First published 2005 by Cornell University Press
First printing, Cornell Paperbacks, 2005

Library of Congress Cataloging-in-Publication Data
Antisemitism and its opponents in modern Poland / edited by Robert Blobaum.
    p. cm.
  Includes bibliographical references and index.
  ISBN 0-8014-4347-4 (cloth : alk. paper)—ISBN 0-8014-8969-5 (pbk. : alk. paper)
    1. Jews—Persecutions—Poland—Congresses.   2. Antisemitism—Poland—History—
Congresses.   3. Poland—History—20th century—Congresses.   4. Poland—History—19th
century—Congresses.   5. Poland—Politics and government—Congresses.   6. Poland—Ethnic
relations—Congresses.   I. Blobaum, Robert.
DS135.P6A72 2005
305.892′40438′09—dc22
                                                    2005002688

Printed in the United States of America

Cornell University Press strives to use environmentally responsible suppliers and materials to the fullest extent possible in the publishing of its books. Such materials include vegetable-based, low-VOC inks and acid-free papers that are recycled, totally chlorine-free, or partly composed of nonwood fibers. For further information, visit our website at www.cornellpress.cornell.edu.

Cloth printing   10 9 8 7 6 5 4 3 2 1
Paperback printing   10 9 8 7 6 5 4 3 2 1

Contents

Preface

Antisemitism in late nineteenth- and twentieth-century Poland was part of a larger and especially European hostility toward Jews and their place in the modern world. Practically all the attitudes and behaviors associated with antisemitism in Poland could be found elsewhere in modern Europe to varying degrees, and indeed its ideological expressions were often imported and adapted to a changing Polish environment. Thus, there is nothing peculiarly "Polish" about antisemitism, and claims to the contrary have served only to encourage present-day antisemites. It is accurate, however, to speak of antisemitism "in modern Poland": that is, its multiple and shifting contexts from the mid-nineteenth century to the present. Since these Polish contexts have not remained static, antisemitism in modern Poland has taken on different meanings, content, forms of expression, and social range. A chief purpose of the chapters in this volume is to examine this constantly moving target at different moments in time, in various contexts, and in relation to other factors. At the same time, the fact that the relative strengths and weaknesses of resistance and opposition to antisemitism in Poland during the modern era have been similarly situational has in turn affected their capacity to be heard and acted upon. The goal of this collaborative effort, therefore, is not to provide a definitive history either of antisemitism in modern Poland or of opposition to it but to bring the larger picture into better focus.

This collection of original essays and articles is the final product of a collaborative research project that has involved fifteen scholars from the United States and Poland since the autumn of 2001. Its origins, however, date to the summer of 2000 and a roundtable—"The Politics of Antisemitism in Early Twentieth-Century Poland"—involving Jerzy Jedlicki, Theodore R. Weeks, and Brian Porter at the World Congress of Central and East European Studies in Tampere, Finland. As the organizer of the roundtable, I sought to put my own conclusions about the emergence of a modern, politicized antisemitism in Warsaw on the eve of the First World War to the test of a larger scholarly debate before they appeared in print.[1] At the same time, the Tampere roundtable provided an opportunity to discuss topics and areas in the rapidly expanding scholarship of Polish-Jewish relations in the twentieth century which nonetheless demanded new exploration or further consideration.

Subsequently, and in consultation with several U.S. and Polish colleagues, I began to organize a team of scholars whose past research had helped define or whose current work had the potential to redefine the contours of study of Polish-Jewish relations in the modern era. After several mutations, the research team whose work appears in this volume comprised a group of individuals fairly diverse in academic rank, professional training, methodological approach, and specific period of historical interest. Such diversity was necessary in light of the project's goal of bringing chronological breadth, thematic depth, and a balanced treatment of actors to this complex and controversial subject. On the one hand, the work presented here synthesizes an enormous amount of recent research since 1989, in Poland and the United States as well as in Israel and Western Europe—work reflected in the selective bibliography compiled for this project by Stephen D. Corrsin. On the other hand, contributors have sought to break entirely new ground in their discussion of specific issues and topics not previously or prominently featured in the scholarship of Polish-Jewish relations.[2]

Most members of the research team presented, shared, and discussed preliminary versions of their contributions at a conference held in Morgantown, West Virginia, June 16–18, 2002. This conference, free and open to the public, drew in interested parties from the Pittsburgh and Washington, D.C., areas (including a representative from the Polish Embassy) as well as from the West

1. Robert Blobaum, "The Politics of Antisemitism in Fin-de-Siècle Warsaw," *Journal of Modern History* 73, no. 2 (2001): 275–306.

2. For example, the roles of gender, sexuality, and notions of social deviance in shaping perceptions of the ethnic and religious "other" in modern Poland are discussed here for the first time. In contrast, the more general study of antisemitism in modern Europe has long included such approaches; see George L. Mosse, *Nationalism and Sexuality: Respectability and Abnormal Sexuality in Modern Europe* (New York, 1985), and Sander Gilman, *The Jew's Body* (New York, 1991). In Polish, Bożena Umińska's recent discussion of the images of Jewish women in Polish literature begins to address the role of gender and sexuality in Polish stereotypes, but only in respect to women; see her *Postać z cieniem: Portrety Żydówek w polskiej literaturze od końca XIX wieku do 1939 roku* (Warsaw, 2001).

Virginia University and local communities. Those team members who were unable to attend the conference made separate trips to Morgantown to present their research to and take questions from a mixed academic and public audience. These individual contributions were then extensively critiqued by fellow collaborators on the research team, which in turn led to some lively electronic exchanges. The most contentious issues revolved around the definition of antisemitism itself and the relationship between traditional Judeophobia and more modern hatreds; the role of Jewish assimilation (or lack thereof) in the deterioration of Polish-Jewish relations; reasons for the relative ineffectiveness of Polish opposition to antisemitism over most of the modern era; the social range of antisemitic ideology and of specific images and stereotypes (positive and negative) of Jews; interpretations of the causes and meanings of pogroms and other forms of anti-Jewish violence; and the role of the Roman Catholic Church and its clergy in the spread of antisemitism in Poland as well as the prospects for success of recent Catholic efforts to deal with that legacy.

The space constraints of a single volume have left some obvious chronological and thematic gaps, the coverage of which can be entrusted to future research in the rapidly growing field of Polish-Jewish studies. A hypothetical second volume could include, for example, separate contributions on the role of Jewish issues in the "Polish October" of 1956 and Solidarity's self-limiting revolution of 1980–81. Moreover, nearly all the discussion in these pages is about Poles, although modern Poland (especially before 1945) contained both antisemites and opponents of antisemitism who were not Polish—especially Ukrainians, who outnumbered Jews by two million in interwar Poland, but also Germans, Belarusians, and Lithuanians. To do any justice to Ukrainian and other Christian minority perspectives, however, would require additional chapters and therefore must also be set aside for future study.

Finally, with the exception of the Zionists in the interwar Polish parliament, Jewish opponents of antisemitism receive relatively little attention in this volume. An additional chapter or two devoted to the various strategies pursued by different Jewish groups, ranging from the Orthodox members of the conservative Agudas Israel to the radical socialists in the Bund, in dealing with and responding to antisemitism would certainly have been of value.[3] Again, constraints tend to impose their own priorities. The opposition of Jewish groups and parties to antisemitism, interesting though its variations and dilemmas might be for scholarly analysis, can ultimately be assumed—unfortunately, that opposition also came to little effect—whereas not only

---

3. This is not to suggest the existence of a historiographical vacuum in this area, although in English most attention in this regard has been paid to early Jewish socialist and Zionist political formations. See, for example, Joshua Zimmerman, *Poles, Jews, and the Politics of Nationality: The Bund and the Polish Socialist Party in Late Tsarist Russia, 1892–1914* (Madison Wis., 2004); Ezra Mendelsohn, *Zionism in Poland: The Formative Years, 1915–1926* (New Haven, Conn., 1982); and Joseph Marcus, *Social and Political History of the Jews in Poland, 1919–1939* (Berlin, 1983).

could opposition among the Christian Polish majority not be assumed, but its relative absence or presence at critical moments counted a great deal. Even then, it can be argued that not all Polish actors—for example, the socialist and communist movements and the leftist political tradition that remained relatively open to Jews (in any case, before 1950)—have received their appropriate due in this volume.

At the same time, although some limited attention is paid to Jewish society and institutions, this is not a book about Jewish communal life. On the one hand, an extended discussion of the Jewish community and Jewish actors would be more appropriate to a work on Polish-Jewish relations generally.[4] On the other hand, in a book about antisemitism that treats only one aspect of Polish-Jewish relations, Jews necessarily appear as objects rather than subjects. That said, readers should not expect this book to be about the Holocaust in Poland, though it can hardly be ignored. Tempting though it might be to view Polish-Jewish relations and even the history of antisemitism in modern Poland from its low point during World War II, this is something that serious scholarship should resist. Instead, this book looks at the Holocaust as an episode, however important and tragic, in a much longer history of social and cultural attitudes that have shaped and reshaped Polish-Jewish relations.

This project has been generously supported by major funding over a two-year period from the National Council for Eurasian and East European Research. Additional support at critical moments has come from various units of West Virginia University, including the WVU Research Corporation, the Eberly College of Arts and Sciences, and the Office of International Programs. I thank Feliks Tych and Alina Cała of the Jewish Historical Institute in Warsaw and Padraic Kenney of the University of Colorado for their advice during early stages of the project; Włodzimierz Rozenbaum, John Markoff, Małgorzata Markoff, Maciej Pisarski, and William Brustein for their encouraging comments and insights during the June 2002 conference in Morgantown; and Lisa Di Bartolomeo of the University of Pittsburgh for her timely assistance with the translations. My wife, Victoria Gruber, has for long been the most faithful reader of my own manuscripts and has lent her discerning eye to the editing and indexing of this work. And, finally, I thank all my collaborators whose names and work appear in this volume and who helped transform a personal vision into a collective one.

---

4. In fact, a relatively unknown but important two-volume work consisting of such contributions already exists: *The Jews in Poland*, vol. 1, ed. Andrzej K. Paluch (Kraków, 1992), and vol. 2, ed. Sławomir Kapralski (Kraków, 1999).

ANTISEMITISM AND ITS OPPONENTS IN MODERN POLAND

Introduction

ROBERT BLOBAUM

S ince the chapters of this volume follow a rough chronology—from
Theodore R. Weeks's discussion of "what went wrong" in Polish-Jewish
relations in the late nineteenth century and to Janine P. Holc's analysis
of competing Polish and Jewish memory of Auschwitz (and by extension of
Polish-Jewish relations) at the close of the twentieth—a brief overview of
Polish-Jewish relations before and during these hundred-odd years is necessary in order to provide a backdrop to the scholarship featured in these pages.
Polish-Jewish relations through most of the nineteenth century were not characterized by the animosities that would mark the subsequent era and that had
already appeared in western and central Europe, despite the persistence in
Poland of a religion-based Judeophobia (also inherited from Poland's western
neighbors) and the familiar stereotypes associated with it (such as those of
Jewish deicide, profanation of the Eucharist, and ritual murder). In this regard,
Poland was a relative latecomer to the spread of more "modern" forms of
antisemitism from west to east, as it was to the economic penetration and
social disruptions of modern capitalism that were firmly set in motion only
after the January 1863 insurrection and the final emancipation of the Polish
peasantry in territories then under Russian imperial rule.

Noting this relative lack of hostility in Polish-Jewish relations before the
end of the nineteenth century is not meant in any way to characterize those
relations as cordial or friendly, or to suggest that Poland prior to its capital-

ist transformation was an oasis of ethnic and religious tolerance. Though the reasons for the Jewish presence in Poland long predate the modern era, they may be briefly summarized. Jewish migration to Poland, which began in earnest in the fourteenth century, was the result of both the push factor of religious turbulence and persecution to the west, particularly in the German states, and the pull factors of economic opportunity and cultural autonomy granted by the Polish monarchy in order to populate and increase the revenues of its lands. These relative advantages to Jewish settlement in medieval Poland would last more or less until the eighteenth-century partitions of the Polish-Lithuanian state, brought on by a series of wars and chronic political instability.[1] Nonetheless, long before its demise, the Polish-Lithuanian Commonwealth had become the center of European and perhaps even world Jewry.

Although their relations were not devoid of tensions in the early modern era, most Poles and Jews had what one Western observer later described as a "mutual good natured contempt" for each other that allowed them to live in grudging coexistence rather than conflict.[2] Despite the centuries-long presence of both groups in Poland, Poles and Jews actually knew very little about each other. Apart from practicing different religions, they spoke different native languages, wore different dress, and for the most part led separate existences. It was a rare occasion indeed when a Polish Christian entered the Jewish sphere or vice versa, though it might, infrequently, happen at wedding celebrations, for example. This segregation of Poles from their Jewish neighbors was mainly the result of a castelike social structure with its origins in the early Middle Ages.[3] Until the middle of the nineteenth century the Christian population itself was divided into castes, or feudal estates, that defined the privileges and obligations of each estate (clergy, nobility, burghers, and peasantry) in respect to the whole, including the state. Jews for all intents and purposes constituted a separate estate with its own rights and obligations. Though the Jewish caste did not share the privileges of the first three Christian estates, it did have more rights than the Christian peasantry, including the right not to be enserfed or enslaved. Jews also possessed their own self-governing institutions, the most important of which was the *kahal*, which regulated the religious affairs of the Jewish community and represented it in its dealings with the state and the Christian estates.

1. For a classic study of Poland's Jewish community from its origins to the partitions, see Bernard D. Weinryb, *The Jews of Poland* (Philadelphia, 1973).

2. This observation, part of the British ambassador's description of relations between Polish peasants and Jews in interwar Poland, was then already losing its currency but is certainly applicable to an earlier period; see William W. Hagen, "Before the 'Final Solution': Toward a Comparative Analysis of Political Antisemitism in Interwar Germany and Poland," *Journal of Modern History* 68, no. 2 (1996): 356.

3. For an examination of the role of medieval castes in the subsequent evolution of Polish-Jewish relations in the modern era, see the pioneering study of Aleksander Hertz, *The Jews in Polish Culture*, trans. Richard Lourie (Evanston, Ill., 1988).

Such contact as there was between Jews and the Polish estates was primarily economic. Since Jews could not own land (a monopoly of the Polish nobility, or *szlachta*), hold public office (also a monopoly of the *szlachta*), or otherwise leave their caste unless they converted, they served mainly as a "middleman minority" in an agrarian and manorial economy within which the Christian burgher estate had been seriously weakened over the centuries.[4] Thus Jews dealt with both nobles and peasants, as agents and managers for the former and as purveyors of goods and services to the latter.[5] Yet by virtue of their religion, Jews would never be granted the rights and privileges of a Christian burgher estate and therefore could never constitute an embryonic middle class of the Western type. Moreover, economic and social differentiation *within* the Jewish community was sharp—ranging from poor, itinerant peddlers at the bottom to wealthy merchants and lenders at the top. Indeed, in terms of wealth, these distinctions were sharper among Jews than among Christians. In any case, within this structure of castes, which began to break down in Poland only at the end of the eighteenth century, Poles and Jews largely tolerated each other's existence, and in an economic sense, each was dependent on the other.

This relative calm was disturbed by several developments, beginning with the late eighteenth-century partitions of Poland, which affected Poles and Jews alike. The latter saw their autonomous communal institutions, particularly the *kahal*, either emasculated or ultimately eliminated by the partitioning powers, only to be problematically revived in the early twentieth century by the interwar Polish state. Although Poland's political dismemberment originally left the existing social order intact, successive but failed uprisings led by the Polish nobility and the retributions that followed considerably weakened the noble estate. The decline of the *szlachta* was accompanied by a decades-long process of emancipation of both peasants and Jews from their medieval castes, initiated not by the Polish political class but by the powers—Russia, Prussia, Austria—that had partitioned Poland.[6] The completion of emancipation in the middle decades of the nineteenth century was followed by the arrival of modern capitalism, industrialization, urbanization, and mass migrations, all of which occurred within a relatively short period of time and were socially destabilizing for both Poles and Jews. The dilemmas of economic moderniza-

4. For more on "middleman minorities," see *Essential Outsiders: Chinese and Jews in the Modern Transformation of Southeast Asia and Central Europe*, ed. Daniel Chirot and Anthony Reid (Seattle, 1997).

5. According to Hillel Levine, the origins of antisemitism in Poland can be found in the very structure of these economic relationships, particularly as they evolved from the end of the sixteenth century against a general backdrop of economic stagnation and decline; see Hillel Levine, *Economic Origins of Antisemitism: Poland and Its Jews in the Early Modern Period* (New Haven, Conn., 1991).

6. On the processes of peasant and Jewish emancipation, see Stefan Kieniewicz, *The Emancipation of the Polish Peasantry* (Chicago, 1969); and Artur Eisenbach, *The Emancipation of the Jews in Poland, 1780–1870* (Oxford, 1991), respectively.

tion, as Theodoce Weeks argues in chapter 1, led to a "blurring of categories": the rejection of old distinctions and the challenging of traditionally accepted "Polish" and "Jewish" identities. At the same time, as the new social and economic environment took shape, the earning of livelihoods became increasingly based on competition rather than interdependence, and many of the ties that had bound Polish Christians and Jews unraveled.

In the countryside the now emancipated peasantry, first in the Austrian crownland of Galicia and subsequently in the Russian-ruled Polish Kingdom, in order to make a living from small parcels of land, needed cash and credit, and demand for both drove up prices and interest rates. Jews traditionally had served as lenders to peasants and, in the absence of modern credit institutions, would continue to do so. As Keely Stauter-Halsted shows in her discussion of the causes of the pogroms of 1898 in western Galicia (chapter 2), the demand for cash and the consequent pressures on prices and interest rates now made Jewish lenders and purveyors of basic goods, mainly in their capacity as inn- and tavernkeepers, appear to an increasing number of rural Poles as exploiters rather than benefactors. It is against this background that pogroms, something relatively unknown to the previous history of Poland, began to break out at the end of the nineteenth century.

The first pogroms were basically riots that had an economic rather than racial or religious character. To be sure, they targeted Jews, but Jews *as* Jews much less than as owners of inns, taverns, and distilleries. Significantly, it was these points of Jewish economic contact with Poles that were attacked and looted, rather than Jewish community or religious institutions. Synagogues were not touched, for example, and rabbis remained respected by many Polish peasants who continued to seek their counsel in settling disputes in their own village communities.[7] And although property damage in these riots could be quite considerable, injury, let alone death, to persons was much rarer. The application of an "antisemitic" label to these anti-Jewish pogroms is therefore questionable. Compared with the Lwów pogrom of November 1918 (analyzed in chapter 6 by William W. Hagen)—itself a harbinger of the now infamous massacre of the Jews of Jedwabne in the summer of 1941[8]—the late nineteenth-century interethnic violence was not based on a view of the world that defined Jews as universally alien and evil. Nonetheless, as Stauter-Halsted argues, the structures of economic life in Galicia had placed Jews and Catholics

---

7. Indeed, anthropologist Alina Cała notes the persistence of positive images of Jews in rural Polish popular culture, mixed with negative images of an "anticapitalist" nature and ongoing belief in Jewish participation in ritual murder, well into the mid-1980s; see Alina Cała, *Wizerunek Żyda w polskiej kulturze ludowej* (Warsaw, 1987).

8. On Jedwabne, see the much debated work of Jan Tomasz Gross, *Neighbors: The Destruction of the Jewish Community in Jedwabne, Poland* (Princeton, 2001), originally published in Polish as *Sąsiedzi: Historia zagłady żydowskiego miasteczka* (Sejny, 2000). The publication of *Neighbors* has given rise to a fairly substantial literature that has debated its contentions (see the section on Jedwabne in Stephen Corrsin's bibliography, chapter 15).

"on a sociological collision course" whose consequent politicization helped "position rural Poles on the cusp of a more modern era in their expression of antisemitism."

That collision occurred earlier in Poland's cities and larger towns, where "modern" forms of antisemitism originated more striking than in rural environments. In the first place, Jews had long made up a predominantly urban rather than rural population, even if in many instances their "urban" area is better described as a rural small town. Indeed, the "Polish" small town (*miasteczko*) was often almost entirely Jewish in population and character, especially in the east, and hence is often known by the Yiddish appellation *shtetl*. But with the onset of industrialization in the late nineteenth century, Jewish migration from shtetls and Polish migration from the countryside in search of employment altered the urban landscape. At first, Jewish migration from small towns to large cities occurred at a more rapid rate and was accompanied by the movement of Jews to central Poland from the western provinces of the Russian empire which constituted the Pale of Settlement.[9] The immediate demographic consequence of these Jewish migrations was that emerging industrial centers such as Warsaw and Łódź became for a time nearly 50 percent Jewish. Although in the first decades of the twentieth century the Jewish percentage declined relative to the Polish, these proportions would eventually lead Poles to raise questions about who "really owned" or "ruled" Polish cities, Poles or Jews. Similar questions would be raised about the urban industrial economy more generally, since Jews, whether as skilled artisans, merchants, or commercial agents, seemed better situated to compete in the new capitalist environment than Poles of either noble or peasant background. At the same time, the "failure of assimilation," as Weeks puts it—that is, the retention by Jews of a separate identity, however transformed by economic modernization—aroused additional Polish suspicions and fears of an existential threat to their own national and cultural development.[10]

Let us now be more precise about which Poles, motivated by their anxieties over the appearance of a "separate nation" on the Vistula, were raising these questions or—taken collectively—the Polish version of modern Europe's "Jewish question." The nineteenth century saw the emergence of the Polish intelligentsia, a new urban social stratum of mixed origins whose ethos of moral and national leadership was both derived from and collided with the

9. The Russian Empire's harsh and discriminatory "May Laws" of 1887, along with the pull factor of the Polish Kingdom's industrial development, were the principal causes of the migration of Jews from its western provinces, particularly from Lithuania and Belarus. Branded as "Litwacy" (Litvaks) regardless of their place of origin, they were often better skilled and educated than native Polish Jews, and their fluency in Russian became the source of antisemitic consipiracy theories; see Francois Guesnot, " 'Litwacy' i 'Ostjuden' (Żydzi ze Wschodu). Migracja i stereotypy," in *Tematy żydowskie: Historia, literatura, edukacja*, ed. Elżbieta and Robert Traba (Olsztyn, 1999), 73–80.

10. For more on Jewish assimilation and its "failures" in the eyes of Poles, see Alina Cała, *Asymilacja Żydów w Królestwie Polskim (1864–1897)* (Warsaw, 1987).

traditional value system of the *szlachta*. With the emancipation of the peasantry and as the agrarian economy began its transformation into an industrial one, offspring of the nobility also migrated to the cities in search of employment. Yet although they were often endowed with a classical education that made them fit for holding public office or serving in the bureaucracy, in the largest of the partitioned Polish territories under tsarist rule the best offices and positions were reserved for Russians. Thus, this well-educated but relatively large and job-hungry social group, the intelligentsia, looked to commerce and the free professions for potential employment. And there it faced Jewish competition. It was from such economic and political frustrations of the Polish intelligentsia that modern forms of antisemitism were first given voice in the public arena.[11]

Earlier, throughout most of the nineteenth century, the Polish national movement had spoken of liberation in universal terms: that is, of liberating the country and its inhabitants, regardless of religion or ethnicity, from the oppression of the partitions. The battle cry of nineteenth-century Polish insurgents was "For Your Freedom and Ours!" Earlier, it had been considered political bad taste to propagate anti-Jewish views openly. The idea of a political nation that included Jews, inspired by Polish romanticism, peaked with the 1863 insurrection, when Poles appealed for the support of Jews in the language of "brotherhood."[12] By the beginning of the twentieth century, however, the Polish national movement, now more or less synonymous with the National Democratic political machine (known by its popular acronym as the *Endecja*) led by Roman Dmowski, was already speaking less of liberating the country from the partitions than of liberating Poland from the Jews, whom it now identified not only as a cultural and religious "other" but as an alien internal enemy.[13] Particularly after the failed 1905 revolution, important aspects of the Endecja's interpretation of the "Jewish question" came to be shared by many "liberals" and "progressives" and by representatives of the Roman Catholic Church in Poland as well, the former having abandoned their earlier faith in "assimilation," the latter as part of the wide-ranging Catholic confrontation with modernity and its presumed evils.[14] By the time of the out-

11. For a discussion of the relationship between the Polish intelligentsia's economic and political frustrations at the end of the nineteenth century, see Jerzy Jedlicki, *A Suburb of Europe: Nineteenth-Century Polish Approaches to Western Civilization* (Budapest, 1999), particularly part 2: "Ambiguities of Progress from 1864 through the 1880s"(171–291).

12. See Magdalena Opalski and Israel Bartal, *Poles and Jews: A Failed Brotherhood* (Hanover, N.H., 1992), for a discussion of the "honeymoon" in Polish-Jewish relations during the insurrection and its subsequent breakdown.

13. This transformation of Polish nationalist thought is the subject of a recent study by Brian Porter, *When Nationalism Began to Hate: Imagining Modern Politics in Nineteenth-Century Poland* (New York, 2000).

14. On mainstream Polish liberalism's movement toward the radical right after 1905, see Theodore R. Weeks, "Polish 'Progressive Antisemitism,' 1905–1914," *East European Jewish Affairs* 25, no. 2 (1995): 49–68. On the Catholic Church and the place of antisemitism in its efforts to meet the challenges of modernity, see Brian Porter's contribution to this volume (chapter 5).

break of the First World War, nationalists, "progressives," and Catholic clergy had joined forces to proclaim a boycott of Jewish-owned shops and businesses in Warsaw and other Polish cities in an effort to dislodge Jews from their positions in the urban economy.[15] And to promote this boycott, its more radical proponents employed the language of hatred, a language that demonized Jews.

Already in the first decades of the twentieth century, the attitudes, language, and behaviors associated with modern antisemitism in Poland, whatever its links to old-fashioned Judeophobia based on religion (particularly in its recycling of chimerical images of Jews), encountered resistance and opposition. In chapter 13, on the "anti-Zionist" campaign of 1968, Dariusz Stola makes a distinction between passive resistance and conscious opposition which is useful in looking at the entire period. Although the relative range, proportionality, and forms of both responses were situational, like that of antisemitism itself, resistance and opposition *were* present throughout the twentieth century. There is considerable evidence of popular resistance before the First World War to campaigns of political mobilization against Jews. In western Galicia, as Stauter-Halsted notes, it was a *failed* election campaign based on openly antisemitic rhetoric that formed the immediate backdrop to the 1898 pogroms. In both Galicia and the Polish Kingdom, attempted campaigns of economic boycott collapsed for lack of popular support, and efforts to "dislodge" Jewish trade, lenders, and handicrafts through the formation of Christian cooperatives made at best slow progress, as Poles maintained their interactions with Jews out of economic self-interest.[16] And, as I argue in my own contribution to this volume (chapter 4), there was a good deal of cultural resistance, particularly in the Polish countryside, to the spread of the demonizing images contained in the urban-based construction of a phantasmagoric Jewish criminality or, for that matter, of global Jewish conspiracies based on *The Protocols of the Elders of Zion*, a tsarist police fabrication, which had recently been imported to Poland from Russia.

Active opposition to antisemitism, particularly in the public and political sphere, came primarily from the same social stratum that had formulated the "Jewish question" in the first place and sought increasingly radical "solutions" to it—namely, the Polish intelligentsia. Jerzy Jedlicki's chapter 3, while noting the courage and strength of character of the intellectual opponents of antisemitism on the eve of the Great War, also highlights the obstacles they faced in confronting the first wave of anti-Jewish hostility in Poland's modern era—obstacles that would only mount in subsequent decades. Beginning with individuals such as Eliza Orzeszkowa and Jan Baudouin de Courtenay through

15. On the 1912–14 boycott, see Robert Blobaum, "The Politics of Antisemitism in Fin-de-Siècle Warsaw," *Journal of Modern History* 73, no. 2 (2001): 291–305.

16. The proponents of economic boycotts of Jews continued to complain of popular Polish indifference to their campaigns well into the interwar period; see Szymon Rudnicki, "Towarzystwo Rozwoju Handlu, Przemysłu i Rzemiosł," in *Gospodarka, Ludzie, Władza: Studia Historyczne*, ed. Michał Kopczyński and Antoni Mączak (Warsaw, 1998), 315–36.

the likes of Zofia Nałkowska, Tadeusz Boy-Żeleński, Czesław Miłosz, Leszek Kołakowski, Jan Błoński, and Maria Janion, the intellectual opponents of antisemitism in twentieth-century Poland have counted many of the leading lights of Polish literature, culture, and scholarship. Nonetheless, like many more of their lesser-known intellectual colleagues, these Polish "defenders of Jews" exposed themselves to indiscriminate insults and vilification as anti-Polish, anti-patriotic, or anti-Catholic "Judaicized Poles." Weeks, in reference to the eloquent propositions of Polish-Jewish condominium of Baudouin de Courtenay and Kazimierz Kelles-Krauz, laments that "two swallows do not make a spring."[17] Perhaps a more appropriate analogy would suggest that there were actually many more swallows but that they could not often be heard over the raucous crowing of antisemitism. During much of the communist era, as we see in chapters 12 and 13 by Bożena Szaynok and Dariusz Stola, opposition voices were suppressed and silenced, at least in public.

At the same time, as Jedlicki shows, the swallows were "soloists" in the sense that they came from across the political spectrum and in some cases did not subscribe to any particular ideological orientation, whereas the antisemites increasingly constituted a "choir." Second, Jedlicki notes that many opponents of early twentieth-century antisemitism nevertheless shared several of its stigmatizing categories and stereotypes; thus, the issue of opposition to antisemitism cannot be reduced to a simple question of "for or against" but involved a variety of factors and motivations. Jedlicki's point is even more strikingly evidenced in the stark contrast between the interwar antisemitic attitudes and the wartime humanitarianism of several Catholic founders of *Żegota*, the popular cryptonym for the underground Council of Aid to the Jews that assisted Jews seeking to hide on the "Aryan" side during the Holocaust.[18] Those like Baudouin de Courtenay, whose tolerant multiculturalism negated the very premises of Poland's "Jewish question," were indeed exceptional. Unfortunately, arguments such as his were conducive not to changing the minds of contemporaries but rather to the antisemitic right's transformation of their most principled Polish opponents into "artificial Jews," as noted by Antony Polonsky (chapter 9) in reference to attacks on Boy-Żeleński.

Larger geopolitical issues associated with the outbreak of the First World War temporarily overshadowed the war of words among the Polish intelligentsia over the Jewish question. Nonetheless, the cataclysm of war, although it led to the restoration of an independent state, had a further negative impact on Polish-Jewish relations. As the new Polish state fought to establish postwar borders with its Lithuanian, Ukrainian, Soviet, and German neighbors, terri-

17. For more on the response of Kelles-Krauz to the "Jewish question," see Timothy Snyder, "Kazimierz Kelles-Krauz, 1872–1905: A Polish Socialist for Jewish Nationality," *Polin* 12 (1999): 257–70.

18. This ambivalence, personified in the figure of Zofia Kossak, is discussed in some detail by Dariusz Libionka in chapter 11.

tories passed back and forth between armies that more resembled militias and paramilitary groups than regular disciplined formations. Jews, who frequently sought to find in neutrality shelter from the ensuing chaos, were instead considered collaborators of the enemy on one side or the other. In the city of Lwów a bloody pogrom accompanied its Polish conquest from the hands of the Ukrainians in November 1918, when approximately 150 Jews were murdered and more than 500 Jewish shops and businesses were ransacked. William Hagen's analysis (in chapter 6) of the Lwów pogrom is concerned, however, not with the empirical extent of its anti-Jewish violence or with its social-political triggers but rather with the "mythic meanings and messages in its perpetrators' eyes." The evidence he musters from the pogromists' own words shows that on many occasions the perpetrators, as they engaged in plunder and violence, moved within a self-chosen framework of symbolic action which, in carnival-like form, gave expression to a collective sense of celebration, triumph, cruel playfulness, and joy at the dispossession, humiliation, and even murder of Jews. Of even greater concern to Hagen, however, is how such brutal behavior and particularly its genocidal overtones could be understood by its perpetrators as justifiable or righteous. The "moral economy" that sanctioned such ethical calculus, Hagen argues, was in part contained in the conviction that the Jews *owed* pogromists the goods and even the lives of which, by moral right, they were being dispossessed. At the same time, Hagen attributes the "phantasms of mass murder" that stalked on the margins of the anti-Jewish actions to "an apocalyptic imagination" that framed the pogromists' self-understanding as Christians. Such popularly conceived retributive justice thus marks the addition of a new and deadly element to existing Polish hostility toward Jews.

Visions of apocalyptic warfare, according to Brian Porter (chapter 5), also came to dominate thinking in the highest circles of Poland's Roman Catholic Church, making it possible for Catholics to find much common ground with antisemites in their epochal struggles for survival against evil and against the conspiracies of open and secret enemies. Until the beginning of the twentieth century, Porter argues, the Church's "traditional antipathy toward Jews because of their refusal to convert" did not preclude a rejection of the secular racism and conspiracy fixations we frequently associate with modern antisemitism. Such resistance, however, would erode first into ambivalence toward and then wide acceptance of the Spencerian rhetoric of racial antisemitism in Polish Catholic circles by the 1930s. Within a larger European Catholic framework, beginning with the papacy of Leo XIII, Porter finds the key to this change in the Church's approach to Jews in its abandonment of an earlier and raging opposition to modernity in favor of attempts to reconcile itself with the modern world. The adoption of an "aggressive militant model of Catholicism" that sought to meet and defeat enemies of the faith from within that world was accompanied by the conviction that the satanic enemy had penetrated Polish society and culture in Jewish guise. According to Porter, this Manichean view of the modern world created considerable space within the Church for accommodating modern, racial antisemitism.

This transformation of the Church's perceived religious mission in relation to Jews (i.e., from one of conversion to one of "struggle") was accompanied by institutional and occupational motivations for its steadfast opposition to Jews, according to Konrad Sadkowski in his discussion of clerical nationalism and antisemitism in the Lublin region during the interwar period (chapter 8). The Church as an institution in interwar Poland, Sadkowski argues, encountered a secular and pluralistic Polish state that by its very nature defined citizenship on the basis of legal equality (though as we see in Szymon Rudnicki's chapter 7, definition and implementation were two different things). The idea of the civic nation, although indispensable for interwar Poland's Jews, Sadkowski sees as particularly threatening to the Church's own power and authority in society. That threat in turn drew the Church ever more visibly into "a politics of cultural construction" that insisted on Catholicism as the central element of Polish identity. From the more mundane perspective of priests, Sadkowski argues, the Jewish "demand" for a secular and civic Poland would, if realized, erode the ideological and cultural importance of the clergy and therefore its economic and social standing. Thus Sadkowski concludes that both the ideological development of Polish Catholicism and institutional and professional motives of self-preservation, power, and prestige were behind the Church's drive to "Catholicize Poland" during the interwar years, to realize an imagined Poland with space for only a limited number of converted Jews.

As Church attitudes toward Jews changed in the first decades of the twentieth century, so too did attitudes toward Jewish assimilation and acculturation. If, as Weeks and others have noted, assimilation's "failure" was an important factor in the rise of antisemitism before the First World War, then its "successes" during the interwar years provided new fuel for the radical right's anti-Jewish rhetoric and polemics. Indeed, Antony Polonsky (chapter 9) argues that Jewish integration and acculturated Jews became the main targets of antisemitic hostility in the 1920s and 1930s. Writing on Julian Tuwim and other Polish writers of Jewish origin, as well as other Polish writers of the era such as Boy-Żeleński, who shared their cosmopolitanism, irony, sophistication, and eclecticism, Polonsky offers a case in point. Tuwim especially became a bête noire to the Nationalist right, in part because he and his poetry represented everything the right hated about the culture of the big city, in part because of his merciless ridicule and mockery of the Nationalist right itself. Polonsky sees Poland's cultural wars of the interwar period as part of a wider dispute that continues into the present. There can be little doubt, however, that by the end of the 1930s the first round of this conflict had been won by the much louder and rhetorically violent champions of an art that stressed national, Catholic, and rural values and who branded their Polish opponents as Jews in Polish cloth, or "artificial Jews."

Increasing antisemitism in Church, culture, and society eventually assumed the form of legislation. Following the First World War, independent Poland was established as a parliamentary democratic state that pledged itself to respect the rights of national minorities in international agreements and its own constitution of March 1921. Yet as Rudnicki demonstrates, it took a decade, until 1931, to abrogate all laws and regulations from the era of the partitions which discriminated against Jews. Ironically, once Jews had finally achieved equal civil rights, they found themselves immediately confronted with new legislation that sought to undermine or strip them of those rights. Rudnicki focuses in particular on the legislation passed at the national level in the second half of the 1930s, whose target, even if it didn't mention Jews by name, was clear. Although Rudnicki does not suggest that the interwar Polish *Sejm* passed anything approximate to the Nuremberg laws of Nazi Germany, he shows that parliamentary deputies did attempt to introduce legislation in the Nuremberg spirit which would have effectively disenfranchised the vast majority of Poland's Jews, while the government itself began to consider projects of forced mass Jewish emigration.

As Poland approached the "ghastly decade" (or *upiorna dekada*, as Jan Gross puts it)[19] of the Second World War and its aftermath, antisemitism was reaching its height: Jews and Poles of a liberal humanist bent found themselves in a defensive position, confronting an increasingly "eliminationist" antisemitism that threatened the security of persons and property in violation of both Polish law and public morality.[20] As noted in my preface, the temptation to view the entirety of Polish-Jewish relations from its low point in the 1940s, particularly through the lens of the Holocaust, should nonetheless be resisted; as we have seen, Polish-Jewish relations had begun to deteriorate only at the end of the nineteenth century and would improve again by the end of the twentieth. Yet much of the literature that deals with Poles and Jews is focused on the "ghastly decade," as we can see from the proportionately large section devoted to the war years in Stephen Corrsin's bibliography (chapter 15), which itself contains only a small representative sampling. Most recently,

19. See Jan Tomasz Gross, *Upiorna dekada: Trzy eseje o stereotypach Żydów, Polaków, Niemców i komunistów, 1939–1948*, 2 ed. (Kraków, 2001), which has been translated into English as "A Tangled Web: Confronting Stereotypes concerning Relations between Poles, Germans, Jews, and Communists," in *The Politics of Retribution in Europe: World War II and Its Aftermath*, ed. Istvan Deak, Jan T. Gross, and Tony Judt (Princeton, 2000), 74–129.

20. The term "eliminationist" antisemitism was coined by Daniel Jonah Goldhagen in *Hitler's Willing Executioners: Ordinary Germans and the Holocaust* (New York, 1996). Goldhagen's thesis in regard to the nature and extent of antisemitism in Germany has been strongly criticized by historians; however, "eliminationist" seems to describe best the main direction of antisemitism in Poland on the eve of the Second World War in the sense that its long-term goal was to eliminate the Jewish presence in Poland. Extermination, it should be emphasized, was not among the means considered to accomplish this goal, even among the most radical of antisemites. The Church, in particular, consistently warned against a resort to violence as a means to remove Jews from Polish society.

following the publication of *Neighbors*, Gross's book on Jedwabne, the years of war, occupation, and genocide (which had already figured prominently in the Western-language literature) became the object of months of intense academic and public debate, as well as both soul-searching and denial, in Poland itself.[21] With a sense of proportionality in mind, this volume consciously contains only two contributions devoted to Polish-Jewish relations during the years of the Second World War, both of which, however, seek to open new vistas for future scholarship. The first, by Katherine R. Jolluck (chapter 10), casts wartime relations between Poles and Jews in a somewhat different light by exploring the attitudes of Polish women toward their Jewish counterparts in the circumstances of Soviet exile. The second, by Dariusz Libionka (chapter 11), tackles the controversial response of the Roman Catholic Church and its clergy to the extermination of their fellow countrymen on Polish soil, which until recently has been a practically taboo subject in Polish discourse.

Jolluck's study, in particular, shows that antisemitic stereotypes—like national identity itself—are relational and dependent on context. In this case, that context is provided by the shared but differently interpreted experiences of female citizens of both groups exiled to the interior of the USSR after the Red Army invasion of eastern Poland in September 1939. By examining women's testimonies collected by the Polish army commanded by General Władysław Anders following its evacuation of the Soviet Union in 1942, Jolluck is able to analyze the role of gender in Polish depictions of Jews and in the articulation and reception of antisemitic stereotypes in the particular and calamitous experience of wartime exile. She finds that two-thirds of these Polish testimonies did present negative or hostile depictions of the Jewish women with whom they lived and worked. Yet although many of the anti-Jewish attitudes inherited from the interwar period persisted in exile and were compounded by new stereotypes of Jews as enthusiastic supporters of the Soviet invasion, they did not contain the old and modern chimerical images of Jews as ritual murderers, criminals, and sexual perverts (discussed in my chapter 4). The main charge against Jewish women, Jolluck demonstrates, was that they were unfit and selfish members of the Polish national collective, conceived in terms of the family, and therefore fell far short of the Polish ideal for womanhood. These same Polish testimonies, however, depict Russian females as perverted, "unnatural" women, primitive and Asiatic. Thus, although in Polish eyes Jewish women failed as citizens, Russian ones failed more fundamentally as women. Ultimately, Jolluck attributes this mitigation and partial dissipation of Polish hostility toward Jews, which she finds among Polish male testimonies as well, to the fact and character of Russian domination. For the Poles who had experienced Soviet rule in exile, in other

---

21. In English, see *The Neighbors Respond: The Controversy over the Jedwabne Massacre in Poland*, ed. Antony Polonsky and Joanna B. Michlic (Princeton, 2004); and *Thou Shalt Not Kill: Poles on Jedwabne*, ed. William Brand (Warsaw, 2001).

words, Jews suddenly ranked well below Russians in the hierarchy of Poland's enemies.

Libionka, for his part, challenges the paradigm established in Polish Catholic journalistic and academic literature of the late 1960s and early 1970s—one that continues to exercise a strong influence on present-day discourse—of the Church's very serious involvement in the rescue of Jews. Although Libionka acknowledges the engagement of individual members of the clergy in aiding Jews and their courage in doing so, he argues that those individual cases have served as the basis for a number of "replicating myths" in the Polish literature. And although he is careful to note the dire situation in which the Polish Church and its clergy found itself under German occupation, he clearly refutes claims that the Church and its representatives did everything in their power on behalf of Jews. According to Libionka, the Church hierarchy's interventions with the German authorities were limited to unsuccessful efforts on behalf of converts; otherwise, he finds "a profound gulf separating the Church from the mass crimes perpetrated in its Polish dioceses." Libionka attributes the narrow dimensions of the Church's actions on behalf of Jews to the ongoing influence of antisemitism, based on the ideological transformation earlier described by Porter and its institutional and material interests delineated by Sadkowski. Thus, though Libionka finds instances of "authentic compassion" for Jews within the wartime Church, he sees a far larger proportion of Church representatives as indifferent to the victims of genocide, an attitude that continued into the postwar period.

The multiple traumas of the war, the social chaos and political confusion of the immediate postwar period, and the subsequent inhibitions imposed on scholarly debate and publication by Poland's communist authorities gave rise to a number of "half-truths" about Polish-Jewish relations during and after the Second World War.[22] According to Bożena Szaynok (chapter 12), one of these half-truths is contained in the use of "antisemitism" as the sole descriptor of Polish attitudes toward Jews or its designation as the sole cause of a seemingly final polarization in Polish-Jewish relations in the immediate postwar period. For example, Szaynok attributes the initial desire of Jewish survivors of the Holocaust to emigrate to profound ideological and psychological reasons—particularly their perception of Poland as a cemetery where the continuation of Jewish life was impossible—rather than to antisemitism. Nonetheless, Szaynok does not view antisemitism as a marginal phenomenon, particularly given the strength of the stereotype of the *Żydokomuna* (Jewish communism) in postwar Poland. This powerful myth, born in the interwar period and intensified by perceptions of Jewish collaboration with the Soviet invasion of eastern Poland in 1939, now held that Jews were responsible for introducing the unpopular communist regime to Poland.

22. In this regard, see Krystyna Kersten, *Polacy, Żydzi, komunizm: Anatomia półprawd, 1939–1968* (Warsaw, 1992).

Mounting violence against Jews, regardless of its motivations, culminated in the Kielce pogrom of July 1946, for Szaynok the "turning point" in postwar Polish-Jewish relations, after which Jewish emigration from Poland increased dramatically.[23] Moreover, the subsequent entanglement of Jewish issues and antisemitism with postwar Poland's political conflicts would leave those relations "frozen in time" for several decades, according to Szaynok. Meanwhile, the communist regime effectively co-opted, silenced, or suppressed independent initiatives that aimed at a genuine rapprochement, for example, that of Władysław Bartoszewski and the League for the Struggle against Racism in the late 1940s. Within a larger context, Soviet-bloc communist parties, taking their cue from Moscow, would soon launch their own anti-Jewish campaigns against "rootless cosmopolitanism," culminating in the trial of Rudolf Slánský in Czechslovakia in 1952 and the "Doctors' Plot" in the Soviet Union on the eve of Stalin's death, a purge which targeted Jews in the medical profession. The subsequent attempts of Leszek Kołakowski and the journal *Po prostu* to counter the postwar revival of antisemitic tendencies during the "Polish October" of 1956, and the efforts of liberal Catholic intellectuals in the 1960s to readdress various issues of Polish-Jewish history, would suffer a fate similar to that of Bartoszewski's earlier initiative.

The instrumentality of Jewish issues in Polish communist politics, the pattern for which had already been established by the late 1940s, reached its apogee in the anti-Zionist campaign of 1968, which also marked the last major gasp of antisemitism in the history of modern Poland. Before the campaign originated in 1967 in the aftermath of the Arab-Israeli Six-Day War, there remained in Poland approximately 25,000 to 30,000 Jews whose purported sympathies for Israel made them the target of claims by Władysław Gomułka and other communist party leaders that they constituted a subversive Zionist fifth column. Yet the main and most dramatic phase of the anti-Zionist campaign occurred the following March in reaction to a wave of student protests. Dariusz Stola (chapter 13) argues that the campaign served several purposes: to fight the student rebellion, to prevent the spread of political unrest to other social groups, to change the political balance in the party leadership, and to launch a "preventive strike" against potential Polish followers of the Czech "Prague Spring."[24] Despite evidence of the cynical and multifunctional exploitation of the "Jewish card" in pursuit of "rationally defined interests," Stola also finds in Polish government and party documents an antisemitic paranoia and irrational impulses too sincere to be cynical.

These were expressed, above all, in the images of the "March Jew" that dominated the anti-Zionist propaganda campaign and its "symbolic aggres-

---

23. Szaynok deals with the Kielce pogrom in much greater detail in *Pogrom Żydów w Kielcach, 4 lipca 1946 r.* (Warsaw, 1992).

24. For more on the politics of the anti-Zionist campaign, see Dariusz Stola, *Kampania antysyonistyczna w Polsce, 1967–1968* (Warsaw, 2000).

sion" and "verbal pogrom" against Jews. As I do in my own essay about the "criminal Jew," Stola links the chimerical images of March 1968 to their origins in medieval Christendom, although with a difference. In the early decades of the twentieth century, those images were transformed into the language of "moral panic" that demonized the Jewish outsider as a sexual predator, moral pervert, and most dangerous of felons—images that had little or no basis in statistical evidence. According to Stola, the old chimeras were recycled yet again in the spring of 1968, only now in the language of communist newspeak. Thus the hydra-headed "March Jew" was depicted simultaneously as a "Jewish nationalist" and "rootless cosmopolitan," as both a "Stalinist" and an "agent of American imperialism."

The anti-Zionist campaign would lead to the final wave of mass Jewish emigration and the reduction of the community of survivors in Poland by half. Yet, as Stola argues, the campaign also led to the thorough discrediting of a communist regime that had placed its faith no longer in historical determinism, class instinct, or workers' loyalty to "People's Poland" but in demonic monsters. Subsequent communist efforts to play the "Jewish card," most notably in the regime's attempts to counter the challenge of Solidarity in the crisis of 1980–81, would come to naught. Meanwhile, Polish-Jewish relations began to move into the new and contested terrain of memory. Already in the last years of communist rule, the main sites of that contest had become located in the years of the Second World War and the issue of Polish behaviors during the Holocaust.[25] On the one hand, the collapse of communist rule in Poland in 1989 opened the door to new scholarly research and public discussion of issues ("blank spots," as Szaynok calls them) in Polish-Jewish relations that had been previously been taboo. On the other, it enabled the enactment of previously unstated tensions in Polish and Jewish memory of their recent common history in directions that at times partially legitimized antisemitism and at other times allowed for the voicing of strong Polish opposition to antisemitism. By the late 1990s the Auschwitz museum and memorial site had become the principal location for a highly publicized and much-debated controversy that pitted Poland's past against its future.

In chapter 14, Janine P. Holc analyzes competing Jewish and Polish memories and interpretations of Auschwitz by focusing on the affair of the Auschwitz crosses, the public discussion of which, like that of the Jedwabne massacre shortly thereafter, generated new opportunities for revisiting and renarrating Catholic-Jewish relations in Poland. The controversy was sparked in 1998 when the radical nationalist Kazimierz Świtoń asserted the right to

25. For a discussion and presentation of these debates, particular those surrounding the January 1987 publication of Jan Błoński's "Biedni Polacy patrzą na getto (Poor Poles Look at the Ghetto)" in the liberal Catholic periodicial *Tygodnik Powszechny*, see *My Brother's Keeper? Recent Polish Debates on the Holocaust*, ed. Antony Polonsky (London, 1990). Michael Steinlauf follows these debates into the early postcommunist period in his *Bondage to the Dead: Poland and the Memory of the Holocaust* (Syracuse, N.Y., 1997).

maintain a theologically dubious and recently transplanted "papal cross" on the grounds of the Auschwitz memorial site. When plans to relocate that cross were announced, Świtoń responded by illegally filling the space with hundreds of crosses in what eventually became an explicit countermemorial to Auschwitz as a uniquely Jewish symbol of the Holocaust. The ensuing months of controversy and debate were important, according to Holc, not least because antisemitic voices were able to reenter the Polish public arena in an "injured mode" at a time when the government was negotiating Poland's NATO membership and eventual entry into the European Union. At the same time, the affair forced Polish opponents of antisemitism to grapple more directly with the link between Catholicism and the painful experience of Jews in Poland in their articulation of the reasons why a cross might be an unwelcome symbol at Auschwitz. In this regard, Holc highlights the efforts of several well-known Catholic clergy and intellectuals, particularly Fathers Stanisław Musiał and Stanisław Obirek, to listen and respond to Jewish voices in the controversy. The affair's denouement—the ultimate forced removal of Świtoń and his symbols, though not the papal cross he had "defended"—seemed both to relieve and to satisfy an ambivalent public opinion that viewed him as an "extremist" but believed that the papal cross should stay. This apparent compromise, Holc argues, demonstrates the limits to a specifically Catholic opposition to antisemitism imposed by the "supersessionist" basis of Christianity itself—that is, by its historical claims to primacy and universality.

Thus the ghosts of the recent past accompanied Poland's entrance into the twenty-first century, symbolized by the reaction of an increasingly polarized public to the revelations and conclusions contained in Jan T. Gross's *Neighbors*. Like the affair of the Auschwitz crosses before it, *Neighbors* served to reanimate antisemitic voices in the public sphere, voices that found partial support in a more general and defensive "obsession with innocence" (a phrase Holc borrows from Joanna Tokarska-Bakir). At the same time, the book provided an opportunity for opponents of antisemitism to reckon with the realities of twentieth-century Polish-Jewish relations and promote efforts toward reconciliation. Again, the results of the debate over what happened at Jedwabne were mixed. Sincere and widespread public sympathy for the victims of the Jedwabne massacre coincided with an equally widespread reluctance to accept the bitter truth that Poles had willingly participated in the mass murder of their Jewish neighbors.

The presence and strength of antisemitism in contemporary Poland suggests an equally mixed picture. As elsewhere in Europe, there was a notable decline in the number of those declaring antipathy toward Jews in the 1980s and 1990s. Opinion and sociological surveys taken in Poland shortly after the collapse of communism seemed to confirm that antisemitism, if not a totally marginalized phenomenon in Polish society, was not a general one either. Its relative strength among identifiable age, occupational, residential, and educa-

tional cohorts and its relative weakness among others were optimistically eval-
uated and interpreted to predict a further weakening of antisemitic attitudes in
Polish society in future decades.[26] Early in the new century, however, this
process appears to have come to at least a temporary halt, as it has elsewhere
in a Europe marked by the striking reemergence of antisemitic symbols and
stereotypes. Coinciding with the public controversies over the Auschwitz
crosses and Jedwabne was a general upsurge in antisemitic publishing activity
and its reception in Poland, whether in print form or over the Internet.[27] Thousands tune in daily to the antisemitic Radio Maryja, which is supported by
Catholic priests in opposition to the official pronouncements of the hierarchy,
if not to several bishops. Many of its listeners voted for candidates of the
League of Polish Families (Liga Polskich Rodzin, or LPR), the largest among
several antisemitic parties, in the September 2001 parliamentary elections. The
support of 6 percent of the electorate for the LPR has been followed by the
multiplication of incidents of vandalism in Jewish cemeteries and synagogues,
and antisemitic graffiti on public buildings and in the halls of apartment com-
plexes meet the eye on a daily basis. According to a recent article, this recent
upsurge of antisemitism is not so much condemned as it is denied, particularly
in Poland's political arena, while the clearly illegal activities and social pathological behaviors associated with it often go unpunished.[28]

Throughout this volume we have sought to examine antisemitism in its
proper historical context and in relation to other factors; it is necessary to do
so in regard to the apparent resurgence of antisemitism in present-day Poland
as well. Since communism's collapse in central and eastern Europe a good deal
of scholarship has been devoted to the problems of economic and political
transition to market economies and functioning pluralistic democracies. A
more profound and painful transition, however, has been occurring in Poland
and elsewhere in the former Soviet bloc—that is, the transition from industrial to postindustrial societies. That transition had been delayed by the
rigidities of communist rule, placing these societies in a position of relative
disadvantage, since an increasingly global economy favored the rather rapid
penetration of multinational corporations, not to mention "foreign" cultural
influences. Thus, the recent visibility of antisemitism is a reaction in part to
an increasingly pluralized Polish culture, in part to the economic disparities
and high unemployment rates of this transitional phase, all of which have
fomented anxieties about national identity and its disruption by "globaliza-

26. See *Czy Polacy są antysemitami? Wyniki badania sondażowego*, ed. Ireneusz Krzemiński
(Warsaw, 1996).

27. Indeed, even before the preliminary results of this research project were presented in
Morgantown, it was attacked on the Internet as a "Polish nation libel." See "Next Jewish Attack
on Poland in the Guise of a 'Conference,'" http://www.papurec.org (June 10, 2002).

28. Alina Cała, Dariusz Libionka, and Stefan Zgliczyński, "Antysemityzm bez Żydów i bez
antysemitów: Patologia antysemityzmu w Polsce w 1999–2001 r.," *Nigdy Więcej* 13 (spring
2003), 29–34.

tion" and "Europeanization." The direct relationship between antisemitism and these larger fears was made explicit during Świtoń's "defense" of the crosses at Auschwitz, as his supporters carried banners proclaiming "Jews out of Poland" on the one hand, and "No to NATO" and "Europeans out of Poland" on the other. The conflict between antisemitism and its opponents has long been part of a wider dispute between two visions of Poland, one nativist and xenophobic, the other outward-looking and European, according to Antony Polonsky, and "its outcome will determine the place of Poland in the twenty-first century."

To an extent, that outcome has been decided. In the 2003 referendum on membership in the European Union, a sizable majority of the participating Polish electorate voted in favor of joining the EU, this well after the euphoria of the immediate postcommunist period and exaggerated expectations of economic prosperity associated with a "return to Europe" had subsided. Despite growing evidence of popular indifference and antipathy toward the European Union since the referendum, Polish withdrawal from the EU, as advocated by Andrzej Leper and his Samoobrona (Self-Defense) party, is most unlikely.

There are other encouraging signs as well. Whereas in early twentieth-century Poland, Warsaw's leading dailies and magazines were dominated by the anti-Jewish camp, thus reducing the outlets for the expression of opposing opinions and the capacity of those opinions to reach a wider audience, the mainstream media in present-day Poland give little space to voices of hatred and far more to their opponents. As I mention in my own chapter, antisemitic literature in Poland today, however shocking its appearance and distribution, is bottom rather than top shelf. That a major site for the sale of antisemitic publications in Warsaw is the leased basement of the All Saints' Church can be read in either of two ways: one, that antisemitism resides just below the surface of Polish society or, contrarily, that antisemitism has been pushed by its publicly perceived illegitimacy into less prominent locations. In any case, antisemites can no longer rely on the institutional support of the Roman Catholic Church, which since the Second Vatican Council has undergone major changes in Poland (contrary to certain appearances) and whose ecumenism has aimed at Catholic-Jewish reconciliation, if arguably on its own terms. Those members of the clergy who support antisemitic activities, particularly in association with Radio Maryja, do so in opposition to the stated positions of the majority of the Polish episcopate and the Vatican.

Last but not least, the enormous upswing in the volume and quality of publishing related to Polish-Jewish themes, which partly inspired this project, has dwarfed the recycling of antisemitic titles such as *Poznaj żyda* (Know the jew) and reprints of *The Protocols of the Elders of Zion*. As Stephen Corrsin points out in the introduction to his bibliography (chapter 15), this increase in Polish interest in the country's Jewish heritage has been reflected in the rapid development of a Jewish Studies infrastructure in the form of newly founded centers, societies, university departments, and scholarly journals. There is no question, he argues, that the field of "Polish-Jewish studies" has developed into a significant area of study in its own right, thanks in no small part to the Poles' own "voyage of self-exploration." That self-exploration can often be painful, a recent example of which can be found in the official investigation of the Jedwabne massacre entrusted to the Instytut Pamięci Narodowej (Institute of National Remembrance, or IPN) following the publication of *Neighbors*. Despite constant hounding from right-wing politicians and general disbelief in Polish responsibility for the destruction of Jedwabne's Jewish community, the IPN, originally set up to "investigate crimes against the Polish nation," confirmed Gross's main assertion that Poles, themselves victimized during the war, could also act as perpetrators of mass murder.[29] Thus, as this volume goes to press, one can reasonably argue that for the first time since the late nineteenth century the opponents of antisemitism in Poland have regained the upper hand. Whether they can maintain it depends much on the success or failure of Poland's transition to a postindustrial order and on perceptions of its future experience in integrated European structures and its role in a global economy.

29. See the studies and documents contained in *Wokół Jedwabnego*, 2 vols. ed. Paweł Machcewicz and Krzysztof Persak (Warsaw, 2002).

I

Assimilation, Nationalism, Modernization, Antisemitism

Notes on Polish-Jewish Relations, 1855–1905

THEODORE R. WEEKS

The nineteenth century witnessed a massive revolution (indeed, revolutions) in the way Europeans viewed themselves, their communities, and their countries. Whereas in 1800 most Europeans derived their sense of identity from local, religious, and social categories (i.e., resident of a certain village, Catholic, peasant), by 1914 nationality as a principle of self-definition had in most places overwhelmed these old defining characteristics. The combined effects of industrialization, railroads, state educational systems, military service, and simply a higher degree of personal mobility created a situation in which large numbers of Europeans came to perceive their identity primarily in ethnic and national terms. Nor should ideological factors be ignored: by the late nineteenth century (and, in many areas, earlier) it had come to be broadly accepted that a nation deserved if not its own state, then at least far-reaching cultural autonomy. The nation (i.e., the cultural, linguistic, ethnic group) thus came to legitimize the state (the political entity) in a way that would have been incomprehensible to Louis XIV or Tsar Nicholas I. The idea that ethnically homogenous nation-states on the French model were the natural expression of progressive democracy challenged the very fundaments of dynastic, multinational states such as the Russian Empire.

In Eastern Europe, whose industrialization, urbanization, and general political rights lagged behind those of Central and Western Europe, the ideology of nationalism and the reality of national consciousness among broad social groups nonetheless made significant strides in the generations before 1914. The development of national identity in Eastern Europe was complicated by the low level of literacy, the presence of a large number of mainly peasant ethnicities, and fundamental disagreements on the definition and "limits" of given nationalities. To take one well-known instance, the Russian government (and quite possibly most Russians) refused to accept the existence of the Belarusian and Ukrainian nations, seeing in them mere subgroups of the Russian nation. And there was, of course, the tricky issue of whether the Jews constituted a nation. The historical process by which nations were defined and the masses were "nationalized" was extremely complicated; in the Polish and Jewish cases this process was certainly not completed by 1914. Increased national feeling, particularly in areas of mixed nationality, has generally been accompanied by feelings of antagonism toward the "national other." In the Polish case, the creation of modern nationalism and the rise of modern antisemitism were inextricably linked.[1] This connection makes it necessary here to hazard some tentative definition of the key term "nationalism."

Nationalism

Nationalism is perhaps best—if simplistically—defined as that political ideology which holds that each nation deserves its own independent or autonomous political unit, the state. But what constitutes a nation? Depending on the case, a historical state, historical memory, culture, language, religion, shared customs, or shared social status can be decisive.[2] In East-Central Europe on the whole the growth of national identity was primarily a phenomenon of the mid- to late nineteenth century, when previously "submerged" nations such as Lithuanians, Slovaks, and Ukrainians began to demand cultural and political rights.[3] But in this respect the Poles form a distinct exception. Unlike certain neighboring national groups, the Poles could hark back to a powerful histor-

---

1. This is not, of course, to argue that such a development was inevitable. Nonetheless, some of the key figures in modern Polish nationalism—in particular Roman Dmowski—as well as *the* Polish nationalist grouping, the National Democratic Party, were deeply hostile to the Jews, seeing them as a negative element in the Polish past and present.

2. For a far more sophisticated discussion of nationalism than can be given here, see Ernest Gellner, *Nations and Nationalism* (Ithaca, N.Y., 1983); E. J. Hobsbawm, *Nations and Nationalism since 1780: Programme, Myth, Reality* (Cambridge, U.K., 1990), and the stimulating texts collected in *Becoming National: A Reader*, ed. Geoff Eley and Ronald Grigor Suny (New York, 1996).

3. For an interesting, if perhaps overly schematic, attempt to describe the process of nation-formation and the rise of nationalism in East-Central Europe, see Miroslav Hroch, *Social Preconditions of National Revival in Europe: A Comparative Analysis of the Social Composition of Patriotic Groups* (Cambridge, U.K., 1985); and Józef Chlebowczyk, *O prawie do bytu małych i młodych narodów: Kwestia narodowa i procesy narodotwórcze we wschodniej Europie środkowej w dobie kapitalizmu (od schyłku XVII do początków XX w.)* (Warsaw, 1983).

ical state, a highly developed and sophisticated literature, and a strong and wealthy noble estate. As Andrzej Walicki has pointed out, the concept of modern Polish nationhood, already well developed in the late eighteenth century, was based much more on political than ethnic identity.[4] Nonetheless, it is also a fact that Polish nationalism as a modern political movement dates not from the time of Tadeusz Kościuszko but from nearly a century later when the Polish Socialist Party (PPS) and National League (Liga Narodowa) were formed in 1892 and 1893 respectively.[5]

When Polish nationalism assumed modern form in mass political organizations, it did so under highly unfavorable circumstances. As is well known, Poland disappeared from the European map at the time of the third partition in 1795 and would not reappear until 1918. Lacking an independent state, Poles were thrown back on their language and religion as bearers of *polskość* or Polishness. In the Russian Empire, where cultural, political, and religious restrictions on them were greatest, Poles were justified in seeing a real threat to their religious and cultural traditions. In particular after the failed insurrection of 1863, the Russian authorities did their best to limit and stymie the development and spread of Polish culture and to assure the predominant position in the empire of Russian culture and the Orthodox religion.

Throughout this period, state power (whether Austrian, Russian, or Prussian) was entirely detached from—and often hostile to—the Polish nation and Polish culture. In many other instances, the state (e.g., France or Britain, Italy or Germany from the 1870s) expended enormous energy to bring together nation and state. For Poles and their culture, state power was at best alien and aloof (Austria) and more frequently (Prussia and Russia) actively working to weaken the Polish nation. Without their own state Poles had to construct their national survival strategy around language, faith (Catholicism), and history. Feeling persecuted and weak, Polish patriots were extremely sensitive to any hint that non-Poles were "allying with the other side." Such suspicions were to strain Polish relations with Jews and Lithuanians by the early twentieth century.

At the same time, one should not exaggerate the extent and success of Russification (as the policies of that era are usually called). Polish literature and journalism continued to be published in the Russian Empire, and despite all restrictions Poles somehow managed to pass their culture and traditions on to the younger generation. Indeed, a Pole—Henryk Sienkiewicz—was

4. Andrzej Walicki, *The Enlightenment and the Birth of Modern Nationhood: Polish Political Thought from Noble Republicanism to Tadeusz Kościuszko* (Notre Dame, Ind., 1989).

5. On these two currents within Polish political thought, see *Narodowa Demokracja: Antologia myśli politycznego "Przeglądu Wszechpolskiego" (1895–1905)*, ed. Barbara Toruńczyk (London, 1983); and Ulrich Haustein, *Sozialismus und nationale Frage in Polen* (Cologne, 1969). For a stimulating recent attempt to explain the development of "integral nationalism" in its Polish form, see Brian Porter, *When Nationalism Began to Hate: Imagining Modern Politics in Nineteenth-Century Poland* (New York, 2000).

awarded the Nobel Prize for literature in 1905. Warsaw remained, even in the dark years of the late 1860s and 1870s, the cultural capital of a nonexistent state.

If the Polish nation was unusual in the context of East-Central Europe, the Jewish nation is arguably unique, a case unto itself. Indeed, even at the end of the nineteenth century there was no clear consensus as to whether the Jews constituted a nation at all. Many Jews, especially in the more assimilated milieus of France and Germany, vehemently denied the existence of a "Jewish nation," preferring to define their Jewishness in exclusively religious terms.[6] And yet, in the particular context of Eastern Europe, the stark differences in language, culture, dress, and everyday life that separated the Jewish masses from the surrounding population made their self-definition as a nation logical, if not necessarily inevitable. Furthermore, Jews had enjoyed communal autonomy in the Polish Commonwealth. Although the Jewish *kahal* was abolished by Nicholas I in 1844, Jewish institutions continued to exist in the form of schools, burial societies, and religious organizations. To state matters baldly, in the mid-nineteenth century most Polish Jews lived in a quite separate world—social, cultural, institutional, even to a great extent economic—from their Christian Polish neighbors. The partitioning powers had, of course, absolutely no interest in breaking down the barriers between Polish and Jewish societies.

The unusual nature of the Jewish nation, defined primarily in religious terms (at least initially) and living dispersed among other ethnic groups, finds no parallel among other European nationalities. And the disputed nature of Jewish identity (cultural, national, or religious?) could only further complicate relations between Jews and Polish nationalists. In particular, Poles could hardly be expected to welcome Jewish cultural and especially political nationalism (e.g., in the form of the Yiddish-speaking socialist Bund, or throughout Zionism—both products of the 1890s).

Although nationalism is certainly possible without antisemitism, the link between the two ideologies is far from accidental. In a sense, any kind of exclusivist nationalism ("Poland for the Poles," "Russia for the Russians," and the like) would seem inevitably to lead to restrictions (or worse) on Jews. But this inevitability is only apparent and depends on the nation's definition. That is, if (for example) a "Pole" is defined as a person who supports Polish cultural, political, and national aspirations, then a Jew ("Pole of the Mosaic Law," to use the contemporary phrase) can easily be accepted into the fold of Polishness. This conception of Jews gradually shedding their linguistic, cultural, and

---

6. See, for example, Michael R. Marrus, *The Politics of Assimilation: The French Jewish Community at the Time of the Dreyfus Affair* (Oxford, 1980). For an excellent collection of essays discussing various conceptions of Jewish identity after legal emancipation, see *Paths of Emancipation: Jews, States, and Citizenship*, ed. Pierre Birnbaum and Ira Katznelson (Princeton, 1995).

external differences and becoming integrated into the Polish nation was, in fact, the most prevalent proposed solution for the "Jewish question" before the very end of the nineteenth century.

On a practical or even conceptual level, however, it was a solution fraught with difficulties. Jewish identity was closely tied to scrupulous observance of traditional modes of behavior and dress, even when these were not, strictly speaking, religious precepts. Thus any Jew who dared to go against tradition by, say, dressing in "European" clothing or shaving his beard could very easily find himself treated as an apostate by his own community.[7] Similarly, a Jewish woman who wished to live an independent existence rather than marry would have a difficult time fitting into the community. Conceptually, the over-whelming identification of Catholicism with the Polish nation made it quite difficult for Jews, even if Polish-speaking, Western-clad, and "enlightened" in religious practices, to be accepted as entirely Polish. This brings us to a central question of this chapter: the concept of assimilation and its diverse forms and definitions.

Assimilation

Assimilation—both then and now—has often been linked with emancipa-tion, modernization, and "Europeanization."[8] From the time of Moses Mendelssohn, at least, the general assumption held that political emancipa-tion and social acceptance of Jews into the mainstream would have the effect of weakening "medieval," "Asian" traditions while strengthening elements of Western, progressive culture within the Jewish community. It is hardly by chance that these arguments were framed in Europe-versus-Asia rhetoric. The

---

7. This possibility of alienation from one's native society is also reflected in contemporary Yiddish literature, in particular in the works of Mendele Moykher Sforim (real name Sholem Abramovich), whose literary pseudonym, Dan Miron argues, was far more than a mere literary diversion; Dan Miron, *A Traveler Disguised: A Study in the Rise of Modern Yiddish Fiction in the Nineteenth Century* (New York, 1973), 130–68. In his report on Jewish small towns in Tomaszów district (eastern Lublin province), I. L. Peretz noted with heavy irony that in "Tishe-vitz" to be a *maskil*—an "enlightened Jew," for conservatives only a step from apostasy—a man did not even have to shave: "It's enough that he trims his beard": "Impressions of a Journey through the Tomaszow Region," in *The I. L. Peretz Reader*, ed. Ruth Wisse (New York, 1990), 30. For more examples of frictions between "reformers" and traditional Orthodox communities, see François Guesnet, *Polnische Juden im 19. Jahrhundert: Lebensbedingungen, Rechtsnormen und Organisation im Wandel* (Cologne, 1998), 281–331.

8. The title of one of Jacob Katz's essay collections is indicative of this link: *Emancipation and Assimilation* (Farnborough, U.K., 1972). On a broad theoretical level, see the stimulating essays by Zygmunt Bauman, "Exit Visas and Entry Tickets: Paradoxes of Jewish Assimilation," *Telos* 77 (Fall 1988): 45–77; Amos Funkelstein, "The Dialectics of Assimilation," *Jewish Social Studies* 1, no. 2 (Winter 1995): 1–14; and (a contemporary discussion, first published in 1893) Ahad Ha-Am, "Imitation and Assimilation," in *Modern Hebrew Literature*, ed. Robert Alter (New York, 1975), 90–101.

late nineteenth century was, after all, the period of European world hegemony, and certainly few Europeans questioned the predominance and superiority of European culture and even "race" over the rest of the world—at least, not before the defeat of the mighty Russian army in Manchuria by the Japanese in 1904. Assimilation did not necessarily mean abandoning the traditional rites and restrictions of the Jewish religion. Mendelssohn, as is well known, remained Orthodox, as did most of the first generation, at least, of assimilated Jews both in Germany and elsewhere. The difficulty, however, of maintaining a Jewish identity while integrating oneself into a self-confident and dynamic Christian culture is illustrated by the fact that the second and third generation of assimilated Jews often became indifferent to (or even contemptuous of) the religion of their fathers, and more than a few converted to Christianity.[9]

Even within the Russian Empire, where the harsh legal restrictions and consistently anti-Jewish attitudes of the Russian authorities worked against assimilation, the writer Judah Leib Gordon advocated (in Hebrew): "Be a man in the streets and a Jew at home." In other words, and in contrast to traditional Jewish culture and religious practice in Eastern Europe, Jews were to restrict their visible religious practices to the private sphere and in public adopt the modern, progressive, and European culture of their surroundings. As Michael Stanislawski points out, Gordon was not advocating a compartmentalization of Jewish culture and its restriction to the private sphere but the integration of its most fundamental spirit into every aspect of life—for how could one be a "man" without being a good Jew?[10] It needs to be remembered as well that Gordon wrote his famous line in Hebrew, the only language in which he composed his poetry. Ideally, "enlightenment" (in Hebrew, *haskalah*) would strengthen Jewish morality and identity while simultaneously transforming Jews into good citizens.

Still, and despite the excellent intentions of those aiming to integrate Jewish culture into the European mainstream (read: progressive, scientific, basically secular) culture, the obstacles to any such integration were very great indeed. On the one hand, the traditional Jewish community remained hostile to these innovations, seeing criticism of traditional modes of dress, ritual, and everyday behavior as attacks on Judaism itself. On the other, it remained to be seen whether the European mainstream was really prepared to accept Jews *as Jews* on equal terms. The almost universal denigration of Yiddish is just one indication that it was not. Another example is the failure to acknowledge (except among the extreme left) that Christian dogmas such as the Trinity or the Virgin Birth are no less "absurd" than religious commands to avoid the flesh of

9. This phenomenon in the Polish context is discussed in Alexander Guterman, "Three Generations of Warsaw Assimilationists and Their Attitude toward Conversion, 1820–1918" (in Hebrew), *Gal-Ed* 12 (1991): 57–77 (Hebrew numeration).

10. Michael Stanislawski, *For Whom Do I Toil? Judah Leib Gordon and the Crisis of Russian Jewry* (New York, 1988), 50–52.

certain animals, to abstain from labor on the Sabbath, or to dress in a modest and traditional manner.

All of this is not to say, of course, that assimilation (even in the extreme sense of retaining only the Jewish *religion* while taking on the surrounding population's *culture*) was impossible, but the great difficulty of balancing Jewish and "European" identity should not be underestimated; both progressive Europeans and Jews certainly did not adequately appreciate this in the nineteenth century.[11] One indication of this difficulty was the tendency, documented by Aleksander Guterman and others, for cultural assimilation (i.e., learning Polish and outwardly conforming to Polish norms of dress and behavior) of the first generation to "culminate" in conversion and a total loss of Jewishness in the second or third. Consider the lament of Aleksander Kraushar in 1886: "What kind of future awaits my poor child? He was born a Pole, the Muscovites demand that he be a Muscovite, [the antisemite] Jeleński forbids him to be a Pole, he doesn't want to be a German, and he's incapable of being a Jew [żydem już być nie może]."[12]

Even the definition of the term "assimilation" is vague and changing, covering a range of meanings from total cultural and ethnic extinction ("total assimilation") to a creative integration of Jewish and non-Jewish cultures embodied in such figures as Moses Mendelssohn and Judah Leib Gordon.[13] The distinction between "assimilation" and "acculturation" has been proposed to designate two quite dissimilar processes: one that sees Judaism as exclusively a religious matter, the other retaining a broader conception of Jewish identity and culture but taking on many aspects of surrounding culture and language.[14] In the context of Eastern Europe, however, I question the utility of this distinction. The Polish term *asymilacja*, it seems to me, was used from the 1850s to the early twentieth century in a rather imprecise manner, probably quite unconsciously. In the 1860s, for example, the idea that Polish Jews as a community would completely shed their language, distinct cultural markers, and way of life was obviously utopian. In such a context, "assimilation" could mean only the absorption of a certain level of the surrounding Polish culture: for example, language and possibly, in some modest respect, attire. In any case, although some individuals foresaw the gradual total absorption of Jews into

11. On assimilation in the European context, see (inter alia), *Assimilation and Community: The Jews in Nineteenth-Century Europe*, ed. Jonathan Frankel and Steven J. Zipperstein (Cambridge, U.K., 1992); and *Jewish Assimilation in Modern Times*, ed. Bela Vago (Boulder, Colo., 1981). The latter volume contains a suggestive though short and necessarily general article by Ezra Mendelsohn, "A Note on Jewish Assimilation in Polish Lands," 141–49.

12. Originally published in *Kraj*, 1886, quoted in Jan Kołodziejczyk, *Jan Bloch (1836–1902): Szkic do portretu "Króla polskich kolei"* (Warsaw, 1983), 180.

13. For a recent discussion of Mendelssohn and the Haskalah ("enlightenment") movement, see David Sorkin, *Moses Mendelssohn and the Religious Enlightenment* (Berkeley, Calif., 1996).

14. The first to make this distinction (acculturation vs. assimilation) was apparently Milton M. Gordon in *Assimilation in American Life: The Role of Race, Religion, and National Origins* (New York, 1964).

European nations, theirs was a minority opinion.[15] Even the weekly *Izraelita*, the foremost "assimilationist" journal in Poland from the later 1860s to the eve of World War I, aimed not at an obliteration of Jewishness but at the transformation and further development of Jewish religious and cultural traditions as "Poles of the Mosaic Law." Here "integrationist"—a term preferred by Ezra Mendelsohn—seems closer to the mark than "assimilationist," with its implication of total cultural and ethnic effacement.[16]

Alina Cała has pointed out the imprecision of the concept of assimilation at the time: "Approaches to it were, on the whole, intuitive. Assimilation, many publicists assumed, meant the same as the attainment of citizenship, emancipation or, for that matter, progress."[17] While agreeing with this statement on the whole, I would shift the emphasis: contemporary Poles (and progressive Jews) tended to see the processes of political emancipation, modernization, and cultural assimilation as inextricably and inevitably intertwined. When it became clear, during the last decades of the nineteenth century, that Jews were becoming "modern" (modifying religious observance, dressing in "Western" garb) yet holding fast to Jewish identity, the Polish reaction was one of surprise and, soon thereafter, anger. Polish dissatisfaction at "Jewish separatism" revealed a fundamental lack of respect for Jewish culture, based primarily on ignorance and a Christian-European feeling of superiority that was all but universal in this period.[18]

A further complication of assimilation in the context of the Russian Empire was the subordinate position of Polish culture within that state. Traditionally Jews had followed the precept that "the law of the state is the law": that is, Jews too must obey the laws of the state where they reside. But political power had been taken from the Poles and was firmly in the hands of the Russians. Culturally and even economically, Jews who wished to prosper needed to know Russian—the only language, for example, used in education above the primary level. During this period, assimilation also affected Russian Jewry; take the example of Lev Trotsky (born Lev Davidovich Bronstein in 1879).[19] By the early twentieth century a thriving community of Russian-speaking Jews existed in many cities of the Pale of Settlement and in the Russian interior, a

15. On two such figures, see Ezra Mendelsohn, "Jewish Assimilation in Lvov: The Case of Wilhelm Freidman," *Slavic Review* 28, no. 4 (December 1969): 577–90; and Jacob Shatzky, "Alexander Kraushar and his Road to Total Assimilation," *YIVO Annual of Jewish Social Science* 7 (1952): 146–74.

16. Ezra Mendelsohn, *On Modern Jewish Politics* (New York, 1993), 16.

17. Alina Cała, "The Question of Assimilation of Jews in the Polish Kingdom (1864–1897): An Interpretive Essay," *Polin* 1 (1986): 131. This short essay is an attempt to sum up the conclusions reached in Cała's detailed and pathbreaking *Asymilacja Żydów w Królestwie Polskim (1864–1897)* (Warsaw, 1989).

18. Some of these ideas are developed further in Theodore R. Weeks, "Poles, Jews, and Russians, 1863–1914: The Death of the Ideal of Assimilation in the Kingdom of Poland," *Polin* 12 (1999): 242–56.

19. On the Russian case, see the stimulating work by Benjamin Nathans, *Beyond the Pale: The Jewish Encounter with Late Imperial Russia* (Berkeley, Calif., 2002).

community which, even when rejecting the political status quo (Trotsky again), accepted the Russian language.

Poles could view such a development only with suspicion and fear, in particular as a threatening precedent for the Jews of ethnic Poland.[20] Polish irritation at the failure of the "Jewish question" to solve itself was thus considerably exacerbated by the widespread feeling that Jewish migrants from the Pale (generally termed "Litwacy" or Litvaks) to Warsaw and other Polish cities served (consciously or otherwise) as agents of Russification. The perception of the Jew as St. Petersburg's ally helped to propel Polish-Jewish relations over the abyss after 1905 and utterly to discredit assimilation—at least as a conscious program of Jewish integration into the Polish nation. After that point, the only kind of assimilation still possible was an absolute and unconditional denunciation of one's roots: only the Jew turned antisemite could be accepted fully into the Polish national community.[21]

This is not, of course, to suggest that Jews after 1905 failed to assimilate in the sense of learning Polish, donning modern fashions, or participating in Polish political and cultural life in the interwar period. In fact, a quick look at photographs of Polish-Jewish communities taken in the 1930s shows the opposite to be the case. Jews certainly learned Polish, became less religiously observant, and "blended" more easily with their Christian neighbors in the two generations between 1905 and the Shoah. In describing Wilno in 1938, Lucy Dawidowicz notes that most middle-class Jews spoke Polish—if perhaps with an accent—and were trying to adapt to the modern world, "in search of ways to reconcile their dual identity as Jews and as Poles."[22] On the other hand, one finds scant evidence in the post-1905 years of assimilation in the sense of becoming integrated into the Polish nation or—crucially—having even a Polish-Jewish identity validated by their non-Jewish neighbors. That is the true meaning of assimilation's failure.

Antisemitism

The failure of assimilation, one may posit, helped pave the way for the growth of modern antisemitism. Or, alternatively, one may blame antisemitism for cre-

---

20. Although Poles never constituted more than a few percent of the total population in the Pale of Settlement, most of that area had belonged before 1772 to the Polish-Lithuanian state, and high culture continued to be dominated (in particular in the Northwest Belarusian and Lithuanian provinces) by Polish even to the early twentieth century. The Polish national poet Adam Mickiewicz also came from "Lithuania" (in the geographical, not the ethnic sense).

21. There were, of course, Poles who even up to 1914 (and beyond) continued to advocate more humane relations based on bilateral Polish-Jewish respect. In particular after 1912, however, in Polish society the dominant opinion toward the Jews was a far more chauvinistic and hostile one—which nonetheless never entirely excluded the possibility of individual assimilation, though under the condition of breaking one's ties with all things Jewish.

22. Lucy Dawidowicz, *From That Place and Time: A Memoir, 1938–1947* (New York, 1989), 107.

ating an atmosphere in which assimilation could not prosper. Whichever factor is placed first, it is clear that the two cannot be separated. The term "anti-semitism" is generally traced to 1870, when it was coined by the Judeopho-bic journalist Wilhelm Marr to describe a nonreligious movement—advocated by Marr and others like him—aimed against the Jews. While some have attempted to link up "antisemitism" with a Judeophobia dating back to the early Christian church and even to pagan times, most scholars see a signifi-cant and ominous shift among the "haters of Israel" during the second half of the nineteenth century.[23] Up to that point, hatred of the Jews had been based primarily on religious grounds: the Jews refused to acknowledge and accept the new covenant of Jesus Christ or, in the more radical version, were them-selves responsible for his crucifixion. Now stress shifted to the alleged delete-rious effects of Jewish penetration into modern life. Jewish involvement in the press, stock exchange, commerce, and politics took on a far greater impor-tance than (to take just one medieval charge) the "blood libel," the accusa-tion that Jews used Christian blood in the making of Passover matzos.

In the context of East-Central Europe and especially the Russian Empire, the distinction between religious Judeophobia and mainly secular, often racist antisemitism does not always work. After all, to bring up the grotesque example of the blood libel, the unfortunate Mendel Beilis was tried for pre-cisely this crime in Kiev barely a year before the outbreak of World War I.[24] Indeed, even after the Holocaust at least one researcher found that Polish folk prejudices against Jews continued to exhibit a very strong religious element.[25] On the one hand this is hardly surprising: at the turn of the century most Poles were peasants, illiterate or semiliterate, and very devoted to the Catholic Church. The main Polish antisemites, however, were not peasants themselves, or writing for a peasant audience; they were middle-class men (rarely women). And despite their "all-Polish" rhetoric, they were not particularly successful in gaining peasant support for their movement, even in the interwar years. Speaking in general terms, even though Polish peasants certainly didn't see Jews as their brothers or potential Polish compatriots, neither were many peas-ants active antisemites. Bad or good, Jews simply belonged to the landscape that the Polish peasant inhabited.

Polish antisemitism could not avoid Western influences. Although Catholi-cism certainly played a far more important role in the ideology of Polish anti-

23. On Wilhelm Marr, see Mosche Zimmermann, *Wilhelm Marr: The Patriarch of Anti-semitism* (New York, 1986). For a highly interesting attempt to argue the case of continuity between religious (medieval) Judeophobia and modern antisemitism, see Gavin Langmuir, *Toward a Definition of Antisemitism* (Berkeley, Calif., 1990).

24. On the Beilis trial, which ended in acquittal for Beilis (although the peasant jurors insisted that a ritual murder had taken place, despite all evidence to the contrary), see Hans Rogger, "The Beilis Case: Anti-Semitism and Politics in the Reign of Nicholas II," in his *Jewish Policies and Right-Wing Politics in Imperial Russia* (Berkeley, Calif., 1986), 40–55 and Albert S. Lindemann, *The Jew Accused: Three Anti-Semitic Affairs; Dreyfus, Beilis, Frank, 1894–1915* (Cambridge, U.K., 1991).

25. Alina Cała, *Wizerunek Żyda w polskiej kulturze ludowej* (Warsaw, 1992).

semitism than in Germany, Austria, or France, the image of the Jewish capi-talist, journalist, and "free thinker" began to appear in Poland, too.[26] No less important, the social disruption engendered by the birth pains of capitalism in the Kingdom of Poland encouraged the search for scapegoats, and the highly visible Jewish community was only too convenient a selection. At times it is difficult in Polish anti-Jewish rhetoric to distinguish actual Jews engaged in moneylending, retail sales, and the like from the image of "Jew" as a metaphor for modernity: loving money, breaking down old social hierarchies and iden-tities, dominating the press, and spreading socialism.

Antisemitism appears to have been endemic in late nineteenth-century Europe.[27] Generally speaking, scholars accept that the rise of modern, nonre-ligious antisemitism is linked with at least two larger phenomena: the legal emancipation of European Jewry and "modernization"—a term that brings together a number of factors, including industrialization on the economic front, democratization on the political, and secularization on the spiritual. As far as the law went, in the 1860s Jews in Prussia and Austria were granted equality in most respects. The Jews resident in the Kingdom of Poland, though not those living in the Russian Pale of Settlement, were granted legal emanci-pation in 1862.[28] A generation or two later, many Polish antisemites would argue that the "prematurity" of this law had severely strained Polish-Jewish relations because Jews had exploited their equal rights to enrich themselves, primarily at the expense of Poles. In fact, legal equality remained for most Polish Jews something of a fiction, as restrictions on Jewish entry into higher education and government employment continued to be practiced. This reality, however, did not prevent Polish antisemites from claiming that Jews enjoyed "double rights": as Jews (in the form of being allowed separate Jewish schools and community organizations) and as "citizens."

Modernization

From Berlin to Moscow the years 1855–1914 witnessed a boom in railroad building, the rapid development of textile and other industries, and a rise in literacy (in particular in the second half of this period). Nowhere were the

26. On one of the earliest Polish antisemites who deemphasized the religious issue, see Theodore Weeks, "The 'International Jewish Conspiracy' Reaches Poland: Teodor Jeske-Choiński and His Works," *East European Quarterly* 31, no. 1 (March 1997): 21–41.

27. For an excellent general history of the phenomenon, see Léon Poliakov, *The History of Anti-Semitism*, trans. Miriam Kochan, 4 vols. (New York, 1965–85). Other basic sources are the many works of Shmuel Ettinger, most of which have not been translated from Hebrew: e.g., *Ha-anti-shemiut ba-et ha-hadasha* (Tel Aviv, 1978). A recent and controversial look at the rise of antisemitism as a reaction to the "rise of the Jews" is Albert S. Lindemann, *Esau's Tears: Modern Anti-Semitism and the Rise of the Jews* (Cambridge, U.K., 1997).

28. The generations-long discussions that culminated in the law of June 5, 1862, are discussed in Artur Eisenbach, *The Emancipation of the Jews in Poland, 1770–1870* (Oxford, 1991).

changes wrought by such modernization more evident than in Russian Poland, where cities like Warsaw and Łódź grew at breakneck speed, bringing hundreds of thousands of peasant Poles and impoverished Jews (not a few from the bordering Lithuanian and Ukrainian provinces) into these Polish boomtowns. At least one researcher has made the argument that conservative fear of change formed the largest single element in the growth of antisemitism in late Imperial Russia.[29] And conservatives were indeed eager to make use of the Jewish scapegoat in their campaign against social and political change, but that is only one part of the story: in the Polish context, the most conservative element, the so-called Realists, were in fact quite reluctant to play the Jewish card, whereas progressive and at least ostensibly democratic groups such as the National Democrats spearheaded anti-Jewish rhetoric and action.

Modernization means many things: urbanization, technological advances, the rise of "the masses" in both political and economic terms, the advance of the secular over the religious.[30] In all these areas the Polish lands did modernize in the second half of the nineteenth century. Warsaw almost quadrupled in size between 1850 and 1914, and Łódź expanded almost tenfold.[31] The Polish capital was connected to St. Petersburg by rail in 1862 (a connection already existed to Vienna), and the railroad net expanded considerably in the ensuing half-century. Not incidentally, Jews played a very significant and visible role in financing and building the railways. As large-scale manufacturing and modern transport expanded, many Jewish peddlers, carters, and petty retailers—finding their livelihoods directly threatened—would be forced to abandon their villages and join the exodus to the growing industrial cities.[32] In the Austrian and Prussian partitions, however, much less change took place: that is, industrialization drove Jews out of their shtetls, too, but it drew them to Vienna, Budapest, Berlin, the Rhineland—not to Lwów or Poznań.

In the cities, the traditional separation of religious groups was harder to maintain. To be sure, Jews congregated in certain parts of towns—Nalewki

29. Heinz Dietrich Löwe, *Antisemitismus und reaktionäre Utopie: Russischer Konservatismus im Kampf gegen den Wandel von Staat und Gesellschaft, 1890–1917* (Hamburg, 1978). The book, somewhat amplified, has also appeared in English translation as *The Tsar and the Jews: Reform, Reaction, and Antisemitism in Imperial Russia, 1772–1917* (Chur, Switz., 1992).

30. A brilliant study of Polish intellectuals' attempts to deal with the challenge of modernity in the nineteenth century (concentrating on the first half of the century and ending in the 1880s) is Jerzy Jedlicki, *A Suburb of Europe: Nineteenth-Century Polish Approaches to Western Civilization* (Budapest, 1999), originally published under the title *Jakiej cywilizacji Polacy potrzebują* (Warsaw, 1988).

31. Stephen D. Corrsin, "Warsaw: Poles and Jews in a Conquered City," in *The City in Late Imperial Russia*, ed. Michael F. Hamm (Bloomington, Ind., 1986), 127; Wiesław Puś, "The Development of the City of Łódź," *Polin* 6 (1991): 7, 11–12.

32. For an excellent discussion of "modernizing" in Warsaw and Russian Poland around the turn of the century and the rise of Polish antisemitism, see Robert Blobaum, "The Politics of Antisemitism in Fin-de-Siècle Warsaw," *Journal of Modern History* 73, no. 2 (2001): 275–306.

Street in Warsaw is the most famous example[33] —but on a day-to-day basis Jews and Christians came into contact with each other more and more. By the early twentieth century it was no longer so easy to distinguish Jews, in particular those from the educated middle class, from Poles. This "blurring of categories" was denounced by antisemites in the same terms of outrage that conservatives bewailed the tendency of servant girls to dress like their mistresses: in both cases, old categories and distinctions were being rubbed out. It needs to be remembered that in this period both "Polish" and "Jewish" identities were being challenged. Not by chance was one of Polish nationalism's canonical texts titled *Thoughts of a Modern Pole* (1903). In this work, the National Democrat Roman Dmowski sketched out a modern Polish nation defined not by Catholic faith and *szlachta* (noble) blood but by a strong middle class and shared national feeling. Attempting to forge a secular—or at least "modern religious"—Jewish identity was even more difficult, although Theodor Herzl's *Jewish State* (1896) and modern Zionism were precisely steps in that direction. Along with economic and social dislocation, modernization called into question traditional religious and national-religious categories. The challenging of accepted identities was perhaps the single most important effect of modernization on Polish-Jewish relations.

What Went Wrong? Some Tentative Conclusions

Throughout the nineteenth century, Poles felt themselves to be under threat as a national and cultural entity. Having lost their political independence at the end of the eighteenth century, they formed an anomaly in East-Central Europe. To be sure, many "nations without states" lived in the region during this era. In no other case, however, did a nation develop sophisticated high culture and political independence in the early modern period only to be subjugated politically precisely at the time of the French Revolution, as ideologies of modern nationhood were developing. This peculiar historical circumstance, combined with the very large numbers of Jews living on historical Polish lands, cannot be ignored when considering the direction in which Polish-Jewish relations developed.

In the pre-modern Polish Commonwealth (*Rzeczpospolita*), Jews had lived more or less autonomously among their Polish (and Lithuanian and Belarusian) neighbors. In a society dominated by estate structures and noble privileges, as the Commonwealth was, the separateness of Jews was not a problem. Each estate—and the Jews were one, for all intents and purposes—lived according to its own duties and privileges. It was only with the coming of

---

33. For a memoir of a slightly later period, see Bernard Singer (born 1893), *Moje Nalewki*, 2d ed. (Warsaw, 1993).

modern ideologies of democratic, homogeneous national societies—ideologies that had begun to filter eastward in the late eighteenth century—that the separate corporate existence of the Jewish community in Poland began to be seen as a problem in and of itself. In other words, only when Polish society (which in this context meant, of course, noble society) began to posit the need for a relatively fluid, uniform, and "democratic" (at least in the sense of abolishing estate-based rights and privileges) Polish nation did the Jewish question assume new and crucial significance. Rather than a primarily religious problem, now the Jews posed a *national* conundrum for Polish society. Simply put, the question that arose in the last decade of the eighteenth century was how to incorporate Jews into the Polish nation (or "society"—in the 1790s these terms were often used interchangeably).

Such issues, it must be admitted, concerned only a small number of Poles—even of educated Poles—until the mid-nineteenth century. From that point on, however, and with growing intensity from the 1880s, Polish society could not ignore the Jewish question. In the earlier period, at least to the 1870s, Polish society (the peasantry, of course, is a different matter entirely) generally supported the solution loosely termed assimilation; that is, as education and knowledge of Polish culture spread, Jews would shed "medieval" practices and, outside of the religious sphere, become more or less indistinguishable from Poles. The idea of Poles and Jews sharing common interests as mutual inhabitants of one country reached its apex during the January Insurrection of 1863, when in Warsaw—but also in other localities—Polish and Jewish demonstrators *together* opposed Russian occupation and repressive policies. The broad masses of Jews did not participate directly in the uprising, as was noted at the time, but neither did most Polish peasants. As the positivists later noted, although the peasantry and Orthodox Jews both remained outside the Polish nation, education and progress would gradually "lift" both groups into a consciousness of Polish identity.

From the start, assimilation presumed an inherent superiority of Polish or "European" culture over "Asiatic" Jewish customs. Even a writer as sympathetic to the Jews as Eliza Orzeszkowa clearly expected that over time, Jews would alter their religious practices, shed "superstitions," and recognize the greater "logic" and attractiveness of modern Polish culture (itself only just developing in those years). Assimilation always retained a colonial aspect, the presumption of a more advanced, superior culture (Polish/European) "generously allowing" a more backward group to join it. It must be stressed that the negative views of traditional Jewish culture were expressed not so much by antisemites—who took such things for granted—but by liberals who compared today's backwardness with tomorrow's enlightenment. In an earlier period such an ideology might well have succeeded; after all, in many ways the French, for example, did succeed in assimilating or at least subordinating regional ethnic, linguistic, and (pagan) religious differences. In the late nineteenth century, however, when Polish culture was itself under attack from

Russian officialdom, the chances of large numbers of Jews accepting the Polish "offer" of a superior culture were, to say the least, very slim indeed.

The political and cultural position of the Poles is thus of crucial importance. The majority of Poles lived within the Russian Empire, where the threat to Polish culture was arguably the greatest. Although Prussian policies resembled those farther east in anti-Polish content and possibly exceeded Russian measures in the amount of government resources expended upon them, the cultural importance of Prussian Poland paled when compared with that of the Kingdom of Poland. Meanwhile, from the later 1860s the province of Austrian Galicia enjoyed autonomy, with Poles dominating local politics and culture. Thus it was the context of Russian Poland during the two generations after the crushing of the 1863 insurrection that set the tone for modern Polish nationalism and Polish-Jewish relations.

After 1863 Polish society perceived, rightly or wrongly, an existential threat to its further cultural development. Under Russian rule, Poles were deprived—at least until 1905—of all control over instruments of cultural replication and national indoctrination (to put matters baldly): the school system was dominated by the Russian language and even imported Russian teachers; no Polish-language university was allowed in the Empire; private education was forbidden; and even the use of Polish in public and official places was curtailed. To be sure, many of these restrictions were not enforced with particular efficiency (this was, after all, the Russian Empire), but the moral impact was the same: in a period of burgeoning national feeling, Polish society in the Russian Empire lacked the most basic institutions of cultural development. It is hardly surprising that at the time and in retrospect, many Poles viewed this period of Russification as an all-out attempt by St. Petersburg to prevent the development of a modern Polish nation.

Fears for their own cultural development help to explain some of the stridency of Polish reactions to any Jewish reservations toward the cultural "offer" presumed by assimilation. It was far easier to accept an abstraction like "assimilation" or "modernization" than the real-life complications and contradictions of Jews who took on Polish culture. It was easy to point out the personal limitations of specific individuals and extrapolate these to "prove" the failure of assimilation. But in fact, even the most liberal Poles rarely stopped to question exactly why Jews should adopt Polish culture in the first place. After all, Polish culture did not enjoy the international prestige of, say, its French or German counterparts, and from a practical point of view Russian culture would have been more immediately useful. Further complicating the situation was the growth of Jewish national consciousness from the 1880s, and the very notion of Jews as a modern nation—not simply a religious group—violated the conceptual categories held dear by nearly all members of Polish society. The very novelty of this concept rendered it impossible to accept for nearly all non-Jewish contemporaries, from Aleksander Świętochowski to Eliza Orzeszkowa to Stalin. How on earth could the Jews, lacking their own territory, national culture, or even language (so it was argued), constitute a nation? Through the outrage and anger expressed against Jewish nationalism one senses profound feelings of betrayal: we (Poles) offered them what is most sacred to us, and they rejected us.

By the eve of World War I, relations between Poles and Jews had become extremely strained, and in a certain sense they never recovered. It needs to be emphasized once again that no one factor caused Polish-Jewish relations to go sour, nor was this development inevitable. Several long-term factors from the 1860s, however, combined to increase strains between Poles and Jews, among them, economic change, political and cultural repression, and the general intensification of national consciousness during the period—which affected not just Russians, Poles, and Jews but similarly Latvians, Lithuanians, Ukrainians, and many other groups. These long-term factors served to "turn up the heat," so to speak, in interethnic relations (compare, for example, contemporary Estonian-German or Lithuanian-Polish controversies).

One "large" and one "small" event brought Polish-Jewish relations to the boiling point. The "large" event was the 1905 Revolution or, more precisely, the disappointment at its failure to deliver on Polish aspirations. This intense disappointment, combined with a general perception that Jews now opposed Polish interests, paved the way for a "small" event: the Fourth Duma elections in Warsaw, which ended in the general Polish boycott of Jews. Considering how little the Polish representatives in the Third Duma (1907–1912) had accomplished, it might seem absurd that anyone cared who represented Warsaw in the Russian semiparliament. But Poles, of course, cared very much indeed because of the symbolic value of Warsaw as the capital of a country that existed only in the hearts of Polish patriots. Thus when Jewish electors in Warsaw demurred at the idea of sending to St. Petersburg a representative who would not promise to uphold Jewish equal rights, their rather timid protest unleashed massive outrage in Polish society, including its liberal segments.[34]

Economic change in the Kingdom of Poland brought together large numbers of Poles (of peasant origin) and Jews (coming from impoverished shtetls) in growing industrial cities such as Warsaw and Łódź. Even more important, industrialization, the opening of railroads, and the inclusion of Russian Poland in a larger economic system directly threatened the livelihoods of both Polish peasants and traditional Jews. This economic shift was even more threatening for the cultural and everyday life of Poland's Jews. Traditional Jewish religious practices had been predicated on a close-knit, relatively unchanging local com-

34. On the 1912 Duma election, see the articles by Stephen D. Corrsin, "Polish-Jewish Relations before the First World War: The Case of the State Duma Elections in Warsaw," *Gal-Ed* 11 (1989): 46–53, and "The Jews, the Left and the State Duma Elections in Warsaw in 1912: Selected Sources," *Polin* 9 (1996): 45–54. For background on the long-simmering issues that "came to a boil" in 1912, see Theodore R. Weeks, *Nation and State in Late Imperial Russia: Nationalism and Russification on the Western Frontier, 1863–1914* (Dekalb Ill. 1996), 152–71.

munity, but now families were forced to emigrate to cities or even abroad, and individuals left their communities to seek a livelihood in the cities. As economic imperatives forced individuals to leave their birthplaces, they were exposed to new influences and ideas—all of which called into question traditional practices and authority. The development of modern Jewish nationalism may be seen as a reaction to this breakdown (or the perceptions of a future breakdown; one should not exaggerate the frailty of the traditional communities before the twentieth century) and an attempt to create a form of identity better attuned to modern life.

Poles as well certainly felt the disruption of economic change as millions of them emigrated to cities and the New World, or worked as seasonal laborers in the Prussian Empire. That bulwark of Polish identity, the Catholic Church, clearly perceived its own position as under threat from "modernity," as is reflected in both the reactionary assertions of Pope Pius IX and the attempts at reconciliation by his successor, Leo XIII. Certainly the temptation was great for patriotic Polish priests to locate the ills of "modernity" in one concrete and easily identifiable figure: the Jew. Throughout his career the clerical antisemite Jan Jeleński emphasized the fusion of economic and religious struggle against the Jews. As good Catholics, Jeleński argued, Polish peasants must isolate themselves from Jewish economic interests and strengthen themselves by founding their own Polish cooperatives, savings banks, and stores. In a land where petty commerce and retailing were overwhelmingly dominated by Jews, the economic arguments of Jeleński must have made sense to more than a few Poles. Along similar lines, the entry of (relatively) large numbers of Jews into the free professions in the late nineteenth century could be perceived as a direct threat to Polish livelihoods and hence, in Roman Dmowski's formulation, a weakening of the very sociological foundations of the Polish nation. Following such arguments, the health of the Polish nation was dependent upon Polonizing commerce, trade, banking—in short, the middle classes.

All these socioeconomic arguments played out against the background of a highly unfavorable political situation. The Russian authorities were deeply suspicious of Poles and Polish culture and, it must be said, equally distrustful of Jews. After 1863, Poles were never the "masters" in the Kingdom of Poland, despite their overwhelming numerical and cultural presence there. Although few—either Polish or Russian—seriously thought that the Russians could really Russify the Polish nation, there was nonetheless the threat that they might stunt and retard its "healthy development." One of the fundamental assumptions of assimilation was that Jews would help strengthen the Polish position; it was explicitly for this reason that Marquis Aleksander Wielopolski had pushed for the Jewish civil equality, which was granted in 1862. Following such logic, the Poles "needed" the Jews as allies against Russian predominance. By the end of the century, however, Polish society was increasingly viewing the Jews as either indifferent to Polish interests or actively conspiring against them. Fatally, this perception was considerably strengthened after the failed revolution of 1905, in particular with the spread of accusations that Jews coming from the Pale (the so-called Litvaks) were consciously spreading the Russian language, to the detriment of Polish.

Intensification of national consciousness and the spread of nationalist assumptions were general throughout Europe in the nineteenth century, particularly in its second half. In the repressive antidemocratic and antinational (even anti-Russian-nationalist!) atmosphere of the Russian Empire, national sentiment developed all the more fervently in the face of government suspicion and restrictive policies. The new forms of national identity—both Polish and Jewish—developed closely intertwined with democratic and even socialist movements. The Polish Socialist Party specifically called for the resurrection of an independent Polish state, though with full toleration and even autonomy for non-Poles. The National Democrats (whose name we should take seriously) rejected as impractical such national tolerance, pursuing a more Spencerian line of aggressive, exclusionary nationalism. But one should not lose sight of the fact that modern nationalism, whether "liberal" or "integral," *must* define the limits of the nation. By defining who is "in," modern nationalism also excludes. The National Democrats were quite forthright in their exclusion of Jews (with few exceptions) from the Polish nation. But *any* definition of a nation must ipso facto exclude, and by the late nineteenth century it was questionable indeed whether the Jewish community in Poland was truly interested in abandoning its own cultural (or "national") characteristics in favor of Polish culture. Thus some form of friction was to be expected.

This is not to say that a rupture in relations and generalized mutual hostility had to triumph; nevertheless, the historical fact remains that by 1913 few positive signs of Polish-Jewish cooperation could be discerned. The outbreak of World War I the following year prevented the breach from healing, and the short and troubled period of interwar Polish independence brought little relief. Only time could have healed Polish-Jewish relations or at least allowed some sort of compromise solution to develop. Instead, the murderous Nazi occupation destroyed Poland's Jewish community. We should not, indeed must not, draw a direct line between the anti-Jewish boycott of 1912–14 and genocide. We must remember that Polish antisemites—Jeleński and Dmowski, for example—always condemned physical violence toward the Jews. For all their faults, Polish antisemites, unlike the Nazis, had not entirely discarded that quintessentially Jewish list of precepts, the Ten Commandments. And yet, by refusing to recognize for Jews the national rights they demanded for themselves, Polish antisemites certainly do bear the guilt of encouraging indifferent, hostile, and even murderous (one thinks of Jedwabne) Polish attitudes toward their Jewish neighbors under Nazi occupation.

Some Poles, like Kazimierz Kelles-Krauz and Jan Baudouin de Courtenay, had spoken eloquently in favor of some kind of Polish-Jewish condominium that would have respected the cultural and national differences of both sides.[35] Again it must be admitted, however, that two swallows do not make a spring; in a period of anti-Polish cultural repression, few members of Polish society were ready to complicate the issue by attempting any such creative negotiation. Several generations later, it is both superfluous and self-indulgent to concentrate overmuch on "what the Poles—or Jews—should have done." Rather, may their long-past shortsightedness and moral shortcomings serve as a negative lesson for all of us as we interact with ethnic and religious "others."

35. Timothy Snyder, *Nationalism, Marxism, and Modern Central Europe: A Biography of Kazimierz Kelles-Krauz (1872–1905)* (Cambridge, Mass., 1997). Baudouin de Courtenay, linguist and free-thinker, deserves more scholarly attention; meanwhile, see Robert A. Rothstein, "The Linguist as Dissenter: Jan Baudouin de Courtenay," in *For Victor Weintraub: Essays in Polish Literature, Language, and History, Presented on the Occasion of his Sixty-Fifth Birthday* (The Hague, 1975), 391–405; and Jan Baudouin de Courtenay, *W kwestji żydowskiej: Odczyt wygłoszony w Warszawie 7 lutego 1913 r.* (Warsaw, 1913).

2

Jews as Middleman Minorities in Rural Poland

Understanding the Galician Pogroms of 1898

KEELY STAUTER-HALSTED

In June of 1898 the thirty-three western districts of Austrian Galicia erupted in a wave of violence against Jewish establishments. Beginning in the district of Myślenice, south of Kraków, on the eve of the Corpus Christi holiday, landless laborers and local artisans smashed windows in Jewish homes and taverns. Farmers from villages surrounding the market town of Kołaczyce, Jasło district, gathered the next day to plot revenge for the arrest of several potters accused of planning similar disruptions. They formed roving bands that looted and destroyed taverns in villages on the outskirts of Jasło and set fire to a distillery the night of June 11. By June 13 the rioters' targets had expanded to include manorial offices of Jewish estate owners and managers. Oil workers in Gorlice district laid waste to a string of Jewish taverns, prompting the intervention of troops garrisoned in Nowy Sącz. Over the next several nights the violence spread to Krosno, Sanok, Łańcut, Jarosław, and Tarnów districts. Throughout the historically violent district of Nowy Sącz (locus of the peasant uprising of 1846), Jewish establishments were systematically

I am grateful for the support of the Frank and Adelaide Kussy Scholarship for the Study of the Holocaust, administered through James Madison College at Michigan State University, in researching this article. I also thank Kenneth Waltzer, Anna-Maria Orła-Bukowska, and Robert Blobaum for their commentary on earlier drafts, and Daniel Unowsky for help in understanding the 1896 imperial electoral reform.

demolished from June 19 to 24. Jews fled their taverns and shops to seek refuge with the Austrian army and gendarmerie. The governor of Nowy Sącz district threatened capital punishment for anyone caught and convicted of inciting riots. By the time the Austrian government imposed martial law at the end of the month, several dozen rioters had been killed and some 3,500 arrested. Over a thousand participants, Jews and Christians alike, would stand trial on charges of attempted murder, plunder, arson, and destruction of property.[1] The intensity of the anti-Jewish violence was unprecedented in Galician history and found little reflection in the crownland's major urban centers.[2] Instead, the unrest remained concentrated in the small towns and villages south and east of Kraków, many of them engaged in a heated campaign for a seat from the peasant curia to the Viennese *Reichsrat*.

The anti-Jewish attacks of 1898, signaling the eruption of new and dangerous forces in the Polish provinces, have yet to receive the level of historical attention granted the 1881 Russian pogroms, let alone to be treated as a defining moment in Jewish-Gentile relations in eastern Europe. Nonetheless, the varied backgrounds of the pogromists, combined with the widespread occurrence and relative simultaneity of the violence and its exclusive manifestation in the crownland's Polish settlements, point to an important realignment of social forces in the Polish countryside. This discussion is intended to map out the components of a changing landscape in provincial Polish-Jewish affairs at the turn of the twentieth century. The gangs of angry young men rampaging through the towns and villages of western Galicia were not driven by anti-Jewish homilies in parish churches, nor were they preoccupied with the racist rhetoric of contemporary social Darwinists. Their resentment was neither exclusively "medieval" in its religious impulse nor predominantly "modern" in its dependence on "scientific" racial epithets. Rather, the anti-Jewish animosity that burst forth during the summer of 1898 grew out of the rising economic tensions that characterized rural and small-town Poland. The profound contradiction that lower-class Poles were experiencing between their

1. *Związek Chłopski*, the newspaper edited by peasant deputy Stanisław Potoczek, provided a detailed account of the June disturbances (*rozruchy*) in the countryside, carefully chastising rioters for their displays of violence yet at the same time expressing sympathy with the mob's frustration with Jewish merchants and landholders; *Związek Chłopski* (July 1, 1898), 147–56. On specific sites of violence in this year, see Franciszek Bujak, *Żmiąca: Wieś powiatu Limanowskiego: Stosunki gospodarcze i społeczne* (Kraków, 1903), 105–7; Karoł Marcinkowski, *Krwawe niespory we Frysztaku w 1898 r.* (Philadelphia, 1983); and Zygmunt Hemmerling, "Stronnictwa ludowe wobec żydów i kwestii żydowskiej," *Kwartalnik Historyczny* 96, nos. 1–2 (1989): 160–61. The election districts in question were the south-central *powiaty* of Krosno, Jasło, Sanok, Dobromil, Stare Miasto, Lisko, and Brzozów.

2. Interestingly, no anti-Jewish excesses took place either during the peasant actions against manor houses in February 1846 or during the revolutions of 1848 in Galicia. Artur Eisenbach has argued that Galician Jews at this time may have enjoyed greater confidence among the peasants than did the landowning class; see his *The Emancipation of the Jews in Poland, 1780–1870* (Oxford, 1991), 348–50.

aspirations for social mobility, on the one hand, and the very real barriers to economic advancement, on the other, found reflection in increasingly self-conscious ethnic attachments. As economic deprivation came increasingly to be attributed to the advancement of the religious "other," mutual resentment and hostility bred a tinderbox atmosphere in which attacks on Jewish property could be conceived as acceptable. The antagonism directed against Jewish establishments displayed none of the exclusionary nationalist impulses of peasant activists a generation later, nor were Jewish individuals physically attacked as they would be during the pogroms of the Polish-Soviet War.[3] Instead, these property-oriented anti-Jewish excesses can be viewed as part of a transitional moment in the evolution of Jewish-Polish interactions before the First World War. Changing attitudes toward the Jews' status as economic middlemen meant that the 1898 violence unfolded as part of a sharp break in relations between lower-class Polish Christians and provincial Jews. A series of pointed anti-Jewish articles in the rural press combined with an election campaign focused on the Jews and a general atmosphere of legitimized public violence to create conditions in which the destruction of Jewish establishments was deemed an acceptable outlet for provincial frustrations.

The June days of 1898 are typically portrayed as part of an ongoing cycle of violence against Jews that include the Russian pogroms of the early 1880s and the Kishinev pogroms of 1903, each of which had reverberations in the Polish countryside. Historians have pinned responsibility for the 1898 events on the leadership of the newly founded Peasant Party (Stronnictwo Ludowe) and its explicitly antisemitic election campaign for seats in the Viennese Reichsrat. Months of speeches, public debates, and newspaper commentary stirred up an already hostile peasantry and laid the ground for the outbursts of public violence. Contemporary peasant observers, for their part, told of rumors circulating in the countryside that Crown Prince Rudolf was still alive, that the prince had warned of an impending Jewish attack against the emperor himself, and that he was authorizing two weeks (some said three months) of unchecked attacks on Jews.

Perhaps the most forceful linkage of the anti-Jewish attacks with the rise of the Peasant Party was made by contemporary historian Simon Dubnow, who wrote that in this election year "the candidate of the anti-Semitic People's Party, the Jesuit priest, [Stanisław] Stojałowski . . . carried on a wild agitation against Jews, which soon led to pogroms in thirty towns and villages of that region."[4] Stojałowski, according to Dubnow, "followed the customary strategy of the Christian Socialists, and he steered the discontent of the people

---

3. See, for example, Isaac Babel, *1920 Diary*, ed. Carol J. Avins (New Haven, 1995).

4. Father Stanisław Stojałowski, a former Jesuit, had actually been elected in 1897 but campaigned vigorously during the 1898 special election in support of Lewicki, a nonpeasant, against the more radical peasant Jan Stapiński; see Simon Dubnow, *History of the Jews from the Congress of Vienna to the Emergence of Hitler* (New Brunswick, N.J., 1973), 5:491–93.

against the Jews."[5] More recently, Piotr Wróbel has suggested that "peasant hostility toward the Jews" in 1898 was motivated "by political propaganda" and a sense of unfair economic competition.[6] Yet organized and explicitly anti-Jewish economic initiatives had circulated in the countryside since the early 1880s, with the birth of the agricultural cooperative movement, and peasant campaigns for political office had employed economics-based anti-Jewish rhetoric for decades.

Although the contentious campaign season and rumors of the archduke's return clearly played a role in encouraging the rioters, several deeply rooted causes help explain the breadth and passion of these anti-Jewish excesses. Ongoing perceptions of economic exploitation provided the backdrop to a more profound crisis of identity both within the Galician Jewish community and among Polish peasants. Jews had long functioned in an entrepreneurial capacity throughout the Polish lands, selling scarce manufactured goods and offering short-term loans to a cash-strapped peasantry. Under serfdom, Jews frequently served as estate managers (*arendarzy*) for absent landlords. With peasant emancipation in 1848 and the removal of legal restrictions on Jewish activities in the 1860s, however, the Jews' position as a middleman minority grew increasingly vulnerable. As Hillel Kieval has noted with reference to Ukrainian villagers: "To a ... peasant ... the fact that ... the innkeepers, moneylenders and estate managers spoke Yiddish ... and were Jews amounted to little more than an obvious description of the world. At crucial moments in time, though, a sea change occurs, as a result of which the very same traits are radically reinterpreted. ... By definition, they now are no longer 'natural,' and their main significance may also now be understood to lie in the realm of economics."[7] The latter years of the nineteenth century appear to have been one of the "crucial moments" that brought about a reinterpretation of Jewish cultural characteristics and helped convert the perceived status of Galician Jews from middleman minority to something more hostile and threatening.

Sweeping changes had come to the East-Central European socioeconomic landscape in the second half of the nineteenth century, causing strain on

5. Stojałowski led the first substantial effort to organize Galician Polish peasants politically, editing two newspapers for villagers (*Wieniec* and *Pszczółka*) beginning in 1875 and encouraging peasants to run for the Galician parliament after 1861. He was involved in efforts to establish a formal peasant political party, the Stronnictwo Ludowe in 1895, but soon left the party with his supporters to found the more socially conservative Christian Peasant Party (Stronnictwo Chrześcijańsko-Ludowe). For more on this complex character, see Keely Stauter-Halsted, *The Nation in the Village: The Genesis of Peasant National Identity in Austrian Poland, 1848–1914* (Ithaca, N.Y., 2001).

6. Piotr Wróbel, "The Jews of Galicia under Austrian-Polish Rule, 1869–1918," *Austrian History Yearbook* 25 (1994): 130–31.

7. Hillel Kieval, "Middleman Minorities and Blood," in *Essential Outsiders: Chinese and Jews in the Modern Transformation of Southeast Asia and Central Europe*, ed. Daniel Chirot and Anthony Reid (Seattle, 1997), 213.

Jewish-peasant relations. Peasant emancipation set off an intense battle for land in the overcrowded Galician countryside, a battle that reached its zenith after the late 1860s abolition of the final restrictions on the Jews' right to purchase property.[8] The absence of industry as an outlet for the overcrowded rural population left peasants and Jews alike with few options. Contemporary historian Simon Dubnow noted that in the early twentieth century, as "pauperism mounted from year to year . . . [Jews] were reduced to a state of poverty that was unknown anywhere else in Europe."[9] The misery of the Galician Jews was becoming legendary, with much of the crownland's Jewish community supported by donations from Viennese Jews.[10] Thousands of families each year emigrated to Palestine or America, yet this exodus had little effect in reducing the poverty of those who remained.[11] Conditions were so desperate that the numbers of Jews leaving Galicia (some 36,000 in the 1880s and 114,000 in the 1890s) made up a disproportionately high portion of total emigrants: 60 percent in the 1880s and 40 percent in the 1890s, although the Jews represented only 12 percent of the population.[12]

Galician peasants also saw their position reduced to that of paupers in these years. Over 80 percent of them subsisted on farms of less than five acres by 1899, and the population of embittered landless day laborers and servants was rising dramatically.[13] Peasants left Galicia in droves during the last two decades of the century, nearly 200,000 of them leaving behind unpaid debts to Jewish moneylenders as they relocated to North America.[14] Yet the rural population of Galicia increased dramatically, from 5.4 to 8 million inhabitants between 1869 and 1910, and Jews and Christians increasingly competed in trade, banking, handicrafts, and other nonagricultural niches.[15] Leaders of Polish peasant organizations and Jewish communities alike argued with increased stridency that their very survival depended on the expansion of their economic presence beyond their traditional occupations.

8. On the long and halting process of Jewish emancipation in the Polish lands, see Eisenbach, *Emancipation of the Jews.*

9. Other contemporary observers had similar comments about both Jewish and peasant society of the time; Dubnow, *History of the Jews,* 5:493.

10. Naftali Schipper, *Dzieje Żydów w Polsce oraz przegląd ich kultury duchowej (z uwzględniem krajów ościennych),* p. 2 (Lwów, 1927), 66.

11. Ibid., 96, 101; Ignacy Schiper, *Dzieje handlu żydowskiego na ziemach polskich* (Warsaw, 1937), 442–43.

12. Schiper, *Dzieje handlu żydowskiego,* 443.

13. Franciszek Bujak, "Wieś zachodnio-galicyjska u schyłku XIX wieku," in *Wybór pism,* vol. 2, *Z dziejów społecznych i gospodarczych Polski X–XX w.,* ed. Helena Madurowicz-Urbańska (Warsaw, 1976), 281–83; see also Stefan Inglot, *Historia chłopów polskich* (Warsaw, 1972), 248–56.

14. Emily Greene Balch, *Our Slavic Fellow Citizens* (New York, 1910), 137–40.

15. On population growth, see Bohdan Wasiutyński, *Ludność żydowska w Polsce w wiekach XIX i XX* (Warsaw, 1930); *Die Habsburgermonarchie 1848–1918,* ed. Adam Wandruszka and Peter Urbanitsch, vol. 3, *Die Volker des Reiches,* p. 2 (Vienna, 1980), 882–83; and Włodzimierz Wakar, *Rozwój terytorialny narodowości polskiej* (Kielce, 1918).

To be sure, Jews could be found at all rungs of the social hierarchy in late nineteenth-century Austrian Poland, an economic omnipresence that was not lost on lower-class Poles. Beginning with reforms introduced in 1859, Habsburg Jews were permitted to practice all artisan professions and to purchase real estate anywhere. The Austrian Constitution of 1867 granted equal civic rights to Jews, permitting them to serve on town councils and in other elected offices and eliminating all residence restrictions.[16] Jews were thus significant landholders in the last third of the century, owning up to 8 percent of the arable land in western Galicia and 14 percent in the eastern part of the crownland, in addition to renting or serving as managers on estates throughout the province. They were frequently elected to public office in these years; by 1874 some 83 percent of Galicia's three hundred city councils had Jewish representation, and ten cities in Galicia had elected Jewish mayors.[17] Thus, despite the continued limitations on Jewish social mobility—reflected in the underrepresentation of Jews in the Polish civil service and in universities—and the economic pressures placed on them by peasant competition in certain fields, Galician Christians may well have perceived the Jewish position as one of economic success. To emancipated peasants who faced land shortages, growing prices for arable land, and difficulty breaking into trade, Jews appeared to be enjoying a more fluid economic status.

From the 1870s on, then, a combination of land hunger, redoubled efforts to enter trade and handicraft professions, and a general competition for scarce rural resources increased the mutual resentment between the two groups. The pattern of transitional group identities and parallel but conflicting attempts to bring about economic improvements confounded relations, setting the stage for the violence of June 1898. Economic expectations in both communities, in turn, were tied to expanding ethnic identities: peasants came to view themselves as members of the Polish nation (partly through the engine of the new peasant party, Stronnictwo Ludowe) and notions of Zionism began to circulate among rural Jews.[18] The evolving sense of national Polish identity helped to harden attitudes toward ethnic "outsiders." The Jews who, functioning as an entrepreneurial minority, had earlier "been seen as just one among many ethnic groups that existed in complex pre-modern agrarian societies" as sociologist Daniel Chirot argues, "now became in the eyes of these new nationalists, something more threatening."[19] For peasants and Jews alike, then, pressure for social and economic mobility combined with nascent nationalism to produce fear, resentment, hostility, and eventually violence.

---

16. Eisenbach, *Emancipation of the Jews*, 404–6; Majer Bałaban, *Dzieje żydów w Galicyi i Rzeczypospolitej Krakowskiej 1772–1868* (Warsaw, 1914), 192; Wróbel, "Jews of Galicia," 103.

17. *Żydzi w Polsce Odrodzonej*, ed. Ignacy Schiper (Warsaw, 1932), 1:392.

18. On the importation of Zionist ideas to Galicia in the 1890s, see Schipper, *Dzieje Żydów w Polsce*, 99–101.

19. Daniel Chirot, "Conflicting Identities and the Dangers of Communalism," in Chirot and Reid, *Essential Outsiders*, 8.

Imperial Preconditions: Famine, Violence, and Crisis of Confidence

Mass unrest, such as that in Galicia's summer of 1898, often grows out of a population's enraged and desperate sense that it lacks effective access to formal channels of authority, that its voice is not being heard through conventional, peaceful means. To what extent was this the case during the Galician June days? Although the electoral franchise in the crownland had been extended to a limited group of tax-paying smallholders after the introduction of Polish self-government in 1861, the curia system and indirect elections meant that even those smallholders with voting rights had only very limited influence on political life. Almost four decades of peasant voting had resulted in the election of only a handful of villagers to the Galician Sejm. Meanwhile, the imperial government had opened up a fifth curia with universal manhood suffrage (age twenty-four and older) in elections to the Viennese Reichsrat as of 1897. The 1897 elections had been the first in imperial history to involve mass participation. Why then would peasants, having so recently gained the opportunity to participate in civic life at this level, riot and attack Jewish neighbors? Part of the explanation may lie in a combined sense of abandonment by the imperial regime and the legitimation of public violence in this election year.

The near-famine conditions in Galician villages during the spring of 1898 set the stage for the summer's rioting. Most of the June attacks on Jewish shops and taverns focused first on looting foodstuffs and only later on the destruction of buildings. The annual pre-harvest shortfall had been exacerbated that spring by heavy rains which prevented even the heartiest of crops from growing, and deep mud meant that farmers could not transport their cattle to market. Appeals from peasant farmers to the Austrian state for assistance fell on deaf ears, prompting a sense of general abandonment among starving villagers. The monarchy, of course, was distracted with unrest elsewhere, as Larry Wolff has shown in his study of events surrounding the September 1898 assassination of Empress Elizabeth.[20] Meanwhile, village readers were inundated with reports of anti-Jewish attacks, from the Viennese City Council to the streets of Paris, Hungary, and Bohemia.[21] Ritual murder accusations in the

20. Larry Wolff, "Dynastic Conservatism and Poetic Violence in Fin-de-Siècle Cracow: The Habsburg Matrix of Polish Modernism," *American Historical Review* 106, no. 3 (2001): 735–64.

21. In November 1897, *Związek Chłopski* published an account of a screaming match in the Viennese City Council prompted by the proposal that Christians not serve on juries of Jewish judges because "Jews do not have a feeling for the religious ethics or national sentiment like Aryans." See "Burza antysemicka," *Związek Chłopski* (November 1, 1897), 242. The ongoing Dreyfus affair and the Tiszla Eszlar case also received regular coverage in the peasant press, including an account of the February 1898 crowd violence against Jews and Jewish establishments. "The Frenchman hates the Jews," the paper commented, in a familiar parallel to Polish peasant attitudes, "because he suspects them of favoring the Germans": *Związek Chłopski* (February 1, 1898), 31–32.

crownland itself had increased dramatically from the much publicized Ritter case of 1881 to a pitch of some six officially investigated accusations of ritual murder in 1899 alone.[22] An atmosphere of generalized violence and anti-Jewish attacks throughout Europe helped to legitimize Jews as a target, while hunger and economic desperation raised the level of tension throughout the countryside.

Finally, peasants thought they perceived clear examples of Austrian favoritism toward the Jews both before and during the riots. Imperial troops called in to quell the violence shot at dozens of Christian peasants and artisans and arrested thousands for perpetrating the violence, but very few Jews were included in the arrest reports. Peasant leaders condemned the imposition of martial law in the wake of the riots as arbitrary and unnecessary. The imposition of the death penalty for those convicted of taking part in the pogroms exacerbated the general sense that the monarchy supported the cause of the Jews over that of the peasants.[23] The widespread belief that "the Austrian courts were under the influence of Jewish financiers" was adduced as an explanation for the forced auction of the homes and farms of Christians accused of having taken part in the hostilities. Trials and accusations by Jews against village neighbors continued for several months after the pogrom. Peasants believed they were randomly accused by local Jews—perhaps as vindication for earlier slights—and brought to trial. Memoirists reflected that "it was enough in these times for a harmed Jew to accuse a completely innocent peasant neighbor for him to end up in jail."[24]

The perception of favoritism on the part of Habsburg officialdom helped to reinforce new categories of public identity among the peasantry. While some villagers remained loyal to the empire until its collapse, grateful to have received emancipation from serfdom and support against the gentry in their massacre of 1846, the advent of Home Rule after 1869 changed the distribution of power in the crownland. The growth of Polish-language schools, the reopening of the Sejm in Lwów, and the dramatic expansion of Polish-language economic and cultural institutions meant that a major component

22. For a summary of officially investigated ritual murder accusations, see Andrzej Żbikowski, *Żydzi krakowscy i ich gmina w latach 1869–1919* (Warsaw, 1994), 292–93. Simon Dubnow depicts the controversy surrounding the four-year trial of the Ritter family for the ritual murder of a Christian girl in a west Galician village: Dubnow, *History of the Jews*, 5:490–94. And in October of 1897, Jakób Jarmark, a Jew from the village of Łodzina, Sanok district, was sentenced to death for the murder of Michał Pasturski by poison (arsenic mixed with cheese); see "Na karą śmierci," *Związek Chłopski* (October 11, 1897), 223.

23. A proclamation from the Galician viceroy of June 28, 1898, distributed to all sheriffs (*starosta*) in Galicia announced that anyone found guilty "by a unanimous jury of the crimes of murder, plunder, burning, or otherwise destroying the property of others in accordance with section 85 of the criminal code will be sentenced, according to section 442 of criminal procedures, to the death penalty, which will be carried out within three hours. There is no right to appeal" (reprinted in *Związek Chłopski* (July 1, 1898), supp.

24. Marcinkowski, *Krawe niespory we Frysztaku*, 15.

of the Galician peasantry's "coming of age" after emancipation involved an unprecedented accommodation with their Polish identity.[25]

Targets of Rural Violence: Taverns, Estates, and Distilleries

What did rural Jews represent to Galician villagers in the 1890s and how did they choose the specific targets of their violence during the June days? A close look at the foci of attacks in 1898 reveals consistent patterns. Easily the most frequent target was the village tavern, symbol of Jewish dominance over the peasantry. Tavern windows were smashed, inventory plundered, furniture destroyed, liquor and food consumed or hauled away. In some cases the buildings themselves were set ablaze. The vast majority of the court cases brought against Christian rioters stemmed from violence in and around Jewish taverns. Twenty-five peasants in Rzeszów district were tried for attacking the inn in the village of Godowa, for example, and three day laborers were convicted of "attacking the tavern in Wola Duchacka armed with sticks." The Jewish tavern manager in the latter case testified that the attackers "threatened his wife, Minie Goldberg and their serving girl, Annie Barak, into giving them drinks."[26] Here as elsewhere, the rioters broke windows, damaged or destroyed furniture, smashed cupboards, stole cigars and tobacco. Liebe Goldberg fled the tavern in search of help and returned to find the men "stealing tobacco and breaking furniture." By the time the guards arrived, fire had broken out, and the men had gone on to the next tavern. Similarly, an eighteen-year-old male servant was convicted for "threatening to kill the tavern keep in Wzary and his wife if he and his friends were not given vodka and cigarettes."[27]

Jewish-owned shops, booths, and homes were also targeted. But rioters had to search out the other two main objects of their discontent: Jewish estate owners and managers (whose manor houses and barns they stoned and burned) and distilleries and breweries under Jewish management. Throughout Nowy Sącz district, for example, crowds first attacked Jewish shops and taverns and then set out toward Jewish-owned estates in the countryside. In Dąbrowice, Stary Sącz district, a Jewish barn was burned. In Tokarz, however, the village mayor and local residents defended the Jewish-owned estate and disbursed an angry crowd.[28] There is no record of attacks on local synagogues or other community buildings, and no major injuries to Jewish residents are recorded in the press.

What can we make of the selective targeting of Jewish business enterprises and the relative avoidance of religious and cultural institutions? First, it is

25. See Stauter-Halsted, *The Nation in the Village.*
26. "Sprawy sądowe," *Czas* (August 8, 1898), 3.
27. *Czas* (August 13, 1898), 2.
28. *Związek Chłopski* (July 1, 1898), 155–56.

important to recognize that the tensions surrounding Jewish management of village inns were of relatively recent vintage in 1898. Prior to peasant emancipation and on into the immediate postemancipation years, the innkeeper served a vital role in the village community, functioning as a conduit for information from the world outside the village, a go-between in peasant relations with the landlord, and a source of advice and assistance on issues ranging from medicine and familial relations to financial and legal affairs. Despite the peasantry's inherently suspicious view of commerce and business, contemporary sources emphasize that under serfdom, peasants spoke openly with the Jewish barkeep, "listened to his advice, sought his help, escaped to his protection."[29] The innkeepers, in turn, "patiently listened to the peasant's complaints, often wrote down prescriptions, or bled him." Villagers often looked with suspicion on their lords, while finding trust in this classic middleman relationship with the Jew.[30]

Well into the 1880s, Jews were perceived to be useful sources of information for the newly emancipated peasants.[31] Meetings of the village council traditionally took place in the bar, with the innkeeper influencing proceedings. Over time the Jewish tavernkeepers helped encourage local Jews to run for council office, a phenomenon that was much lamented in the peasant press by the 1870s.[32] Admittedly, then, relations between village innkeepers and their peasant customers did not always proceed on the basis of mutual trust and reciprocity, and certainly, the two groups maintained firm divisions between their religious and cultural communities. Yet the existence of separate spheres did not breed violence and hostility as it did later in the century.

29. On the animosity often expressed toward Jews as merchants, see "Lucy Dawidowicz" in *Negro and Jew: An American Encounter* (New York, 1967), 15–18; and Ewa Morawska, *Insecure Prosperity: Small-Town Jews in Industrial America, 1890–1940* (Princeton, 1996), 3–30.

30. Stanisław Schnur-Popławski, *Cudzoziemcy w Galicyi, 1787–1841* (Kraców, 1893), 50–51. More generally, on the changing role of innkeepers in village life, see Józef Burszta, *Społeczeństwo i karczma: Propinacja, karczma i sprawa alkoholizmu w społeczeństwie polskim XIX wieku* (Warsaw, 1951). Wincenty Witos, reflecting on his childhood in the village of Wierzchosławice in the late nineteenth century, noted that "many peasants went to the Jew for advice not only on economic, political, and familial matters and usually received specific instructions": Wincenty Witos, *Moje wspomnienia* (Warsaw, 1978), 197.

31. Jewish innkeepers were often in a position to pass on valuable information, especially about land sales and auctions, to prospective peasant buyers. In one case, a tavern manager in Myślenice district informed the memoirist and his neighbors of the impending sale of a nearby estate and helped them organize villagers to buy and parcel up the land; see "Wyrobnik (muzykant), a później dorabiający się gospodarz w pow. Myślenickim, który po wojnie przeniósł do pow. Inowrocławskiego," *Pamiętniki chłopów*, 1, no. 43 (Warsaw, 1935): 600–606.

32. Passionate peasant letters to the rural press complain that local Catholics were "paid by the Jews" to support them in elections or that Jewish members of village councils refused to enforce drunkenness laws. Readers began to encourage one another to "elect one of our own" in order to improve the welfare of the *gmina* (commune). At least one peasant letter included a request that the emperor himself establish an imperial commission to investigate the ostensible monopoly of local power by village Jews; see letters of Izdebki to *Wieniec* (May 26, 1876), 5; Jazłowiec to *Pszczółka* (August 8, 1878), 3; and F. K., Jazłowiec to *Wieniec* (March 24, 1876), 5.

This relationship of at least limited cooperation between peasants and Jewish bartenders was, of course, maintained in the context of the peculiar status of public houses and liquor sales in Galician Poland.[33] Imperial law provided a monopoly in alcohol production and sale to the nobility (the system of *propinacja*). Gentry landholders leased to local Jews the right to manufacture and sell liquor. Jewish leaseholders (*arendarzy*), in turn, rented distilleries and taverns on an annual basis and lived on the profits from village customers. Although most of the income from alcohol sales ended up in the pockets of gentry landholders, peasants perceived "the responsibility for getting the peasants drunk and separating them from their cash" as that of the Jewish bartenders.[34]

Apart from being a site for transmitting information and the locus of political activity in the village, the inn was also the center of economic transactions. The few material objects peasants purchased—salt, tobacco, matches, simple tools—were often available locally only through Jewish tavernkeepers. Moreover, as small farmers found themselves required to pay taxes and indemnities after emancipation, their need for cash rose, and innkeepers functioned as the only source of local credit. Because of the high level of risk associated with lending money to peasant farmers (and the absence of competition), moneylenders (both Jews and non-Jews) charged interest rates as high as 100 percent per annum. Peasants whose debts mounted—whether through loans or on their alcohol tabs—frequently saw their farms and homes auctioned off to pay the debt. The association of the tavernkeeper with peasant indebtedness, usurious interest rates, and the high incidence of rural auction helped heighten the hostility and mistrust between Jew and Christian.

The changes wrought by emancipation gradually reduced the Jewish tavernkeeper's position as an invaluable element in the nexus of peasant-lord relations to the function of credit provider. The cash-strapped and land-hungry peasantry directed much of its anxiety toward the tavern itself, or *karczma*. Although the image of the village Jew as informant and adviser continued through the 1880s, alongside it arose a new set of stereotypes. Jewish merchants and small businessmen came to be associated with the notion of "exploitation," of making money from peasants through trickery rather than honest labor. Perceptions of the Jews as profiting unfairly at the expense of the impoverished peasants began to upstage the more cooperative aspects of this relationship.

The transition in the status of the village tavern thus accounts at least partially for the focus of crowd violence during the June 1898 events. In many respects, the village inn had ceased to function primarily as a communal meeting place and center of peasant social life and had instead come to rep-

33. On the tangled web of reciprocal relations between rural Jews and peasants, see Anna-Maria Orła-Bukowska, "*Shtetl* Communities: Another Image," *Polin: Studies in Polish Jewry*, vol. 8, *Jews in Independent Poland, 1918–1939* (London, 1994), 89–113.

34. Witos, *Moje wspomnienia*, 36–37, 193–94.

resent the locus of an alien economic power that could be attacked, robbed, and even destroyed. The rage against this site of perceived exploitation was expressed through collective violence.

A similar transition in Jewish ownership patterns may explain the destruction of manorial buildings and factories. The *arenda* system expanded dramatically in the years following peasant emancipation as gentry landholders struggled to stay afloat financially. By 1893, some 30 percent of estate land—including distilleries, breweries, and manorial offices themselves—was rented by Jews.[35] Another shift in land ownership occurred after 1867, when the Habsburg government abolished restrictions on Jewish purchase of property, and rural Jews began to buy arable and forest lands outright from impoverished Polish gentry. By the 1890s, Jews owned some 10 percent of what had been estate land, in addition to the property they rented.

The acquisition of estates embittered peasants toward their Jewish neighbors partly because they resented the lost opportunity to buy lands adjacent to their own. Dozens of letters to rural papers complain of estate lands being sold to Jews despite the willingness of eager peasants to make competitive offers.[36] In addition, Jewish control over local pastures or forests meant the conversion of customary uses of these lands to cash transactions. Instead of permitting villagers to graze their cattle on local meadows or collect kindling from forests, Jewish landholders leased out the lands for these purposes and clear-cut the forest for lumber. In some cases, landless peasants worked as farmhands on Jewish estates or transported wood from logging operations in Jewish-owned forests.[37] Complaints of nonpayment of wages occurred when wages went directly to cover previous debts.

Finally, the loss of "Polish" land—of "traditional" gentry meadows, pastures, forests, and fields—to "foreign" hands precipitated protonationalist hostility in the countryside. Having come to see themselves as sharing a common culture and political future with Polish-speaking landholders, peasants regarded the sale of these lands to non-Poles as a physical blow against Poland. Not only did peasants view Jews as wielding economic power to which they themselves somehow did not have access, but they were also preoccupied with land acquisition as a nationalist enterprise. In their effort to assess and explain the sources of the anti-Jewish sentiment expressed during the riots, peasant leaders explained that "all the capital finds itself in Jewish hands. . . . [I]t is no surprise that in this unequal battle [for land] our peasant loses. [The Jews] began to take away ownership of his native land holdings; land began to flow into the hands of the Jews. Every tavern, every Jewish home, every toll possessed by a Jew became a fire, from which the Jewish spider spun its web of economic ruin and moral destruction."[38]

35. Hemmerling, *Stronnictwa ludowe*, 156–58.
36. See, for example, the letter of Michał Tworek to *Przyjaciel Ludu* (May 1, 1899), 201–2.
37. Hemmerling, *Stronnictwa ludowe*, 162.
38. Stanisław Potoczek, "O przyczynach zaburzeń i likarstwach na nie," *Związek Chłopski* (August 11, 1898), 177–78.

In a sympathetic summation of what motivated peasants to attack Jewish establishments, peasant leader Stanisław Potoczek accused Galician Jews of "getting our peasants drunk," "tormenting them with usury," and "forcing the peasant to sell his plot for peanuts (*za bezcen*) [to pay off debts] and go to America to starvation, disease and death." This Jewish "spider" was becoming all the more threatening for its alien, non-Polish status.[39] Villagers' frustration and resentment at all these transitions help explain why distilleries and manor houses became a focus of crowd violence during the 1898 events.

The Challenges of Rural Capitalism

In many respects, Polish peasants were not as equipped to respond to the challenges of nascent capitalism as were their Jewish neighbors.[40] A combination of competition, envy, and disapproval contributed to a heightened sense of anxiety and tension. Rural Jews functioned in a wide variety of professional positions and economic niches, from itinerant peddlers to legal counselors. Although their status as small shopkeepers, tavern managers, and estate owners drew the most violent attention during the June days of 1898, the diversity of professional activities Jews performed made them appear omnipresent in public affairs; little could be accomplished in rural life without the intervention of a Jew at some level. Economic scarcity had led to a position of greater visibility for Jewish inhabitants in the minds of Polish small farmers, landless laborers, and artisans.

In the litigious postemancipation days, for example, Jewish *proceśnicy*, or advocates, had filled the law courts, representing the peasant in land claims against his former lord or his peasant neighbors. Lawsuits that dragged on for years benefited mainly the Jewish scribe. Peasants complained about these *proceśnicy* who "roam[ed] around the courts" all day and prolonged cases until the peasants were "completely ruined"; the Jews, they said, had "caused more unhappiness than it was worth."[41] Some even believed that the Jewish communities themselves initiated the June 1898 riots partly to bring business to these informal scribes. One apocryphal estimate set the number of Jewish lawyers trying cases associated with the pogrom at around a thousand, each earning some 5 million *zloty* a year![42]

---

39. Ibid.

40. For a discussion of the resentment expressed by German farmers toward rural Jews because of the insecurities produced by capitalism, see the articles by Reinhard Rurup, "Jewish Emancipation and Bourgeois Society," *Leo Baeck Institute Year Book* 14 (1969): 67–91, and "Emancipation and Crisis. The 'Jewish Question' in Germany, 1850–1890," *Leo Baeck Institute Year Book* 20 (1975): 13–25. See also David Peal, "Antisemitism by Other Means? The Rural Cooperative Movement in Late Nineteenth-Century Germany," *Leo Baeck Institute Year Book* 32 (1987): 135–53.

41. Stanisław Michałczyk, Dąbrowski district, to *Przyjaciel Ludu* (March 10, 1899), 118–20.

42. Tworek to *Przyajciel Ludu*, 201.

The hyperbolic terms in which the earnings of Jewish litigators were expressed provide an insight into the attitudes of peasant farmers regarding the "work" of local Jews. The problem, as one rural correspondent expressed it, was that Jews "don't work [physically] or at least not from dawn till dusk like the peasants."[43] Small farmers and their craftsmen neighbors operated in a conceptual universe in which value resulted directly from the application of labor to a product. Selling services or making money from court transactions struck the peasant as unjust, since no physical object was produced in the process. For the peasantry, moreover, objects possessed universally accepted values such that the concept of buying and reselling the same item to gain profit was unfamiliar and threatening. Instead, peasants intuitively believed that the Jews' profit was their loss and held these money and trade-related occupations in utter contempt—not least because they were performed by a different ethnic group.[44] Thus, the work of Jews, who made up some 85 percent of all merchants in turn-of-the-century Galicia, became inherently suspicious.[45]

The concept of "illicit profit" is central to the shifting relations between Jews and Christians in the Galician countryside. Already in the 1870s the majority of village councilmen, for example, characterized local Jewish occupations as primarily "usury, litigation, exploitation of the peasants, purchasing stolen goods, accomplices to theft, smuggling, swindling, and clandestine alcohol sales."[46] Peasants in general distrusted the Jews' ability to "wander about the countryside buying odds and ends and eventually set up a shop, then a home, and then an estate." While "we work with our bodies," the Jews "only traded" and yet had "things better."[47] For small farmers, whose sense of value was rooted in a precapitalist conception, the notion of profit was both foreign and a source of suspicion.

The whole process of capitalist acquisition and of the laws of supply and demand remained mysterious to many peasant farmers. In particular, the long-standing practice of Jewish merchants buying grain in the fall at relatively low prices and reselling it at higher rates during the pre-harvest famine prompted a sense of communal violation among many villagers.

As one village schoolteacher remarked somewhat naively during the June rioting: "And now a word about the sale of grain! We all know that in the spring the grain is usually cheaper, and many villagers take it to markets in towns to sell naturally to no one else but the Jews. We know that the Jews buy up a great reserve of grain for some reason! And that reason is so that

43. Ibid.
44. Kieval, "Middleman Minorities," 216; Morawska, *Insecure Prosperity*, 12.
45. Schiper, *Dzieje handlu żydowskiego*, 443–49.
46. This list represents a composite of comments from several hundred heads of village commune and commune counselors; see Tadeusz Pilat, *Wiadomości statystyczne o stosunkach krajowych* (Lwów, 1881), 19–20.
47. Letter of J. Świątek, village of Kamienica, to *Związek Chłopski*, July 1, 1898, 158–59.

when the pre-harvest shortfall comes [*przednówek*] and in the peasant cottages the grain has been weeded out, they can sell for twice the price. And look how they ingeniously conspire."[48] As the earning of profit came to be viewed as an "ingenious conspiracy," Jewish attempts at economic survival in the countryside were pitted against peasant conceptions that such transactions violated an unstated moral code.

Peasants likewise expressed discomfort about the tradition of bartering at Jewish stores and market stalls. Jewish memoirists tell us that "for Jew and peasant alike, to pay the price asked or to refuse to modify the first price named would be contrary to custom."[49] Yet in fact, peasant leaders found bargaining so distasteful that one of the key goals of the Christian stores established by agricultural circles (kółka rolnicze) in the 1880s was the establishment of "fair," stable prices. Peasant insecurity about Jewish business and about the notion of profit contributed to the easy characterization of Jewish businesspeople as "thieves," "cheats," "swindlers," and "con artists." By the 1890s, well before the riots, letters published in village newspapers were depicting taverns as "nests of thievery and holes of brigandage" and innkeepers as "instruments of the devil," vampires, spiders, and "moral poisoners of rural people."[50]

Since the characteristics often required of a business person were associated with breaking a rural code of conduct, Jewish tradesmen were easily labeled as "immoral" and accused of a willingness to commit unethical, outrageous acts in their shameless pursuit of cash. Villagers lamented that their Jewish neighbors were "greedy for money, which made [their] hearts beat for joy." The majority of Jews, they explained, "worship the golden calf like their own God and don't ask if it is a sin or not to consider cheating someone out of a grosz."[51] The preoccupation with material wealth was often associated with an ironic assumption that Jews also lacked a sense of community and family values, something Catholic peasants prided themselves on.

Backwardness and Self-Hatred: Dueling Nationalisms in the Galician Countryside

Out of the language of anticapitalism and charges of Jewish immorality and crass materialism emerged another current that helps explain the passion behind peasant accusations. Gradually, the Jew and the tavern were blamed for the tenacity of peasant backwardness. Populist activists who edited rural

48. Ibid.
49. Mark Zborowski and Elizabeth Herzog, *Life Is with People: The Culture of the Shtetl* (New York, 1952; reprint, 1995), 65–66.
50. See *Związek Chłopski* (February 21, 1898), 42–43; (July 1, 1898), 148–49; (July 21, 1898), 161–62; and (August 11, 1898), 178.
51. Michałczyk to *Przyjaciel Ludu*, 119.

papers, gave speeches to village gatherings, and campaigned for communal office were adamant in their opposition to the institution of the tavern. Consuming the body and spirit of small farmers, sucking away their scarce resources, destroying families and ruining farms, the inn, they contended, was becoming symbolic of the negative aspects of postemancipation village life. Even more than under serfdom, small farmers had the freedom and the cash to waste long days in the tavern. This habit, activists argued, was the most important factor preventing cultural and economic progress in the countryside. For peasant editors, political activists, and priests, the tavern represented all that was retrograde in the Polish peasantry. Rather than dealing with alcoholism as a social problem, then, peasant leaders began using the tavernkeeper as a symbolic reference for all that was backward and in need of reform in the villages.

Indeed, the peasant press virtually justified the attacks of June 1898 by reference to the ills of the tavern environment. In a direct appeal to the emperor himself, peasant editor Stanisław Potoczek argued that the damage perpetrated against a few village inns was nothing compared with the daily harm inflicted on innocent peasants in the tavern itself. Anthropomorphizing the village inn and endowing it with the most malevolent of intentions, Potoczek begged:

> Excellency! Look at this "tavern." You see a cottage with doors and windows—is this the tavern? Oh no. The "tavern" is an arrogant and malicious force, in which the strength of a person's body and soul [are consumed]. The tavern is a power which has at its disposal countless abominable means, through which the whole person with his body and soul are lost to a horrible cold darkness, where he is imprisoned not in iron chains but with the weak magical threads of a hellish shrew!—and although she is weak when she imprisons him, he already does not have the strength to break away from her—he looks but does not see, listens but does not hear, not the groans nor the suffering of his hungry children and wife! Because the tavern is a hellish force. . . . Oh, how many painful examples are here, striking the eye in the view of the multitudinous proletariat in the countryside, deprived of cottage and land, and how many tears of widows and orphans, emaciated and slowly dying from hunger! And all of these are because of the *karczma*![52]

Rife with satanic symbolism, such descriptions cast "the Jew," the manipulator of tavern practices, in the role of messenger from the underworld, ascribing to him peasant weakness, poverty, landlessness, and lack of power and painting the institution of the tavern and the person of the village Jew as the direct causes of peasant misery and backwardness. Without the tavern and the temptations it represented, such arguments implied, Galician peasants would

52. *Związek Chłopski* (July 1, 1898), 148.

proceed uninhibited on the road of progress, modernity, and upward mobility. So long as the "still simple and dark rural population" continued to "help the Jew" in his journey to prosperity and power, however, little improvement could be expected.[53] The tavern had to be eliminated, along with the influence of the rural Jew—and the capitalist exploitation he represented—in order to open a space for peasants in the moral universe of postemancipation Galicia.

In a peculiarly double-edged pattern of argument, peasant reformers—among them, parish priests, rural teachers, village council members, and activists in the budding agricultural cooperative movement—accused Jews and peasant masses alike of being caught up in a mutually reinforcing system of backwardness. They criticized "as dark and unenlightened" the peasants who wasted time in taverns and ran up huge debts with Jewish moneylenders. At the same time, they portrayed Jews themselves as representatives of a more primitive age that would be washed away by the "modern" Austrian government and Galician administration. Coverage of Jewish culture in crownland papers consistently portrayed conditions in Jewish communities as filthy, lacking in hygiene, overcrowded, and even prone to violence. Stanisław Koźmian wrote in 1871 that "the characteristic trait of Jewish culture is dirt"; Jewish factories in Galicia suffered "low sanitary conditions and employed children under the age of twelve," presumably something only an "uncivilized barbarian" would do in the "modern" Habsburg monarchy. Elsewhere, journalists referred to the "dark masses of Jews" flooding into Kraków from the countryside, the "scuffles constantly breaking out in Jewish-run taverns," and the Jewish merchants who illegally sold vodka by the glass in their shops. Thus, what Polish Catholics read about Galician Jews spoke of filth, violence, crime, the practice of base professions, and primitive working conditions.[54]

Interestingly, this sense of cultural and economic backwardness among the masses of unreformed Galician Jewry was also reflected in the attitudes of contemporary acculturated *Jewish* observers. In an 1893 pamphlet, Wilhelm Feldman characterized the bulk of Galician Jewry as tradition-bound, uneducated Hasidim. Both "Galician Hasidism," he proposed, and "Rabbinical Jewry are decrepit and have been reduced to but a spark of their dying souls."[55] Similarly, the interwar Jewish historian Naftali Schipper viewed Galician Jews in the 1880s as a superstitious and insular rabble: "The mass of Jews crammed into the towns and cities of Galicia had lived for ages in the gloom of the ghetto, governed by the miracle-worker Hasids. European culture had made no inroads here; the spirit of enemies of the educated reigned. Fanaticism and intolerance with regard to progress reigned throughout the region."[56] The solution put forth by both writers lay in increased education, to be supported

---

53. Świątek to *Związek Chłopski*, 158–59.

54. A thorough analysis of *Czas* coverage of Jewish culture can be found in Żbikowski, *Żydzi krakowscy*, 272–82.

55. Wilhelm Feldman, *Asymilatorzy, syoniści i polacy* (Kraków, 1893), 11–12.

56. Schipper, *Dzieje Żydów w Polsce*, 94.

by the Habsburg state.[57] Provincial Galician Jews in their vast majority *were* Hasidim, however, and largely uninterested in a secular education that would encourage occupational diversity and acculturation into Polish-speaking society.

Ironically, the tensions that would lead to violence in 1898 may have been caused partially by rising expectations among Jews and peasants alike. The expansion of rural education after 1870, the mass circulation of rural newspapers in Polish and Yiddish, the introduction of more cash into the local economy through migration and return migration, and the transition out of traditional occupations meant that both groups were more aware of the competitive presence of the "other" than ever before. At the same time, the conceptual divisions between the two groups had hardened. By the 1890s the reform efforts of Jewish enlighteners (*maskilim*) had been superseded by the Zionist impulse coming from Vienna. In 1892 the assimilationist newspaper *Ojczyzna* ceased publication, and by 1898 a pro-Palestine newspaper, *Przyszłość*, was promoting a return to Zion.[58] The spread of Jewish nationalist efforts created turmoil within the Jewish community itself, as Orthodox and Hasidic leaders alike expressed their opposition to this "modern" movement. At the same time, some rural Polish speakers came to resent the Zionist movement for its lack of interest in Jewish assimilation.

The ongoing prevalence and visibility of Hasidism combined with the very exclusivity of the Zionists to make Jews appear increasingly alien and hostile to the project of Polish nation-building. At the same time, popular Polish nationalism was on the rise in the Galician countryside, reflected most clearly in the fortunes and platform of the Stronnictwo Ludowe. One of the Peasant Party's primary objectives was the organization of Christian trade cooperatives intended to displace Jews from their near monopoly over Galician business. Beginning already in the late 1870s, this network of Christian agricultural cooperatives and credit unions sought to promote the founding of Christian shops in order to sidestep the Jewish middleman. The agricultural cooperative circles were correctly perceived by rural Jewish businessmen as a direct threat to their livelihoods.

Efforts to compete with Jewish storeowners largely failed, since the more experienced, better-connected Jews could offer items at lower prices, and peasants refused to boycott the stores even when their leaders encouraged them to do so (as in the failed boycott of 1893). Even after forty years of effort, the antisemitic peasant newspaper, *Piast*, could comment in 1914 that "local trade, although small, is exclusively in the hands of the Jews."[59] Nonetheless, despite the slow gains made in entering the rural bourgeoisie, peasant and Jew alike felt the signs of rural "progress" and saw in it the decline of Jewish eco-

57. Feldman, *Asymilatorzy*, 44–45.
58. Schipper, *Dzieje Żydów w Polsce*, 2:99–100.
59. "Ludowcy, a Żydzi," *Piast* (January 4, 1914), 2.

nomic dominance. The peasants' heightened confidence found reflection in the increased fear and mistrust of them among provincial Jews.[60] Jewish migrants to the United States in the late nineteenth century expressed the near-consensus view, for example, that Christian peasants were driven primarily by corporeal instincts, that they were unrestrained in their aggressive nature, that peasant customers were "uncivilized and backward" and potentially violent in their dealings with Jewish business people. Peasant aggression (or potential aggression) bred Jewish insecurity.

Peasant confidence grew with even the limited success of Christian stores, and peasants came to believe that the Jews felt threatened by the peasantry's rising economic strength. One peasant poet's parody of rural Jews on the eve of the riots claimed:

If it weren't for those circles
We would be in better shape
We would be able to cheat all the goyim, . . .
That peasant education is harming us
It is ruining us . . .[61]

In many senses, then, the advent of implicitly anti-Jewish institutions such as reading rooms, credit unions, and cooperatives were indeed signs of economic and cultural "progress" in Galician Polish villages. Education and the economic diversification of rural professions meant the tragic displacement of village Jews as Polish Catholics set out to "dislodge" Jewish trade, Jewish lenders, and Jewish handicrafts. Meanwhile, writes Feldman, the Jewish population fought desperately "for its own land and for government positions."[62] Jews and Catholics were on a sociological collision course as the structures of economic life in Galicia established important preconditions for antisemitic outbreaks.

Early advocates of Polish nationalism among the peasantry thus associated the "nation" with economic advancement and cultural progress. The "moral community" established between peasant nationalists and their intellectual and notable allies rested on assumptions of industry, sobriety, and enlightenment—values both modeled on and juxtaposed against stereotypical Jewish qualities. As national identity came to be rooted increasingly in a common culture of Polish language and Catholic religion, peasant leaders saw rural Hasidism and rabbinical Jewry outside the boundaries of their national community and threatening to its future agenda. Jews, rather than gentry office-

60. Morowska, *Insecure Prosperity*, 16.
61. "Lament żydowski na kółka rolnicze i czytelnie," *Związek Chłopski* (September 11, 1897), 201.
62. As Wilhelm Feldman put it, "The Polish residents want to dislodge Jewish trade, Jewish banks, Jewish handicrafts [while] the Jewish bourgeoisie [seeks] to gain all the property and . . . to control the bureaucracy." See Feldman, *Asymilatorzy*, 45–54.

holders, could be attacked as symbols of the hated *propinacja* system. Jewish membership in village councils could motivate smallholders to campaign for local office. And the Jewish-run tavern could serve the rural temperance movements as a horrible example. The image of the Jew was increasingly held up as a symbol of the dark and primitive village past, his ouster painted as a symbol of progress and enlightenment. The combination of the Jews' perceived affinity for German culture and their retrograde influence on Polish villagers were enough to ostracize rural Jews from the moral universe of Peasant Party activists.[63] The next step would be the explicit demand for the physical removal of Jews from the countryside—the final development in the evolution of "modern" antisemitism in prewar rural Poland.

Antisemitism and Peasant Politics

The antisemitic rhetoric of the 1898 election campaign was clearly not the only impulse pushing impoverished Poles to attack Jewish homes and businesses, but these elections do represent a sharp breaking point in peasant attitudes toward Jews. In the early years of the new century the Polish Peasant Party (Polskie Stronnictwo Ludowe, or PSL) would split into a left wing (PSL-Lewica) led by the socialist Jan Stapiński and a right wing (PSL-Piast) headed by a future prime minister, Wincenty Witos. In the opening pages of Piast's new press organ in 1914, soon after the party's formal alliance with Roman Dmowski's National Democrats, there appeared in bold letters the announcement that the new party "aimed and [would] succeed in the goal that there be no more Jews in the countryside."[64] Likewise, for the conservative Christian Peasant Party (Stojałowski's wing, which predated the Piast split), the only solution to the "problem" of Jews in the countryside on the eve of the Great War and Poland's reemergence as a state was the physical separation of peasant from Jew. Such a proposal represented an admission that peasants could neither compete with Jews nor include them in their community. The longstanding issues of Jewish economic dominance, and of the peasantry's discomfort at exposure to their "backward" ways, could be resolved only by eliminating Jews from interactions with villagers.

Whether Polish farmers were threatened by rural Jews as vestiges of a primitive (isolated, uneducated, dependent, even irrational and satanic) past or as the foreshadowing of a crass, materialist, individualist future is not clear. What does seem true is that the peasants, workers, and artisans who took part in

---

63. By 1903, the program of the Polish Peasant Party included a reference to the Jews as a "tribe gravitating . . . toward German culture—a tribe that views Polish society as foreign and which we on our side encourage . . . to fulfill its program of emigrating to Palestine": Stanisław Lato, *Programy Stronnictw Ludowych* (Warsaw, 1969), 73.

64. "Ludowscy, a żydzi,"1.

the violence of the summer of 1898 felt somehow displaced by recent developments and believed that removal of the Jews was the way to restore order to their disrupted universe. Intemperate articles in periodicals circulating throughout rural and small-town Galicia, combined with electioneering that brought the "Jewish Problem" into sharp relief, plus an atmosphere of generally legitimized anti-Jewish violence, led provincial Galicians to express their anxieties and frustrations against the only group that could be painted as responsible for their situation: those economic middlemen, the Jews. In a sense, then, evidence from the 1898 pogroms helps position rural Poles on the cusp of a more modern era in their expression of anti-Jewishness. The June days of 1898 suggest that premodern antagonisms were evolving into a more sinister variety of antisemitism based on economic and exclusionary nationalist rationales.

3

Resisting the Wave

Intellectuals against Antisemitism in the Last Years of the "Polish Kingdom"

JERZY JEDLICKI

F or the Polish intelligentsia, antisemitism in the late nineteenth and early twentieth centuries was primarily a political phenomenon. It had, of course, its ancient religious roots and an important economic dimension in certain periods; it drew racist notions and justifications from Germany or France; and it often manifested itself as an aversion to a strange and incomprehensible culture. Nevertheless, political fears were its basic and permanent component. By this I simply mean that the Polish intelligentsia became uneasy or reacted with hostility whenever the Jews claimed any collective rights and demanded recognition as a separate, autonomous nation.

Before 1862, whenever the question of equal rights for Jews arose, the main argument was that cultural and political integration of Jews with the Polish nation must become either a condition or an outcome of legal equality, because Poles—who had been deprived of their own freedom—could not permit the existence of a "nation within the nation."[1] Every manifestation of Jewish separatism outside the religious sphere was regarded with suspicion, considered an act of disloyalty and a threat to Polish efforts toward national liberation.

In the two decades following the tragic defeat of the anti-tsarist January Insurrection of 1863, when Polish dreams of autonomy, let alone indepen-

---

1. See Artur Eisenbach, *Wielka Emigracja wobec kwestii żydowskiej 1832–1849* (Warsaw, 1975), as well as my review of this book, "Narod w narodzie," *Więź* 11 (1976): 134–41.

dence, were stifled and then abandoned, Polish-Jewish relations remained relatively free of direct conflict, since there was no public arena in which Poles and Jews could compete and no political goals in sight for which they could fight. Assimilated Jews were welcomed by the Polish educated classes, whereas traditional Jews were viewed as an exotic tribe that had an undeniable right to live in its own way. Only in the 1880s did blatant antisemitism gain a foothold in the censored Warsaw press. It was virulent enough but limited itself mainly to economic struggle and moral slander and did not manage to influence mainstream public opinion.

Only at the beginning of the twentieth century and especially in the wake of the 1905 Revolution, did the Jew become a powerful personification of a mysterious "enemy from within," conspiring to deprive the Poles of their expected self-rule. These native aliens who demanded equal civic rights supposedly could not be satisfied with equality; instead they would strive to prevail over Poles in towns and cities, to humiliate them, and finally to turn Poland into a Judeo-Polonia. It is no wonder that such a myth was subsequently activated during every political crisis or electoral competition.[2] It certainly reflected a Polish national feeling of uncertainty and the fear of being manipulated—as a national entity—by the great powers, secret societies, or other forces beyond people's knowledge and control. The image of the conspiring Jew made this mysterious world clearer, simpler, and more comprehensible. It was precisely this image that had captured the imagination of a large part of the Polish educated class by the early twentieth century, representing a peculiar turn of events. Until the end of the nineteenth century, for all the occasional outbursts of animosity or even pogroms, the Jews were believed to constitute a recognized segment of the Kingdom's society and were not suspected of entertaining any political ambitions of their own.

To be sure, the liberal or socialist intellectuals of the late nineteenth century did not appreciate ethnic and cultural diversity, but who did? The stereotype of the ghetto or shtetl as a hotbed of ignorance, viciousness, and religious fanaticism was shared by all Polish intellectuals and they were not particularly anxious to learn more about these strange neighbors. Only a few individuals such as Klemens Junosza or Eliza Orzeszkowa tried to penetrate a little deeper into the Jewish society and way of life. The liberals from the positivist "young press" in the 1870s believed that the progress of education would Europeanize and at the same time Polonize these alien masses, making them abandon their distinctive features and become faithful Polish patriots.[3] The assimilated (or assimilating) Jews usually shared this outlook which entangled them in an

2. Moreover, this myth has recently been revitalized; see Andrzej Leszek Szcześniak, *Judeopolonia: Żydowskie państwo w państwie polskim* (Radom, 2001), and his *Judeopolonia II: Anatomia zniewolenia Polski* (Radom, 2002).

3. A good introduction to this subject is Stanislaus Blejwas, *Realism in Polish Politics: Warsaw Positivism and the National Survival in Nineteenth-Century Poland* (New Haven, 1984).

inescapable paradox: the more eagerly they renounced Jewish tradition, the more willingly they were accepted by the Polish intelligentsia, yet the less able they were to work for a cultural emancipation of the Jews whose very language they did their best to forget and by whom they were regarded as renegades.[4]

The emergence of Zionism and other forms of Jewish nationalism in the Kingdom and Galicia was immediately recognized by Polish liberals as a challenge to their own optimistic theory and patronizing practice. Aleksander Świętochowski, the leader of the liberal camp, put the point bluntly in 1902. In his opinion, Jews were lacking any "cultural material needed to create their homeland and to build a separate nation"; if they were nevertheless to pursue such an ideal, then a friendly coexistence with an alien nation on the same soil would become impossible. The spread of Zionism would thus result, Świętochowski warned, in the rise of Polish hostility toward Jews, even in those segments of society that previously had been free of prejudice.[5] It was a clear sign that the liberal Polish intelligentsia, tolerant toward Jews so long as they were the object of its proselytizing, was not prepared to recognize Jewish national identity and partnership.

Nor did the socialists differ much in this respect. Kazimierz Kelles-Krauz, an intellectual gifted with exceptional wisdom, was rather isolated in his understanding that the Jewish national revival was a natural outcome of the democratization of culture and a manifestation of awakened collective dignity.[6] Still, the leaders of both wings of the Polish socialist movement renounced ethnic and religious prejudices and welcomed Jewish comrades and revolutionaries who were ready to fight the common enemy—the propertied classes of any nationality, protected by the imperial state and its police forces.

Assimilators such as the journalists Stanisław Kempner, editor of *Nowa Gazeta* in Warsaw, and Wilhelm Feldman, editor of *Krytyka* in Kraków, took the lead in the struggle against Zionism. In their view, if Polonization meant progress, then every separatist striving must be considered a retrograde process, a return to the ghetto, since a return to Zion or even Jewish cultural autonomy elsewhere were regarded as idle dreams.[7]

4. See Alina Cała, *Asymilacja Żydów w Królestwie Polskim (1864–1897): Postawy, konflikty, stereotypy* (Warsaw, 1989).

5. A. Świętochowski, "Odpowiedź p. Jahrblumowi," *Prawda* 15 (1902): 176; see also his "Ostrożnie z ogniem," *Prawda* 5 (1903): 52.

6. Kazimierz Kelles-Krauz, "W kwestii narodowości żydowskiej," in his *Pisma wybrane* (Warsaw, 1962), 2:318–341; see also Timothy Snyder, *Nationalism, Marxism, and Modern Central Europe: A Biography of Kazimierz Kelles-Krauz (1872–1905)* (Cambridge, Mass., 1997), 197–201.

7. [Wilhelm Feldman], "Utopia," *Krytyka* 2, no. 12 (1902): 345–55; Stanisław Kempner, *Syonizm: Kilka uwag polemicznych* (Warsaw, 1903).

So long, however, as Polish national interests were dimly defined, the area of conflict remained indeterminate. It was the Revolution of 1905 that opened the era of mass politics, marked by the unprecedented savagery of interparty struggles.[8] It thus established a favorable climate for antisemitism, which always spreads in periods of political strife and instability.

In the wake of the revolution and the October Manifesto of 1905, Poles in the Kingdom gained access to a range of long-forgotten rights and benefits: education in the national language, voluntary associations, trade unions, increased freedom of the press, and limited voting rights. That all these were granted to Jews as well created new areas of rivalry. The same people who were struggling for Polish schools, political representation, or autonomy of the Kingdom were taken aback when confronted with much more restrained demands from the Jewish community. Any signs of Jewish collective self-esteem—the development of the Yiddish-language press and literature, the emergence of Jewish political parties, demands for cultural autonomy—were looked upon with suspicion as prejudicial to the newly promised and not yet implemented Polish rights and liberties. Understandably, restrictions imposed on these rights by Petr Stolypin's government resulted in a widespread feeling of frustration and insecurity which could only magnify the fear of a Jewish deluge. In particular, the National Democrats (Endecja) pointed to the Jews as the main obstacle to the political emancipation of the Poles.[9]

The liberal press also rang the alarm. True, it continued to voice hopes for assimilation, yet assimilation conceived as *digestion* of the alien element by the national organism. Compromise with Jewish "separatists" came to be regarded as impossible, and their pledges of loyalty to the "interests of the Polish nation" were distrusted. There was a feeling in the air that the hour of struggle for Poland's independence was near, in the context of which the perception that "a second nation has appeared on the banks of the Vistula!" (as an alarmed Antoni Chołoniewski wrote from Kraków) provoked a sense of horror.[10] In this atmosphere a demand of certain rights for Yiddish was understood as a design to transform the future Poland into a bilingual state, a Judeo-Polonia.

The Endecja, of course, heated up the atmosphere, and the Russian regime's announcement of an imminent granting of self-government to the municipalities of the Kingdom brought matters to a head, since it was obvious that in some towns Jews would gain a majority. The liberals, now following in the nationalists' footsteps, advocated a life-and-death struggle. "Whatever

8. See Robert Blobaum, *Rewolucja: Russian Poland, 1904–1907* (Ithaca, N.Y., 1995).

9. See "Listy Warszawskie" by Ignotus in *Przegląd Wszechpolski* (1903), reprinted in *Narodowa Demokracja: Antologia myśli politycznej "Przeglądu Wszechpolskiego" 1895–1905*, ed. Barbara Toruńczyk (Warsaw, 1981), 96–98.

10. Antoni Chołoniewski, *W sprawie żydowskiej: Trzy listy polemiczne* (Kraków, 1914).

weakens the nation's instinct for self-preservation is a challenge to its very existence," wrote Iza Moszczeńska, one of the best pens in the progressive camp.[11] Equal rights, however, were a nonnegotiable postulate of all Jewish parties, and thus matters moved inexorably toward collision. In 1910, Bronisław Grosser of the Jewish socialist Bund foresaw that "the setting up of the first representative institutions in the country may mark the beginning of an internal struggle in the Kingdom with results fatal for the country and for both nationalities living together."[12] And so it came to pass.

The story of the Warsaw elections to the Fourth Duma in November 1912 is fairly well known.[13] Jan Kucharzewski, a historian and moderate national-ist, was defeated after he refused to support equal rights for Jews; Jewish pro-prietors, landlords, and shopkeepers cast their votes for a Polish socialist worker instead. The whole affair had more symbolic than practical impor-tance, yet a large segment of Polish public opinion viewed the outcome of the balloting as a Jewish insult and provocation. "The jelly-like mass of Polish society," wrote Świętochowski, "is just becoming crystallized as a nation. And now the Jewish nation has for the first time stood against this Polish nation as its equal. This is no longer an ignorant ghetto rabble . . . nor the amorphous mass I need to digest and absorb, but our rival and enemy."[14]

Once they entered the orbit of nationalism, the "progressives" cast aside their inhibitions. Many a writer, from the liberal as well as the nationalist trenches, now went into raptures over "the miracle of unity" of the entire nation after years of interparty struggles. The miracle was not to last long, but the myth of the Jewish enemy had seemed to act as a unifying factor. The tide was rising, wrote Stanisław Pieńkowski in 1913, and now "no more sentiments, no more bridges, no more agreements!" The relentless though nonviolent Polish-Jewish war "marks the beginning of a new era for Poland."[15]

And so on the eve of the First World War all political and social concerns had been overshadowed by the Jewish question. It became a foremost issue in the Polish press of all political colors, an obsession out of any proportion to

11. Iza Moszczeńska, *Postęp na rozdrożu* (Warsaw, 1911), 28; for more on Moszczeńska's arguments, see Theodore R. Weeks, "Polish 'Progressive' Antisemitsm, 1905–1914," *East Euro-pean Jewish Affairs* 25, no. 2 (1998–99): 55–62; and Jerzy Jedlicki, "The End of the Dialogue: Warsaw 1907–1912," in *The Jews in Poland*, vol. 2, ed. Sławomir Kapralski (Kraków, 1999), 119–20.

12. Bronisław Grosser, "Pro domo sua," *Wiedza* 9 (1910), 277–78; Jedlicki, "End of the Dia-logue," 115–17.

13. A good account can be found in Stephen D. Corrsin, *Warsaw before the First World War: Poles and Jews in the Third City of the Russian Empire, 1880–1914* (Boulder, Colo., 1989); see also Robert Blobaum, "The Politics of Antisemitism in Fin-de-Siècle Warsaw," *Journal of Modern History* 73, no. 2 (2001): 294–98.

14. H.D. [A. Świętochowski], "O Żydach," *Kultura Polska* 12 (1912): 5.

15. Stanisław Pieńkowski, *Dwa żywioły (Głos w sprawie żydowskiej)* (Warsaw, 1913), 21.

its real importance for the rebirth of Poland. The phantom of the intruder, however, once generously allowed in the Polish home but now scheming against its hosts' rights and interests, had revealed its powerful *symbolic* significance.

That part of the Polish intelligentsia in the Kingdom (in practice confined mainly to Warsaw) that was mentally prepared to resist this tempest did not have an easy task. Entering the polemical lists exposed one to the risk of indiscriminate insults from the journalists of the anti-Jewish front. Moreover, there were few outlets for the expression of opposing opinions. In fact, the only Warsaw daily that remained loyal to the traditional liberal program of gradual assimilation and respect for Jewish equal rights was *Nowa Gazeta*, published by Stanisław Kempner. Generally considered a Jewish organ, it went out of its way to accent its Polishness and was consequently derided by both sides, Polish antisemites and Jewish nationalists. It defended its views quite cautiously, attempting to maintain a moderate polemical tone so as not to excite its opponents even further. In 1914 *Nowa Gazeta* drew closer to the Piłsudski camp, which at the time did not enjoy much popular support in the Russian partition.[16]

I am purposely omitting Jewish voices here—that is, the reactions of representatives of different Jewish orientations, from assimilators to Zionists, to the campaign in the Polish press and to the Endecja boycott agitation—as well as the mutual and sometimes rough-spoken polemics between them. This is a separate subject, one that reflects sharp differences in Jewish political and cultural strategies in Poland after the 1905 Revolution. These disputes, nota bene, did not manage to dislodge from the Polish debate statements entirely incongruent with reality about the political tendencies and intentions of Polish Jews as a whole. Such exaggerations and generalizations can also be found in the responses of opponents of the anti-Jewish action.

They also accepted several stigmatizing categories and biases that were strongly situated in the language of the period. To these belong in particular the words *żargon* and *żargonowy* (jargon, gibberish) in reference to Yiddish, used by almost all participants in the debate, not excluding those authors appearing in *Izraelita*, the organ of Jewish assimilators. Also practically in general usage was the insulting term *Litwacy* (Litvaks), which embraced all Jews who had migrated to the Kingdom following pogroms and expulsions from the western provinces of the Russian Empire, whether or not they had anything in common with Lithuania. The stereotype of the *Litwak* as a vulgar and arrogant agent of Russification of the Kingdom was taken at face value, and the proponents of assimilation also took for granted the dislike and even

16. Barbara Petrozolin-Skowrońska, "'Gazeta Handlowa' i 'Nowa Gazeta' (1864–1918)," *Rocznik Historii Czasopiśmiennictwa Polskiego* 7, no. 1 (1968): 47–72.

enmity of honest local Jews toward the alien newcomers.[17] There were few efforts to look objectively at the cultural conditioning of the Jewish migrants who mostly spoke Russian as a matter of course (which in itself extremely irritated Poles as well as Jews in Warsaw) but in any case had no reason whatsoever to support a tsarist project for the final incorporation of the Kingdom into the Russian Empire. It has been noted several times that the opinion of Polish Jews regarding the *Litwacy* recalls the attitudes of German Jews about their Polish counterparts as *Ostjuden*.[18] Both stereotypes were gladly repeated by publicists outside the Jewish world, particularly those who wanted to define by such means the territorial or cultural boundaries of their tolerance.

The positions occupied in this bitter civil war of words in 1910–14 cannot be uniformly associated with political-social orientations. As already mentioned, the mainstream part of the liberal camp headed by Świętochowski went over to a stance of "progressive antisemitism" during these years. These liberals differed from the Endecja only in that they did not recognize openly the determinism of ancestry as something that would hinder at least their declarative approval for the Polonization of Jews, which nonetheless was saddled with increasingly rigorous conditions.[19] The left as well did not lack voices— to be sure, they were exceptional—that betrayed favorable attitudes toward a program of reducing or eliminating Jews and Jewish influences in the Kingdom.

Opponents of such a program and the rhetoric behind it also came from across the political spectrum; they could be found among the conservative right (in particular the publicists and sympathizers of the Stronnictwo Polityki

17. The novel by Artur Gruszecki, *Litwackie mrowie* (Warsaw, 1911), and several other literary works were based on this stereotype. On the role of the image of the "Litwak" in antisemitic hysteria, see Lesław Sadowski, *Polska inteligencja prowincjonalna i jej ideowe dylematy na przełomie XIX i XX wieku* (Warsaw, 1988), 233–40; and Theodore R. Weeks, "Fanning the Flames: Jews in the Warsaw Press, 1905–1912," *East European Jewish Affairs* 28, no. 2 (1998–99), 73–75. This stereotype also made its way into later academic historiography; see, for example, Henryk Wereszycki, *Historia polityczna Polski 1864–1918*, 2d rev. ed. (Paris, 1979), 249. The extent of Jewish migration from the Empire, as well as the role of the migrants in Jewish life in the Kingdom, requires additional scholarly research.

18. Belaryusz [Bernard Lauer], "W tak zwanej sprawie 'litwackiej': Przyczynek do kwestyi żydowskiej w Królestwie Polskim," *Krytyka* 3 (1909): 274–88. See also François Guesnet, "'Litwacy' i 'Ostjuden' (Żydzi ze Wschodu): Migracja i stereotypy," in *Tematy żydowskie*, ed. Elżbieta Traba and Robert Traba (Olsztyn, 1999), 73–80.

19. In the resolution adopted at a meeting of the *Polskie Zjednoczenie Postępowe* (PZP, Polish Progressive Union) in Warsaw on April 5, 1910, it was announced that "political assimilation— that is, active support for the strivings of the Polish nation—is the condition of peaceful coexistence. Groups not standing on this ground must be fought as an alien, and sometimes hostile, element": *Prawda* 15 (1910): 8. Two years later a resolution of the Society of Polish Culture, which in principle represented the same group of liberals, contained an even stronger formulation: "By assimilation of the Jews is meant unconditional incorporation into the Polish nation": *Kultura Polska* 12 (1912): 12. These definitions, similar to the editing of postulates related to cultural assimilation, were preceded by long discussions, and every word in them was subjected to careful crafting.

Realnej (Party of Realistic Politics), the liberal center, and the two main wings of the socialist movement.[20] In several instances, however, it is impossible to ascribe to these individuals any ideological direction. As was true of such opposition many times later in the twentieth century, vocal protest against the propaganda of hatred was more frequently a function of personal character than of world view.

One cannot fail to note, however, that among those voices of protest the Catholic clergy was conspicuous by its complete absence. It is true that *Przegląd Katolicki*, *Posiew*, and *Polak-Katolik*, press organs under the patronage the Warsaw curia, resigned naturally enough from anthropological justifications of antisemitism and warned against resorting to coercion and violence, but they did not try to halt the campaign of the Endecja and its allies—quite the contrary.[21] Moreover, no one apparently expected the Church to appeal any longer to Catholics for conscientious reflection.

On the other hand, at some point at the end of 1909 or beginning of 1910, as the temperature of the conflict rose but had yet to reach its peak, the largest Jewish daily in Warsaw, *Hajnt*, requested an interview with the foremost (in Jewish eyes) Polish authority, the ailing Eliza Orzeszkowa. The writer—irritated that the reporter sent by *Hajnt* did not know Polish and wanted to speak with her in Russian—declined to be interviewed and instead began to write an article which, unfinished, appeared soon after her death in *Kurjer Warszawski* as well as in Yiddish translation in *Hajnt*. This text, titled "On Jewish Nationalism," can be likened to the last word of a departing epoch. The article is meditative, an attempt to answer the question posed by the author to herself: why had the positivist program of assimilation basically failed?

Orzeszkowa defended her conviction that this program was fundamentally realistic; history, after all, did not lack examples of separate peoples taking on for themselves the higher culture of nations among which they had come to live. Differences of a physical type and of language and religion did not necessarily pose insurmountable obstacles in this regard. The main tool of this kind of assimilation was education, the first gust of which dispatched separate characteristics: "Are there Jews, if only a little educated, who would be moved by the brightness of candles burning on the Sabbath table, or brought to tender pride by the sight of the gaberdine? The distinctiveness that so easily, so quickly, disappears without a trace is not the distinctiveness that has penetrated the blood and marrow of a people and determines their specific national individuality." If therefore this process of convergence has not met expectations, it is because Polish society itself has not possessed the means of public education (in such vagueness one feels the influence of the censor or the author's self-censorship). But it is also because an awakened Jewish nation-

20. Blobaum, "Politics of Antisemitism," 301.

21. For more on this issue, see the richly documented work of Krzysztof Lewalski, *Kościoły chrześcijańskie w Królestwie Polskim wobec Żydów w latach 1855–1915* (Wrocław, 2002).

alism has acted as a brake on assimilation. Orzeszkowa's stance toward Jewish nationalism reflects understanding and respect: no tribe can be denied the right to regard itself a nation, especially Jews in the atmosphere of enmity and insults that surrounds them. The fact is, nonetheless, that an inevitable collision between two equally justified national aspirations has arisen as a result: "The organization of Jews on Polish land in a separate nationality, in a nationality indifferent to Polish struggles, aspirations and desires, to Polish ideas and culture—represents a serious and threatening danger for Polish society" and may become even more threatening if indifference is transformed into hostility.[22]

One can only conjecture that had the author managed to complete her article, she would have considered ways of bringing the two aspirations into agreement, of avoiding a ruinous confrontation between them, although she was conscious that she was dealing with "the thorniest subject" of the Polish debate.[23] But even as it stands, her text is noteworthy for the mentality of positivism's epigones that did not appreciate popular ties to traditional culture and religious customs and were completely unprepared to accept either the ideal of the multinational state or modern multicultural civilization. The conviction that civil society could not be maintained without cultural and sociopsychological homogeneity was at the base of almost all reasoning in the dispute described here. Religious and ethnic diversity was permitted, but the greater the diversity, that much stronger the bonds that cemented a nation should be, particularly a nation that had yet to gain recognition of its own right to political existence.

For those who accepted such assumptions, the politics of repelling and reviling the Jews appeared counterproductive, even absurd and, beyond that, offensive in its vulgarity. In the most vocal protests there is the sense of offense to healthy logic together with a reflex of moral and esthetic revulsion. In what apparently was a self-published brochure, the little-known writer Teresa Lubińska fervently asked, "Is it permissible for us to excommunicate the Jewish masses for separatism when we have done nothing for them since the post-insurrectionary period?—when we declare to them at every step that we are the landlords here—they are tenants; when we have not attempted to remove the walls of division and [promote] their Polonization?" It was as if this task had been left to Jewish assimilators, who themselves however—even if they have been the greatest of Polish patriots—had to confront at every turn *zoological antisemitism*. And now hatred had been unleashed, creating an abyss "which may be forever impossible to bridge."

Lubińska viewed the boycott campaign as political suicide, since Jews had brought to Polish life their energy, resourcefulness, and intellectual vigor—all

22. Eliza Orzeszkowa, "O nacyonalizmie żydowskim," in her *Pisma* (Warsaw, 1913), 9:213–34.

23. From a letter of Orzeszkowa to Tadeusz Bochwic cited in Edmund Jankowski, *Eliza Orzeszkowa* (Warsaw, 1980), 579.

of which contributed to economic progress and cultural development—and were not interested at all in political power, as was apparent in Galicia. Therefore, the boycott ran contrary to Polish interests, impoverishing industry and capital, agriculture and science: "Poverty will spread in the villages, it will grow in the cities—theaters, conference halls and bookstores will stand empty." The author addressed herself directly to Polish women "who with noble bravado and thoughtlessness conduct a campaign of persecution." It would be in vain, however, to speak to them in the name of justice, love for one's neighbor, compassion, responsibility, and finally conscience, the last of which can be found in the title of her booklet, *Do sumienia waszego mówię!* (I speak to your conscience), so "I appeal to you in the name of sobriety, which comes from the conscientious study of history and the premises for tomorrow that can be drawn from it. . . . Let's not boycott the Jews, because they are . . . the yeast from which grows the bread of the nation's economic strength."[24]

No less emotional was the reaction of Stefania Sempołowska, a distinguished representative of the Polish left, a woman who always came out in defense of the persecuted. Besides her sympathy for the wrongs suffered by the Jewish poor, she found extremely painful the sense of moral disgrace that had fallen on her country, where "voices were resounding that dared to equate patriotism with nationalism, the Polish idea with anti-semitism." In no way, she wrote, could the participation of Jews in Polish culture be effaced or the rights of Jews to Poland be taken away. Therefore, the only result of the boycott campaign of the Endecja would be the unleashing of hatred: "You are digging a precipice between two peoples who are forced to live on the same land. You are corrupting your souls, you are building a barrier to the Polonization of individual Jews, you are pushing the Jewish crowd toward poverty and ignorance instead of raising its level of civilization and preparing it for coexistence with us in solidarity." The only hope was to consider the present struggle as only a "temporary movement of reaction," because after all, "humanity in its development is aspiring toward the ideal of justice, national animosities are fading away, brotherhood is building."[25]

Similar in tone, though not free of stereotypes, was the pronouncement of the well-known journalist from the conservative and "conciliationist" Party of Realistic Politics, Ludomir Grendyszyński, written immediately after the elections to the Fourth Duma.[26] In his introduction the author—as Lubińska

---

24. Teresa Lubińska, *Do sumienia waszego mówię!* (Warsaw, 1913).

25. Stefania Sempołowska, "Z powodu nastrojów chwili" *(Nowa Gazeta,* 1912), in Sempołowska, *Publicystyka społeczna (Pisma,* vol. 4), ed. Żanna Kormanowa (Warsaw, 1960), 49–53.

26. In Polish terms, "conciliationist" politics aimed at reconciling Polish society to the reality of the partitions. "Conciliators" also hoped to wring concessions from the partitioning powers, particularly in the national and cultural sphere, in exchange for demonstrated acts of Polish loyalty and moderation.

had done, for that matter—stammered out the ritual accusation against "the impertinent *Litwak* politicians" who had supposedly pushed Jewish electors in Warsaw to reject the candidacy of Kucharzewski. This justified, in Grendyszyński's opinion, the outburst of national anger but could not provide the basis for a program. Two million Jews, after all, would not emigrate. It was necessary instead to rebuild Poland's small towns, create industry, found credit societies and vocational schools, and publish books and journals in order to provide employment, education, and cultural advances for both the Polish and the Jewish people, a people that is otherwise indifferent to political matters and that in its majority finds electoral combinations incomprehensible. "Therefore, I protest against the forcing of all Jews into one camp, . . . I protest against borrowing from the Prussian 'Hakatists' the hypocritical argument of 'self-defense,' I protest against the lighthearted trampling on the humanitarian traditions of our country. And, finally, I protest against the turning away of reformist social thought from real work on the progress of civilization in the entire country and among all groups of the population inhabiting it. . . . Every citizen who sees how his nation is heading down a dangerous slope is obligated to protest. They write about *struggle* and they make a *commotion*. They write about *defense* and they mean *boycott*. They say *boycott* and they make *terror*. And from terror it's only one step to the *pogrom*, and after the pogrom, as we know from sad experience, comes *robbery and banditry*. I don't want this disgrace for my nation and therefore I protest!"[27]

This lone protest had a certain echo in the Warsaw press. Even Świętochowski devoted a moment of his attention to it in his next of a series of press organs, *Humanista Polski*, where he wrote maliciously that in protesting, Grendyszyński "felt in himself the strength and calling of Zola." He connected Grendyszyński to Lubińska and the learned sociologist and socialist Ludwik Krzywicki, who was known to have written in *Nowa Gazeta* that it only remained to hand out knives to the promoters of the campaign. But "when the Żabotyńskis and, following their example, the Jackans[28] defiled the Polish nation, not one of these present avengers of wronged Jews 'protested,' 'spoke to conscience' and 'handed out knives,'" sneered the aging leader of the progressives.[29]

Świętochowski himself, however, lost during these years the remnants of his once significant authority. Despite his polemical eloquence he was unable to outbid the National Democrats in attacks on Jews, while the glibness and pathos of his nationalism repelled the leftist intelligentsia.[30] Several of its rep-

27. Ludomir Grendyszyński, *Protestuję!* (Warsaw, 1912).
28. Jackan was the name of the owner of *Hajnt*. The contemptuous form of pluralized names was and remains today a favorite rhetorical device of antisemitic libels.
29. H.D. [Aleksander Świętochowski], "Po drodze," *Humanista Polski* 1 (1913): 5.
30. See Ludwik Krzywicki, *Wspomnienia* (Warsaw, 1959), 3:158–59.

resentatives gave him tit for tat, observing that this publicist of once great renown had fallen in the end to the level of the antisemitic libelers.[31]

The division of Polish opinion was therefore profound, but it would be a simplification to reduce it to a straight *for* or *against*. If the anti-Jewish choir was fairly monotonous in its accusations, the soloists who came out against it were guided by various motives and turned attention to different aspects of the conflict. There were also critics who lashed at both sides and who didn't consider the Jewish parties to be at all innocent victims in the war of words. Thus, for example, Leo Belmont, a popular author and leading Warsaw free-thinker, considered the Jewish rejection of Kucharzewski's candidacy—for the sole reason that he had not agreed to equal rights in future municipal self-governing institutions—an error fatal in its consequences. Belmont (himself of Jewish descent) demanded of the leaders of the Jewish community an understanding of the sources of Polish fears about the loss of majorities in city councils and the councils' coming under the control of Jewish nationalists who, moreover, were not familiar with the existing needs of the population. He was of the opinion that the electoral property qualifications introduced by the Russians needed to be replaced with educational qualifications that were, of course, Polish. Yet at this point the direction of his polemic turned to the Polish press, which knew only how to instruct Jews how to vote and to threaten them instead of reliably presenting the person and program of the candidate. In turn, Kucharzewski himself had not perceived "that in a time when at Dmowski's meetings there were slogans of starving out the Jews with a boycott and of chasing them away from Polish culture, he, the candidate for delegate, should have uttered his own weighty word of condemnation addressed at the anti-semitic cannibalism, this word from him for which Jewish Poles thirsted like rain, driven out as they were by Dmowski and his followers."[32]

If the Jews did not always want to understand the reasons for Polish sensitivity, Polish progressives nonetheless should try, declared Belmont, to consider the profound religious and psychological reasons for Jewish resistance to an assimilation that one way or another sentenced an ancient nation to self-annihilation. The serious work of assimilation could not be based on a repudiation by Jews of their own identity but must build a "supranational humanitarian consciousness" connected, naturally, with Polish national consciousness. This idea was not clearly formulated, nor was it very practical, but the task of such texts was to shape sensitivity rather than advance scripts of political action to an audience that, moreover, was not identified. Belmont's pamphlet began and ended by pointing out the absurdities of the boycott that was pushing even those Jews who were becoming secularized and Polonized

31. Jerzy Huzarski, "Handel pianą," in Leo Belmont and Jerzy Huzarski, *Zwycięstwo Romana Dmowskiego* (Warsaw, [1912]), 11–39.

32. Leo Belmont, "Dlaczego przepadł p. Kucharzewski," in Belmont and Huzarski, 40–70.

back to the ghetto, "and this hostile *ghetto* will paralyze the strength of the Polish nation that is being reborn in difficult conditions."[33]

This last argument was repeated by opponents several times in their writings, as was the thesis that one nationalism promoted the development of the other in a law of equal and opposite reaction. "Dmowski and Jackan can shake each other's hand," wrote Wilhelm Feldman, the editor of the Kraków-based *Krytyka* and a declared proponent of assimilation.[34] In any case, such arguments could only serve the organizers of the anti-Jewish campaign as a confirmation of their strategy. Antisemitism always acts on the principle of the self-fulfilling prophecy.

As one might expect, the most consequential critics of the logic of nationalism were the publicists from both wings of the socialist left. Yet they were also surprised by the volcanic eruption of tribal emotions that were supposed to disappear as capitalism progressed. Since they had not disappeared, it was apparent that capitalism had yet to perform its tasks. Antisemitism—whether in Russia or in Austria, in France or in Poland—is everywhere the ideology "of the Christian shopkeeper," argued Ludwik Krzywicki.[35] The petite bourgeoisie and clerical reaction, others wrote, have grasped this idea as a weapon in an intensifying competitive struggle. In Western Europe as well as in Germany, the "Jewish question" had already been resolved or was in decline because Jews had been almost completely incorporated into respective social classes. The racist form of antisemitism, although it had gained a certain popularity in Germany, was of little significance; at most it makes "some noise in circles of the intelligentsia, it gives vent to the emotions of those who frequent the literary-artistic cafes."[36]

It was different in Russia and in the Polish districts that it governed, where Jews as a result of their larger number had become a separate caste subordinate to the *kahal*, and where the petite bourgeoisie, whether Christian or Jewish, continued to occupy an important place in the social structure; on such foundations nationalism had developed on both sides, holding back the clarification of class divisions.[37] This analysis—let us admit—was not particularly penetrating. Marxist doctrine, to be sure, demanded the smashing of stereotyped characterizations of Jews and the bringing of their economic stratification out into the open.[38] But at the same time it made its adherents insensitive to the psychology of people permanently humiliated as a consequence of their identification. Of course, the socialists did not possess an ounce of sympathy

33. Leo Belmont, "Pod znakiem bojkotu" and "Myśli na czasie" in ibid., 4–5, 85–88.

34. [Wilhelm Feldman], "Asymilacja," *Krytyka* 1 (1910): 177. Feldman, for his part, was an assimilated ex-Jew who considered himself a Pole.

35. Ludwik Krzywicki, "Sprawa żydowska: pobudki bojkotu," *Nowa Gazeta* 7 (1913): 2–3.

36. Julian B. Marchlewski, *Antysemityzm a robotnicy* (Kraków and Chicago, 1913), 21–23.

37. Leon Wasilewski, *Kwestya żydowska na ziemiach dawnej Rzeczypospolitej* (Lwów, 1913), 6–9 and elsewhere.

38. Marchlewski, 64.

for the customs of the ghetto or shtetl; they saw in Jewish religious rules only medieval superstition and in their hearts and minds were in favor of assimilation. Yet it was difficult for them to understand that Zionism and—more broadly—the affirmation of Jewish national identity were not necessarily synonymous with the solicitous conservation of tradition and backwardness.

The socialists condemned all forms of national and religious oppression but nonetheless considered the cultivation of national distinctness a historical error. Julian Marchlewski, a leading Marxist intellectual, spoke out—as did Rosa Luxemburg—against the Bundist demand of equality for the Yiddish language in mixed communities and against the idea of any sort of cultural autonomy for Jews; after all, "social development leads to the assimilation of Jews as an unavoidable necessity: a racial group that is a minority living in the habitat of another race becomes sucked in by that habitat, so long as it doesn't artificially maintain its separateness."[39] Marian Bielecki perceived only a choice between the archaic culture of Judaism and modern cosmopolitan culture: "What this means is that this nation must rid itself of the traits of a *nation-caste*, that its national culture—as much as it endures and about which there can be different opinions—must rid itself of the traits of *ghetto* culture, of tribal-religious culture, and become part of the general culture of humanity."[40] Since separatist tendencies, the intention of reviving Jewish nationality, are the fantasies of people wanting to reverse history, the working-class movement should come out "with all of its strength against nationalism, both Polish and Jewish, against this infection that poisons life!"[41]

From such an ideological position it was possible to view the antisemitic campaign with a most profound repugnance, seeing in it not only a national disgrace but a manifestation of counterrevolutionary reaction and, on top of it all, "the utter depravity of Polish liberalism," that bourgeois formation which the left had always treated with particular disdain. Marchlewski had no inhibitions in describing the boycott actions and the cowardice of the Warsaw intelligentsia: "Never before has Poland been the spectacle of such a monstrosity, such moral barbarism, such debauchery of the basest of instincts."[42]

Yet there were troubling question: "Why has antisemitic propaganda succeeded in stifling all other dissonances in our public life? Why have even progressive and intellectual circles partially submitted to the leadership of reaction?" In responding to such questions already during the war, Jan Stróżecki from the PPS Left came to the conclusion that the peculiar conditions of those years were responsible: "Antisemitism could find favorable soil

39. Ibid., 78.
40. Kmicic [Marian Bielecki], *Przesądy antysemickie w świetle cyfr i faktów (Przyczynek do kwestji żydowskiej)* (Wilno, 1909), 71.
41. Marchlewski, 91.
42. Ibid., 60–64, 80.

for its development only under the reactionary government which after the [revolutionary] movement of 1905–1906 burdened all of Polish public life. This was a period of counterrevolution, of military courts, of terrible and bloody repressions. Prisons and fortresses were overflowing, the scaffold was not idle even for a moment. . . . The working class, weakened and decimated, was unable to exert its influence in the following years. It has remained, however, loyal to its principles and managed to resist the antisemitic infection. This is most encouraging as a guarantee of the future."[43]

Thus the socialists, although they felt isolated in these years, had preserved their faith in historical progress. "The hysterical tumult"[44] would pass, a few more Jews would emigrate to America or, if only the Pale of Settlement were abolished, into the heart of Russia, and then assimilation, the only road to European civilization for eastern Jews, would resume its work: "The liberation of all peoples and countries oppressed by the yoke of autocracy and assuring them normal conditions of development," trusted the PPS expert on nationalities, Leon Wasilewski, "will bring about as a result in the lands of the old Commonwealth a resolution of the Jewish question according to those principles, which Western Europe has realized in deed."[45]

One could, moreover, refer to various other theories. Mateusz Mieses, a learned Judaicist, sketched a history of racist concepts in order to come to the conclusion that they were only superficial rationalizations and that religions had created the most profound divisions between nations and civilizations, for which he provided dozens of examples. Hatred for Jews was therefore also purely religious in its source. Although the vestige of divisions once grooved into the consciousness of generations could last a long time even in a completely secularized society, as the great religions had done in their time, so today culture would unify people and remove the remnants of hatred: "Intellectuals of all faiths, nations, peoples, tribes, or races should feel the common bonds of friendship, a common striving toward a higher ideal, to brotherhood, to the ennoblement of the human type, to superhumanity."[46]

Józef Lange, a member of the Progressive Union, a left liberal excellently read in European literature, viewed the Jewish issue more soberly. He considered it against the background of the development of modern nationalism, the model for which in his opinion was the "Action Française" founded by Charles Maurras, with its hatred for everything that was new and ethnically or religiously different. Lange acknowledged that nationalism could capably utilize and appease human stupefaction with the turmoil of modern civilization and the resulting fear of a coming ruthless struggle for existence and search for "existential truth." The weary individual strives in this torrent of change to

43. La Question juive en Pologne, enquête (Paris, 1915?), 55.
44. Krzywicki used this expression in his "Sprawa żydowska," 2.
45. Wasilewski, 41.
46. Mateusz Mieses, W kwestyi nienawiści rasowej (Kraków, 1912), 129.

find strong material, moral and emotional support; he tries to belong to a corporate body, to a group, to his own kind, to subordinate himself to authority, to define the source of evil. And now come the nationalists "exploiting every pain, longing, thirsting, need, all unsatisfied national aspirations that may have become the most real element of our lives. . . . They use work for national culture, aspirations to retrieve from it the native elements, in order to cover themselves with the cloak of defenders of the national soul, to cast the slogan of struggle with foreign accretions in a false way, and to acquire the label of the only true patriots."[47]

Thus Polish nationalism, Lange argued, had almost nothing in it that was peculiarly Polish. Nationalism is everywhere the same: it draws from positivism and social Darwinism; it proclaims the principles of national egoism and of political realism, which in practice exemplifies conciliatory and conservative politics. And the Jews? "Nationalism is not really concerned with Jews as such; rather it needs, coûte que coûte, 'internal enemies' in order to justify, strengthen, and above all propagate its social-political program. Among us, the most important 'internal enemies' just happen to be Jews." The National Democrats, taking up antisemitism—which was older than their movement—in order to turn it into a useful instrument of "national politics," proclaimed Jews to be an agent of moral corruption, then took it upon themselves to uncover "defenders of the Jews" and "Judaicized Poles," so that finally "everything in the country is Jewish, with the exception of National Democracy."[48]

The secession of Świętochowski, Andrzej Niemojewski, and other luminaries from the "camp of progress," Lange wrote, supplied Polish nationalists with biting pens; they had now acquired the feuilleton, "a particularly valuable means of shaping the mood, of preparing the ground for agitation." In exchange, the progressives from *Prawda* and *Humanista Polski*, seduced by the pathetic slogan of "Polonization of the cities," had lost any kind of ideological autonomy; what remained to differentiate them at the very most was anticlericalism, but they would eventually shed that as well, since after all one couldn't conduct politics of "national unity" without the clergy.[49]

Lange did not underestimate the agitational capabilities of nationalism. In the conclusion of his book he reiterated once more that nationalism nourished itself on real issues of the epoch, particularly dislocations in the "bonds of human communities." The democratic movement had to find its own response to these needs. "Nationalism, which exploits them for its own aims through a total barbarism and immorality of means, is a ruthless, implacable opponent with whom any discussion is senseless, with whom any compromise is impossible." It has proclaimed in the Kingdom "a kind of state of war, a state

47. Józef Lange, *Postęp a nacyonalizm* (Warsaw, 1913), 42–59, 98.
48. Ibid., 78, 79–84.
49. Ibid., 115–21.

of emergency, [whereby] principles of honesty, ethics, and truth are no longer obliging." The time has come, therefore, to join all truly progressive democratic forces against it, particularly now that "society is terrorized by the nationalists, when very many people either do not express their opinion, or speak contrary to it."[50]

Józef Lange's book, bringing together penetrating social analysis with critical passion, was one of most developed and distinctive responses in the moral-ideological war that peaked in 1912. It is worth noting that this author was soon completely forgotten, and his book went unread—to a certain extent because the outbreak of the war marked a sharp break with the previous period. But similar memory lapses would repeat themselves in the history of Poland in the twentieth century, in which a sometimes surprising continuity of mental attitudes and styles of action tend to stand out—a primarily unconscious continuity, however: the mechanism of repetition, a codified reflex, and not therefore memory or knowledge of predecessors. Still one more example of this phenomenon is the fate of the intellectual legacy of Jan Baudouin de Courtenay.

The descendant of a family settled in Poland since the eighteenth century, a linguist of international reputation, a professor at St. Petersburg University, and every inch an intellectual, Baudouin de Courtenay would again and again throw his authority onto the scale of public debate. His lectures and brochures, to my mind, constitute the voice with the most weight in the Polish resistance to antisemitism prior to the recovery of independence.[51]

His criticism aimed both at the lowering of the level of political discourse in Poland and at the main arguments upon which the entire campaign depended. With his peculiar sarcasm he wrote about the libels of the journal *Myśl Niepodległa,* suggesting in due course that its editor (Andrzej Niemojewski) was acquiring from suspect sources "personal data about all his literary opponents [so that] he can use this information as bullets in polemical clashes." The slanderous articles in this journal (accusing, for example, that the Social Democratic Party, the SDKPiL, was directed by Jews who had called Polish workers to demonstrations and the barricades in 1905 in order to push them into the range of Cossack fire and disorganize the country's life) were "fanning the flames of herd hatred" and "giving incitement to pogroms," wrote Baudouin de Courtenay.[52] He was particularly incensed that "many edu-

---

50. Ibid., 60, 127, 128. See also Lange's *Sprawa żydowska jako zagadnienie ekonomiczne* (Warsaw, 1914).

51. Of at least twenty-six titles devoted to this theme before 1918 by the author's own count, not a single one of them was included in the fourth volume of his *Dzieła wybrane* (Warsaw, 1983), containing the publicist literature of this great scholar; there one finds only the author's articles on the Jewish question in independent Poland.

52. Jan Baudouin de Courtenay, *W sprawie "antysemityzmu postępowego,"* offprint from *Krytyka* (Kraków, 1911), 16–18.

cators are bringing the antisemitic tumult into the schools," and that in magazines for youth "Polish" children were being encouraged to torment their colleagues of "Jewish" descent (the author's quotation marks). The boycott's concept of "de-Judaization" of the economy and culture, schools and hospitals, was scurrilous and would soon collapse, the author foresaw, but it would leave behind in its wake "an intensification of the war of all against all—and there somewhere in the distance of the future new bloody specters."[53]

The conviction that ideas and words may have dangerous consequences may be found among other authors, but no one equal to Baudouin in competency could carry out such a vivisection of the foundations and rhetorical devices of the language of hatred. To their front rank belonged "wholesale thinking": that is, operating on the basis of collective notions and ascribing some kind of characteristic traits to Poles in general, Jews in general, or Christians in general. Such language serves to condemn and in the end kill people for sins they didn't commit, for simply belonging to some category. "The obscure 'apocalyptic' style, threatening in an indefinite way, . . . permits one to assume anything and, even without much fertile fantasy, pogroms above all else." This was also the language of Vladimir Purishkevich and Russian pogrom literature.[54]

Baudouin de Courtenay devoted particular attention to the aspiration to acquire an exclusive national right to a particular ancestral territory, that is, to "the savage theory, that a certain part of the inhabitants of a given state or country have the right to consider themselves 'hosts,' while another at most can lay claim to the role of tolerated 'guests.' This is 'zionism' *sui generis*. Polish Zionists dream of a purely Polish land, just as Jewish Zionists dream of a land that is purely Jewish." In this way, the author scoffed, the entire globe should be divided into cages of immaculate national fatherlands with the most uncontaminated *purebreds* in each. But who, he asked, is the host and who is the guest in, for example, eastern Galicia? He continued: "The Polish Progressive Union [Polskie Zjednoczenie Postępowe, or PZP] in Warsaw has decreed that Poles do not recognize the rights of Jewish nationality, do not recognize the civil and national-cultural rights of Jews. . . . The PZP should remember that the Russians treat all *inorodtsy* [non-Russians], and therefore Poles as well, in the very same way. Yet the Jew even more so has always been perceived as an innkeeper and a peddler, as a pariah deprived of the right of choice and self-identification. The Jew, simply because he is a Jew, does not have the right to personal dignity, does not have the right of the individual citizen."[55]

Baudouin was one of the few writers of the time who considered *żargon*, the stigmatizing label for Yiddish, to be nonsense. There were no criteria, he

53. Jan Baudouin de Courtenay, W *"kwestyi żydowskiej,"* odczyt wygłoszony w Warszawie 7 lutego 1913 r. (Warsaw, 1913), 46, 57.
54. Baudouin de Courtenay, W sprawie *"antysemityzmu postępowego,"* 18–19.
55. Ibid., 30–31, 32.

explained, for distinguishing *żargon* from a language, and therefore Yiddish was as normal a language as all others. The fact also needed to be recognized that a rich Yiddish press, literature, and theater existed in both Russia and Poland. This position was not in the least drawn from philosemitism, which was completely foreign to the professor. As a rationalist, a freethinker, and a radical in the early twentieth-century sense of the word, he felt contempt for any kind of exclusive nationalism, whether Russian, German, Polish or Jewish, because in each one he could sniff the potential preparation to remove from "their" country any elements that were considered insufficiently native or harmful. "To mutually slaughter and eradicate each other," he wrote in 1913, "that is the aim of our 'patriotic' dreams. In the name of tribal unity and racial purity we are supposed to sacrifice several or dozens of millions of human beings."[56]

For now, although Polish progressives had not gone beyond the slogan of "de-Judaizing Polish progressivism, Polish socialism, Polish independent thought," official antisemites had already taken it upon themselves to remove Jews from Polish associations, schools, and the press. This was not yet enough, wrote Baudouin caustically; it would still be necessary to remove Jews from Polish history; to erase the participation of Jews in Polish political movements (in other words, the uprisings); to de-Judaize science, art, and literature; to introduce a "pale" in the area of thought and creativity, an internal passport system, and an order requiring proof of ancestry at least to the third generation. De-Judaize socialism, why not? And Christianity too, beginning with Jesus and Mary. Besides, the professor perceived, the prototypes of the idea of tribal exclusion and of the practice of exterminating members of alien tribes could be found in the Old Testament, whose spirit of intolerance had been taken over by Christianity.[57]

Baudouin de Courtenay was a historical pessimist and saw little of promise in the still-new century. He did, however, have his own positive program, on the surface scanty and minimalist. Nationalities did not have to love each other or come closer together; it would be enough if they could learn to tolerate each other, respect their differences, and admit their equal rights. It would require only a reform in education to replace nationalist patriotism with territorial patriotism and the loyalty of citizens to the state in a way that was not national but perhaps federal. Doing so would be a great task for the schools—nondenominational, of course, because cults of devotion, whether religious or national, should remain a completely private matter. Here Baudouin, reflecting that perhaps this project of reform was too bold, indicated that he wouldn't wish to introduce changes by Jacobin methods; in the end, denominational schools could also remain if that was the desire of those interested in them—so long as they did not fill heads with the poison of hatred

56. Ibid., 30.
57. Ibid., 38–41.

and stupefy their pupils to excess. Maybe these were only fantasies, maybe tasks that would last untold years, but in politics, Baudouin stipulated, it was worthwhile to establish aims based on certain principles in order to have a gauge of ethical conduct.[58]

He had little faith in the efficacy of persuasion, in the possibility of sobering up intoxicated minds, and therefore tried to speak not to conscience but to practical reason. In one of his public lectures he cynically weighed all previously proposed solutions to the forever vexing "Jewish question," beginning with the slaughter (yes!) of all Jews, going on to their expulsion ("but would that sufficiently frighten them from returning? and besides, where should they go? and at what cost? and would 'others' allow us to do it?") and then further to uncompromising boycott, forced and 100 percent assimilation (but "what is the criterion? what are requirements for the 'examination in correct Polish thinking'? and who will analyze this purity of Polishness?"), and Zionism (the mirror image of antisemitism). Only after rejecting all these solutions as impractical did the author present his own fourteen-point project, the most important part of which was point 3: "The resolution of the 'Jewish question' depends on its denial or negation. There are no 'Jews' and 'non-Jews.' There are only individual people, personally responsible for themselves." Perhaps it is worthwhile to quote the postscript to his final point: "But why can't a person simultaneously feel connected to two human communities, why can't he draw from the treasures of two cultures, two traditions, why can't he be made enthusiastic by the memories of one and the other nation—this I completely fail to understand. Nationalities are not religions, and they do not have dogmas that are outright opposed to the dogmas of other faiths."[59]

The ethical individualism of Baudouin de Courtenay was, of all the acts of opposition discussed here, the most ethically profound refutation of nationalism. By the same token, however, it had little chance of reaching the minds of the intelligentsia in this age of sanctifying national loyalty, always and unconditionally paramount and indivisible. His was also the most radical, unsentimental deconstruction of antisemitic ideology, invalidating its issues at their very core. Again, however, such an operation could not count on popularity. The learned professor was acutely aware of the contrariness of his position, and he did not have a high opinion of the ethical and rational capacity of human nature, yet despite everything he continued to appeal to its potential.[60]

The "Jewish question" in central Poland was not "solved" in any sense of the word as it was understood at the time. It only became overshadowed for four years by wartime concerns and excitements—only to return with new force in 1918. Always, however, then and later, its embarrassing manifestations called forth the opposition of those who had the courage to think and

58. Ibid., 47, 52.
59. Baudouin de Courtenay, W "kwestyi żydowskiej," 62–96.
60. See his "Myśli nieoportunistyczne" (1898) in Dzieła wybrane, 4:70–79.

proclaim the truth despite the obsession of the herd—courage for themselves
and for others who preferred to remain quiet. Their objections were naturally
based to a certain extent on a given ideology, and in this regard the Polish left
had a relatively clean record. As I have tried to show, however, not everything
can be explained systematically by reference to ideological convictions. Accepting the challenge and giving testimony in difficult times was above all a matter
of character and of irreducible attributes of personality.

Translated by Robert Blobaum

4

Criminalizing the "Other"

Crime, Ethnicity, and Antisemitism in Early Twentieth-Century Poland

ROBERT BLOBAUM

He [Szatkiewicz] knew that he had to provide the *Kurier Narodowy* with a sensational piece about some Jewish villainy, something about usury and its terrible effects—in short, something "new" and "piquant" on that subject known and used by all those organs that supported themselves by rousing the passions and fanning racial hatred.

Gabriela Zapolska, *The Anti-Semite* (1897–98)

As antisemitism transformed the religious and cultural Jewish "other" into the alien internal enemy of the nation it defined as Polish, it developed a well-honed propaganda of hatred that was well in place at the beginning of the twentieth century. The mortal enemy with whom the imagined Polish nation of the antisemites was locked in a struggle of life and death had to be demonized in order to be hated as well as feared. That demonization took a number of forms, not the least of which was the image of the Jew in the role of dangerous criminal. To the early twentieth-century antisemite there was no crime of which the Jew was incapable. In addition to older images of Jews as usurers, swindlers, and petty thieves—not to mention diabolical ritual murderers—modern antisemites created new images and fantasies that held Jews responsible for prostitution, the "white slave trade," pornography, the scourges of burglary and armed robbery, receiving and fencing stolen goods, perjury, fraud, embezzlement, counterfeiting, racketeering, cruelty to animals, and much more.

At the end of the twentieth century the image of the "criminal Jew" remained part of the antisemitic repertoire, although a reconfiguration beginning in the interwar period and completed following the Second World War, when the dominant antisemitic stereotype became that of the *Żydokomuna* (Judeo-communism), had deprived the image of much but not all of its original content. In Alina Cała's interview with a self-proclaimed antisemite from Strzyżów in 1984, her respondent declared: "What did they [the Jews] bring with them to Poland? Only theft [*złodziejstwo*] and communism."[1] At the end of 2001 the *Ruch* media outlet distributed a small book titled *The Polish Holocaust: Documentation of Jewish Crimes in the History of Poland, Parts IV and V*, which likewise tied Jewish "criminality" to the real and imagined ills of the communist era.[2] Although still demonized, the "criminal Jew" in this publication was also associated with the political power exercised in post-communist Poland by "the contemporary *Żydokomuna*," which was said to have "gigantic international financial and political means" at its disposal and as its main agent the "president-swindler" Aleksander Kwaśniewski. Fortunately, such literature finds few readers in Poland today, which is why it is confined to the bottom shelves of kiosks. The same cannot be said, however, of the top-shelf antisemitic print journalism of the early twentieth century.[3] Here too, though, we should take care not to exaggerate the range and impact of the demonic images of the "criminal Jew" it sought to propagate.

That these images gained currency at all had much to do with the onset of Poland's socioeconomic transformation from a rural to an industrial society at the end of the nineteenth century. My discussion begins by exploring the

1. Alina Cała, *Wizerunek Żyda w polskiej kulturze ludowej* (Warsaw, 1987), 60.

2. *Polski Holokaust: Dokumentacja żydowskich zbrodni w dziejach Polski, cz. IV i V* (Warsaw, 2001).

3. In this regard, I have examined several titles from the Warsaw-based mass-circulation press for the period before the First World War, including Poland's oldest daily newspaper, *Kurjer Warszawski*, as well as the nationalist dailies *Gazeta Warszawska* and *Gazeta Poranna 2 grosze*. The latter, in particular, rivaled *Kurjer Warszawski* in its number of subscribers by 1914. For this early period, I have also looked at *Przegląd Katolicki*, the semiofficial weekly of the Roman Catholic Church in Russian Poland, and the influential "literary-cultural" monthly *Myśl Niepodległa*, initially established by Andrzej Niemowejski to promote anticlerical "freethinking." Although the weekly *Rola*, Poland's first antisemitic periodical, established in the 1870s, would cease publication on the eve of the Great War, its views were no longer treated as marginal among a large segment of the Warsaw press after 1905. For the interwar period, I have also examined the nationalist weekly *Myśl Narodowa* and the Catholic weekly *Kultura* published in Poznań, in addition to the aforementioned *Przegląd Katolicki*. If one agrees with Aleksander Hertz that antisemitism "introduces a definition of the Jew as an enemy who should be hated and combatted," then all these periodicals, regardless of their other ideological proclivities, can be defined as antisemitic; see Aleksander Hertz, *The Jews in Polish Culture*, trans. Richard Lourie (Evanston, Ill., 1988), 75. For a discussion of antisemitism in the fin-de-siècle Warsaw press, see Theodore R. Weeks, "Fanning the Flames: Jews in the Warsaw Press, 1905–1912," *East European Jewish Affairs* 28, no. 2 (winter 1998–99): 63–81.

fears, particularly among the Polish intelligentsia, generated by a modern era perceived by many as morally corrupt, a *świat zwyrodniały* ("degenerate world"), in Jerzy Jedlicki's words, a world of darkness and foreboding associated with the city, one of whose major features was urban crime.[4] Indeed, the exaggerated perception of ever rising crime rates in the degenerate environment of the city contained many features of a moral panic, as defined by contemporary sociologists and criminologists. And since Poland's Jews constituted a substantial proportion of the urban population, this moral panic would eventually turn its gaze on Jews, already cast in the role of strangers and outsiders. I then compare the resulting images of the "criminal Jew" and their role in antisemitic discourse with actual statistics on criminality in the late partition and interwar periods. Here the goal is to determine not simply whether the images can withstand statistical measurement but whether the statistics themselves and the criminal justice systems that produced them were influenced by ethnic profiling. Finally, I attempt to determine the social and cultural range and influence of the imagined "criminal Jew" among the general population of early twentieth-century Poland. In particular, did counterimages in Polish culture, including the philosemitic one of "honest Jew," prove sufficiently durable to neutralize, if not defeat, that of the demonized "criminal Jew?"

A Modern Plague: The Construction of the Criminal Jew

By the end of the nineteenth century the optimism of the early Warsaw positivists in the progress of modern civilization had given way to a criticism of modernity in Polish intellectual circles. Among the substantial component of the Polish intelligentsia that eventually constituted the radical right, according to Brian Porter, this entailed a loss of faith in the soothing promises of historical time.[5] Suddenly, the world of modernity became a dark place, nowhere more so than in its principal enclave of the city. Such cultural pessimism, moreover, was hardly confined to the radical right. Even positivist literature about the city had been ambivalent; Warsaw in particular was portrayed interchangeably as a center of progress and civilization and as a location of immorality and evil. Yet the evils of the city as depicted by the positivists were, in the words of one scholar, "private rather than social."[6] For modernist

4. Jerzy Jedlicki, *Świat zwyrodniały: Lęki i wyroki krytyków nowoczesności* (Warsaw, 2000); see especially the chapter "Proces przeciwsko miastu," 83–112. "The accusation against the city and its defense," according to Jedlicki, "were [in Poland] fragments of a much wider process: the choice of nationality against cosmopolitanism, of tradition against a too rapid modernization of life and customs according to western models" (90).

5. See Brian Porter, *When Nationalism Began to Hate: Imagining Modern Politics in Nineteenth-Century Poland* (Oxford, 2000).

6. Ewa Ihnatowicz, "Miasto kryminalne?" in *Miasto, kultura, literatura; wiek XIX*, ed. Jan Data (Gdańsk, 1993), 124.

writers such as Gabriela Zapolska, however, the city was a prison, a labyrinth, and a monster that devoured its victims, physically and morally. Zapolska's city, according to Irena Gubernat, was a source of human depravity—of the moral degeneration, collapse, and disgrace of its individual inhabitants—in both its public and its private spaces. Noble and good character allowed positivist heroes to survive in the city; Zapolska's city spit out people of such character because they were weak.[7]

Zapolska herself was a self-declared "anti-antisemite," but her vision of the city as a locus of darkness and crime was shared by the nationalist press. Burglary in Warsaw, according to the Endecja's *Gazeta Warszawska*, had reached the proportions of a "plague."[8] Elsewhere, *Gazeta Warszawska* sounded the alarm about the criminal "trade" of "banditism" (armed robbery), one "involving minimal risks and significant profits" and plied by "professionals" who also trained a growing number of "journeymen and apprentices."[9] The metaphor of the plague was also employed by *Kurjer Warszawski*, the largest mass-circulation daily in Russian Poland, to describe the "almost daily" attacks of "gangs" and "bandits" at the beginning of 1912.[10] "We no longer recognize life without crime," declared *Kurjer Warszawski* several months later; elsewhere, the daily claimed that the "flood of crime" had reduced Poland to the level of "the wildest regions of the Balkans, even worse." Such a country, according to *Kurjer*, "cannot call itself civilized."[11]

Moral panic theory, formulated originally by British sociologists Stanley Cohen and Stuart Hall in the 1970s and firmly established in the conceptual apparatus of criminologists by the 1990s, has been used in recent decades to explain public anxiety about and reaction to increases in the reported rate of specific offenses. The notion of a "moral panic" suggests that the scale of the public response is disproportionately greater than the scale of the problem and is overblown by media exaggeration and hyperbole. According to Cohen, the mass media are "especially important carrier[s] and producer[s] of moral panics" in industrial societies. "The media have long operated as agents of moral indignation in their own right," he has argued, "[and] can create social problems suddenly and dramatically" by devoting a great deal of attention to "sensational crimes, scandals, bizarre happenings and strange goings-on."[12] A wave of irrational public fear can also be said to exist, according to Philip Jenkins, when media representatives and public "experts" appear to talk "with one voice" about rates, diagnoses, problems, and solutions; stress the

7. See Irena Gubernat, "Miasto Zapolskiej," in *Data, Miasto*, 213–25.
8. "Plaga złodziejstwa," *Gazeta Warszawska* 41 (August 10, 1912): 2.
9. "Recydywa bandytyzmu," *Gazeta Warszawska* 65 (September 3, 1912): 1.
10. "Ciężka plaga," *Kurjer Warszawski* 24 (January 24, 1912): 1–2.
11. "Powódź zbrodni," *Kurjer Warszawski* 240 (August 30, 1912); see also "Rozbójnictwo," *Kurjer* Warszawski 203 (July 24, 1912), 1, and "Jak w dzikim kraju," *Kurjer Warszawski* 81 (March 22, 1913): 4–5.
12. Stanley Cohen, "Deviance and Moral Panics," in *The Sociology of Crime and Deviance: Selected Issues*, ed. Susan Caffrey (Kent, U.K., 1995), 213–14.

"novelty" of deviance; and adopt medical and biological metaphors (of plague, epidemic, virus, etc.) to describe deviant acts.[13] Of course, not every public concern, anxiety, or alarm about a crime problem can be labeled a moral panic, as one critic of the theory has cautioned.[14] The public discourse in Warsaw on the eve of the First World War, however, certainly bears many of its principal features.

One such feature is the heightened fear of sexual offenses and crimes, which is in turn closely related to other fears of deviance, partly explaining, according to Jenkins, "why concerns about sex crimes have frequently acquired similar ideological directions, emphasizing external monster figures, psychopaths, and predators." In addition, Jenkins argues that claims about the sexual menace in the United States in the middle decades of the twentieth century "focused ill-defined fears resulting from the social upheavals of this time, which were causing a radical redefinition of gender roles and family obligations."[15] Indeed, the moral panic in much of the Western Christian world at the end of the nineteenth and beginning of the twentieth centuries was caused by demographic change and gender turbulence: that is, by a declining birthrate in marriage, which in turn was seen as related to grave moral sins—the practice of birth control and the use of contraceptives. Such concerns were particularly acute in societies with mixed population such as Poland, where the dominant group felt threatened not only by the "other" but by the increasing visibility of professional, educated women in the "threatened" group who exemplified the conscious limitation of fertility, challenged existing gender roles, and symbolized social disorder and "race suicide."[16] Consequently, another main feature of moral panics, according to Erich Goode and Nachman Ben-Yehuda, is the fabrication by "one symbolic-moral universe [of] a negative, morally evil symbolic universe" and its campaigns against "arch-enemies who supposedly helped support this deviant, heretical symbolic-moral universe."[17]

It is in this light that one should view the widespread Polish discourse on prostitution, the image of which represented all the dangers of social chaos felt to be inherent in human sexuality and the emancipated female.[18] More-

13. Philip Jenkins, *Moral Panic: Changing Concepts of the Child Molester in Modern America* (New Haven, 1998), 6, 21.

14. Peter Waddington, "Mugging as a Moral Panic: A Question of Proportion," in Caffrey, *Sociology of Crime and Deviance*, 235–47.

15. Jenkins, *Moral Panic*, 16. See also his *Intimate Enemies: Moral Panics in Contemporary Great Britain* (New York, 1992) for a discussion of Britain's moral panic of the 1980s, which featured widespread allegations of sexual abuse of children in sex rings and satanic cults.

16. See Alison Mackinnon, *Love and Freedom: Professional Women and the Reshaping of Personal Life* (Cambridge, U.K., 1997), 12–15, 21.

17. Erich Goode and Nachman Ben-Yehuda, *Moral Panics: The Social Construction of Deviance* (Oxford, 1994), 200.

18. For a similar discussion as it relates to fin-de-siècle Germany, see John C. Fout, "Sexual Politics in Wilhelmine Germany: The Male Gender Crisis, Moral Purity, and Homophobia," in *Forbidden History: The State, Society, and the Regulation of Sexuality in Modern Europe; Essays from the Journal of the History of Sexuality*, ed. John C. Fout (Chicago, 1992), 259–92.

over, from the point of view of fin-de-siècle Warsaw's publicists, prostitution in particular came to symbolize all the criminal evils of the city. According to Stanisław Milewski, it was said that "theft, armed robbery, even murder, embezzlement and bribery grew in its shadow. . . . It led to the compromising of organs of authority and the police. It developed without restriction—the gangrene of the city. It led to the moral collapse of women and their capture by dealers in human flesh."[19] In the minds of such publicists, who included many from Poland's first generation of feminists, prostitution acquired legendary dimensions.[20] Wildly exaggerated claims that one of every three women in Warsaw between the ages of twenty and thirty-five practiced prostitution were matched only by depictions of Warsaw as the center of yearly meetings of the "white slave traders" who supposedly supplied brothels around the globe with dozens of thousands of women annually from the Polish Kingdom and Galicia.[21]

The brothel was thus imagined as the primary setting of urban crime. In the positivist era of the 1870s and early 1880s, images of the brothel were connected to attitudes toward lower-class sexual behavior as part of a perceived social pathology. By the early twentieth century, however, Jews were increasingly held responsible for the "prostitution industry" and its "spread of demoralization," not to mention the "white slave trade." The association of the male Jew with the prostitute was commonplace throughout modern Europe, according to Sander Gilman, as it was believed that Jews and prostitutes had a common interest: namely, "the conversion of sex into money and money into sex."[22] Moreover, Jews and prostitutes were both associated in public discourse with the spread of venereal disease, especially syphilis, which was much feared in the early twentieth century. Finally, the association of Jews with "white slavery," particularly the kidnapping of Christian girls for export to foreign brothels, recalled the centuries-long chimerical assertion of Jewish predators kidnapping Christian children in order to use their blood in acts of ritual cannibalism.[23]

---

19. Stanisław Milewski, *Ciemne sprawy dawnych warszawiaków* (Warsaw, 1982), 100.

20. According to George L. Mosse, what began as a Europe-wide campaign against inspections of prostitutes, their treatment and exploitation, was originally conceived as part of a feminist struggle for women's dignity and rights. Yet once that campaign went beyond the mere abolition of inspections to a crusade against prostitution itself, the feminist context dissipated, while the crusade for social purity forged ahead. "The transition from the advocacy of women's rights to a crusade against all forms of vice," Mosse argues, "helped reconcile the feminist movement with both respectability and nationalism": George L. Mosse, *Nationalism and Sexuality: Respectability and Abnormal Sexuality in Modern Europe* (New York, 1985), 100–111.

21. Jolanta Sikorska-Kulesza, "Prostitution in Congress Poland," *Acta Polniae Historica* 83 (2001): 127, 131.

22. Sander Gilman, *The Jew's Body* (New York, 1991), 122.

23. Gavin Langmuir's argument that antisemitism, whether medieval or "modern," should not be defined by shifts in its rhetorical form over the centuries, but by the chimerical assertions contained therein, is particularly applicable to the "modern" association of Jews with "white slavery"; see Gavin Langmuir, *Toward a Definition of Antisemitism* (Berkeley, Calif., 1990). In

In the Polish context, antisemites would exploit already widespread concerns about prostitution and white slavery to cast the Jew in a dual role as the personification of the plague of urban crime *and* the main source of moral and sexual perversion. According to George L. Mosse, the sexual abnormality with which modern European society supposedly endowed the Jews was very much a "part of their putative criminality."[24] Not surprisingly, the antisemitic press also linked Jews to the "explosion" of pornography in Warsaw and other major Polish cities before the Great War.[25] In Poland, however, "pornography" was often equated with the spread of birth control literature. It was also widely believed that Jews had invented birth control, particularly the condom. And since the condom was used as much for the prevention of venereal disease as for contraception, it too was frequently associated with the presumably "Jewish" brothel and the crimes it inspired.

These beliefs raise the question of whether assertions of Jewish sexual immorality, particularly the association with prostitution, possessed a "kernel of truth" or were simply the contorted fantasies of antisemites.[26] In fact, following the lifting of a ban on Jewish residence in certain parts of Warsaw in 1862, Jews would play a significant role in the establishment of legally sanctioned "public houses," so that by 1874 two-thirds of all registered prostitutes in Warsaw were Jewish. As late as 1905, Jews continued to own the majority of public houses in Warsaw—yet Jewish participation in prostitution had already declined precipitously before 1905 and would continue to do so in subsequent years. In part, this decline was due to the growth of illegal prostitution at the expense of the licensed bawdy houses and the influx of Polish migrants into the illegal trade at the turn of the century.[27] Of the registered prostitutes in Łódź, the Jewish percentage declined from 35.7 to 29.8 percent between 1902 and 1904. Of the 2,843 illegal prostitutes arrested by the Łódź police in the 1920s, 20.9 percent were Jews. Well before that time, illegal prostitution in Łódź was several times larger in scale than the open and registered

---

this regard, it is interesting to note that the British moral panic of the late 1980s particularly alarmed Jewish groups who feared a revival of the antisemitic blood libel in the hysteria surrounding the imagined sexual abuse of children in pedophile rings and satanic cults: Jenkins, *Intimate Enemies*, 171–72.

24. Mosse, 147.

25. Milewski, 78, 108–9, 113.

26. According to Langmuir, the possession of a "kernel of truth" in hostile assertions toward Jews distinguishes mere xenophobia from antisemitism: Langmuir, 341–49. Others, like Helen Fein, include xenophobic hostility toward Jews as well as chimerical assertions in a broader definition of antisemitism: see Helen Fein, "Dimensions of Antisemitism: Attitudes, Collective Accusations, and Actions," in *The Persisting Question: Sociological Perspectives and Social Contexts of Antisemitism*, ed. Helen Fein (Berlin, 1987), 67–85.

27. Sikorska-Kulesza, 127. According to a report by the Department of Urban Economy of the Russian Ministry of Internal Affairs, there were 2,512 "controlled" prostitutes in the Polish Kingdom in 1910, more than half of whom were registered in Warsaw province. The report also included data on 1,795 women arrested for illegal prostitution; see "Statystyka prostytucji," *Wiedza* 2, no. 30 (July 24, 1910): 122.

variety, and Jewish participation in the trade was lower than the Jewish proportion of the city's general population.[28] In Warsaw, the culminating point of this transformation was marked by the violence of a May 1905 ransacking of the public houses by gangs associated with the illegal trade, eliminating most of their legal competitors.[29]

But nothing stopped the antisemitic press, particularly before the First World War, from claiming that prostitution in Poland, whether legal or illegal, was dominated by Jews, who were therefore responsible for all of the criminal "evils" associated with the "industry." Such claims were conveniently based on 1870s statistics on the public houses and registered prostitutes. Similarly, antisemites claimed that the global "trade in human flesh" was "practically a Jewish monopoly," while ignoring evidence that Jewish girls were the principal victims of traders whose ethnic composition, like that of Poland's criminal underground more generally, was multinational. When Polish feminists, who themselves exaggerated the scale of the "white slave trade," sought to raise public awareness of the issue, they were accused by *Przegląd Katolicki* of "burdening the Polish nation with the responsibility for the trade in women, when everyone knows that this disgraceful practice is conducted exclusively by Jews."[30] Andrzej Niemojewski's *Myśl Niepodległa*, for its part, demanded that Jewish feminists in the Polish movement "stick to their own kind" and concentrate on the "barbarisms" of the Jewish community rather than spread demoralization among Polish women.[31] "A Jew arrives from South America

28. Edward Rosset, *Prostytucja i choroby weneryczne w Łodzi* (Łódź, 1931), 9–10. Thus, earlier suppositions of medical "experts" of a higher rate of prostitution among the Jewish population, based solely on data compiled on registered prostitutes, cannot be substantiated; for example, see B. Margulies, "Prostytucya w Łodzi," *Zdrowie* 22, no. 8 (1906): 539–47. On the other hand, proportional Jewish participation in registered prostitution was much higher in provincial towns, where Jews often formed the majority of the population; for Piotrków province, see Stanisław Skalski, "Prostytucya w gubernii piotrkowskiej," *Zdrowie* 22, no. 8 (1906): 547–56.

29. In this regard, Laura Engelstein's feminist interpretation of Warsaw's "Great Cathouse Massacre" as a pogrom staged by Jewish workers to assert their masculinity against brothelkeepers fails to account for the fact that the "pogrom" affected only the registered public houses, and it completely ignores the role of the criminal underworld in driving their legal competitors out of business: see Laura Engelstein, *The Keys to Happiness: Sex and the Search for Modernity in Fin-de-Siècle Russia* (Ithaca, N.Y., 1992), 309, 330. That said, her chapter "Sex and the Anti-Semite" (299–333) contains many valuable insights.

30. "Spychanie win żydowskich na polskiej głowie," *Przegląd Katolicki* 10 (March 7, 1914): 156. For a classic statement of the Polish feminist position on the "trade in women," see Marya Turzyma, "Handel kobietami," in *Głos kobiet w kwestyi kobiecej*, ed. Marya Turzyma and Kazimiera Bujwidowa (Kraków, 1903), 143–62. In Russia as well, according to Laurie Bernstein, the discourse on forced prostitution "reinforced the deep strains of antisemitism in Russian society": see Laurie Bernstein, *Sonia's Daughters: Prostitutes and Their Regulation in Imperial Russia* (Berkeley, Calif., 1995), 161.

31. "Kobieta w Talmudzie," *Myśl Niepodległa* 265 (January 1914): 28. On the "liberal antisemitism" of Niemojewski and others, see Tadeusz Stegner, "Liberałowie Królestwa Polskiego wobec kwestii żydowskiej na początku XX wieku," *Przegląd Historyczny* 80, no. 1 (1989): 69–88; Theodore R. Weeks, "Polish 'Progressive Antisemitism,' 1905–1914," *East European Jewish Affairs* 25, no. 2 (1995): 49–68; and Jerzy Jedlicki, "The End of the Dialog, Warsaw, 1907–1912," in *The Jews in Poland*, ed. S. Kapralski (Kraków, 1999), 2: 111–23.

and literally persuades domestic servants, village girls, and workers to do anything," according to the eminently respectable *Kurjer Warszawski*. Claiming that the Jewish trade in Polish women "has become one more aspect of the Jewish Question in Poland," the author of that article argued that Polish feminist efforts to exert moral pressure on "the dealers in human flesh" would inevitably fail because "they are all Jews, as far removed from us as the Hottentots."[32]

As already noted, the sexual dimensions attributed to Jewish criminality by the antisemitic press before the First World War extended beyond prostitution and the "white slave trade" to brand Jews as pornographers, often by innuendo. Thus, the confiscation of a "filthy" press in Warsaw "belonging to a certain Zimmerman," which presumably distributed pornographic postcards and photographs to all larger cities of the Russian Empire, was singled out by *Przegląd Katolicki* in 1913 as a particularly "Jewish atrocity."[33] And although the association of Jews with prostitution appears to have declined slightly in the antisemitic discourse of the interwar period, the image intensified of the Jewish pornographer, who was now spreading his "moral filth" not only through the sale of stamps and postcards but also through the cultural vehicles of literature, cinema, dance halls, the visual and dramatic arts, fashion, and popular music—all of which supposedly had been conquered by Jews. The objective of this "abominable pornography," according to Jan Wszebor in *Myśl Narodowa*, was "to poison our souls."[34] "Let's admit it openly," wrote a contributor to *Przegląd Katolicki* in 1936, "the spread of evil and demoralization has been and continues to be overwhelmingly the work of Jews" who "derive tremendous profits from the trade in pornography... uninhibited by liberal judges."[35] For Jerzy Bondrowski, the segregation of Jews from Christians in the public school system was a matter of defending public morality, since Jewish teenage males were naturally the main "collectors of pornography" as "sons of cheaters, owners of bars and nightclubs, and dealers in flesh."[36] Adam Romer went even further in the pages of *Przegląd Katolicki*, calling for the gradual but involuntary emigration of the "numerous Jewish throngs" who make their livelihood from "moral depravation": that is, from "pornography, pimping, dance halls, and other means of exploiting human weakness."[37]

32. "Handel kobietami," *Kurjer Warszawski* 330 (November 29, 1913): 2–3.

33. "Żydowska ohyda," *Przegląd Katolicki* 28 (July 12, 1913): 444.

34. Jan Wszebor, "Film w Polsce," *Myśl Narodowa* 24 (June 5, 1938): 375–76; see also Józef Stanisław Czarnecki, "Seksualizm w literaturze," *Kultura* 25 (June 19, 1938): 2; Ks. Henryk Weryński, "Walka z bezwstydem i pornografią," *Przegląd Katolicki* 42 (October 30, 1932): 659–62; Wacław Sas-Podolski, "Zażydzenie kultury umysłowej w Polsce," *Przegląd Katolicki* 28 (July 9, 1933): 437–39.

35. Spartanin, "Na marginesie walki z pornografią," *Przegląd Katolicki* 30 (July 26, 1936): 514–15.

36. Jerzy Bondrowski, "Żydzi we wspomnieniach," *Kultura* 28 (July 11, 1937): 5.

37. Adam Romer, "Zagadnienie kolonialne a sprawa żydowska," *Przegląd Katolicki* 36 (September 20, 1936): 615–16.

Before the First World War, according to *Myśl Niepodległa*, not only pros-titution, "white slavery," and pornography but divorce, polygamy, premarital sex, incest, and sodomy were peculiarly Jewish vices.[38] *Rola*, with its pride of place as the Poland's first mass circulation antisemitic publication, called upon the Polish press to cease its advertisements of birth control devices, a "dis-graceful commodity" the distributors of which were "exclusively Jews" intent on encouraging "criminal debauchery."[39] Father S. Popławski, a frequent prewar contributor to *Przegląd Katolicki*, went so far as to warn that Polish women risked moral contamination by reading Jewish female authors.[40] By the 1930s the imagined linkage between the "supremacy of eroticism" in Polish literature and Jewish cultural influences was so firmly established in the antisemitic mind-set that a proposal to ban from the public schools all text-books, lectures, and literature written by Jews seemed to follow naturally.[41]

The antisemitic press of the early twentieth century linked Jewish sexual abnormality to a larger moral perversion that, in the words of *Myśl Niepodległa*, "permits anything."[42] For Andrzej Niemojewski, the monthly's editor, modern Jewish criminality was directly derived from the depraved moral code contained in the Talmud, a "simply criminal" book "blindly fol-lowed by the Jewish plebeian masses" that conflicted with the penal codes "of all civilized nations." The Talmud, according to Niemojewski, contained instruction that "directly or indirectly approves every kind of immoral and criminal behavior," including murder, criminal conspiracy, fraud, counterfeit-ing, the "trade in flesh," blackmail, "hooliganism," defamation of character, and livestock poisoning.[43]

In this regard, Niemojewski belonged to an older tradition of "enlightened" Polish criticism and condemnation of the Talmud, one that includes such lumi-naries as Stanisław Staszic and Julian Ursyn Niemcewicz.[44] It would be an exaggeration to claim, however, that anti-Talmudism was a defining feature of Polish liberalism. Most Polish liberals of the late nineteenth and early twen-tieth centuries shared the views of Bolesław Prus: "The Talmud is not at all a dogmatic book, but rather a collection of interpretations. Even without that, however, one must assume that it does not exert too decisive an influence on

38. "Kobieta w Talmudzie," 24–26.
39. "Ogłoszenia żyda-optyka," *Rola* 29 (July 20, 1912): 529.
40. Ks. S. Popławski, "Żydówka dla Polek," *Przegląd Katolicki* 8 (February 21, 1914): 114–17.
41. Jan Szczęsny Rogala, "O wprowadzenie kwestii żydowskiej na tory realne," *Przegląd Katolicki* 22 (May 28, 1939): 343–45.
42. "Etyka Żyda w stosunku do goja i jego urządzeń społecznych," *Myśl Niepodległa* 260 (November 1913), 1499–1500.
43. For a sampling of Niemojewski's writings about the Talmud, in addition to the article cited above, see "Kodeks złodziejski a szlachetni," *Myśl Niepodległa* 266 (January 1914): 49–58. Practically every reference to Jews in *Myśl Niepodległa* from 1912 to 1914, however, contained an attack on the Talmud.
44. For Staszic and Niemcewicz's writings on the Talmud, see *Stranger in Our Midst: Images of the Jew in Polish Literature*, ed. Harold B. Segel (Ithaca, N.Y., 1996), 40–41, 53.

the character of Jews. If books truly had an effect on people, then how honorable would Christians have to be!"[45] Nor did liberal antisemites such as Iza Moszczeńska and Aleksander Świętochowski, focused as they were on Jewish economic and political competition before the Great War, use the Talmud as their foil or claim that Jews lived according to a criminal moral code. Niemojewski, on the other hand, would argue after the First World War that the criminal Jew was not the product of the Talmud but that the Talmud was a product of Jewish criminality.[46] In this regard, Niemojewski moved much closer to the position of *Przegląd Katolicki*, which before the Great War did not need to claim "expertise" in the Talmud in order to refer to "crimes specific to this 'nation'"—which it listed as usury, smuggling, the trade in women, the leadership of armed bands, speculation, horse theft, and the fencing of stolen goods—or to denounce "the social solidarity of the Jewish community with criminal organizations," resulting from "their lack of any scruples, of any ethics."[47]

Nevertheless, in the interwar period, Stanisław Jerzy Nowak in *Kultura* retreated to the argument that the Christian struggle with Jews was actually anti-Talmudic rather than antisemitic. "It's not about the shape of the nose," he claimed, but about the "ethical double standard of the Talmud," which permits "even perjury, theft, and fraud" in Jews' relations with Christians; therefore, the struggle against it was one of Christian "idealism" against the "immorality" of Jewish "materialism"—thus echoing the prewar Niemojewski.[48] It may not have been "about the shape of the nose," but articles by Catholic clergy appearing in *Myśl Narodowa* and *Przegląd Katolicki* linked Jewish religious texts and practices to "Satanism" or referred to Jews themselves "as instruments of Satan," evidence that the chimerical assertions within antisemitism could exist, even prosper, outside a "modern" racist agenda.[49]

During the years of the 1912–14 Warsaw-centered boycott of Jewish shops and retail stores, the first of its kind led by the National Democrats, the press made much of Jewish criminality in the economic sphere.[50] Jewish economic competition with Poles during these years was by its very nature branded as "unfair" and "deceitful."[51] *Przegląd Katolicki* went furthest in this regard,

45. Ibid., 216–17.
46. Hertz, 204.
47. "Z najnowszej literatury o Żydach," *Przegląd Katolicki* 8 (February 22, 1913): 114–20, and "Etyka żydowska," *Przegląd Katolicki* 47 (November 22, 1913): 748–49.
48. Stanisław Jerzy Nowak, "Antysemityzm czy antytalmudyzm?" *Kultura* 15 (July 12, 1936): 4.
49. See particularly Ks. Franciszek Błotnicki, "Chrześcijaństwo i antysemitzym," *Myśl Narodowa* 9 (February 28, 1937): 189–190; and M. Skrudlik, "Źródła lucyferianizmu masonerii," *Przegląd Katolicki* 35 (September 11, 1938): 568–69.
50. On the boycott and its sociopolitical aspects, see Robert Blobaum, "The Politics of Antisemitism in Fin-de-Siècle Warsaw," *Journal of Modern History* 73, no. 2 (2001): 275–306.
51. "W kwestji wolnej i podstępnej konkurencji," *Myśl Niepodległa* 231 (January 1913): 136–38.

claiming that "for years the Jews have resorted to terror in the provinces against even the slightest attempt to establish Polish commerce. Denunciations, the poisoning of horses and livestock, even arson are means of normal competition from the Jewish side when its monopoly is threatened."[52] If the anstisemitic press discovered instances of higher-than-average interest rates or prices, Jewish lenders and wholesalers were accused of "usury," "speculation," and monopolistic trade practices.[53] And when Jewish prices were lower, it could only be the result of a "swindle," "manipulation," or "fraud."[54] Jewish bankruptcies, the presumed goal of the boycott, were always considered fraudulent from the perspective of the antisemites.[55] The association of Jews with counterfeiting and "speculation" on lottery tickets (known in the United States as the "numbers racket") also forms part of the constructed image of Jewish economic criminality spread by the antisemitic press before the Great War. *Gazeta Warszawska*, in particular, ran several articles about an "entire falange" of Jewish lottery ticket traders who supposedly swindled Polish "amateurs" out of "thousands of rubles."[56]

Such themes became commonplace during the interwar period, which by the 1930s featured annual anti-Jewish boycotts. Jewish "criminal activity" extended "to all organs of the nation," according to *Myśl Narodowa* at the end of 1937, including the economic field where "Jews collect their yields by robbery and fraud."[57] The previous year, the same periodical turned its gaze on the "plague" of "filthy" Jewish peddlers in Warsaw: "We can assume how many fences of stolen goods are among them ... and [their] assistants in the revitalized criminal 'movement'" who "sell used clothing as new to naive people." Calling for the forced removal of Jewish peddlers from Warsaw "for reasons of hygiene and public order," *Myśl Narodowa* also invoked the purity of the Polish language: "The Jews are destroying and deforming Polish in such a criminal way that it simply should be punished!"[58] Remarkably, antisemitism in Poland by the late 1930s had come to criminalize even the most basic element of human behavior: the use of the tongue.

52. "Przyczynki do kwestji żydowskiej," *Przegląd Katolicki* 14 (April 5, 1913): 222.

53. "Z praktyk lichwiarskich," *Gazeta Warszawska* 144 (November 21, 1912): 2; and "Drożyna mięsa i widoki eksportu, *Gazeta Warszawska* 159 (December 6, 1912): 1.

54. "Taniość żydowska," *Gazeta Poranna 2 grosze* 20 (October 12, 1912): 3; and "Sztuczki żydowskie," *Gazeta Warszawska* 78 (March 20, 1913): 2.

55. "Oszustwa 'firmowa,'" *Gazeta Warszawska* 23 (January 24, 1913): 2; and "Nowa 'plajta' żydowska," *Rola* 7 (February 7, 1912): 107.

56. "Przed ciągnieniem loteryi," *Gazeta Warszawka* 158 (December 5, 1912): 2. See also "Reforma loteryi klasycznej," *Gazeta Warszawska* 174 (December 21, 1912): 2; "Popłoch wśród spekulantów loteryjnych," *Gazeta Warszawska* 9 (January 10, 1913): 2, and 36 (February 6, 1913): 2.

57. "Co robią w Polsce żydzi," *Myśl Narodowa* 51 (December 5, 1937): 775–76.

58. Fel. Lach, "Plaga handelsmanów," *Myśl Narodowa* 34 (August 16, 1936): 536–37. For a discussion of long-standing Christian perceptions of the Jew's "voice" or language (whether Yiddish or Hebrew, "hidden" or "polluted") as pathophysiological, see Gilman, 10–37.

Statistics

The image of the "criminal Jew," which would figure so prominently in anti-semitic discourse of the interwar period, was constructed more or less in its entirety in the last years of partitioned Poland, particularly in Warsaw. But did this image reflect any, even partial, social reality. To create at least a facade of fact, antisemites often resorted to statistics. I have already suggested how very sporadic and limited data from the 1870s were used to create the impression after the turn of the century that prostitution was a "Jewish industry." Similarly, the antisemitic press cited statistics taken from questionable sources for the 1870s and 1880s to indict the Jewish community as a whole for a laundry list of crimes. Based on such sources, both *Gazeta Poranna 2 grosze* and *Myśl Niepodległa* in the summer of 1914 published figures which suggested that for every thousand cases tried in the Russian courts, Jews constituted an overwhelming majority of those accused of livestock poisoning (82.4 percent), armed robbery (65.5 percent), fencing stolen goods (79.7 percent), perjury and false denunciations (86.2 percent), fraudulent bankruptcies (92.1 percent), commercial fraud (78.9 percent), and the trade in women (93.7 percent).[59] Niemojewski's monthly, in particular, had no qualms about publishing such data, despite the fact that two years earlier it had published far more recent statistics from the Russian Ministry of Justice that showed Jewish criminality to be less that of the Christian population.[60]

It is likely, however, that Jewish criminality had been higher in the 1870s and 1880s than it was a generation later on the eve of the Great War. I believe this can be explained by the fact that the social and economic dislocations caused by Poland's capitalist transformation, then in its initial phase, first affected the existing urban population and therefore Jews engaged in small-scale commerce, retailing, and manufacturing. As in the case of prostitution, however, subsequent waves of migration from the Polish countryside to the cities dramatically reduced the proportion of Jewish participation in urban crime—as is reflected in qualitative evidence, as well. In his two volumes of memoirs written in prison in the early 1930s, the often convicted felon Icek Farbarowicz lamented that in the old days "all of the good crooks were Jews" and fences "primarily Jews." The influx of "others" into the criminal underworld, Farbarowicz complained, had destroyed his "profession" and its moral code of "honor among thieves." Similarly, Farbarowicz defended the old (i.e., Jewish) relationship between professional criminals and registered prostitutes, based on mutuality and a shared "rejection by society," against the "new"

59. "Przestępość śród Żydów," *Gazeta Poranna 2 grosze* 160 (June 12, 1914): 1–2; and "Talmudyczny kodeks złodziejski a statystyka," *Myśl Niepodległa* 284 (July 1914): 956–57.
60. "Spostrzeżenie nad stanem kultury naszego ludu," *Myśl Niepodległa* 214 (August 1912): 1022–23. In this instance, Niemojewski's purpose in publishing such data was anticlerical, to ridicule the Catholic Church's claims to moral inspiration of the Polish population.

(i.e., Polish) relationship between pimps and prostitutes, based on the economic exploitation of street girls.[61]

Thus, at the same time that the image of the criminal Jew was being constructed in Polish antisemitic discourse, actual Jewish criminality was experiencing a rapid decline, a trend that would continue into the interwar period. Yet even official data present a distorted picture, because Russian and eventually interwar Polish statistics on criminality included misdemeanors. These were often minor infractions of administrative regulations, which affected in particular Jews who made their livelihoods from trade and commerce and whose infringement of various codes often resulted in small fines. For example, 13.3 percent of the sentences by the courts under Russian rule in 1910 involved such administrative violations, which effectively raised the rate of punished crime among Jews to 1.6 per thousand, compared with 1.3 per thousand among Roman Catholics. When this category is removed from consideration, however, the Jewish felonious crime rate for 1910 was almost 20 percent lower than that of the Catholic population.[62]

Polish criminal statistics from the mid-1920s, presenting a far more accurate picture in that minor transgressions (*wykroczenia*) were excluded from the compilations, continue to demonstrate rapidly declining rates of crime among the Jewish population. In 1924 a total of 184,355 individuals were punished for criminal offenses by the Polish courts; of these, 72 percent were Poles, 21 percent were "Ruthenians (i.e., Ukrainians)," and a mere 3.4 percent were Jews. The highest rate of Jewish criminality was recorded in the central provinces, which accounted for 53 percent of all Jews punished by the Polish courts. The central provinces (Warsaw, Łódź, Kielce, Lublin, and Białystok) corresponded roughly to the former Polish Kingdom under Russian rule and included the largest urban concentrations of Jews. Here, of 45,288 punished individuals, Poles accounted for 91 percent of those sentenced by the courts, Jews for 8 percent.[63]

In 1925 the Polish courts sentenced a total of 184,964 individuals for criminal offenses, of whom 67 percent were Poles, 26 percent were "Ruthenians," and 2.9 percent were Jews. In the central provinces, of the 37,994 individuals punished by the courts, Poles continued to account for 91 percent of the

61. Urke-Nachalnik (Icek Farbarowicz), *Życiorys własny przestępcy* (Łódź, 1989), 208, and his *Żywe grobowce* (Łódź, 1990), 135–38. These accounts of the criminal underworld and prison life under Russian, German, and Polish rule are unique for their articulated insights, due largely to the literacy Farbarowicz acquired as a Yeshiva student. Although they offer a somewhat sensationalized confession for public consumption, designed to promote both the sale of his memoirs and reform of the penal system, Farbarowicz's description of the changing demographics of criminality on the eve of the Great War has no observable agenda and is verified by quantitative evidence.

62. *Rocznik Statystyczny Królestwa Polskiego: Rok 1914* (Warsaw, 1915), 243–44.

63. *Statystka Polski (Seria dawna)*, 9, pt. 1, *Statystyka kryminalna: Osoby prawomocnie skazane i uniewinnione w 1924 roku* (Warsaw, 1930), 215.

total, whereas the Jewish proportion declined to 5.7 percent.[64] Overall, the crime rate among Jews from 1924 to 1925 declined by 14.3 percent for Poland as a whole and by 35 percent in the central provinces.

Thus the ratio of Jewish to non-Jewish criminality in Poland during the 1920s had fallen to well below 1-to-2—perhaps too low for official purposes, because in August 1931 the Ministry of Justice introduced "new" methods of compiling criminal statistics, similar to those of the earlier Russian compilations that had lumped misdemeanors and minor administrative offenses together with felonies. And like the Russians, the Polish Ministry would thenceforth seek to characterize criminality in terms of religious affiliation. That reorganization of criminal statistics was strongly criticized by Karol Czernicki in *Gazeta Sądowa Warszawska*, the leading organ of the interwar Polish bar—a bar, one might add, that had yet to be corrupted by anti-semitism.[65] Czernicki argued that the new methods "will not reflect the factual state of affairs" and condemned the ministry's "waste of time and money on an experiment that already contains within itself mistaken foundations."[66]

On such foundations, however, were Polish criminal statistics built in the 1930s, and they immediately produced the desired results, reflected in the summary figures of the *Mały Rocznik Statystyczny* (Small Statistical Annual). Though the fact is not often noticed, even that publication notes the incongruity of its own data with criminal statistics published in previous years and attributes it to "changes in methods of calculation."[67] Liebman Hersch, who studied Polish criminal statistics for the period 1932 to 1937 and published

64. Ibid., pt. 2, *Statystyka kryminalna: Osoby prawomocnie skazane i uniewinnione w 1925 roku* (Warsaw, 1930), 641.

65. As late as 1936 the law journal would warn of "dangerous currents" among younger members of the bar, whose calls for a break with positive law and the adoption of the idea of "state totalism" and the "collectivist" application of the law were viewed as threats to the "legal order in the state" and the "legal consciousness of society": Ignacy Kondratowicz, *Gazeta Sądowa Warszawska* 26 (June 29, 1936): 401–3, and 27–28 (July 13, 1936): 417–21. Two years later, however, the wolves were not only at the door of the Polish bar but well inside it. By that time the principal nationalist organization among Polish lawyers, the *Związek Adwokatów Polskich*, represented nearly 40 percent of all Polish members of the bar. Its purpose was to wage a "decisive struggle to defend the bar against the alien flood and to restore to it a real Polish face and character": see "Zjazd Związku Adwokatów Polskich," *Gazeta Sądowa Warszawska* 19 (May 10, 1937): 285–86. That agenda was partially realized in the spring of 1938 when new statutes regulating the legal profession restricted applications and admissions to the bar from "certain categories" of the population. Though Jews were not specifically singled out by the new legislation, it was clear that it applied to them.

66. Karol Czernicki, "Kilka uwag o nowej organizacji statystyki przestępości," *Gazeta Sądowa Warszawska* 48 (November 30, 1931): 699–701.

67. For the most accessible version, see *Mały Rocznik Statystyczny Polski*, ed. Ewa Estreicher-Grodziska and Ludwik Grodzicki (Warsaw, 1990; reprint of 1939 and 1941 editions), 152. Actually, the *Mały Rocznik Statystyczny* contains very little information on Jewish criminality. The annals of 1936–38 furnish only half a page of information about certain types of crime for the convicted of various denominations in the years 1934–36. Only for the year 1937 (in the 1939 edition) is there more detailed information (pages 365–66) concerning the types of crimes and the religious affiliation of the convicted in Poland.

his findings in the *Yivo Bleter* in 1942 (translated into English in 1946), shows that the inclusion of minor transgressions effectively multiplied the 1932 Jewish crime rate by 11 to 12 times the annual average for the mid-1920s and raised the percentage of Jews among the convicted to 12.7 percent and the ratio of Jewish to non-Jewish criminality to 135-to-100. Needless to say, such statistics provided much-needed ammunition to the antisemitic press of the interwar period in its efforts to maintain and substantiate the image of the criminal Jew. What is most interesting about Hersch's findings, however, is their demonstration that even *with* these statistical manipulations, Jewish criminality in both the actual sense and in terms of *wykroczenia* continued their rapid decline, so that by 1937 the percentage of Jews among the convicted *for both* crimes and minor transgressions had declined to 6.5 percent and the ratio of Jewish to non-Jewish criminality to 63.9-to-100. In 1932, 95,578 Jews had been convicted for a variety of offenses; by 1937, that number had dropped to 23,131.[68]

Although exact statistics are not available for the prison population, there is enough information to argue that Jews did not constitute more than 2 to 4 percent of the inmates of interwar Poland's penal institutions from the mid-1920s to the end of the 1930s. In this regard, it would be inaccurate to claim that Jews were victims of ethnic profiling by the criminal justice system of interwar Poland, which maintained its relative independence vis-à-vis the government and especially the attempted encroachments of the Ministry of Justice. Before leaving the realm of statistics, however, there is one other category of crime that I need to mention: namely, the political. In 1924, according to a report of the International Red Cross, Jews accounted for slightly more than 39 percent of Poland's 951 political prisoners.[69] It is safe to argue that the majority of Jewish political prisoners in 1924 had been arrested for their involvement in illegal communist formations. According to the *Mały Rocznik Statystyczny* for 1936, Jews accounted for about 35 percent of those sentenced for "crimes and transgressions against the state and social order," a veritable hodgepodge of the most diversified offenses ranging from treason to a host of violations of administrative regulations, including failure to register one's residence with the authorities (a common urban transgression). By comparison, when the 1937 annual sorted out actual political offenses from other crimes and transgressions against the state, Jews accounted for only 7.7 percent of all those convicted for the former, a percentage lower than the 9.8 percent Jewish share of the total population.[70]

Thus, like the myth of the criminal Jew more generally, the myth of the

68. Liebman Hersch, "Jewish and Non-Jewish Criminality in Poland, 1932–1937," *Yivo Annual* 1 (1946): 183.

69. A. Mogilnicki, "Bezstronny głos o więzieniach polskich," *Gazeta Sądowa Warszawska* 3 (January 17, 1925): 33–35.

70. *Mały Rocznik Statystyczny* (1937/1939), 365–366; see also Hersch, 186. The figure of 9.8 percent for the Jewish proportion of the total population, moreover, is derived from the 1931 census, which most experts agree tended to understate the shares of the non-Polish minorities.

criminal *Żydokomuna* gathered steam in the public repertoire of antisemitism against countervailing social realities.[71] As recent research of voting patterns in Poland's parliamentary elections of the 1920s has shown, communist and pro-Soviet parties drew their popular support primarily from the Orthodox Belarusian and Ukrainian minorities rather than from Jews, whose support for communists was proportionally less (4 to 7 percent) than their representation of the total population and only slightly higher than that of Polish Roman Catholics.[72] Yet perhaps because of this minor difference between Jewish and Roman Catholic support of communist political formations, and because Jewish political offenses were higher than the overall rate of Jewish criminality, the discursive boundaries of antisemitic demonology began to shift, putting increasing emphasis on Jewish political crimes and "treason." In a 1937 *Myśl Narodowa* article that recounted five recent incidents of Jewish "criminal activity," drawn from Polish dailies "in the course of half an hour," three trials of communists in Kielce, Lublin, and Warsaw topped the list, followed by the arrest of suspects in the "trade in human flesh" in Warsaw and in Kraków the breakup of a ring of thieves with presumed connections to Jewish fences.[73]

The invocation of Judeo-communism as a main source of Jewish criminality in Poland was more than a simple addition to the older xenophobic images constructed earlier in the century. Together they formed the increasingly chimerical character of antisemitism in Poland on the eve of the Second World War, fantasies increasingly removed from whatever "kernels of truth" they may have originally been based upon. "In few areas of myth-making," as Aleksander Hertz put it, "were the magical elements as explicit and prevalent as in anti-Semitism."[74] In the case of the invented myth of the criminal Jew, however, did countervailing reality prove strong enough to limit the range of at least one element of magic?

Who's Afraid of the Big Bad Wolf? The Criminal Jew in Polish Culture

In discussing the range and influence of the antisemitic invention of the criminal Jew, a good place to begin is with the Polish underworld itself. Icek Farbarowicz, in reference to the Łomża prison (known to inmates as "the

71. Françis Guesnet traces the myth of Judeo-communism to stereotypes of the "Litvak" migrants from the Pale of Settlement to the Polish Kingdom at the end of the nineteenth century. In particular, he refers to a pamphlet written by Julian Unszlicht (himself a Jew whom Guesnet mistakenly refers to as a member of the PPS) ominously entitled *O pogrom narodu polskiego: Rola socjallitwaków w niejednej rewolucji* (Kraków, 1912), which claimed that the internationalism of the SDKPiL was a cover for a new Jewish nationalism: François Guesnet, " 'Litwacy' i 'Ostjuden' (Żydzi ze Wschodu): Migracja i stereotypy," in *Tematy żydowskie: Historia, literatura, edukacja*, ed. Elżbieta and Robert Traba (Olsztyn, 1999), 77.

72. See Jeffrey S. Kopstein and Jason Wittenberg, "Who Voted Communist? Reconsidering the Social Bases of Radicalism in Interwar Poland," *Slavic Review* 62, no. 1 (2003): 87–109.

73. "Co robią w Polsce żydzi," *Myśl Narodowa* 51 (December 5, 1937): 775–76.

74. Hertz, 16.

Czerwoniak" because of its red brick facade), where he served more than one
sentence during the First World War, claimed, "The Jewish Question didn't
exist here. We were all brothers."[75] After the war Farbarowicz was transferred
to the Mokotów prison in Warsaw, where he even took under his tutelage a
"pogromist" (that is, a man given a long-term sentence for having participated
in a pogrom, one of the many that wracked Galicia in 1918 and 1919). What
counted in prison, according to Farbarowicz, was recognition and respect for
one's criminal profession and place in the inmate hierarchy, not nationality.[76]
If the "Jewish Question" did not exist in prison, the same could be said of
the underworld more generally. Farbarowicz himself had many Polish
partners during his long career. Whatever conflicts occurred among criminal
gangs, moreover, were over territory rather than nationality. In Arnold
Mostowicz's semifictional account of the legendary Łódź gangster "Blind Max"
Borensztajn, the "bandit of Bałuty" rises to the top by eliminating a Jewish
competitor in a revenge killing. Borensztajn's closest associates, moreover, were
Poles, one a trusted older adviser, the other a hit man who had befriended him
in boyhood.[77] Clearly, the Polish underworld did not share the magical and
mystified "ethics" of "national egoism" that manufactured the criminal Jew.

At the opposite end of the social spectrum as well, the image of the criminal Jew did not penetrate Polish high culture appreciably more than it did the
culture of the socially marginalized. Many years ago Aleksander Hertz argued
that the image of the Jew in Polish literature "is, most frequently, friendly and
at times even warm and affectionate." Such literary tendencies, Hertz went on
to say, often poorly reflected Jewish reality in Poland, and thus the images they
presented were also "stereotyped, fragmentary, and inadequate" but not, by
and large, antisemitic.[78] There were, however, exceptions, including, according to feminist literary scholar Bożena Umińska, Władysław Reymont's *The
Promised Land* (1899) and especially Michał Choromański's "pornographic"
Jealousy and Medicine (1933), novels noted for their combination of racism
and misogyny. Surprisingly, given her later principled opposition to antisemitism, the young Zofia Nałkowska's character of Raissa in *Serpents and
Roses* (1913) is the daughter of a wealthy Jew rumored to have made his fortune from prostitution.[79] Nonetheless, in contrast to much of early twentieth-

75. [Farbarowicz], *Życiorys*, 197.
76. [Farbarowicz], *Żywe grobowce*, 73, 88–90.
77. Arnold Mostowicz, *Ballada o Ślepym Maksie* (Łódź, 1998). What particularly fascinated
Mostowicz about "Blind Max" was Borensztajn's reputation during the depression years as the
"Robin Hood" of Łódź. For example, Borensztajn established an office of requests and petitions
to advise and help the poor Jews of Bałuty materially and to right their wrongs, often by employ-
ing violence.
78. Hertz, 207, 221.
79. Bożena Umińska, *Postać z cieniem: Portrety Żydówek w polskiej literaturze od końca XIX
wieku do 1939 roku* (Warsaw, 2001), 126–48, 187–208, 238–56. In Nałkowska's case, however,
her conception of Jews and their sexuality had undergone a fundamental transformation already
by the early 1920s and shed its mythical dimensions.

century Polish political journalism with its dark images of Jewish criminality, the criminal Jew hardly figures among the stereotypical images of Jews in either the positivist or modern Polish literary traditions.[80]

The cultural demography of modern Poland, however, has not been dominated by underworld criminals, by creative intellectuals, or even by the highly politicized urban and small-town intelligentsia. Rather, until 1960, Poland remained predominantly a peasant society. Most commentators argue that ambivalence has been the defining characteristic of images of the Jew in Polish popular culture. "Even though Polish folklore treated the Jews with ridicule and aversion," according to Aleksander Hertz, "it also expressed its respect for the Jew's intelligence and his positive qualities."[81] In normal times, argues Alina Cała, such ambivalence made possible a relatively peaceful coexistence. In times of crisis, on the other hand, the anti-Jewish mechanisms contained in Polish popular culture, including the fantastic belief that Jews performed ritual murders, could be activated and mobilized in the form of violent pogroms.[82] Even so, both Hertz and Cała are reluctant to define such popular attitudes in their entirety as antisemitic, primarily because, lacking ideological cohesion, they do not consist of uniformly negative value judgments that define the alien "other" as a hated enemy.

If ambivalence marked general popular images of Jews, the same can be said of the popular image of Jewish criminality. On the one hand, rural popular culture was capable of typecasting outsiders as villains. According to Keely Stauter-Halsted, "The role of petty crook or swindler in Polish *szopki* [Christmas plays] was played interchangeably by a villager dressed as a Gypsy or a Jew."[83] In part, this was due to the peasant view that *handel* (trade) was something inherently dishonest, compared with the higher calling of working the land. In the peasant mind, the Jew was synonymous with *handel* and therefore guilty of something in the nature of a lesser sin in the popular system of values. On the other hand, respondents to a mid-1870s rural survey (cited by Stauter-Halsted) who characterized the main occupations of rural Jews as "usury, litigation, exploitation of the peasants, purchasing stolen goods, accomplices to theft, smuggling, swindling and clandestine alcohol sales" likely represented the emerging village intelligentsia and local elites rather than the rank-and-file peasantry.[84] In Alina Cała's interviews with rural inhabitants in southeastern and eastern Poland, most of whom were born before the Second World War and could recall personal contacts with Jews, there was an overwhelming consensus that "Jews didn't steal" and that "there were few

80. In Segel, *Stranger in Our Midst*, the discourse on Jewish criminality figures only in selections from the political brochures included in the volume.

81. Hertz, 202.

82. Cała, *Wizerunek Żyda w polskiej kulturze ludowej*, 102, 191.

83. Keely Stauter-Halsted, *The Nation in the Village: The Genesis of Peasant National Identity in Austrian Poland, 1848–1914* (Ithaca, N.Y., 2001), 38–39.

84. Ibid., 41.

criminals among them." Cała concluded on the basis of such evidence that the demonizing of the Jew was "an urban creation" which made its way to the provinces only through print propaganda and affected only those who read the antisemitic press on a semiregular basis—in other words, a small minority, found more in small towns than in villages.[85]

In this regard, popular views coincided with everyday social reality and everyday personal contacts. For example, Jewish moneylending, defined uniformly by antisemites as usury (*lichwa*) and the prime example of the "crimes of material exploitation" peculiar to Jews, was viewed far more favorably by peasant borrowers. Perhaps they encountered much more onerous rates of interest on short-term loans from their more well-to-do coreligionists.[86] Jewish moneylending, as Ginowefa Milewska later recalled, "was very useful and very helpful for Polish farmers" in the difficult years of the Great Depression. Milewska's father, the owner of twelve hectares between Płonsk and Ciechanów, "had confidence in Jews" who marketed his milk cows and whose loans spared his wife and children from hunger. Milewska, who didn't finish elementary school, sincerely lamented the disappearance of the Jewish moneylender from the Polish countryside. "If the Jews were in Poland now," she reasoned, "farmers wouldn't be hungry, because Jews always came to their aid, which was good for Jews and good for the farmers."[87]

Thus the criminal Jew, the dishonest trickster and swindler of antisemitic propaganda, was forced to confront the "honest Jew" of the Polish popular experience, the Jew of personal observation who "didn't steal." And precisely because Jews in reality didn't steal, or did so at a rapidly declining rate in the first forty years of the twentieth century ("there were few criminals among them"), antisemitic fantasies of Jewish criminality failed to establish themselves firmly in the Polish popular mind. For a peasant, the Jew may have killed Christ, may have murdered Christian children in accordance with a mysterious and evil ritual, may have even faced divine retribution during the Shoah, but at least the Jew was someone who could be trusted.

Fed by an exaggerated fear of crime among the urban intelligentsia in what was essentially a moral panic, the "criminal Jew" was constructed by the publicists of the emerging radical right at the turn of the last century and connected to the crystallization of a set of hateful, hostile, and uniformly negative

---

85. Cała, *Wizerunek Żyda w polskiej kulturze ludowej*, 28–29, 31–33.

86. Hertz, 56–57. Evidence that economic self-interest proved stronger than the myth of Jewish exploitation can be found in the lack of response and opposition to anti-Jewish boycotts among the rural and urban lower classes, not only in early twentieth-century Poland, but also in the Third Reich; see Blobaum, "The Politics of Antisemitism," 302–5; and Ian Kershaw, "German Opinion on Persecution of the Jews in the Third Reich," in Fein, *The Persisting Question*, 323–25.

87. Ginowefa Milewska, "Ktokolwiek pamięta," in *Żyli wśród nas: Wspomnienia Polaków i Żydów nadslane na konkurs pamięci polsko-żydowskiej o nagrodę imienia Dawida Ben Guriona*, ed. Stanisław Sierkierski (Płońsk, 2001), 88–91.

views toward Jews that moved from the xenophobic to the irrational and fantastic. Demonized images of Jews had always been a defining element of antisemitism. Its early twentieth-century iteration was in part based on the linking of older assertions of Jews as ritual murderers and poisoners of wells with "modern" anti-Jewish images of sexual predators, white slave traders, and poisoners of public morality. At the same time, the image of prostitution as both a Jewish industry and the locus of urban crime enabled antisemites to take another leap in logic: that is, to associate crime generally with Jews and to claim that Jewish immorality and criminality were culturally and, eventually, racially derived. The implication behind the construction of universalized Jewish criminality was both clear and ominous: to fight the "plague" of crime and its ill effects on Polish society, the Jew, morally perverse and criminal by his very nature, had to be eliminated from Polish society—an even greater necessity once the criminal Jew assumed political dimensions in the myth of Judeo-communism during the interwar period. That the propagation of the image of the criminal Jew in the Polish press coincided with a steady and ultimately dramatic decline in crime rates among Jews in the first decades of the twentieth century was merely one of many magical moments in the modern history of antisemitism in Poland.

Usury and fraud, associated with Jewish commercial activity, had long formed part of the stereotype of Jews in Polish culture and should be considered a means of expressing an agrarian society's cultural opposition first to the idea of trade and eventually to the encroachments of capitalism. Beyond that, however, the modern images of Jewish criminality as constructed by the radical right failed to take firm root in either Polish literary or popular culture or to implant themselves as stereotypes—in part because of the continued strength of older chimeras, particularly those related to ritual murder and cannibalism, which were not easily supplanted by modern ones in the popular imagination. At the same time, Polish culture also contained strong counterimages of Jews, primarily because the vast majority of Poles did not encounter Jewish leaders of criminal prostitution rings, traders in female flesh, armed robbers, arsonists, horse thieves, blackmailers, hooligans, and murderers in their everyday lives and interpersonal contacts. Statistically speaking, they were far more likely to be cheated, accosted, robbed, or murdered by fellow Poles. Even usury and fraud were destined to disappear from the stereotype of Jews once it lost its anticapitalist component after the Second World War. Consequently, as recent public opinion polling has revealed, criminality plays a much larger role in the contemporary negative stereotype of Poland's Roma population than in the stereotype of the Jew. Indeed, criminality appears to be of greater significance to the contemporary Polish auto-stereotype.[88] The

---

88. Alina Cała, "Autostereotyp i stereotypy narodowe," in *Czy Polacy są antysemitami? Wyniki badania sondażowego*, ed. Ireneusz Krzemiński (Warsaw, 1996), 199–228.

criminal Jew lingers mainly in association with the myth of the *Żydokomuna* and its purported political atrocities against the Polish nation.

The range of the image of the criminal Jew was limited, then, even during the highwater mark of antisemitism in Poland: that is, during the *upiorne dekady* (ghastly decades) of the 1930s and 1940s.[89] First and foremost, it was embraced by the true believers in the gospel of hatred among the radical right, to a somewhat lesser extent by the urban intelligentsia as a whole, and to a still lesser extent by the industrial working class whose belief system had not been entirely transformed by migration from village to city before the Second World War (although here more research clearly needs to be done).[90] As an urban creation, the image of the modern criminal Jew failed to penetrate the consciousness of the peasantry to any significant extent and remained confined to the rural intelligenstsia and professional groups—the parish clergy, teachers, pharmacists, political activists, and local administrative officials and employees who constituted the semiregular readers of antisemitic propaganda. Whether the same can be said of the range of antisemitism in modern Poland more generally, and of cultural resistance to it, is an open question.

89. The obvious reference here is to Jan Tomasz Gross, *Upiorna dekada: Trzy eseje o stereo-typach na temat Żydów, Polaków, Niemców i komunistów, 1939–1948* (Kraków, 1998). I have pluralized the short title of Gross's book to extend its meaning to two decades rather than one.

90. A promising start in this direction is the work by Laura Crago, "The 'Polishness' of Production: Factory Politics and the Reinvention of Working-Class National and Political Identities in Russian Poland's Textile Industry, 1880–1910," *Slavic Review* 59, no. 1 (2000): 16–41; and by Padraic Kenney, "Whose Nation, Whose State? Working-Class Nationalism and Antisemitism in Poland, 1945–1947," *Polin* 13 (2000): 224–35.

5

Antisemitism and the Search for a Catholic Identity

BRIAN PORTER

The role of Christianity in the growth of modern antisemitism has become a contentious topic. It used to be widely accepted that antisemitism was quite different from older forms of Judeophobia: the former marked by biological metaphors and overblown conspiracy theories, the latter distinguished by charges of deicide and a theological hostility toward those who refused to recognize Jesus as the messiah. Most fundamentally, the racial essentialism of modern antisemitism used to be sharply contrasted with the relative mutability (via conversion) of Christian Judeophobia. Christianity contributed to the foundation of modern antisemitism, but it was argued that the Church's evangelical theology made it difficult to advocate the more extreme forms of twentieth-century hatred. Meanwhile, modern secular thought presumably had difficulty absorbing old prejudices rooted in Christian theology, and thus Judeophobia had to be fundamentally transformed to find a place in the modern world.[1]

---

1. On modern antisemitism, see Shmuel Ettinger, "The Modern Period," in *A History of the Jewish People*, ed. H. H. Ben-Sasson (Cambridge, Mass., 1976), 875–79; Jacob Katz, *From Prejudice to Destruction: Anti-Semitism, 1700–1933* (Cambridge, Mass., 1980); Léon Poliakov, *The History of Anti-Semitism*, vol. 4, *Suicidal Europe, 1870–1933*, trans. George Klim (New York, 1985); Peter Pulzer, *The Rise of Political Anti-Semitism in Germany and Austria*, rev. ed. (London,1988); *Hostages of Modernization: Studies on Modern Antisemitism, 1870–1933/39*, ed. Herbert A. Strauss (Berlin, 1993).

The Vatican's Commission for Religious Relations with the Jews endorsed this view in a 1998 text titled *We Remember: A Reflection on the Shoah*, which affirmed that modern antisemitism was "essentially more sociological and political than religious." The commission concluded that "we cannot ignore the difference which exists between anti-Semitism, based on theories contrary to the constant teaching of the Church on the unity of the human race and on the equal dignity of all races and peoples, and the long-standing sentiments of mistrust and hostility that we call anti-Judaism, of which, unfortunately, Christians also have been guilty. . . . The *Shoah* was the work of a thoroughly modern neo-pagan regime. Its anti-Semitism had its roots outside of Christianity and, in pursuing its aims, it did not hesitate to oppose the Church and persecute her members also."[2]

Despite this authoritative statement (or perhaps because of it), several scholars have challenged the dichotomy between modern and premodern, secular and Catholic antisemitism. The most famous critic is David Kertzer, whose book *The Popes against the Jews* argues that the Church propagated all the major tenets of modern antisemitism, thus serving as "antechamber to the Holocaust." Kertzer has shown that all the elements we typically associate with modern antisemitism—including belief in racial immutability and a global "Jewish conspiracy"—were found in the official proclamations of the Church, the internal documents of the Vatican, and the approved Catholic press.[3]

A survey of Polish Catholic writings would seem, at first glance, to verify the more traditional view distinguishing religious Judeophobia from modern antisemitism. This chapter explores these distinctions and shows how they gradually eroded in the early years of the twentieth century, as Catholic rhetoric and modern antisemitism became increasingly compatible. The key shift came in the period immediately before World War I, but we cannot pinpoint any specific moment, text, or writer who inspired a sudden change; instead, we witness a slow but steady accommodation between Catholic authors and the theories of modern antisemitism. The basic question is how such a reconciliation could have been possible. Instead of simply assuming some inexorable antisemitic essence to Catholic thought, I want to stress the

2. Commission for Religious Relations with the Jews, *We Remember: A Reflection on the Shoah* (http://www.vatican.va/roman_curia/pontifical_councils/chrstuni/documents/rc_pc_chrstuni_doc_16031998_shoah_en.html). Some examples of Polish authors who have repeated the distinction between Catholic and modern "racial" antisemitism are Bogumił Grott, *Nacjonalizm Chrześcijański: Myśl społeczno-państwowa formacji narodowo-katolickiej w Drugiej Rzeczypospolitej* (Kraków, 1991), 221, 228; *Dzieje Żydów w Polsce: Ideologia antysemicka, 1848–1914; Wybór tekstów zródłowych* (Warsaw, 1994).

3. David I. Kertzer, *The Popes against the Jews* (New York, 2001). Less noticed outside the field of Polish studies was Ronald Modras, *The Catholic Church and Antisemitism: Poland, 1933–1939* (Chur, Switz., 1994). Modras unflinchingly documents the rhetoric of the Catholic press in interwar Poland, blurring almost beyond recognition previous assumptions about the lines between the secular right and the Catholic right.

profound gaps between the theology of Roman Catholicism and the deeply secular teachings of racialist antisemitism. From this starting point, though, I examine the way those gaps were downplayed, ignored, denied, or avoided. The particular configuration of Catholic thought at the start of the twentieth century did indeed open some points of entry for racialist antisemitism, despite all the doctrinal and theological obstacles. By the 1920s those entry points had been thoroughly exploited, setting the stage for an interwar history of Catholic antisemitism that remains troubling to this day.

The first prominent exponent of modern antisemitism in Poland, the Warsaw publisher and journalist Jan Jeleński, was greeted with hostility by the leading Catholic magazine of the Warsaw Archdiocese, *Przegląd Katolicki*. An anonymous editorial in that publication warned Jeleński against "descending from the position of Christian love" and "soaking his pen in hatred." The antisemitic doctrine of the "struggle for survival" was, according to this editorialist, unacceptable for a Christian author, who should always keep in mind that "the German, and the Jew, and every human is a brother to the Pole, if the Pole recognizes God as his Father."[4] In the next issue, *Przegląd Katolicki* reiterated that it was acceptable to criticize the specific actions of any individual or group, but one must "never forget that the Jews are our neighbors."[5] This approach remained typical of the Warsaw Catholic press for several years. In 1896 an author identified only as Father A. Z. urged Jeleński to "act more cautiously and delicately, not drawing blood, not inciting the estates, not stirring up hatred, preserving the limitations that the Holy Faith and Christian love impose. Christian periodicals should be distinguished by two things: truth and love. Let us defend the truth without violating love; let us love while respecting the truth."[6] A 1903 article in *Przegląd Katolicki* was even more emphatic in rejecting antisemitism. "Not all Jews are bad," argued Father A. Kwiatkowski. "It isn't right to lump them all together. Antisemitism does that. . . . Such one-sidedness and exaggeration is certainly not in accord with the principles of justice, which are dear to every priest. . . . Using generalizations to build dislike of the jews [sic][7] in the parish is surely dangerous, insofar as

4. "Walka o byt," *Przegląd Katolicki* 7 (February 3/15, 1883): 105.
5. "Objaśnienie 'Roli,'" *Przegląd Katolicki* 10 (February 24–March 8, 1883): 155.
6. A.Z., "W odpowiedzi 'Roli,'" *Przegląd Katolicki* 44 (October 29, 1896): 702–3.
7. Kwiatkowski, like many authors of his day, did not capitalize "żyd" but did capitalize "Polak." As a general rule, Polish orthography calls for the capitalization of national labels but not religious ones (thus "Polak" but "katolik"). The word "Jew" constitutes a special case: although it is always capitalized today, in the nineteenth and early twentieth centuries it was sometimes written in the lower case. Initially this was simply to mark Judaism as a religion, not a nation or ethnicity, and it followed that religious authors would use the lower case while racial antisemites would use the capital "Ż." By the interwar years this strict distinction was starting to blur, as otherwise secular antisemites used the lower case in order to deny the Zionist claim that the Jews were a nation, equal to the Poles. In my translations, I have followed each author's capitalization.

it kindles hostile impulses that make people unaccustomed to looking at
certain social phenomena rationally. It even entitles them to resolve certain
difficulties with rather violent means. After all, it is more comfortable to hide
your own inability and incompetence with someone else's malice."[8]

Similar reluctance to embrace modern antisemitism could be seen in Galicia.
At the Catholic Congress in Kraków in 1893 the audience greeted with "loud
bravos and applause" a speech by Count Stanisław Tarnowski, in which he
condemned antisemitism as "fundamentally evil, and practically dangerous.
Evil, because it is un-Christian, unjust, and uncharitable. It is unjust to hate
one's neighbors merely because God created them in the way he created them:
different from me. Moreover, this so-called antisemitism could be very dangerous in practice, because one can never know and never predict where it will
end, where it is going, once such hatred between one part of humanity and
another has been incited and unbridled. . . . May God defend us against antisemitism."[9]

One could still hear such voices in Catholic circles after World War I. For
example, Father Józef Lubelski published a book in 1924, *Nacjonalizm w
świetle etyki katolickiej*, which was graced with the *nihil obstat* and *imprimatur* stamps. Although Lubelski repeated the idea that "our national minorities, and particularly the jews, often behave with hostility toward the Polish
state and nation," he stressed that "we will not resolve the jewish question,
which is indeed a burning issue here, with shouted antisemitism. Moreover,
we ought to remember that by applying injustice to others and violating their
innate rights, we bring the greatest harm to ourselves, because we destroy in
ourselves and in our nation that greatest of human qualities: a sense of justice
and honor."[10]

By the 1930s, however, most Catholic authors were more equivocal, and a
great deal of undisguised antisemitism had penetrated the Church in Poland.
Even the remarks of August Cardinal Hlond, the Primate of the Roman
Catholic Church in Poland, showed signs of a more modern form of antisemitism. A passage from his pastoral letter of 1936 has become infamous:
"It is a fact that the jews are struggling against the Catholic Church, that they
are penetrated by free-thinking, that they constitute the avant-garde of god-
lessness, of the Bolshevik movement, and of subversive activities. It is a fact
that jewish influences on morality are pernicious, and that their publishing
enterprises propagate pornography. It is true that in the schools the influence
of the jewish youth on the Catholic youth is, in general, religiously and ethi-

8. A. Kwiatkowski, "Kaplan i stronnictwa," *Przegląd Katolicki* 4 (January 28, 1904): 58–61.

9. Tarnowski's speech was reprinted as part of the published proceedings of the conference
in *Księga pamiątkowa wiecu katolickiego w Krakowie odbytego w dniach 4, 5 i 6 lipca 1893 r.*,
ed. Władysław Chotkowski (Kraków, 1893), 163. For another example of Galician Catholic
opposition to antisemitism, see Włodzimierz Czerkawski, "Refleksye nad stanem kwestyi
żydowskiej u nas," *Przegląd Powszechny* 236 (August 1903): 190–213.

10. Józef Lubelski, *Nacjonalizm w świetle etyki katolickiej* (Lwów, 1924), 45–46.

cally harmful." Alongside these arguments, Hlond added a condemnation of violence and a willingness to accept conversion that was typical of statements by the Catholic hierarchy: "But let's be fair. Not all jews are like that. . . . I caution against an ethical stance imported from abroad that is fundamentally and ruthlessly anti-jewish. This is incompatible with Catholic ethics. It is permissible to love one's own nation more, but it is not permissible to hate anyone. Not even the jews. . . . It is not permitted to attack the jews, beat them, wound them, slander them."[11] Hlond could be variously interpreted when he said "the jewish problem exists, and will exist as long as the jews remain jews." We could take this to mean that the problem would cease to exist after the conversion of the Jews (as is suggested by his used of the lower case), but it was also possible to understand this as an affirmation that Jewishness was an immutable and irredeemable racial quality.

An openness to racial categories would be the marker of the transition to a more modern form of hatred. Back in 1896, Father Maryan Morawski had tried to balance his own antipathy toward the Jews with the Church's principled opposition to racial antisemitism. It was not easy. Writing in *Przegląd Powszechny*, Morawski affirmed that Jews were guided by a moral code "lower than that of Christianity," and he repeated conspiratorial myths familiar to all antisemites. Significantly, however, his article was titled "A-Semitism," and he struggled to find a way to fit his prejudices within the limitations of Catholic teaching by creating a form of Judeophobia distinct from the antisemitism of his day. This was difficult, for as Morawski himself stated, "The Christian conscience, to which both philosemites and antisemites appeal, sometimes vacillates, not knowing where duty lies." It was important to recognize, he argued, that "Jews, from the Middle Ages all the way to the present day, have persistently fought (with some success) against the Christian faith, and they have prepared for the rule of freethinking and atheism." In this struggle they were aided by their adherence to a single coherent leadership, to "a concrete, vital organization" that allowed them to sustain "amazing strength and resilience." Liberalism was appealing to the Jews because it facilitated their economic domination, insofar as they could pursue their interests "unrestrained by the principles of Christian ethics." But the Jews did not stop there: they penetrated and came to dominate the socialist movement as well: "The foresight of Israel compelled them to have their own people [in the socialist movement], so that, in case that party triumphs, they would be shielded from its blows, and maybe to explore whether it might not also be possible to exploit that movement somehow, for the benefit of the chosen people." Morawski was ambivalent about racialist thinking. A Jew could be defined, he wrote, as "the creation of a specific race, under the influence of a specific history," but he cautioned that racial thinking could perpetuate unjust

11. August Hlond, *Na straży sumienia narodu: Wybór pism i przemówień*, ed. A. Słomka (Warsaw, 1999), 165–65.

overgeneralizations. Trying to balance his racism and his Catholicism, he rejected the possibility of secular assimilation (which he believed would only backfire, turning religious Jews into "materialists and atheists"), but he repeated the Church's long-standing argument that converts from Judaism must be welcomed into the Christian community. All the tensions between old and new forms of antisemitism came out in an intriguing passage about conversion:

> It is even more unjust and irrational—but unfortunately it happens often among us—to refuse in advance to trust every Jewish convert. Only those who themselves lack all religious convictions, and regard every religion as a purely traditional form, could consistently deny the possibility of all conversions from conviction; but those who believe that Christianity is the truth cannot doubt that other people might also come to this truth and, with divine help, be convinced. . . . It is understood that sincere conversion quashes at once all negative Talmudic principles. Regarding those features of the Jewish character we do not like: those will not in fact be erased immediately, but only over the course of several generations.

Thus conversion was possible after all, but not because it could really change the individual convert's nature. Instead, only after "several generations" of intermarriage would the corruption be sufficiently diluted to truly "erase" the marks of Jewishness.[12]

This ambivalent resistance to modern, racial antisemitism would gradually erode in Catholic circles. Another important transitional moment came with a series of articles titled "On Antisemitism," published in May and June 1900, in Warsaw's *Przegląd Katolicki*. Like Morawski before him, the anonymous author (who signed his name only as J.b.P.) initially insisted that Catholicism had nothing in common with antisemitism, which was "a specifically Protestant product."[13] With each successive installment in this series, however, J.b.P. slid closer and closer to an identifiably modern antisemitism. In the second article he argued that the papacy had long been sympathetic towards the Jews, on the grounds that "the justice that is owed to everyone is also owed to the Jews," but he went on to itemize the many reasons the Jews might merit persecution from less virtuous institutions than the Holy Church. Among these Jewish vices, the author maintained, were unethical trading practices, profanation of the Sacred Host, and ritual murder (a charge he considered "proven").[14] As odious as all this was, it was nothing new; indeed, what is striking here is the anachronistic nature of J.b.P.'s charges. But soon he took

12. Maryan Morawski, "Asemityzm," *Przegląd Powszechny* 49 (February 1896): 161–89. Note that Father Morawski capitalized the word "Jew," implying that he perceived Jews as a national or ethnic group, not a religion.

13. J.b.P., "Coś o antysemityzmie," *Przegląd Katolicki* 22 (May 31, 1900): 339.

14. J.b.P., "Coś o antysemityzmie," *Przegląd Katolicki* 23 (June 7, 1900): 360.

the step that distinguished traditional Catholic Judeophobia from modern antisemitism: the conviction that human communities were immutable, that conflict was inevitable and eternal, and that sin resided in races rather than individuals.

> The Jews are entirely distinct; they are a society which, in their opinion, is the only one that deserves to exist, because they believe that they possess the absolute truth. They demand power for themselves in the name of that truth, and since they do not have their own fatherland under their feet, they regard the whole earth as their fatherland and want to be supreme on [the earth] and command others. Money, for them, is never a goal, only a means for attaining power. . . . There is really only one path to the conquest of the earth for the Jews: . . . the steady destruction of Christianity in its religious and social aspect. There is, put simply, not a single method for undermining Christianity which the Jews have missed. Be it anti-Christian periodicals or newspapers, or pornography, or providing the means for decadence or drunkenness, or the trade in live human products, or providing the means for minors to cheat their parents, or the bribing of public and private servants and bureaucrats— in all these areas the leaders, if not the only practitioners, are Jews.[15]

Also like Morawski, wanting to retain his self-image as a man free of anti-semitic sentiments, J.b.P. insisted that Christians must never employ violence or hatred in their struggle with the Jews. He even cautioned that economic struggle was both futile and morally problematic, because immoral means would be needed to beat the Jews at their own game. In the last installment of his series, however, J.b.P. fell into the dangerous Spencerian language that Catholics had previously tried to avoid: "This is a struggle, a struggle which will be a matter of life or death."[16]

Such language soon spread. By 1905, Teodor Jeske-Choiński, a contributor to the once shunned *Rola*, was writing articles for *Przegląd Powszechny*, unapologetically propagating his vision of a Spencerian battle between Poles and Jews. As he put it, "Two entirely distinct forces now confront each other in a struggle for survival. . . . [The Jews], unrestrained by a Christian conscience, freed by the Talmud from all considerations in their relations with the hated aliens and infidels, greedy for gold, thrifty, resourceful, undiscouraged by failure, stand in the struggle for survival ideally adapted, armed with cleverness and the ruthlessness of a predatory animal." Not only did Jeske-Choiński openly draw upon a "struggle for survival" vocabulary, but he undermined the Catholic faith in the power of conversion:

---

15. J.b.P., "Coś o antysemityzmie," *Przegląd Katolicki* 23 (June 7, 1900): 361.
16. J.b.P., "Coś o antysemityzmie," *Przegląd Katolicki* 25 (June 21, 1900): 395.

Polish neophytes can be divided into two categories: those who accepted Christianity from religious conviction or merged with the native population with a desire to assimilate [*uobywatelnienie się*—literally, make themselves citizens]; and those who got baptized for practical reasons, with the goal of attaining the right to get a job in the civil service or to attain other privileges closed to israelites. The first of these strove to erase as quickly as possible the traces of their origins, entering into the native population by way of marriage, the union of blood; they truly assimilated and produced many useful, worthy people. The second, having received baptism with a sense of repugnance, for material reasons, entered only nominally into Christian society. . . . One must beware of them, because, concealed by baptism, they work directly upon Christian society.[17]

Like Morawski, Jeske-Choiński was compelled to accept the theoretical possibility of baptism, but he found a way to integrate this doctrine into his racialist views: Jews could convert, he argued, but those who were sincere would be inspired to intermarry so as to eradicate their racial distinctiveness in a "union of blood." Conversion, in this vision, must entail racial obliteration to be genuine. Since Jeske-Choiński did not consider this likely, he never imagined that it could be instituted on a mass scale.

By the interwar years, racialized antisemitism had thoroughly penetrated the Catholic community (in Poland as well as elsewhere). It is true that the Church hierarchy remained publicly at arms length from the more vulgar and violent forms of hatred propagated by the extreme right-wing groups of the 1930s; no matter how close they may have seemed at times, we cannot simply equate the attitudes of the clergy with (for example) those of the National Democrats, and it would be an even more profound mistake to assume that self-identification as a Catholic implied an embrace of modern antisemitism. Catholic authors and the clergy would typically try to contain or domesticate the implications of antisemitic rhetoric, usually by saying that the struggle for survival with the Jews had to be limited to nonviolent means. Such protestations, however, faded alongside a multitude of expressions of barely restrained hatred and fear. It became a truism among Catholics that (in the words of Father Joachim Raczkowski) "capitalists—that is, the jews—hold the press in their hands."[18] Moreover, most took it for granted (as stated in the passage quoted above from Cardinal Hlond) that the Jews were implicated in liberal capitalism, atheism, Freemasonry, and pornography. But even more than any of this, Catholic authors were preoccupied with the perceived link between Judaism and Bolshevism.

17. Teodor Jeske-Choiński, "List z Warszawy," *Przegląd Powszechny* 259 (July 1905): 165–76.

18. Joachim Raczkowski, *List otwarty wiejskiego proboszcza do Pana Antoniego Szecha* (Warsaw, 1908), 10.

Father Józef Kaczmarczyk captured the grandiosity and the scope of anti-semitic conspiracy theories in a 1935 essay arguing that the Jews were the "soul of [Bolshevism], its directors." Jews were drawn to communism by their desire to steal the wealth of the bourgeoisie, their quest for revenge against the Russians for nineteenth-century oppression, and their hope to redirect the threat of an anti-Jewish revolution. All these motives were at work, mused Kaczmarczyk, "but none of this would be a sufficient answer. In order to understand today's participation of the Jews in the Bolshevik revolution, one must penetrate more deeply into the secrets of the Jewish soul." The most fundamental desire of the Jews, he said, is for a messiah—not a spiritual savior like Jesus but "a messiah who is supposed to establish the dominion of the jews over the *goyim* (that is, the non-jews)—over the entire world. This messianic idea, which is joined with the most base materialism and imperialism, is consumed by every jew with his mother's milk." This fundamental drive leads the Jews to exploit "every movement—not just every political or social movement but every current of human thought, even every religious manifestation. . . . They support everything that brings them closer to their goal, such as revolutionary strikes, so-called liberal education, nondenominational schools, godless and demoralizing literature, and the press." Strikes in particular, we are told, are fertile ground for Jewish intrigue, because "they know well that work moralizes and enriches mankind, so it lies close to their heart to reduce that work, to sicken the workers, to demoralize and revolutionize them, and in doing all this, weaken society." Thus "nearly all strikes" could be traced to Jewish agitation. Lest his readers retain any doubt about the immutability of the Jewish drive for world domination, Kaczmarczyk assures us that "if we survey the history of the jewish movement from the time of Christ right up to the present day, we notice that nothing has changed, that the jewish soul has remained the same."[19]

Significantly, Father Kaczmarczyk discussed religion only insofar as it constituted a field of battle in the eternal war against Jewish domination. Jews attacked Christianity—or more specifically, they "supported with all their soul every international sociopolitical movement that strives to weaken national distinctiveness and fight against religion"—not because of any theological difference, but because "the strength and cohesiveness of a society lies in its nationality and religion." Clearly, we have come a long way from the more traditional antipathy toward the Jews because of their refusal to convert; indeed, conversion is not even at issue here. Kaczmarczyk was fighting a battle not to bring salvation to the Jews but to defeat them in an epochal struggle for survival.

Obviously, Catholic antisemitism had its own particular features. Even those who would follow John Cornwell's sensationalist labeling of Pius XII as

19. Józef Kaczmarczyk, "Bolszewizm a mesjasz żydowski," *Biblioteka Spraw i Zagadnień Narodowych i Polskich* 2/3 (1935): 104–12.

"Hitler's Pope" would never go so far as to suggest that the Nazis and the Catholics shared identical approaches to the "Jewish question."[20] Most scholars would surely agree that antisemitism is far from a monolithic ideology, that it has many origins and is marked by its own internal tensions. Moreover, it should go without saying that the Catholic Church is an enormous institution whose members include people with a wide variety of attitudes, ideas, goals, and beliefs. Recognizing this diversity, and accepting that secular racism and Catholic antisemitism remained different, recent scholarship has nonetheless been pushing toward an acknowledgment that the Church provided fertile ground for modern antisemitism to flourish, and that there was a lot of overlap between these two forms of Judeophobia.

But this observation raises more questions than it resolves, because Catholic antisemitism seems paradoxical when set alongside Catholic theology. How can the universalism embedded in the very name of the faith be reconciled with biological racism? How can a religion preach love and hatred at the same time? To answer these questions, we must pose one that is even more basic: when we read hate-mongers such as Kaczmarczyk, are we dealing with antisemites who happened to be Catholics, or with a specifically Catholic intellectual framework that somehow bred antisemitism? In other words, are we confronting simple intellectual inconsistency—antisemitic Catholics who ignored some of the basic tenets of their faith—or should we try to work out the seeming incongruity between universalism and racism so as to discover the ways in which Catholicism may have actually *caused* antisemitism? Jan Błoński, in his famous essay "A Poor Pole Looks upon the Ghetto," argued that Christianity held the Poles back from the worst forms of hatred and violence, protecting them from the genocidal desires that drove the Nazis into such a moral abyss. As he put it, "If we did not take part in that crime, it is because we were still a little bit Christian, because at the last moment we realized what a satanic undertaking it was."[21] It would be comforting to think that Catholicism could have this effect. But did it?

Undeniably, for some it did. The story of Zofia Kossak is the most often cited and intriguing example. Though a nationalist and antisemite before World War II, her deep-seated faith drove her to risk her life by rescuing Jews during the war.[22] At the other extreme is the now infamous story of Jedwabne, where the parish priest did nothing to stay the hands of his murderous parishioners.[23] There are examples of individual Catholics both resisting and com-

20. John Cornwell, *Hitler's Pope: The Secret History of Pius XII* (New York, 1999).

21. Jan Błoński, *Biedni Polacy patrzą na getto* (Kraków, 1994), 23.

22. Kossak's story is discussed in ibid., 38–53; Anna Landau-Czajka, "Image of the Jew in the Catholic Press," *Polin: Studies in Polish Jewry* 8 (1995): 165–66; and Israel Gutman, *The Jews of Warsaw* (Bloomington, Ind., 1985). There is an interesting exchange regarding Kossak between Abraham Brumberg and Czesław Miłosz in *New York Review of Books* (June 22, 1995).

23. Jan Tomasz Gross, *Neighbors: The Destruction of the Jewish Community in Jedwabne, Poland* (Princeton, 2000).

mitting acts of antisemitic violence, but enumerating them will bring us no closer to answering our question. Indeed, it may be impossible to do so, insofar as "Catholicism" (as an abstract category) functioned in idiosyncratic ways among the millions of people who called themselves "Catholic." On one level, it is impossible even to speak of "Catholicism" as a totality. But if we formulate the problem in terms of the conceptual and perceptual framework delineated by "official" Catholic rhetoric (that seen in Vatican statements, the formally sanctioned Catholic press, pastoral letters, and publications with the *imprimatur*), we can approach a resolution. The point is not to identify any deterministic force within Catholicism that *compelled* the faithful to act in one way or another. The Church itself teaches that God and "natural law" merely establish standards, which people freely accept or deny (with grave consequences, of course). The model of human behavior offered by Catholic doctrine is one that recognizes human inconsistency; it is presumed that even the faithful will occasionally succumb to temptation and sin, thus requiring the sacrament of confession. Methodologically, this model serves as a reminder that ideology and theology may mandate certain behaviors and attitudes, without any assurance that a particular adherent will actually exhibit them. Any statement made about "Catholicism" may not necessarily apply to any specific Catholic individual (and vice versa).

Nonetheless, at the boundaries of any religion there are more or less coherent tenets of faith and doctrine, and for Catholicism these tenets are quite explicitly delineated and enforced. The ideas expressed in the Nicene Creed exemplify such a boundary: one could hardly deny the existence of God, the resurrection of Jesus, or the Virgin Birth and still be a Catholic. This is not saying much, however, because these tenets do little to explain the actions or attitudes of Catholics. More interesting but much harder to pin down are the myriad ways in which Catholicism advances a set of perceptual filters through which the faithful understand the world. Such filters give content to fundamental beliefs and structure (without strictly determining) the worldviews of those who consider themselves Catholic. The metaphor of the filter is useful, because it suggests a network of imperfect constraints (even the best filters are not 100 percent effective) which allow a wide range of ideas (some of which might even be mutually contradictory) to penetrate. Still, the filters of ideology and theology *do* structure the ways in which adherents see the world, thus making some ideas and attitudes more likely and others less so. How, then, should we characterize the filters woven by the official voices of the Catholic Church in the early twentieth century which shaped the way the faithful approached the "Jewish question"? The key, I would argue, can be found by exploring Catholicism's encounter with the range of social, intellectual, and cultural transformations we customarily lump together under the label "modernity."

It is a truism that the Catholic Church was, until Vatican II, a quintessentially antimodern institution, but that label is more useful in anticlerical polemics than in scholarly analysis. Although there were strains of overtly antimodern thinking within the Church, a blanket rejection of the post-Enlightenment, industrial, capitalist world was hardly a prerequisite to being Catholic. It is certainly possible to find those who would try to roll back the changes of the modern era and return the Church and European society to what they see as a pristine, uncorrupted age. Prior to the papacy of Leo XIII (1878–1903), it is probably fair to say that such views were even dominant within the Church. But after Leo, Catholicism would never be the same again. It would remain a profoundly conservative institution, but in the 1880s Catholics began building their own distinctive vision of modernity, one that would accommodate and try to Christianize, not merely anathematize, the new world.

A Polish example of the older, more rigid viewpoint is the anonymous book *Kościół i postępowość* [The Church and Progress], published in 1868 in Poznań. This small volume, originally serialized in *Tygodnik Katolicki*, sets out the whole array of openly antimodern attitudes. The author had little respect for the era in which he lived: "Today narcissism, not God, governs the world, so everyone thinks only of themselves, and of the harm they can do to others. . . . Every political movement today is a sin, so it is better for us that we do not participate in them."[24] Freedom was just a "delusion," this author argued, and the goal in this life was just to figure out "to whom one ought to be subordinated, and to what degree." Ultimately, one had to decide "whether to obey God or surrender to Satan."[25] The reference to the divine is crucial, because this author believed that "human self-governance [*samowładztwo ludzkie*] is always godless, whether it rests in the hands of a single man, or the hands of hundreds or thousands."[26] This statement makes sense within a worldview rooted in the immanent presence of God in all things—not excluding the state. To deny that God is the foundation of all authority and that (as follows) Christ's Church must hold an honored place in the political order is to repudiate that immanence, and thus to deny God Himself. The ideal system, continued *Kościół i postępowość,* would be *kościołowładztwo*, literally "rule by the Church." Such a system would recognize that "the spirit of a Christian society is the Church, so the Church ought to be the vital force within every human system. . . . If, then, the Church would be obeyed, if it had the power to restrain falsehood and evil, then the world would be happy."[27] The alternative was a dark vision indeed: "If the progressives win in the end, if they entirely govern the family (which they are trying so resolutely to accomplish), then the law of property would be immediately abolished, or subordinated to the force of greedy conquest and occupation. Whoever is stronger

24. *Kościół i postępowość* (Poznań, 1868), 82.
25. Ibid., 5.
26. Ibid., 15.
27. Ibid., 60–61, 64.

than his neighbors, he alone would be owner and lord. . . . The governments of the progressives are not governments but only disorder. Their legality is merely the decay of universal legality. They have no faith, so what is supposed to guide their governance? Probably their own sick imaginations, broken off from the totality of the living mental force in man."[28]

What does this overtly antimodern rage have to do with antisemitism? Very little—and that is precisely the point. The Jews as such did not enter this 1868 text, although "judaism" did, as a metaphor. Ideas such as the separation of church and state, we are informed, are "jewish theories" because they "exclude Christ from the life of mankind." In other words, just as the Jews refused to accept Christ as their savior, so do these modern ideologies refuse to grant Christ His rightful position in the world. It follows that progressives were "modern jews," not because they were literally Jewish but because they were to modern society what the Jews had been to the ancient world: the deniers of Christ.[29] For all its vehemence and vitriol, *Kościół i postępowość* did not exhibit the features we typically associate with modern antisemitism.

It was not, then, antimodernism that drove Catholics to antisemitism so much as their quest to *reconcile* themselves with modernity. Catholics, like everyone else, sooner or later had to come to terms with the new world of the nineteenth century. They did indeed reject the specific adaptations of the liberals, but they came to acknowledge that new circumstances required new ideas. So, instead of categorizing Catholics as antimodern, it is much more useful to consider the search for a Catholic modernity, to ask how their means of understanding the changes of the modern world differed from those of their secular opponents. Taking this approach, we discover how Catholicism wove that lace of filters through which they perceived the Jews. The Catholic framework for understanding modernity did not mandate any specific antisemitic ideas, and it certainly did not lead directly to biological racism, much less to any genocidal desires. Nonetheless, it did offer a Manichean worldview that fit antisemitism nicely. Ultimately, the Catholic understanding of modernity introduced an almost unbearable tension into the Church, and leading Catholics were driven to torturous doctrinal arguments that tried to reconcile two seemingly irreconcilable ideas: on the one hand, a belief in a universal potential for salvation and a commandment to work for the conversion of all humanity; on the other hand, an acceptance of biological racial categories and a commitment to defeating Catholicism's (increasingly racialized) enemy. One consequence was yet another tension, between an opposition to violence and a conviction that the Church was confronting a danger (from the Jews, among others) that threatened its very existence.

28. Ibid., 47, 54.
29. Ibid., 10.

Leo XIII is famous for bringing the Catholic Church into the nineteenth century.[30] In the 1885 encyclical *Immortale Dei* he argued that it was "a ridiculous and groundless calumny" to charge the Church with a blanket hostility to modernity. "Our eyes are not closed to the spirit of the times," he wrote. "We repudiate not the assured and useful improvements of our age, but devoutly wish affairs of State to take a safer course than they are now taking, and to rest on a more firm foundation without injury to the true freedom of the people; for the best parent and guardian of liberty amongst men is truth."[31] More famously, Leo's 1891 encyclical *Rerum novarum* offered a distinctly Catholic framework for coping with—and not merely denouncing—the brutality of nineteenth-century capitalism. He remained resolutely conservative: he continued to defend the existence of social inequality as natural and inevitable, and he affirmed that "if the Church is disregarded, human striving will be in vain."[32] Leo XIII certainly did not approve of what had happened to the world in the nineteenth century, but neither did he advocate, like earlier Catholics, the total rejection of modernity.

If liberal Catholics today, desperate for a papal hero, sometimes exaggerate Leo XIII's reputation as a reformer, they construct an equally one-sided myth about Pius X (1902–14) as a dark reactionary. Certainly, encyclicals such as *I supreme* and *Lamentabili sane* were among the harshest attacks on modernity the Vatican has ever issued. In the former text, published shortly after assuming the papacy, Pius bemoaned the condition of the world: "For who can fail to see that society is at the present time, more than in any past age, suffering from a terrible and deep-rooted malady which, developing every day and eating into its inmost being, is dragging it to destruction?" This sickness was the product of a "sacrilegious war which is now, almost everywhere, stirred up and fomented against God." In order to counter this danger, Pius announced that "we have no other program in the Supreme Pontificate but that 'of restoring all things in Christ.'"[34] Nonetheless, Pius X also spoke repeatedly about adjusting to "the needs of modern society." In 1905 he made it clear that there was no going back: "It is well to remark that it is impossible today to re-establish under the same form all the institutions which have been useful and even the only effective ones in past centuries, so numerous the

30. The historian Thomas Bokenkotter wrote that Leo's pontificate "was one long and somewhat successful effort to place the Church on a new footing in regard to modern secular culture"; Thomas Bokenkotter, *A Concise History of the Catholic Church*, rev. and exp. ed. (New York, 1990), 297, 311.

31. Leo XIII, *Immortale Dei: On the Christian Constitution of States* (November 1, 1885), in *The Papal Encyclicals, 1903–1939*, ed. Claudia Carlen (Raleigh, N.C., 1981), 2:115–16.

32. See Leo XIII, *Rerum novarum: On Capital and Labor* (May 15, 1891), in *Papal Encyclicals*, 2:249, 252, 256.

33. Ibid., 247–48.

34. Pius X, *I supreme: On the Restoration of All Things in Christ* (October 4, 1903), in *Papal Encyclicals*, 3:6.

new needs which changing circumstances keep producing."[35] Condemnations of modernity and modernism were plentiful under both Leo XIII and Pius X, but so were efforts to engage the new world and offer Catholic solutions to its problems.

This duality is particularly evident in the Polish Church of the time, despite its reputation for conservatism. There are certainly plenty of texts that could be used to bolster a picture of Polish Catholicism as the bastion of antimodernism. When August Gorayski was elected marshal of the Catholic Congress that met in Kraków in 1893, he expressed his wish "that, in the face of the struggle that nondenominationalism [*bezwyznaniowość*] and all modern theories have declared against the Catholic Church, our meeting may lead to our successful defense and their defeat."[36] A 1906 book titled *Liberal Catholicism*, by the Jesuit priest Jan Rostworowski, summarized the reasons many Catholics felt themselves unable to reconcile with the dawning twentieth century. The goal of the modern era, wrote Rostworowski, was to "eradicate God from the life of humanity" by offering a view of religion as a human institution, like any other. "That which the proponents of coming to terms [with modernity] will never be able to understand fully enough," he wrote, "is that the very *spirit*, the very direction of mind and heart that modern education produces, is anti-Christian. . . . The Church . . . if it allowed that spirit in any form, in even the most holy and lustrous garment, to penetrate its ranks, would have to deny [the Church's] very essence as the Kingdom of God on Earth."[37]

Before long, however, a different trend began to emerge, and eventually it became routine for Polish Catholics to deny vociferously that they were opposed to modernity *as such*. Among the first to call enthusiastically for the Church to work within rather than against modernity was Archbishop Józef Bilczewski of Lwów. In 1900 he gave a speech at Jan Kazimierz University in Lwów (where he had previously served as rector) in which he praised the just-completed century:

"More life, more light, more freedom," proclaimed the eighteenth century. The nineteenth century took up that slogan and wrote it down as the emblem for the historical card that it would enter into the history of humanity. Universal progress—that, too, is its distinguishing characteristic, its defining physiognomy. No other century could match it in this regard, no other could display such a rich harvest of intellectual accomplishments, such deep discoveries in theoretical science, and the application of these to practical goals. In a word, no other century has accomplished as much as the nineteenth in that eternal striving to raise

35. Pius X, *Il fermo proposito: On Catholic Action in Italy* (June 11, 1905), in *Papal Encyclicals*, 3:39–40.

36. *Księga pamiątkowa wiecu katolickiego w Krakowie*, 56.

37. Jan Rostworowski, *Liberalny katolicyzm* (Kraków, 1906), 48.

society to the summit that we call civilization. As an accomplishment of our century I hold up, alongside the deepening of science, the establishment of a more equitable division of rights and duties among the various rungs of society, greater respect for the individual in social life, a distribution of the attainments of civilization to the entire society so that all may benefit from its treasures—not just the upper stratum but also the child of the beggar. . . . There have been, and perhaps still are, some shortsighted people who are frightened by the triumphs of science and fear for the fate of religion. For me, every step that takes science forward is a victory for truth over error, light over darkness.

Bilczewski recognized that there were many enemies of the Church among those responsible for all this progress, but his response was almost flippant: "What of it? Truth is always truth, even in the mouths of those who blaspheme, just as gold is always gold, even in the hands of someone who abuses it."[38]

No one exemplified this new line better than Cardinal Hlond himself, who is widely credited with effectively adapting the Polish Church to the conditions of the interwar years.[39] Even before becoming the Polish Primate, he was trying to take the slogan "progress" away from the progressives, arguing that "true culture means progress, and above all moral progress, which one can accomplish only on the foundation of faith. . . . Let us not, therefore, be afraid that faith might restrain the march of culture. Let us instead be convinced that it is precisely religion that will lead the way to true progress." He admitted that the shift from rural to urban life, from an agrarian to an industrial economy, sometimes led to a decline in faith: "True, that happens—but it does not have to happen. Indeed, it ought not happen."[40] He stated even more clearly in 1932 that it was a mistake to think "that the task of the Church was to withdraw from the current moment to some previous form, to yesterday's institutions, to a frozen romanticism, to the baroque, to a lively medieval era. It is not the Church's goal to hold back the march of humanity."[41] A few years later he stressed that the Church was not an enemy of progress and modernity, since it "acknowledges everything that is new, progressive, and cultured, insofar as it does not conflict with Christ, with God's law, and with the ethics of the Gospels."[42]

38. Józef Bilczewski, "Przemówienie rektorskie przy otwarciu nowego roku szkolnego 1900/1, dnia 11 października 1900," in Józef Bilczewski, *Listy pasterskie i mowy okolicznościowe* (Mikołów-Warszawa, 1908), 1: 528–31.

39. See, for example, Jerzy Lukowski and Hubert Zawadzki, *A Concise History of Poland* (Cambridge, U.K., 2001), 218.

40. "O życie katolickie na Śląsku: List pasterski z dnia 1 marca, 1924 r., Katowice," in Hlond, *Na straży sumienia narodu*, 17.

41. "O zadaniach Katolicyzmu wobec walki z Bogiem. List pasterski w Środę Popielcową r. 1932, Poznań," in Hlond, *Na straży sumienia narodu*, 42.

42. "Z życia Kościoła Chrystusowego. List pasterski z dnia 12 marca 1935, Poznań," in Hlond, *Na straży sumienia narodu*, 137.

All this was, in part, a rhetorical nod to the demands of the twentieth century, when unrelenting conservatism no longer seemed to be a viable public stance—and that is precisely the point. By the interwar years, most Catholics (in Poland and in the Vatican) were recognizing that they had to engage the modern world, and that to do so they would have to make some revisions in their practices and their rhetoric. As Hlond put it in 1932, Catholics "had to be familiar with modern political thought and with the changes taking place in the world, and had to derive from that all that was fresh, vital, and creative."[43] Before Leo XIII we see a siege model of Catholicism, according to which the faithful would defend themselves while hoping for a restoration of *kościołowładztwo*. Afterward, we see an aggressively militant model of Catholicism, according to which the Church should actively enter into the modern world and defeat the enemies of the faith. As Cardinal Hlond put it, "Defense is not everything. It is not enough to cover ourselves and ward off blows. . . . The leading imperative of the current moment is to launch a general Catholic offensive."[44] This was to be not an offensive *against* modernity but an aggressive war against Catholicism's foes *within* the context of the modern world.

Launching such an "offensive" would not be easy, because Catholics had to find a way to describe this battle that would make sense both within a traditional Catholic framework and within newer frameworks for perceiving social reality. Thus emerged the twentieth-century version of a very old Catholic theme: the apocalypse. From within a revived imagining of the apocalypse, in turn, would emerge spaces for talking about modern, racial antisemitism. We generally use the expression "apocalyptic" as a metaphor, and it is hard for secular scholars to grasp fully that millions of people consider the end-time to be an undeniable, impending reality. As Pius X put it forebodingly, "There is good reason to fear lest this great perversity may be, as it were, a foretaste, and perhaps the beginning of those evils which are reserved for the last days; and that there may be already in the world the 'Son of Perdition' of whom the Apostle speaks."[45] Elsewhere he wrote: "We have grounds for fear, with so many storms gathering on every side, with so many hostile forces massed and advancing against Us, and at the same time so utterly deprived are We of all human aid to ward off the former and to help us to meet the shock of the latter. But when We consider the place on which Our feet rest and on which this Pontifical See is rooted, We feel Ourself perfectly safe on the rock of the Holy Church. . . . Supernatural force has never during the flight of ages been found wanting in the Church, nor have Christ's promises failed."[46]

---

43. "O Chrześcijańskie zasady życia państwowego. List pasterski z dnia 23 kwietnia 1932 r., Gniezno," in Hlond, *Na straży sumienia narodu*, 265.
44. "O zadaniach Katolicyzmu wobec walki z Bogiem," 44.
45. Pius X, *I supreme*, 6.
46. Pius X, *Lucunda sane: On Pope Gregory the Great* (March 12, 1904), in *Papal Encyclicals*, 3:21.

The inability to recognize the centrality of this supernatural vision is a common problem, faced by all those who search for rational causation by studying social forces, economic interests, political alliances, and the pursuit of material self-interest. For devout Catholics, however, the transcendent matters at least as much as the mundane. As one early twentieth-century Polish Jesuit put it, in a comment that applies just as well to secular scholars as to liberal Catholics, "It seems to me that one general mistake penetrates to the very essence of liberal Catholicism: the liberal Catholic does not know how to look upon the Church and everything that is in the Church from a sufficiently *supernatural* point of view. That which is mundane and human absorbs his whole attention. . . . Catholicism is a religion from top to bottom and through-and-through *supernatural.* . . . So everything that is in the Church has one goal, one task, one reason for existence: to instill, preserve, and perfect the supernatural life in human souls."[47]

The apocalyptic subtext of these early twentieth-century comments were accompanied by a conviction that the enemy—who must ultimately be Satan himself—had penetrated the very heart of the Church. During the first years of the twentieth century a vibrant intellectual movement that came to be called "Catholic modernism" shook the Church far out of proportion to its actual size or influence. When a handful of intellectuals—most prominently Alfred Loisy, Maurice Blondel, and George Tyrrell—advocated a more metaphorical reading of the scriptures and a more ecumenical attitude toward alternative Christian traditions, the Vatican responded with fear and fury. Umberto Benigni, a Vatican official and creator (in 1909) of the infamous antimodern religious order, the Sodality of Saint Pius V, led a campaign to root out all traces of "modernism" within the Church. He utilized secret informants, anonymous denunciations, and other unsavory techniques in his zealous effort to purge Catholicism of anyone who might question his rigid interpretation of doctrine. His description of the danger faced by the Church captured the prevailing view at the time: "The danger of Modernist propaganda is always present, and it is all the more to be feared because it is often in a fluid state, inconsistent, so as to be overlooked by those who are unprepared for it, who do not pay close attention, who are seduced by their own optimism to see everything in a rosy light. It is a tactic employed by the most cunning to speak of the 'failure' of Modernism. Quite frankly, they want us to go to sleep. . . . Good Catholics must beware of falling into this trap. Modernism spreads and organizes by means of the malice of some and by the naiveté of others."[48]

To this call for eternal vigilance, Pius X added an image of a secret enemy within: "They put into operation their designs for her undoing, not from

---

47. Rostworowski, *Liberalny katolicyzm,* 51.

48. As quoted by Marvin R. O'Connell, *Critics on Trial: An Introduction to the Catholic Modernist Crisis* (Washington, D.C., 1994), 361–62. For a Polish discussion of modernism, see *Studia o modernistach katolickich,* ed. Józef Keller i Zygmunt Poniatowski (Warsaw, 1968).

without but from within. Hence, the danger is present almost in the very veins and heart of the Church, whose injury is the more certain from the very fact that their knowledge of her is more intimate. . . . Further, none is more skillful, none more astute than they, in the employment of a thousand noxious devices; for they play the double part of rationalist and Catholic, and this so craftily that they easily lead the unwary into error; and as audacity is their chief characteristic, there is no conclusion of any kind from which they shrink or which they do not thrust forward with pertinacity and assurance."[49]

In these texts we see the two basic elements of Catholicism's engagement with modernity: first, a belief that the Church should enter the modern world to do battle with Satan, recognizing the epochal nature of the struggle; second, an injunction to the faithful to be on guard against the devious tricks of the enemy, because the Evil One was nothing if not deceptive. Within this vision of apocalyptic warfare, Catholics could find much common ground with anti-semites and with other modern thinkers. Indeed, the differences between the secular, social Darwinist struggle for survival and the Catholic struggle against Satan could easily be overlooked.

The link between the more positive approach to modernity and the apoc-alyptic rhetoric of struggle is readily visible in the writings and statements of Church leaders of the early twentieth century. In Archbishop Bilczewski's ode to modernity's accomplishments, cited above, he was discussing the value of education; in 1911 he addressed the same theme in a pastoral letter headed (without much subtlety) "Learn, learn, learn!" Catholics needed to devote more attention to education, he argued once again, but not merely because enlightenment brought progress. Here his rhetoric became overtly militant and the education in question more precisely defined: "It is all the more necessary that everyone strive to attain a fundamental knowledge of the teachings of the Church [nauka Kościoła], because recently the enemies of Catholicism—the Masons, the socialists, and also the Kozłowska heretics or Mariavites, the Protestants and the Orthodox schismatics—have been ever more vigorously expanding their activities." Of these foes, Bilczewski continued, the most dan-gerous were the Masons, "an international union of nonbelievers, who, under the lofty mask of the slogan, 'equality, freedom, brotherhood,' work secretly and openly for the destruction of all religions, above all Catholicism." The archbishop went on at great length to itemize the threats posed by these many enemies, but (significantly) there was only one passing reference to Jews: "The socialist organizations, particularly those led by jews, go hand in hand with the Masons."[50]

49. Pius X, *Pascendi dominici gregis: On the Doctrines of the Modernists* (September 8, 1907), in *Papal Encyclicals*, 3:71.

50. Józef Bilczewski, "Uczyć, uczyć, uczyć! List pasterski do kapłanów i wiernych" in Józef Bilczewski, *Listy pasterskie, odezwy, kazania i mowy okolicznościowe* (Lwów, 1922), 2:126–44.

An image of the Jews was *not* what held this worldview together, and Polish Catholics in 1911 had not yet fixed on antisemitism as the keystone of their conspiratorial fears (it seems that the Vatican was ahead of them in this regard). Generally, the Polish Catholic press of the day simply wasn't interested in the Jews. There were plenty of articles attacking liberalism, urban growth, and capitalism, but in almost all cases the connection between these evils and Judaism was left in the silent margins—perhaps implied to those reading between the lines but rarely articulated. Even extended critiques of that old Catholic bête noire, Freemasonry passed without reference to the Jews.[51] The search for a Catholic modernity led many in the Church to a militant rhetoric that depicted a struggle against the forces of Satan over the shape of the new world; this vision, in turn, made them increasingly preoccupied with enemies open and secret, which finally drew their rhetoric closer to the previously shunned secular racists.

An exploration of Cardinal Hlond's writing further reveals this pattern. In the very same pastoral letter in which he extolled the potential for a Catholic future in the industrialized world, he expressed his concern regarding "the enemies of the Church and of faith, whose secret network encompasses Poland as well, and whose hidden conspiracy is preparing for a great, open struggle with Christ." Like Bilczewski before him, Hlond mentioned the Masons and the communists, whom he accused of spreading pornography, civil marriages, divorce, "romance novels," "illustrated magazines," and fashion that is "un-Polish . . . immodest and sinful." His pastoral letter was a call to arms: "There is no doubt that a great struggle, a general test of souls, is emerging, the result of which will determine for a long time whether Silesia is to remain Catholic or not. That struggle has already begun. It is being fought along the entire front of life, and is most violently raging in people's souls. The goal of the enemy is to destabilize the Catholic idea so as to then replace Christ with some sort of Masonic naturalism, and turn our lives from the line of Christ a long way back, to paganism of a pronounced anti-Christian character."[52] A few years later Hlond released a pastoral letter titled, "On the Tasks of Catholicism vis-à-vis the Struggle against God." Here he specified the enemy:

There are those who look with joy upon the red dawn that is coming upon the world, and see in it a desirable omen of the moment when faith, moral principles, natural law, revelation, Christianity, and the Church will fall. They greet that bloody dawn as their hour, as the hour of confusion and ferment among the people, the hour of struggle and murder,

51. See, for example, the long series of articles from 1897 on "Masonry and Socialism" by Cam. Segr., "Masonerya i socyalizm," *Przegląd Katolicki* 1–8 (January 7, 1897–February 24, 1897); or, from the same year, Wł. M. Dębicki, "Owoce pozytywizmu," 1–4 (January 7, 1897–January 25, 1897).

52. "O życie katolickie na Śląsku," 23–25.

of hunger and despair. In that hour they want to spread over the world the black banner of Satan. The future, in their expectation, will be built on the principle of humanity, ruthlessly freed from the Creator. These are the goals not only of the Bolsheviks and the Godless Soviets. Such goals tempt the freethinkers, the rationalists, the Freemasons, the adherents of atheistic materialism, the nondenominationalists.[53]

Nowhere here do we find the Jews; it would be up to others to insert them into the picture, and others did indeed eventually make this move. It was not hard to do so, and all too many interwar Polish Catholics made the leap from this apocalyptic struggle for spiritual survival to the antisemite's biological struggle for survival. These two visions were not, strictly speaking, compatible, since the former entailed a battle for souls, whereas the latter would prove to be all too material. And this distinction was not incidental, as Żegota activists like Zofia Kossak would demonstrate. In a way, Jan Błoński was right: it was Catholicism that stayed the hand of such Catholics as Kossak. But it was also the Church's well-sanctioned apocalyptic rhetoric that gave her a conceptual framework allowing her to make peace with antisemitism prior to World War II. Catholicism did not "cause" modern antisemitism, but it did develop in such a way as to negate what had been—and what would eventually be again—strong barriers keeping devout Catholics from expressing the more vulgar forms of modern hatred. As late as the 1880s, Catholicism (at least in Poland) offered a way of viewing the world that gave its adherents firm ground for rejecting modern antisemitism. By the 1920s a Catholicism more engaged with the modern world was simultaneously closer to those same antisemites. It would require yet another dramatic reconfiguration of Catholicism in the 1960s to pull the church away once again.

---

53. "O zadaniach katolicyzmu wobec walki z Bogiem," 41.

6

The Moral Economy of Popular Violence

The Pogrom in Lwów, November 1918

WILLIAM W. HAGEN

mblematic of my theme here is an incident that survivors of the 1918
Lwów pogrom reported to a delegation of pro-Polish Jewish "assimilators" from Warsaw, who had come to survey their coreligionists' losses
in the ravaged east Galician capital known to them as Lemberg. "The attorney Levin," the appalled visitors heard, "was forced to load the objects plundered from him onto a wagon and then he was hitched to the wagon together
with the horses. After pulling his way as a beast of burden through several
streets he was gunned down together with his wife and old mother."[1] Taking
Lwów's streets as their stage, the pogromists had enacted three rituals: first
they robbed attorney Levin of his property and high social standing; then they
stripped him of his humanity; finally they killed him and his kinswomen. It
remains to confirm the authenticity of this pitiless picture, though eyewitnesses
vouch for other similar scenes. In any case, because contestation of ethnic violence's memory and popularly received narrative is no less central to its historical force than the tangible losses it inflicts, or than a disinterested account
of its causes, the very circulation of such stories as attorney Levin's forms part
both of the pogrom itself and the problem requiring explanation.[2]

1. Quoted from "Warsaw Jewish press" by Leon Chasanowitsch, in *Die polnischen Judenpogrome im November und Dezember 1918: Tatsachen und Dokumente* (Stockholm, 1919), 103.
2. See Paul R. Brass, "Introduction: Discourses of Ethnicity, Communalism, and Violence,"
in *Riots and Pogroms*, ed. Paul R. Brass (New York, 1996), 1–55; Robert Darnton, "Reading a
Riot," *New York Review of Books* 39, no. 17 (October 22, 1992): 44–46.

This chapter interprets the Lwów pogrom as social ritual, playing out—in a deeply sinister sense of the word "play"—public dramas designed to repair a society fallen out of the rightful order that communal convictions assigned to it. Such social norms Edward Thompson memorably termed the popular classes' moral economy.[3] It is tempting to think of the actions dramatizing and enforcing them as a carnival of violence, in analogy to early modern European communal rituals symbolically reversing social hierarchy and punishing offenders against cultural codes. Those rites, usually playful though sometimes rough, occasionally gyrated out of control into bloody violence, as symbolical contention turned real.[4]

Whether they meditated it beforehand or not, some among the Lwów pogromists did inflict physical violence and even murder on their Jewish victims. Others contented themselves with plunder, and still others, as spectators, engaged vicariously in the Jews' collective torment. This chapter's central theme is not the empirical extent of the Lwów pogrom's anti-Jewish violence (though it describes this briefly, as it does the pogrom's political setting) but rather such violence's ritualized *forms* or *stagings*, the social and cultural *scripts* it followed, and the *messages* it conveyed. The argument is that these stagings and scripts constituted the pogrom as a communal act, whose carnivalesque elements were central to its character and purpose. At the level of meaning, the violence exacted retribution from its Jewish victims for the losses World War I was seen to have inflicted on the Poles of Lwów, not the least of which was a breakdown of their sense of mastery over Jews and Ukrainians alike. The pogrom punished the Jews for having transgressed a widely embraced expectation in Polish Catholic society that the Jews should not defend themselves with arms in hand, especially not against the Poles themselves. Shaken in their collective power, Poles were prey to fears of communal eclipse or even bondage. In the shadow of such dangers, murderous impulses quickened.

As attorney Levin's fate shows, the inescapable destructiveness and brutality of pogroms make them unfit for categorization as mere carnivals gone awry.

3. Edward P. Thompson, "The Moral Economy of the English Crowd in the Eighteenth Century" (originally published in 1971), and "The Moral Economy Revisited," in Thompson, *Customs in Common* (London, 1991), 185–351. On medieval Christian anti-Jewish violence sustaining and defining unequal Christian-Jewish relations, see David Nirenberg, *Communities of Violence: Persecution of Minorities in the Middle Ages* (Princeton, 1996). See also Julius R. Ruff, *Violence in Early Modern Europe, 1500–1800* (Cambridge, U.K., 2001); and Michel Foucault, *Discipline and Punish: The Birth of the Prison* (New York, 1977 [French original, 1975]). Innovative approaches to the discursive and social construction of anti-Jewish violence, supportive of this chapter's objectives, are offered in *Exclusionary Violence: Antisemitic Riots in Modern German History*, ed. Christhard Hoffmann, Werner Bergmann, and Helmut Walser Smith (Ann Arbor, Mich., 2002).

4. Natalie Z. Davis, *Society and Culture in Early Modern France* (Stanford, Calif., 1975); Emmanuel Le Roy Ladurie, *Carnival in Romans* (New York, 1980 [French original, 1979]); Robert Darnton, *The Great Cat Massacre* (New York, 1984); further bibliography and analysis in Edward Muir, *Ritual in Early Modern Europe* (Cambridge, U.K., 1997).

Yet the violence they displayed, however much it flowed from anti-Jewish animus and even hatred, does not speak for itself but requires decipherment and intepretation both of its form and its meaning to perpetrators and in wider social perception. This applies alike to random killings and to threats of comprehensive murder, which the Lwów pogromists also occasionally voiced. The idea of mass murder seemingly gained warrant for expression from Polish nationalists' sense that their own community had fended off disaster in a moment of crisis during which, in their view, the Jews deserted them. In the exaltation of victory, the thought seized many Poles, not merely to punish the Jews humiliatingly and bruisingly, but even—wishfully imagining the Jews now irrelevant to Polish survival—to eliminate them altogether from their midst. This idea surfaced as a threat of expulsion or of localized slaughter, sometimes with genocidal overtones.[5]

On the surface, the Lwów pogrom was a military sack by victorious armed forces of civilians marked as enemies. On November 1, 1918, Ukrainian fighters surprised the city's narrow Polish majority—in 1920, 51.3 percent of a total population of 219,000, the remainder numbering three Jews to every Ukrainian—by seizing power over much of the city, including the predominantly Ukrainian and Jewish quarters (though the city displayed considerable ethnic intermixing).[6] The Ukrainians' aim was to make Lwów (L'viv to them) the capital of a post-Habsburg West Ukrainian republic. Polish nationalists counterattacked, first in waves of youthful armed volunteers, then in locally recruited units of the army in process of formation throughout the Polish lands, reinforced by soldiers of the preexisting Polish legions that had arisen on both sides of the front during World War I. The arrival from Kraków of regular army troops secured a Polish victory in the early hours of Saturday, November 22. Power now reposed ill-definedly in the armed forces' hands, with the Polish municipal authorities standing deferentially on the sidelines.[7]

5. See the approach to Polish anti-Jewish violence during World War II proposed in William W. Hagen, "A 'Devilish Mixture' of Motives: A Critique of Explanatory Strategy and Assignment of Meaning in Jan Gross's *Neighbors*," *Slavic Review* 61, no. 3 (2002): 466–75.

6. Christoph Mick, "Nationalisierung in einer multiethnischen Stadt. Interethnische Konflikte in Lemberg, 1890–1920," *Archiv für Sozialgeschichte* 40 (2000): 144.

7. On Polish-Ukrainian hostilities and Polish society in Lwów, see Maciej Kozłowski, *Zapomniana wojna: Walka o Lwów i Galicję Wschodnią, 1918–1919* (Bydgoszcz, 1999); Leszek Podhorodecki, *Dzieje Lwowa* (Warsaw, 1993), 153–72; Wlodzimierz Bonusiak et al., *Galicja i jej dziedzictwo*, 2 vols. (Rzeszów, 1994–95), esp. 1:83–115; Peter Fäßler et al., *Lemberg-Lwów-Lviv: Eine Stadt im Schnittpunkt europäischer Kulturen*, 2d ed. (Cologne, 1995), 46–112; Philipp Ther, "Chancen und Untergang einer multinationalen Stadt: Die Beziehungen zwischen den Nationalitäten in Lemberg in den ersten Hälften des 20. Jahrhunderts," in *Nationalitätenkonflikte im 20. Jahrhundert: Ursachen von interethnischen Gewalt im Vergleich*, ed. Philipp Ther and Holm Sundhausen (Wiesbaden, 2001), 123–46; Mick, "Nationalisierung"; Frank Golczewski, *Polnisch-jüdische Beziehungen, 1881–1922: Eine Studie zur Geschichte des Antisemitismus in Osteuropa* (Wiesbaden, 1981), 184–204 and chaps. 8–10. See also David Engel, "Lwów, 1918: The Transmutation of a Symbol and Its Legacy in the Holocaust," in *Contested Memories: Poles and Jews during the Holocaust and Its Aftermath*, ed. Joshua D. Zimmerman (New Brunswick, N.J., 2003), 32–46.

On November 9–10, in the midst of the Polish-Ukrainian fighting, the Poles' military and civilian leaders had joined the Jews and Ukrainians in sanctioning creation of a Jewish militia numbering some two hundred riflemen, who would patrol the central Jewish district, warding off looters in the food-scarce, darkened, and lawless city and maintaining access to Jewish shops, where such essential goods as were on hand were sold at municipally fixed prices.[8] Already on October 28 a mass meeting of Lwów's Jews, many inspired by Zionist nationalism, had embraced the principle of neutrality in the gathering Polish-Ukrainian conflict.[9]

Except to a narrow stratum of Jewish assimilationist notables, there seemed no compelling argument for taking the Poles' side. Most of Galicia's 900,000 Jews lived in the midst of the Greek Catholic Ukrainian majority of 3,300,000 inhabiting the eastern half of the land (along with 1,350,000 Roman Catholic Poles). Lwów itself was largely a Polish-Jewish island in a rural Ukrainian sea. Ukrainian reprisals for pro-Polish Jewish partisanship were imaginable. In largely Polish-inhabited western Galicia, anti-Jewish violence began in early November to explode in many small towns and across the countryside. This was a pogrom-wave propelled by political lawlessness and perpetrated by armed bands of looters, many of them army deserters or demobilized soldiers. Yet Polish civilians' connivance in them, both for material and political gain, was glaring and deeply dispiriting to the Jews, who saw the Polish phoenix rising out of pogrom flames.[10]

Lwów's Poles burningly resented Jewish neutrality. They widely believed not only that Jewish militiamen had collaborated with Ukrainians in fire-fights against Polish forces but that Jewish civilians also furtively fought them, shooting or pouring boiling water from their windows. Under Habsburg rule, Polish officialdom in Galicia had resisted acknowledging the Jews' right—not claimed by all Jews—to be recognized in law as a separate, linguistically and religiously defined nationality. In the Polish intelligentsia's eyes, the Galician Jews' destiny was to be civilized and modernized through Polonization. Otherwise—and this was especially the view of the ultranationalistic Polish National Democrats, increasingly strong in Lwów—they would face exclusion from the province's Polish-dominated public life by an economic and social boycott of such rigor as to drive the Jews, ever more impoverished, into emigration.[11]

8. For the text and signatories, both Polish and Jewish, of the neutrality agreement, and the Lwów Zionists' interpretation of it, see Central Zionist Archives, Jerusalem [hereafter CZA], A127/74 (Grünbaum Papers), Memorjal w sprawie pogromu we Lwowie, 1.XII.1918, folios. 1–6.

9. CZA, L6/119 (Ostjudenfrage, 1919), "The Pogroms in Poland: Report by Israel Cohen, Special Commissioner of the [British] Zionist Organisation," 30.

10. On west Galician anti-Jewish violence in 1918 (and 1919, which is a subject for a different study), see Chasanowitsch, Judenpogrome; Golczewski, Beziehungen; and Cohen, "Pogroms."

11. Exemplary is Franciszek Bujak, The Jewish Question in Poland (Paris, 1919). For further reference, in addition to the works cited above, see Jerzy Tomaszewski, with Józef Adelson, Teresa Prekerowa, and Piotr Wróbel, Najnowsze dzieje Żydów w Polsce w zarysie (do 1950 roku)

Rumors circulated during the Polish-Ukrainian fight over Lwów that in the aftermath of Polish victory the Jews would suffer for their neutrality. On the morning of November 22 the Polish army disarmed and interned the Jewish militia, whereupon a sacking of the Jewish quarter commenced that lasted through Sunday. On Monday, November 24, an army order dated the previous day proclaimed martial law, halting what had become increasingly bloody mayhem. In later depositions many victims and eyewitnesses testified that rioting soldiers said their officers had given them, in reward for defeating the Ukrainians, forty-eight hours of freedom to sack the Jews. Thus, a man told of meeting a soldier known to him and asking him for help in arresting a plunderer. The soldier replied, "Too bad, but you won't be able to do anything about it, because it has been permitted to rob for forty-eight hours."[12]

The nearest thing to an official Polish government account of the pogrom was an unpublished report of December 17, 1918, prepared for the Foreign Ministry, on the causes and consequences of the "anti-Jewish transgressions" (wystąpienia antyżydowskie) in Lwów. Its authors were Leon Chrzanowski, a Foreign Ministry legal specialist, and assimilationist Jewish journalist Józef Wasercug. They emphasized the role played among the locally recruited Polish armed forces of criminals released from local prisons in the chaos of the war's end. These men, together with others drawn from Lwów's sizable social underworld, seized the weapons Polish authorities were offering all volunteer fighters so as both to repel the Ukrainians and to engage in plunder, especially of the large Jewish shop-owning and business class. A "tragic and vicious circle" arose, for such a soldier, though he fought bravely for the Polish cause, also "robbed at every opportunity and wherever he could."[13]

Chrzanowski and Wasercug determined that even though the army leadership formally ordered no "punitive expedition" against the Jews, the existence of such a command was so generally accepted that soldiers and many officers joined the uniformed criminals in attacking the Jews. When Israel Cohen, "Special Commissioner of the [British] Zionist Organisation," visited Poland

---

(Warsaw, 1993); and Andrzej Żbikowski, Żydzi (Wrocław, 1997). The standard Polish-language historical literature on National Democracy is cited in William W. Hagen, "Before the 'Final Solution': Toward a Comparative Analysis of Political Anti-Semitism in Interwar Germany and Poland," Journal of Modern History 68, no. 2 (1996): 351–81. See also Brian Porter, When Nationalism Began to Hate: Imagining Modern Politics in Nineteenth-Century Poland (New York, 2000); Theodore R. Weeks, Nation and State in Late Imperial Russia: Nationalism and Russification on the Western Frontier, 1863–1914 (DeKalb, Ill., 1996); Keely Stauter-Halsted, The Nation in the Village: The Genesis of Peasant National Identity in Austrian Poland, 1848–1914 (Ithaca, N.Y., 2001).

12. Josef Bendow (pseudonym of Joseph Tenenbaum) Der Lemberger Judenpogrom November, 1918–Jänner 1919 [hereafter cited as Bendow] (Vienna, 1919), 56 (eyewitness protocol 263); see also 56–57, 114.

13. "Raport delegacji Ministerstwa Spraw Zagranicznych R. P. w sprawie wystąpien antyżydowskich we Lwowie," reproduced in full in Jerzy Tomaszewski, "Lwów, 22 listopada 1918," Przegląd Historyczny 35, no. 2 (1984): 281–85, quotations from 282.

in January 1919 to investigate the pogroms, Jewish notables in Lwów told him that on the morning of November 22, Army Chief of Staff Jakubski had said explicitly to a Jewish delegation protesting the pogrom: "It is a punitive expedition into the Jewish quarter, which cannot be stopped."[14] In any event, Chrzanowski and Wasercug determined that "truly hellish orgies" and "terrible things" followed, which they proposed to detail in a subsequent report— no trace of which, unfortunately, has ever been found. "It was a true bestialization [*istne zezwierzęcenie*], altogether medieval." They concluded that "during the days of the pogrom"—a characterization of the violence the Polish government avoided in its public pronouncements—"the authorities did not fulfill their responsibilities." Polish officials in Lwów had dismissed delegations, both Christian and Jewish, seeking to halt the violence. They had publicized inflammatory charges against the Jews and waited too long to declare martial law. In mid-December, Lwów's military and civilian courts had yet to pronounce a verdict against the forty soldiers and some one thousand "criminals" jailed for participation in robbery and murder. "Most lamentable, however, is the lack of any clear evidence of real desire to immediately throttle the pogrom."[15]

Chrzanowski and Wasercug reckoned the Jewish community's losses at "at least 150 killed or burned to death," together with "over 50 two- and three-story apartment buildings lost through fire." In the Jewish quarter alone, more than five hundred shops and businesses suffered total plunder. Homeless, and only partly lodged in temporary shelters, were two thousand people. The Jewish Rescue Committee, an umbrella organization that had taken recovery in hand, discovered seventy orphans who had lost both parents. "A dozen and more rapes of women have been reported by parents," while "a certain number of others have been concealed out of shame." Altogether, some seven thousand victims of violence, theft, and destruction had by December 13 registered with the Rescue Committee, which, in a seemingly early reckoning, counted the dead lower, at 73, and the wounded at 437. Material losses totalled 103 million kronen, the equivalent of about 4 million British pounds or 20 million contemporary U.S. dollars. Half this sum represented stolen commercial-industrial inventories. The pogromists seized cash and jewelry valued at some 18 million kronen and, perhaps surprisingly, bedding worth not much less at 16 million. There remained lost housing, workshops, furniture, clothing, and linen.[16]

14. Cohen, "Pogroms," 38.

15. From Chrzanowski and Wasercug's report in Tomaszewski, "Lwów," 283–85.

16. Ibid., 284. CZA, L6/119, "Der polnisch-ukrainische Konflikt und die Juden," n.d., reporting the Jewish Rescue Committee's statistics, which reckoned among the 73 dead 36 merchants or traders, 11 artisans, 4 members of the intelligentsia, and 22 without occupation. Among 437 wounded were 121 merchants or traders, 26 artisans, 5 workers, 14 commercial employees, and 271 "private persons" and children. The Jewish Rescue Committee (*Komitet Ratunkowy Żydowski*) originally called itself *Rettungs-Komitee für die Pogrom-Opfer* or *Żydowski Komitet*

The 1918–19 Piłsudski-Paderewski provisional governmental condo-minium and the Polish mainstream rightist, centrist, and socialist political parties supporting it were at pains to deny official instigation or toleration of pogroms. They pleaded inability, amid the turbulence and armed clashes of national rebirth, to control those they blamed for anti-Jewish violence: bandits and criminals (including Ukrainians and even the Jewish underworld), and demobilized soldiers and deserters from the Habsburg, German, and Russian armies. The Polish authorities obliquely conceded the common people's involvement by interpreting pogroms as hunger riots and expressions of war-induced immiseration, not shrinking from attributing them also to Jewish war-profiteering. Prominent, too, was the official charge that Jewish support for Bolshevism in Poland and the eastern borderlands had provoked the Polish common folk's righteous fury. Still, the government and the Polish political parties, including the National Democrats, condemned anti-Jewish violence, if for no other reason than that highly visible Jewish protest meetings and press denunciations were doing harm to Poland's reputation, on the eve of the Paris Peace Conference, in Western Europe and the United States.[17]

Polish historiography has proposed few interpretations of this pogrom, the most destructive and brutal among the many that attended the Polish state's war-torn birth. Historians long echoed the interwar political establishment's defensive and denial-ridden arguments, but in recent years the factual accu-racy and moral rectitude of Chrzanowski's and Wasercug's report have gained acknowledgment, though not without provoking nationalist backlash.[18] German historian Frank Golczewski's pioneering 1981 study—dealing broadly both with Polish-Jewish political relations in the period 1881–1922 and with Polish violence against Jews in these years—offers the one modern analysis of the post–World War I pogroms. Golczewski interprets Polish antisemitism as a rhetorical expression of political and economic self-interest issuing from a

---

dla Niesienia Pomocy Ofiarom Rozruchów i Rabunków w Listopadzie 1918, but under govern-ment pressure dropped the references to pogrom and plunder. Cohen ("Pogroms," 38) reported that the Jewish Rescue Committee had collected signed eyewitness testimony to 500 cases in which patrols led by officers wrongfully injured Jews, and another 2,300 cases in which individual sol-diers took part. Names were known of 18 culpable officers and 72 soldiers. Cohen (16) reckoned the krone at 25 to the British pound. Tomaszewski ("Lwów," 280) appears to have overvalued it at 4 to the pound.

17. See Chasanowitsch, *Juden pogrome*, 72–97; Cohen, "Pogroms," 44–48; and the reports of Polish views on the 1918–19 pogroms (including Henry Morgenthau's) assembled in *The Jews in Poland: Official Reports on the American and British Investigating Missions*, published by the National Polish Committee of America (Chicago, n.d. [1919]). On reactions in Germany, see William W. Hagen, "Murder in the East: German-Jewish Liberal Reactions to Anti-Jewish Violence in Poland and Other East European Lands, 1918–1920," *Central European History* 34, no. 1 (2001): 1–30.

18. See the works cited above by Kozłowski, Tomaszewski, and Tomaszewski et al. (notes 7, 11, 13). Aggressive Polish nationalist denial, replete with anti-Jewish accents, is on display in Leszek Tomaszewski, "Lwów—Listopad 1918: Niezwykłe losy pewnego dokumentu," *Dzieje Najnowsze* 25, no. 4 (1993): 164–73.

social-cultural matrix of ethnic prejudice explicable in universal psychoanalytic terms.[19]

The broad literature on both Russian pogroms and interethnic rioting on a world scale concentrates on issues of causation, searching for those political configurations that "trigger" violence, and especially on the role of civil and military authorities in unleashing or tolerating pograms, seeking to scapegoat victims for governmental gain. This literature commonly traces causation to Durkheimian crises of social coherence and solidarity, bringing forth pogromists or rioters from circles suffering status tensions and economic want with particular intensity. Yet another focal point is extragovernmental political agitation stigmatizing "target populations," fomenting ethnic violence to gain power by whipping up popular prejudice against culturally or religiously heterodox subcultures, especially those engaged in trade and commerce.[20]

Such approaches are valuable and necessary. But the questions these pages pose point in other directions—above all, toward the interpretation of ethnic violence's *meanings* and *messages* in its perpetrators' eyes. It seems probable that no one, apart from the hardened professional criminal, commits murder and mayhem or even theft without believing it justifiable or even righteous.[21] But how, precisely, did Lwów pogromists see their handiwork in this light, and what ideas or judgments did they intend it to express or symbolize? Anthropologists and other scholars have depicted social life as a stage on which narratives and rituals expressing a culture's constitutive values and meanings are enacted and reenacted. The political scientist James Scott has shown how a repertoire of behavioral *scripts* structured peasant resistance to landlords and officialdom. The sociologist Irving Goffman and many others have highlighted the performative, role-playing dimension of individual identities and social groups.[22]

19. Golczewski, *Beziehungen*, 1–15. By contrast, Andrzej Żbikowski stresses the religious-cultural and socio-political roots of specifically Polish antisemitism in his *Dzieje Żydów w Polsce: Ideologia antysemicka, 1848–1914; Wybór tekstów źródlowych* (Warsaw, 1994). On large-scale interpretations, with extensive bibliography, see Hagen, "Before the 'Final Solution.' "

20. On the social science literature, see Donald L. Horowitz, *The Deadly Ethnic Riot* (Berkeley, Calif., 2001). See also Norman Naimark, *Fires of Hatred: Ethnic Cleansing in Twentieth-Century Europe* (Cambridge, Mass., 2001), and Brass, *Riots and Pogroms*. On Russia, see *Pogroms: Anti-Jewish Violence in Modern Russian History*, ed. John D. Klier and Shlomo Lambroza (Cambridge, U.K., 1992), especially Hans Rogger's "Conclusion and Overview," 314–72; Henry Abramson, *A Prayer for the Government: Ukrainians and Jews in Revolutionary Times, 1917–1920* (Cambridge, Mass., 1999).

21. See Jack Katz, "Criminals' Passions and the Progressives' Dilemma," in *America at Century's End*, ed. Alan Wolfe (Berkeley, Calif., 1991), 396–420.

22. James Scott, *Weapons of the Weak: Everyday Forms of Peasant Resistance* (New Haven, 1985). On enduring, if historically evolving, cultural structures, see Sherry Ortner, *High Religion: A Cultural and Political History of Sherpa Buddhism* (Princeton, 1989); and *Culture through Time: Anthropological Approaches*, ed. Emilo Ohnuki-Tierney (Stanford, Calif., 1990). On reading history as social theater, see Rhys Isaac, *The Transformation of Virginia, 1740–1790* (Chapel Hill, N.C., 1982).

Difficult questions about cultural structures' coherence and durability face historians concerned with timebound change, yet it is common human experience that much of communal life is enactment of social scripts or scenarios. Participation in them is doubtless constitutive of individual identity, though social and cultural hierarchies channel individuals into many different group dramas, while the subjective self emerges into society from a kaleidoscopic realm of family, kinship, and class that fits or unfits it for participation in one or another social ritual.[23] The 1918 Lwów pogrom witnessed the enactment of several collective scripts or scenarios, all together holding the keys to the pogrom's meaning in its perpetrators' eyes. The violence was causally overdetermined, for more social dramas found expression than were necessary to inflict the physical and material injuries Lwów's Jews suffered. Military plunder and attendant aggression alone wrought great havoc. Yet viewed from the perspective of Polish-Jewish coexistence, noninstrumental and symbolical violence cut the deepest wounds.

The behavior of the Lwów pogrom's perpetrators and the motives they gave for their actions are well documented. The Jewish Rescue Committee, administered by local Jewish notables and chaired by Lwów's assimilationist leader, Tobias Ashkenazy, scrupulously recorded some five hundred or more depositions from victims and eyewitnesses in the violence's immediate aftermath. Some of these appear in full, while others were selectively drawn on, in books published in early 1919 in Stockholm by Zionist publicist Leon Chasanowitsch and in Vienna by pogrom witness Galician Zionist and social analyst Joseph Tenenbaum (writing under the pseudonym Josef Bendow).[24] The Central Zionist Archives in Jerusalem house additional unpublished testimony, and the Central Archive for the History of the Jewish People, also in Jerusalem, holds microfilm of Polish judicial records assembled by the Extraordinary Governmental Investigative Commission (*Nadzwyczajna Komisja Śledcza Rządowa*), which in 1918–19 gathered evidence on the pogroms.

Altogether, this documentation brings to light the pogromists' actions, the scripts they staged, and often too the explanations their own words offer for anti-Jewish aggression. The question looms whether each reported word and deed mirrors empirical reality, but even though some may not, the mosaic picture that comes into view certainly displays widely enacted patterns of pogrom violence and rhetoric. It is characteristic of crime that the victim usually reports it, while the perpetrator seeks to conceal it. Most of the evidence marshaled here is of Jewish provenance; Polish and other scholars might question the extent of pogrom injuries, but few anymore are disposed to deny

23. On social applications of psychoanalytic and social psychological theory useful to the historian, see Sudhir Kakar, *The Colors of Violence: Cultural Identities, Religion, and Conflict* (Chicago, 1996); Joshua Searle-White, *The Psychology of Nationalism* (New York, 2001).

24. See Chasanowitsch's and Bendow-Tenenbaum's works cited above. Tennenbaum's skills in socioeconomic analysis, and his deep knowledge of the Galician scene, are on display in his *Żydowskie problemy gospodarcze w Galicyi* (Vienna, 1918).

them. The vital questions revolve instead around interpreting the Lwów upheaval's meanings and significations.

The carnivalesque rituals of early modern Europe repudiated social hierarchy, "turning the world upside down." Among the common people, Rabelaisian feasting and costumed finery temporarily banished hunger and want. As Polish expulsion of Ukrainian troops from Lwów drew nigh, Jewish bystanders observed a festive mood among Polish fighters, in anticipation of the widely foreseen sacking of Jewish shops clustered around Kraków Square, which was to be their reward for the risks they had run. Tenenbaum characterized their mood in the phrase, perhaps often repeated: "We're going into the land of Eden."[25] A thirty-six-year-old woman, member of a family owning a "big clothing warehouse" that supplied—among other things—army uniforms, saved herself by convincing the pogromists that she was "a poor housemaid and Pole." She testified that a band of some thirty Polish soldiers, speaking in "west Galician dialect" and accompanied by a sister (a nurse) of the Polish Red Cross, burst into her familial apartment, crying "give us gold, silver, diamonds, millions." Thus did the Jewish El Dorado appear to such plunderers (and murderers, for they killed this witness's sister). "The Red Cross sister," she added, "kept shouting 'shoot.' "[26]

A forty-eight-year-old merchant recalled that at five o'clock in the pogrom's first morning, "I heard a harmonica playing while [soldiers] pounded on the door."[27] A Jewish "temple servant" told of a Polish officer who searched a synagogue for evidence that Jews had fired from it on Polish troops: "The officer struck a brutal pose. He had a cigar in his teeth and whistled a popular tune."[28] A still more sinister musical note resounded the next day when soldiers, having plundered a Jewish family and killed the father, repaired to the landlady's apartment. There, as the victim's sister testified, "the murderer played the piano very expertly for about an hour and a half, while his comrades danced. The murderer was thus a member of the intelligentsia from better circles, since I play the piano and I must characterize his playing as very good."[29]

Such evidence points to the pogrom's musical accompaniment. That it also possessed, in Polish participants' and observers' minds, the character of a public spectacle or drama emerges from a Jewish lawyer's recollection that as he was walking on Saturday morning near Lwów's Jesuit Garden, he observed at its entrance "an elegantly dressed gentleman wearing the town militia's armband and shouldering a gun. He spoke to the crowd that was standing about: 'Why are you strolling here? You should go to Kraków Square, where

25. Bendow, 30.
26. Bendow, 155 (protocol 363).
27. Bendow, 143 (protocol 114).
28. Bendow, 160 (protocol 265).
28. Ibid.
29. Bendow, 158 (protocol 265).

a performance is being given free of charge.' Someone asked, 'Has the play already begun?' The guardian of order replied, 'It has begun and it will go on.' "[30] A Viennese Jewish journalist of Galician origins who found himself trapped in Lwów, having first taken a look in the mirror to assure himself that his "physiognomy" did not brand him as "suspicious," ventured "with beating heart" onto the street on Saturday morning, hunger-driven to buy provisions. He encountered "an elegant lady" handing out pastries to the Poles' liberators, asking them, "Will there now be a pogrom [*Bendzie teras pogrom*]?" Into a barber shop, where he was having his (seemingly telltale) mustache shaved, a young woman happily burst with two bottles of wine, given her by soldiers who had plundered a Jewish liquor shop. "And now I'm going to see what else there is to be fetched."[31]

Looting occurred as carnivalesque street theater. The mustache-shorn observer watched the plunder of a furrier's shop. The soldiers threw precious goods into the street "and in a flash the ladies of the working-class suburbs and the population of the Lyczakow district, which houses notorious street people [*Plattenbrüder*] and *Rowdies*, were scrambling for them. Washerwomen and housekeepers threw off their shawls and padded work coats and wrapped themselves in Persian lamb and seal jackets." Nearby, "gentlemen of the higher classes and society ladies watched these scenes and laughed."[32] A female plaintiff, having accosted a woman dressed in clothes looted from her shop, followed her into a barracks, where she found "many legionnaires running about in furs stolen from her." In response to her demand for return of her goods, the legionnaires threatened to shoot her, advising the female plunderer, if the plaintiff further harrassed her, "to stone her."[33]

Another witness saw how "some civilians, foremost among them lame 'Edek,' a knacker's apprentice," identified Jewish-owned businesses to a band of civilian militia. Joined by some sixty soldiers, they threw themselves into plundering. "Then the rabble arrived, among them many ladies [*Damen*] with elegant hats, veils, and gloves. The legionnaires fetched packages from the shops, each giving one to his lady" in an act doubtless often signifying more than Polish gallantry.[34] A third plaintiff, a twenty-five-year-old female bank clerk, told how her family's apartment house was sacked by soldiers. Apart from her own painful loss of a rich bridal trousseau, "which when acquired cost 5000 kronen but now is not to be had," her uncle surrendered his jewelry

---

30. Bendow, 91 (protocol 56).

31. CZA, Z3/179: handwritten copy of article published November 26, 1918, in *Neue Freie Presse*, Vienna. The ungrammatical Polish was the Germanophone journalist's.

32. Ibid.

33. Bendow, 62 (protocol 479). Jewish eyewitness reports often designate Polish fighters as "legionnaires," a term generally associated with the armed followers of Józef Piłsudski, whose wartime units were not present in Lwów. It seems, however, to have been a local synonym for irregular soldiers recruited against the Ukrainians.

34. Bendow, 144 (protocol 114).

and cash. Among the robbers of their building her uncle "recognized a [gymnasium] professor, who was very happy, and who said: my boys too"—that is, his students—"have already got enough, they've stuffed their pockets full."[35]

The carnival tradition warranted sexual license, too, which in the pogrom's brutalized scripts sometimes issued in rapes. Of those, direct eyewitness evidence is lacking, but Tenenbaum reported that as army reinforcements—the "Krakusy"—arrived on the pogrom's eve, the local irregular soldiers sang out: "Here comes General Roja with his boys, the Jews will be having a wedding" (that is, they would be deflowered).[36] About the pogrom itself, he wrote that "women had to disrobe and stand naked, to the delight of the crude mob. Lawyers' wives were treated like whores, university attendees grossly besmirched, their womanly dignity shamelessly trampled on."[37]

An eyewitness told how soldiers came across several girls in a house they were plundering. "One said, 'It's a shame to murder these girls. It's better to cuddle them [liebkosen],' whereupon the soldiers threw themselves on the girls, to make them do their bidding." A young woman who refused suffered a blow to her face: "They had, under threat of death, to kiss and cuddle with the soldiers."[38] On November 22 a Jewish lawyer asked a group of "elegant gentlemen" if the streets were clear. They told him, evidently taking him for a Pole, "You may safely go ahead. The Ukrainians are gone and along with them 'the neutrals.' Now we're going to flirt with the Jews"—but they used the word anbandeln, meaning both to flirt and to start a real fight.[39]

Other scenes cruelly dramatized carnivalesque social reversals. A Jewish lawyer suffered maltreatment recalling attorney Levin's fate when five armed youths burst into his apartment at 1:00 A.M., dragging him and his family from their beds and stealing, "apart from a fur, a large sum of money, which the lawyer was obliged to hand them on his knees."[40] Scenes occurred of humiliations the German National Socialists would later engrave on historical memory, as when the Polish army, in the pogrom's aftermath, seized Jewish gymnasium students on the streets for compulsory labor, including two "who were ordered to wash the floors" at a command post, "where pranks were played with them and they were forced to jump over tables." The Jewish Rescue Committee lodged another complaint about the army's "rounding up of the Jewish intelligentsia and their assignment to the lowest kinds of work, such as stuffing straw sacks and cleaning latrines." In such ritualized form did Polish nationalists castigate Jews—especially, presumably, Zionists and religious quietists—for their distance from Polish military exertions. Many

35. CZA, Z3/181: deposition dated 28.XI.1918. See also Bendow, 91 (protocol 78).
36. Bendow, 31.
37. Bendow, 35.
38. Bendow, 50 (protocol 425).
39. Bendow, 91 (protocol 56).
40. CZA, Z3/179 (see note 31).

"assimilators" among the Jews, who in 1918 had taken up arms throughout the Polish lands for the Polish cause, also suffered rebuffs and humiliations, though on this the Lwów pogrom documentation is silent.

Many Poles entered the charred and plundered Jewish district on Monday, November 24, after the proclamation of martial law had ended violence and tumults. Of them, Zionist Max Reiner, another journalist from Vienna and a pogrom witness, wrote bitterly that they "streamed in as to a festival scene, to survey their handiwork," even as corpses still lay in the streets.[41] Elias Nacht, another observer, wrote in the German-Jewish liberal press of seeing "a mob thirsting for a lynching leading Jews through the streets in chains," and of "the enthusiasm of the Polish population, which streamed to the resting place of thousands [*sic*] of innocent victims like pilgrims to a holy shrine."[42] Doubtless such language reflected rhetorical choice, yet this *was* a time of numerous mass meetings, marches, and demonstrations on all sides. Reiner observed, at the time when Lwów's Jewish community resolved on neutrality in the imminent Polish-Ukrainian fighting, "a great [Jewish] parade, comprising thousands of persons, among them hundreds of Jewish officers and soldiers in uniform, that moved from the theater through the city's main streets. The Zionists celebrated this day as a holiday. Weavings and blue-white pennants hung from many windows, everywhere Herzl pictures were displayed. Men and women had pinned blue-white cockades on their hats, coats, and blouses."[43]

The evidence so far mustered shows that on many occasions the pogromists, as they engaged in plunder and violence, moved within a self-chosen framework of symbolic action which, in carnivalesque form, gave expression to a collective sense of celebration, triumph, and cruel playfulness and joy at the dispossession, humiliation, and even murder of the Jews. Widening the focus to encompass other Polish pogroms of 1918–19 would bring many more such scenes into view. The question arises, how could such brutal behavior be understood by its perpetrators as justifiable or righteous? What moral economy sanctioned such ethical calculus?

The answer lies in part in the pogromists' self-understanding as Christians, and in the conviction that the Jews *owed* them the goods (and even the lives) of which, by moral right, Christian violence was dispossessing them. Before the pogrom, Tenenbaum reported, "a Polish city functionary consoled those assembled before a shop: 'a few days' patience, people [*Kinder*]. As soon as we get to Kraków Square we'll take everything from the Jews and the poor children of Christ will have everything in abundance.' "[44] After the pogrom,

41. CZA, Z3/180: Max Reiner, "Die Pogrome in Lemberg," n.d., 22.
42. "Das Blutbad in Lemberg," *Allgemeine Zeitung des Judenthums* 46 (November 14, 1919).
43. Reiner, "Die Pogrome in Lemberg," 4.
44. Bendow, 31.

on Christmas Eve 1918, Poles seized a Jewish candle dealer's stock "and distributed it among the Christian population."[45] A Jewish merchant reported that at 7:30 A.M. on pogrom Saturday, "financial official Zielinski" burst into his family quarters accompanied by a son, exclaiming, "Now it's the Last Judgment for you, today you'll lose your heads." Later in the day Zielinski, joined by soldiers "and the Christian tenants of Rutkowski Lane 23," plundered the plaintiff's stocks.[46]

Jewish victims sometimes appealed to their tormentors' Christian sentiments. A girl successfully pleaded with her father's murderers not to kill her mother too, saying "the Mother of God would have taken mercy on us, but you don't." One of the soldiers, "visibly moved, said to [the killer]: 'Come, Jasiek, let's get out of here.'"[47] A less fortunate girl, fourteen-years old, "with folded hands knelt before the sergeant," the one whom the above-mentioned Red Cross sister was urging to use his gun, "and received a [fatal] shot through the mouth."[48]

Christian self-righteousness found expression in brutal street theater desacralizing and destroying Jews (whether symbolically or in actuality) in their specifically religious identity and holy sites. A common element of the post–World War I Polish pogroms, and later of National Socialist practice, were scenes such as one in Lwów on December 26, 1918, in which, led by a corporal, "legionnaires seized whiskered Jews, tugging them by their beards into the Żółkiewska Lane barracks where, to the delight of the rabble, they were made to dance."[49] A journalist reported that during the pogrom, soldiers drunkenly attempted to sever an elderly man's earlocks with their bayonets. When he resisted, a sergeant among them shot him dead and robbed the corpse.[50]

Polish nationalist complaints that the Jewish militia had fired on Polish soldiers during the fighting, and that other Jews had furtively shot at the Poles, point to the hostility and anxiety that the ideas of Jewish self-defense and armed power elicited. Soldiers often justified their entry into Jewish dwellings as a search for illicit weapons, and ransacked synagogues on the same pretext. After the pogrom, Polish armed forces halted Jewish funeral processions, opening caskets to search for weapons. At the Jewish cemetery new graves remained undug because military patrols commandeered workers to open older graves and crypts in further arms hunts. Soldiers looking for weapons tore up the floor of the hall in which pogrom victims' corpses lay awaiting burial and "meticulously" searched hearses returning empty from the cemetery. The British Zionist Israel Cohen, a not uncritical researcher, accepted that

45. Bendow, 119.
46. Bendow, 91 (protocol 229).
47. Bendow, 168 (protocol 265).
48. Bendow, 156 (protocol 363).
49. Bendow, 116.
50. CZA, Z3/179 (see note 31).

numerous such incidents occurred in Lwów, including one in which soldiers opened the graves of thirty pogrom victims and ended their work "by flinging mud upon the desecrated dead."[51]

The perpetrators of these acts doubtless intended to distress Jewish mourners and further humiliate the Jewish community. They sought too to prove their charges of Jewish perfidy, though in arms-cache searches they came up empty-handed. Such behavior signaled not just the deep paranoia lodged in many Polish minds about Jewish self-defense and loyalty but projected Polish aggressions—real enough (as the pogroms showed)—onto the Jews, whose boldest gesture in reality was not foolhardily to attack Polish forces, but only to assert a right to armed neutrality.[52]

Physical assaults on synagogues and their sacred paraphernalia packed a murderous symbolic charge. The profanation worked upon Judaism seemingly sought to rob it in anti-Jewish minds of its magical aura and spiritual legitimacy. In Lwów the pogromists put two synagogues to the torch, one a historic structure from the seventeenth century and the other the "progressive temple." An eyewitness reported that "at the Great Synagogue I saw legionnaires hacking at the torah roll with sabers"—sublimated human slaughter— "while Christian women wore the 'Projches' [torah cabinet veil] on their heads." At the progressive temple "the officers led the action, playing the clown with the Procheth on their heads. Silver objects were put in rucksacks and carried off."[53]

The pogrom's theatricalized violence—some largely symbolical, some discharged on property, some bloody or murderous—expressed its perpetrators' satisfaction and even joy at taking righteous revenge for the temporal and spiritual faults they ascribed to their victims. The pogromists' complaints, arising from a popular moral economy governing Christian-Jewish ties, form a long litany, of which only some have come to voice and whose further choruses the pages below summon up. This interpretive perspective, as earlier suggested, lies beyond the perimeter of established research on Polish-Jewish relations and on east European pogroms, which concentrates—leaving apologies and denials aside—on sociopolitical triggers and causes and on identifying perpetrators, rather than on ethnic violence's mythic meaning. Discovering the popular moral-political concepts, more or less deep-rooted in past practice, that the pogrom's scripts dramatized leads beyond the themes so far explored—the pogrom as celebratory street theater, and the pogromists' self-understanding as Christians—to violence's various modalities and their separate significances. For on the margins of anti-Jewish actions, even when staged within culturally defined boundaries, there stalked, in many minds and perhaps in wide social consciousness, phantasms of mass murder.

51. Bendow, 121–22; Cohen, "Pogroms," 42.
52. On projection of aggression, see the works by Kakar and Searle-White cited in n. 23.
53. Bendow, 42, 146 (protocol 114).

Why this was so is a question that goes beyond Polish mentalities to the problem of Jewish presence and absence in Christendom's historically evolving self-understanding, and of Christian interpretations of Jewish social roles. The Lwów evidence reveals that many perpetrators and onlookers readily transformed discrete instances of violence into metaphors of comprehensive Jewish death. The Holocaust might seem to show that Nazi mass murder followed from highly ideologized political antisemitism. Yet there is little evidence that the genocidal shadows hovering around the Lwów pogrom arose from ideological intoxication, though doubtless the anti-Jewish propaganda of Polish National Democrats and right-wing peasant populists legitimized hostile attitudes among east Galician Poles, both townspeople and villagers.

The idea, whether dreaded or embraced, of death effacing whole cultures seems to flow, when it shows itself, from an apocalyptic or millennialist imagination (or potentiality) in Christian—or perhaps human—civilization. In Lwów, as elsewhere in the Polish–east European borderlands, the Poles, fearing subordination to Ukrainian rule or a bloodier fate, could imagine themselves, however exaggeratedly, as having escaped a kind of collective mortal threat. On deliverance from such menace, the wish to inflict crushing punishment on the Jews quickened among some of the pogromists and their sympathizers, whose aggressions toward Ukrainians faced the obstacle that bloody counter-reprisals against the scattered east Galician Poles were likely.

Some of the Lwów pogromists succumbed to visceral murderous impulses. Stella Agid, a twenty-four-year-old schoolteacher, reported to Bronisław Wisznicki, the public prosecutor in Płock assigned to the Governmental Investigative Commission on the Lwów pogrom, that four army patrols stormed into her apartment on November 22: "The fourth patrol was the most ruthless: they robbed and destroyed everything, and one of the soldiers gave the impression of an enraged wild animal. Bloody, sweaty, with a broken rifle, he ran about shouting that he had to kill a Jew." Agid and other women escaped to the neighboring apartment house by climbing down a ladder, "but my husband Moses Agid, an older person, couldn't risk taking this route," and the enraged soldier murdered him with four bullets. Antonina Piątek, nineteen years old, witnessed the shooting and recalled that "before the murder, that person ran about the whole apartment, shouting that he had to kill one of the Jews, no matter whom. After the murder, when one of the soldiers condemned him, saying he'd killed an innocent human being, he kicked the dead man and left the room."[54]

What possessed him this murderer may not himself have known, or known how to express. His action's message, like that of many other killings, is

54. Central Archive for the History of the Jewish People (hereafter CAHJP), microfilm HM2/8299.11, frame 81. This and other CAHJP microfilm cited below derive from the Ukrainian state archive in L'viv, bearing the Soviet-era signature, GALO/g.Lvov/FOND 271/Opis.1/Od. 3B.446.

unreadable. Conversely, other pogrom murders bore the stamp of a seemingly one-dimensional banality, cynicism, and greed. Jetta Donner, merchant Chaim Sender's twenty-nine-year-old widow, told the Investigative Commission's director, Zygmunt Rymowicz, how she and her husband had fled their apartment to take refuge with her sister. Returning, they met a neighbor, Ludwik Ciesiak, "a troublemaker [bosiak] who constantly quarreled with my husband." She added that Ciesiak "also speaks fluent Yiddish." Ciesiak again picked a fight, "threatening [Sender] by saying, 'You just wait, I'll show you where the Poles stand.'" Later, Ciesiak appeared in their apartment with soldiers, to whom he said, pointing to Sender, "That's the one." Sender's body turned up twelve days later among the corpses at the execution grounds (góra stracenia). Six bullets had killed him. Jetta lamented: "My husband had 1,000 kronen on him, all our assets. This money disappeared, and so did the shoes he was wearing. . . . Out of malice an innocent man was murdered." She added that "Ciesiak also used the prostitute Halke Lang to threaten me. [Jetta] said people told her that Ciesiak boasted that 'he treated Sender to some good plums,'" a cruelly ironical claim. Though Ciesiak dressed his denunciation of Sender in nationalist colors, theft and malevolence were his guiding stars. His command of Yiddish—and the emotional-psychological intimacy it conveyed—left him cold to his Jewish victims.[55]

More typical was violence justified by lurid or fantastic charges of Jewish misdeeds and aggression. Among these, Tenenbaum listed selling poisoned candy and cigarettes, giving millions to the Ukrainians, and causing—together with "their Kaiser"—the war.[56] When a Jewish robbery victim went to the Polish army command post at the city hall to file a complaint, he was told, "It's right what's happening to you. People have to rob the Jews. You Jews robbed long enough, now it's time you were plundered."[57] Such comments were legion. But the "main legend," Tenenbaum wrote, "that never fell silent and like a thousand-headed hydra, though once slain, came again to life," condemned the Jews for firing on the Poles. This seemingly violated a deep-seated insistence within Polish popular culture that the Jews remain passive, powerless, and defenseless—reminiscent of a similar pattern in the segregated American South, where black self-defense provoked lynchings. This appears to have been a condition Polish popular culture imposed on Jewish life to balance or neutralize the perceived power, both material and magical, that the Jews wielded in the Poles' midst.[58]

---

55. CAHJP, HM2/8299.11.: frames 76/760d.

56. Bendow, 101–2.

57. Bendow, 76 (protocol 253); see also 77.

58. This is not a point made in the pioneering and invaluable works by Aleksander Hertz, *The Jews in Polish Culture* (Evanston, Ill., 1988 [Polish original: Paris, 1961]); and Alina Cała, *The Image of the Jew in Polish Folk Culture* (Jerusalem, 1995). See also Michael Steinlauf, "Whose Poland? Returning to Aleksander Hertz," *Gal-Ed* 12 (1991): 131–42.

So serious was the charge of furtive Jewish shooting and arms stockpiling that on December 6, Philipp Waschitz recorded having taken part as Jewish Rescue Committee representative in the Polish civilian city militia's search of the Jewish quarter for arms caches. Present were some forty militiamen "from the best Polish social circles (lawyers, senior judges, etc.)," and many policemen, under their Commissioner Piątek. For three hours they combed a passage formed by three intersecting streets, but "nowhere was any trace of weapons or ammunition found."[59]

The provocation that Jewish self-defense posed to Polish nationalists appears in the testimony of a Jewish typist employed in an engineering firm. She told how on November 1 a colleague, engineer Gier, excitedly exclaimed to "the assembled villagers and [prisoner-of-war] Italians"—seemingly the firm's workers—that "we have to arm ourselves. I saw a Jewish boy with a gun." Another engineer colleague said the Jews weren't fighting, only protecting themselves. Later, when she questioned Gier's anti-Jewish vehemence, he said, "The Jews are siding now with Ukrainians, and then they'll go with us, but we'll drive them away like dogs." During the pogrom, soldiers killed this same witness's brother in his apartment, even though he had protested that he and his family should be spared, since he had just returned as a Austrian prisoner of war from Russian captivity; he was still, his sister recalled, wearing his military trousers. "We kissed the murderer's hands and fell at his feet, but he pushed us away, saying, 'It's a shame to leave such a strong man alive, we have to kill him.'"[60]

A more magical level of anxiety over imagined Jewish malevolence emerges from the Governmental Investigative Commission's interrogation of a Polish market saleswoman, who reportedly said she witnessed "a legionnaire's murder by Jews, who plucked out his eye." She admitted only hearing it from others but that both eyes were "dug out."[61] A female apartment house supervisor, seemingly projecting Polish aggression onto the Jews, warned a band of soldiers breaking through defenses behind which neighboring Jews had barricaded themselves that "here live nothing but brutes [Hamans], who rob, steal, and shoot at the legionnaires."[62] A family father told how soldiers stormed into his apartment at 3:00 A.M. The commanding lieutenant ordered the victims shot, stipulating that "these disgusting Jews [Rotzjuden] are worth only one bullet." Rescinding the death threat, the soldiers drove the witness's sons into the street, telling late-night passersby and other legionnaires, that "'these Jews wanted to kill us with axes,' whereupon everyone starting beating our children."[63]

59. CZA, Z3/181: 6.XII.1918, deposition 6.
60. Bendow, 159 (protocol 265).
61. CAHJP, HM2/8299.11:53: frames 103/1030d.
62. Bendow, 112.
63. Bendow, 150 (protocol 268).

Coldly Machiavellian was the response a Jewish apartment house owner received when she implored firemen to save her burning building. She first approached a Jewish firefighter, but he directed her to the Polish sergeant, whom "I begged on my knees for rescue, offering him whatever payment he wanted. But [he] replied: We have orders not to save any Jewish houses. You Jews demanded 20 kronen for a loaf of bread, and now you're getting it."[64] Such willful destruction of Jewish property, apart from any motive of theft, represented, among other things, symbolic violence against the Jews themselves, and occurred widely during the post–World War I pogroms. A female medical student said of soldiers' repeated plunder of her family's dwelling: "What they couldn't carry off in sacks they maliciously demolished like Vandals, with an unbelievable fury, venting their hatred of the Jews."[65] "Repaying" perceived Jewish misdeeds in the coin of violence often extended beyond property damage to physical injury. Before murdering the Jewish veteran returned home from Russian captivity, his killer was heard to tell him, "You people killed three legionnaires, and in return we're taking out a loan of [ausborgen, i.e., shooting] 300 Jews."[66]

Pogrom fire consumed not only Jewish property but, like the premodern burning at the stake of those condemned as heretics, many Jewish lives as well. Government investigators Chrzanowski and Wasercug acknowledged that Polish authorities had denied Jews fire protection during the November crisis. One witness recalled that on November 7, army officials told a Jewish family alarmed by the spread of fighting-ignited fire, "We don't have any time for you," adding that "anyway, the Jews can burn for the Polish cause," that is, burn to death (verbrennen) if they wouldn't burn with zeal.[67] During the pogrom a fireman dismissed a woman's plea for help, saying, "Let the Jews warm themselves up."[68]

Witnesses told of soldiers' and other pogromists' efforts to enclose Jews in burning buildings, or prevent their escape from them. Troops kept a woman's elderly grandmother trapped in her third-floor apartment until finally, on Sunday, unidentified persons helped catch her on the street in a "rescue sheet."[69] Other reports told of a Jewish passerby thrust into a burning apartment house, and a woman with two children forced into a burning prayer house.[70] In another instance, soldiers staged a potent script of Jewish doom: an eyewitness recounted that some seventy Jews took refuge in a synagogue (the "Chaduschim-Shul"). Marauding soldiers discovered them and demanded two thousand kronen, but the poverty-stricken group possessed only a few

64. CZA, Z3/181: 3.XII.1918, deposition 8.
65. Bendow, 151 (protocol 475).
66. Bendow, 158 (protocol 265).
67. Bendow, 139 (protocol 69).
68. Bendow, 49 (protocol 725).
69. CZA, Z3/18: deposition 2, dated 2.I.19.
70. Bendow, 49, 81.

hundred. The soldiers then erected a gallows and announced that executions would begin. "As the distraught victims began lamenting and pleading to be shot rather than hanged, the Polish killer-boys [*Mordbuben*] carried the holy scriptures and Talmudic books to the middle of the room, piled them up, and set them all aflame. They then left the synagogue, locking the door from the outside. Only thanks to the existence of a concealed passage through the wall, unsuspected by the legionnaires, could these people, condemned to death by fire, save their lives."

The scenario of heretic-burning also displayed carnivalesque elements, especially in allusions to the cooking of food. The above-mentioned female medical student asked a Polish officer to enable her to leave her family's burning apartment building, menacingly ringed by soldiers "who were shouting, 'Now we'll roast them alive.' "[71] Tenenbaum reported several "stereotyped answers" which the pogromists threw in the face of Jews threatened by fire. "One heard the Polish crowd rejoicing: 'Now they're getting roasted,' " and soldiers chanted, "Let the Jews fry, there'll be Jewish bacon."[72] In this macabre vision, Jews would vanish, transformed by fire into a prized but eminently Gentile food.

Such deathly theater was prologue to a last act of imagined aggression against the Jews, encompassing their systematic murder. As many of the cited incidents show, other pogrom scripts, including mere plunder, entailed murder or its threat, as when marauding soldiers chased a woman from her apartment with the words "Lay down your head, Jew."[73] Even after the November pogrom, military patrols ostensibly searching for weapons caches robbed individual Lwów Jews. One victim reported that the officers and soldiers stripping him of his possessions "shouted, 'There are too many of you Jews here. Go to Palestine or we'll wipe you all out.' "[74] A woman who saw Polish troops escorting Jewish militiamen taken prisoner, including one who was wounded, said that a monk observing the scene cried out, "It's a shame to waste time with them. It'd be better to mow them down right away."[75]

Threats of murder easily led to real killings. Tenenbaum heard of an incident in which "an officer, exclaiming, 'What's the sense in keeping the Jewish brood alive?' proceeded to bash in the infant's skull."[76] An eyewitness told of a young officer who, in the course of plundering an apartment, "seized a four-week-old infant by the legs from its cradle and twirled it around a few times with the intention of hurling it to the ground. He asked the mother, 'What are you doing with so many Jewish bastards?' " She rescued the child "only with greatest effort."[77]

---

71. Bendow, 152 (protocol 475).
72. Bendow, 39–40.
73. CZA, Z3/181: 3.XII.1918, deposition 8.
74. Bendow, 120.
75. Bendow, 24 (protocol 674).
76. Bendow, 35.
77. Bendow, 46 (protocol 28).

Such words, typical of anti-Jewish scripts, concealed Polish aggression behind the rhetoric of Jewish guilt, threatening murder perhaps only to avoid facing the consequences of pogrom crimes (though the words directed against the infants suggest ideological inspiration). Other such threats issued from hearts choked with wartime hatred. The father whose sons a street crowd pummeled reported that soldiers then forcibly joined his boys to a column of Ukrainian, German, and Jewish captives. As a military escort marched them through the streets, "the Polish public dealt them continual blows. Elegant ladies, who themselves didn't strike out, exclaimed 'Away with the Jews! Hang them! Slaughter them! Shoot them down!'" When the father later sought his sons' release from military custody, an officer threatened to shoot him, while "the other officers called out, 'For the Prussians a bullet, for the Jews a noose.'"[78]

The thought of mass murder hung in the air even before the pogrom erupted. A Jewish witness reported that a Polish acquaintance, a cavalry captain, told him that it was a good thing he lived outside the Jewish quarter, "because a slaughter of the Jews is approaching."[79] Another told of leaving the Jewish quarter with his family on November 5 to buy food in a Polish government–controlled shop, where, "standing in line," seemingly unrecognized, "we heard things that gave us a chill: 'the Jews, that pack of Jews, they're to blame for everything, these lepers [another ancient memory], just wait until we conquer the city, not one of them will escape alive,' and many other similar statements."[80] On the same day another Jewish family found itself caught in its apartment between Polish and Ukrainian fire. The Poles captured the apartment building, and their captain "laughed grimly" at the father, saying, "'So, now we'll blow this house in the air with our cannons. Why did you give the Ukrainians signals, and shoot from your windows at us?' And the soldiers cried out, 'We don't want, we don't need any Jews. Let them all disappear. What good are these traitors? We'll show them, we'll murder them all.'"[81]

During the pogrom, legionnaires burst into a Jewish merchant's dwelling, led by city gasworks employee Banderowski and followed by "a crowd of men and women." They shouted, "We'll shoot you all, we'll burn the house down. . . . You stood with the Ukrainians, you shot at us." Other soldiers delivered Banderowski to an official for interrogation, at which the plundered merchant was present. He heard Banderowski say, first, that the Polish authorities had permitted forty-eight hours of robbery and, second, that the Jews had suffered too little for opposing the Polish army and pouring boiling water on soldiers. For this "they will now all be slaughtered." Later, though the merchant under-

78. Bendow, 150 (protocol 268).
79. Bendow, 57 (protocol 705).
80. Bendow, 139 (protocol 69).
81. Bendow, 139 (protocol 69).

stood that Banderowski had been condemned to be shot, he met him on the street. Banderowski "sought to excuse his robbery," saying he was in military service at the time, and that if the merchant needed anything, "he would gladly be of service."[82] Banderowski had, seemingly, sobered up from whatever intoxication it was that had gripped him during the pogrom.

Teresa Stadler reported to the Investigative Commission that one of the three Polish fighters who robbed her on November 22 was twenty-three-year-old trader Stanisław Boni, one of a poor Polish tailor's six sons. When the commission confronted Boni with Stadler, "the injured party bore witness, looking into Boni's eyes, that she recognized him as the robbery's third perpetrator, and repeated [her original charge] that even though she appealed to him, as someone she knew by sight, for rescue, he had replied, 'It's an order [to rob you] and after that they're going to shoot you all!' "[83]

All such assertions that the Jews would suffer or die because of their culpable actions during Polish-Ukrainian hostilities were, ultimately, political in inspiration and, given their basis in generalizations about the Jews as an undifferentiated community, implicitly antisemitic. Yet there were also instances of violence whose derivation from ideological antisemitism is more or less explicit. A Jewish woman witnessed three soldiers storming a neighbor's apartment on November 22; the band included, as occurred in other cases, the apartment house manager's son (for such people knew the tenants well). "Replying to the plundered victims' plea for mercy, one of the robbers declared in a Kraków accent: We don't need any Jews. Why are they living in this world? We'll slaughter you all. We didn't come here from Kraków for nothing."[84]

When on Monday, November 24, the Lwów Polish army command issued a proclamation imposing martial law, it charged that during the fighting the Jewish militia had broken its neutrality. The Jews "treacherously" resisted—with guns, stones, and boiling water—the Poles' "victorious advance." Nevertheless, "the Polish army command is suppressing the Polish population's and army's spontaneous [anti-Jewish] action," for everyone, including the Jews, stands under "the protection of the law." "Responsibility rests on the Jewish population in general, however, to exert a moderating influence on that fraction among their coreligionists that has not yet ceased to act as if it were determined to bring an *incalculable catastrophe* upon the whole Jewish population. [The command counts on the Jews, in their own interest,] to restrain their coreligionists from outbursts of hatred against the Polish government and, by correct and loyal behavior, to enable the authorities *and the rest of the Polish population* to introduce and uphold order based on right and law" (emphasis added).[85] Like many contemporary Polish political pronouncements

---

82. Bendow, 149 (protocol 147).
83. CAHJP, HM2/8299.11: frames 59–61, 22.XI.18.
84. CZA, Z3/181: 3.XII.1918, deposition 7.
85. CZA, L6/114: German text, released by the Polish Press Bureau in Bern.

about the Lwów tragedy, issued by both officials and political parties, this one cold-bloodedly and terrifyingly threatened the Jews with "incalculable catastrophe" even as it denounced the pogrom violence brought on by the Polish common people's righteous and uncontrollable fury at the Jews' alleged disloyalty and hate. The psychological projection such documents reveal was, it seems, invisible to their authors.

Further study of Polish reactions to the Lwów pogrom is necessary, but even such explicitly antisemitic newspapers as the Poznanian Postęp avoided taking any satisfaction in it, stressing instead the anti-Polish aims of Germans and Zionists in exaggerating the losses it occasioned.[86] Among the established political parties it was not opportune, in the shadow of the Paris peace conference, with Polish frontiers and other vital interests at stake, to ventilate antisemitic sentiments. But in Lwów an obscure populist Polish organization styling itself, cryptically, the "Red Guard" composed two threatening letters and posted them to the Jewish Rescue Committee in December 1918. After intercepting them, the military censorship, perhaps callously, delivered them to the addressees. They express wounded feelings about imagined Jewish power and well-being which, in many minds, it was pogrom violence's purpose to "turn upside down." One letter warned that "the Red Guard Committee demands you leave Lwów free of Jews [judenrein] by New Year's. And all your grand gentlemen can travel with you to Palestine. Leave! All your assets will be devoted to rebuilding Galicia, for without your millions, without your Kaiser with his Jewish mistresses, no such misfortune as now prevails would have come into the world." The second letter decreed that "you may take nothing with you. You have caused the present universal misfortune [Weltunglück]. By New Year's Lwów must be free of Jews. Your baggage may consist of only a small package. In all of East and West Galicia blood boils for revenge for the long years of the Christian population's exploitation. A pogrom against the Jews must be the result, come what may. Let all the burghers, the merchants, lawyers and doctors, go buy land in Palestine."[87]

Striking, apart from the desire to reduce Jewish property to "small packages," is these letters' invocation of the "misfortune" and "universal misfortune" of which the Polish nation as a whole had been a victim, in these unsophisticated Polish eyes, until the war's end and Lwów's reconquest. These statements conjure up the moral economy upon which many of the November pogromists acted: Polish suffering warranted pogroms and the Jews' banishment from city and land. It was a worldview that was political in a moral-absolutist sense rather than the expression of a strategy aiming for advantage within the Polish party and parliamentary system. Pogromists

---

86. CZA, Z3/180: notes on Postęp, 3.XII.18.
87. Bendow, 122–23.

acting on such feelings had few or no words for the state and its officialdom, conceiving themselves instead as executors of a righteous people's will.[88]

Whatever its origins may have been in prewar social conflict and nationalist politics, and in wartime suffering and radicalization, the Lwów pogrom took the form of brutal street drama and intimate scenes of symbolically charged violence. Both modes of torment claimed a warrant in popularly conceived retributive justice. Just as the Holocaust's murderous setting—in Nazi encampments disguised as sites of public health and industrial labor—holds keys to its understanding, so too the scripts enacted in Lwów proclaimed the meanings the pogromists aimed their actions to convey. Though understanding ethnic violence's historical context and sociopolitical setting is vital, invoking them will never wholly explain why its perpetrators attacked their victims precisely as they did. Historical acts and events are intersections of multiple causal tendencies or lines of development, no one necessarily reducible to the other, though all may be intertwined. Aggression toward cultural outsiders is but one choice available to those subjectively gripped in crisis or postcrisis exaltation. There is no way to comprehend their embrace of violence except to decipher the words accompanying it and to read the meaning of the execution of its physical forms.

Pogrom violence and its present-day equivalents flow from ordinary people's convictions about righteous and redemptive action when communally faced with menacing turbulence, particularly when cultural outsiders suddenly loom as perceived enemies. Such convictions are historical legacies perpetuated in practice, and often uncritically embraced with existential, identity-buttressing fervor. To witness them cruelly enacted, as they were in Lwów in November 1918, is to glimpse the trail of destruction that Walter Benjamin's dark angel of history horrifiedly contemplated. To imagine them dispelled presumes that humanity will abandon victimization of outsiders and learn to oppose suffering and injustice in peace, so as to enable the righteousness of law finally to banish the righteousness of violence.[89]

88. On traditions of populist subordination of pragmatic politics to sweeping moral-religious-ideological visions, see Thomas Simons, *Eastern Europe in the Postwar World*, 2d ed. (New York, 1993), esp. chaps 1–2; see also George Schöpflin, *Politics in Eastern Europe, 1945–1992* (Oxford, 1993).

89. Walter Benjamin, "Theses on the Philosophy of History" (1940) in Benjamin, *Illuminations*, ed. Hannah Arendt (New York, 1968), 257–58. On "redemptive" promises of antisemitism, see Saul Friedländer, *Nazi Germany and the Jews*, vol. 1 (New York, 1997). On the modern world's "moral resources," see Jonathan Glover, *Humanity: A Moral History of the Twentieth Century* (New Haven, 2001).

7

Anti-Jewish Legislation in Interwar Poland

SZYMON RUDNICKI

Legal restrictions on Jews in Poland during the years 1918–39 can be divided into two categories: the anti-Jewish laws initiated by the partitioning powers which remained in effect until 1931, and those introduced by the Polish authorities, particularly in the second half of the 1930s.

As far as Jews themselves were concerned, the key to understanding the essence of equal rights can be found in the first speech of Mojżesz Koerner in the Senate in 1923: "We demand nothing more, we strive for nothing more than simply this—that the same laws apply to all citizens without distinction of religion and nationality, so that no one may benefit from a law that doesn't exist for others."[1] Jewish parliamentarians understood the principle of equality before the law on three levels. First, they understood it to mean the removal of all restrictions placed on the Jewish community by the partitioning powers. In this regard, the greatest legal discrimination had existed in the Russian partition, although with wide variations between the *kresy* (eastern borderlands of the pre-partition Polish state) and the former Polish Kingdom under tsarist rule in central Poland. Second, they viewed legal equality as a guarantee contained in the constitutional law of independent Poland. And third, Jewish deputies emphasized the importance of compliance with already existing law (this last issue, however, extends beyond the scope of this chapter).

---

1. Sprawozdanie Stenograficzne Senatu (SSSen) I (February 15, 1923), 11:29. Koerner, a Warsaw engineer, was elected to the Senate in 1922 and reelected to a second term in 1928.

With few exceptions, the legal restrictions of the partitioning powers affecting Jews were individual rather than collective in nature, although in rare instances they did touch the entire community: for example, in Austrian Poland there existed a general ban on the public use of Yiddish and Hebrew. The number of prohibitions and injunctions for Jews in the Russian Empire is difficult to determine but is estimated to have reached into the several hundreds.[2] One among them, for example, made all Jews doubly responsible for the costs of medical treatment, a matter to which I will return.

In other instances the prohibitions were most frequently felt in the realm of consciousness, as discriminatory regulations, rather than as burdens affecting daily life. A significant number of these were contained in civil law: for example, a ban imposed on the composition of civil or commercial documents in Hebrew or Yiddish. At the same time, administrative legal regulations forbade Jews to take up occupations in the mining industry, or to serve in elective office in townships and villages. In addition, rabbinical students did not share the same legal exemption to military service as their counterparts in the Roman Catholic seminaries. In Russian Poland, Jewish inhabitants in the *kresy* confronted specific forms of discrimination that were not shared by Jews in the former Polish Kingdom, although the majority of restrictions affected both communities. Among the former was a regulation that banned guardianship over persons of any Christian denomination by non-Christians.

In independent Poland the fundamental documents that defined the legal condition of national minorities were the so-called Small Versailles Treaty and the 1921 constitution. The treaty regulated citizenship and guaranteed to the each national minority complete equality of rights in the use of its language for private, economic, and public purposes, including in the school system.[3] Above all, the preservation of religious and, to a lesser extent, national distinctiveness was meant to serve as a guarantee of equal rights. These components of the treaty were incorporated into several articles of the Constitution of March 1921. Article 96 specifically declared that "all citizens are equal before the law." The Constitution of 1935 retained in unaltered form the articles guaranteeing equal rights to national minorities.

During the discussion over legislation to change in civil law regulations that had been binding in the former Polish Kingdom, Jewish deputies demanded the abolition of all statutes and decrees that discriminated against Jews. Speaking in support of a motion to that effect, Apolinary Hartglas referred to Article 111 of the constitution, which guaranteed freedom of conscience and religious

2. An official document of 1888 refers to 650 decrees and regulations of this type in the Russian legal code; S. Dubnov, *Noveishaia istoriia yevreiskogo naroda*, vol. 3, *Epocha antisemitskoi reakcii i natsionalnogo dvizheniia* (Moscow, 1881, 1938; 2002 reprint), 123. In subsequent years several dozen more were added.

3. "Traktat między Głównymi Mocarstwami Sprzymierzonymi a Polską," in *Współczesna Europa polityczna: Zbiór umów międzynarodowych*, ed. W. Kulski and M. Potulicki (Warsaw, 1939), 146–50.

worship.[4] The Sejm did not accept this motion, which Hartglas considered the first violation of the recently voted constitution. In the course of discussion over draft legislation on the post, telegraph, and telephone services,[5] Jewish deputies criticized both the rejection of telegrams composed in Hebrew and Yiddish, even when written in the Latin alphabet, and the ban on telephone conversations in those languages. Emil Sommerstein, in particular, used the occasion to note the absence of a statute protecting the confidentiality of private correspondence.[6]

At the beginning of activity of the Legislative Sejm, without waiting for the enactment of a constitution and acting on the initiative of Icchak Gruenbaum, Hartglas proposed the acceptance of a law proclaiming that "all regulations of the civil and military authorities and all court sentences yet to be executed, issued on the basis of restrictive statutory regulations [of the partitioning powers], lose their force from the moment of [its] announcement." On May 23, 1919, in the name of the Free Union of Deputies of Jewish Nationality, its chairman, Ozjasz Thon, presented a motion to abolish the legal and administrative regulations that had restricted Jews under Russian rule.[7] Hartglas, the author of this project as well, retrospectively came to consider it not only needless but a legal and tactical error: since all restrictions would become extinct upon the basis of a law passed by parliament, a separate project could only complicate the situation. But once Jews had filed such a motion, in his opinion, they were compelled to fight seriously for its realization. Meanwhile, with the passage of the constitution, as Hartglas maintained, the existence of a separate motion to abolish restrictions against Jews meant that these restrictions would continue to be applied, however rarely, because certain Polish lawyers and deputies adopted the position that all legal limitations could be abrogated only by means of a separate law that actually listed them.[8] In subsequent years the Jewish deputies renewed their motion, preparing successive legal projects in its support.[9] (These efforts at nullifying particular regulations are discussed below.)

In its assessment of the Hartglas project, the legislative section of the Presidium of the Council of Ministers noted that some of the regulations mentioned in it no longer remained in force, that the project itself was redundant in light of the provisions of the Versailles Treaty, and that the remaining propositions of the Jewish delegates were not of real significance; for that very reason a proposal to eliminate all continually existing legal restrictions, one that

---

4. Sprawozdanie Stenograficzne Sejmu Ustawodawczego (SSSU), (July 1, 1921), 239:15–17.
5. Sejm I kadencji (March 12, 1924), druk 1060.
6. Sprawozdanie Stenograficzne Sejmu (SSS) I (April 4, 1924), 115:20–23.
7. Apolinary Hartglas noted the details of this motion in "Walka o równouprawnienie," Miesięcznik Żydowski 1 (1931): 152.
8. Apolinary Hartglas, Na pograniczu dwóch światów (Warsaw, 1966), 201.
9. I discuss the fate of these projects in Szymon Rudricki, "The Jewish Battle in the Sejm for Equal Rights," in The Jews in Poland, ed. S. Kapralski (Kraków, 1999), 2:147–62.

embraced all citizens of the state and institutions, including the Catholic Church, would have been more appropriate. To place before the Sejm a project devoted exclusively to restrictions on the Jewish population was considered by the legislative section as an affront to the Polish people who, it was argued, should not be held responsible for the consequences resulting from legal succession to the Russian partition.[10] The authors of this analysis of the Hartglas project were not bothered by the internal contradictions of their reasoning. Equally mind-boggling was the contention that the lifting of tsarist restrictions on Jews could somehow be an insult to the Polish population, which should have been offended instead by the continuing existence of tsarist regulations that violated the equality of citizens.

During the Sejm's discussion of a bill to normalize the legal-political status of lands incorporated into the Polish republic following the October 1920 armistice signed in Riga ending the Polish-Soviet war, Gruenbaum demanded the inclusion of a formulation earlier proposed by the constitutional committee: namely, the invalidation of all regulations issued to the advantage or disadvantage of any national or religious group. The Sejm, however, empowered the Council of Ministers to issue separate and appropriate legal decrees regarding this matter.[11] Within the Sejm, the prevailing view was that the commission's formula was too general and objectively offered the Polish administration too many opportunities to act arbitrarily. Many Polish delegates argued that it was first necessary to ascertain which concrete Russian legal norms and regulations were to be abrogated before actually passing legislation to do so. Determining those would require, in their view, time and familiarity with the particular legal provisions that discriminated against Jews in the former Russian Empire, a compilation of which was best entrusted to the Polish administrative apparatus subordinate to the Council of Ministers. The main problem, however, was that these provisions were scattered in hundreds of legal documents, and no one could ever be certain that all of them had been abolished. The Council of Ministers, moreover, was in no hurry to prepare such a list, although Jewish delegates had specified those regulations that were of particular concern and had presented their own lists to the Sejm in the form of bills or motions. (More than ten years later, ironically, the government did follow the original recommendations of the constitutional commission and the postulates of the Jewish parliamentary delegation for a wholesale abrogation; see below.)

In February 1921 the Council of Ministers proposed that some of these restrictions should be considered as abolished for all practical purposes. The council offered as a prime example the regulations regarding the costs of medical treatment for Jews, for which a tsarist decree of 1841 had placed the

10. J. Fałowski, "Posłowie żydowscy w Sejmie Ustawodawcyzm 1919–1922," Instytut Filozoficzno-Historyczny WSP w Częstochowie *Biuletyn* (July 25, 2000), 89.

11. SSSU (February 4, 1921), 206:6, 14–15.

financial burden on Jewish communal institutions. Jews had long complained about the injustice of this regulation as a form of double taxation, since members of the Jewish community already paid the same dues as other citizens, which were intended to include the costs of medical treatment. Already in a circular of August 15, 1918, issued by the wartime Regency Council sponsored by the Central Powers, it was explained that this decree should no longer be applied to Jews, because they paid general municipal taxes and made separate contributions to hospitals as well. A circular of the new Polish administration of January 14, 1919, however, recognized this regulation of the 1841 decree as still in force.[12]

Following negotiations of the government with representatives of the Jewish community, on March 23, 1921, a communiqué of the Presidium of the Council of Ministers was published in the unofficial section of the government bulletin, *Monitor Polski*. In it the government presented its interpretation of several regulations of administrative law that were no longer binding, among them the tsarist decree of 1841 about the double costs of medical treatment, noting that it had lost its force on the basis of a decree of February 4, 1919.[13] The Ministry of Internal Affairs, however, maintained that the costs of hospital care should be borne by Jewish communal institutions and instructed that these costs be incorporated into their budgets.[14] On June 9, 1921, the Council of Ministers adopted a resolution stating that the regulations of the 1841 decree remained in force and that its abrogation required the passing of a special law.[15] After three years of inconsistent and conflicting administrative decisions, the issue had returned to its original unresolved status.

Language questions fared similarly. On March 15, 1919, the Ministry of Internal Affairs issued a circular to the effect that the use of Yiddish was not restricted by any legal provisions and that the dissolution of meetings conducted in Yiddish or Hebrew, for example, violated the law.[16] Nevertheless, officials in many localities continued to dissolve such meetings, refused to grant permission for them, or issued their own proclamations banning the use of Yiddish in public communication, meanwhile ordering the publication of all announcements and posters exclusively in Polish, even when they related to Jewish political and cultural events.[17] In a letter to the Presidium of the Council of Ministers, the Minister of Internal Affairs Stanisław Wojciechowski

12. S. Hirszhorn, "Żydzi a koszta lecznicze," *Dziennik Nowy* 178 (September 18, 1919).

13. "Z Prezydium Rady Ministrów," *Monitor Polski* 67 (March 23, 1921).

14. Hartglas, "Walka o równouprawnienie," 154.

15. Stanisław Downarowicz to the Marshal of the Legislative Sejm, January 17, 1922, in *Materiały w sprawie żydowskiej w Polsce* (Warsaw, 1922), 6:240.

16. "Z Ministerstwa Spraw Wewnętrznych," *Monitor Polski* 61 (March 15, 1919); *Materiały*, 5:8.

17. Interpelacja Hirszhorna i innych do Ministerstwa Spraw Wewnętrznych w sprawie prześladowania jezyka żydowskiego w Grodnie oraz wprowadzenia tamże cenzury prewencyjnej, Archiwum Sejmowe, Interpelacje (ASI), June 14, 1921.

supported such behavior, maintaining that until the publication of a special statute, the law of the partitioning powers still applied; therefore, the use of Yiddish and Hebrew at assemblies, he argued, could not be permitted.[18] Future governments would also reject recognition of Yiddish as a separate language, considering it only as "jargon" or a local dialect.

In 1923 the matter became the subject of an analysis conducted by the General Prosecutor's Office, which maintained that in legally *private* matters (and therefore coming under the civil code) the use of Yiddish and Hebrew could not be restricted,[19] but that in *public* affairs this question continued to be regulated by the old legal provisions from the period of the partitions. The analysis agreed with the interpretation that both of these Jewish languages "do not possess the traits of a countrywide language and in general do not possess the character of a national language of the Jews, who do not use Hebrew in conversation, while Yiddish is simply a primitive form of German." It explained further that as a public institution in the Polish state, the Jewish communal assembly should conduct its proceedings in Polish.[20] Such an interpretation was supported by the earlier practice of state administrative organs, but Jews did not agree with this position and continually sought to use their own languages in Jewish institutions. Compulsion to speak Polish during sessions of the communal religious board or in telephone conversations was to them a vexation that could be justified only in a police state, not in a presumably democratic Polish state. The freedom to use native languages guaranteed in the Versailles Treaty therefore became yet another issue that caused unnecessary tensions between the Polish administrative authorities and the Jewish community. It outlived the first term of the Sejm only to return to that forum many times thereafter.

In January 1922 the government, in line with the constitution as well as a resolution of the Sejm, introduced draft legislation to remove all legal restrictions on the Jewish population, based almost verbatim on the contents of the earlier motion of the Jewish delegation. In the name of the People's National Union (Związek Ludowo–Narodowy, or ZLN), Father Kazimierz Lutosławski demanded in the *Sejm's* legal commission that restrictions on the Roman Catholic Church be eliminated simultaneously.[21] His motion was accepted by

---

18. Letter no. 6174/pr of Kazimierz Gałecki, general government delegate for Galicia, to the Minister of Internal Affairs, March 19, 1920, Archiwum Akt Nowych (AAN), Prezydium Rady Ministrów (PRM), Rkt. 64, 4:5–7; see also the letter of S. Wojciechowski of April 27, 1920, in the same file, 15–17.

19. Elsewhere, however, the General Prosecutor's Office indicated that the ban on composing civil and commercial documents (wills, contracts, etc.) in the Hebrew alphabet did remain in force; see confidential letter no. 13849/1901/23.I of the General Prosecutor to the Minister of Internal Affairs, June 27, 1923, in ibid., 49.

20. Confidential letter no. 23791/3001/22.I of General Prosecutor to the Press Section of the Ministry of Foreign Affairs, February 26, 1923, in ibid., 44–49.

21. SSSU (February 21, 1922), 287:78.

a majority of the lower house. The success of Lutosławski's demonstrative motion led, as intended, to a postponement of discussion on the government's project to the next term of the Sejm.

Only the government of Władysław Grabski, formed in late 1923 and early 1924, was prepared to negotiate with moderate Jewish politicians in exchange for a pledge from the Jewish caucus not to oppose the government in parliament.[22] These contacts led to a change in the balance of forces within the Jewish parliamentary bloc: namely, to a weakening of the position of the Zionist delegates from the former Russian partition in favor of their colleagues from Galicia, proponents of more elastic political tactics. The government signaled a change in its position when in February 1924 it submitted to the Sejm a draft law on Jewish medical expenses. Its second article stated: "The costs of hospital treatment for Jews . . . will be covered by the general funds of local communities in their place of permanent residence."[23] In practical terms, this meant an almost complete realization of the Jewish postulates that had been addressed to successive Polish governments. At the same time, however, the government noted that should such communities be unable to meet these expenses, Jewish communal bodies would be responsible for any unpaid costs.

In addition to the ongoing issue of abrogating the legislation of the partitions, there was also the matter of new legislation. Some of these laws had a direct negative impact on Jews, regardless of the original intentions of those who introduced them. Such was the case of a law that banned work on Sundays, which was defended not only from a Catholic but also from a socialist position. Jewish arguments that the reduction of the working week to five days for Jews, who for religious reasons did not work on Saturdays, would have injurious effects on both workers and tradesmen, not to mention the state budget, fell on deaf ears. Similar in nature was a law on officially recognized holidays. The presidential decree of November 15, 1924, foresaw state recognition of seventeen Catholic holidays, one state holiday, and two local holidays—twenty holidays all together in a calendar year. The parliamentary recorder, Jan Rudnicki from the People's National Union, noted that the decree did not embrace holidays of "foreign religions."[24] Ignacy Schipper declared immediately that the Jewish delegates did not intend to participate in a discussion of the number of Catholic holidays and moved that the government prepare within a month a complete solution of this matter as it affected the national minorities.[25] The Ukrainian delegate Rev. Mikołaj Iłków made a similar motion.

22. Protocol of the 69th session of the Political Committee of the Council of Ministers of February 7, 1924, AAN, Komitet Polityczny Rady Ministrów (KPRM), 2:39.

23. "Ustawa o pokrywaniu kosztów leczenia ubogich Żydów, będących stałymi mieszkańcami gmin na obszarze b. Królestwa Kongresowego," Sejm I kadencji (February 18, 1924), druk 1007.

24. SSS I (February 12, 1925), 177:22.

25. Ibid., 39–44.

Meanwhile, a controversy occurred that complicated both the interpretation of the constitution and the rights of Jews. Article 126 of the constitution foresaw that "all existing legal regulations and practices not in accord with the provisions of the Constitution will be presented to the legislature within a year of its enactment in order to pass compatible legislation." In the case of restrictions against Jews contained in the legal regulations of the partitioning powers, this provision was not implemented. Therefore, on February 16, 1924, the General Assembly of the Supreme Court announced that the constitution had removed all restrictive regulations from the time of its proclamation, so long as no gaps in the law were created in the process. This decision should have ended the question of legal disabilities. On October 30, 1924, however, the Supreme Administrative Tribunal took a different position, stating that the constitution only proclaimed but did not introduce equal rights. From that time on, the two courts referred to different interpretations in their adjudications, a contest in which the decisions of the Supreme Administrative Tribunal frequently held more pertinent sway.[26]

One example of such an interpretation was the tribunal's verdict maintaining a Russian legal ban on the purchase of peasant lands by Jews in Krasocin, Kielce province, indicating that the constitution had not specifically annulled this regulation.[27] Such restrictions affected the inhabitants of the former Polish Kingdom and the eastern territories; in other parts of the country they were preserved in fragmentary form, as administrative practice rather than legal norms.[28] In this situation the General Prosecutor's Office prepared an expert opinion for the government in which it maintained that all legal restrictions affecting Jews "had lost their force because they contradicted the provisions of Chapter V of the Constitution."[29] In order to remove any further doubt whether a regulation violated the constitution, the opinion advised the abolition of all legal restrictions by means of a separate act.

The issue of Jewish enrollment in institutions of higher education, which would increasingly absorb public attention, was first raised on January 16, 1923. In the name of the delegation from the People's National Union, Władysław Konopczyński introduced a motion to change the law on academic institutions, motivated by the necessity to "contain the Jewish flood in our higher schools."[30] Supporters of the motion proposed to give academic depart-

26. Hartglas, "Walka o równouprawnienie," 159.

27. Communique of the Club of Delegates and Senators of the Jewish National Council, Central Archive of Zionism in Jerusalem (CAZ), A 127/208 Gruenbaum; *Historia państwa i prawa Polski, 1918–1939*, ed. F. Ryszka (Warsaw, 1962), 1:128; Jerzy Ogonowski, *Uprawnienia językowe mniejszości narodowych w Rzeczypospolitej Polskiej, 1918–1939* (Warsaw, 2000), 135–36.

28. *Najnowsze dzieje Żydów w Polsce*, ed. J. Tomaszewski (Warsaw, 1993), 182.

29. The General Prosecutor to the Presidium of the Council of Ministers, page four of draft letter of May 12, 1924, Archiwum Polskiej Akademii Nauk (APAN), III/180, 97:17.

30. Władysław Konopczyński, *Sejm 1922–1927 bez osłonek* (Kraków, 1928), 56.

ment councils the right to restrict the number of accepted students in agreement with the Ministry of Religion and Public Education.[31] A few months earlier the All-Polish Youth organization had attempted to publicize the slogan *numerus clausus*, or quota, which would limit Jewish student enrollment to the Jewish proportion (slightly less than 10 per cent) of the total population.[32] Procedural formalities led to the postponement of a discussion of this proposed law in plenary sessions of the Sejm. There was no urgency to take up the matter of quotas, moreover, since Minister of Religion and Public Education Stanisław Głąbiński had already issued an appropriate circular, one that did not directly violate the law on academic institutions but created well-justified fears that the principle of *numerus clausus* was being introduced by other means.

The attempts of Jewish delegates to abolish provisions of the law that restricted Jews, as well as their protests against the illegal actions of the authorities at different administrative levels, were without any apparent result. Even when the authorities declared that they would take steps in this area, their promises remained largely unfulfilled. The government would move only partially in the desired direction, gradually removing successive restrictions in the course of passing particular laws or implementing separate legal acts.[33] This process lasted years, despite constitutional law, as the behavior of the authorities vacillated according to the current needs of governing circles. For this reason the Jewish minority found itself in an isolated situation, since many problems of the Slavic minorities had been regulated by suitable statutes or by international agreements that were more effective than the provisions of the Versailles Treaty.

Several issues affecting the Jews were resolved following the May 1926 coup d'etat carried out by Józef Piłsudski and the establishment of a regime of political purification known as the "Sanacja." On February 2, 1927, Minister of Internal Affairs Felicjan Sławoj-Składkowski restored the right to use Yiddish without restrictions in public assemblies.[34] He similarly concluded the matter

31. The only country that passed a law restricting the number of students of different "races and nationalities" according to their proportion in the general population was Hungary in 1920. This existed, however, only on paper and the number of Jewish students in Hungary continually exceeded their percentage among the total population; see Ezra Mendelsohn, *Żydzi Europy środkowo-wschodniej w okresie międzywojennym* (Warsaw, 1992), 150–51.

32. Szymon Rudnicki, "From 'Numerus Clausus' to 'Numerus Nullus,'" *Polin* 2 (1987): 246–68. According to Vice Minister of Education Miklaszewski, in the 1923–24 academic year, Jews made up 25.04 per cent of the students at Kraków University, 33.78 per cent at Lwów University, 32.91 per cent at Warsaw University, 19.57 per cent at Wilno University, and 1 per cent at Poznań University. In the Lwów and Warsaw Polytechnical Institutes, Jews constituted 15.91 and 14.79% of the student bodies, respectively, along with 1.8 per cent in the Mining Academy, 13.6 per cent in the Veterinary Institute, 8.39 per cent in the Academy of Fine Arts, 62.88 per cent in the Dental Institute, and .01 per cent (one student) in the Higher Agricultural School.

33. For a list of abolished restrictions, see A. Frenkiel, *Sytuacja Żydów w chwili obecnej* (Warsaw, 1923), 27–32.

34. *Monitor Polski* 47 (1927): 98.

of recognizing citizenship, which had dragged out since the first days of independence. In this regard a series of instructions of the Ministry of Internal Affairs had been issued, beginning in 1924, to overcome the resistance of local administrators who had applied their own narrow interpretations of citizenship to earlier directives.[35] Głąbinski's circular on Jewish student enrollment was also rescinded at this time.

In his first speech in the new Sejm, Gruenbaum stated: "Our legal situation in the Polish state has changed little. Those changes that have occurred affect secondary questions that are not of decisive importance to the condition of the Jewish community in Poland. Legal restrictions burden us as in the past. As in the past we receive documents informing us that tsarist and other restrictions continue to exist, that there are no equal civil rights in Poland."[36] As proof he cited a document of January 26, 1928, issued by a land commissar who, on the basis of 1891 regulations, had refused permission to Jankiel Szechter to purchase land from a peasant. Nor was this the only case in which the administration acted according to tsarist regulations. Worse still was the Supreme Court ruling of November 14, 1928, that the provisions of an Austrian law of 1814, which invalidated documents written in the Hebrew alphabet, were still binding.[37] On November 6, 1928, the Ministry of Religion and Public Education forbade the conversion of a Catholic to Judaism on the basis of a tsarist decree of April 17, 1905.[38] On June 11, 1929, the Supreme Administrative Tribunal issued a ruling that nullified the enfranchisement of a long-term lease of approximately 7.6 hectares of land in Stołpie county, referring in its decision to the provisions of a Russian law of 1884 that prohibited Jews from leasing land. These individual cases were insignificant in and of themselves, particularly the matter of converting the Catholic, since Judaism did not seek to proselytize; taken together, however, they meant that Jews were confronted with provisions in the law that did not apply to other citizens.

The need for final legal abrogation of restrictions on Jews dating from the partition era was not a matter of particular controversy within post–May 1926 governments. In January 1930, Prime Minister Kazimierz Bartel recommended to the minister of justice that he expedite the issue in the Sejm.[39] The Sejm began to discuss the projected law on February 8, but as a result of the legislature's dissolution, the bill did not make it to a third and final reading. The legislative commission of the Sejm returned to the government's bill at its

35. Jerzy Tomaszewski, "Mniejszości narodowe w prawie polskim, 1918–1939," *Więź* 2 (1972): 126.

36. SSS II (March 29, 1928), 3:12.

37. Hartglas, "Walka o równouprawnienie," 161.

38. Speech of Gruenbaum in report of the Budget Commission of December 18, 1928, CAZ 127, 118:1–2. The minister was questioned specifically on this matter in an interpellation.

39. "Rząd znosi ograniczenia żydowskie pozostałe z czasów zaborczych: List premiera Bartla do ministra sprawiedliwości," *Chwila* 3898 (January 30, 1930).

session of January 26, 1931. The Senate reviewed it at its sessions of February 3 and 27, and on March 13 the Sejm accepted the Senate's revisions without discussion. Finally, on April 10, 1931, the law became binding. Delayed by more than a decade, the legislation removed all restrictions pertaining to Jews from the laws of the partition era.[40] Formal equal rights had finally been accomplished in law. As Gruenbaum noted, however, equal rights still had to be realized in practice.[41] Jews still faced economic discrimination, restricted access to employment and higher education, and obligatory observance of Sunday as a day of rest, among other matters.

Ironically, the 1931 law was enacted at a time when Jews were being forced to wage a new struggle against the first projects launched by the National Party (the successor of the National Democratic Party) that aimed at restricting their rights. In March a Sejm commission considered a law on "Jewish corpses," or bodies supplied to anatomical laboratories at university medical schools. Soon the educational commission was compelled to consider a motion filed by the nationalist parliamentary group that called for the introduction of the *numerus clausus* for students in academic institutions.

Meanwhile, the nationalist press repeatedly came out in favor of depriving Jews of equal political rights. In 1934 one the leading figures of the Nationalist camp, Stefan Kozicki (the onetime chairman of the People's National Union and for many years the editor of *Gazeta Warszawska*), argued in the Senate for the necessity of restricting Jewish political rights and for the removal from Poland of as many Jews as possible. *Myśl Narodowa* (the monthly of the ZLN), for its part, stressed with approval the prominence of Kozicki's speech, which "for the first time in the Senate of the Republic openly and expressly put forward a program of rejecting equal rights for Jews and a plan for their expulsion from our state."[42] These were still declarations, however, and not concrete legislative proposals.

The global economic crisis, from which Poland only began to recover in the mid-1930s, aggravated the "Jewish question." Hundreds of thousands of unemployed Poles, countless others working for a pittance in the shops and

40. The basic provision of this law declared that "restrictions of rights contained in legal provisions issued prior to the recovery of Polish statehood, as well as civic privileges based on origin, nationality, language, race or religion, contrary to the legal state resulting from independent Polish statehood or the provisions of the constitution regarding the equality of citizens before the law, are no longer binding, even if these particular regulations have not been specifically abolished by legal decree": *Dziennik Ustaw Rzeczypospolitej Polskiej* (DURP) *1931*, 31:214.

41. Icchak Gruenbaum, "Równouprawnienie formalne a faktyczne," *Nowe Słowo* 1 (May 17, 1931).

42. "Głosy," *Myśl Narodowa* 11 (March 11, 1934). Kozicki, referring to the experience of Nazi Germany, maintained that "every citizen and every government in Poland . . . must strive to restrict the political rights of Jews and to remove the largest possible number of Jews from Polish lands": SSSen III (March 2, 1934), 63:21.

stores of their parents in the city, as well as millions of peasants and farm-workers frequently living in unfathomable rural poverty, sought out those responsible for the condition in which they found themselves. The slogan that Jews occupied all places of work was very easy to grasp in this situation. The nationalists' propaganda of struggle with the Jews thus offered a panacea for all economic and social illnesses. The nationalist camp also used antisemitism as a weapon in its struggle with the Sanacja regime for political power by accusing the government of caving in to Jewish interests. After Piłsudski's death the Sanacja itself also came to see as a solution to many problems the reduction by emigration of the number of Jews in Poland. Thus, for Jews, priority had to be placed on security of persons and property. Instead of fighting to ensure equal rights, Jewish parliamentarians were now compelled to protest efforts to introduce new legal restrictions, as well as anti-Jewish propaganda, the currency no longer only of the nationalist camp but also of representatives of the ruling Sanacja regime.

In his inaugural speech in the Sejm on July 4, 1936, new Prime Minister Sławoj-Składkowski, though condemning assaults on Jews, opined, "Economic struggle yes [owszem], but no [physical] injury." This owszem became very popular and was interpreted as government approval for an economic boycott. Within the Sanacja, discussions began on the "Jewish question" to the effect that its resolution could no longer be left to "irresponsible fire-brands" but had to be solved by "authoritative elements in the state and only and exclusively within the boundaries and on the basis of the constitution."[43] Jan Walewski, who made that statement in a speech, did not precisely define what he meant by the "Jewish question" or indicate how it might be resolved other than by recognizing the equal rights of Jews, which was the only way that accorded with the binding law of the constitution. Nonetheless, two of his colleagues, Janusz Radziwiłł and Wojciech Rostworowski, appeared at the same time before the Senate budget commission with a project for the emigration of one million Jews.[44]

In the course of a Sejm debate about ritual (kosher) butchering, Mojżesz Schorr presented his view of the difference between the Endecja and the Sanacja in the methods to resolve the Jewish question: "Some want to deal with us quickly and crudely—I would call this the machine method of slaughter. Others opt for a gradual approach, slowly and in stages, above all in a so-called civilized manner—therefore, we can call it humanitarian slaughter." He continued, "I realize that I don't attach much importance to these subtle differences, these delicate shades separating savage from civilized extermination. The latter seems to me to be even more dangerous, because it is done coldly, in a planned, organized, even refined way, and therefore it is even more alarm-

43. SSS IV (February 24, 1936), 16:11.
44. SSSen IV (March 9, 1936), 8:72.

ing and contemptible in that it resorts to the concept of culture for these purposes. Consequently there is no difference between the system of savage extermination and slow death by starvation, at least from the perspective of the
future victim."[45]

A group of Sanacja deputies connected at this time with the periodical *Jutro
Pracy* began to proclaim the need to find a common language with radical
nationalism.[46] One of them, Juliusz Dudziński, devoted an entire speech to this
development and concluded that the only difference between the Sanacja and
the radical nationalists was in the former's substitution of the word "state"
for "nation."[47] Meanwhile, Bronisław Wojciechowski maintained that the
question of "squeezing out" the Jews had become the most important national
and economic issue for Polish youth, although he warned that a resort to violence could not be tolerated by the government: "We may condemn and repress
excesses, but nothing will change our feelings toward the young generation,
which is and always will be close to our heart."[48]

On February 7, 1937, the Camp of National Unity that had emerged from
the Sanacja following Piłsudski's death came out with a declaration of its
program in which for the first time Jews were treated separately from other
national minorities. This declaration was further developed in a brochure of
the camp's Office of Research and Planning, which referred to Jews as an
"element alien" to the Polish nation, by reason of which they "cannot participate in its 'present' or in the making of its 'future.'" Its basic demand,
therefore, was "the significant reduction of the number of Jews in Poland."[49]
Thus emerged the idea in governing circles that the Jews did not have the right
to live in Poland and, hence, had to leave it.

During the debate of the Sejm's budget commission on January 24, 1938,
Składkowski, now acting as Minister of Internal Affairs, declared that "any
physical outbursts that lead to anarchy in Poland, whether in retaliation or
for lack of patience, are extremely harmful and demeaning to the Polish
nation." Yet he also claimed that the struggle against the Jews was not based
on racism but was "about overpopulation, that is, a struggle against the short-
age of bread, a struggle of economic necessity." He accused the Jews of not
wanting to look truth in the eye; the government had to support the transition of peasants migrating to the cities "because these are the higher economic

---

45. SSSen IV (March 5, 1937), 22:60.
46. J. Bardach, "Grupa 'Jutro Pracy' a idea konsolidacji narodowej w latach 1935–1939,"
Acta Universitatis Vratislaviensis, Historia 36 (1981): 42.
47. SSS IV (December 2, 1936), 30:34.
48. SSS IV (February 15, 1938) 69:7.
49. *Wytyczne polityki narodowościowej*, pt. 1, *Sprawa żydowska* (Warsaw, 1933), 21, 33,
42. The policies of the governing camp found their most radical form in the memorial "The Jewish
Question in 1938," most likely prepared in the Consular Department of the Ministry of Foreign
Affairs; see Jerzy Tomaszewski, "Memoriał z 1938 r. w sprawie polityki państwa polskiego wobec
Żydów," *Teki Archiwalne (Seria nowa)*, 1 (1995): 119–30.

values of the Polish nation. Therefore the Jews have to understand that economic struggle against them is not a violation of their rights, nor is it an attack on them as citizens of the state."[50]

On May 19–21 the congress of the Supreme Council of the Camp of National Unity convened in Warsaw to consider among other matters its position on the "Jewish question." At the congress there were many references to Składkowski's speech. A special resolution declared that "Jews in the present situation are a factor weakening the development of forces in the nation and the state and create an obstacle to the evolution of society currently taking place in Poland." It called for the reduction of the number of Jews employed in certain professions "through the introduction of general legal regulations, creating the possibility of selection from the point of view of state interests." It also called for the freeing of Polish culture from Jewish influences.[51] In commenting on these resolutions, Bogusław Miedziński, one of the closest collaborators of Edward Śmigły-Rydz (the inspector general of the armed forces, considered by many as Piłsudski's successor), wrote that "There is no way out other than planned, organized emigration." In the Sejm the deputy chief of the Camp of National Unity, Zygmunt Wenda, justified the necessity of emigration in terms of the "culturally alien nature of the Jews and as an element burdening the economy."[52] Indeed, the government would undertake a number of steps to gain international support for emigration, to find a suitable terrain for emigrating Jews, and to facilitate Jewish emigration to Palestine.

Jewish politicians could only protest against these kinds of stated intentions. On February 23, 1938, Sommerstein read the official declaration of the Jewish parliamentary delegation, assessing the government's policy toward the Jews: "It can be reduced to actual civil and political inequality, in clear violation of the provisions of the constitution, to the slander of the Jewish nation and religion with impunity, to the open legal discrimination as seen in the rectors' instructions in the matter of the so-called bench ghetto [see below], to the lack of security of life, health, and property of the Jewish citizen; we see the official proclamation of slogans of economic extermination in the form of economic struggle against the Jews supported and realized with the help of public funds, the toleration of boycotts and pickets, the presentation of emigration as the only way to solve the Jewish question in Poland, the introduction of the *numerus nullus* [i.e., the principle of total elimination] for Jews in

---

50. "Mowa premiera gen. Sławoja-Składkowskiego," *Gazeta Polska* 24 (January 25, 1938); "Sprawy mniejszościowe w expose Pana Premiera RP," *Sprawy Narodowościowe* 1–2 (1938): 97–99.

51. *Uchwały Rady Naczelnej OZN* ([Warsaw, 1938]), 18; *Polska Gospodarcza* 22 (1938): 846; *Uchwały Rady Naczelnej OZN: Sesja pierwsza 19, 20, 21 maja 1938 roku* (Warsaw, 1938), 18–22; "Rezolucja Rady Naczelnej Obozu Zjednoczenia Narodowego w sprawach żydowskich," *Sprawy Narodowościowe* 1 (1938): 278–79.

52. Bogusław Miedziński, *Uwagi o sprawie żydowskiej* (Warsaw, 1938), 16; for Wenda's remarks, see SSS V (February 16, 1939), 11:9.

state offices and enterprises and self-governing institutions."[53] On the other hand, Bernard Singer, parliamentary commentator for *Nasz Przegląd*, quipped bitterly in one of his columns that antisemitism had become a state enterprise and, like every other state venture, was running a deficit.[54] If antisemitism indeed was a deficit undertaking, it was above all the Jews who incurred the losses, although Polish society suffered as well—not only economically but also in its social psychology and the upbringing of future generations.

Beginning in 1936, several bills were put before the Sejm that were designed to root out Jews from different fields of economic activity. The first and best known of these projects, which pertained to the issue of ritual slaughter, was filed by Janina Prystorowa.[55] Under the pretext of humane treatment of animals, this bill would have made ritual slaughter—and, therefore, the consumption of meat by Jews—impossible. Jewish representatives thought it no accident that the bill was introduced at a time of heightened antisemitism, which in turn incited further support for the project. Besides, it was not a new idea. National Democratic deputies had made a similar motion in the Sejm on May 26, 1923, but had failed to justify it with humanitarian arguments.

Representatives of the government tried to soften the bill, and the Sejm commission for administrative self-government tried to amend it with an article that to a limited extent would permit ritual slaughter.[56] Dudziński, the commission's recorder, noted that Rev. Bronisław Zongołłowicz, deputy minister of religion and public education, had indicated that an outright ban on this type of slaughter was contrary to Articles 110, 111, 113, and 115 of the constitution. On the other hand, representatives of the Ministry of Agriculture and the Ministry of Industry and Commerce, whose names Dudziński did not provide, declared that ritual slaughter had made the regulation of the meat market impossible.[57] This was hardly true, especially since Minister of Agriculture Juliusz Poniatowski himself defended the government's proposed alterations to the bill in the Sejm. Minister of Industry and Commerce Roman Górecki also supported the changes, pointing to the irony that "neither cartels, nor the lowering of prices or etatism were capable of evoking such an atmosphere and such unbelievable interest as this problem [of ritual slaughter]."[58] The parliamentary debate over this issue unambiguously indicated that humanitarian goals were a mere slogan; in reality, as deputy Józef Morawski

---

53. SSS IV (February 23, 1938), 75:153.

54. Bernard Singer, "Duch czasu," *Nasz Przegląd* 149 (May 28, 1938).

55. "Projekt ustawy złożony przez posła Janinę Prystorową o uboju zwierzat gospodarskich w rzeźniach," February 7, 1936, Sejm IV kadencji, druk 59. For more on the debate in the Sejm and outside it, see Szymon Rudnicki, "Ritual Slaughter as a Political Issue," *Polin* 7 (1992): 147–60.

56. "Sprawozdanie Komisji Administracyjno-Samorządowej o projekcie ustawy . . . ," March 18, 1936, Sejm VI kadencji, druk 143.

57. SSS IV (March 17, 1936), 21:70–71.

58. SSS IV (March 20, 1936), 22:60.

admitted, "the bill was designed to attack a cartel, the [Jewish] monopolization of the meat trade."[59]

Jewish deputies pointed out that the bill was clearly directed against the Jews, since it did not address in similar fashion the matter of regulating the slaughter of hogs. Moreover, they estimated that forty thousand individuals would be thrown out of work if the bill came into law. Yet all attempts to convince fellow deputies that Jewish ritual slaughter was no less humanitarian than other forms, that it had no influence on beef prices, that it was purely a religious requirement and therefore protected under the constitution, were unsuccessful.

Dudziński filed a motion to amend this statute, which practically eliminated ritual slaughter, basing his proposal on the inability to enforce such a ban.[60] The parliamentary commission on administrative self-government accepted the most important points of Dudziński's motion.[61] The Sejm, however, rejected all amendments to the original bill and voted down the commission's version. Thus, the ban on ritual slaughter was slated to come into effect on January 1, 1939.

In July 1938 an amendment to the law regulating sales of farm animals and poultry and the meat wholesale trade was debated in the Sejm and the Senate. Lejb Mincberg criticized it in the Sejm, arguing that the amendment harmed the interests of both peasants and merchants because it made direct purchases from farmers impossible and created new middlemen in the form of licensed brokers, something that wasn't required even of the currency trade. In the Senate, Jakub Trockenheim cited the statement of one of the senators who argued that the bill's introduction had been "due to existing circumstances"— in other words, because of Jewish participation in the meat trade.[62] In this case as well, all Jewish attempts to amend the bill were defeated.

Of similar character were the Sejm's deliberations in March 1937 of a bill introduced by Rev. Stefan Downar the previous January concerning the manufacture and trade of devotional and religious objects.[63] The first article of the bill declared that "only persons physically and legally belonging to that faith for which the articles are intended" could be engaged in such activities. To this, the commission on industry and commerce added a second point: namely, that "religious affiliation is to be determined by the person's status as recorded in the civil registry."[64] In justifying the bill, Downar argued that the produc-

---

59. At the same session, Miedziński declared, "I openly acknowledge that matters of a humanitarian nature are not decisive for me." Józef Głowacki added that ritual slaughter was one form of economic slavery in which Polish society found itself: SSS IV (March 20, 1936), 22:24, 34, 37.

60. "Ustawa o zmianie ustawy o uboju zwierząt gospodarskich w rzeźniach," February 1, 1938, Sejm IV kadencji, druk 675.

61. "Sprawozdanie komisji administracyjno-samorządowej . . . ," March 22, 1938, Sejm IV kadencji, druk 792.

62. SSS IV (July 6, 1938), 85:75–77; SSSen III (July 14, 1938), 52:36–38.

63. Sejm IV kadencji, druk 307.

64. "Sprawozdanie komisji przemysłowo-handlowej o projekcie ustawy . . . ," March 17, 1937, Sejm IV kadencji, druk 456.

tion by Jews of Christian devotional objects offended Christian sensitivities, but he did not conceal the legislation's other objective: "It is high time to strive for complete economic freedom from alien elements, without which there cannot be economic independence in the total sense."[65] Thereafter, no one asked to speak on the issue, and the bill passed without any further discussion.

Another bill, this one about the structure of the Polish bar, had more than an economic character. It not only imposed obligatory court training for applicants to the bar but also empowered the minister of justice to limit the number of practicing attorneys to a list determined by the ministry.[66] This restriction was meant to deny future entrance to the Polish bar to members of the country's national minorities and above all to Jews, thus depriving them of yet another place of employment in the legal profession, since they had little chance of finding work in the judiciary or prosecutor's office. The bill was protested not only by Jewish delegates but also by their Ukrainian counterparts, both of them familiar with the attitude of Minister of Justice Witold Grabowski in this regard. Their fears were well founded. With the passage of this legislation, Grabowski issued an order on June 4, 1938, that closed the list of lawyers and applicants to the bar in all judicial districts until the end of 1945; in the meantime, he would determine the annual contingent of new applicants and lawyers. On the first such list, of sixty-three individuals there was not a single Jew.[67]

The new law thus made it practically impossible for young Jewish lawyers to acquire the necessary training in the court system for entrance to the bar. If that were not enough, in the applications of law school graduates for such training, the young lawyers were divided into separate categories, Christians and Jews, and Polish attorneys were urged to reject Jewish candidates. Nonetheless, despite pressures exerted by a significant part of their professional milieu, personal relations among Polish and Jewish members of the legal profession frequently remained unaffected, and Jewish attorneys continued to appear in court. But the atmosphere had definitely changed. For example, nationalist defendants were occasionally advised by their attorneys to refuse to answer questions posed by Jewish lawyers.

Legislation to strip citizenship from those who had resided for some time outside the Polish state had an expressly anti-Jewish flavor.[68] The bill for doing so was passed expeditiously. The first reading of the bill took place on March 18, 1938 and the second and third (and final) readings occurred a week later. On March 24, Tatomir Drymmer, director of the consular department of the

65. SSS IV (March 20, 1937), 51:52.
66. *DURP 1938*, 33:289.
67. *DURP 1938*, 40:334; K. Gutowski, *Wystąpienia antyżydowskie w Polsce w latach 1938–1939* (diss., Institute of History, Warsaw University, 1994), 158.
68. *DURP 1938*, 22:191.

Ministry of Foreign Affairs, noted that the legislation was directed above all against Jews and also Polish members of the international brigades from Spain currently residing in France.[69] On this basis, the minister of internal affairs issued an instruction that required those living abroad to present their Polish passports to consular officials for the purposes of onetime control, effective October 29.[70] This regulation, in turn, enabled the Nazis to deport to Poland any Polish Jews residing in Germany under the pretext that they would otherwise lose their citizenship. As is evident from the correspondence of German officials, the Nazis were quite concerned about the problem posed by Jews who had been deprived of their citizenship and were thereby rendered stateless. It is not apparent how they intended to deal with foreign Jews in general, but in this instance the Polish government made that much easier their decision to expel all Polish Jews from the Reich.[71]

The measures taken by the government and the Sejm during these years coincided with an effective boycott campaign led by the nationalist camp. The actions undertaken by several municipal councils to ban markets within city limits or to proclaim Saturdays as market days had a clearly anti-Jewish character. In addition, the minister of industry and commerce issued an order on April 19, 1937, requiring that business signs include, besides the name of the enterprise, the full name of the owner of the store or shop—an action directly assisting the boycott by helping to identify its Jewish targets. In the second half of the 1930s, Poland began to recover from the depression, but for the Jewish community hope for an improvement in the situation became further removed as a result of the combined, if not coordinated, efforts of the Sanacja and Endecja.

Particularly debilitating in this regard is the history of the "bench ghetto," the division of places in lecture halls between Christians and Jews. The first to submit to the segregationist demands of nationalist students were the Engineering and Mechanical Department faculty councils of the Lwów Polytechnical Institute, which on December 8, 1935, adopted the appropriate resolutions; these were quickly imitated elsewhere. In conceding to the demands of the nationalist camp, which were supported by student strikes and

---

69. AAN, Ambasada RP w Berlinie, 3278:119, Protocol of the First Session of the Consular Conference in Berlin, May 24, 1938. The published text of this document may be found in Jerzy Tomaszewski, "Obrady konferencji konsularnej w Berlinie w maju 1938 w sprawie pozbawienia Żydów obywatelstwa polskiego," *Teki Archiwalne (Seria nowa)*, 2 (1997): 72–88 and in *Zjazdy i konferencje konsulów polskich w Niemczech: Protokoły i sprawozdania, 1920–1939*, ed. H. Chałupczak and E. Kołodziej (Lublin, 1999), 341–54.

70. *DURP 1938*, 80:543.

71. See the order of the SS command of October 1938 in the Bundesarchiv (Coblenz) R58/276:121, 122, and R43/II/14, 826:62, as well as the correspondence of the Foreign Ministry contained in Politisches Archiv, Auswärtiges Amt, Polen, Band I. This order and its consequences have been analyzed in detail by K. Jońca, *"Noc kryształowa" i casus Herschela Grynszpana* (Wrocław, 1992), 86–90; and Jerzy Tomaszewski, *Preludium zagłady: Wygnanie Żydów polskich z Niemiec w 1938 r.* (Warsaw, 1998), 75–113.

anti-Jewish demonstrations that paralyzed the system of higher education, the Sejm on July 2, 1937, amended the law on higher education, granting greater authority to rectors and strengthening disciplinary measures in relation to students.[72] Based on this amendment, Minister of Religion and Public Education Wojciech Świętosławski granted permission to rectors at their congress on September 24, 1937, to issue regulations establishing separate places for Polish and Jewish students to maintain order in institutions of higher education.[73]

Consequently, Christian students at Warsaw University received on their identification cards a stamp reading "place on even-numbered benches," while their Jewish colleagues were assigned a "place on odd-numbered benches" (at the Warsaw Polytechnical Institute the stamps were marked "A" and "B"). Other institutions of higher education in Poland followed suit, and thus was official segregation by nationality introduced. (It appeared even in the Wawelberg and Rotwand School of Machine Construction and Electrical Engineering, a formerly private academy that had been turned over to the Polish state in 1919 by Hipolit Wawelberg and his son-in-law Stanisław Rotwand on condition that it would never apply restrictions against Jews.)[74] In the Sejm, Emil Sommerstein cited other professional and middle schools, even elementary schools, where similar measures of segregation had been introduced. In the meantime, the new disciplinary provisions approved by the Sejm enabled the punishment of students who did not submit to the segregation regulations. As a result of this systematic anti-Jewish campaign, the number of Jewish students in institutions of higher education fell from 20.4 per cent in the 1928–29 academic year to 7.5 per cent in 1937–38.[75] Indeed, in some institutions and departments not a single Jew was enrolled.

Although the emergence of the bench ghetto disturbed part of the Polish community, it produced outrage and disillusionment among Jews. This was not simply a matter affecting the self-esteem or offended dignity of students; the more general fear was that it was just the first step along the road to segregation in other walks of life. Such concerns had a real basis. One need only recall the division of markets into Jewish and "Aryan" and the resolutions of professional organizations to exclude Jews. Prohibitions also appeared that made municipal parks off-limits to Jews.[76] And as early as 1934, a Czas editorial commented thus on the progaganda of the nationalist camp: "The Endeks know full well that we have 3 million Jews, that these Jews will not

72. DURP 1937, 52:406.

73. Andrzej Pilch, Studencki ruch polityczny w Polsce w latach 1932–1939 (Warsaw, 1972), 154.

74. See Emil Sommerstein's speech to the Sejm in SSS IV (December 1–2, 1937), 60:126–27.

75. "Z materiałów liczbowych MWRiOP," Oświata i Wychowanie 6 (1938). Of 1,672 professors in 1936, only 36 (2.2 per cent) were Jews. Most of them had attained their positions in Galicia before the recovery of independence; see E. Melzer, No Way Out (Cincinnati, Ohio, 1997), 189.

76. AAN MSW 967, Der Moment, as cited by the Nationality Department of the Ministry of Internal Affairs, Komunikaty dzienne, 166 (August 5, 1938).

disappear overnight—though it is desired—that they cannot emigrate even if they wanted to. In other words, we are doomed to coexist with them, probably for long centuries to come, unless the National Democrats propose to sterilize this mass of millions."[77] By the second half of the 1930s, the same words could have been applied to the Sanacja as well.

On December 21, 1938, Stanisław Skwarczyński, as head of the Camp of National Unity, filed an interpellation signed by 116 of 167 of the camp's delegates to the Sejm. This first instance of mass signatures under an interpellation was most probably designed to underscore the seriousness of the question and the extent of agreement among the Camp's parliamentary deputies. It maintained that "Jews are a factor weakening and blocking the normal development of Polish forces in the nation and state. In the structure of our economy, they constitute a highly undesirable element, making it difficult for the Polish rural and urban population to stand on their own feet." The signers, therefore, asked the prime minister whether the government intended "to use all available means to organize the emigration of Jews" with the goal of radically reducing their numbers in Poland.[78] The prime minister responded that the government was thinking along similar lines, that "for the solution of the Jewish question in Poland, one of the most important means is the significant reduction of the number of Jews through emigration," and that this goal was shared as well by a "unanimous Polish public opinion." Therefore, the government would do everything possible "to create conditions that would enable an increase in this emigration."[79]

Meanwhile, deputies put before the Sejm several projects to separate Jews from Poles or that were otherwise anti-Jewish, though few were actually considered by that body. Dudziński came out with the idea of mobilizing 600,000 Jews between the ages of eighteen and forty in work battalions. They were to dig canals, build roads, and drain marshes, thus preparing themselves for work outside of Poland. The costs of maintaining these battalions would be borne by the Jewish population.[80] Józef Bakon, who had been elected in part by Jewish voters,[81] presented the thesis in the budget commission that laws pertaining to Jews should take into account the peculiar Jewish mentality. Jews, in his opinion, always managed to evade universal law; legal norms that were considered sufficiently binding for Poles were not necessarily so for Jews.[82] In line with these views, Bakon introduced a bill to relieve Jews of one of the most important obligations of citizenship: the obligation of military service.

77. "Zwalczanie endecji," *Czas* 61 (May 3, 1934).

78. ASI, Interpelacja posła Stanisława Skwarczyńskiego i 116 innych posłów do Pana Premiera Rady Ministrów (December 3, 1938).

79. "Odpowiedź Prezesa Rady Ministrów gen. Sławoja-Składkowskiego na interpelacje posła Stanisława Skrawczyńskiego i tow.," *Wszystkie Stronnictwa* 1, no. 1 (January 1939): 547–48.

80. SSS V (February 16, 1939), 11:21–23.

81. "Kim był poseł Bakon," *Nasz Przegląd* 21 (January 21, 1937).

82. "Niesłychane wystąpienie żydożercze posła Bakona," *Nasz Przegląd* 13 (January 13, 1937).

Neither of these projects was considered by legislative commissions, because they failed to receive the requisite number of signatures (although at a session of the Warsaw City Council, a combined vote of members representing the Camp of National Unity, the National Party, and the National Radical Party did manage to remove Jews from military recruitment boards).[83]

The project of Franciszek Stoch shared a similar fate. Stoch proposed to treat as displaced persons "all those who in the civil registry or similar records up to December 1, 1938, or later are or will be registered as adherents of the Mosaic faith or were born in wedlock to a father or out of wedlock to a mother and on November 1, 1918, or later were registered as adherents of the Mosaic faith." This status would not affect those who had converted to Christianity before November 11, 1918, or participated in the Polish struggle for independence. The number of those in both categories, together with their families, who would be excluded from the status of displaced persons, would not be allowed to exceed fifty thousand. The remainder would lose the possibility of employment in many professions and would be deprived of the right to retirement pensions.[84] Stoch's scheme was the most far-reaching anti-Jewish project prepared by a deputy in the Sejm.

Again, it is important to note that many of these legal projects did not even make it to the Sejm commissions. Jacek Majchrowski wrote about a project of Colonel Wenda that foresaw changing the law on citizenship by incorporating racial categories; it was presumably supported by Witold Grabowski, then minister of internal affairs.[85] Likewise, Stanisław Ratajczyk, in an interpellation of January 23, 1939, urged the government to strip citizenship from those Jews who, along with members of other non-Polish nationalities, had earlier resided outside the borders of the interwar Polish state and had not acquired citizenship until November 27, 1928. Stanisław Jóźwiak, for his part, proposed changes in several provisions of the law of October 24, 1919, regulating the alteration of surnames.[86] Jóźwiak's basic intent was to make it impossible for Jews to change their names.

Similar thinking appeared in official circles. The Ministry of Internal Affairs considered the introduction of anti-Jewish laws "which should have not only as their formal but also actual goal the elimination of part of Jewish society from our political and economic life." It was proposed that such legislation should have four components: (1) the revision of Polish citizenship, which would embrace approximately a half-million Jews; (2) economic laws emphasizing the exclusion of Jews from a range of professions; (3) a law enabling the government to introduce by administrative means the principle of proportionality for Jewish participation in particular professions—in other words, the *numerus clausus* priniciple; and (4) the introduction of a Jewish emigra-

83. J. Majchrowski, *Silni, zwarci, gotowi* (Warsaw, 1985), 128.
84. *Warszawska Informacja Prasowa* (January 1, 1938), 6.
85. Majchrowski, *Silni, zwarci, gotowi*, 137.
86. SSS V (February 13, 1939), 8:103.

tion tax, which, it was expected, would raise 10 million *złotys* for that purpose. The design of such imagined legislation, to force Jews to emigrate, envisioned not only the departure of 1.5 million Jews over the course of thirty years but the securing of loans amounting to $300 and $500 million from Jews abroad in order to help finance it.[87]

For several parliamentary deputies, particularly those from the nationalist camp but also from the Sanacja in the late 1930s, the "solution of the Jewish question" became a sui generis incantation. One can only agree with the argument that the more frequently a given deputy spoke on Jewish matters, the worse became his assessment of the Jewish community.[88] All of them began by emphasizing that Poles were the only rightful owners of the country; that Jews should not try to affect state policies; that Jews should restrict their influence in all aspects of the country's life; that Jews were not and should not be citizens with equal rights. With the passage of time such speakers became increasingly convinced that the Jews were an undesirable element and as such ought to leave the country.

In this environment the Jewish deputies had no other recourse than to urge the authorities to provide assistance in the organization of emigration to Palestine. To the Sanacja as well as the Endecja, where the Jews went was immaterial so long as they left Poland. The only matters to consider were the means to force their emigration and the costs of such an undertaking. No attention was paid to the fact that emigration was a mere slogan and that its use was sheer demagogy, if only because there was no place for Jews to emigrate to. That these proposals concerned fellow citizens belonging to a people who had lived in Poland for centuries and whose ejection was desired in violation of both law and public morality were also matters of no consequence to their proponents. As Senator Zdzisław Żmigryder-Konopka accurately put it, the real issue was not about emigration at all but about banishment.[89]

The activities of both camps and their political elites, as represented in parliament, contributed to the emergence of a situation thus described by Polish Socialist Party leader Zygmunt Żuławski, commenting in January 1939 on the aforementioned interpellation of the Camp of National Unity and the Prime Minister's sympathetic response: "It is terrible [for an individual] to live in conditions where legislation guarantees identical rights to all, but to feel nonetheless that one is 'tolerated' as if it were an act of mercy, to be treated as if one had the plague and separated from society like a leper, only because he was born a Jew. It is terrible for this person to wait until they 'emigrate' him from his native city and land—'voluntarily' or through coercion—depend-

---

87. AAN MSW 10004:80–82, manuscript copy of a note to the director of the consular department for Jewish affairs of the Ministry of Internal Affairs.

88. A. Landau-Czajka and Z. Landau, "Posłowie polscy w Sejmie 1935–1939 o kwestii żydowskiej," in *Rozdział wspólnej historii: Studia z dziejów Żydów w Polsce ofiarowane prof. Jerzemu Tomaszewskiemu w siedemdziesiątą rocznicę urodzin* (Warsaw, 2001), 212.

89. SSSen III (March 11, 1939), 8:28.

ing on whether an 'international agreement' will make it possible to solve this problem."[90]

At the end of the 1930s a number of measures were taken also against Ukrainians: their places of religious worship and social organization were closed, and Ukrainian peasants were persecuted by various means. All these measures—designed to accelerate their Polonization or, in the vocabulary of the time, their re-Polonization, since a significant proportion of Ukrainians was considered to consist of ruthenianized Poles—were carried out by the state administration and particularly by the army; they found no reflection in any legal statutes of the time. Different methods were used in relation to Jews. Although the nationalist camp's actions against them were at times condemned by the government, the Sanacja did accept the tactic of passing laws that in practice closed off to Jews more and more fields of activity.

In Poland, it is important to note, there was no law passed that applied universally to all Jews. Restrictions specified certain groups and certain spheres of activity. For these groups, however, such restrictions were humiliating or onerous or, as in the case of young law school graduates, prevented them from practicing their profession. Moreover, none of these laws or regulations mentioned Jews specifically by name. On the surface they applied to all citizens, with the possible exception of the law on ritual slaughter, though even it did not refer to Jews by name. The government and the majority in parliament did not submit to the pressures of the more radical deputies and to the very end torpedoed attempts at more formal restrictions of civil rights, including the division of such rights into separate racial categories. Thus, the state authorities guaranteed to Jews formal equality and consistently proclaimed the state's obligation to defend these citizens from violence—though in practice they were often unable or unwilling to carry out this obligation.

To be sure, as Jerzy Tomaszewski has written, the new laws discriminated against only one (even if unnamed) ethnic group.[91] Other scholars, though, have noted that "the most far-reaching projects were not followed up with legislative initiatives. Even those projects that were greeted with loud applause [on the floor of the Sejm] were not put to a vote in the end for lack of sufficient support."[92] Still, the very consideration of legislation that would have effectively disenfranchised nearly the entire Jewish community—similar to the Nuremburg laws in the Third Reich—in itself did much to undermine the spirit of civil equality. Meanwhile, in everyday life, extralegal actions such as the boycott, restrictions in employment, and the lack of a sense of personal security took an ever greater toll.

Translated by Robert Blobaum

90. Zygmunt Żuławski, *Refleksje* (Warsaw, 1939), 225.
91. Tomaszewski, *Najnowsze dzieje Żydów w Polsce*, 197.
92. Landau-Czajka and Landau, "Posłowie polscy," 224.

8

Clerical Nationalism and Antisemitism

Catholic Priests, Jews, and Orthodox Christians in the Lublin Region, 1918–1939

KONRAD SADKOWSKI

The Catholic clergy had a major impact on interwar Polish society. One of their most profound but deplorable actions was the propagation of antisemitism. That most Polish priests steadfastly opposed the Jews is not in dispute.[1] The motivations for their behavior, however, are less understood. Undoubtedly, their antisemitism stemmed in part from the Vatican's continuing anti-Jewish stance.[2] Yet the Vatican condemned nationalism, however obliquely,[3] whereas the Polish clergy strongly coupled nationalism with antisemitism. Clerical antisemitism in interwar Poland, therefore, with tacit encouragement from the Vatican, also derived from the clergy's vision for the Polish nation and state, which itself was tied to the clergy's belief that it

1. See, for example, Ronald Modras, *The Catholic Church and Anti-Semitism: Poland, 1933–1939* (Amsterdam, 1994); and Krzysztof Krasowski, *Episkopat katolicki w II Rzeczypospolitej: Myśl o ustroju państwa; Postulaty, realizacja* (Warsaw, 1992).

2. See David Kertzer, *The Popes against the Jews: The Vatican's Role in the Rise of Modern Anti-Semitism* (New York, 2001). See also Rosemary Radford Reuther, *Faith and Fratricide: The Theological Roots of Anti-Semitism* (New York, 1974).

3. For example, in 1932, in the encyclical *Caritate Christi compulsi*, Pope Pius XI criticized "'undue exaltation' of patriotism," and in mid-1938, in response to the introduction of racial laws in Italy, decried "'exaggerated nationalism' as detestable and unchristian." See Modras, 130–33. See also Czesław Strzeszewski, "Chrześcijańska myśl i działalność społeczna w dwudziestoleciu, 1918–1939," in *Historia katolicyzmu społecznego w Polsce, 1832–1939*, ed. Czesław Strzeszewski (Warsaw, 1981), 295.

occupied a special position in society. This chapter investigates the connections between priests' occupational and economic concerns, their nationalism, and their antisemitism. My geographical focus is the pre-1939 Lublin region (coextensive with the Lublin diocese), which constituted a microcosm of the complex multinational and multiconfessional interwar Polish society.

I argue that a significant contributing motive for pre–World War II clerical antisemitism—and nationalism—was priests' own material and professional interests as the Church confronted the prospect of a secular and democratic society and state. Specifically, in late 1918 the clergy of the Lublin region faced two principal tasks: the propagation of the Catholic faith and expansion of the Church's institutional structures, and the improvement of their professional status and material well-being. But the clergy also encountered a secular Polish state and various national and religious minorities, as well as a vigorous societal debate on who was and who could be a "Pole." Their dogmatic conviction that Catholicism was the "true faith," coupled with their status and needs as a social elite, compelled priests to attempt to Catholicize Polish society, which in the face of a secular state and disputed national identity boundaries amounted to an attempt to build a Catholic Polish nation.

Catholic priests viewed the Jews especially as a threat to the Catholicization of Poland and, implicitly, to Church and clerical power in Polish society. In particular, accepting the Jews as "Poles" would have meant acceding to a nation (and state) constructed on the legal equality of all peoples and religions in the state, which would have undermined not only the Church's institutional raison d'être but also priests' own status and interests. More to the point, because of their high distinctiveness the Jews symbolized the "indispensability" of a civic Polish nation and state, implying a social, political, and cultural order that represented an ideological threat to the Church. Such an order also represented an occupational threat to the clergy in that it pointed toward an ultimate reduction in Church participation and membership, on which the clergy especially relied for their status and livelihood. Inherently, then, the clergy perceived the Jews as a threat to their occupational and professional status, though priests did not—and indeed could not, being ostensibly unconcerned with "status"—articulate this threat. Rather, tapping into their pre-partition-era tradition as defenders of the (ethnic) nation, and following the National Democrats, the clergy of the Lublin region presented the Jews as not only a moral but an economic threat to the Catholic Poles. Fundamentally, however, this equally represented the clergy's utilization of the modern nation as a "field" of political action, to maintain power and authority in society.[4]

4. Rogers Brubaker writes: "Nationalism is not engendered by nations. It is produced—or better, it is induced—by *political fields* of particular kinds. Its dynamics are governed by the properties of political fields, not by the properties of collectivities. . . . [We] should focus on nation as a category of practice, nationhood as an institutionalized cultural and political form, and nation-ness as a contingent event or happening, and refrain from using the analytically dubious notion of 'nations' as substantial, enduring collectivities. . . . To understand the power of nationalism, we

My analysis linking clerical nationalism and antisemitism with priests' occupational and economic concerns rests largely on indirect evidence. In some ways, it would be quite surprising to find direct evidence showing that the clergy opposed Jews because they represented the "necessity" of a secular and pluralistic order in Poland, and that it was this order that threatened to undermine the clergy's status and interests. Though Poland's bishops and priests had to address the Church's fiscal interests directly with their parishioners, publicly the stance of the Church was—and had to be—that it existed in the name of a higher truth. Church leaders and clergy simply could not publicly convey the strong interest in the Church's financial situation that they undoubtedly felt—especially the clergy, who had to squeeze out a living from their often meager parishes. Ultimately, the evidentiary links between priests' occupational and material concerns and the Polish social order are not explicit, yet priests assuredly linked the two, since the Polish nation by the early twentieth century was rapidly becoming a "derivative" of cultural attributes, and the position of the Church and clergy in the Polish state rested on a successful cultural presence and politics.

The first section of this chapter devotes considerable space to how the Church and clergy in the Lublin region saw their mission and future after 1918, since only by examining the way priests themselves regarded their role and status in interwar Poland can we understand their actions. Based on this discussion, the second section explores the Church and clergy's position toward the Jews. The third section then places the discussion in a comparative context, expanding it, however briefly, to the Ukrainian minority in the Lublin region.

The Church, Clergy, and Their Interests

The starting point for considering the clergy's actions in the Lublin region after 1918 is the Church's institutional raison d'être. The fundamental goal of the Church was to order society around itself—or, more innocuously, to create "societal unity," which was also to lead to salvation in the afterlife. Both the goal of societal unity and the idea of salvation through the Church derived from the belief that Jesus Christ was God's chosen son and the "redeemer," and that the Catholic Church was the "true Church."[5] The Polish hierarchy confirmed this ideological framework shortly after independence: "We . . . call

---

do not need to invoke nations. Nor should we, at the other extreme, dismiss nationhood altogether. We need, rather, to decouple categories of analysis from categories of practice." See Brubaker, *Nationalism Reframed: Nationhood and the National Question in the New Europe* (Cambridge, U.K., 1996), 17, 21–22. More generally, my thinking on nations and nationalism is informed by the classic works of Benedict Anderson, Ernest Gellner, Anthony Smith, and Miroslav Hroch.

5. Krasowski, 172–73.

upon everyone . . . to be united . . . *ut unum sint*—will it, o Lord, that they be one! We will come together in this unity to construct the edifice of our fatherland."[6] The new Lublin bishop, Maryan Leon Fulman, likewise expressed this thinking in his "program" to the Lublin diocesan faithful and clergy in December 1918. "I come to you to fulfill the will of the one who sent me so that everyone . . . has eternal life. . . . My greatest task is to organize ministerial work and religious life . . . so that everything is renewed in Christ. The spiritual and material good of our fatherland will be permanent only if it is constructed on the idea of Christ. What for so long has been divided and almost crushed into dust now must be brought together and united, and must live."[7]

Yet Bishop Fulman and his clergy recognized that creating unity around the Church would be difficult, though it had apparently once existed. Throughout the Middle Ages, as Father Marjan Peryt declared, the Church had exerted a unifying force. Then came Renaissance humanism, which initiated the "secularization and paganization of the collective human soul." The Reformation further undermined the authority of the Church, as the concept *cuius regio, eius religio* (i.e., with the monarch rests religious choice) was propagated, and the French Revolution "removed God from the life of nations." The result was the "modern person, who in many ways is a pagan, a product of a godless and irreligious state that removes from civic education the influences of the Church and family."[8] Therefore, against the siege of numerous visible and invisible enemies—secularists, Masons, socialists, communists—the Church and clergy now had to work long and hard to reestablish societal unity as the earthly foundation of ultimate salvation. Thus, Bishop Fulman also declared in December 1918, "Especially today, the enemy of God's work inflames an infernal struggle against the Church and her servants and faithful. We will be oppressed, persecuted, and slandered."[9] Nevertheless, "the establishment of the Catholic faith in the nation, the defense of national interests, . . . the development of religious and civic virtues, and the unity and vitality of the nation will be especially close to my heart. Against enemies of the faith, against unjust and atheistic legislation, against the incitement of discord among citizens, against moral corruption . . . and [all] oppression will I act unconditionally. . . . A mighty and impenetrable bulwark must surround the Polish soul, so that the filth of an immoral world does not engulf it."[10]

6. This Episcopal letter, "Biskupi Polscy do Duchowieństwa i Wiernych," is dated December 10, 1918. It very likely appeared in a number of publications; however, I discovered it at the Catholic University of Lublin Library in the bound volumes of *Wiadomości Diecezjalne Lubelskie*, between nos. 3 and 4, 1919. This particular citation is from pages 14–15 of the letter.

7. *Wiadomości Diecezjalne Lubelskie* 1 (December 1918): 1, 7–8.

8. Ks. Marjan Peryt, "Warunki ekonomiczno-społeczne a praca duszpasterska w diecezji lubelskiej," *Wiadomości Diecezjalne Lubelskie* 11 (November 1935): 338–39. Father Peryt echoed the sentiments of numerous Church publicists of his time. See also Alec R. Vidler, *The Church in an Age of Revolution, 1789 to the Present Day* (1961, 1971; reprint, Middlesex, U.K., 1974).

9. *Wiadomości Diecezjalne Lubelskie* 1 (December 1918): 10.

10. *Wiadomości Diecezjalne Lubelskie* 1 (December 1918): 8.

However well intentioned, the goal of ordering society around the Church was deeply self-righteous. It encouraged clerical paternalism and led to an effort by the Church to dominate the lives of both Catholics and non-Catholics. Bishop Fulman's "program" suggests this paternalism, as does the language with which priests often addressed their parishioners, such as "little peasant" (chłopek), "little ones" (maluczkie), "little sheep" (owieczki), or, more derogatorily, "our illiterates." Non-Catholics, conversely, were considered heretics, schismatics, unbelievers, sectarians, and godless, and were staunchly opposed as the Church looked forward to a time, however distant, of unifying these people with the "True Church."[11] For example, Bishop Fulman wrote to the Lublin voivod (provincial governor) regarding the activities of the recently arrived "Followers of the Teachings of the First Christians" (Zwolenniki Nauki Pierwszych Chrześcijan): "The Church's relationship to this small Protestant sect is the same as it is to Protestantism as a whole. . . . Poland must defend itself in the face of this new deception . . . with all its legal resources so that unenlightened Polish people do not become a sacrifice of foreign sectarians."[12] And a model for a sermon on mission work declared: "If here [in Poland], where Christian culture dominates, we still encounter so many religious falsehoods [błędów religijnych] and ignorance, what can be said for the pagan world? It is true that we find among the pagan nations—in particular the Asiatic, thus especially in China and India—cultures several thousand years old, but in light of their ignorance of the true God and Christianity, their centuries-old beliefs equal a centuries-old wandering."[13]

Finally, occupational factors combined with historical memory and mythology to strengthen the clergy's tendency toward domination. Priests long had been and still were an elite in society; that Catholic workers and peasants were largely uneducated encouraged among priests a feeling of superiority toward their parishioners.[14] As well, memories of past Russian repression and the Polish-Ukrainian and Polish-Bolshevik wars encouraged the clergy to associate the Christian Orthodox Ukrainians with the "hostile East" (not only the Great Schism); and Jewish cultural uniqueness encouraged them to associate the Jews with secularism, Bolshevism, and communism (not only the crucifixion of Jesus Christ).

The Church's confrontation with various "visible and invisible" enemies and its effort to "surround the Polish soul" against "the filth of an immoral

11. Such expressions are found in Wiadomości Diecezjalne Lubelskie throughout the interwar period; see also Spójnia 1 (January 10, 1923): 1–2.

12. Archiwum Archidiecezjalne w Lublinie (hereafter AAL), Rep. 61.XIII.I, 16–[16b].

13. "Szkic kazania o misjach na przedostatnią niedzielę 20 października," Wiadomości Diecezjalne Lubelskie 8–9 (August–September, 1935): 260.

14. On the complaints of parishioners against priests, see Archiwum Państwowe w Lublinie, Urząd Wojewódzki Lubelski—Wydział Społeczno-Polityczny (hereafter APL, UWLWSP), syg. 630. See also Jan Słomka, From Serfdom to Self-government: Memoirs of a Polish Village Mayor, 1842–1927, trans. William John Rose (London, 1941). On the pre–World War I period specifically, see Józef Ryszard Szaflik, O rząd chłopskich dusz (Warsaw, 1976).

world" concerned the rise of the secular, constitutional state in Europe in the nineteenth century. As the Roman Catholic Church in Europe confronted the modern state, priests were drawn into a politics of cultural construction (i.e., control) ostensibly to "save" society as well as to defend the Church. After 1918 the clergy of the Lublin region also were drawn heavily into this politics, which fundamentally concerned shaping state laws and policies and societal attitudes in a pro-Catholic manner. The clergy engaged in party politics as well as utilized the Church's broad array of institutional resources and structures to foster this culture. For example, Bishop Fulman told his priests that alongside their apostolic responsibilities they also had civic duties; thus they should "even be mindful of political matters."[15] But since the Church eschewed establishing a Church-based political party,[16] priests could work only through pro-Church political allies to influence state law and policies. In the Lublin region, and throughout Poland, the clergy sided strongly with the highly nationalistic, antisemitic, and pro-Catholic National Democrats.[17] Additionally, the Church and clergy attempted to define a pro-Catholic societal culture through religious education in the public schools; Church-based religious, charitable, and social organizations; and publishing and radio broadcasts.[18]

---

15. *Wiadomości Diecezjalne Lubelskie* 1 (December 1918): 11. More forcefully, prior to the 1930 parliamentary elections Bishop Fulman declared that priests "can and must speak" against anti-Church parties "from the pulpit, though very carefully": *Wiadomości Diecezjalne Lubelskie* 8 (October 1930): 262–63. Another example is Father Edward Fijołek who, exhorting his fellow priests "to work," wrote that "[the Church] by necessity must have an influence on social and state organizations. . . . We will wholeheartedly support religious-social associations, and all those organizations that, in their programs and in their political, social, and educational work have taken the slogan 'God and Fatherland.' We will oppose the organized strength of the enemies of the faith with Catholic organizations." See "Do Pracy!" *Wiadomości Diecezjalne Lubelskie* 4 (March 1919): 112–13.

16. See Strzeszewski, 293–94. See also Ks. Władysław Goral, "Z okazji wyborów do Sejmu i Senatu," *Wiadomości Diecezjalne Lubelskie* 8 (October 1930): 265–67.

17. A central goal of the National Democrats was to "cleanse non-Polish elements from Polish social and state life." See Alicja Bełcikowska, *Stronnictwa i związki polityczne w Polsce* (Warsaw, 1925), 61. For a more detailed discussion of the political preferences of the Lublin regional clergy in the interwar years, see Konrad Sadkowski, "Church, Nation, and State in Poland: Catholicism and National Identity Formation in the Lublin Region, 1918–1939" (Ph.D. diss., University of Michigan, 1995), 91–110, 171–90. See also APL, UWLWSP, syg. 2080, 27–83. On the late 1930s in particular, see APL, UWLWSP, syg. 627 and 2081. After the 1928 elections, the People's National Union (*Związek Ludowo-Narodowy*, ZLN), under which the National Democrats were united in the Sejm, was transformed into the National Party (*Stronnictwo Narodowe*—SN), to which priests who had earlier supported the ZLN transferred their loyalties.

18. *Wiadomości Diecezjalne Lubelskie* devoted enormous attention to the development of the Church's local young people's, men's, women's, and religious organizations; as well as umbrella organizations: at first the Catholic League and then Catholic Action. An article titled "Association of Polish Working Women" summarized well the great importance of these organizations to the Church: "Social action is the most important work for us because only through it can we develop such human material that no politician will be able to corrupt. Social action will exercise the minds of the people and develop in it a Catholic national character. No one with any fine-sounding, radical, or revolutionary slogans will find easy success among such people." See Ks. Walerjan Markl, "Stowarzyszenie polskich kobiet pracujących," *Wiadomości Diecezjalne Lubelskie* 8 (July–August 1919): 241–50.

This "social Catholic" organizational activity increased dramatically after 1927–28, a partial reaction to Marshal Józef Piłsudski's 1926 coup d'état, which reduced the possibilities for Church influence through politics, though it was also a form of surrogate political action. For example, Father Antoni Szymański, addressing a meeting of the Chełm deanery clergy in February 1928, called for a broad Catholic education of society—that is, a Church politics conducted by other means—that would yield Catholics in all sectors of society who would abide by a Catholic way of life and defend the Church completely.[19] Predictably, the number of Church-sponsored organizations in the interwar Lublin diocese increased significantly, though it is difficult to gauge their overall impact.[20]

Bishop Fulman and his clergy were concerned with the salvation of everyone in society, Catholics and non-Catholics. But in the late nineteenth century the Polish intelligentsia began to forge a new Polish nation on the Polish ethnic core, though its broader characteristics were still very open to question (e.g., could non-Catholics be "true" Poles?). At this time, the Polish Church's position was complex. On one hand, Catholic priests had long stood as defenders of Polish (ethnic) culture and language. On the other, the Polish Church, like the Roman Catholic Church throughout Europe, confronted growing anticlerical and secularizing forces. Now, and in concert with the National Democrats, Polish bishops and priests increasingly began to support the development of the Polish nation on a narrow ethnic principle that maintained Catholicism as a central element of Polish identity. It might appear that this was only natural; Catholicism, as religious practice, fundamentally also was cultural practice, which intersected with the idea that the nation should reflect a shared

19. Fr. Antoni Szymański, the rector of the Catholic University of Lublin from 1933 to 1942, was a leading theorist of the social Catholic movement in interwar Poland. In support of the Catholic League (precursor to Catholic Action) he also forcefully declared to the Chełm deanery priests: "We cannot always expect help from the Polish state, because the government is indifferent to the expansion of religious life. . . . The Catholic League as a social organization always has strength. . . . The Catholic League also helps to develop educational activities and politically take advantage of them. In the area of state law the League is alert and informs people that schools should be Catholic, divorces are harmful, the Concordat is necessary, state law should not offend God's law, secular cemeteries are disgusting, and so on. In critical times, the League organizes protests against crematoria, informing society that the state must defend the rights of the Catholic Church. Just let a cross [disappear] from a school or office or other similar place. Immediately, the Catholic League mounts a protest without a party struggle, but only from a religious point of view." See AAL, Rep. 61.I.7, Chełm deanery clergy conference, February 16, 1928. See also Sadkowski, "Church, Nation, and State," 176–80; and Ks. Zbigniew Skrobicki, "Szymański, Antoni" in Słownik polskich teologów katolickich, 1918–1981, ed. Ks. Ludwik Grzebień (Warsaw, 1983), 7:264–71.

20. For example, in 1920 there were 23 religious and social organizations for 13 parishes in the Chełm deanery, and in 1939, 131 such organizations for 21 parishes. In 1920, then, there were about two (1.8) religious and social organizations per parish in the Chełm deanery; in 1939, about six (6.2). Similar growth occurred in the other deaneries of the Lublin diocese during the interwar period. On the other hand, the clergy were frequently criticized for not doing enough to develop the Church's social Catholic institutions. See Sadkowski, "Church, Nation, and State," 110–22, 191–234, 268–82; and APL, UWLWSP, syg. 2081, 156–76.

culture. But considering that the Church felt increasingly besieged at this time, the insistence on Catholicism as a central element of Polish identity and the attempt to exclude non-Catholics from the nation equally constituted an attempt by the Church to maintain its traditional and authoritative position in society.[21]

After 1918 the clergy of the Lublin region indefatigably promoted a Catholic Polish nation. Because of their conviction that Catholicism was the true faith, as well as their opposition to non-Catholic faiths, the clergy could not support the definition of the nation on the basis of legal equality: (that is, that non-Catholics and non-ethnic Poles could also be "Poles"). This would make Catholicism just another faith in the Polish state and inherently undermine the Church's religious raison d'être, its authority and power, as well as the clergy's own standing in society. Thus, the clergy's nearly exclusive support of the National Democrats was not merely an expression of their desire to shape a Catholic Polish nation for religious-ideological reasons, but an expression of their desire to maintain their own authority and power in society. Indeed, after 1918, rhetoric coupling the Church with the nation was omnipresent in the hierarchy's pronouncements, Catholic publications, and clergy's sermons.[22] Yet it is important to remember that this rhetoric of Church-nation identification also derived from what the clergy perceived as a genuine defense of the Polish ethnic community.[23] From a sociological perspective they saw the Catholic faith and the Church as providing the values and rituals on which Polish ethnic identity and social cohesion were constructed.[24] Thus, after 1918 the Lublin church and clergy (and Polish Church generally) also attacked such so-called "evils" as secularism, liberalism, socialism, and communism because, on a certain level, they truly believed these were mortal threats to the Polish people.

The Catholicization of Poland was driven by religious faith and conviction, yet also by institutional and professional self-preservation and power. That the latter often overshadowed the former and defined the Church's and especially the clergy's interactions with society and vision of the nation is evident when one considers money matters. The Lublin diocese (like all dioceses) was a

21. See Konrad Sadkowski, "Catholic Power and Catholicism as a Component of Modern Polish National Identity," *Donald W. Treadgold Papers in Russian, East European, and Central Asian Studies* 29 (January 2001): 7–10, 13–16, and 32–35; on the "intentionality" of coupling Catholicism with Polish identity, see especially 34–35.

22. For example, Poland's bishops declared in 1919 that "it is in the Catholic Church that [over the centuries] Poland united spiritually into one body and one organism. Poland longed and wept in the Church, and through it sought God's justice. In the Church supernatural faith and national feeling gathered in one indissoluble bond and union." "Bispuki Polscy do Duchowieństwa i Wiernych," 1.

23. On the role of national elites in nineteenth-century nation building, see Miroslav Hroch, *Social Preconditions of National Revival in Europe: A Comparative Analysis of the Social Composition of Patriotic Groups among the Smaller European Nations*, trans. Ben Fowkes (Cambridge, U.K., 1985).

24. Sadkowski, "Catholic Power and Catholicism," 28 n, 45–46.

major organization, and Bishop Fulman was concerned with funding and maintaining the curia, the Lublin cathedral, diocesan meetings and conferences, the parish network, state taxes, the Lublin seminary, the Catholic University of Lublin, Catholic organizations and publications, and missionary activities.[25] Primate Hlond addressed these fiscal concerns in his 1935 pastoral letter, "On the Church's Financial Matters":

> Leading [you] to eternal riches, [the Church] cannot survive without earthly riches. The Church needs them to build and maintain its churches and buildings, to propagate its religious cult, for its apostolic work and works of mercy, for the education and earthly existence of those who serve the altar and preach the Gospels [i.e., priests]. . . . The riches of the Church are today only a memory and a legend. The truth and reality today is a continuing impoverishment of the Church. . . . With sacrifice and perseverance *we will continue to build that which is "first" and "necessary"* [emphasis added] because in our personal lives, in the life of the Nation and State, we are erecting "God's Kingdom".[26]

Concerned to develop the institutional Church, the bishops of Poland, at least, thanks to their positions, did not worry about their personal material needs, which were well cared for. The same cannot be said of the parish clergy. Parish priests likewise were administrators, though of far smaller organizations (i.e., parishes). Their main work was satisfying the pastoral needs of their parishioners (such as performing masses, confessions, baptisms, funerals, and marriages) and, more generally, strengthening the ties between the Church and society. They had to maintain the parish church, cemetery, and other properties; purchase devotional items such as candles and wine; contribute monies to the curia for its needs; pay state taxes; pay the salaries of the parish organist and other staff; finance the parish's religious, social, and charitable associations; and purchase publications for the parish. They also paid for their own food, entertainment, travel, and other personal items. Yet priests found it difficult to fulfill these obligations because their salaries were low, and they could not rely on their parishioners for contributions because the 1920s–30s was a period of intense economic hardships.[27]

25. A reading of *Wiadomości Diecezjalne Lubelskie* throughout the interwar period amply attests to these concerns. See also Ks. Leon Balicki, *Dzieje gospodarcze Diecezji Siedleckiej, 1918–1939* (Lublin, 1991).

26. August Kardynał Hlond, *Na straży sumienia narodu: Wybór pism i przemówień z przedmową Prof. Dr. Oskara Haleckiego* (Ramsey, N.J., 1951; reprint, Warsaw, 1999), 144–45, 148, 153.

27. AAL, Rep. 61.I.6–10. The deanery conference minutes (1919–39) in these reports clearly attest to these responsibilities and burdens. Another important indication of the clergy's concern with financial and material conditions is the friction that existed between pastors and associate pastors (*proboszcz* and *wikariusz*) over such things as payments for food and housing. This tension in their relations continued over the entire interwar period, with younger priests often complaining about older ones, and is reflected in *Wiadomości Diecezjalne Lubelskie*.

Consequently, priests often compromised themselves in various ways as they sought to maintain their parishes and to satisfy their personal material needs and preserve their elite social status as well. The months and years immediately after independence saw a great effort at clergy reform by Poland's bishops, and self-organization by priests to protect their "interests." *Wiadomości Diecezjalne Lubelskie* (Lublin Diocesan News) frequently published information on these efforts, also painting a good picture of how priests behaved in their parishes and what they valued. For example, at a conference of deans on January 9, 1919, Bishop Fulman noted that there is "great opposition" in society to priests entering the Constituent Assembly of the reborn Polish state. People are "accusing priests of leading immoral lives," and of "avarice and material self-interest." He cautioned his deans to be on the lookout for these "errors" and to "closely examine" whether priests were not charging excessive fees for religious services or exploiting their parishioners in other ways.[28] The bishop also warned his priests against "hazardous card playing." In March 1919, *Wiadomości Diecezjalne Lubelskie* reported that "an exceedingly painful fact is that today's clergy do not pray enough, and some do not pray beyond their official duties." "At [deanery] conferences pay attention to and warn against materialism and the pursuit of money; and examine each other to see that you do not disgrace our position through a dirty social life [*brudnem pożyciem*] or scandalous behavior, or that you do not insult the pulpit or any holy place with your private interests, vindictiveness, or tactlessness."[29]

The same issue of *Wiadomości Diecezjalne Lubelskie*, in an article on the need for the clergy to engage in Catholic social work, reported that some priests "are traders, workers, economists, and wheeler dealers. The only thing they lack is a priestly spirit, love for God's work, and desire to spread God's kingdom on earth! The only remaining thing they carry from the priesthood is their frock, which is sometimes even too heavy to wear. . . . May God defend His Church from such priests." Finally, an article on the need for a priests' association in the Lublin diocese reported:

Now we are scattered and divided. Each [priest] tries to find happiness for himself, most often clumsily and not infrequently with harm to himself, and to the outrage of many and discredit to our priestly dignity. . . . Instead of looking at the world idealistically, and being eager to seek new heights and to pull others along with ourselves, we so strangely entangle ourselves in a crass materialism, putting on our own necks a noose that strangles us. And so our lives as priests pass so poorly that at the twilight of our lives we remain at the mercy of, or disgraced by, the bad company we keep. In addition, our moral state suffers increas-

28. *Wiadomości Diecezjalne Lubelskie* 3 (February 1919): 88–89, 92.
29. "Kongregacja dekanalna," *Wiadomości Diecezjalne Lubelskie* 4 (March 1919): 102–3.

ingly from the hard blows of the world. The secular company we keep dulls our delicate priestly feelings, which are so highly developed at the beginning of our careers.[30]

Finally, it is highly revealing that Poland's bishops themselves put the defense of the Church in terms of the defense of priests' material interests. In the turbulent months following independence, when the Church especially feared a socialist order in Poland, the Polish hierarchy appealed to the clergy with the following:

In fact, you [priests] will be unable to avoid difficulties and dangers even if one of you wanted to temporarily hide for personal reasons. If the enemy is not defeated today, he will more boldly raise his head tomorrow. . . . From the socialist government's program and actions we can clearly see that a great movement is in place here that is very similar to the Bolshevik movement in Russia. . . . *And who does not see that so-called Bolshevism endangers not only the culture of the society and the nation, but also the personal property of everyone, especially the priest. Thus, if one of you should not feel strong enough to be virtuous from conviction, then your own personal consideration and closest [material] interests should convince you of the need for bravery and sacrifice* [emphasis added].[31]

The quotations are from a period when the Church had just begun to reform and rebuild after years of repression, revolution, and World War I. In 1925 the Concordat between Poland and the Vatican established new, though insufficient state salaries for priests.[32] Over time, Bishop Fulman and his deans imposed greater discipline on the clergy through better oversight, improved training, the introduction of new priests, and periodic mandatory retreats. Priests became more "priestly"—yet no doubt they also became more skilled in evading their superiors' watchful eyes. It is important to recall that a major reason for the spread of the schismatic Polish National Catholic Church throughout Poland in the middle to late 1920s was the over changing for religious services by priests, just as the emergence of the sectarian Mariavite movement had been in the 1890s. Thus, whether they abused their positions or not (and many did), priests worked for financial gain on behalf of the Church as well as themselves. Their choice of political allies and treatment of national minorities—i.e., nation and state building—surely reflected these interests. The

30. "Związek księży," *Wiadomości Diecezjalne Lubelskie* 4 (March 1919): 114–15.
31. "Biskupi polscy do duchowieństwa," *Wiadomości Diecezjalne Lubelskie* 6 (May 1919): 162–63.
32. See Ks. Bogdan Stanaszek, *Duchowieństwo Diecezji Sandomierskiej w latach, 1918–1939* (Lublin, 1999), 137.

clergy may have believed they were protecting the nation, yet they also used it to advance their own personal, professional, and material status and condition, a reflection of their greater concern to maintain power in society.

The Jews

As Bishop Fulman and his clergy worked to order society on Catholic principles and around the Church, how did they regard the Jews, an important segment of society?[33] For centuries, Polish Jews had remained culturally and socially distinct, by and large, and emphatically rejected conversion to Catholicism.[34] Not surprisingly, after 1918 the Catholic Church of the Lublin diocese considered the Jews "outsiders," a people that willingly separated itself from "Christian society."[35] The Church in the Lublin region, as an extension of the Roman Catholic Church, desired the conversion of the Jews[36] but hardly expected it to happen soon; as a result, it viewed the Jews as a major obstacle to its work of ordering society around itself.

By this time, however, opposition was based on far more than fundamental religious differences; by the early twentieth century the Roman Catholic Church had heavily entangled the Jews in its greater confrontation with "modernity." Generally, enormous political, economic, and social change followed in Europe on the heels of the French and Industrial Revolutions, including a massive growth of cities and unprecedented technological and communication advancements, as well as the progressive enfranchisement of the masses. Liberalism and socialism, firmly based on Enlightenment rationalism and secularism, drove the latter. Thus, as European societies transformed under the pressure of enormous economic, technological, and intellectual change, traditional political and religious authorities faced increasing attack and the loss of power. The Jews, on the other hand, were among the main beneficiaries of this massive societal change, achieving political emancipation throughout Europe and frequent economic success because of their historic location in the urban commercial world (even though Jewish poverty

33. According to the 1931 census, 8.6 percent of Poland's total population (31,916,000) was Jewish by "nationality," 9.8 percent by religious affiliation, whereas 16.8 percent of the population in the Lublin region was Jewish by religious affiliation. See Henryk Zieliński, *Historia Polski, 1914–1939* (Wrocław, 1983), 124–26; and Główny Urząd Statystyczny Rzeczypospolitej Polskiej, *Statystyka Polski*, Seria C, Zeszyt 85 (Warsaw, 1938), 26–35. Approximately 3.25 million Jews were living in Poland on the eve of World War II.

34. On the Jews' "caste" status, see Aleksander Hertz, *The Jews in Polish Culture*, ed. Lucjan Dobroszycki, trans. Richard Lourie (Evanston, Ill., 1988).

35. See Peryt, 344; and Ks. I. Władziński, *Lublin w walce o swoją polskość* (Lublin, n.d. [1916–20]), 60.

36. See the instruction from Bishop Fulman, "Modlitwa mszalna za nawrócenie odszczepieńców," dated September 25, 1924, in *Wiadomości Diecezjalne Lubelskie* 5 (October 1924): 89.

was endemic). In response, such traditionalist forces as the Catholic Church blamed the Jews for the "evils" of modern society. Nationalists, who now constructed new identities on the basis of ethnic tradition, including religion, even more vehemently opposed the Jews, whom they saw as racially and culturally inferior and an obstacle to the economic development of their specific nations. Consequently, by the turn of the twentieth century the Jews throughout Europe were frequent scapegoats for the political, economic, social, and psychological dislocations that accompanied "modernity."

After 1918, then, opposition to the Jews was rooted in historic religious differences and prejudices, but following the Europe-wide Roman Catholic Church, the Church in the Lublin region also opposed the Jews because they were allegedly promoting secularism, liberalism, socialism, and communism and were corrupting society. The clergy's opposition to the Jews is clearly evident through their extensive support of the highly nationalistic and antisemitic National Democrats. *Wiadomości Diecezjalne Lubelskie* also gave semi-official support to clerical antisemitism in references to Jewish-Masonic and Bolshevik-Jewish conspiracies and to Jews as propagators of atheism and communism. These references grew in frequency in the 1930s as the Church's anticommunism campaign intensified. For example, the reports of an anticommunism conference for the clergy held in December 1936 strongly coupled Jews to communist activity and announced that the participants had agreed to "systematically and with determination free Poland of Jewish cultural and economic influences."[37]

Yet as a diocesan publication *Wiadomości Diecezjalne Lubelskie* also tried to distance the Church—and inhibit the clergy—from aggressive actions. For example, in March 1919, *Wiadomości Diecezjalne Lubelskie* reported that "in the matter of the Jewish question, [priests] should not incite hatred. They should speak prudently and in the spirit of Christian love, but also warn people of the bad influence of the Jews."[38] And in 1937 the periodical reported that although Jews had a "tendency toward revolution, cheating, and swindling," the Lublin diocesan clergy could not and "would not even know how to" use these methods to oppose the Jews. "Let us retrieve from within ourselves all of those abilities and that strength that God has placed in the souls of Poles and victory will be certain, without resorting to sneers and caricatures, which we find too frequently to the harm of the Polish psyche."[39] These statements seeking to inhibit the clergy's aggressive antisemitic activities could not but be

37. *Wiadomości Diecezjalne Lubelskie* 1 (January 1937): 3–17.

38. *Wiadomości Diecezjalne Lubelskie* 3 (February 1919): 95.

39. S., "O metodę walki," *Wiadomości Diecezjalne Lubelskie* 6–7 (June–July 1937): 227. Interestingly, the article was directed against the advice given by Fr. Stanisław Trzeciak. According to Fr. Trzeciak in a more recent *Głos Lubelski* article, Poles should use the same methods to fight the Jews as the Jews use against the Poles. Though Fr. Trzeciak's advice was criticized, *Wiadomości Diecezjalne Lubelskie* did encourage its readers (i.e., the clergy) to read his publications by advertising them in its bibliography section.

unsuccessful, however, since at their core they still condoned antisemitism. More commonly, priests were encouraged to boycott Jewish merchants (of wine, Catholic devotional items, and publications) and to read such Church publications as *Rycerz Niepokalanej* and *Mały Dziennik*, which were stridently antisemitic.[40]

In actuality, the clergy's condemnation of the Jews for bringing the "evils" of modernity and for corrupting society—layered over the Church's religion-based hostility to the Jews—concerned the progressive erosion of Church and clerical power in society and the clergy's consequent attempt to define a Catholic Polish nation to counter this trend. Essentially, secularism, liberalism, socialism, and communism represented different programs of societal transformation and modern nation and state building, and each was inimical to religion to one degree or another. Since these programs had helped to emancipate the Jews after the French Revolution, and since the Church equally suffered because of them, it was easy for the clergy to blame them on the Jews, an ancient "enemy." Specifically, in light of their mission to Catholicize society by defining a Catholic Polish nation, the clergy and the Church in general opposed the Jews at three levels. First, for fundamental religious-ideological reasons—i.e., Catholicism was the True Faith—the Church could not practically condone a Polish nation (and state) built on legal equality and cultural pluralism. Yet because of their high distinctiveness, compounded by their relatively large numbers, the Jews represented the "indispensability" of just such a nation. It was because of this inherent indispensability, which translated into a direct challenge to the Church's religious raison d'être, that the clergy vehemently opposed the Jews. For example, Father I. Władziński wrote of "democracy" in *Lublin w walce o swoją polskość*, an antisemitic brochure: "It was the [Russian post-1905] constitutional era that fully showed us the greed of these ["Litvak"] newcomers, who in the guise of rabid Chasids, Zionists, and Bundists began to declare that Poland is their country, a new Palestine in which the Jewish people, standing equal with all others, have a right to demand recognition for their jargon and their nationality and Talmudic superstitions. . . . Religious disbelief, discouragement toward life, contempt for national ideals are stealing themselves into our hearts under the cloak of democratic slogans."[41]

Yet, second, the Jews, in representing the indispensability of a civic nation, were not only a religious-ideological threat to the Church but also an eco-

---

40. *Rycerz Niepokalanej* and *Mały Dziennik* were recommended at deanery conferences and in the pages of *Wiadomości Diecezjalne Lubelskie*. See AAL, Rep. 61.I.9–10. *Wiadomości Diecezjalne Lubelskie* also advertised "Christian" merchants, for example, of wine for the Mass. On the issue of devotional items, see also Modras, 238–42.

41. Władziński, 5, 7–8. I believe this author is Fr. Jan Władziński, a frequent contributor to *Głos Lubelski*, the Lublin nationalist and antisemitic daily, and author of such brochures as *Semici* and *Skarga*. He was also the editor of *Wiadomości Diecezjalne Lubelskie* from 1924 to 1927. He died in 1935.

nomic one. Specifically, the development of a civic and secular Polish nation (and state) would have meant a dilution of Church influence and power in society, involving fewer churchgoers and a reduction in revenues. The Church, however, presented the Jews as a direct economic threat not to itself but rather to the nation. Thus, Father Władziński also declared: "Through our own blindness we have not realized that we are voluntarily giving away to the Jews everything that represents the existence of the entire nation—houses, squares, capital, trade, industry, the press."[42] On one hand, this reflected the fact that priests truly believed they were defending the nation by opposing the Jews, yet on the other, we must remember that after 1918 the Church had to ensure its ideological as well as its economic survival through the secular state. Ultimately, the Church's condemnation of the Jews for threatening the economic survival of the nation was also intended to strengthen the bonds between ethnic Poles and the Church in order to enhance the Catholicization (or suppress the secularization) of the state administration and authorities. That is, by working through the nation to shape "the state," specifically as a defender of the livelihood of the ethnic nation, the Church equally sought to defend its own economic-financial position. The argument can be made as well that by working to strengthen the nation economically, the Church sought to ensure its own economic survival, since an increasingly prosperous nation tied to the Church would "share" its prosperity with the Church.

Third, the clergy in particular, as an occupational group, felt threatened by the Jews. Again, more than any other social, religious, or ethnic group the Jews symbolized the indispensability of a Polish civic nation, which would mean the erosion of commitment to the Catholic Church and specifically the weakening of parishes. Yet the clergy had to live off their parishes, and it was equally they who had strong materialistic impulses. Catholic priests, then, perceived the Jews as a threat to their professional and economic status through the Jews' unmistakable "demand" for a Polish secular and civic nation, which would erode both the ideological and cultural importance of the clergy and their economic standing. In condemning the Jews for threatening the nation (on economic and moral grounds), Catholic priests equally revealed that they needed a Catholic Polish nation to protect their professional and economic status. This attack was not unlike that of other occupational groups who in the nineteenth and early twentieth centuries perceived the Jews as an impediment to their professional advancement and embourgeoisement.[43] In the case of the Catholic clergy, the Jews obviously did not challenge priests by competing with them for their parishes; they did so by their need for a particular kind of nation and state, one that represented a direct challenge to the Church, and especially its clergy.

42. Władziński, 7.
43. See William Hagen, "Before the 'Final Solution': Toward a Comparative Analysis of Political Antisemitism in Interwar Germany and Poland," *Journal of Modern History* 68, no. 2 (1996): 351–81.

The Ukrainians

In addition to the Jews, the Lublin region contained a relatively large population of Ukrainians along its eastern border in the Chełm subregion.[44] How did Bishop Fulman and his clergy regard this population? Did their actions toward it resemble those toward the Jews?

The relations between the Catholic Church, and the Ukrainians and their religious institutions—the Greek Catholic (Uniate), Orthodox, and Byzantine Slavonic Churches—in the Lublin region are too complex for more than the most basic summary to be given here.[45] Before the Union of Brest of 1596 the Ukrainian population of the Chełm region was Christian Orthodox. With the Union, the Orthodox joined the Roman Church and became Greek Catholics, or Uniates. In 1839, following the partitions of Poland, the Russian authorities abolished the Greek Catholic Church throughout the Russian Empire except the Kingdom of Poland, which included the Chełm region. In 1875, however, Russia extended its suppression to the Kingdom, forcing many Uniates to become Orthodox. In 1905, Tsar Nicholas II's Toleration Edict allowed the residents of the Chełm region to choose their religion, though not to return to the Uniate Church, which was still banned. Taking advantage of the edict, many former Uniates in the Chełm region converted to Roman Catholicism; however, many others remained Christian Orthodox. Ultimately, with Polish independence in late 1918, the Church in the Lublin region faced two serious questions: first, would it concede to a return of the Uniate Church to the Chełm region in light of the fact that the Uniate Church had become a "Ukrainian church"—in Austrian Galicia—in the nineteenth century? Second, would the Church concede to a strong Orthodox presence in the Chełm region, considering the harsh suppression of the Uniate Church in 1875? Suffice it to say that Bishop Fulman and his priests strenuously opposed the return of the Uniate Church or further development of the Orthodox Church. The great majority of Catholic priests even opposed the new Byzantine Slavonic rite as an instrument intended to reclaim the Orthodox for the Roman Catholic Church. Essentially, as with the Jews, most Catholic priests and Bishop Fulman

44. According to the 1931 census, the districts of the eastern Lublin region with the heaviest Orthodox population were Biłgoraj, 17.9 percent; Chełm, 23.1 percent; Hrubieszów, 37.8 percent; and Tomaszów Lubelski, 27.3 percent. See Główny Urząd Statystyczny Rzeczypospolitej Polskiej, *Statystyka Polski*, Seria C, Zeszyt 85 (Warsaw, 1938), 26–35. In the 1920s–30s in the Lublin region, the Ukrainians were still often called "Rusini."

45. For a fuller discussion, see Konrad Sadkowski, "Catholic Power and Catholicism." As well, see Sadkowski, "The Roman Catholic Clergy, Byzantine Slavonic Rite, and Polish National Identity: The Case of Grabowiec, 1931–1934," *Religion, State & Society* 28, no. 2 (2000): 175–84; "From Ethnic Borderland to Catholic Fatherland: The Church, Christian Orthodox, and State Administration in the Chełm Region, 1918–1939," *Slavic Review* 57, no. 4 (1998): 813–39; and "Religious Exclusion and State Building: The Roman Catholic Church and the Attempted Revival of Greek Catholicism in the Chełm Region, 1918–1924", *Harvard Ukrainian Studies* 22 (1998): 509–26.

were aggressive toward the Ukrainians, especially the Orthodox Church and clergy, as they pursued their goal of Catholicizing Polish society. The most outstanding example was the collusion with the state authorities and the military in eliminating 127 so-called superfluous Orthodox (many of which were pre-1875 Uniate) churches in 1938.

The clergy's actions toward the Jews and the Ukrainians were not identical, however, because priests perceived the Ukrainians as a significantly lower ideological—consequently, economic—"threat" to the Church and themselves. On one hand, as with the Jews, the clergy could not accept the Ukrainians—whether Uniate, Orthodox, or Byzantine Slavonic—as "Poles," because doing so would de facto signify the abandonment of their conviction that (Latin rite) Catholicism was the True Faith, as well as their desire to build a Catholic Poland. On the other hand, the clergy held out the hope that since the Ukrainians were fellow Christians and Slavs, they would convert, or could be converted, to Roman Catholicism and be Polonized. In fact, Bishop Fulman and his clergy worked toward these ends. The hope, even expectation, of conversion and Polonization, therefore, meant that the clergy did not see the Ukrainians, as they did the Jews, as imposing on the Church—and themselves—a recognition or acceptance of a secular and pluralistic Polish nation and state. In other words, the clergy viewed the Jews as a far greater threat than the Ukrainians to their politics of Catholicizing society by associating the Church with the nation.

Clerical nationalism and antisemitism were powerful forces in Poland before World War II. It is highly likely that an important contributing motive for both, though an underlying one, was priests' concerns over their occupational status and material well-being. Specifically, the arrival of the Industrial Revolution in the late nineteenth century and attendant social and political changes also eroded the social and economic status of the Church and clergy. To maintain their status in society, priests in the Lublin region, as elsewhere, endorsed the ethnic model of the nation promoted by the National Democrats and began increasingly to couple Catholicism with Polishness. After 1918 the prospect of a democratic and secular Poland in which all national and religious minorities had an equal voice intensified the challenges the clergy faced. Such an order implied an eventual reduction in Church membership and therefore in parish revenues, from which the clergy derived their livelihood. The clergy's nationalism was directed in particular at the Jews because, more than any other ethnic or religious minority, the Jews symbolized the "indispensability" of a secular and democratic order in the new Polish state.

The clergy also opposed the Ukrainian Uniate, Orthodox, and Byzantine Slavonic populations and churches (and all other religious minorities). Ultimately, the Orthodox Ukrainians also symbolized the need for a secular and pluralistic Polish nation and state, yet Bishop Fulman and his clergy envisioned the conversion and Polonization of this population and thus viewed it as less "threatening." It is important to remember that Bishop Fulman and his clergy saw the entire Jewish people (or "race") as *the* "threat," whereas the Orthodox were Slavic and Christian, and it was leaders (bishops and clergy) especially who were seen as troublesome. Despite these differences, however, the similarities in the Church and clergy's actions toward the Jews and Ukrainians should be recognized. They reflect Church and clerical politics intended to identify Catholicism exclusively with the Polish nation, ostensibly to protect the nation yet unmistakably, in light of the Church's claims to absolute truth, to further the Church and especially the clergy's status and power in society.[46] Undeniably, then, although Catholic ideological exclusivism made priests nationalistic and antisemitic, so did their economic and professional concerns.

46. What Charles Kimball has written on the power of religious nationalism in the world today is applicable to the pre–World War II period: "Religious truth claims about God or the transcendent necessarily rely on language. When the language stiffens into unyielding doctrine, people frequently take on the role of defending God. . . . When adherents lose sight of the symbolic nature of language about God, religion is easily corrupted. Rigid truth claims, particularly in times of conflict, are the basis for demonizing and dehumanizing those who differ. . . . [R]eligious convictions that become locked into absolute truths can easily lead people to see themselves as God's agents. People so emboldened are capable of violent and destructive behavior in the name of religion." See Kimball, *When Religion Becomes Evil* (San Francisco, 2002), 51–52, 70.

9

"Why Did They Hate Tuwim and Boy So Much?"

Jews and "Artificial Jews" in the Literary Polemics of the Second Polish Republic

ANTONY POLONSKY

How did we come to this? How did we lose ourselves
In this vast world, strange and hostile to us?

Julian Tuwim, 1926

It is a terrible burden and hindrance
To be a country created by the prayers
Of poets who dipped their pens
In the bitter inkwell of blood and tears

Julian Tuwim, 1936

One of the most characteristic tropes of modern antisemitism and one that distinguished it from traditional Christian anti-Judaism was its hostility to Jewish integration and to acculturated and integrated Jews. According to the antisemites, although a small number of Jews had kept to the "assimilationist bargain" and had adopted the culture and way of life of the country to whose citizenship they aspired, most saw this acculturation purely in terms of the advantages it brought to them as individuals or as a group. They thus constituted an unassimilable mass, all the more dangerous because they understood the language and customs of the host country and could use this knowledge to advance specific Jewish interests. This disillusionment with the politics of Jewish integration was first articulated in Germany, in the wake of the economic crisis of the 1870s. In his well-known essay "A Word about Our Jewry," written in 1880, Heinrich von Treitschke argued that in Germany, unlike England and France, the number of Jews made assimilation difficult. "[Our] country is invaded year after year by multitudes of assiduous pants-selling youths from the inexhaustible cradle of Poland, whose children and grand-children are to be the future rulers of Germany's exchanges and Germany's press. This immigration grows visibly in numbers and the question becomes more and more serious how this alien nation can be assimilated." Jewish integration could succeed, but only if the Jews sincerely desired it: "What we have to demand from our Jewish fellow-citizens is simple: that they become Germans, regard themselves simply and solely as Germans, without prejudice to their faith and their old sacred past which all of us hold in reverence . . . [for] it cannot be denied that there are numerous and powerful groups among our Jews who definitely do not have the desire to become simply Germans." Germany, he argued, was a young nation and, unlike England and France,

> still lacks national style, instinctive pride, a firmly developed individual-ity—this is the reason why we were defenseless against alien manners for so long. . . . The only way out therefore is for our Jewish fellow-citizens to make up their minds without reservation to be Germans, as many of them have done already long ago, to their advantage and ours. There will never be a complete solution. . . . There will also always be a specifi-cally Jewish education, and, as a cosmopolitan power, it has a historical right to existence. But the contrast can be mitigated if the Jews, who talk so much about tolerance, become truly tolerant themselves and show some respect for the faith, the customs and the feelings of the German people which has long ago atoned for old injustice and given them human and civil rights.[1]

Treitschke's views were supplemented by more extreme spokesmen. Thus the German antisemitic publicist Julius Langbehn made it clear that he did not object to Orthodox Jews; what he disliked were those who *had* attempted to become German. In his words "the modern plebeian Jews are a poison for us and must be treated as such . . . they are democratically inclined and have an affinity for the mob."[2]

One particular aspect of this hostility was the allegedly negative impact that Jewish writers were having on the national culture. According to Richard

1. Heinrich von Treitschke, *A Word about our Jewry*, ed. Ellis Rivkin, trans. Helen Lederer (Cincinnati, Ohio, n.d.), 1–7.

2. Quoted in Fritz Stern, *The Politics of Cultural Despair: A Study in the Rise of Germanic Ideology* (Berkeley, Calif., 1961), 141.

Wagner, the central problem was the "the Judaization of modern Art." Disillusioned by the failure of the revolution of 1848, he argued that this had been caused by the degeneration of German society, which in turn was the product of Jewish cultural influence. He elaborated this idea in his essay "Judaism in Music" written in 1850, in which he claimed that the Jew "rules, and will rule, as long as Money remains the power before which all our doings and dealings lose their force." The Jews were responsible for the "commercialization of art" and had transformed the suffering of artists for their art into financial profit, making genuine creativity impossible. "We have no need to first substantiate the Judaization of modern art; it springs to the eye, and thrusts upon the senses, of itself. . . . The Jew, who is innately incapable of announcing himself to us artistically through either his outward appearance or his speech, and least of all through his singing, has nevertheless been able in the most widespread of modern art varieties, to wit in Music, to become the ruler of public taste." Yet the Jews were unable to be a genuine part of the European community or participate in its culture: "Alien and apathetic stands the educated Jew in midst of a society he does not understand, with whose tastes and aspirations he does not sympathize, whose history and evolution have always been indifferent to him."[3]

Wagner's views were echoed in turn, though in a more moderate way, by Treitschke. In his pamphlet he asserted that

> we do not want an era of German-Jewish mixed culture to follow after thousands of years of German civilization. . . . [However,] recently a dangerous spirit of arrogance has arisen in Jewish circles and . . . the influence of Jewry upon our national life, which in former times was often beneficial, has recently often been harmful. . . . Among the leading names of art and science there are not many Jews. The greater is the number of Semitic hustlers among the third-rank talents. And how firmly this bunch of *literateurs* hangs together! How safely this insurance company for immortality works, based on the tested principle of mutuality, so that every Jewish poetaster receives his one-day fame, dealt out by the newspapers immediately and in cash, without delayed interest. The greatest danger, however, is the unjust influence of the Jews in the press—a fateful consequence of our old narrow-minded laws which kept the Jews out of most learned professions. For ten years public opinion in many German cities was "made" mostly by Jewish pens. It was a misfortune for the Liberals, and one of the reasons of the decline of the party, that their papers gave too much scope to the Jews.

Given the much slower pace of Jewish acculturation on the Polish lands, it is not surprising that these motifs surfaced here a generation later than in

---

3. *Neue Zeitschrift für Musik* 33, (September 3 and 6 1850): 19, 20.

Germany. The emergence of the "new Jewish politics" in the Kingdom of Poland around the turn of the century, with its stress on ethnicity rather than religion as the marker of Jewish difference, contributed to a growing loss of faith on the part of the Polish positivists in Jewish integration. The increased strength of Zionism in the Kingdom of Poland was taken by them as a rejection of their bona fide offer of integration by a significant section of the Jewish elite. It provoked Aleksander Świętochowski, probably the most important of them, to rethink his previous views on the Jewish question. He did not believe, he wrote in *Prawda* in April 1902, that Jews possessed the "cultural material needed to create their own homeland or to build a separate nation." If, however, they were to pursue such an ideal, then friendly coexistence with such an alien and separate nation would become impossible for the Poles. In a second article, in February 1903, significantly titled "Take Care with Fire," he warned that the spread of Zionism would result in the rise of hostility to the Jews in segments of society which until then had been free of hatred; this anti-Zionism would quickly turn into antisemitism and would destroy all hope of Polish-Jewish reconciliation.

Świętochowski's views were expressed in more extreme form by Roman Dmowski, who in *Myśli nowoczesnego Polaka* (Thoughts of a Modern Pole) doubted whether the Polish nation could absorb more than a few unusually acculturated Jews:

> There, where we can multiply our strength and our development as a civilization by absorbing other elements no law forbids us that, and we even have an obligation to do so. . . . This does not mean that we should willingly absorb any elements we find along the road. The national organism should aim to absorb only that which it may tame and convert into an expansion bringing growth and strength to the whole group. The Jews are not such an element. They have an individuality too distinct, too crystallized by tens of centuries of life as a civilization to allow themselves to be tamed in greater numbers by one as young as ours, only now forming its national character; rather they would be capable of assimilating our majority [to themselves] spiritually, and, in part physically.[4]

In a lecture a few years later, Dmowski expanded on this idea of the superficiality of assimilation as a mass phenomenon. After asserting that in the Kingdom of Poland, even after the January uprising, Polish intellectual life still held attractions for Jewish youth, he continued:

> Nevertheless, to the extent that the Jewish intelligentsia grew in size— and it grew with unbelievable speed—assimilation, while gaining in extent, lost in intensity. The enormous production of assimilated Jews

4. R. Dmowski, *Myśli nowoczesnego Polaka* (Lwów, 1904), 214–15.

began to be distinguished by that which often denotes mass production, namely, a degree of superficiality. The ranks of Poles of Jewish descent increased enormously, but these Poles were ever more superficial. Because of its numbers, it was simply not possible for this new Polish-Jewish intelligentsia to enter into the Polish sphere as deeply as had the few persons assimilated earlier. It created its own Jewish sphere with a separate spirit, a separate attitude toward life and its mysteries. Besides that, it felt increasingly strong, and in the natural course of things, consciously or unconsciously, aimed to impose its ideas and aspirations upon Polish society.[5]

Along with this belief that the Jews as a group were unassimilable and that the consequences of attempts at assimilation had been more harmful than beneficial went a rejection of what was regarded as the negative impact of Jewish influences on Polish cultural life. This influence was also slower to develop in Poland than in German-speaking Europe. Although the first literary works by Jews in the Polish language date back to the middle of the nineteenth century, it was only in the interwar period that Polish-Jewish literature began to flourish on a significant scale. The phenomenon now became bifurcated. On the one hand, there were those writers whose backgrounds were Jewish but who considered themselves to be Polish writers, dealing with specifically Jewish themes only rarely if at all. On the other hand, there were the consciously Jewish writers who made the choice to use Polish as their language of expression. Their point of view was well articulated by one of their number, Stefan Pomer, who wrote in 1933: "Here live and create multitudes of writers . . . who, while making their contributions to the treasury of Polish culture, while enriching and developing it, remain conscious Jews shaping Jewish themes in their works and raising ideas and problems that pervade Jewry. This seemingly imperceptible and abnormal phenomenon is actually strong and normal, and results not only from numerous social and political reasons, but, above all, from the very structure and spirit of the Jewish nation."[6]

Of the interwar writers who saw themselves as primarily part of the central Polish literary tradition, the most important were Bolesław Leśmian, Julian Tuwim, Antoni Słonimski, Józef Wittlin, Aleksander Wat, and Bruno Schulz, a writer who should perhaps be placed in an intermediate position between this group of writers and those who thought of themselves as Jewish writers producing their work in Polish.

The group of consciously Jewish writers did not attain the artistic level of Tuwim or Schulz but emerged as a distinctive presence in the interwar years. Their point of view was well articulated by Roman Brandstaetter, perhaps the

5. R. Dmowski, *Separatyzm Żydów i jego źródła* (Warsaw, 1909), 12.
6. Quoted in E. Prokop-Janiec, *Międzywojenna literatura polsko-żydowska jako zjawisko kulturowe i artystyczne* (Kraków, 1992), 22.

most gifted of their number. In his words: "We express our own Jewish long-
ings in the Polish language, we set the pain of a Jewish heart to the sound of
[Jan] Kochanowski's words for the first time on Polish land, we associate the
words of [Adam] Mickiewicz with the holy words of the Bible. . . . We are a
group that rehabilitates with its output the activity of the renegade [Julian]
Klaczko, which contradicts [Józef] Feldman's ideology [of assimilation] with
existence. . . . The soul of the Polish Jew speaks through us for the first time."[7]

The group, whose leading members were Władysław Szlengel (1914–43),
Maurycy Szymel (1903–42), and Hersz Avrohom Fenster (1908–42), was seen
by some leading Polish critics as a new phenomenon in Polish literature.
Although the authors tried to address their writings to Polish readers in
general, however, their audience was recruited mainly from linguistically acculturated but otherwise unassimilated Jews. Its members—who have been
subject of an extensive study by Eugenia Prokop-Janiec[8]—were mostly not of
the first rank. They favored poetry as their principal medium and in their
works limited themselves to several common motifs: the problem of two moth-
erlands, Poland and Erets Yisrael; Zionist ideology; their relationship to Jewish
history and tradition; and the decay of the shtetl and the transformation of
the Jewish family under the influence of acculturation and secularization.

The Polish-Jewish writers found they had to defend themselves on two
fronts. On the one hand, within the trilingual world of Polish Jewry they were
still a minority, although one that was growing as the linguistic acculturation
of Polish Jewry proceeded rapidly in the interwar period.[9] This phenomenon
was commented on by Adolf Rudnicki in 1938: "The Jewish masses for the
most part speak Polish, this is their everyday language, this is the language
they use to express their emotions."[10] In spite of this, the Polish-Jewish press
and the Polish-Jewish writers had to defend themselves constantly against the
accusation that their choice of Polish, rather than Yiddish or Hebrew, constituted a betrayal of their Jewishness.

The Polish-Jewish writers were also at odds with the principal Polish writers
"of Jewish origin" and above all with their main organ, *Wiadomości Literackie*, the leading literary weekly in Poland throughout the interwar period.
Wiadomości, edited by the Jewish convert Mieczysław Grydzewski
(1894–1970),[11] adopted impeccably liberal and universalist positions. It supported cosmopolitan literary models, strongly opposed integral nationalism
and Catholic intolerance, and backed the Piłsudski coup, although some of its

7. *Opinia* 25 (1933), quoted in E. Prokop-Janiec, "The Sabbath Motif in Interwar Polish
Literature," in *The Jews of Poland between Two World Wars*, ed. Yisrael Gutman, Ezra
Mendelsohn, Jehuda Reinharz, and Chone Shmeruk (Hanover, 1989), 417.

8. See note 6.

9. According to the *Mały Rocznik Statystyczny* of 1921, 750,000 Jews used Polish as their
mother tongue.

10. Adolf Rudnicki, *Lato* (Warsaw, 1959), 116.

11. His name was originally Grycendler.

contributors, including Tuwim and Słonimski expressed their outrage at the violence that accompanied the 1930 election and the treatment meted out to the leaders of the "Centrolew" (center-left) opposition.[12] But though it mocked unsparingly the crudities of the antisemites, *Wiadomości* also castigated the Jews for their "separatism" and attributed many of their problems to the oppression of the "backward rabbinate." The journal was bitterly hostile to Jewish nationalism and to most aspects of Yiddish culture. In 1934–35 a bitter polemic took place between the two concepts of Jewish writing in Polish. Responding to Brandstaetter's attempt to formulate his idea of a "Polish-Jewish literary culture," Słonimski and an associate, Stanisław Rogóż, did not hesitate to describe it as "pathological" and Brandstaetter as a racist and a "Jewish Nazi." The concept of "Jewish culture" was dismissed as typical of chauvinist thinking, whether Polish, German, or Jewish, something that would cut the Jews off from the benefits of the European tradition.

In spite of their hostility to Jewish nationalism, it was this group that was most strongly attacked by Polish nationalists and antisemites. They concentrated their attacks above all on the "Skamander" group, which had emerged as the dominant literary clique in Poland in the optimistic years of the 1920s. As the first generation of writers to come to maturity in an independent Poland, they were eager to throw off the heavy burden of commitment to the Polish cause, which had weighed down literature in the nineteenth century. In the words of one of their members, Jan Lechoń, "And in the spring let me see spring, not Poland."[13] Another, Julian Tuwim, the subject of this essay, put it more sharply: "I don't want tombs, I don't want a sad Orthodox chapel, the lamentations of crows, owls, and other night birds."[14]

Their artistic credo spelled out clearly their optimism and lightheartedness:

> We believe deeply in the present, we feel we are all its children. We understand there is nothing easier than to hate this "today" of ours, not acknowledged by anybody as his own. We do not wish to pretend that evil is non-existent, but our love is stronger than all evil: we love the present with a strong first love. We are and we want to be its children.

---

12. Kazimierz Koźniewski, *Historia co tydzień* (Warsaw, 1976), 43. On the detention of the regime's political opponents in the Brześć fortress, see Antoni Słonimski, "List otwarty do Wacława Sieroszewskiego and J. Kadena-Bandrowskiego," *Robotnik* (December 21, 1930). Słonimski's attitude toward the Piłsudski camp after Brześć is outlined in his memoirs, *Jedna strona medalu: Niektóre felietony, artykuły, recenzje, utwory poważne i niepoważne publikowane w latach, 1918–1968* (Warsaw, 1971). Słonimski also wrote about Brześć in his *Kronika Tygodniowa*. See *Wiadomości Literackie* 1 (January 4, 1931), 5; and 34 (August 23, 1931), 4. Tadeusz Boy-Żeleński, Julian Tuwim, and Kazimierz Wierzyński, among others, expressed their criticisms of Brześć in "Pisarze o Brześciu," *Wiadomości Literackie* 2 (January 11, 1931), 3. See also Juliusz Wirski, "List otwarty," *Robotnik* (December 21, 1930).

13. Jan Lechoń, "Hierostrates" in *Poezje*, selected and introduced by Matylda Wełna (Lublin, 1989), 30.

14. Quoted in J. Ratajczyk, *Julian Tuwim* (Poznań, 1995), 87.

And this day is not only a day of the seven plagues, it is also a day when a new world is being born. That new world has not yet emerged from the earth; its shape is still a guess, but the trembling we feel under our feet proves it is rising already. . . .

We want to be poets of the present and this is our faith and our whole "programme." We are not tempted by sermonizing, we do not want to convert anybody, but we want to conquer, to enrapture, to influence the hearts of men. We want to be their laughing and weeping. . . .

We know that the greatness of art does not appear in subjects, but in the forms through which it is expressed, in that most light and elusive game of colors, of words transforming a rough experience into a work of art. We want to be honest workers in that game, through our efforts hidden under frivolous shapes.[15]

The group included a number of poets and writers, most notably Jan Lechoń, Kazimierz Wierzyński and Jarosław Iwaszkiewicz who were not Jewish. But in the eyes of the right its Jewish character was confirmed by several factors: by the leading role in it of Antoni Słonimski, who, though the son of a socialist and baptized in infancy, had many distinguished Jewish antecedents and regarded himself as a "Jew of antisemitic antecedents"; by the key role played in the propagation of its ideas by *Wiadomości Literackie*; and above all, by the central position in the group of Julian Tuwim. Tuwim, in particular, was a major literary talent and one of the two or three most outstanding Polish poets of the first half of the twentieth century. It may seem paradoxical that the right could tar with the "semitic" brush writers like Lechoń, Iwaszkiewicz, and Wierzyński, but in the eyes of its ideologists, this "guilt by association" was a consequence of the right's inability to expand the definition of "Pole" to include people such as Tuwim and Słonimski. Indeed, as we shall see, it was the right that invented the concept of "artificial Jew" as distinct from "born" Jew to deal with this problem.

Certainly, with his cult of the modern city and its crowds of anonymous people seeking both a living and new diversions—a cult that made him seem most akin to the American poet Walt Whitman—Tuwim embodied more than any of his contemporaries the Skamander aesthetic. He was born into a middle-class Jewish family in the textile town of Łódź and had a remarkable gift for verse, writing not only serious poetry but also verse for cabarets and for children. He was obsessed with verbal coinages and innovative rhymes and expressed in his poetry a sensual love of life and nature. A liberal and a bitter opponent of antisemitism, he savagely castigated the nationalist right, whom he addressed thus in a poem he wrote after the assassination of President

15. Quoted in Czesław Milosz, *The History of Polish Literature* (Berkeley, Calif., 1983), 385–86.

Gabriel Narutowicz in December 1922: "You have a Cross around your necks and a Browning in your pockets."

At the same time, though, he attacked what he described as the "materialism" and "philistinism" of the Jewish bourgeoisie.[16] Yet his sense of identification with the Jews was strong. In 1924 he wrote: "With me the Jewish question lies in my blood; it is a fundamental element in my psyche. It is like a powerful wedge cutting into my view of the world, affecting my deepest personal experiences. . . . For me the "Jewish problem" is a tragedy, in which I myself am one of the anonymous actors. What will be the end of this tragedy and when it will occur, I cannot at present predict."[17] He expressed his Jewish feelings even more clearly in his poem "Jewboy"(*Żydek*).

He sings in the courtyard, clad in rags
A small, poor chap, a crazed Jew.

People drive him away, God has muddled his wits
Ages and exile have confused his tongue

He wails and he dances, weeps and laments
That he is lost, is dependent on alms.

The gent on the first floor looks down on the madman.
Look my poor brother at your sad brother.

How did we come to this? How did we lose ourselves
In this vast world, strange and hostile to us?

You on the first floor, your unhinged brother
With his burning head dances through the world

The first floor gent fancies himself a poet
He wraps up his heart, like a coin, in paper

And throws it out from the window, so that it will break
And be trampled and cease to be

And we will both go on our way
A path sad and crazed

And we will never find peace or rest
Singing Jews, lost Jews.[18]

16. See, for instance, the poems on Jewish themes in Julian Tuwim, *Utwory nieznane ze zbiorów Tomasza Niewodniczałskiego w Bitburgu, Wiersze, Kabaret, Artykuły, Listy*, ed. Tadeusz Januszewski (Łódź, 1999), and those in *Jarmark Rymów* (Warsaw, 1983), especially "Bank."

17. Tuwim, *Utwory nieznane*, 105–6.

18. All poems excerpted in this chapter are from Tuwim's *Dziela*, 5 vols. (Warsaw, 1955). Translations are by the author.

Tuwim was certainly the most bitterly assailed member of the Skamander group. The intellectuals of the right denounced him for "debasing" the Polish language and for his "semitic" sensuality. Thus Józef Mackiewicz, a Vilna journalist, asserted bluntly that Tuwim was not a Polish poet, while the Kraków writer and critic Karol Hubert Rostworowski described him as a "Jewish poet writing in Polish." The right-wing journalist Adolf Nowaczyński referred to him as "Jozue" Tuwim. When a Yiddish translation of a Tuwim poem appeared, *Gazeta Literacka* crowed that Tuwim had finally decided to write in Yiddish. The right-wing literary weekly *Prosto z mostu* abounded in such headlines as "Tuwim and Słonimski Are One Hundred Percent Jews," "A New Center of Masonry Has Been Established in Warsaw," "The Literary Ghetto," and "Jewish Poetry in the Polish Language."[19]

Why was Tuwim such a bête noire for the nationalist right? It is not my intention here to address the question of the general critical reception of Tuwim in Poland, which also raises many complex questions about both Polish cultural life in the twentieth century and the Jewish role in it. Rather I want to set out those elements in Tuwim's creativity which aroused the particular ire of antisemites.

In the first place, they were outraged by his political views. Tuwim's attitude to politics was, above all, emotional and probably never went deeper than a facile sympathy for the common man and a rather simpleminded pacifism that saw war as a result of capitalist machinations. Despite his love for Russian literature, he seems never to have been attracted by communism, at least not before the late 1930s. Indeed, as he himself admitted in an interview with *Robotnik* in 1928, his sympathy with the common man could not even be described as socialist:

> I was born in Łódź, in that city of factory chimneys, where the misery of the conditions of the workers was most apparent. I know the worker and his life. I know how early he has to rise to go to exhausting work and how he returns home in the evening tired and worn out. As a young boy, I witnessed the 1905 revolution in Łódź. To me, what is most important is the awareness of the injury to which people are subjected. . . . Pain, injury, and human misery always arouse the most vigorous response from me. Whether I am writing about a poor clerk, a hunchback, or an old maid, my point of departure is general human sympathy, without any clearly socialist concept.[20]

As he was to write later, "Politics is not my profession. It is a function of my conscience and temperament."[21]

19. For these and other attacks on Tuwim, see Ratajczyk, 102–3.
20. Quoted in Ratajczyk, 82.
21. Quoted in I. Ehrenburg, *Memoirs, 1921–1941* (Cleveland, 1964), 28.

What offended the right which led its adherents to describe Tuwim as a "Judeo-communist" was what Artur Sandauer has described as his attack on "traditional sanctities: private property, the family, the army, maidenly virtue."[22] His poem "To the Common Man" (*Do Prostego Człowieka*), in which he expressed his pacifist views, led the right-wing poet Jerzy Pietrkiewicz to call for him to be tried for treason.

> When they begin to plaster the walls
> With freshly printed proclamations,
> When black print sounds alarm
> Calling "To the People" and "To Soldiers"
> And ruffians and adolescents
> Are taken in by their recurring lies
> And believe that you should start firing cannons
> Murder, poison, burn and plunder . . .
> It means that somewhere they have struck oil
> Which will bring them riches;
> That something has gone wrong in the banks they own
> That they scent cash somewhere
> Or that those bloated rascals have now thought up
> A higher duty on cotton.
> Throw down your rifle on the pavement!
> The blood is yours, and the oil theirs!
> And from one capital city to another
> Cry out in defense of your hard-earned bread:
> "Gentlemen—peddle your lies somewhere else!"

Similar offense was caused by his poems "To the Generals" (*Do generałów*), "Litany," "Quatorze juillet," and "The Funeral of President Narutowicz" (*Pogrzeb Prezydenta Natutowicza*). In "To the Generals," he wrote:

> They scowl, menace, threateningly raise their eyebrows
> These former Generals, covered with stars.
> —Gentlemen! Stop pretending to be lions!
> You should know finally that now—we,
> Thoughtful passersby
> We are the Generals here! . . .
>
> None of you has risen
> To the rank of—Free Poet!
> I gentleman have power, indeed I do!
> —The whole world belongs to me!

22. Artur Sandauer, *O sytuacji pisarza polskiego pochodzenia żydowskiego w XX wieku* (Warsaw, 1982), 27.

Tuwim reveled in the attacks on him, seeing himself as the scourge of the nationalist right. As he put it in one of his poems:

> History gave a crash—and there jumped out
> From his alchemist's retort
> Rubbing his eyes in astonishment
> The poet—very political

In his "Request for a Song" (*Prośba o piosenkę*), he wrote:

> If, O God, I have Thy splendid gift, the Word,
> Cause my heart to beat with the wrath of oceans;
> Give me the ancient poets' noble sword,
> To strike at the tyrants with raging emotions.

He turned his scorn on his detractors in a series of deadly ripostes. This is one of his responses to the nationalist critic Stanisław Pieńkowski:

> Spitting poison and froth from his mouth
> He spits, snorts and splutters
> And writes that I am a butcher
> A yid and bolshevik
> Jewboy, bacillus
> A baboon and a Skamandrite
> That I sell out the Fatherland
> That I deform the Polish language
> That I provoke and profane
> And the Devil knows what else.
>
> And to think that from all
> The fine activity
> Of this gentleman—from the spittle
> Wheezing, screaming, scribbling,
> Spewing, kicking and wailing
> On which he has lost half his life
> From the books and articles
> From the words, sentences and titles
> From the reviews, from the sneering paragraphs
> In a word from that whole
> Journalistic mess
> Will remain . . . one poem
> And that will be—mine, not his.

Indeed *this* very poem ... O stern revenge
Inspired by a Jewish God.
Here is a phrase, a few words with which I toy
To immortalize my enemy.

He could be equally devastating in his attacks on conventional pieties, as in his poem "Protest," written shortly after the May coup:

About this Poland, about our Fatherland
Most painfully afflicted
(O Thou Merciful God,
What will happen, O Our Lady?)
Seeing her appallingly shamed,
Alarmed about her fate
Thinking of those who suffered for her in the *tajga*
Those exiled in Siberia and in the heavens;
And those Bards, those Prophets
Who sang of her in their poems,
And those children who in Września
And that Drzymała, and so on;
And that Silesia, and our own access
And because miasma are constantly
Poisoning us from the East.
And because the Spirit of the Nation is dying;
And because of the passivity, and especially
Because of the revolutionary elements
Who are thoroughly depraved,
Because of the wearing of low-cut dresses;
Because respect for order is dying
And not words but action is needed
(O Thou Merciful God!
Look down, Kościuszko on us from Heaven!)
And the destructive party spirit
And these personal governments
And the lack of respect
Also in relation to the Pastoral Letter;
Moreover that there is blasphemy
And those who perpetrate it are undiscovered
That the Sanacja runs wild,
A disgrace—bandits.
—Because of all these conditions and reasons
(What will happen, O Our Lady!)
All we who append our signatures

Solemnly protest:
[there follows a grotesque list of names and places full of puns that
defy translation].[23]

Tuwim, who like Słonimski believed that the the antisemitic right was essentially ridiculous, was convinced that the best way to deal with it was through
mockery. Słonimski imagined a special Endek autonomous area, where Endek
principles could be implemented but where a few token Jews would have to
be allowed in so that the inhabitants could satisfy their antisemitic urges.
Słonimski's 1933 play *Rodzina* (Family) revolves around two brothers, both
fervent exponents of totalitarian ideologies, one a racist and fascist, the other
a communist; at the climax they both confront the fact that they are in reality
the sons of a prosperous Jewish miller! The belief that scorn was the way to
undermine antisemitism proved politically naive, however, underestimating the
danger of a phenomenon that neither author was able to take seriously, given
the obvious absurdity and stupidity of most of its exponents.

The right was also shocked by Tuwim's open exaltation of physicality and
sexuality. Tuwim was, above all, a sensual poet. He gloried in the depiction
of nature, described his poetic creativity in almost physical terms, and vividly
depicted the joys of sexual love (he even wrote a poem describing sexual
union). In his poem "Spring—a Dithyramb" (*Wiosna*), written in 1915 and
published in 1918 in the student magazine *Pro Arte et Studio* (a poem that
owes a great deal to both Whitman and to Rimbaud), and above all in his
"Paris s'eveille," Tuwim gave fervent, if ironic, expression to this sense of physicality. This poem with its exaltation of the physical world and of sexuality
was the first to draw attention to Tuwim and to make him the bête noire of
the nationalist and Catholic right. They took literally this basically ironic
hymn to the lustful emotions provoked by spring in the city. Read in this way,
the poem was certainly shocking. As its opening two stanzas show:

Today they praise the Mass
The Crowd is praised
And the City.

23. Ładwinowicz z Czerbichowa,
Kłyś z Podwodzisk, Szurguń z Wierpska,
Z Białych Mogił Hacelkowa
I z Czerwiny Kwasisierpska.
Antałkowski z Dobrogajców
Cudak z Żółczki, Płantaś z Wiezbian
Dymba z Rykwi, Frynd z Murajców
I Kordulec z Górnych Świerzbian.
Dułdujewicz z Malgocina,
Rańcuchowski z Księżych Skalek
Ksiądz Kapucha z Węgorzyna
I Buchajski z Odrzygałek

In the squares they kindle pyres
And a throng pours out on to the streets,
They crawl out of their corners, they dash out of their lairs
To celebrate spring in the city,
To celebrate the lustful holiday.
And they praise You,
With your belly above broad loins
Woman!

It rocks—it bursts forth—and it flows—
Little feet shuffle on the ground, hips rock,
Noise, noise, noise, giggling,
Noise, noise, noise, squealing,
Polished mouths joke,
The countless, gaudy mob pours out,
Little feet shuffle, hips rock
Shuffle, shuffle, shuffle, noise, noise, noise
Thousands of unrestrained couples glide
—and further! Further! Further!
To the dark greenery, to the alleys,
On a bench, you rascals, on the grass,
Create little brats for Poland,
Writhe, you rascals, writhe,
Drink in corner bars,
Discard more of those 'bachelors' illnesses'!
O! Later they will writhe with shame,
Those factory tarts, those big-bellied mares,
Those deformed kids, those lustful trollops!
Violate them! Let all partake of a meal
In your colored shirts
And your paper collars!
Crowd, be savage!
Crowd! RIGHT is on your side!!!

This poem was certainly provocative in the somewhat puritan atmosphere of a Poland about to achieve its long-desired independence. *Myśl Narodowa* asserted that far from condemning debauchery, the verses extolled it and, in addition, praised those things which "Henryk Sienkiewicz condemned in literature as rutting and bestialization." Another right-wing weekly, *Goniec*, described the poem as made up of "the sewage of pornographic and debauched experiences, full of depictions of licentiousness and sadism." Father Marian Pirożyński drew attention to the Jewish character of this provocation: "Julian Tuwim who has been widely touted as the poet who will revitalize [Polish] poetry . . . has placed himself on a footing of equality with the Lord God. In this there is no lack of racial insolence. It is no accident that this sort of poet also involves himself with Satanism."[24]

The aesthetic of the Skamander was not particularly radical; in fact, the group was regarded by the exponents of modern poetry in Poland as excessively conservative. But what marked it above all was its desire to appeal to a wider audience, "to bring poetry to the street." Tuwim in particular wrote extensively for the cabaret, and his desire to bridge the gap between high and popular culture was deeply suspect to the right, brought up on the concept of the poet as Prophet (*Wieszcz*) expounding weighty truths to the Nation.

Finally the right saw this poet as a blasphemer. Tuwim seems to have been a pantheist, believing in an immanent force in nature. Like a number of Jewish artists at this time, he was also attracted by the personality of Jesus, whom he may have seen as a Jewish figure. An early poem, "Manifesto" (1914), describing his pantheon, culminates in the line "A rosebud dawn spoke to me—Christ."

That Christ figured in a number of poems in Tuwim's first collection, *Czyhanie na Boga* (In wait for God), served merely to provoke the nationalist right, whose members saw it as another example of "Jewish insolence"—particularly one poem in which Jesus addresses God, explaining that he will not complain of the sufferings he has to undergo, provided only that God "soon, in a miracle, makes the good, quiet people understand me." In another poem, "The Christ of the City," the only person to recognize Jesus is Mary Magdalen.

Tuwim was not above using religious and Christian language in a new and deliberately shocking way. The first section of "The Word and the Flesh" reads:

And the Word was made flesh
And it has dwelt among us,
I feed the starving body
With words as if they were fruit;
I drink the words with my mouth,
Swallow them like cold water,
I breathe them like young leaves,
I grind them with sweet odors

The word is wine and honey,
The word is meat and bread
It is the word that guides my eye
Along the starry sky.
O joy of the sacred gift,
O eternal fondness
O Lord, grant me today
My common word!

24. Quoted in Ratajczyk, 35.

Artur Sandauer has argued that Tuwim seems to have responded to his "demonization" by opponents with "self-demonization"[25]—possibly the origin of his fascination with the devil, who appears in many of his poems, as Father Pirożyński noted. The obsession was strengthened by the large strawberry mark he had on his face, which contributed to his sense of being an outsider and which he sometimes referred to as a consequence of an encounter with the Devil.

Tuwim seemed to embody everything the right hated about the intellectual culture of the big city. In opposition to the literary aesthetic of the Skamander group and also of the Modernists in Poland, rightist literary ideologues called for an art that would stress national, Catholic, and rural values and would sustain group solidarity. They admired in an uncritical way the great Polish romantic poets, such as Mickiewicz and Słowacki, whose work they effectively bowdlerized. Among more recent writers they favored Sienkiewicz and, to a lesser extent, Reymont. They admired above all the poetry of Jan Kasprowicz, a metaphysical and nature poet of peasant origins whose later work had a strongly Catholic character.

The only other figure in the 1920s who was subjected to the sort of vilification meted out to Tuwim was Tadeusz Boy-Żeleński, who had already made his reputation in Kraków before the First World War as a translator and as the *spiritus movens* of the *Zielony Balonik* cabaret.[26] There were many similarities bewtween Boy and Tuwim. Boy campaigned for an improvement in the status of women in Polish society, calling for civil marriage and divorce, easy access to contraceptive methods, and legal abortion. Like Tuwim, he was a bitter foe of ethnic nationalism and provincialism, which he mocked mercilessly, and he welcomed the May coup as the only way to bar the Catholic and nationalist right from achieving power. As he wrote shortly after the coup to the women's rights activist Helena Staniewska, "You have no idea of the extent to which, since the May coup, and despite everything that was painful and tragic in the event, the air has become easier to breathe; this must be a sign that something is changing for the better."[27] Boy also rejected the

25. Sandauer, 28.

26. In the large literature on Boy, I am particularly indebted to chapter 5 of the University of Toronto 2001 doctoral thesis of Eva Plach, "'The Clash of Moral Nations': *Imponderabilia* in the Second Polish Republic, 1926–1935." See also Tadeusz Bereza, "Formajca Boya," *Nowa Kultura* 51–52 (1951); Zofia Starowiejska-Morstinowa, "Zagadnienie Boya," *Tygodnik Powszechny* 22 (January 13, 1952): 7–9. For a review of articles written about Boy in the 1950s, see Mirosława Dołęgowska-Wysocka, *Poboyowisko* (Warsaw, 1992), 71–152. See also Andrzej Stawar, *Tadeusz Żeleński (Boy)* (Warsaw, 1958); Stanisław Sterkowicz, *Tadeusz Boy-Żeleński: Lekarz-pisarz-społecznik* (Warsaw, 1959; reprint 1974); Andrzej Makowiecki, *Tadeusz Żeleński (Boy)* (Warsaw 1974); and Wojciech Natanson, *Boy-Żeleński: Opowieść biograficzna* (Warsaw, 1977).

27. Biblioteka Narodowa, Pałac Krasińskich, Listy Boya do M. H. Staniewskich, File III 11.143, 31: letter dated June 16, 1926, quoted in Plach, 276. A fragment of Boy's letter to Staniewska is reprinted in Barbara Winklowa, *Tadeusz Żeleński (Boy): Tworczość i życie* (Warsaw, 1967), 214–15, and in *Tadeusz Żeleński (Boy): Listy*, ed. Barbara Winklowa (Warsaw, 1972),

filiopietistic way in which the great literary figures of the past, above all the Romantic poets such as Mickiewicz and Słowacki, were treated in Polish life. And he too was closely associated with *Wiadomości Literackie*, where he published many of his most controversial pieces, some of which were subsequently reprinted in book form; these included *Dziewice Konsystorskie* (1929), *Piekło kobiet* (1929), and *Jak skończyć z piekłem kobiet* (1930), which attacked clerical hypocrisy on divorce and defended a woman's right to birth control and safe and legal abortion. *Nasi okupanci* generalized the attack against the clericalism which in Boy's view prevented the adoption of sensible policies in these matters. In his *Brązownicy* (1929) he sought to dispel the aura with which patriotic mythmakers had surrounded Mickiewicz. Boy also attempted to put his views into practice: he was one of the founders of Poland's first family planning clinic in 1929, and he helped to establish the journal *Życie Świadome* in 1932, which was devoted to exploring family planning, "free love," and eugenics.

Like Tuwim, Boy mercilessly derided his critics, describing himself as "the anti-Christ . . . under the pseudonym Boy."[28] In a letter to one of his detractors he admitted that he became "nervous" when he failed to arouse passionate response in others: "I begin to fear . . . that I am no longer necessary for the nation. . . . This is my role—to be an antidote to your charming lies."[29]

The attacks on Boy were similar in character to those on Tuwim. Thus Adolf Nowaczyński denounced Boy as a "slum intellectual" who deliberately turned his back on "the Nation" and made himself an "apologist for sexual prostitution."[30] The Catholic and nationalist publicist Czesław Lechicki, editor of a volume in which many earlier newspaper articles condemning Boy were reprinted, wrote that Boy's goal was to replace "family life with herd life and Christian morality with the morality of the brothel."[31] According to Mieczysław Piszczkowski, Boy's "catechism of pansexualism" enjoyed support only because of the persistence of the atmosphere of "moral hypocrisy" which had prevailed under the partitions.[32] Boy's critics claimed that his views, like

---

250–51. The same quotation is also used in J. Hen, *Błazen—wielki mąż; opowieść o Tadeusza Boyu-Żeleńskim* (Warsaw, 1998), 196, and in Barbara Winklowa, *Nad Wisłą i na Sekwaną: Biografia Tadeusza Boya-Żeleńskiego* (Warsaw, 1998), 121.

28. Boy, preface to *Nasi Okupanci*, as quoted in Dołęgowska-Wysocka, *Poboyowisko*, 51.

29. Boy to Izabela Moszczeńska, dated October 12, 1928, as reprinted in Boy, *Listy*, 277. The letter is also reprinted in Tadeusz Żeleński (Boy), *Pisma*, vol. 16, *Felietony* (Warsaw, 1958), 327–31.

30. Nowaczyński, "Boyszewizm" in *Prawda o Boyu-Żeleńskim: Głosy krytyczne*, ed. Czesław Lechicki (Warsaw, 1933), 110–11, 115. For a similar view that Boy popularized base tastes and appealed to the lowest common denominator, see Jerzy Braun, "Atakujemy Boya," in Lechicki, *Prawda o Boyu-Żeleńskim*, 5; reprint from *Zet* 16–17 (November 15, 1932).

31. Czesław Lechicki, *W walce z demoralizacją: Szkice literacko-społeczne*, vol. 1 (Miejsce piastowe, 1932), 65.

32. Mieczysław Piszczkowski, "Krytyka obyczajowości współczesnej," *Myśl Narodowa* 54 (November 22, 1931), 316. The term "pansexualism" is also used by Lechicki in "Wstęp," *Prawda o Boyu-Żeleńskim*, xxxvii.

those of Tuwim, were particularly attractive to women. In Piszczkowki's judgment, since they lacked men's "self-control," women's minds had been "upset by the war, which makes them vulnerable to Boy's argument that abortion and divorce are the eighth heaven of Mohammed."[33] According to the editor of the Christian Democratic *Głos Narodu*, the typical female supporter of Boy (*kobieta boyowska*) "is a bitch and only a bitch. Her purpose is . . . to satisfy sexual appetite."[34] The accusation of "sexual depravity," as we have seen, was also applied to Tuwim and to *Wiadomości Literackie* as a whole. Thus Father Charczewski referred to the weekly as *Wiadomości Literacko-ginekologiczne*, and Lechicki called it *Wiadomości Ginekologiczno-weneryczne* to underline its obsession with matters of sex.[35]

The fact that Boy was not Jewish did not prevent his opponents from ascribing to him a Jewish origin. According to Lechicki, Boy's mother was a Frankist (follower of an eighteenth-century Jewish mystic).[36] Kazimierz Morawski, writing in *Pregląd Katolicki*, described Boy as an "artificial Jew," a category distinct from and even more dangerous than a "born Jew."[37] An anonymous writer described Boy's writings as pervaded by *wolnomyśliciestwo Nalewkowskie* (Nalewki-style freethinking), in an allusion to the main street of Warsaw's Jewish district.[38]

The literary polemics I have described here were, above all, a feature of the 1920s. Tuwim's optimistic belief that chauvinism and antisemitism could be dispelled by mockery was shared by the other members of the Skamander group. Tuwim was also seen as a bridge between Jews and Poles. Kazimierz Wierzyński has recounted a conversation with Tuwim: "The Orthodox Cathedral on Saxon Square was still standing when one winter night, as we were returning from the 'Picador' cabaret by our usual roundabout way, we sat down on its snowy steps and Tuwim burst out into tears. I told him that he was the Polish Heine and that he would help to give the Jews new significance in Poland and would help bridge the deep divide."[39] Indeed, one might wonder whether the rather naive optimism of the Skamandrites and their belief that the antisemites were common, ignorant, and, above all, ridiculous did not perhaps lead to their underestimation of the danger from the radical right in

33. Piszczkowski, 316.

34. W. Z. [Father Jan Piwowarczyk], "Przeciw poniżeniu macierzyństwa," in Lechicki, *Prawda o Boyu-Żeleńskim*, 155.

35. Father Charczewski, as quoted in Dołęgowska-Wysocka, *Poboyowisko*, 64 and Czesław Lechicki, *W walce z demoralizacją: Szkice literacko-społeczne*, vol. 2 (Miejsce piastowe, 1933), 554 (Lechicki used *Gynecological-Venereal News* as the subtitle of a section of the appendix in vol. 2).

36. Lechicki, *Boy-Żeleński we wklęsłem zwierciadle* (Lwów, 1933), 10–11, 87; Lechicki, "Wstęp," in *Prawda o Boyu-Żeleńskim*, x–xi; and Świecki, "Pamflet antyklerykalny," in Lechicki, *Prawda o Boyu-Żeleńskim*, 168; reprinted from *Gazeta Kościelna* 40 (1932).

37. Morawski, "Na marginesie polemiki z Boyem" in Lechicki, *Prawda o Boyu-Żeleńskim*, 29, reprint from *Przegląd Katolicki* 3 (1929).

38. Anon., "Zielony balonik," *Myśl Narodowa* 8 (February 24, 1929), 123.

39. Quoted in Ratajczyk, 111.

Poland. In other words, Tuwim's provocations may well have sown an anti-semitic whirlwind.

The atmosphere was much more threatening in the 1930s; with Nazism and Stalinism on Poland's borders, intensifying antisemitism in Poland led to a significant lowering of the the the temperature of the dispute between the two groups of "Jewish" writers. As Mieczysław Braun, a prominent Polish-Jewish writer and journalist, wrote in an article "*Wiadomości Literackie* under Fire," published in *Nasz Przegląd* in late 1937, the antisemitic attacks on the journal "are an indication that we are faced with a tremendous conflagration, one which threatens not only Grydzewski's acolytes."[40] Tuwim felt this change of atmosphere very painfully. He identified strongly with the urban ordinary man, yet in Poland the very petit bourgeois element for whom he wished to produce was strongly affected by antisemitism. "I am going down, it is very difficult, it is awful for me in this country," he wrote in the 1930s, and on another occasion, "It is difficult to be a stepson with a stepmother."[41]

He responded by writing *Bal w Operze*, one of the most remarkable of the apocalyptic visions produced in the doom-laden years leading up to the outbreak of the Second World War, though because of its strongly antigovernment and possibly blasphemous character, it could not be published in full until after the war. "A Ball at the Opera" is a savage description of a corrupt fascist dictatorship, written by an individual in despair. Unlike some other Polish "catastrophist" writers of the 1930s, such as Konstanty Ildefons Gałczyński and Stanisław Witkiewicz, Tuwim clearly situates this fascist dystopia in Poland. This was the last significant poem that he wrote before the outbreak of the war; only after the Polish defeat and his arrival in Brazil in August 1940 did poetic inspiration return, in spite of his sense of guilt at being in such an idyllic spot at such a tragic time. He explained the end of his creative block in a letter to his sister: "How do I explain, dear Irena, that in Poland in the past five years I was able to write practically nothing whereas here I have been writing non-stop. I think that (1) the atmosphere in Poland was so unbearable that it seeped into my subconscious and blocked my "poetic orifices" [and] (2) that here—I feel compelled to rebuild in some measure that unbearable but, above all, most beloved Poland."[42]

From today's perspective the cultural conflicts of the 1920s are part of a wider dispute, which has continued until today, between two visions of Poland: one pluralistic, outward-looking, and European; the other nativist and hostile to foreign influences, identifying Polishness narrowly with Catholicism and the tradition of Poland as a victim and martyr. From this standpoint the antisemitism of Tuwim's critics seems like one of those elements in nature which

40. M. Braun, "*Wiadomości Literackie* w ogniu," *Nasz Przegląd* 267 (1937), quoted in Prokop-Janiec, *Międzywojenna literatura*, 114.
41. Quoted in Ratajczyk, 95, 96.
42. Quoted in Ratajczyk, 115.

can exist only in combination with others. It was part of an integralist and Catholic nationalist view of Polish society and culture which it saw as profoundly threatened by the cosmopolitanism, irony, sophistication, and eclecticism of those whose literary works seemed to set the tone for cultural life in the newly independent Poland. Thus it was perfectly natural for the exponents of such a view to attack the "born Jew" Tuwim, who was masquerading as a Pole, along with the "artificial Jew" Boy-Żeleński, the exponent of "Nalewki-ite" views, who had become "Jewish" by osmosis. This conflict is, of course, still with us, and its outcome will determine the place of Poland in the world of the twenty-first century.

10

Gender and Antisemitism in Wartime Soviet Exile

KATHERINE R. JOLLUCK

T his chapter focuses on a discrete experience of the Polish nation during the Second World War: the exile of Polish citizens to the interior of the USSR after the Red Army invasion of September 1939. This was a time when the Polish nation, its independent state once again obliterated by its enemies, faced a threat to its continued existence. The crucible of war typically provides an opportunity, even necessity, for testing, developing, and articulating national identity; in the Polish case, its preservation became both the goal and a means for survival. This episode of Polish wartime history also produced unique sources that enable us to examine the attitudes of a cross-section of ethnic Polish society toward the Jews. The testimonies of women are especially fruitful: charged with maintaining national identity and culture in times of crisis, Polish women are particularly expressive about the struggles they faced and their efforts to overcome them. Additionally, in their discussions they focus on the behavior and character of women as indicators of national difference.

My investigation proceeds from the assumptions of recent scholarship on nationalism: namely, that national identity is an invented category, highly

Some of the material for this article is taken from *Exile and Identity: Polish Women in the Soviet Union during World War II*, by Katherine R. Jolluck, © 2002 by University of Pittsburgh Press. Reprinted by permission of the University of Pittsburgh Press. Special thanks to Norman Naimark for his comments and suggestions.

dependent on the creation of "others" for its definition.[1] There has also been considerable recent research into the role of gender in the construction of national identity and of stereotypes of "others," who are frequently defined in terms of perceived deviations from sexually based social norms.[2] Such analysis, however, has rarely been applied to the phenomenon of antisemitism in Poland or elsewhere.[3] I seek to do just that, examining the role of gender in Polish depictions of Jews in the calamity of wartime exile and asking whether gender-based differences exist in the articulation or reception of antisemitic stereotypes. Do men and women present their national "enemies" differently? Do the targets of such hostility experience it in different ways, depending on their sex?

Background and Sources

The Molotov-Ribbentrop Pact, signed on August 23, 1939, provided for the partitioning of Poland between its two powerful neighbors, Nazi Germany and the Soviet Union. The Wehrmacht invaded Poland from the west on September 1, quickly defeating attempts at national self-defense, and the Red Army entered from the east on September 17. After a period of initial chaos, Soviet authorities set out to institute their own order in the occupied area, which was quickly annexed. The process of Sovietization included the elimination of elements of society deemed hostile—or potentially so—to the communist regime. Immediately after the invasion, NKVD officials began arresting those consid-

---

1. The classic works on this topic include Ernest Gellner, *Nations and Nationalism* (Oxford, 1983); E. J. Hobsbawm, *Nations and Nationalism since 1780: Programme, Myth, Reality* (Cambridge, U.K., 1990); Benedict Anderson, *Imagined Communities: Reflections on the Origin and Spread of Nationalism* (London, 1991). On the construction of Polish national identity, see Brian Porter, *When Nationalism Began to Hate: Imagining Modern Politics in Nineteenth-Century Poland* (New York, 2000); and Miroslav Hroch, "From National Movement to the Fully-Formed Nation: The Nation-Building Process in Europe," in *Becoming National: A Reader*, ed. Geoff Eley and Ronald Suny (New York, 1996), 60–77. For a study of the evolution of Polish antisemitic myths, see Aleksander Hertz, *The Jews in Polish Culture*, trans. Richard Lourie (Evanston, Ill., 1988).

2. See, for example, *Woman-Nation-State*, ed. Nira Yuval-Davis and Floya Anthias (London, 1989); and *Nationalisms and Sexualities*, ed. Andrew Parker et al. (New York, 1992).

3. The most attention to the issue can be found in the growing literature on gender and the Holocaust. See, for example, *Different Voices: Women and the Holocaust*, ed. Carol Rittner and John Roth (New York, 1993); and *Women in the Holocaust*, ed. Dalia Ofer and Lenore Weitzman (New Haven, 1998). For more on gender and antisemitism, see Judith Friedlander, "The Anti-Semite and the Second Sex: A Cultural Reading of Sartre and Beauvoir," in *Women in Culture and Politics: A Century of Change*, ed. Judith Friedlander et al. (Bloomington, Ind., 1986), 81–96; Laura Engelstein, "Sex and the Anti-Semite: Vasilii Rozanov's Patriarchal Eroticism," in *The Keys to Happiness: Sex and the Search for Modernity in Fin-de-Siècle Russia* (Ithaca, N.Y., 1992), 299–333; Sander Gilman, *The Jew's Body* (New York, 1991). For a rare discussion of gender and Polish views of Jews, see Bożena Umińska, *Postać z cieniem: Portrety Żydówek w polskiej literaturze od końca XIX wieku do 1939 roku* (Warsaw, 2001).

ered "enemies of the people": army officers and reservists, government officials, social and cultural leaders. The thousands of individuals who tried to flee
the Soviet occupation, often only to the other side of Poland, ended up in
Soviet prisons, as did many who joined the developing underground resistance.

Early in 1940, Soviet officials started removing the families of arrested
persons and others considered "socially harmful" elements. These included
individuals whose social origins, occupation, or relationships to other Polish
citizens rendered them suspicious: landowners, military colonists (*osadnicy*),
civil servants, police officers, forest workers, small farmers, tradespeople,
refugees from western Poland, and relatives of individuals who had fled
abroad, gone into hiding, or been interned during the fighting. Beginning in
February 1940 these persons, often entire families, were loaded into train
cars and transported deep into the Soviet Union. Not charged with any crime,
they were removed from their homes by decree and designated "special settlers," "administratively exiled," or "exiled settlers." Throughout this chapter
I refer to them as "deportees," as opposed to "prisoners," who ended up in
Soviet prisons and labor camps; the term "exiles" denotes both groups as a
whole.

The total number of exiles is now a matter of dispute; currently, it is possible to give only minimum and maximum figures. The number of arrested
persons (prisoners) lies between 100,000 and 250,000, 8 to 10 percent of
whom were women.[4] The low estimate of civilian deportees is approximately
320,000; traditional estimates place their number at nearly one million.[5] In
contrast to the prisoners, most deportees were women and children. Though
the deportations primarily targeted ethnic Poles, Polish citizens of other
nationalities were also arrested and deported, suffering similar maltreatment
and deprivation. Ethnic Poles made up approximately 60 percent of the dis-

4. For high estimates of the number of persons arrested, see Hoover Institution Archives (hereafter HIA), Władysław Anders Collection (hereafter AC), Box 68, No. 62c, Bohdan Podoski,
"Polskie Wschodnie w 1939–1940," 29; Bronisław Kuśnierz, *Stalin and the Poles: An Indictment
of the Soviet Leaders* (London, 1949), 80. For low estimates, see Krzysztof Jasiewicz, "Obywa-
tele Polscy aresztowani na terytorium tzw. zachodniej Białorusi w latach 1939–1941 w świetle
dokumentacji NKWD/KGB," *Kwartalnik Historyczny* 101, no. 1 (1994): 125–30; Albin
Głowacki, "Organizacja i funkcjonowanie więziennictwa NKWD na Kresach Wschodnich II
Rzeczypospolitej w latach 1939–1941," in *Zbrodnicza ewakuacja więzień i aresztów NKWD na
kresach wschodnich II Rzeczypospolitej w czerwcu-lipcu 1941 roku* (Warsaw, 1997), 39.
5. For early estimates, see Władysław Wielhorski, *Los Polaków w niewoli sowieckiej
(1939–1956)* (London, 1956), 11–15; Kuśnierz, 80. For revised estimates, see Albin Głowacki,
"Widmo Berii w statystyce," *Polityka* 6 (February 5, 1994); Aleksander Gurjanow, "Cztery deportacje 1940–41," *Karta* 12 (1994): 114–36. For challenges to the revised figures, see "Sprawozdanie z dyskusji dotyczącej liczby obywateli polskich wywięzionych do Związku Sowieckiego w
latach 1939–1941," *Studia z dziejów Rosji i Europy Środkowo-Wschodniej* 31 (1996): 117–48;
Małgorzata Giżejewska, "Deportacje obywateli polskich z ziem północno-wschodnich II Rzeczypospolitej w latach 1939–1941," in *Studia z dziejów okupacji Sowieckiej (1939–1941): Obywa-
tele polscy na kresach północno-wschodnich II Rzeczypospolitej pod okupacją sowiecką w latach
1939–1941*, ed. Tomasz Strzembosz (Warsaw, 1997), 87–88.

located population, and Jews 20 percent.[6] Many Jews deported to the USSR came from the western part of Poland, which fell under Nazi occupation. Tens of thousands of Jews had fled eastward to avoid the Germans, only to find life under the Soviets too difficult to bear. In the spring of 1940, many of them applied for repatriation to their homes in the German zone but soon found themselves on trains headed eastward, as the Soviets considered their registration to leave an act of disloyalty to the new regime. They ended up, along with ethnic Poles, in deportation settlements and collective farms in Siberia, Central Asia, or the Arctic region of the USSR. Assuring the exiles that they would never leave Soviet territory, the authorities taunted them with the phrase, "Your grave is here."

Even Stalin did not foresee the surprise attack on the USSR by the Germans in June 1941. The debacle that followed "Barbarossa" forced his government to sign an agreement with the Polish government-in-exile, located in London, which provided for the release of Polish citizens from their places of detention. The Sikorski-Maiskii Pact of July 30, 1941 also called for the creation of a Polish army under General Władysław Anders, from among the "amnestied" Polish citizens, to help fight the Germans. In 1942 this army succeeded in evacuating 115,000 of the exiles across the Caspian Sea to Iran. The evacuees included members of the military, their families, and orphans. Ethnic Poles were favored by both Polish and Soviet authorities in determining whom to include on the transports: Jews represented 5 percent of the evacuated military personnel and 7 percent of the civilians—a total of 6,570 individuals.[7] After brief stays in Pahlevi and Teheran, many of these Jews moved on to Palestine.

The Anders army immediately asked the evacuees to write about their experiences under the Soviet regime and collected roughly thirty thousand handwritten documents. Some individuals responded to questionnaires; others wrote free-form memoirs from several pages to several hundred pages long. They contain a wealth of detail and description, as well as emotional outpourings. One might wonder whether the Poles felt free to express their feelings about such subjects as the national minorities. But the orders given to the authorities overseeing the documentation process, stating that the authors should be encouraged to write freely and expansively of their ordeals, are reflected in the content of the testimonies, particularly in regard to Jews.

6. Zbigniew Siemaszko, "The Mass Deportations of the Polish Population to the USSR, 1940–41," in *The Soviet Takeover of the Polish Eastern Provinces, 1939–41*, ed. Keith Sword (London, 1991), 231. The exact percentages are 58 and 19, respectively. According to recent research on the deportees based on NKVD documents, 63 percent were Poles and 22 percent Jews: Grzegorz Hryciuk, "Deportacje ludności Polskiej," in *Masowe deportacje radzieckie w okresie II wojny światowej*, 2d ed., ed. S. Ciesielski, G. Hryciuk, and A. Srebrakowski. (Wrocław, 1994), 68.

7. Joanna Hanson, "Questionnaire and Protocols," in *Jews in Eastern Poland and the USSR, 1939–46*, ed. Norman Davies and Antony Polonsky (New York, 1991), 301.

Indeed, members of the Bureau of Documents of the Polish Army in the East, formed to prepare the statements for use with the Allies in an expected peace conference, later quarreled over whether to use the testimonies as written or to edit out prejudiced sentiments that could harm the Polish case. One bureau member noted: "There is not a single statement in which one could not find at least one episode, paragraph, or sentence containing antisemitic or anti-Ukrainian sentiments, or describing how some segments of our population took the side of the Reds in October 1939."[8] The original documents, which I used for this research, often contain marks indicating sentences to be omitted in typed versions. The authorities' uneasiness with some of the sentiments contained in the documents suggests that the authors did not restrain themselves.[9]

These sources are especially valuable for the ground-level view of Polish nationalism that they offer. In particular, they provide a unique window on the way Polish women related to their nation. Elite women are well represented among the authors, and they offer the most eloquent and lengthy accounts of their lives in exile, but individuals of all social classes were included on the eastbound transports: wives and daughters of army officers and policemen, village schoolteachers, artisans, lawyers, clerks, midwives, homemakers, and peasants. The documents reflect the varied background and levels of education. Some are semiliterate, full of grammatical mistakes; others were apparently dictated by individuals unable to write. Some testimonies are written in stream of consciousness and some as emotional laments; others are well-organized, articulate memoirs. Such sources offer insight into how Poles viewed their Jewish neighbors, especially the threats they perceived to their own national identity and unity. Focusing on women from varied walks of life can expand our understanding of modern Polish antisemitism, which has been studied mostly from the perspective of elites and males. Like all stereotypes, Polish antisemitic ones tell us more about their holders than about their objects. The fears and needs of the Poles played a paramount role in determining their depiction of their adversaries.

Polish Views of Jews

Polish women did not unanimously express anti-Jewish views. Of the statements I examined that discussed the Jews at all, 15 percent contained positive and 18 percent neutral assessments of them. Still, the majority, 67 percent, did

8. AC, Box 76, Akta Wewnętrzna Biura Dokumentów, "Notatka Służbowe" 080543, May 8, 1943.

9. Jan Gross makes the same argument regarding the reliability of the sources: Jan Gross, *Revolution from Abroad: The Soviet Conquest of Poland's Western Ukraine and Western Belorussia* (Princeton, 1988), xviii–xx.

present negative or hostile depictions of the Jews.[10] Most of the comments by Polish women refer specifically to Jewish women. The practical explanation for this lies in the fact that their communities in exile were largely composed of women: prison cells, camp barracks, and labor brigades tended to be segregated by gender, and groups of deportees were overwhelmingly female. More important, given the dislocation and trauma of exile, Polish women demonstrated a need to articulate a distinct and unified identity that both endowed them with honor and esteem, and opposed those around them. This identity centered on traditional notions of proper womanhood, which Polish females invoked as a key ordering element of their nation, a hallmark of its level of civilization. They therefore continually compared themselves with females of other nationalities.

In discussing the Jews exiled with them, Polish women concentrate almost exclusively on one issue—their reputed disloyalty. No other aspect of their lives appears noteworthy or relevant. It is important to note that Poles present nothing regarding Jewish life or their particular plight; even differences in looks and dress, religion, customs, or education draw no attention. The value used to define, and largely denounce, the Jews is the paramount Polish one—patriotism; the women report only on how the Jews fit into the Polish scheme.[11] They demonstrate no awareness or understanding of abuse suffered by Jews in the interwar state, and they react to any complaint or suggestion that the Jews' lot might improve under the Soviets as outright betrayal.

Their evidence for the Jews' lack of patriotism lay in their speech—both the language Jews used and the sentiments they expressed. According to one deportee, when her transport arrived at the place of exile, "the Jews already forgot how to speak Polish." They preferred to speak Russian instead, insist others.[12] Even worse, the Jews continually slandered the Polish state, "spreading lies" about how they had been mistreated. One woman reports bitterly that the Jews in her cell insisted that life was very bad for them in Poland; another one states that the Jews conducted an "anti-Polish campaign."[13] Poles write with anger and disbelief that their fellow citizens gloated over the fall of Poland and announced that they had no desire to return. For the Poles,

---

10. Current views have changed this balance. An analysis of Polish stereotypes of Jews, drawn from an extensive survey conducted in Poland in 1992, found that 52 percent of the respondents mentioned positive traits of the Jews and 31 percent negative ones. According to Alina Cała, the stereotypes did not depend on the sex of the respondent, "although women singled out the negative traits of the Jews a little more often": Alina Cała, "Autostereotyp i stereotypy narodowe," in *Czy Polacy są antysemitami? Wyniki badania sondażowego*, ed. Ireneusz Krzemiński (Warsaw, 1996), 217, 221.

11. This attitude parallels Polish treatment of Jews in literature of the late nineteenth and early twentieth centuries, which, as Aleksander Hertz and Bożena Umińska point out, shows little about the realities of Jewish life and attitudes, focusing rather on their participation in Polish life: Hertz, 209, 216–22; Umińska, 93.

12. AC, Box 43, Vol. 10, No. 11918; Box 54, Vol. 35, No. R7157.

13. AC, Box 38, Vol. 5, No. 5638; Box 48, Vol. 21, No. R2160.

such statements constituted unwarranted and painful rejections of the father-land, evidence only of the Jews' disloyalty and deliberate cruelty. A dressmaker from Krzemieniec relates that the Poles had no peace because of the Jews in their barracks, who always spoke to them of "your Poland." A woman deported to Kazakhstan reports being taunted by "our Jews," who insisted "that everything is over for you, that you'll see Poland when you see your ear."[14] According to a compatriot, "The Jews offended our national feelings at every step." "It's hard to find the words to describe how they abused our Fatherland," concludes another.[15]

Jews reportedly went beyond offending the Poles to causing them great harm by informing on them to the NKVD. The label of informer is the most common one applied to Jews.[16] Describing a "quiet war" between the Poles and Jews in her settlement, Małgorzata Kazimierczak fully blames the latter: "The Jews were constantly going to the Commandant of the camp and inform-ing what the Poles were saying and doing."[17] "Our greatest curse was several Polish-Jewish women who denounced us to the authorities for any opinion we expressed," writes an office worker sent to the Gulag.[18] In this way the Jews allegedly broke from the community of exiles. "We lived as friends," writes one woman of her compatriots in the camp, "except for the Jews, who denounced us, and for which we suffered terribly."[19] Maria Pieszczek offers a similar view, explaining that in her camp "many ladies found themselves in the punishment cell [karcer] because of the Jewish women."[20] In the settle-ments they allegedly caused many "good Poles" to be arrested by the NKVD.[21] Although it is impossible to establish the truth of these claims, old stereotypes of Jews as harmful to the nation clearly played a role. One arrested woman, writing that her interrogators produced a list of witnesses who had reported on her activities, inserts parenthetically, "of course, Jews."[22]

The Polish documents complain of other forms of Jewish collaboration with the Soviets. In the camps they obtained positions of authority, for which they were rewarded.[23] According to many Polish women, the Jewish women always secured the best conditions, including lighter work, larger food rations, and hard-to-obtain medical care. They used their positions not only to their own advantage but to cause the Poles grief: Jewish doctors refused to grant Poles

14. AC, Box 48, Vol. 21, No. R2001; Box 48, Vol. 21, No. 2240.
15. AC, Box 48, Vol. 20, No. R1868; Box 36, Vol. 2, No. 1561.
16. AC, Box 36, Vol. 2, No. 1871; Box 36, Vol. 2, No. 1610; Box 36, Vol. 2, No. 1956; Box 48, Vol. 20, No. R1890.
17. AC, Box 48, Vol. 21, No. R1963.
18. AC, Box 48, Vol. 21, No. 2207.
19. AC, Box 48, Vol. 21, No. R2177.
20. AC, Box 48, Vol. 21, No. R2172.
21. HIA, Poland, Ambasada (Soviet Union), Records, 1941–1944, Box 33, tom 3, A. Siemińska.
22. AC, Box 50, Vol. 25, No. R3588.
23. AC, Box 39, Vol. 5, No. 6812; Box 43, Vol. 10, No. 11912; Box 52, Vol. 30, No. R5654.

necessary medical releases from work; Jewish brigade leaders ruthlessly drove the women in their labor.[24] "The conduct of the Jews toward us was significantly worse than that of the Soviet authorities," concludes one deportee.[25] Additionally, Jews participated in the cultural activities—plays, concerts, and lectures—staged by the Soviets and loathed by Poles.[26] Such characterizations easily fit prevailing stereotypes of the Jews. Discussing their behavior, Poles note that some of these women simply sought to ingratiate themselves with the authorities–aligning themselves with the prevailing winds for their own benefit. "The Jews, as usual, looked out for themselves," declares a woman from Brzozów, explaining that they served the Soviets for their own interests.[27] Other women, we are told, were "Bolshevized" or devoted communists. According to Ada Domianewska, many "devotees of the Soviet regime" could be found among the Jews.[28] Such women gave particular offense in the initial aftermath of the Red Army invasion: then, we are told, they not only welcomed the Soviets but took the jobs of Polish schoolteachers, actively participated in the elections, accepted Soviet passports, and worked for the NKVD.[29] Regardless of their motives and ideological convictions—not to mention diversity among their reactions to the occupation—Jewish women were largely seen by Poles as collaborators and traitors.

Polish women voice particular anger at what they report as the Jewish reaction to the amnesty in 1941: after slandering Poland, antagonizing its adherents, and collaborating with its enemy, Jewish women again changed their colors and embraced it. Many women complain that suddenly the Jews all wanted to return to Poland. One woman elaborates: "Only after announcement of the amnesty, several of them were ingratiatingly polite, and in contact with the authorities they all emphasized that they were Polish women. To the angry comment of an NKVD agent that several months ago during interrogation one of them said that she was a Jew and not a Pole, and now changed her nationality, she answered that one had to obey the authorities: the Soviets ordered us to put ourselves down as Jews and not Poles—so we said that; now you're allies with Poland—so we are Poles [*Polki*]."[30]

The precariousness of the Jewish position and the reality of Soviet pressure exerted on them to disavow Polish nationality receive no comment—only the apparent changeability of the Jews. For Poles, injury was added to insult. They maintain that Soviet authorities released the Jews from detention first, allow-

24. AC, Box 41, Vol. 8, No. 9968; Box 41, Vol. 8, No. 10052; Box 48, Vol. 20, No. R1571.

25. AC, Box 48, Vol. 20, No. R1868.

26. AC, Box 52, Vol. 30, No. R5654.

27. AC, Box 41, Vol. 8, No. 10623.

28. AC, Box 54, Vol. 35, No. R7157. See also AC, Box 47, Vol. 19, No. R1280; Box 48, Vol. 21, No. R1950.

29. AC, Box 45, Vol. 14, No. 14238; Box 54, Vol. 36, No. R7835; Box 52, Vol. 31, No. R6105; Box 55, Vol. 39, No. R8585; Box 75, No. D1267.

30. AC, Box 36, Vol. 2, No. 1610.

ing them to reach the newly formed Anders army quickly and take the spots of "real" Poles.[31] From the Polish perspective, the Jews were once again manipulating the situation to their own advantage, at the expense of more deserving Poles.

There is evidence of some truth to the claims of hostility toward ethnic Poles and support for the Soviet invasion on the part of some Jews, although it cannot be taken as the rule.[32] Without trying to make any conclusions on the extent of these phenomena, we can gain much from examining Polish perceptions. The picture of the Jews that emerges from the Polish accounts combines old stereotypes and the specific context of their encounters. Thrown into crowded cattle cars and sent to remote locations, where they lived in close proximity, the Poles could not ignore their Jewish compatriots, whose presence, complaints, and activities often challenged Polish notions of their interwar state and the identity of its inhabitants. Having lost their statehood and sovereignty, Poles faced questions about the legitimacy of the Polish state, the unity of its populace, and the certainty of its future. Jews provoked these fears and also bore the brunt of them. Projecting disloyalty, disunity, and indifference to the future of Poland on the Jews en masse served to exclude them from the Polish collective: they could be dismissed as undeserving and irrelevant to the future so desired by ethnic Poles. This view also affirmed the Polish perception that Poles alone were blameless victims.

On the surface, the claims made about Jews seem to have little to do with gender. The stereotype of the Jew as disloyal or as a subversive element in the nation had long been applied to Jews of both sexes by Poles of both sexes. Likewise, the coupling of the terms Communist and Jew, which also originated before the war and was popularized by the term *Żydokomuna* (Judeocommunism), was not gender specific. Nor do these accusations present the Jewish people as a feminized "other," which late nineteenth-century discourse sought to do.[33] And yet, if we examine these claims about Jewish women in the context of Polish women's descriptions of their own behavior in exile, we can see the work of gender. The aims and emphasis of Polish women's descriptions of their Jewish counterparts are all attached to gendered notions of the nation as family.

Faced with repression from Soviet authorities, hostility from the local population, and daily challenges to their ideas of normality, Polish females

---

31. AC, Box 36, Vol. 2, No. 1610; Box 43, Vol. 10, No. 11748.

32. On this much-debated topic, see Jan Karski, "The Jewish Problem in the Homeland," in Davies and Polonsky, *Jews in Eastern Poland*, 260–74; Gross, *Revolution from Abroad*, 28–35; Jan Gross, "A Tangled Web: Confronting Stereotypes Concerning Relations between Poles, Germans, Jews, and Communists," in *The Politics of Retribution in Europe: World War II and Its Aftermath*, ed. István Deák, Jan Gross, and Tony Judt (Princeton, 2000), 92–104; Norman Naimark, "The Nazis and 'The East': Jedwabne's Circle of Hell," *Slavic Review* 61, no. 3 (2002): 476–82.

33. See Gilman, esp. 76, 134; Umińska, 36–42.

turned to the group as a means of survival. Whether a handful of Poles in a labor camp, a larger community in a deportation settlement, or the entire nation, the group variously offered women material assistance, moral support, an esteemed identity, and a clear sense of difference from what they saw as the debased peoples around them. The women rejected the dismal living conditions, brutal social relations, hard labor, and cultural repression that defined Soviet life for them. Maintaining the distinctiveness and the unity of the group bolstered their interlocking identities as women and as Poles.

In their depositions Polish women clearly articulate the duties of a proper woman, drawing on the traditions of their foremothers during the partition era and the social norms of the interwar period.[34] History, religion, and popular opinion extolled the mother as the epitome of Polish womanhood, idealized as the *matka-polka*. Her duties extended from her own family to the nation: she bore responsibility for raising the nation's children by bringing her own offspring up as "honorable citizens" and patriots; she was also to uphold the morality and the reputation of both family and nation. Entrusted with sustaining the unity of the fatherland, she was to be a source of "faith, hope, and strength of the soul."[35] The Polish woman served the nation through others and, as a popular interwar magazine advised, was expected to demonstrate "pure service to the idea of the nation, free of ambition and personal viewpoints."[36] Self-sacrifice was the key to female heroism.

Socialized according to these notions and steeped in the legends of their ancestors, women coped with the trials of exile by bonding with others. Young women describe being cared for by a mother figure in prison cells; deported women recount taking in children orphaned in exile. Groups of women, particularly those with children, banded together to help one another survive, invoking the term "family." Some deportees refer to their entire communities in exile, numbering even into the hundreds, as "one big family." Poles frequently called themselves the descendants of those exiled to Siberia under the tsars. Such connections gave the exiles a sense of belonging to something bigger and, with it, hope and the strength to survive.

Jews were expected to contribute to this communal effort at survival. Many women refer to "our" Jews, and some use the term "Pole of the Mosaic faith," suggesting the more inclusive view of the nation, not determined by ethnicity,

34. On the period of partitions, see Barbara Jedynak, "Dom i kobieta w kulturze niewoli," in *Kobieta w kulturze i społeczeństwie*, ed. Barbara Jedynak (Lublin, 1990), 70–105; and *Women in Polish Society*, ed. Rudolf Jaworski and Bianka Pietrow-Ennker (Boulder, Colo., 1992). On the interwar period, see *Równe prawa i nierówne szanse: Kobiety w Polsce międzywojennej*, ed. Anna Żarnowska and Andrzej Szwarc (Warsaw, 2000); Katherine R. Jolluck, *Exile and Identity: Polish Women in the Soviet Union during World War II* (Pittsburgh, 2002), 48–56, 91–98.

35. Kazimiera Neronowiczowa, "Nowe prawa—nowe obowiązki," *Bluszcz* 53, no. 52 (December 28, 1918): 391; Henryk Sienkiewicz, quoted in Matka-Polska, "Gdzież są?" *Bluszcz* 53, no. 30 (July 27, 1918): 216.

36. "Na dzień Matki," *Moja Przyjaciółka* 3, no. 10 (25 May 1936): 180; Dr. E. R., "Cel pracy kobiecej," *Bluszcz* 54, no. 1 (October 15, 1921): 2.

that was characteristic of the first two-thirds of the nineteenth century.[37] It may be that the Poles regarded the Jews as poor and distant relatives, but they believed they shared the same fatherland and thus expected loyalty to Poland and solidarity with its citizens before what was presumed to be a common enemy. The women's shock at learning of the Jews' dissatisfaction with the Polish state underscores this expectation. But it is further underscored by those women who accepted their Jewish counterparts as part of the collective. Wanda Dzierżanowska describes several Jews in her settlement who, "in their behavior, civic attitude, ethical principles, and helpfulness could serve as a model for many others."[38] A handful of women report living in harmony with the Jews.[39] Good relations were predicated on the Jews' expressions of respect for the feelings of the Poles and for the "true" worth of the fatherland; such Jews displayed solidarity with the Polish women and came to their assistance by, for example, standing guard while they met to pray.[40] With time, one woman notes, some of the Jewish women who had initially informed on their cellmates "turned out to be good Poles."[41] In explanation, she states that they ceased their informing and united with the Poles. Patriotism and solidarity thus defined Polishness, and these Jews met the requirements.

Cases of harmonious relations are the exceptions, however. Most women present the Jews as deliberately breaking from their fellow citizens with their uncooperative and antagonistic behavior. Referring to them possessively in this context paints the Jews as ungrateful relatives. Describing their lives in exile, Polish women stress the unity of the collective and the selflessness of its members, and depict Jewish women as violating all the cardinal virtues that the effort at collective survival required. Their actions are said to be not only selfish but harmful to others in the group. Rather than cooperating or even keeping to themselves, the Jews spoiled relations in the cells and barracks, turning women of other nationalities against the Poles. "They managed to incite the Soviet women against us, telling them lies about conditions in Poland," writes Eugenia Schmidt. Maria Arciszewska recalls such an incident: "Masha Kraska, a Jewish woman from Grodno—Trojecka Street—said in prison in Petropavelsk that Jews in Poland didn't have any rights at all, that they were beaten and tortured, that there were pogroms, and when I pointed out to her that it was all slander, that the Jews had it very well in Poland, she turned the whole cell against me and the communists almost killed me."[42] In

37. See Porter, 37–39.

38. AC, Box 39, Vol. 6, No. 7829.

39. AC, Box 41, Vol. 8, No. 10056; Box 48, Vol. 21, No. 1968; Box 52, Vol. 30, No. R5626.

40. HIA, Poland, Ministerstwo Informacji i Dokumentacji (hereafter MID), Box 198, Folder 5, "I Am Forced to Leave My Country"; AC, Box 48, Vol. 21, No. R1974; Box 44, Vol. 12, No. 12631.

41. AC, Box 36, Vol. 2, No. 1610. See also AC, Box 38, Vol. 5, No. 6084; Box 48, Vol. 21, No. R1950.

42. AC, Box 41, Vol. 8, No. 10623; Box 39, Vol. 5, No. 6812. See also: AC, Box 54, Vol. 36, No. R7842; Box 36, Vol. 3, No. 2163; Box 47, Vol. 19, No. R1278.

every case the women describe, the Jews are the aggressors, the Poles the victims.

Reports of such selfish and hostile actions of Jews are almost always counterposed to assertions that Polish women acted differently. According to a teacher from Lwów, "The Jews informed about everything that went on in the cell. They were often called for interrogations, from which they returned in good moods, having been given sugar, cigarettes, and even white bread. Poles in interrogations were beaten in the face, kicked." Most women insist that in contrast to Jews, Poles rarely were put in positions of authority; some report refusing such duties as brigade leader so as not to contribute to the misery of fellow workers, but if they accepted such positions, they used their influence to try to improve the situation of their compatriots. Consequently, "it was characteristic that Polish women rarely lasted long in that function," explains a former clerk. "This came from the fact that they could not be ruthless in relation to their companions subordinated to them."[43] Women similarly report losing their positions as doctors for granting too many exemptions from labor, which they did to provide some relief to fellow exiles.

Former prisoners recall their impassioned reactions to the cries of beaten men in NKVD prisons: they screamed, banged on doors, and staged hunger strikes in attempts to end the maltreatment of compatriots who, though unknown to them, were considered relatives. "Many times an uprising arose in the women's section when the ear-piercing screams of tortured men reached us. The Jews did not take part," explains one woman. She continues: "We yelled then, 'Don't beat them!' The women in other cells did the same thing. The next day we did not eat breakfast. The Jews ate."[44] "We were all patriotic," asserts another woman, "except for the Jews."[45]

By their declarations and actions, these Jews seemed to exclude themselves from the Polish collective. Furthermore, their reported behavior rendered them lesser women. Accusations of having an antisocial nature, long applied to Jews, bear particular meaning for women—even more so in the context of national crisis. If women were to foster the unity of the collective, to put the interests of others above their own, maintain the morality and the hope of the group, then Jewish women fell far short. In fact, some Poles claim that the Jews failed to cooperate not only with the Poles but among themselves as well. A teacher deported from Łuck writes: "There was a case of death by starvation (a Jew)—after that the Jewish community only insignificantly assisted its needy. The Poles saved each other and helped each other."[46] Describing life in a prison camp in the Mordovsk ASSR, one woman notes: "There were very bad relations among our Polish Jews and in their relation-

43. AC, Box 44, Vol. 13, No. 13970.
44. AC, Box 41, Vol. 8, No. 10052. See also AC, Box 39, Vol. 5, No. 7481.
45. AC, Box 52, Vol. 30, No. R5656.
46. AC, Box 38, Vol. 5, No. 6086.

ship toward us."[47] The internal cohesion often attributed to Jews in other contexts is absent here.[48]

In the Polish telling, Jewish women, incapable of demonstrating solidarity, also distinguished themselves by their lack of hope. Whereas Polish women emphatically state that they refused to surrender their faith in a just future and a return home, the Jews were different. Kazimiera Bola writes that the NKVD often summoned Poles to discussions aimed at destroying their hope for the future: "They succeeded only with the Jews." Even worse, some Jews tried to destroy hope in others. One prisoner recalls, "They wanted to kill in me the hope, or rather belief, which intensified every day, that Poland would rise and that Poland had to rise."[49] Far from uplifting the morale of others, as an ideal woman was charged to do, Jews ruined it.

In comparison with their Polish counterparts, Jewish women are clearly presented as reproachable. Some Poles go further, suggesting that the Jewish females were improper women, casting aspersions on their sexual morality—again, in contrast to the high moral standards allegedly upheld by Polish women. "No one would accept any kind of relief which would have been the result of the favor of the Commandant of the settlement, and for which one would have to forsake the honor of a Pole or the reputation of a woman," asserts one deportee. But, she continues, "the Jews were lower in this respect; they often (not all, there were some courageous ones among them as well) searched for and found better living conditions, they exploited the situation and tried to live easier—not damaging their health—beyond the voice of conscience."[50]

The intimation of impropriety can be found also in descriptions of Jewish women's behavior at the time of the Red Army invasion. It is neither detailed nor explicit but implies that the standards of honor and chastity—important elements of female patriotism—of Polish women were not upheld by female Jews. Jewish women wearing bright clothes, we are told, greeted the soldiers of the Red Army on the streets with flowers and cheers—acts of welcome and submission. In contrast, Polish females put on mourning clothes, in the tradition of their foremothers under the partitions. "Their officers expected smiles from our girls, but not one wanted even to look in their direction," recalls one young Pole, "We all dressed as modestly as possible, wearing black scarves on our heads." Hermina Halicka reports that "a great number of Jews and Ukrainians threw bouquets of flowers at their feet." Some reportedly kissed the soldiers.[51]

47. AC, Box 48, Vol. 21, No. R1965. See also AC, Box 48, Vol. 21, No. R1996; Box 52, Vol. 31, No. R6091.

48. Alina Cała, *Wizerunek Żyda w polskiej kulturze ludowej* (Warsaw, 1992), 16.

49. AC, Box 48, Vol. 20, No. R1880; Box 48, Vol. 21, No. R2200.

50. AC, Box 39, Vol. 5, No. 7365.

51. AC, Box 43, Vol. 10, No. 11942; Box 41, Vol. 8, No. 10439; Box 65, Vol. 69, No. 15797. See also, AC, Box 45, Vol. 14, No. 14442; Box 45, Vol. 15, No. 14470.

One woman makes an explicit condemnation: "The moral standards of the Jews—dissolute."[52] Such comments on the sexual morality of Jewish women appear rarely in the documents, however. Simply put, it was not the main issue Polish women used to differentiate themselves from Jewish ones. Signaling the low esteem in which they held their Jewish counterparts, some Polish women assert that their "own" prostitutes, whom they considered the lowest element in society, deserved greater praise. Why? Because they were properly patriotic. Though the prostitutes mistreated their compatriots by stealing from them and monopolizing the best spots in the cells, they did not spy or inform on cell-mates. "They didn't let the communists speak badly about Poland and came to our defense," explains one woman. She continues the list of "proper" behaviors: "They related kindly to pregnant women, children, and the sick. They did not like the Jews or the Ukrainians." In a similar vein, another woman writes that the Ukrainian and Jewish women "harassed us so much that even the prostitutes, outcasts from everything, of whom there were several, turned out to be better Poles and came to our defense."[53] Patriotism thus raised even Polish prostitutes, considered in other contexts the "dregs of society," to a higher moral level than that of disloyal Jewish women. Jewish women judged as lesser because they failed to uphold the standards of patriotic female behavior thus fell far short of the ideal Polish woman—even below Poland's "fallen women."

At other times, in their home communities, Polish women had expressed their resentment of Jewish women by remarking on their fabled beauty (attributed to their lack of hard work) and their seductive power over Polish men, or they attributed sexual deformity to Jewish women as a way of signaling their difference and inferiority.[54] In these wartime documents, though, blanket condemnations of Jewish females specifically as *women* do not occur. In exile, issues of Jewish women's beauty or sexuality, of their hygiene, mothering, or affinity for work—which might matter at other times—have no relevance.[55] What truly mattered in this context was the attitude of the Jews to the Polish nation—its people and its state. And all that was needed to render the Jews different was to demonstrate their lack of loyalty; other stereotypes were not activated in this setting. Even the few hints of sexual impropriety are conflated with issues of patriotism, so that the real focus of these statements is the

52. AC, Box 48, Vol. 20, No. R1868.

53. AC, Box 41, Vol. 8, No. 10052; Box 44, Vol. 12, No. 12629.

54. See, for example, Cała, *Wizerunek Żyda*, 25, 55, 66; Claude Lanzmann, *Shoah: An Oral History of the Holocaust; The Complete Text of the Film* (New York, 1985), 88. The figure of the Jewish beauty who charmed Christian men was a basic type in Polish literature; see Umińska. The notion of the sexual deformity or perversity of the Jews was a common element of European antisemitism of the late nineteenth and early twentieth centuries. See, Gilman; and Judith Friedlander, "Anti-Semite" in Friedlander, *Women in Culture*, 82.

55. I have found among the women's documents only one reference to the Jews as "dirty and lice-infested": AC, Box 41, Vol. 9, No. 10743.

women's disloyal or treasonous behavior. Proper citizenship takes the highest priority, and Polish women use gender only indirectly to undermine their Jewish counterparts.

We can see the importance of this approach when we examine the Polish depiction of Russian women, for in contrast, the Poles do employ gender as a central means of denouncing Russian women and, by extension, their entire nation. In this way the Poles express their utter disdain for the Russians and their way of living. Issues of proper citizenship and the loyalty of Russian women to their own nation have no impact whatsoever on the Poles' self-perception and draw no attention in the women's accounts, and insulting comments from Russian females about Poland are typically dismissed as ignorance. Instead, Russian women are described in much more intimate terms: on the basis of their personal hygiene, ability to perform heavy (masculine) labor, fitness as mothers, and sexual morality—characteristics critical, for the Poles, in defining the civilized and proper woman. On each of these accounts Russian women are found to be so perverted and "unnatural" that, as one Pole puts it, they can hardly be called women at all. Russian females swear like men and ably perform the same hard physical labor. As mothers, they show little care for their offspring; as wives, little fidelity. Unconcerned about personal hygiene, Russian women reportedly manifest an excessive, even abnormal, sexuality.[56]

The sharp contrast between the devastating picture drawn of Russian women and the relatively mild one of Jewish women reveals the varying type and degree of threat that these "others" posed to the Poles. In view of the calamities that had befallen eastern Poland since September 1939, Jews paled in comparison to the Russians as enemies of the Poles; none of the exiles blames the Jews for causing the catastrophe. Jews challenged the authority and solidarity of the Polish exiles; they threatened the women's views of the past and their hopes for the future in the context of their own nation-state; but the Russians (seen as synonymous with the Soviets) represented a graver challenge. Not only could they determine whether the Polish state existed, but they had the power to displace hundreds of thousands of its citizens. Even more dangerous was the order that the Russians imposed on the exiles, one that threatened to deprive them of their identity as Poles and as proper, civilized women. Polish women feared succumbing to the Soviet system and becoming what they saw around them—labor animals, toiling for the communist state, unable to fulfill the functions they associated with being female and Polish. They also feared rape and sexual degradation. The lack of respect for "proper" gender roles, above all visible in the character, behavior, and treatment of Russian women, to the Poles marked Soviet society as profoundly aberrant.

Gender is one of the most fundamental ordering categories of human societies, basic to both individual and collective identity. Accusing Russian women

56. Jolluck, 253–78.

of not resembling "true" women constitutes a profound insult. In so doing, Polish women denounce them as alien and uncivilized, unequivocally inferior to Poles, whereas the Jews, though damned as fellow citizens, are nonetheless presented as akin to the Poles. Their most intimate identity, as individuals and as a people, does not receive criticism. Though seen as disloyal to Poland and perhaps falling short of the ideals of womanhood, Jewish women are not dismissed as uncivilized or unnatural; they still belong to the same world as the Poles. Jews are not labeled Asiatic or primitive, as are Russians. Jews are thus left with a humanity not accorded the women of that more dangerous "other."

Gender plays a similar role in Polish women's divergent accounts of Jewish and Russian men. Jewish males receive less attention than females in these documents, though they are included in some of the broad denunciations of Jews as communists and collaborators. Women's accounts of Jewish men focus on the period immediately following the Soviet invasion: they condemn Jewish men for welcoming the Red Army, serving in Bolshevik militias, replacing Polish administrators, denouncing their Polish neighbors, and assisting the NKVD in the arrest and deportation of Poles.[57] Such men come across as either ideological enemies or as lackeys and opportunists. Images of the "criminal Jew," popular in the interwar years, do not surface here.[58] Furthermore, these stereotypes are not sexualized. The documents contain no accusations of rape or suggestions of sexual aggression on the part of Jewish men, nor do Polish females cast aspersions on their masculinity. Such condemnations and insults are made only about the Russian (and Central Asian) men who wielded greater political and physical power over the exiled women. Jewish men did not present the most dangerous threat to Polish women or their nation. They are denounced as disloyal and as communists but otherwise are not discussed.

Polish men tend to make the same basic complaints as the women about Jewish behavior, both in response to the invasion and in exile. Men also accuse the Jews of welcoming the Red Army into Poland and serving the new regime there. They state that, full of hatred, the Jews criticized Poland, instigated fights with Poles in prison, and allegedly collaborated with the NKVD, informing on Poles and taking positions of authority in the camps, serving the Soviets with enthusiasm.[59] And Jews reportedly attended propaganda meetings and cultural events that Polish men boycotted. In short, like the women, Polish men characterize the Jews as hostile and traitorous to the Polish cause, but their descriptions do not have the same coloration as those by women. The framework of the family and its attendant expectations appear less frequently, and Polish men do not stress the unity of their collective to the same degree that women do. Male identity and self-esteem seem to be more based on indi-

57. See AC, Box 41, Vol. 8, No. 10623; Box 42, Vol. 10, No. 11245; Box 43, Vol. 10, No. 11922; Box 44, Vol. 12, No. 12699.

58. See chapter 4 by Robert Blobaum in this volume.

59. AC, Box 43, Vol. 10, No. 11897; Box 45, Vol. 14, No. 14315; Box 36, Vol. 2, No. 1904; Box 45, Vol. 14, No. 14262.

vidual characteristics and achievements, to depend less on relationships and the harmony of the group. Polish men can admit to difficult relations with other Poles, to "bad" Poles in their midst, and to the psychological or moral collapse of their compatriots without having this information compromise their own identity. In men's testimonies, these negative behaviors do not so exclusively mark the Jews. Not charged with serving the nation by devoting themselves to others, men do not look for selflessness in their communities, or describe the behavior of the Jews as selfish—it is merely hostile and hateful. And their criticism is not a question of manhood. Gender is not used as an instrument of exclusion or denigration in men's accounts of the Jews. Jewish males, though presented as treasonous, are not belittled as men: only one man uses the word "cowardly" to describe them.[60] Nor do the older stereotypes of Jews as bad soldiers or as the instigators of Poland's calamities surface in these documents.[61] Polish men, too, recognize the Russians as their main enemy.

Jewish Views

The final issue to consider is the Jewish description of relations with Poles in exile. The so-called Palestine Protocols, written by Jewish evacuees who moved from Iran to Jerusalem in 1943, are the equivalents of the documents written by ethnic Poles discussed above. The Jewish documents are far fewer than the Polish ones, numbering approximately three hundred, nor can we be as confident regarding the freedom of expression felt by Jews who wrote their testimonies. Many of their depositions do report facing antisemitism from Poles, but few dwell on it—probably to be expected, as they were writing under the auspices of the Polish army. Some Jews may have felt too constrained to voice their complaints; others may have wanted to express their gratitude to the Polish army for removing them from the USSR and thus underplayed their encounters with Polish antisemitism. Additionally, most of the Jews who wrote had suffered the ravages of the Nazi occupation before their deportation to the USSR. Though they did not witness the Final Solution, in the first days and weeks—in some cases, months—of the German occupation they did endure acts of humiliation and physical violence, from beatings and the ripping of beards off men's faces to the murder of relatives—traumas they depicted at length. No doubt Polish antisemitism experienced in exile faded before the Nazi version. Indeed, the stories of what they faced under the Germans and their escape to the Soviet side often dominate the accounts written by Jews,

---

60. AC, Box 44, Vol. 12, No. 12611.

61. These stereotypes do surface in records of high-level views at the time, expressed by Generals Sikorski and Anders, as well as Stalin. See Yisrael Gutman and Schmuel Krakowski, *Unequal Victims: Poles and Jews during World War II* (New York, 1986), 316.

even though they spent much more time under Soviet rule. Finally, it must be noted that not all Jews experienced hostility from the Poles, and some have only praise for their fellow citizens.

Anti-Polish sentiments are hard to find in the protocols: blanket characterizations or denunciations of the Poles rarely appear. It may be that the Jews who managed to get out of the USSR with the Polish army were among the most assimilated; their identification with the Polish cause would lead them to feel less distinction between the two peoples. Some Jews leave the ethnic makeup of their communities in exile unclear, speaking only of Polish citizens. Others refer only to Jews, suggesting segregation in the settlements. Even more than Poles, Jews discuss the behavior of fellow citizens only in terms of how they were affected by it; they tend not to extend their comments on ethnic Poles to issues that had no impact on themselves, such as sexual morality, hygiene, family life, religious practice, attitude toward the Soviets, or even patriotism.[62] The sparseness of the comments about Poles and the similarity of female and male documents mean that little can be said about gender in regard to the Jewish protocols, with reference either to anti-Polish sentiments or to the experience of antisemitism.

What can we learn from these protocols? In some cases they support Polish claims about Jewish reactions to the Soviet occupation of eastern Poland: that some Jews (though not all) welcomed the Red Army, accepted Soviet passports, or worked for the NKVD.[63] Some reveal the lack of hope that Poles wrote of, admitting that they never expected to get out of the USSR.[64] More often, however, the protocols refute Polish complaints about the Jews. Regina Treler, for example, explains the response to the Soviet invasion in Równe in a way Poles do not: "Not only Jews went out on the streets to welcome the Soviet army, but also Poles turned out in crowds through the city. It was generally thought that the Russians had not come as occupiers but were hurrying to help Poland, to help her in the fight with the German invaders."[65] The authors frequently note their distress at the Soviet invasion, and some insist that Jews typically met with worse treatment from the Soviets than did others. In fact, one man asserts that Russian antisemitism was worse than any he had experienced before.[66]

Most Jews relate their adamant refusal to accept a Soviet passport after the invasion, which led to their exile. Having fled eastward from Warsaw, Róża Hirsz found that all the refugees were required to accept Soviet citizenship. "I promised myself I would never do that," she states, like many others, explain-

62. For an exception, which discusses Polish women and sex in the camps, see MID, Box 123, No. 47.

63. MID, Box 123, Nos. 31, 214.

64. MID, Box 123, Nos. 45, 77.

65. MID, Box 123, No. 51. See also MID, Box 124, No. 281.

66. MID, Box 123, No. 45. See also AC, Box 46, Vol. 15, No. 15544; MID, Box 123, No. 151.

ing that her arrest followed her refusal to accept a passport.[67] The majority of the Jews writing protocols found themselves on trains headed eastward after applying to return to their homes under Nazi rule, though well aware of the horrible treatment accorded Jews there—unquestionably demonstrating their lack of support for the Soviets and their regime. In further contrast with Polish claims, some Jews stress the lack of ethnic hostility once in exile. One man states that Soviet propaganda had no effect, and efforts to stir up trouble between the Poles, Jews, and Ukrainians failed in his prison, where "a warm communal life" prevailed among Polish citizens.[68] As if aware of Polish accusations, one woman, writing about the demoralization of prisoners, declares, "None of the Jewish women ever denounced anyone."[69] Finally, some Jews make it clear that they regarded Poland as their fatherland, stressing their service to their country in 1918, as well as 1939, and their continued loyalty.[70]

Some of the documents matter-of-factly note good relations between Poles and Jews; others recount assistance, sometimes lifesaving, from Polish friends and even strangers.[71] About one-third of the documents contain such positive comments. Approximately 40 percent of the Jewish protocols I examined do report encountering antisemitism from Poles, and it is in these that we find negative comments about ethnic Poles. One deportee states that in her settlement, Jewish women suffered from "the denunciations of a certain Polish girl, who always accused us of sabotage."[72] Rarely, though, do accounts of antisemitism concern the period of detention in the USSR. It is possible that under conditions of equal powerlessness, in which Polish citizens shared the same fate, Jews found Polish prejudice to be a minor issue. Most complaints of antisemitism stem from the periods immediately after the invasions and the amnesty, when Poles and Jews experienced differential treatment and unequal power. In 1939, some authors assert, Poles beat Jews, looted their property, and even took part in the Nazi killings of Jews.[73] And once freed from detention in the USSR, Jews report discrimination from Polish relief agencies and the army. Children recall having to beg for admittance into Polish orphanages, where Christian children tormented them. Szoszanna Elkes, who was twelve when evacuated from the USSR, states that the Jewish children could only quietly accept the abuse of their Polish counterparts because they needed the bread and soup the orphanage offered.[74] Adults also report facing hostility.

67. MID, Box 123, No. 85. See also MID, Box 123, Nos. 36, 163, 120; Box 124, No. 304.

68. MID, Box 123, No. 149.

69. MID, Box 124, No. 271.

70. MID, Box 123, Nos. 162, 69.

71. MID, Box 123, Nos. 154, 119, 201, 214; Box 124, Nos. 255, 316.

72. MID, Box 123, No. 43. See also MID, Box 123, No. 36.

73. MID, Box 123, Nos. 36, 112, 116.

74. MID, Box 123, No. 132. See also AC, Box 45, Vol. 15, No. 14480; MID, Box 123, Nos. 108, 131.

Starving and exhausted, one woman appealed to the Polish delegation, but "I didn't get help because I was a Jew," she states.[75] Others similarly claim that relief supplies were given only to ethnic Poles, a complaint echoed by Jewish leaders in Palestine and the United States, but called isolated incidents by the Polish government.[76]

Some Jews bitterly recall the troubles they experienced trying to join the Anders army or to secure a place on the evacuation transports. Soviet authorities spread the notion that Polish antisemitism was the cause; Polish officials insisted that the blame fell on the Russians. The stance of Soviet and Polish authorities on this question is the subject of ongoing scholarly research and debate.[77] What concerns me here is how the issue is reflected in conflicting and ambiguous personal testimonies. These documents suggest that both sides played a role in the difficulties encountered by Jews, which David Engel confirms in his study of the Polish London government.[78] In the first months after the amnesty many Jews joined the Polish army, and some Poles, including the head of the army itself, found their high numbers distressing.[79] In December 1941, Stalin's government proclaimed that it did not consider Jews, Ukrainians, or Belarusians from eastern Poland to be Polish citizens, so they should not be recruited into Polish forces. Thereafter, the number of enlisted Jews fell. In the protocols, some Jews state that it was Soviet members of the Polish army recruitment commissions who rejected them; a few go out of their way to make this clear. Emma Lewinowa writes: "Since I've many times heard complaints that Polish antisemitism was the reason for not getting accepted into the Polish army, I want to declare that with my own eyes I saw how, on a mixed commission of Bolsheviks and Poles, in response to the document of my cousin, the Bolshevik commissar said, 'A Jew—no.'" She concludes: "I personally never saw any manifestations of antisemitism in the army, in which my brother and father served."[80] But other Jews declare the opposite. After recounting her son's rejection by the Polish army and the difficulties her family faced getting on the evacuation transport, Róża Buchman states, "It is not

75. MID, Box 123, No. 56. See also MID, Box 123, Nos. 38, 43.

76. MID, Box 123, No. 36. On the issue of discrimination in the relief effort, see Keith Sword, "The Welfare of Polish-Jewish Refugees in the USSR, 1941–43: Relief Supplies and their Distribution," in *Jews in Eastern Poland*, 145–60; see also David Engel, *In the Shadow of Auschwitz: The Polish Government-in-Exile and the Jews, 1939–1942* (Chapel Hill, N.C., 1987), 127–32.

77. Ryszard Terlecki, "The Jewish Issue in the Polish Army, 1941–44," in Davies and Polonsky, *Jews in Eastern Poland*, 162–66; Gutman and Krakowski, 309–46; and David Engel, "The Polish Government-in-Exile and the Holocaust: Stanisław Kot's Confrontation with Palestinian Jewry, Nov. 1942–Jan. 1943; Selected Documents," *Polin* 2 (1987): 269–309.

78. Engel, *In the Shadow*, 133–47.

79. Both General Anders and the Polish ambassador, Stanisław Kot, expressed this opinion; see Engel, *In the Shadow*, 133.

80. MID, Box 123, No. 68. See also MID, Box 123, Rabin Joel Landau. Engel states that the Poles used the Soviet liaison officers to exclude the Jews, covering their own antisemitism: Engel, *In the Shadow*, 138.

true, I affirm, that the Bolsheviks made it difficult for the Jews to leave Russia. Most often it depended on Polish officials."[81]

The picture provided by these documents of the Polish army's attitude toward Jews is thus not as black and white as some subsequent writing suggests.[82] Some Jews state that they had no trouble receiving aid, joining the army, or being evacuated.[83] Others relate that Polish antisemites tried to obstruct their exit from the USSR. One wife of an army officer found her name crossed off the list of evacuees; the captain in charge of military families told her "that he was not devoting his twenty-year military career to saving Jews."[84] But people like her, in the end, managed to get out because of the efforts of Polish individuals who felt compassion for their fellow citizens. When, two days before the evacuation, Dora Werker and her daughter had their tickets taken away and were told, "You're Jews, you can't go," she turned to a Colonel Janusz: "He was deeply moved by my story, the loss of my husband—a member of the delegate's office, and that my son was in the army, and he said that if there was no other way, he'd put us down as his mother and daughter."[85] Here we can see a gender difference. A few Jewish men turned down by the army report sneaking onto the evacuation transport or stating vaguely that they left illegally.[86] Women, who did not need to join the army to be evacuated, had other options, and they explain the ruses they employed to get out: purchasing fake documents, falsely registering as Christians, or having themselves baptized.[87] A few women entered into fictitious marriages with Polish soldiers.[88]

Some Poles may have found in these actions confirmation of their view of Jews as chameleons; clearly, though, Jews had little choice if they wanted to leave the USSR. One woman, recalling her distress at being rejected by the army despite her good health and university education, concludes, "I understood, however, that I had to leave Russia if I wanted to survive."[89] She purchased a passport from a Christian woman and made it to Iran. Just as Poles voice surprise and disappointment at the apparent lack of solidarity among citizens from Poland, so, too, do Jews, suggesting that they had similarly felt they were part of the same collective. Discussing the antisemitism she faced, this same woman elaborates: "I couldn't understand how people who only

---

81. MID, Box 123, No. 69.

82. Gutman suggests that Stalin decided to exclude the minorities only after Sikorski and Anders voiced their anti-Jewish views: Gutman and Krakowski, 316–20. Terlecki blames the Soviets for the exclusion of the Jews, and paints some reports of antisemitism in the army as anti-Polish propaganda: Terlecki, 162–64, 167.

83. MID, Box 123, Nos. 142, 173, 288; Box 124, No. 307.

84. MID, Box 123, No. 41. See also MID, Box 123, Nos. 47, 112.

85. MID, Box 123, No. 27. See also MID, Box 123, Nos. 102, 107; Box 124, No. 312.

86. MID, Box 124, Nos. 304, 305, 275, 315.

87. MID, Box 123, No. 77. See also MID, Box 123, No. 38; AC, Box 46, Vol. 15, No. 15536.

88. MID, Box 123, Nos. 69, 163.

89. MID, Box 123, No. 85.

yesterday were suffering together with us, and who were humiliated like we were, could today persecute and humiliate the Jews." Each side blamed the other for causing divisions.

The depositions of evacuated Polish women show that detention in the USSR served as a hothouse for the development of their overlapping identities as women and Poles. Under the pressures of exile, women's notions of "Polishness" were continually tested and rearticulated in opposition to those around them.

Polish women express considerable animosity toward the Jews exiled with them. Many of the attitudes from the interwar period persisted in exile, compounded by the new stereotype of Jews as enthusiastic supporters of the Soviet invasion of eastern Poland in 1939. But in comparison with the deadly inflaming of Polish hostility toward Jews in other parts of Poland during the war, such hostility was somewhat dissipated in exile. Jewish reports on relations while they were in Soviet detention suggest this conclusion. Poles reporting on Jews in the USSR perpetuate the old motifs of Jews as disloyal and as communists, but other stereotypes of Jews—as criminals, sexual perverts, and ritual murderers; as evil—seemed to fade in the face of the overwhelming shock of being under the power of the Russians. This change created somewhat more cohesion—or resulted in less hatred—than one might expect. In other words, the effects of Polish antisemitic views were mitigated by the fact and character of Russian domination. For the Poles under Soviet rule, in the hierarchy of Poland's enemies the Jews ranked below the Russians.

This situation is reflected in the use of gender in Polish women's descriptions of "others." Gender plays an indirect role in creating the stereotype of Jewish women in exile. Jewish women's behavior as women-citizens is described only insofar as it is necessary to establish them as unfit members of the Polish collective. Polish women map the notion of the good citizen onto the notion of the good mother. In this framework, as disloyal citizens who exhibit no solidarity, put their own interests first, and fail to uphold the morale and hopes of the group, Jewish women fall far short of the Polish ideal for womanhood. Nearly everything Poles report about Jewish women's behavior under the Soviet regime is construed as treasonous—from their attitude to Poland to their sexual morality—rendering them suspect as good women and unequivocally marking them as traitorous.

The blunt way that gender is used to condemn Russians offers insight into the role that gender plays in the categorizing and ranking of "others." Whereas Jewish women, in the Polish depiction, fail as female citizens, Russian ones fail more fundamentally as women. In the Polish view, Russian females are perverted, even "unnatural" women, reflecting the profoundly aberrant nature of their entire nation. The focus on gender norms expresses deep-seated fears raised in a period of national crisis; accusations of gender deviation become an attack on the essence of the Russian people. The Jews are less threatening to the Poles and, in the context of Soviet exile, less hated than the Russians; for this reason, Jewish women are not subjected to the intimate, categorical denunciations made of Russian women. Jews are not labeled primitive or Asiatic; unlike the Russians, they remain a part of the same world of the Poles, though not of its inner circles. The documents show that like national identity itself, antisemitic stereotypes are both relational and dependent on context.

The common Soviet enemy did not, however, lead to a sense of solidarity and common interest between Poles and Jews in exile, nor, as both recent scholarship and some of the Jewish testimonies have shown, were Polish leaders ready to accept the Jews as full citizens. But in the face of the threat posed by Russians and the Soviet way of life, the Poles did recognize, it seems, that Jews were not actually alien.

II

Antisemitism, Anti-Judaism, and the Polish Catholic Clergy during the Second World War, 1939–1945

DARIUSZ LIBIONKA

The Polish Roman Catholic Church's attitude toward the extermination of Jews during World War II has been the subject of considerable controversy. In his essay *Polish-Jewish Relations during World War II* (1944), Emanuel Ringelblum wrote about the near-total indifference of the Polish clergy as the result of deeply rooted antisemitism. "It would have been difficult to expect more effective aid to Jews from such a clergy during the present war," he opined, "since the Polish clergy did not provide assistance even when they were in a position to do so."[1] Although references appear in his notes, either to instances of individual priests' compassion for Jews or their help in converting and hiding Jewish children in monasteries and convents, Ringelblum remained skeptical, seeing in such acts opportunism or, at best, a search for a kind of alibi.[2] Israeli researchers have continued along these lines, not necessarily questioning the engagement of members of the clergy in aiding Jews but rather demanding a deeper analysis of clerical motivations and behavior within a broader historical and social context.[3]

This article is dedicated to the memory of Rev. Stanisław Musiał.

1. Emanuel Ringelblum, *Stosunki polsko-żydowskie w czasie drugiej wojny światowej* (Warsaw, 1988), 147–48.

2. See also Emanuel Ringelblum, *Kronika getta warszawskiego* (Warsaw, 1983), 68, 120, 213, 217, 248.

3. Shmuel Krakówski, "The Polish Church and the Holocaust," in *Judaism and Christianity under the Impact of National Socialism (1919–1945)* (Jerusalem, 1987), 395–99.

Two diametrically opposed views dominate in Polish historical literature. The paradigm of the Church's very serious involvement in acts of saving Jews, and of a connection between the religiosity of Polish society and the scale and effectiveness of aid to Jews, had already formed at the turn of the 1960s and 1970s in the Catholic press, supported by research conducted under the auspices of Church academic institutions.[4] Given the limitations on scholarly discussion in the People's Republic of Poland on the one hand, and the need to commemorate the Church's own wartime martyrs on the other, the strength of this paradigm is completely understandable. With the perspective afforded by time, however, it is already obsolete. In the more recent historiography, particularly since 1989, doubts have arisen about the kind of historical narrative promoted by this approach, the type and selection of source materials (particularly the disproportionate use of Church archives as primary sources), the method of their interpretation, and the reliability of materials of dubious provenance and quality.[5] Nonetheless, the works that emerged at the end of the 1960s, clearly shaped by political preferences and lacking methodological sophistication, continue to influence scholarly discourse to this day.[6] As a result, unverified and erroneous information introduced at that time remains in wide circulation. After 1989, unfortunately, treatment of the subject was resumed often in a polemical rather than scholarly manner and lacked the depth of genuine reflection. Certainly the topic still awaits its own historian. In this chapter, I concentrate on two poorly defined and simultaneously mystified issues: the Catholic bishops' reactions to the extermination of Jews, and the wartime attitudes of clergy who had participated in anti-Jewish activities before the war.

One distinguishing feature of Polish literature treating the Church's position on the annihilation of Jews is its almost complete neglect of the manner in which the Church perceived Jews and the "Jewish question" before the war.[7]

4. See *Ten jest z Ojczyzny mojej: Polacy z pomocą Żydom, 1939–1945*, ed. Władysław Bartoszewski and Zofia Lewin (Kraków, 1969); Franciszek Stopniak, "Katolickie duchowieństwo w Polsce i Żydzi w okresie okupacji niemieckiej," in *Polskie podziemie polityczne wobec zagłady Żydów* (Warsaw, 1988); and Stopniak, "Katolickie duchowieństwo w Polsce i Żydzi w okresie niemieckiej okupacji," in *Społeczeństwo polskie wobec martyrologii i walki Żydów w II wojnie światowej*, ed. Krzysztof Dunin–Wąsowicz (Warsaw, 1996), 19–42; Zygmunt Zieliński, *Problem ratowania Żydów przez polskie zgromadzenia zakonne w okresie okupacji hitlerowskiej* (Warsaw, 1983); and Z. Zieliński, "Activities of Catholic Orders on Behalf of Jews in Nazi-occupied Poland," in *Judaism and Christianity under the Impact of National Socialism*, 381–94.

5. See D. Libionka, "Die Kirche in Polen und der Mord an den Juden im Licht der polnischen Publizistik und Historiographie nach 1945," *Zeitschrift für Ostmitteleuropa Forschung* 2 (2002): 188–214.

6. For example, *Dzieło miłoszerdzia chrześciajańskiego: Polskie duchowieństwo a Żydzi w latach okupacji hitlerowskiej* (Warsaw, 1968) was even reissued recently under the authorship of Franciszek Kącki, *Udział księży i zakonnic w holokauście Żydów* (Warsaw, 2002).

7. This omission is in part due to the tardiness of Polish research. The most important works on this subject came from outside Poland. See Ronald Modras, *The Catholic Church and Antisemitism: Poland, 1933–1939* (Chur, Switz., 1994); and Viktoria Pollman, *Untermieter im*

Familiarity with the position of the prewar Church, however, is necessary for understanding both its actions and its disinclinations in the later period. In the 1930s, and particularly in the second half of that decade, the Church as an institution was tolerant of expressions of antisemitism in public life, although a considerable portion of the clergy and Catholic publicists formally distanced themselves from antisemitic ideology and its most radical proponents. More neutral slogans were used by these Church "moderates" to define appropriate Christian behavior toward Jews: "healthy reflex," "defense mechanism" or "self-defense," and "defense of one's proper rights." Still others, primarily Jesuits, labeled themselves "a-Semites." Nonetheless, even such emphatic distancing from radical positions or theories did not signify a revision of the established view, which asserted that Jews themselves—or, rather, "the type of Jewish psyche" formed by centuries of the doctrinal, ethical, and social "defects" of Judaism—were the cause of antisemitism.[8] Most important, to a significant majority of the diocesan and monastic clergy (and not only sympathizers of the nationalists), the solution of the "Jewish question" appeared to be one of the main challenges confronting the Polish state. Aversion to Judaism, constituting over centuries an immanent part of the Church's teaching, yielded in this period to a "modern" approach that treated the "Jewish problem" in national and racial categories. Theological argumentation was increasingly supplemented by reasoning from the fringes of the philosophy of history, economics, politics, and psychology. The traditional image of Jews as murderers of Christian children gave way to a vision of Bolsheviks and their agents, carrying out murders against the Christian populations of Spain, Mexico, and the Soviet Union. Jewish moneylenders were replaced by the sharks of international financial circles, and Pharisees and Cabalists by the all-powerful "Elders of Zion." Particularly in the Catholic press, anticommunism became the most important engine of antisemitic propaganda.

Obsessions with "Judeo-communism" (Żydokomuna) and the "Jewish conspiracy" were by no means the sole domain of mass-circulation papers such as Mały Dziennik. The press of the Catholic intelligentsia was no less bigoted in its tracts, significantly contributing to the enhancement of anti-Jewish stereotypes and the distortion of reality.[9] Even those supplied with French Catholic intellectual models found it difficult to free themselves of the influ-

---

christlichen Haus: Die Kirche und die "Jüdische Frage" in Polen anhand der Bistumpresse der Metropolie Krakau, 1926–1939 (Wiesbaden, 2001). For Polish work on the subject, see Anna Landau-Czajka, "Żydzi w oczach prasy katolickiej okresu II Rzeczypospolitej," Przegląd Polonijny 4 (1992): 97–113, and "Rozwiązanie kwestii żydowskiej w Polsce w świetle prasy katolickiej lat międzywojennych," Dzieje Najnowsze 1 (1993): 1–13.

8. Ks. Eugeniusz Dąbrowski, "Chrystianizm a judaizm," Warszawskie Studia Teologiczne 10 (1935), 97, 119.

9. Dariusz Libionka, "Obcy, wrodzy, niebezbieczni: Obraz Żydów i 'kwestii żydowskiej' w prasie inteligencji katolickiej lat trzydziestych w Polsce," Kwartalnik Historii Żydów 3 (2002): 318–38.

ence of the antisemitic heritage.[10] Doing so was made even more difficult by the fact that the bishops' pronouncements left no doubt as to the actual position of the Church's hierarchy. A typical list of accusations against Jews is included in the pastoral letter of Bishop Henryk Przeździecki of Podlasie on 15 September 1938, which indeed pointed to the difficult position of the Jewish population in Poland:

> Your [Jews'] biggest enemy is your fellow countrymen, who inculcate in you hatred of other peoples; who throughout the world take part in various disturbances, revolutions, in oppression and murder of people, play the role of their executioner; who promulgate drunkenness, disbelief, debauchery, in conversations, letters, brochures, books, in cinemas, in fashion; who deceive and bring people to degradation; who, in countries where for centuries they have found shelter, want to own property and even to rule those countries; who belong to Masonic, communist, and other similar organizations. You know what your fellow countrymen have done and continue to do in Soviet Russia, Spain. . . . Work, strive harder to stop what they do. Your fate will then change. There will be no hatred toward you. Antisemitism will disappear from the face of the earth.[11]

Likewise in the pronouncements of the highest Church dignitaries, accusations of a purportedly Jewish inclination to political radicalism multiplied, as did warnings against "threats" in political, cultural, economic, and moral spheres.[12] The "Catholic" differed from the "nationalist" approach to the Jewish problem in its critical appraisal of brute force as a method of political struggle. That the Church and the Catholic press "condemned" the increasing violence of anti-Jewish attacks was not, however, synonymous with depriving their instigators and participants of the moral right to come out in defense of the Polish national interest. To a certain degree, even in the columns of *Ateneum Kapłańskie*, the Polish clergy's most important organ in the interwar period, such incidents were justified by the claim that proponents of communism were dominant among Jews, or that "the Pole, in his own country, has been dispossessed of his property, while factories and homes, shops and banks have become Jewish possessions." According to this interpretation, resorting to violence, in itself mistaken and sinful, was "an understandable reaction and healthy self-defense in the face of the terrible expropriation that [the Jews]

10. Dariusz Libionka, "Kwestia żydowska', myślenie za pomocą clichés: 'Odrodzenie' 1935–1939; Przyczynek do historii antysemityzmu w Polsce," *Dzieje Najnowsze* 3 (1995): 31–46.

11. Henryk Przeździecki, *Listy pasterskie 1928–1938* (Siedlce, 1938), 373.

12. See "Delegacja Związku Rabinów Rzeczpospolitej Polskiej u Jego Eminencji Kardynała Aleksandra Kakowskiego," *Wiadomości Archidiecezjalne Warszawskie* 6–7 (1934): 248; August Hlond, "O katolickie zasady moralne," *Przegląd Katolicki* 13, 14, and 16 (1936); "Orędzie Księcia-Metropolity Sapiehy z powodu zajść krakowskich," *Prąd* 30 (1936): 168–70.

themselves have done."[13] Such a position amounted to resignation from creating real alternatives to the nationalist version of militant antisemitism. Thus, on the eve of the war advocates of the "de-Judaization" of culture and the economy, of the introduction of religious schools and *numerus clausus* at universities, of Aryan sections at public institutions, and finally of the emigration of Jews, whether voluntary or forced, dominated among the Polish clergy. And the Catholic press, even of the more elevated variety, did not offer any guidelines for proper Polish-Jewish coexistence but instead anticipated a rapid escalation of the conflict.

The Church Hierarchy and the Extermination of Jews

Beginning in September 1939, occupied Poland became the testing ground for the anti-Jewish policies of the Nazis. Over the course of several months, anti-Jewish measures were introduced on an unprecedented scale. How did Polish Church circles view the situation of the Jewish population? This problem cannot be examined in isolation from the situation in which the Polish clergy found itself under German occupation. After Poland's defeat in the war with the Germans, the structure of the Church was thrown into disarray, while the clergy, like the entire Polish elite, became the object of persecution and repression. The papal nuncio and the Primate left the country. The Gniezno, Poznań, Chełmno, Włocław, and Katowice dioceses, as well as fragments of several others, were incorporated into the Reich. The dioceses of Warsaw, Lublin, Kielce, Sandomierz, Siedlce, and Tarnów, plus the greater portions of the Kraków and Przemysł dioceses, as well as smaller fragments of several other Church provinces, found themselves within the borders of the General Gouvernement (GG), the German occupation regime in central Poland, created in October 1939. The eastern provinces of the Church came under Soviet occupation.

German policies toward the Catholic Church varied. In the territories annexed to the Reich, brutal liquidation of the Polish Church's hierarchy began as early as 1939, followed by mass arrests and the closing of churches and religious orders. Bishops were arrested or forced to vacate their dioceses.[14] The repression of the clergy in the GG occurred on a smaller scale, and all bishops remained in their dioceses, with the exception of the Lublin bishops, Maryan Fulman and Władysław Góral, both arrested in 1939.

13. "Tragedia Żydów," *Ateneum Kapłańskie* 38, no. 2 (1936): 125–26.

14. The Płock bishops, Antoni Julian Nowowiejski and Leon Wertmański, were murdered in the concentration camp at Działdów in 1941. The vicar general of the Włocławek diocese, Michał Kozal, died in Dachau in January 1943. The personnel losses of the Włocławek diocesan clergy totaled 50.2 percent; Chełmno, 46.5 percent; Łódź, 38 percent; Gniezno, 36.5 percent; Poznań, 35.4 percent; and Płock, 30.4 percent.

At the end of 1940, in the face of German plans for enclosing Jews in ghettos, Catholics of Jewish origin became the object of Church concern, since Nazi racist legislation made no distinction between them and practitioners of Judaism. Such efforts on behalf of converts were taken up by Archbishop Adam Sapieha, who became the effective head of the Polish Church after Primate August Hlond fled the country. At the turn of 1940–41, through the intervention of Adam Ronikier, the chairman of the *Rada Główna Opiekuńcza* or RGO (Main Welfare Council, a legally functioning Polish charity organization), Sapieha appealed to the occupying authorities to exempt those persons baptized before 1 September 1939 from forced labor, resettlement into ghettos, and the obligation to wear armbands bearing the star of David.[15] The RGO began to issue certificates of Catholic Church affiliation, provoking a violent reaction from the German authorities, who let it be understood that these actions had no chance of success.[16] Indeed, despite subsequent attempts at intervention, the outcome was a foregone conclusion.[17] Nevertheless, at the end of December 1941 the Germans suddenly proposed to free thirty to forty of those identified by Sapieha as "Catholics of non-Aryan origin" from the rigors of anti-Jewish legislation.[18] This "offer" was turned down, in all likelihood because of fears about possibly unmasking Jewish converts hiding on the "Aryan side."

That such concerns were well founded is confirmed by events in Przemyśl in July 1942. After regulations ordering the creation of a ghetto were issued, Bishop Franciszek Barda of Przemyśl, as a result of requests from Catholics of Jewish origin, appealed to the German authorities asking that these people be allowed to stay in their current places of residence. The Germans demanded delivery of a list of such people, whereupon they were all forced to relocate to the ghetto; several were shot to death in the process.[19] According to other sources, however, the local Gestapo had earlier demanded from the bishop's curia a precise list of those Jewish individuals who had been baptized after January 1, 1933.[20]

In any case, those were the only efforts undertaken by the bishops on behalf of Jewish converts.[21] Nonetheless, the argument for their necessity, included in the letter from Sapieha to Ronikier, is extremely interesting. The Kraków

15. Archiwum Akt Nowych (AAN), RGO (Kraków) 5:6, "An die Regierung des Generalgouvernements Abteilung Innere Verwaltung Bevolkerungswessen und Fursorge in Krakau."
    16. AAN, RGO (Kraków) 5:62–63.
    17. Adam Ronikier, *Pamiętniki 1939–1945* (Kraków, 2001), 95–96.
    18. AAN, RGO (Kraków) 14:45, protocol of the session of the RGO of December 11, 1941.
    19. *Diecezja przemyska w latach 1939–1945*, vol. 3, *Zakony*, ed. J. Draus and J. Musiał (Przemyśl, 1990), 394.
    20. Jan Sziling, *Kościoły chrześcijańskie w polityce niemieckich władz okupacyjnych w Generalnym Gubernatorstwie (1939–1945)* (Toruń, 1988), 129–30.
    21. According to Ronikier, the matter was supposed to be discussed during one of the meetings of bishops from the GG in Kraków, although this is not confirmed by other sources; Ronikier, *Pamiętniki*, 105.

archbishop pointed out that baptized Jews "belong with us in a single community of the faithful" and that their motivations had been examined during their period as catechumens; therefore, the sincerity of their intentions could not be questioned. "Both the Church authorities and the faithful must behave in the same manner toward them as toward other members of the faith, considering them in every way as having equal rights, as brothers in faith," particularly those who had converted to Catholicism years before. "Unfortunately," he wrote further, "the German authorities take a completely different position, treating these Catholics on a par with the entire mass of Jews, who are subjected to far-reaching aggravations according to racist principles." Sapieha considered that it would be a particular misfortune for Jewish Catholics "if they were once again thrown into that environment with which they had voluntarily broken and which had become for them fundamentally alien. In that environment they are met with aversion and hatred. Their situation thus becomes exceptionally difficult and morally painful." For that very reason, "one cannot fail to take their side and attempt to clarify the existing state of things. Those converted from the Jewish faith cannot be considered members of the Jewish community. Their family relations, ideas, and customs are completely distinct from those of Jews."[22]

Several days earlier, a letter on this very matter had made its way to the RGO from the Warsaw superintendent of the Evangelical Reformed Church. It was not out of the question that the letter influenced the Kraków archbishop's actions. The authors of both these letters failed to condemn the anti-Jewish measures as such, but they do differ in their position toward converts. Whereas Sapieha treated them exclusively as Catholics, for the representative of the Evangelical Reformed Church national identity was equally important. He demanded, therefore, that the Germans make "a clear distinction between a Jew and a Christian Pole of non-Aryan origins."[23]

These different opinions reflected differences in the treatment of converts in Catholic and Protestant circles. The latter were relatively open, but among Catholics a negative stereotype of the neophytes remained.[24] In the 1930s, prejudices toward neophytes and converts alike had deepened. The sources of this mistrust included both the traditional conviction that religious conversions would lead to the "judaizing" of the Church and the "takeover" of Christian communities and the nationalist obsession with the necessity of the "defense" of the nation and the "purity" of its culture in the face of an invasion of assimilated intruders. Toward the end of the 1930s, even for many of the clergy the sacrament of baptism was not a ticket of admission to Polishness, a viewpoint

22. AAN, RGO (Kraków) 5:19–20, letter of Archbishop Adam Sapieha to Ronikier, October 30, 1940.

23. AAN, RGO (Kraków) 5:9, letter of the superindendent of the Evangelical-Reformed Church of October 25, 1940.

24. Krzysztof Lewalski, *Kościoły chrześcijanskie w Królestwie Polskim wobec Żydow w latach, 1855–1915* (Wrocław, 2002), 209, 217.

reflected in the Catholic press. On the eve of the war, even in the columns of *Ateneum Kapłańskie*, a racist logic ruled: "No person of another race undergoing baptism, for example, a Negro, will be considered a member of the white race simply because a priest belonging to the white race baptized him. The Jew is no exception here. The more so since he falls under the 'rule' that because he was a Jew *racially* and *ethnically before* undergoing baptism, so *racially* and *ethnically* he remains a Jew even *after* undergoing baptism."[25] Similarly, from the commentary of a widely read weekly for priests, it emerged that the prospect of total assimilation, even in the case of individuals "authentically" converted, was extremely distant. The "inclusion" of such an individual into the nation could be accomplished only exceptionally, for, it was taught, "the undue influence of Jews on Polishness (even those sincerely Polonized) would be harmful for us because the Jewish spirit is different from Polish (and even Aryan) spirituality, and we would be threatened by a perversion of our national psyche, by a pollution of our national type with alien elements."[26]

Even for Zofia Kossak, whose later contribution to the wartime movement to assist Jews cannot be overestimated, the vision of mass conversion looming on the horizon signified a national catastrophe. In 1936, in a dispute with young nationalists of the National Radical camp, she argued: "There is no doubt that the Catholic-Jewish element would force its features on the Polish psyche, that it would create a new nationality. Perhaps that nationality would have many positive attributes, but it would not be Polish. We will have ceased to exist as Poles. The name will remain, but its essence will have changed. And thus the happy solution for the Catholic would not give joy to the Pole."[27] Jan Dobraczyński (who was also unusually active in the effort to aid Jews during the war) was even more emphatic, convinced that "the Jew represents one world view. . . . The Pole may be a Catholic or a Protestant, nationalist or Marxist, but the Jew is always a proponent of the Jewish world view. This binds him more closely than blood ties or national traditions."[28] Greater moderation characterized the stance of the editor-in-chief of the Kraków-based *Głos Narodu*. Although there was no doubt in his mind that baptism did not yet signify acceptance into the national community, because this had to be "earned," yet he declared himself in favor of observing the criterion of national identification subjectively. In his opinion, "vigilance" in "accepting Jews into the nation," although advisable, should not be "exaggerated."[29]

During the German occupation, the Church did not entirely cease its missionary activities. On July 23, 1940, however, the Warsaw archbishop,

25. Ks. Witold Gronkowski, "Chrzest Żydów w świetle nauki Kościoła," *Ateneum Kapłańskie* 43, no. 5 (1939): 452–53.

26. "Żydzi-chrzescijanie," *Gazeta Kościelna* 31 (1938): 1.

27. Zofia Kossak, "Nie istnieją sytuacje bez wyjścia," *Kultura* 26 (1926): 1–2.

28. Jan Dobraczyński, "Niepokojące analogie," *Kultura* 20 (1939): 1.

29. J.P., "Żydzi—Chrzest—Polska," *Głos Narodu* 183 (July 6, 1938): 1.

Stanisław Gall, reaffirmed the general principle behind the requirement of a six-month period of preparation for catechumens. Organized missionary activities therefore proceeded on a large scale only in the Warsaw ghetto, where the preparatory period was shortened to six weeks.[30] Precise information about these Jewish catechumens nonetheless had to be turned over directly to the security police. In October 1942, German authorities finally forbade the baptism of Jews. The Church continued to dispense the sacraments secretly, although the adoption of Catholicism did not protect the persecuted.

The bishops' intervention on behalf of the Jewish population *as a whole* must be regarded differently. In the summer of 1940 the RGO, in concert with Archbishop Sapieha, appeared before the GG authorities requesting suspension of the mass resettlement of Jews from Kraków.[31] Not only did this have no effect, but the rabbis who had appealed to the RGO in this matter were first arrested and then murdered.[32] Possibly for this reason, the Jewish community sought no further intervention by the Church. After the creation of the ghettos, Jews and their problems effectively vanished from the field of vision of representatives of the Church hierarchy, even with the commencement of the Final Solution. A symbolic expression of this state of affairs is the memorial from Sapieha to Hans Frank dated November 2, 1942, protesting the terror on Polish lands. Although the origin of this document coincided with the beginning of the next stage in the liquidation of the Kraków ghetto, it contains no direct reference to that fact, apart from its opposition to the forcible incorporation of Poles into the so-called Construction Service (*Baudienst*) to assist in the murder of Jews.[33] In later notes from representatives of the curia addressed to the German authorities, even this matter was no longer broached. Nonetheless, one may read in Polish historical literature that in his dealings with the German authorities, Sapieha repeatedly appealed to the occupying powers for "the cessation of terror against the Jewish population," and even the statement that he had done everything within his powers to stop the persecution, while the "Jewish lobby" in the United States and Western Europe did nothing to save their own kind.[34]

This is not the only instance where the literature diverges from reality. There is also the widely held opinion that the majority of bishops resident in the GG participated in some way in actions to assist the Jews.[35] A prime example of

30. Antoni Czarnecki, "Przyczynek do duszpasterskiej działalności księży parafii Wszystkich Świętych w getcie warszawskim," *Wiadomości Archidiecezjalne Warszawskie* 7–8 (1973): 303.

31. AAN, RGO (Kraków) 8:76, protocol of the session of the RGO of July 31, 1940.

32. Aleksander Biberstein, *Zagłada Żydów w Krakowie* (Kraków, 1985), 38–39.

33. See J. Wolny, "Arcybiskup Adam Sapieha w obronie narodu i kościoła polskiego w czasie drugiej wojny światowej," in *Księga Sapieżyńska*, ed. Ks. J. Wolny (Kraków, 1987), 2:435. Slightly earlier the press of the *Armia Krajowa* (AK, Home Army) had protested this sort of practice.

34. Stopniak, "Katolickie duchowieństwo," in *Społeczeństwo* 24; Jerzy Ślaski, *Polska Walcząca*, vols. 3–4 (Warsaw, 1986), 518; Jacek Czajowski, *Kardynał Adam Stefan Sapieha* (Wrocław, 1997), 141.

35. Stopniak, "Katolickie duchowieństwo," in *Społeczeństwo* 24–26.

such misinformation is the case of the Łomża bishop, Stanisław Łukomski. This is a matter of particular importance, considering that in June and July 1941, on the territory of that diocese, numerous pogroms and murders of Jews were carried out by the local Christian population, either spontaneously or at German instigation. In Polish publications, several variants of Łukomski's involvement on behalf of Jews are put forward. Attributed to him are interventions with the German authorities in defense of Jews, the issuing of a recommendation to clergy to encourage among their parishioners a positive attitude toward the Jewish population, and words of condemnation from the pulpit for those Poles taking part in the murder of Jews.

In this context, Jan Tomasz Gross's book *Neighbors*, in addressing Łukomski's inglorious role in these events, has provoked deep indignation. According to Jewish accounts cited by Gross, Łukomski did not keep his word to a Jewish delegation that he would restrain the wave of pogroms approaching the town of Jedwabne.[36] What is the real story? Numerous discrepancies in the sources obstruct closer acquaintance with Bishop Łukomski's role. It is known that, living elsewhere in the province since the autumn of 1939, he returned to Łomża on July 8 or 9—in other words, shortly before the pogrom in Jedwabne on July 10, 1941, which brings into question the probability of his contact with representatives of the Jewish community.[37] Reference to such a meeting, however, appears in a report published in *Tygodnik Powszechny* in 1948: disturbed about the fate of the Jews, Łukomski on his own initiative supposedly made his way to the commander of the German military headquarters, attempting to gain assurance that "no atrocities" would occur. According to this account, only later did a delegation of Jews appear before him asking for intercession.[38] The issue appears in yet another light in Łukomski's own memoirs. Here the initiative for the meeting is said to have come from the German side, and the conversation revolves around entirely different questions.[39] It is difficult to believe that if Łukomski *had* taken steps to help the Jews, he would have neglected to remember them.

Equally contradictory are the references to the stance of other bishops regarding Polish participation in anti-Jewish incidents. From March 22 to 29, 1940, when a series of anti-Jewish pogroms occurred in Warsaw, Archbishop Gall is supposed to have expressed indignation at the excesses.[40] One source even claims that Gall intervened in this matter with the German authorities and addressed an appeal to the clergy to condemn the pogroms.[41] Such

36. Jan Tomasz Gross, *Sąsiedzi: Historia zagłady żydowskiego miasteczka* (Sejny, 2000), 49.

37. D. Libionka, "Duchowieństwo diecezji łomżyńskiej wobec antysemityzmu i zagłady Żydów," in *Wokół Jedwabnego*, ed. Paweł Machcewicz and Krzysztof Persak (Warsaw, 2002), 126.

38. Paweł Jasienica, "Jednym płucem," *Tygodnik Powszechny* 26 (1948), 9.

39. Łukomski, "Wspomnienia," *Rozporządzenia Urzędowe Łomżyńskiej Kurii Diecezjalnej* 5–7 (1974): 61.

40. Ringelblum, *Kronika*, 120.

41. Ruta Sakowska, *Ludzie z dzielnicy zamkniętej* (Warsaw, 1993), 236.

accounts in turn are difficult to reconcile with Sapieha's characterization of Gall, sent to the General of the Jesuit Order, from which it appears that Gall was completely intimidated by the Germans.[42] If so, his standing up for Jews hardly seems likely. Perhaps documents may yet be found in the archives that can throw new light on both the Łukomski and Gall cases.

In light of the replicating myths in Polish historical literature, it may seem ironic that the only public declaration by a Polish bishop on the subject of Jews during the German occupation had an antisemitic tone. In the pastoral letter of Bishop Czesław Kaczmarek of Kielce, titled "Religious Training and the Family Home" and published at the beginning of 1942, he asserts that Jewish children exert a "very pernicious influence" on Christian children. That document was read in all churches of the Kielce diocese and subsequently appeared in a diocesan publication.[43] Clear echoes of the Polish episcopate's age-old attempts to create a faith-based educational system in Poland resound here.[44]

At the same time, open protests by the Polish Church's hierarchy against the intensifying persecution of Jews—similar to French and Dutch bishops' statements—or active intervention with German governing circles, given the actual conditions ruling in the GG, would have carried enormous risk. Fears of making the Church's own isolation and persecution worse were not without basis. After October 15, 1941, any aid given to a Jew was punishable by death. It was not difficult for Church leaders to imagine the harsh repressions against priests or even bishops that could result from attempts at intervention on behalf of Jews. The futility of such protests likewise seemed obvious. These facts, however, do not mean that the Church's possibilities for action had been exhausted. Representatives of the hierarchy, remaining in steady contact with the Holy See through informal channels, could have transmitted information, and even initiated some sort of diplomatic action, yet the correspondence published by the Vatican shows that no such opportunities were seized.[45]

Even in the letters of Sapieha, the Vatican's primary informant, there is not a single reference to the extermination of the Jews. There is not even an allusion to the position of Catholics of Jewish origin, although unsuccessful

42. Cited in Wolny, *Księga Sapieżyńska*, 2:257. For a discussion of the attitudes of Archbishop Gall, see also Tomasz Szarota, *U progu zagłady: Zajścia antyżydowskie i pogromy w okupowanej Europie; Warszawa, Paryż, Amsterdam, Antwerpia, Kowno* (Warsaw, 2000), 76–77.

43. Czesław Kaczmarek, "Wychowanie religijne a dom rodzinny," *Kielecki Przegląd Diecezjalny* 3 (1941): 115.

44. In the interwar period, Kaczmarek's opinions on the "Jewish question" were not exceptional in any way. In the texts published in the press organ of the *Akcja Katolicka*, the future bishop called for a separation from "Judeo-Polish culture" and for an "end to coexistence with Jews and half-Jews who are not imbued with Catholic thought and the ideas of Polishness"; see C. Kaczmarek, "Problem inteligencji katolickiej w Polsce," *Ruch Katolicki* 4 (1936): 174, and "Inteligencja katolicka w Polsce i jej organizacja," *Ruch Katolicki* 12 (1936): 560.

45. *Actes et Documents du Saint Siège relatifs a la Seconde Guerre Mondiale* (The Vatican, 1967–81), hereafter cited as ADSS.

attempts had been made to change their legal status. It is no different in the case of other bishops who were in contact with the Vatican.[46] On February 28, 1942, Sapieha wrote to Pius XII and presented in precise terms the tragic position of the Church and the Polish nation, asking for the pope's intervention.[47] That letter was composed before the start of "Aktion Reinhardt"[48] and was sent to Rome on April 15, 1942. A clear convergence between the dates of Sapieha's letters and the developments of "Aktion Reinhardt" does occur, however, in letters addressed to Pius XII and to Secretary of State Cardinal Luigi Maglione dated October 28, 1942. That date marked a tragic moment in the history of Kraków's Jews: the commencement of the next stage of the ghetto's liquidation, accompanied by heretofore unseen barbarity. On this day, 4,500 people were taken to the extermination camp at Bełżec, and six hundred were murdered outright. Among them were three hundred children from the liquidated Institute of Jewish Orphans, who were taken outside the city limits and murdered. In neither of Sapieha's letters is there even a reference to the use of Poles during the liquidation actions, which *can* be found in the slightly later memorial to Frank.[49] Finally, one of his last letters to the Vatican was sent on June 18, 1943, *after* the uprising in the Warsaw ghetto and the final liquidation of the ghetto in Kraków.[50]

Another constant Vatican informant was the bishop of Katowice, Stanisław Adamski, who had been deported to Warsaw. On September 18, 1942, he sent a note and in January 1943 a report informing the Holy See of the fate of Polish bishops and the situation of the Church. He sent another report on this subject in June 1943 to Cardinal Maglione.[51] The dates of these documents were crucial moments for Warsaw's Jews: the first was written in the last days of the "great action" in the ghetto, the second at the moment the Germans were attempting the ghetto's final liquidation, and the third after the uprising had been crushed. A detailed report on the situation in his diocese was also sent by Lwów Metropolitan Archbishop Twardowski on July 12, 1943[52]—just over two weeks after the Galician district SS and police commander reported the "liberation" of his jurisdiction from Jews and the murder of 434,329 people.[53]

46. In a letter of the Przemyśl bishop, Franciszek Barda, however, whose diocese came under Soviet occupation in the autumn of 1939, there is mention of the takeover of the bishop's curia building to provide apartments to Jews (ADSS, vol. 3, pt. 1, no. 39:117–18). After the Germans occupied the territory in 1941, information about Jews ended.

47. ADSS, vol. 3, pt. 2, no. 357:539–41.

48. The operation for the murder of Jews in the GG, which was directed by the Lublin chief of the SS and police, Odilo Globocnik, carried this cryptonym. This action began on the night of March 16–17, 1942, in Lublin.

49. ADSS, vol. 3, pt. 2, nos. 436 and 437:668–70.

50. ADSS, vol. 3, pt. 2, no. 523:813–14.

51. ADSS, vol. 3, pt. 2, no. 413:639–40, no. 472:728–31, and no. 527:818–21. The Vatican documents were translated by Rev. Stanisław Musiał.

52. ADSS, vol. 3, pt. 2, no. 529: 822–24.

53. Friedrich Katzmann, *Rozwiązanie kwestii żydowskiej w dystrykcie Galicji*, ed. A. Żbikowski (Warsaw, 2001), 38–39.

Not one of the Polish Roman Catholic bishops did anything remotely resembling the response of Andrii Szeptyts'kyi, the metropolitan of the Greek Catholic Church in Lwów. Despite his initial delusion that the Germans might be potential allies in the struggle for an independent Ukraine, in late August 1942 he alerted Pius XII to the mass crimes against the Jews.[54] It should also be emphasized that Pirro Scavizzi, an Italian priest and hospital train chaplain through whom Sapieha transmitted his letter of February 28, 1942, to the pope, shortly thereafter acknowledged the necessity of turning the pope's attention to the extermination of the Jews.[55]

Although the problem demands further analysis of source material in Polish and other archives, a preliminary hypothesis of the reasons for the profound gulf separating the Church from the mass crimes perpetrated in its Polish dioceses can be offered. This gulf may be ascribed only partially to a series of unfortunate coincidences and to the individuals holding key bishoprics. The bishops of the Lublin diocese, where the first mass extermination camp in the GG was founded (Bełżec), lived in isolation, whereas the extermination centers at Sobibór and Treblinka were located in the territory of Podlasie diocese administered by Czesław Sokołowski, the only member of the Church hierarchy identified by the Polish underground as an opportunist and collaborator.[56] The Warsaw archbishopric, in turn, was occupied by the ailing Stanisław Gall, who died on September 11, 1942. Such explanations are, however, hardly convincing. One might likewise point to the fact that at least several bishops—certainly including Sapieha, who maintained constant contact with representatives of the Polish government-in-exile inside the country—had to be aware that precise information on the country's situation regularly reached the Vatican through the agency of the Polish ambassador to the Holy See.[57] In any case, that knowledge did not prevent the Kraków archbishop from alerting the pope to the tragic position of the church and the Polish people, but Polish Church circles clearly did not feel a similar moral injunction regarding the Jews. There was likewise no attempt to use the Polish underground in order to deliver information on Jewish issues to the Vatican.[58] It is not out of

54. ADSS, vol. 3, pt. 2, no. 406:625–29.

55. In Scavizzi's letter to the Pope of May 12, 1942, we read: "The fight against the Jews is unrelenting and is constantly getting worse, with deportations and mass executions. The massacre of Jews in Ukraine is already complete. In Poland and Germany the intent is also to conclude it by a system of mass killing": ADSS, vol. 8, no. 374:534. On October 7, 1942, Scavizzi submitted a report on the situation in Poland, including information on the murder of two million Jews: ADSS, vol. 8, no. 496:669–70.

56. AAN DR/202/1–32, 39, "Attitudes and Political Position of the Catholic Clergy in Poland," January 6, 1943.

57. The Polish ambassador to the Vatican, Kazimierz Papée, submitted several reports on the extermination of Jews—among others on October 8, 1942, December 19, 1942, and March 23, 1943.

58. Representatives of the Church were in constant contact with the Polish underground and had transmitted numerous materials affecting the Church to the Polish government-in-exile in London through its auspices. Representatives of the Church also met with Jan Karski, courier of the London government, before his departure from the country.

the question that—just as in some émigré circles[59]—the Kraków curia feared that the topic of Jewish martyrdom could eclipse that of the Church and the Polish population, thereby reducing further the chance for a diplomatic reaction on their behalf from the Holy See, a reaction for which they waited in vain.

There remains the question of whether all materials related to the correspondence of the Polish bishops have been published. It is possible that documents hidden in the Vatican archives could alter the hypotheses presented here. Moreover, it cannot be ruled out that information on the fate of the Jews could have been transmitted orally to individuals who remained in contact with the Polish bishops.[60] Evidence that information did reach Rome by private channels can be found in a note from the Vatican's secretary of state discussing the delivery to Warsaw in May 1943 of lists of Jews, with a request for Bishop Adamski's assistance in attaining information about their fate. That mission ended in failure; Adamski reportedly responded that the Warsaw ghetto had ceased to exist, and the Jews concerned had perished, been imprisoned, or were hiding under false names.[61] Still more mysterious is a note from Adamski from January 1943, discussing the failure of oral and written initiatives with the authorities of the Warsaw ghetto undertaken by Archbishop Gall in the matter of Catholics of Jewish origin.[62]

Materials from the Polish national archives may yet be discovered as well. It is known, however, that none of the three conferences of the episcopate that took place in Kraków during the German occupation (October 14, 1940; May 5, 1941; and June 1, 1943) discussed the condition of the Jewish population or even of converts, although their dates partially overlapped stages in Nazi anti-Jewish policy in the GG. The first conference coincided with the confinement of Jews in the Warsaw ghetto; the second deliberated a month after the Kraków ghetto was established; the third was convened shortly after the Warsaw ghetto uprising was crushed and the ghetto liquidated.

Representatives of the Church hierarchy living in exile, however, reacted differently to the persecutions of Jews. The Wrocław bishop Karol Radoński, residing in London, actively joined the Polish government's efforts to inform the world of the crimes committed in occupied Poland. In a BBC radio address delivered on December 14, 1942, he said among other things that the suffering of the Jewish people in Poland "has surpassed whatever hatred and savagery of the oppressor we are capable of imagining" and that "the murders committed against Jews in Poland . . . must awaken horror and disgust in the

---

59. Dariusz Stola, *Nadzieje i zagłada: Ignacy Schwarzbart—żydowski przedstawiciel w Radzie Narodowej RP (1940–1945)* (Warsaw, 1995), 186–87.

60. Walter Laqueur notes that there is no trace in the archives of much of the information that reached the Vatican by informal channels; see Walter Laqueur, *The Terrible Secret: Suppression of the Truth about Hitler's "Final Solution"* (Boston, 1981), 57.

61. ADSS, vol. 9, no. 255:376.

62. ADSS, vol. 9, no. 39:113.

entire civilized world." As a Polish bishop, he condemned the crimes "most emphatically."[63] Similarly well-informed was Primate August Hlond. His report to the Vatican on the situation in occupied Poland, issued in Lyons at the beginning of 1943, contained information about the confinement of Jews in ghettos and the fatal conditions there, the deportation to Poland of Jews from all occupied countries, and the mass executions and gassings of Jews.[64] These accounts came to him from the Polish government in London.

In Primate Hlond's petitions directed to the Holy See, however, there is no mention of the extermination of the Jews. It is likewise missing from his wartime notes (or at least from the published fragments); when Jews are referred to at all, they appear exclusively in a negative context. In his reflections on the prewar past we read of the "diversions of the national minorities" and "Jewish depravity"; his thoughts about the future contain the statement that industry in postwar Poland must not remain the domain of the "nameless . . . Jewish oligarchy."[65] It is fruitless to search here, moreover, for commentary on the persecution of Jews in France. Although in his postwar enunciations Hlond says that while living in France he aided Jews—Polish, French, and German—the claim is difficult to verify.[66]

In summary, information from what were after all trustworthy Polish Church sources—whether or not they were in a position to alter Vatican policy—could have played a tremendous role in transmitting to the world the truth about the fate of the Jews. Yet although many questions still await answers, everything so far suggests that the Polish Church's hierarchy, in relation to the possibilities it possessed, did very little in this regard—in part, certainly as a result of the perception of Jews as aliens and threats.

The Roman Catholic Clergy and the "Jewish Question" during the Occupation

Equally fundamental is the matter of the diocesan clergy's treatment of the "Jewish question," the stance of its representatives toward the extermination of the Jewish population and toward the provision of aid to Jews. As in the case of the Church hierarchy, reconstruction of the views of the clergy as a whole on the "Jewish question" encounters serious obstacles. Reports of the Polish underground sent to London devote little space to this matter, and the

63. "Przemówienie biskupa Radońskiego," *Dziennik Polski* (December 17, 1942).

64. Kardynał August Hlond, "O położeniu Kościoła katolickiego w Polsce po trzech latach okupacji hitlerowskiej," *Chrzescijanin w Świecie* 70 (1978), 33.

65. *Z notatnika Kardynała Augusta Hlonda*, ed. Wojciech Necel (Poznań, 1995), 148, 159.

66. He supposedly helped them in efforts at emigration, finding safe hiding places and obtaining documents. A similar claim can be found in the proclamation made by the Primate after the Kielce pogrom; see *Antyżydowskie wydarzenia kieleckie 4 lipca 1946 roku: Dokumenty i materiały*, ed. Z. Meducki (Kielce, 1994), 118.

Church-generated documentation accessible to researchers is sparse indeed. Nonetheless, the underground transmissions form a sufficiently compact picture. A report from late summer and early autumn of 1941 provides information on the critical stance of priests linked to the National Party toward the government of Władysław Sikorski, because of his "leftist and philosemitic" tendencies. Their manifestation was supposedly contained in the premier's greetings for the Jewish New Year, as well as in his nomination for Minister of Justice and Sikorski's later recognition of a deceased PPS member of Jewish origin, Hermann Lieberman. This was nothing exceptional, since all declarations of the London government regarding Jews were poorly received inside the country.[67] The report considered that the majority of the clergy was linked to centrist groups, with the younger cohort linked even to the populist movement. Such perceived affiliations, however, had no influence on the report's ultimate conclusion that "antisemitic attitudes among the clergy are rather widespread."[68]

The most capacious document characterizing the clergy's stance on the "Jewish issue" is the *Sprawozdanie Kościelne z Polski* (Church report from Poland), delivered to London through the intermediacy of the government delegation to the Polish underground. Here we read: "It is necessary to consider it a peculiar decree of the Lord's providence that the Germans, alongside the multitude of offenses that they have done and continue to do to our country, have made a good start on one score, in that they have shown the possibility of freeing Polish society from the Jewish plague and have pointed out for us the road which, naturally less savagely and brutally but consistently, we must take." There follows a reckoning of Jewish harm to Poland reiterated from the interwar Catholic press: Jews "suck the nation dry economically"; they render the development of indigenous trade impossible; and above all they are the source of society's demoralization. They are the promoters of corruption and graft; through "their secret influences on governing and administrative bodies they warp our public life, ... they run bawdy houses and trade in human beings as well as pornographic literature, they induce the people to drink, they infiltrate literature, art, and public opinion with immoral and un-Catholic views, and finally they always ally themselves with everything harmful to the Church and to Poland, everything that can weaken and degrade her." It is likewise emphasized that Jews hate the Poles even more than they do the Germans. In this situation, the direction of Polish policy had to remain unchanged, and the solution to the "Jewish question" was a matter of the utmost weight in a future postwar Poland.[69] The proposed solutions, however,

---

67. For more on this subject, see Stola, *Nadzieje i zagłada*, 116.

68. AAN, DR, 202/II-6, 108, "Situation report for the period from August 15 to November 15, 1941."

69. Studium Polski Podziemnej (SPP, Studies of the Polish Underground), MSW, teka 46, L.p. 8/Kosc., 7–8: "Church report from Poland for June and the middle of July 1941."

were not exact replicas of prewar concepts but were instead linked to Nazi models. The proposed means of accomplishing the ultimate goal, which remained Jewish emigration from Poland, included the concentration and isolation of Jews into "closed spheres of settlement," a religion-based educational system, application of the *numerus clausus*, exclusion of Jews from the army and the public sphere, the Aryanization of the free professions, and so on. The realization of this plan was considered a necessary condition for the "health of the re-born Fatherland."[70]

As Tomasz Szarota has correctly stated, that text lacks "any kind of concrete information about the German persecutions of Jews initiated from the very first days of the occupation" or any mention of the tragic situation of the Jewish population in the Warsaw ghetto.[71] Although the author and origin of this work are unknown, the views it expresses must be acknowledged as close to those of a large part of the clergy.[72] On the eve of the war a significant majority of the clergy, regardless of individual political sympathies, demanded swift resolution of the "Jewish question" and supported ideas similar to those found in this report. It is difficult to assume that there would have been a sudden change of convictions within this group, since such a radical transformation did not occur in other segments of Polish society. It is unclear whether this memorial inspired any sort of discussion among the London Poles; however, it is known that Church circles continued to endorse the postulate of Jewish emigration from Poland.[73]

There were, of course, exceptions to the rule, cases in which priests call for Polish-Jewish solidarity in the face of the common Nazi enemy in the GG.[74] Yet clerical hatred for Jews in the Soviet-occupied territories became even more entrenched after September 17, 1939. An NKVD report from the town of Nur in the area of Bielsk Podlaski attests to this radicalization of attitudes: "In October 1939, the Reverend Zarzecki . . . stated: 'The fall of Poland is the fault of the Jews and I shall not die until I myself shoot 50 Jews.' To the question . . . how he, as a priest, could reconcile murder with the teachings of Christ, Zarzecki answered: 'Killing Jews redeems our souls.' The next time, . . . Zarzecki said: 'During the German invasion I was in Vilnius and there I saw the Red Army's invasion, I witnessed how, after the withdrawal of the Polish Army the Jews were shooting from all sides. I shall not die until I kill

70. Ibid.

71. Tomasz Szarota, " 'Sprawozdanie kościelne z Polski za czerwiec i połowa lipca 1941r': Próba analizy dokumentu" (unpublished manuscript in the author's possession).

72. In the SPP archive, besides the document cited here, there is a second major report for July–August 1941, plus several shorter reports for the period from January 1943 to January 1944.

73. Father Zygmunt Kaczyński, prewar director of the Catholic Information Agency and a member of the London National Council representing the Party of Labor, developed a project to solve the "Jewish question" by resettling Jews in Bessarabia, which he presented at the session of the National Council on June 2, 1942; see Yisrael Gutman and Shmuel Krakowski, *Unequal Victims: Poles and Jews during World War II* (New York, 1986), 85.

74. Ringelblum, *Kronika*, 227.

50 Jews.'"[75] Perhaps this is an extreme and drastic case, and the source cited is hardly credible, but there is no reason to believe that the perceptions of Jews by clergy ran counter to the dominant opinions among most Poles in the eastern borderlands.

Did such opinions change in the course of the ultimate phase of the Final Solution? The absence of documents of Church provenance and the nonexistence of an underground Church press obstruct a comprehensive analysis of the clergy's views. For that very reason, "theoretical" discussions of the "Jewish question" among this group certainly came to an end. Still, the possibility cannot be excluded that priests wrote on this subject in the secular underground press. Without committing a huge error, one can assume that the worldview of the clergy harmonized with the ideology of old and new rightist formations with declared ties to the Church as an institution. Here I want to focus on the Front for the Rebirth of Poland (*Front Odrodzenia Polski*, or FOP), a small but influential organization, concentrated in the Catholic intelligentsia, which had close ties to part of the hierarchy.[76] It is precisely this organization that initiated a deeper reflection on the victims, perpetrators, and witnesses of the Holocaust. The language of its discourse, full of antisemitic clichés, attests equally to the authenticity and depth of existing prejudice against Jews within Catholic elites, as well as to their intellectual inability to deal with reality. Even in the first series of texts—manifestos written by Zofia Kossak titled *Proroctwa się wypełniają* (*Self-fulfilling prophecies*), full of passionate condemnation of Nazi policies and instances of indigenous collaboration—there is not the least effort to overcome antisemitic conceptualizations. On the contrary, the idea that the Jews' fate was a punishment justly brought upon them remains beyond discussion. Fittingly, only the "hecatomb of Jewish children, who certainly were not guilty of anything" stirred some slight doubts. There was some evenhandedness, to be sure, in the self-critical accents: the "responsibility" for the fact that Jews remained Jews had in part to fall on Catholics who did not display missionary zeal.[77]

Even the liquidation of the Warsaw ghetto did not weaken the force of antisemitic stereotypes. In the proclamation *Protest* that appeared at the beginning of August 1942, alongside ardent calls to condemn the crime and the conspiracy of silence surrounding it, an unmistakably ideological-sounding declaration is found: "Our feelings toward the Jews have not changed. We have not ceased to consider them the political, economic, and cultural enemies of Poland. What is more, we are well aware of the fact that they hate us more than they hate Germans, that they are making us responsible for their mis-

75. Quoted in Marek Wierzbicki, *Polacy i Żydzi w zaborze sowieckim: Stosunki polsko-żydowskie na ziemiach północno-wschodnich II RP pod okupacją sowiecką (1939–1941)* (Warsaw, 2001), 227.

76. AAN, DR, 202/II-6, 13, Situational report for the period November 15, 1941, to June 1, 1942.

77. "Proroctwa się wypełniają," *Prawda* (May 1942), 5.

fortune. Why, on what grounds?—that shall remain the secret of the Jewish soul, but nonetheless it is a constantly confirmed fact."[78] The text then explains this fact from the antisemitic perspective of an established Jewish "psyche"—the reason Jews hate Poles is the "Jewish ethic"—which is then coupled with the constant reminder of Catholic morality's absolute superiority over Judaism: "Only Christianity is capable of inducing man not to enjoy his enemy's misfortune."[79] Similar thinking governs the text published in another FOP magazine during the fighting in the Warsaw ghetto. And this time the call to aid the Jews is accompanied by extremely antisemitic overtones. It attempts to convince the reader that the ghetto fighters are negating the shameful history of the cursed Jewish nation, dominated by ignominy, trickery, cowardice, and hatred (Jews were supposedly the mechanism of the majority of armed conflicts in Europe). Kossak, the author of the text, is unable to conceal her scorn for those who "walked passively to the gas chambers or to their firing squad"; she hoped with missionary fervor that in the face of death the grace of the True Faith would be given unto Jews and that the "baptism of blood" would thus lead them to salvation.[80]

Another FOP brochure deserving attention is on the subject of missionary activities among Jews who, it was supposed, would remain in Poland for yet some time. Assuming that one ought not to equate baptism with "entrance to the Polish national community," it recognized the necessity of creating a "community [that will be] Catholic by religion, but Jewish by nationality." A Polish chaplain would presumably stand at the head of this Jewish "national parish." Activity of this sort was intended to occur initially in one church in Warsaw, and subsequently in other cities. It was assumed that the liturgy would be conducted in Polish and Hebrew.[81] Similar ideas had already appeared in the 1930s and were treated skeptically by the Church hierarchy.[82] But the authors of this project could have been inspired by the Catholic community of Jews in the Warsaw ghetto which survived until July 1942.

As is generally known, the FOP created an organization to help the Jews. The first step in this direction occurred on September 27, 1942, with the formation of the Provisional Committee of Aid to the Jews, named after Konrad Żegota. On December 4, 1942, it was replaced by the Council of Aid for Jews under the Government Delegation, with the cryptonym "Żegota." The FOP

---

78. Quoted in *Polacy-Żydzi, 1939–1945: Wybór źródeł*, ed. Andrzej K. Kunert (Warsaw, 2001), 213.

79. *Prawda* (September 1942), 9.

80. "Wokół płonącego getta," *Prawda Młodych* (April–May 1943). Zofia Kossak has only subsequently been identified as the author of this text; see Kunert, *Polacy-Żydzi*, 272.

81. *O zadaniach misyjnych katolików polskich*, supplement to *Prawda* (undated).

82. Even a project of the Jewish church organization appeared, based on the Syrian-Chaldean rites in Aramaic. In the opinion of its initiator only a "Jewish" clergy would be able to adapt to the "needs of the Jewish spirit," foreign to a Pole; see S. Stolarz, "Krok naprzód do rozwiązania kwestii żydowskiej," *Ateneum Kapłańskie* 36 (1935): 79–86.

was the only rightist group taking part in its actions.[83] It is uncertain whether representatives of the Church were active in its founding. Numerous Warsaw priests did actively participate, led by FOP activist Jan Zieja.[84] But for the most part the organization was run by the laity.[85] Reactions to Żegota among the priestly ranks varied. The majority of the provincial clergy remained passive, or didn't even know of its existence. Judging by the account of the former AK head of intelligence for several counties in Mazowia, it appears that "the position of the Catholic clergy, both to the liquidation of the Jews and to acts of aid for those remaining, was rather indifferent—and any aid on the clergy's part was practically nil. Of course, there were instances of help, but unfortunately they were barely perceptible. There may well have been kindhearted references [to Jews] in some homilies, but the clergy on my turf did not effectively manifest itself in any visible way."[86]

To a certain extent, this passivity should be linked to a lack of clear instructions from above. The Church hierarchy's ties with the FOP did not translate into support for Żegota; during the council's entire existence none of the bishops sent Żegota a clear sign of endorsement. Only Bishop Radoński, in the aforementioned BBC broadcast, referred to the contents of *Protest*, emphasizing that its composition "is redolent of the true spirit of Christian brotherly love and human compassion and represents an expression of what every Polish Christian feels."[87] Certainly this passive stance arose at least in part from anxiety over the German repression that could result from activity on behalf of Jews. The bishop of the Polish armed forces headquartered in London, Rev. Józef Gawlina, pointed to the Polish Church's limited room for maneuver. His homily of October 3, 1943, dedicated to Polish children and given in the presence of the president and members of the government-in-exile, contained an unusually strong expression of solidarity with the persecuted Jews: "In speaking about the salvation of our persecuted youth, we do not exclude any religious or national group. All are children of God and sons of the motherland. In praying for Polish children, let's not forget about Jewish children, whose severe fate has been prepared by the cruelty of a modern Assyria. We are chilled to the bone when we read of the barbarous system of murder of the Jewish nation. At the very least, as in the Middle Ages, Catholic churches again should have become safe asylums and shelters for the persecuted and displaced. Catholic churches in Poland should have willingly opened

83. The organization comprised representatives of the Polish Socialist, Peasant, and Democratic parties, the FOP, as well as Jewish organizations—the Bund and the Jewish National Committee.

84. Bartoszewski and Lewin, *Ten jest z ojczyzny mojej*, 819–20.

85. The subject of the clergy's ties to Żegota has not yet been treated. A monograph about that organization provides little information in this regard; see Teresa Prekerowa, *Konspiracyjna Rada Pomocy Żydom w Warszawie, 1942–1945* (Warsaw, 1982).

86. Archiwum Żydowskiego Instytutu Historycznego (AŻIH), 301/4164: account of Henryk Mściwoj–Radziszewski (February 6, 1948).

87. "Przemówienie biskupa Radońskiego."

their doors not only to Christians, but also provided comfort to Jews in the safety of our altars out of brotherly love. But the churches are closed, the chaplains have vanished, and the pagan fist of the new Nebuchadnezzars even strike in the house of the Living God."[88]

To be sure, there is evidence that the Wilno archbishop, Romuald Jałbrzykowski, had already issued a recommendation in 1941 that monasteries and convents hide escapees from liquidated ghettos.[89] Individual gestures could also partially compensate for the episcopate's lack of tangible support for Żegota: for example, Sapieha's issuance of a dozen or so baptismal certificates to Jews in need,[90] and the hiding of Jews in a bishop's residence (Lwów).[91] Still, the only member of the episcopate engaged in organized activity on behalf of Jews was the Pińsk suffragan, Karol Niemira. This was carried out far from his home diocese, however, which the bishop was forced to evacuate in September 1939 after the Soviet invasion. Niemira returned to Warsaw, where he had earlier been the parish priest of St. Augustine's, and joined the Korpus Bezpieczeństwa (Security Corps), an underground organization of the AK which maintained numerous contacts with the Jewish Military Union, a Zionist formation, and participated in its activities in support of Jewish resistance inside the Warsaw ghetto.[92]

Despite the lack of encouragement from above, some priests provided various types of assistance to the Jewish population. The scope and forms of their engagement have not thus far been convincingly examined, nor is this the place for their detailed analysis. According to Church historians, it appears that from 1939 to 1945, nearly 800 Catholic clergy took part in activity of this sort, including 265 nuns.[93] The credibility of these figures remains a serious problem, however, and even if accurate, they do not represent more than a few percent of the clergy as a whole. The number of those taking part in long-term aid to Jews could not have amounted to more than a few dozen— which is still significant, considering the Polish Church's difficult situation as well as the character of German policy in occupied Poland.[94] The fact that aid to Jews was punishable by death should not be taken lightly; estimates of the

88. *Józef Feliks Gawlina Biskup Polskich Sił Zbrojnych*, ed. Andrzej Krzysztof Kunert (Warsaw, 2002), 123. I wish to thank Tomasz Szarota for bringing this text to my attention. Bishop Gawlina was overly pessimistic in his evaluation of the situation in the country; churches and cloisters did frequently provide asylum for the persecuted, particularly children.

89. Stopniak, "Katolickie duchowieństwo," in *Społeczeństwo*, 23–24.

90. Bartoszewski and Lewin, *Ten jest z ojczyzny mojej*, 824.

91. Z. Fijałkowski, *Kościoł katolicki na ziemiach polskich w latach okupacji hitlerowskiej* (Warsaw, 1983), 34.

92. AŻIH 301/5792, account of Karol Niemira.

93. Stopniak, "Katolickie duchowieństwo," in *Społeczeństwo*, 34.

94. On the basis of existing sources it is difficult to determine what proportion consisted of aid for coreligionists. In the estimation of the chronicler of the Warsaw ghetto, that activity, although it made for a "lovely chapter in the activity of the Polish clergy," was not a part of the action to aid the Jews; see Ringelblum, *Stosunki*, 149–50.

number of clergy murdered in the course of aiding Jews range from a dozen to several dozen, of which the lower figures seem more likely. In the calculations made by the Main Commission for the Examination of Nazi Crimes in Poland, it appears that eleven priests and monks and ten nuns were executed for precisely this reason.[95]

Of those instances of aid to Jews noted in the sources, a decisive majority come from the territory of GG and the eastern provinces. After the outbreak of Soviet-German hostilities, priests of the eastern dioceses were the first to be confronted with the genocide. Many of them witnessed the eruption of violence against Jews, whether provoked by the Germans or spontaneously prompted by their own parishioners who sought to "avenge themselves" for "wrongs" suffered during the Soviet occupation. In a few places, priests courageously intervened in defense of Jews threatened by such attacks. In Knyszyn, in the Wilno diocese, the priest thwarted preparations for a pogrom and every Sunday appealed for aid to the Jews. The parish priest in neighboring Jasionówka did not succeed in halting the violence, although he repeatedly attempted to restrain his parishioners: "There, where there were no Germans, he hit them [the Poles] with sticks, and, seeing that no speech or admonishment helped, threatened them with damnation if they continued to do such injustices." In a few towns in the Łomża diocese, events came to a similar head, although the clergy there had been distinguished before the war by its profound antisemitism. In the village of Rutki the priest attempted to stop the murder of Jews by a group of armed Poles. At daily mass in Grajewo the local priest admonished parishioners against taking part in antisemitic provocations, though according to Jewish sources, in Goniądz and Szczuczyn (also located in this region) priests refused to help the Jews. The most murderous incidents took place in Radziłów and Jedwabne on July 7 and 10, 1941, respectively. Directed by a mixture of fear and his own view of the world, the Radziłów parish priest did not react to preparations for a bloody settling of accounts with Jews. Only after the wave of violence had rolled through the region did he baptize a Jewish family rescued from the pogrom to increase its members' chances for survival; later he also baptized (for a suitable fee) other Jews. But the parish priest from Jedwabne, although he had stopped anti-Jewish incidents on June 26, 1941, with the argument that "the German authorities themselves are already making order," made no effort at intervention during the tragic events of July 10, which led to the immolation of several hundred Jews in a barn.[96]

Up to the beginning of Aktion Reinhardt, priests in the GG devoted themselves to the care of converts as well as to charitable activity. With the onset

---

95. Wacław Bielawski, *Zbrodnie na Polakach dokonywane przez hitlerowców za pomoc udzielana Żydom* (Warsaw, 1987). In several instances the author's interpretation of facts is at least questionable.

96. All aforementioned cases are described in Libionka, "Duchowieństwo."

of the mass extermination of Jews, the problem of organizing aid to those seeking to hide on the "Aryan side" became paramount. A few priests procured the necessary baptismal certificates and helped find safe apartments for ghetto escapees. Jews were hidden in church buildings, sometimes for many months. This sort of activity was conducted in Warsaw, Kraków, and Lwów, for priests in larger urban centers were as a rule more engaged in underground activity and its causes than the provincial clergy. It was also easier in larger cities to maintain the discretion and security necessary to the provision of effective assistance to Jews. In the majority of cases, aid for Jews took the form of immediate support. Whether the activity was long-term or immediately specific, however, the initiative came from individuals rather than organizations—except in the case of hiding children who, through the efforts of children's department of Żegota, found their way to Church orphanages, boarding schools, and monasteries. Of the approximately 2,500 children saved by Żegota, 500 survived the war in places run by the religious orders. Most engaged in this activity were the sisters of the Family of Mary, in particular the Mother Superior of the Warsaw province, Matylda Getter, as well as the nuns of the Most Holy Virgin Mary. It is estimated that Jewish children found their way into 180 institutions belonging to 37 women's religious communities, though not all of them cooperated with Żegota.[97]

The question arises as to how aiding Jews was generally perceived within the Church and by its lay and monastic clergy. Nechama Tec cites the startling testimony of a Żegota member that one of the bishops, inspecting a convent demanded the categorical removal of all Jewish children located there.[98] Likewise characteristic were the vicissitudes of Genowefa Czubak from the order of Missionaries of the Holy Family, whose convent was located in a rather small building in Prużań; having decided to help a Jewish woman, she confronted aversion from her community and conflict with her superiors, ending with her removal from the assembly.[99] It is difficult to generalize here, but although there is no way to deny the influence of antisemitism on the dimension of aid to Jews, at the same time it is important to remember the objective conditions affecting the scale of this assistance. Members of the clergy were public figures, and as such their activities were closely monitored by the occupation authorities. Any suspicion of providing aid to Jews would have carried serious repercussions.

The idea of the spiritual transformation of Polish antisemites during World War II is strongly rooted in the Polish literature. This sort of assertion arises not from serious analysis of the sources, however, but rather from a general-

97. E. Kurek, *Dzieci żydowskie w klasztorach: Udział żeńskich zgromadzeń zakonnych w akcji ratowania dzieci żydowskich w Polsce w latach 1939–1945* (Lublin, 2001), 118–19.

98. Nechama Tec, *When Light Pierced the Darkness: Christian Rescue of Jews in Nazi-Occupied Poland* (New York, 1984), 139.

99. Genowefa Czubak, *W habicie* (Warsaw, 1986), 117, 140.

ization based on a few individual cases. These cases do not rule out the participation of persons with antisemitic convictions in the acts of aid to Jews already discussed, priests among them. Rev. Marceli Godlewski (1865–1945), who was linked to the Endecja (the National Democratic Party) before the war and active in anti-Jewish activities, was parish priest of the Warsaw Church of All Saints, which fell within the borders of the ghetto during the occupation.[100] Together with his subordinates he led a charitable and pastoral effort for some 2,000 Catholics of Jewish origin. These priests likewise provided the baptismal certificates needed to forge documents and helped place Jewish children in monastic institutions.[101] Even Bishop Niemira had an antisemitic episode in his biography.[102] There is, however, no way to tell what portion of the Catholic clergy underwent a spiritual transformation or, for that matter, acted on behalf of Jews without renouncing their antisemitic views. Representative of the latter is the Reverend Popławski, parish priest of another church in the Warsaw ghetto, who in the summer of 1941 confided to Adam Czerniaków, head of the Jewish Council, that "after the war he would leave the ghetto as the same antisemite he had been when he arrived there."[103] In some of the Church institutions that were hiding Jews, in fact, such views continued to be aired openly; a primary example was the Marian priests' boarding school in Warsaw.[104]

A large group of ideological antisemites among the clergy came from the territories annexed to the Reich. In 1939 some of them managed to emigrate, but others found their way to prisons or concentration camps. Not infrequently they fell among the first victims of Nazi terror. Rev. Ignacy Charszewski was one who suffered such a fate. He belonged to the generation raised by the Theological Academy in Petersburg, Jan Jeleński's *Rola*, and *The Protocols of the Elders of Zion*. Of his few publications, two from the 1930s

---

100. In December 1921 the antisemitic *Rozwój* assosciation organized a "Jewish knowledge" conference, at which it recognized Godlewski for his services by bestowing upon him honorary membership on its presidium. The conference was inaugurated, moreover, by a celebratory Mass at All Saints; see *Pamiętnik I. Konferencji żydoznawczej obytej w grudniu 1921 roku w Warszawie* (Warsaw, 1923), 12.

101. Ludwik Hirszfeld, *Historia jednego życia* (Warsaw, 1957), 306–11. For a characterization of the Catholic community in the ghetto, see Havi Ben-Sasson, "Christians in the Ghetto: All Saints' Church, Birth of the Holy Virgin Mary Church, and the Jews of the Warsaw Ghetto," *Yad Vashem Studies* 31 (2003): 153–73.

102. In 1929 he came into conflict with the Jewish community in Warsaw when he accused Jewish children of vandalizing the surroundings of his church and making it difficult to carry out his religious duties. He interpreted this as evidence of Jewish hatred for the Catholic Church and let it be understood that an active reaction on the part of his parishioners was possible; he also notified the press in this regard. The Ministry of Religion and Public Education deemed his acts to be "misleading public opinion" but nonetheless smoothed matters over: AAN, MWiOP/385, 111–13.

103. Adam Czerniaków, *Dziennik getta warszawskiego*, ed. Marian Fuks (Warsaw, 1983), 202.

104. "Rodzina Grosmanów," *Tygodnik Powszechny* 10 (1964). Before the war the Marians published the radical antisemitic monthly *Pro Christo*.

deserve attention: *Synowie szatana* (Sons of Satan, 1933) and *Królestwo Szatana* (The Kingdom of Satan, 1935). These books, among the most obscurantist in the antisemitic literature of the time, present a vision of Jewish world conquest and "the founding of the kingdom of Satan," based on the best existing models of anti-Jewish demonology. Charszewski, one of the few daring enough to voice publicly his belief in the authenticity of accusations of ritual murder, asserted that for Jews, "murder and drinking the blood of their victims" is the same as Holy Mass and Communion for Catholics.[105] He praised Nazism, seeing in Hitler the savior of the Christian world before its "ultimate poisoning by Jews."[106] Serving as parish priest in Dobrzyń in the Płock diocese, Charszewski was arrested on November 5, 1939, and imprisoned successively in concentration camps at Chełmno, Stutthof, and Sachsenhausen, where he died on April 14, 1940, as the result of a severe beating. Also among those arrested and confined in concentration camps was Rev. Piotr Turbak, author of the antisemitic trilogy *Walka przeciwko Żydom* (The Fight against the Jew), *Czym żydzi nas biją* (What the Jews beat us with), and *Program walki z Żydami* (A Program for struggle against the Jews).[107] Turbak, however, survived the war.

One of the few priests who escaped German repression was Rev. Stanisław Trzeciak (1873–1944). Trzeciak's works, including *Mesjanizm a kwestia żydowska* (Messianism and the Jewish question, 1934), *Ubój rytualny w świetle Biblii i Talmudu* (Ritual slaughter in light of the Bible and Talmud, 1935), *Program światowej polityki żydowskiej* [The Program of Jewish world policy, 1936), and *Talmud o gojach a kwestia żydowska w Polsce* (The Talmud on Gentiles and the Jewish question in Poland, 1939), belonged to the "classics" of interwar antisemitic literature. His message resonated equally with politicians and the widest circles of society. He was a national and international "expert" on the "Jewish question," his international fame resting on his activity in the Nazi-sponsored Institut zur Erforschung der Judenfrage (Institute for Research of the Jewish Question), headquartered in Erfurt. His popularity and recognition were reflected in the homage paid him in the columns of the most important Church publications for priests. For example, in the opinion of the reviewer for *Wiadomości Archidiecezjalnych Warszawskich* (News of the Warsaw Archdiocese), Trzeciak's *Mesjanizm a kwestia żydowska* was a virtual roadmap for conduct with Jews, the "key to understanding the Jewish question," which should guide every priest. Almost identical opinions can be found in *Ateneum Kapłańskie*.[108]

---

105. Ks. Ignacy Charszewski, "Krwawa legenda chrzescijańska czy krwawy zabobon żydowski," *Pro Christo-Wiarą i Czynem* 1 (1935): 44.

106. Ks. Ignacy Charszewski, *Synowie szatana* (Poznań, 1933), 101–27.

107. In *Głosy Katolickie* 4, 6, 7 (1937).

108. *Wiadomości Archidiecezjalne Warszawskie* 6–7 (1934): 265–66; *Ateneum Kapłańskie* 35, no. 2 (1935): 202.

During the years 1939–44, Trzeciak worked in the Warsaw parish of St. Anthony's. He was not disturbed by the Germans as a consequence of his long association with German antisemites. Until recently, little space has been devoted to this figure. In the literature there is a singular account which states that Reverend Trzeciak praised the provision of aid to Jewish children, and for many years this story served to support the argument of his active involvement in the action to aid Jews.[109] Even texts devoid of apologetic tendencies point to a lack of proof that his activities were in any way harmful.[110] The apotheosis of the author of *Polityka żydowska,* however, turned out to be premature. In April 1941 the Gestapo arrested Tadeusz Puder, a Warsaw priest of known Jewish origins. He worked as chaplain of the chapel of the Sisters of the Family of Mary in Białołęka, where he had been placed on the recommendation of Archbishop Gall in light of the danger that threatened him. In accordance with German law, Puder should have found himself in the ghetto, but after a few months in prison, thanks to the aid of the nuns, he managed to escape and survive the war. The matter of his arrest was no secret, although the name of his denouncer was unknown.[111] As it turns out, that person was none other than Trzeciak; during his interrogation, Gestapo agents informed Reverend Puder of the identity of his betrayer and his motives.[112] Trzeciak's treachery was linked to an earlier conflict surrounding the parish priest's position at St. Jacek's church in Warsaw. In July 1938, the parish, which for years had been led by Trzeciak, the idol of antisemitic circles, was taken over by Puder, a chaplain of Jewish ancestry, much to their indignation. Intervention with the curia, a smear campaign in the press, and a brutal attack on Puder—who was slapped in the face while he led Mass on July 3, 1938, by a member of a radical nationalist group—all availed nothing. Trzeciak did not forget the humiliation and later avenged himself.

In Trzeciak's career this was but a single episode. In the first months of occupation, he belonged to the circle of those prepared to collaborate with the Germans, who were used to carry out a series of anti-Jewish pogroms in Warsaw in March 1940.[113] Despite the complete failure of this group's political calculations, Trzeciak did not break contact with the Germans. In July

109. Bartoszewski and Lewin, *Ten jest z ojczyzny mojej,* 108.
110. J. Rokicki, "Ksiądz Stanisław Trzeciak (1873–1944): Szkic biograficzny," *Biuletyn ŻIH* 2 (1999): 53.
111. Information about Puder's arrest was immediately transmitted to London by the Polish underground: "Another form of persecution of the Faith occurs when the administrative authorities create so many obstacles that it is practically impossible for converts, striving to enter the Catholic religion, to do so, at least officially. . . . Moreover, Rev. Puder, a very active chaplain and convert of the Mosaic faith who has done much good in Warsaw, has been arrested for no apparent reason": SPP, MSW/teka 46/9, k.3: "Sprawozdanie kościelne z Polski za lipiec-sierpień 1941."
112. This version comes from a letter of Maria Szletyńska to Tomasz Szarota of February 10, 2001. The information is derived from the closest family member of Father Puder, made privy to the whole matter shortly before his tragic death in January 1945; see Szarota, *U progu zagłady,* 49.
113. For more on this issue, see Szarota, *U progu zagłady,* 48–49.

1940 he sent a request to the German foreign ministry, asking for its intervention on behalf of Dr. Józef Krzywiec and his wife, who had been placed in custody following their unsuccessful attempt to cross the Soviet-German border. Trzeciak referred to Krzywiec's pro-German antisemitic activities before the war (Krzywiec had supposedly informed the German embassy in Warsaw of Jewish plans to assassinate the Führer), suggesting that at present his help in anti-Jewish actions in Warsaw would also be useful. The case was subsequently turned over to Himmler, which shows the range of possible influences and important acquaintances that Trzeciak possessed.[114]

In the Government Delegation materials we find further information about Trzeciak's wartime activities. From a conversation of an underground agent with Trzeciak that took place in the spring of 1943, it emerges that he held no official meetings with the Germans, as he was suspected of doing, but rather engaged in "private and nonbinding conversations on the subject of the Judeo-Communist danger." He is supposed to have "repeatedly emphasized to the Germans that as a result of communist and Jewish denunciations, they [the Germans] often destroy Poles who could have been most useful to the fight against Jewry and communism."[115] We do not know which side initiated these meetings, but their dates were not chosen arbitrarily. The occupier, preparing to publicize the case of the NKVD murder of thousands of Polish officers in the Katyń forest in the spring of 1940 (discovered by German field police in February 1943), was sounding out the possibility of convincing representatives of the Church hierarchy to cooperate against "a common enemy." On April 9, 1943, Warsaw governor Ludwig Fischer turned to Bishop Antoni Szlagowski with the suggestion of publicizing a pastoral letter against communism. This "offer," however, was refused.[116] The bishop's position coincided with the feelings of Warsaw's priests. Against this background, Trzeciak's readiness to collaborate was exceptional. We know of cases of priests interested in taking over Jewish property,[117] discouraging parishioners from helping Jews, expressing recognition for German policy from the pulpit, and even enjoining the denunciation of Jews.[118] Still, only Trzeciak dreamed of continuous collaboration with the Germans for ideological reasons. He was not treated seriously, however. The only result of his endeavors was the publication of fragments of his works in the pages of the occupation regime's "reptile press" and citations of his words appearing on antisemitic

114. ŻIH, Kolekcja Bernarda Marka, no. 220, letter of Trzeciak to the Reich Ministry of Foreign Affairs, July 30, 1940; letter to the Reichsführer SS in the matter of the internment of the Polish military physician, Dr. Jerzy Krzywiec and his wife, September 30, 1940.

115. AAN, DR, DSW, 202/II-37, 34 and 52.

116. AAN, DR, DSW, 202/II-37, 51.

117. Archiwum Państwowe Lublin Oddział Chełm, Atka instytucji wyznaniowych (dekanatu i parafii) powiatu chełmskiego, "Korespondencja wychodząca Dekanatu Chełmskiego w Chełmie: Rok 1940," letter of the dean of the Chełm deaconate to Treuhander in Chełm, February 4, 1941.

118. Tec, 139–40; Krakowski, 395; Prawda (July 1942): 8.

posters.[119] Trzeciak's attempts to legitimize himself with the Germans by providing them documents attesting to his "real" position did not save his life. On August 9, 1944, he died from a German bullet during the Warsaw uprising.

The example of the willing but barely used services of Trzeciak is evidence that from the German point of view, Polish antisemites were completely dispensable. It was no different in the case of Rev. Józef Kruszyński (1877–1953), another recognized "expert on the Jewish question" before the war and administrator of the Lublin diocese from 1940–45. Among Polish antsemites he is an exceptional figure for the very reason that he left memoirs behind. These confessions of an antisemitic ideologue, written shortly before his death in 1953, are at the same time those of a direct witness to the Holocaust and as such constitute a unique source. From 1919 to 1925, Kruszyński was one of the main figures in the debate on the Jewish question in Poland.[120] Although he took up this issue relatively late (at age forty-two), he had been interested in Jewish literature and the Hebrew language already during his studies under the eye of the notorious Rev. Justyn Pranajtis, author of *Christianus in Talmude Judeorum* (1892). Because of these interests his colleagues from the Theological Academy in Petersburg had dubbed him "Rabbi Akiba."[121] In addition to anti-Jewish agitation by means of the written word, Kruszyński also gave unusually spirited public lectures.

In 1925 he was offered the position of rector of the Catholic University of Lublin (KUL) on condition that he cease his public anti-Jewish activity.[122] Despite distancing himself from anti-Jewish activism, however, Kruszyński's rank as a "Jewish expert" remained very high. His task was now to bring this issue closer to the Polish clergy. In a report presented during the "Course for Ministers on Sectarianism and Heterodoxy" (1931), organized on Cardinal Hlond's initiative, Kruszyński presented a vision of Jewish conspiracy against Poland and the entire Christian world, based on *The Protocols of the Elders of Zion*. The text subsequently appeared with others in a volume bearing the *imprimatur* and *nihil obstat*.[123] Kruszyński also made sure that information on the great cognitive values of the *Protocols* found its way into the *Encyklopedia kościelna*.[124] After his duties as rector came to an end in 1933,

119. For example, see "Głos ks. Trzeciaka," *Nowy Głos Lubelski* (June 17, 1943), 1. One of the posters has also been preserved; see AAN, 214/I-17, 2.

120. He was the author of a dozen brochures during this period, beginning with *Żydzi i kwestia żydowska* (Włocławek, 1920) and ending with *Stanisław Staszic a kwestia żydowska* (Lublin, 1926).

121. Józef Kruszyński, "Moje wspomnienia" (Biblioteka Włocławskiego Seminarium Duchownego, undated manuscript), 30.

122. Ibid., 158. Kruszyński's anti-Jewish publications are discussed in Anna Łysiak, "The Rev. Kruszyński and Polish Catholic Teachings about Jews and Judaism in Interwar Poland," *Kirchliche Zeitgeschichte/Contemporary Church History* 16 (2003): 52–75.

123. Józef Kruszyński, "Zgubny wpływ judaizmu na duszę polską," in *Pamiętnik kursu duszpasterskiego w sprawie sekciarstwa i innowierstwa*, comp. B. Ciszak (Poznań, 1931), 101–20.

124. Józef Kruszyński, "Żydzi," in *Encyklopedia kościelna*, ed. Father M. Nowodworski (Włocławek, 1933), 33:476.

Kruszyński, somewhat surprisingly, no longer returned to active journalistic activity. Remaining a professor at KUL all the while, instead of defending the country from the "Jewish threat," he devoted himself tirelessly to a Polish translation of the Bible.[125] Kruszyński's prewar relationship with German anti-semitism is saturated with ambivalence. In 1938, he wrote, "Hitler called Jews the microbe of the world. It is an unusually harsh accusation, but we must recognize that it is correct." At the same time, however, he did not spare words condemning the Third Reich's treatment of Jews. In his opinion, German anti-semitism had grown to monstrous proportions, unworthy of not only human culture but even that of barbarians.[126]

On November 11, 1939, Kruszyński was arrested along with other Lublin priests and remained in prison until mid-April 1940. Several months later he was appointed head of the Lublin diocese. For our purposes, what is most important is what the onetime "Rabbi Akiba" wrote in regard to the fate of the Lublin Jews. On the pages of his memoirs, antisemitic clichés mingle with authentic compassion for the Jews. He describes with horror the anti-Jewish legislation and repression that befell Jews. His condemnation is total: "No measure vindicates the Germans." The murder of hundreds of children from the Lublin Jewish orphanage especially disturbed him.[127] That is one side of the coin. Yet alongside a few piercing judgments on the nature of German policy, Kruszyński's text is full of omissions and inaccuracies. Above all, the lack of any sort of reference to the extermination camp at Bełżec immediately meets the eye; we read only that "before the concentration camps began to function, there was a mass deportation of Jews to the forest where they were murdered. First a forest near Bełżec was selected. A few tens of thousands of Jews were taken there and murdered."[128] In reality, from March to December 1942, no less than 435,000 people were murdered at Bełżec.[129] From Kruszyński's description it would appear that the extermination of Jews was primarily carried out at Majdanek. It is difficult to attribute this to bad memory, especially since he speaks accurately about events even further in the past. Quite likely the details of the extermination of Jews were of little interest to him—certainly less than the "Jewish threat" with which he had grappled during the period of the Second Republic. There may also be a direct causal link between the ignorance of the administrator of the Lublin diocese and the lack of an informed Church position on the extermination of Jews.

---

125. Józef Kruszyński, *Pismo święte Starego Testamentu: Przekład z oryginału hebrajskiego; Komentarz*, 3 vols. (Lublin, 1937–39). From the point of view of contemporary biblical studies, his translations and commentaries are of little value and have been almost completely forgotten.

126. Józef Kruszyński, "W sprawie żydowskiej," *Przegląd Powszechny* 220 (1938): 211.

127. Kruszyński, "Moje wspomnienia," 230–32.

128. Ibid., 230.

129. Peter Witte and Stephen Tyas, "A New Document on the Deportation and Murder of Jews during 'Einsatz Reinhardt,' 1942," *Holocaust and Genocide Studies* 3 (2001): 470.

Bishop Kruszyński does not recall that the Lublin "reptile press," referring to his person and positions, placed him alongside Trzeciak among the ranks of the few oppressed ideologues of prewar Poland who indicated the need for a solution to the Jewish problem.[130] Similarly, he does not write about the fact that on May 22, 1943, he issued an anticommunist pastoral letter that was enlisted in the Nazi propaganda campaign surrounding the Katyń affair. On the other hand, one must nevertheless give Kruszyński his due. He does not hide the fact that within the Polish community there were derelicts who, for 500 marks and a liter of alcohol, betrayed Jews in hiding.[131] It is also not without significance that in the spring of 1942 a Jewish girl, sent by the chancellor of the Lublin curia, hid in buildings scattered throughout the diocese for some time, with the help of perhaps a dozen priests.[132]

For our purposes, the most important question relates to the evolution, if any, of Kruszyński's worldview. To anyone reading his memoirs, it appears that his approach to the Jewish question remained unchanged. Frequent references to *The Protocols of the Elders of Zion* and, above all, his observations uttered with a sarcasm that was difficult to hide would seem to bear witness to this immutability. "I had often thought," Kruszyński wrote, "that the Jews would get theirs from the Germans. I didn't know I would live to see this moment. During the Second World War, the Germans prepared a terrible Gehenna for the Jews. Jews completely lost their political orientation. These great traders, exploiters, demoralizers themselves came to know extremely great disillusionment." Elsewhere he proclaimed: "Of course I believed that this problem would not soon be solved. I did not suppose and did not foresee that Hitler would solve the Jewish problem so quickly and radically. To be sure, he employed barbaric and very inhuman methods, but he solved it."[133]

Epilogue

The sparse amount of autobiographical materials accessible to the historian does not permit the formulation of more categorical statements on the typicality of such figures as Bishop Kruszyński. Both official and private postwar statements by Church representatives may provide a certain indication of antisemitism, but above all they attest to the opinions they formulated on the place occupied by Jews, and Poles of Jewish ancestry, in postwar reality. In the first months after the war a wave of antisemitism swept over the country. The small number of Jews, having survived the war, began to be identified in general

130. "Komu zawdzięczamy rozwiązanie kwestii żydowskiej," *Nowy Głos Lubelski* 141 (June 20–21, 1943): 1.

131. Kruszyński, "Moje wspomnienia," 234.

132. S. Kraus-Kolkowicz, *Dziewczyńka z ulicy Miłej albo świadectwo czasu Holocaustu* (Lublin, 1995), 46.

133. Kruszyński, "Moje wspomnienia," 157–58, 144, 158.

Polish opinion with the communists who had assumed power in Poland. Some died as victims of political assassination, though equally often they fell victim to murders and attacks carried out for antisemitic or criminal motives. Pogroms were yet another category of postwar anti-Jewish violence, erupting under the influence of extremely preposterous pretexts, with accusations of ritual murder in the forefront. From 1944 to 1947, around a thousand Jews were killed.

In face of the threat to their safety, spokesmen for the Jewish community appealed to the Church hierarchy, given its authority in Polish society, with a request for its official condemnation of antisemitism. Possibly the first representative of the hierarchy to whom they turned in this regard was Bishop Kruszyński, for in his memoirs we read: "Particularly unpleasant were the visits of the Jew Somersztajn [Emil Sommerstein]. He absolutely demanded that I issue an appeal for good treatment of Jews. There was not even a need for issuing such an appeal, since after the Bolshevik invasion no one had persecuted or intended to persecute Jews. There were few Jews, they inspired sympathy, and hence there was no need for their special protection. Somersztajn unendingly demanded [such protection]. [He was] [p]romising certain favors, as well as the opposite, threatening various unfriendly consequences if such an appeal were not issued. I explained that I cannot be the first to do this. Let the Polish Episcopate take an appropriate position and I will then submit to its will. I advised him to go to Kraków and that perhaps such an appeal could be published by the Metropolitan, and I would repeat it in my diocese. In these demands there was something so obsessive, that I could not free myself from the importunity of this Jew."[134]

Similarly, Adam Sapieha, Czesław Kaczmarek, August Hlond, and Stefan Wyszyński, among others, were all approached in vain.[135] Bishop Adamski supposedly said that the martyrdom of the Jewish community was known to him and "in accordance with the premises of Christian ethics and the principles of the Catholic Church [he] condemn[ed] most harshly all murders against innocent people."[136] The reasons for this situation were complex. For the communist party the struggle against antisemitism became a convenient instrument for fighting and compromising the political opposition. In this conflict the Church neither wanted nor intended to participate, but in a few pronouncements Church representatives gave voice to anti-Jewish prejudices, in particular to the stereotype of "Judeo-communism." Primate Hlond's declaration, made after the Kielce pogrom, stated that the deterioration of relations

134. Ibid., 252.

135. See Anna Cichopek, *Pogrom Żydów w Krakowie 11 sierpnia 1945 r.* (Warsaw, 2000), 28–29; Michał Checiński, *Poland: Communism-Nationalism-Antisemitism* (New York, 1982), 21; Szmuel L. Schneiderman, *Between Fear and Hope* (New York, 1949), 110–11; Krystyna Kersten, *Polacy, Żydzi, komunizm: Antonomia półprawd* (Warsaw, 1992), 137.

136. "Przedstawiciele społeczeństwa żydowskiego u ks. Biskupa Stanisława Adamskiego, *Głos Niedzielny* 11 (1946).

between Poles and Jews was the fault of Jews themselves, "standing in prominent state positions in Poland, and striving for the imposition of structural forms which the vast majority of the nation does not want."[137] The majority of the Episcopate apparently shared such an interpretation.[138] Ten days after the Kielce pogrom, Bishop Łukomski wrote to Primate Hlond: "The leftist press is using the Kielce crime . . . to undermine Your authority and the authority of the Episcopate. The main Jewish organizations have mobilized themselves, merging in a certain anti-Nazi league, without a doubt primarily Jewish as well, to exert prsssure in the Jewish interest. . . . Where were these 'moralists' in 1939–1941 when the Bolsheviks were murdering thousands of Poles in Poland and deporting thousands to Russia? . . . Not one of these contemporary dictators of Poland, then under Stalin's care in Moscow, nor any of these Jewish organizations, felt any need to condemn those mass crimes."[139] That Polish Jews were the victims of genocide, about which a large portion of Church representatives remained indifferent, the bishop did not wish to recall.

Translated by Lisa Di Bartolomeo and Robert Blobaum

137. Meducki, *Antyżydowskie wydarzenia kieleckie*, 118.
138. The Częstochowa bishop, Antoni Kubina, was an exception whose declarations contained unmitigated condemnation of the crime and of antisemitism.
139. The text of this letter was found in the unorganized diocesan archive in Łomża by Jan Żaryn.

12

The Role of Antisemitism in Postwar Polish-Jewish Relations

BOŻENA SZAYNOK

P olish-Jewish relations after the Second World War, as well as the problem of antisemitism, are among the most difficult subjects of the postwar history of Poland for two fundamental reasons. On the one hand, the communist authorities did not look favorably on research into these issues and inhibited scholarly debate and publication. On the other, every attempt to describe Polish-Jewish relations in less formal circles was accompanied by powerful passions that posited the primacy of personal experience over careful analysis. Quite simply, until 1989 the postwar relationship between the two communities was neither analyzed nor subjected to open public discussion. Consequently, the state of scholarship on Poles and Jews remained for years in a state of suspended animation.

Since the beginning of the 1990s, enormous changes have occurred in Polish scholarship, and a great deal of new evidence has been brought to light. Nonetheless, blank spots continue to exist in the history of Polish-Jewish relations in general and in antisemitism research in particular. Perhaps the best illustration of the latter is that the first monograph on the 1945 pogrom in Kraków was published only recently, in 2000.[1]

In Poland the problem of antisemitism after 1945 has often been considered one of the stereotypes of postwar Polish-Jewish relations. Even if one

---

1. See Anna Cichopek, *Pogrom Żydów w Krakowie 11 sierpnia 1945 r.* (Warsaw, 2000).

agrees that this phenomenon to various degrees has been simplified or over-generalized as a descriptor of Polish-Jewish relations, that fact even further justifies the need for precise, scholarly analysis of the actual essence of this otherwise incomplete reflection of reality. It is also important to consider the circumstances of the postwar period that created an environment where anti-semitism could prosper.

Any analysis of antisemitism in postwar Poland must begin with a defini-tion of antisemitism itself, which, once established, will permit us to examine the postwar attitudes and behaviors of Poles in light of that definition. The *Nowa Encyklopedia Powszechna* (New General Encyclopedia) published in Poland in the 1990s gives the following definition of antisemitism: "An atti-tude of aversion or animosity toward Jews and those of Jewish ancestry result-ing from various sorts of prejudice; the persecution of or discrimination against Jews as a religious, ethnic, or racial group, as well as views that justify such actions."[2]

If we accept this simple encyclopedia definition, then antisemitism undoubt-edly existed in Poland after the Second World War. What remains in question is its scale. And already here we come face to face with the consequences of years of scholarly neglect of the issue. For example, estimates of victims of anti-Jewish violence in Poland after the war range in number from 600 to 3,000 persons.[3] It is important to note, however, that even these data come from a discussion of social phenomena that are broader than antisemitism, which is considered only in part by the studies that produced the data. To this day there does not exist in Poland a scholarly work that is devoted exclusively to the issue of antisemitism or that has subjected the existing estimates of Jewish victims to critical analysis.[4]

As mentioned, we also need to examine carefully the context that shaped Polish-Jewish relations after 1945 and facilitated antisemitism within those relations. Undoubtedly, such a consideration must begin by pointing out the consequences of the war. Poles and Jews, although both were victims of Nazism between 1939 and 1945, nevertheless experienced different fates. The separation of the Polish and Jewish communities by the occupier, the isolation of one from the other by forced resettlement and ghettoization, according to Michał Borwicz, led to a situation in which "the attitude [toward Jews] ceased to be that of one people toward another, and became that of one people toward an abstraction."[5] In his essay about the problem of the Holocaust in Polish

2. *Nowa Encyklopedia Powszechna PWN* (Warsaw, 1995), 1:187.
3. *Dzieje Żydów w Polsce 1944–1968: Teksty źródłowe*, ed. Alina Cała and Helena Datner-Śpiewak (Warsaw, 1997), 15.
4. For an analysis of antisemitism in immediate postwar Poland in English, see David Engel, "Patterns of Anti-Jewish Violence in Poland, 1944–1946," *Yad Vashem Studies* 26 (1998): 43–85. Unfortunately, Engel's study does not extend beyond 1946.
5. Michał Borwicz, "1944–1947," *Puls* 24 (1984–85): 60.

recollections and memoirs,[6] Feliks Tych observed "a characteristic psychological phenomenon in many memoirs: that is, the initial concern of their authors
for the fate of the Jews disappears the moment those same Jews disappear
from their field of vision behind the ghetto walls."[7] The void left by old neighbors was then filled by indifference, and these prewar neighbors, known by
name and on sight, were replaced by a single construct: Jews. Moreover, during
the years of the occupation the ubiquitous German propaganda allowed this
construct—Jews—to appear only in powerfully negative contexts.

Indifference was likewise a reaction to the enormity of a crime that could
not be prevented, and a defense mechanism in a situation that could not be
changed. As Stanisław Ossowski put in his famous essay written after the 1946
pogrom in Kielce: "The inability to be appalled by the crime is in large measure
. . . a result of wartime training: the murder of Jews had ceased to be something extraordinary. Why were those people supposed to be concerned with
the death of forty Jews when they had grown accustomed to the idea that
Hitler had killed them by the millions?"[8]

Besides the socially dominant attitude of indifference, there existed two
others that ran in opposite directions: namely, heroic attempts at rescue and
active participation in the crime. Evidence of the former may be found in the
number of Poles recognized with medals of Yad Vashem (the Holocaust memorial organization established in Jerusalem in 1953) as "Righteous among
Nations"; the latter, linked undoubtedly to the phenomenon known as the
"fatal contamination" of the wartime generation, would continue to make
itself felt after war.

Since different fates divided Poles and Jews in wartime, at war's end the
two communities found themselves with a different baggage of experience,
different expectations of the future, and different evaluations of the postwar
situation. Zionist influences, in particular, dominated Jewish perspectives after
the war; the conviction was practically universal that Poland was a cemetery
where the continuation of Jewish life was impossible. The only solution for
the future that most Jews perceived lay in emigration to Palestine and the
establishment there of a Jewish state.[9] All means and actions that facilitated

6. Translators' note: The term in Polish is *zagłada*, which means "extermination" or "annihilation" but has come to mean "the Holocaust," in the sense of the singular event of genocide
of the twentieth century. Here it is capitalized in Polish. We have chosen to use "the Holocaust"
as the best English approximation of this term from Polish, although "Shoah" would work equally
well.

7. Feliks Tych, *Długi cień Zagłady* (Warsaw, 1999), 21.

8. Stanisław Ossowski, "Koszula Nessosa," *Kuźnica* 38, no. 56 (1946): 3.

9. Palestine was the principal direction, if not always the final destination, of Jewish emigration from Poland after the Second World War. It is important to note the many obstacles encountered by Polish Jews in actually reaching Palestine, especially as a consequence of British policy
toward Jewish emigration as enunciated in the famous "White Paper." Some Jews therefore
decided to wait in DP camps for the legal opportunity to leave for Palestine; others made their
way there illegally; still others changed their decision and went to other countries, particularly

the realization of this program were given priority in the activities of the majority of Jewish political parties, with the exception of the communists and the socialists of the Bund, who argued for the reconstruction of Jewish life in Poland after the Holocaust.

In any case, Jewish issues naturally became paramount for the majority of Jews. For most, Poland and Poles were important only in those instances when they might serve the realization of programs related to the Jewish future, whether by gaining permission of the Polish government for emigration to Palestine or, in the case of those groups wishing to remain in the country, by obtaining aid for rebuilding Jewish life after the Holocaust. Both instances, however, involved only limited engagement with the Polish environment in the immediate postwar period. For the majority of Jews, Polish issues were of marginal importance. As a member of one of the active Zionist groups put it: "We were not seeking a solution for Poland, we were seeking a solution for ourselves. Those were Polish problems, Polish matters, and I didn't concern myself with them."[10]

Similar behavior—that is, association with people of shared experience—characterized the Polish community as well. Here we need to note another significant consequence of the war for Polish-Jewish relations, one that is connected to a broader development that affected other societies as well. Quite simply, wartime divisions based on the criteria of nationality served to reinforce national ties. If, following the war, it was natural to seek out people of similar experience, the easiest means of doing so lay in finding empathy and understanding from people belonging to the same nationality. The appeal to the ties that bind, to commonly shared values, was thus realized among people with shared experiences not only of the war but also of culture, religion, and history. This process of enclosing oneself within the confines of one's own nationality was further strengthened by the wartime and postwar mass migrations. In a difficult situation in which thousands of people were forced to become wanderers, the best means of support for those who abandoned their former "homelands" turned out to be the group that shared the same fate. This was true of both the Jewish and Polish populations.

In addition, we need to consider the psychological and physical state of both communities. Behind these indifferent terms hide colossal human tragedies and disasters, wounded and maimed societies in which every expression of aversion or hostility from individual Poles became for Jews a signifier of attitudes for the Polish whole. In the memoirs of Jews returning to Poland after the war there is the frequent description of unfriendly receptions on the part of the Polish community. Many survivors bitterly recall being greeted by

---

the United States. Nonetheless, it is estimated that some 124,000 Polish Jews arrived in Palestine between 1946 and 1950. See Piotr Wróbel, "Migracje Żydów polskich. Próba syntezy," *Biuletyn Żydowskiego Instytutu Historycznego* 12 (January–June 1998): 28.

10. Author's interview with Hana Szlomi in Israel, September 1995.

their prewar neighbors with comments along the line of "So, you're still alive?" Halina Birenbaum writes, "Having returned to their homeland, [Jews] found none of their own, while their former Polish neighbors, particularly in the small towns, were not overjoyed at their return."[11] For many Jews, these reactions, along with information about the genocide, became their only postwar memory taken from Poland, since soon thereafter they decided to emigrate: such experiences reinforced the desire among Jews to leave Poland, especially once they became aware of the full extent of the Holocaust.

Until 1946, antisemitism—though not a marginal problem for the Jewish population—contributed to Jewish emigration impulses only to a degree. For example, the Central Committee of Jews in Poland—the postwar representative of the Jewish community—in a memorandum of January 1946 stated: "In connection with the experiences and tragedy of the Jewish people, the goal of creating their own national seat in Palestine has been strengthened among a significant proportion of Polish Jews. . . . It is an undeniable fact that at the present moment in this country there are still cases of murder of democratic activists, employees of the security organs, and people of Jewish origin. . . . We strongly emphasize, however, that manifestations of antisemitism are not the main reason for the desire to emigrate. . . . As we have demonstrated, the basic reasons are more profound, objective, ideological, and psychological."[12]

In discussing the consequences of the war, we have yet to recall the matter of Jewish property that had changed ownership during the occupation. Michał Borwicz, in his essay on the years 1944–47, wrote that the takeover of confiscated Jewish property by Polish owners "was a social advance and, even if it turned out that the appropriation had not been planned in advance, the return of the former owners was perceived as harmful."[13] Such a situation was frequently a cause of attacks on returning Jews. A good illustration of this phenomenon may be found in data from June 1945 in Kielce province, where, of thirteen murders committed against Jews, ten were connected to the wartime takeover of their property.

One final consequence of the war that influenced Polish-Jewish relations in the postwar period was the problem of regime change in Poland. The communist takeover, assisted by the Soviet Union, was viewed by many Poles as yet another partition of Poland and a new occupation, and the stereotype of the Żydokomuna automatically implied that Jews were responsible for introducing to Poland the unpopular communist regime. The political conflict and disorder that accompanied the change of regime, moreover, fostered an environment favorable to criminal behavior, particularly banditry.

---

11. Quoted in Ewa Koźmińska-Frejlak, "Nieudana odbudowa. Powroty," *Midrasz* 7–8 (1988): 8.

12. Archiwum Akt Nowych (AAN), Ministerstwo Administracji Publicznej (MAP), 788:51–53.

13. Borwicz, 59.

The pervasiveness of these two factors led to an unusually difficult entanglement for both Poles and Jews. On the one hand, the struggle for independent Poland sometimes became a justification for bandit attacks. On the other hand, Jews often accepted the claim of communist propaganda that those responsible for anti-Jewish actions were the same groups that refused to recognize the authority of the new regime. And all this was complicated by yet a third factor: namely, the participation of several Jews in those very organs of the new state authority whose aim was the pacification of the Polish population.

The complex political situation was bound to yield different evaluations of those incidents in which Jews were victims. One example concerns the events that took place in Przeborze on May 27, 1945, which, according to Jewish representatives, amounted to a pogrom. The commander of a local unit of the Narodowe Siły Zbrojne (NSZ, National Armed Forces), Władysław Kołaciński, offers a different version of events: namely, that there was no pogrom in Przeborze; instead, he claims, during the action "individuals were shot for the persecution and mistreatment of the Polish community, for hunting down former members of the underground, and for tormenting former partisan fighters during investigations and while in prison."[14]

Those two versions well illustrate the polarized views of postwar Polish-Jewish relations. Similar in nature are the descriptions of a "train action" of early 1946 during which Jews returning to Poland were murdered. According to several authors, these activities were conducted mainly by units of the NSZ, and the number of Jews killed by them has been estimated at around 200.[15] By contrast there is the assertion among others that information on the number of victims is based on the account of a single individual and that "in reality we do not know who gave the order for the action or who directed it, but everything points to the spontaneity of the action as well as . . . the criminal element. We repeat, there was no coordinated 'train action.' "[16] There are many more examples illustrating the absence of any consensus regarding those incidents that shaped postwar Polish-Jewish relations. Regardless of the difficulties of explaining all the circumstances surrounding such events, however, there remains the fact that Jews were their victims. For Jewish representatives who provided information about these incidents, it didn't matter whether the described murders were criminally motivated, or part of an organized action, or executed by individuals acting against the interests of the Polish nation. For

---

14. Władysław Kołaciński-Zbik, "Pod okupacją sowiecką," in *Zeszyty do historii NSZ*, no. 3 (Chicago, 1964), 94. David Engel, among others, has challenged the veracity of Kołaciński's account; see Engel, 72.

15. J. Adelson, "W Polsce zwanej Ludowej," in *Najnowsze dzieje Żydów w Polsce*, ed. J. Tomaszewski (Warsaw, 1993), 393.

16. Quoted in Marek Jan Chodakiewicz, *Żydzi i Polacy, 1918–1955: Współistnienie— Zagłada—Komunizm* (Warsaw, 2000), 485.

the Jewish population, traumatized by the Holocaust, the murder of Jews conjured up a single, unequivocal connotation.

Considering the consequences of the war for Polish-Jewish relations, as well as the postwar reality in which both peoples found themselves, it is perhaps easiest to state that almost nothing could have enabled a rapprochement or facilitated a common ground where the two communities could meet each other halfway. Instead, stereotypes filled the void that isolated the two communities from each other; indeed, stereotypes came to represent simplified versions of Polish-Jewish relations. Consequently, Jewish memory of dealings with Poles after the war became characterized by a perceived omnipresent antisemitism in Polish society. Undoubtedly, antisemitic activities in Poland did exist after the war; however, in Jewish memory, antisemitism frequently appears as the only element in Polish-Jewish relations.

In an article devoted to the situation of Jews in Poland after the Second World War, Israel Gutman wrote about four forms of anti-Jewish activity: "(1) attacks having a provocative character resulting from the spread of false accusations against Jews. Incidents or riots following the accusation that Jews had murdered a Polish child for ritual purposes; . . . (2) cases of coercion with the intent of expelling Jews or divesting them of their property; (3) cases of murder during the commission of armed robbery; (4) attacks and murders unconnected to armed robbery."[17]

An analysis of the protocols of the Central Committee of Jews in Poland from 1945 to 1946 shows that to the Jewish population, security was of paramount concern. News came in almost daily of attacks on Jews, of robberies and murders. The threat of violence, moreover, coincided with the appearance of antisemitic propaganda in underground newspapers and flyers. From the bureaucracy, the Jews increasingly encountered harassment on account of their nationality. Danuta Blus-Węgrowska, in her article on the conditions of Jews in Poland after 1945, defined the atmosphere as "pogromlike" and argued that "the pogrom that took place on July 4, 1946, in Kielce could have occurred anywhere."[18]

Anti-Jewish activities grew in intensity during the period of repatriation in the first half of 1946, when approximately 125,000 Jews arrived from the Soviet Union. Some of them returned to those places where they had lived before the war, which led to an intensification both of the attacks connected with property taken over by Poles during the war years and of the perception that Jews constituted a threat to Poland. Moreover, the perpetrators of the anti-Jewish actions were seldom punished.

In the reports of the central Jewish representation from this period, there is a good deal of information on attacks against the Jewish population. In

17. Israel Gutman, "Żydzi w Polsce po II wojnie światowej—akcja kalumnii i zabójstw," in *Studia nad żydostwem polskim* (Jerusalem, 1985), quoted in Cichopek, 35.

18. Danuta Blus-Węgrowska, "Atmosfera pogromowa," *Karta* 18 (1996): 99.

April 1946 alone one notes the murder in Tarnów of a repatriated Jew from Russia, the killing of five people in Nowy Targ, and the disappearance of three Jews from a road near Białystok. Subsequent murders took place in Szczecin and Dzierżoniów, among other places. On April 30, near Czorsztyń, seven people were murdered, including a fourteen-year-old boy.[19]

Before July 1946 and the Kielce pogrom—the event that marked the apogee of postwar antisemitism in Poland—larger anti-Jewish incidents or attempted pogroms had occurred in several places. In August 1945, during one such incident in Kraków, five Jews were murdered. Rumors of ritual murder committed by Jews frequently provided a pretext for anti-Jewish violence, as was the case in Kielce.

The pogrom against Jews in Kielce requires separate treatment, since that event influenced so many aspects of the postwar history of Jews in Poland as well as Polish-Jewish relations.

On July 4, 1946, thirty-six Jews were murdered in Kielce. Most likely, the total number of victims was forty-two, since several died later in the hospital from injuries suffered during the pogrom. Among the victims were a small child, an infant, a pregnant woman, and several youths of sixteen and seventeen who were members of a kibbutz. Originating from a rumor that Jews had kidnapped a Polish child, the pogrom began in the morning and lasted more than six hours, although the anti-Jewish hostility and attempts to provoke new incidents continued into the evening. The bulk of the action took place at a building on Planty Street which housed Jews. Direct action against its Jewish residents was provoked by units of the militia and army who confirmed the rumors of the kidnapped Polish child and did nothing to prevent the assembling of a large and aggressive crowd on Planty Street. The police and soldiers were also the first to fire shots at the Jewish inhabitants of the building, giving civilians a pretext to join the fray.

Any description of the events in Kielce must emphasize the impunity of the perpetrators of the murders and looting, as well as the absence of any sort of countermeasures and the complete incapacity of the city administration, political parties, or (given his possession of repressive means) the head of Kielce's security forces to stop the anti-Jewish violence. Ordinary Polish residents of Kielce also took part in the murder of Jews; the afternoon phase of the pogrom was indeed sparked by the arrival on the scene of workers from a local factory. The number of victims, moreover, does not reflect the atrocities that accompanied the pogrom. Eyewitness reports recall the shooting of innocent victims, the police throwing young girls out of third-story windows, after which they were beaten to death by the crowd below, and the stoning to death of a young man. Moreover, although the violence was played out mainly at the building on Planty Street and its immediate vicinity, there were murders of individual Jews throughout the city as well as on trains passing through Kielce on that day.

19. Ibid., 93, 97.

Even this brief account of the Kielce events provides an indication of the scale of the tragedy.[20] What happened there had enormous implications for Jews living throughout Poland as well as for Polish-Jewish relations. For a Jewish population that had miraculously survived the Holocaust, the events in Kielce served as a confirmation of Polish antisemitism and as evidence of the profound abyss that existed between the Polish and Jewish communities. After July 4, 1946, it became obvious to the majority of Jews that they had no future in Poland. As a consequence, Jewish emigration from Poland increased dramatically and included those who had earlier decided to stay in Poland. They took with them, moreover, the worst possible impressions of Poland and the Poles. The enormity of the crime committed in Kielce against people who had somehow survived the wartime extermination of practically their entire community made impossible any other perception of these events. For the postwar history of Jews in Poland, the Kielce pogrom was a turning point.

In later considerations of the Kielce pogrom, many hypotheses emerged that sought to explain the reasons for this crime. Two alternatives are most frequently repeated: that the pogrom was the apogee of postwar antisemitism, or that it was a provocation of the security forces. Many of the facts surrounding the events of July 4, 1946, in Kielce remain unexplained to this day, persisting blank spots that allow considerable room for highly speculative interpretation. It seems, however, that a comprehensive understanding of the pogrom must take into account both of the major hypotheses mentioned above. Undoubtedly, the anti-Jewish violence in Kielce was to a certain extent provoked, but it is also true that many of the residents of Kielce were more than willing to carry it out. Soldiers, police, and civilians all figured among the murderers. Among the instigators and passive witnesses of the crime were not only representatives of the local authorities but also "ordinary people." Part of the crowd that had gathered in the vicinity of the building that housed Jews not only failed to oppose the killing but actively participated in it. Many exhorted others to violence with loud and aggressive shouts.

The debate over the Kielce pogrom and the exploration of all the circumstances that led to it, however, cannot obscure the most important fact, that more than forty innocent people were murdered. Meanwhile, the Kielce pogrom provided a pretext for different forces in the public arena to influence opinion and to take positions regarding the Jewish situation in Poland. At this point it is worth pointing out how the most important players in Polish political life—the communists, the opposition, the Catholic Church, and the intellectual elites—reacted to the Kielce pogrom. It is also important to look closely at the degree to which antisemitism influenced these players or, alternatively,

20. A far more detailed account may be found in Bożena Szaynok, *Pogrom Żydów w Kielcach, 4 lipca 1946* (Warsaw, 1992).

was perceived or addressed by them, whether before or after the Kielce pogrom.

The position of the communists grouped in the Polska Partia Robotnicza (PPR, Polish Workers Party) regarding the Jewish issue was not uniform. Among the activists of the PPR one can in fact distinguish several positions: backing programmatic assimilation of Jews in realization of the idea of the nation-state; supporting the reconstruction of Jewish life in Poland after the Holocaust; seeking aid for Jewish emigration to Palestine and the attempts of Jews to create their own state. These positions were in flux in the postwar period, and their evolution was, above all, connected with subordination to Moscow and the realization of Soviet policies. During the initial period, attempts by the Polish government to gain the goodwill of international Jewish organizations were of some significance, seeking their support either for Jewish emigration from Poland or for the resurrection of Jewish life in Poland after the Holocaust. These attempts, in turn, were tied to the significant financial aid for Polish Jews that could be acquired from these organizations. In addition, the good favor of such organizations meant a great deal for the new authorities in Poland in their dealings with Western Europe and the United States.

Besides support for different programs related to the future of Polish Jews, however, attitudes of hostility, even antisemitism, were discernible among the communists. Many PPR activists themselves noted the existence of anti-semitism in the party at that time. According to Krystyna Kersten, "they emphasized the necessity of opposing antisemitic tendencies, a disease that . . . was also making itself felt in the party as well."[21]

The stance of leading activists of the PPR was not without significance in this regard. Władysław Gomułka, secretary general of the PPR, repeatedly called for the removal from power of communists with Jewish ancestry; he believed that their presence was harmful to party interests. Gomułka's position was not an isolated one. Many PPR activists were convinced that Jews would have to emigrate from Poland because their presence hindered the struggle against the forces of reaction.[22]

The Jewish problem also made itself known in the activities of the new regime in the context of ongoing political conflict. Allegations of antisemitism were levied by the communists against opposition groups in an effort to discredit them in the eyes of Great Britain or the United States. The most striking evidence comes from documents and commentaries that appeared in connection with the pogroms in Kraków and Kielce. The communist press, as well as the leadership of the PPR, uniformly pointed to the domestic anti-communist opposition and to politicians of the London government-in-exile

21. Krystyna Kersten, "Pierwszy rok," *Midrasz* 7–8 (1998): 29.
22. See the account by H. Smolar, *Oif der lecter pozicje mit der lecter hofenung* (Tel Aviv, 1982).

as responsible for the pogroms at a time when investigations into these events had yet to be completed.[23]

The Jewish issue thus became a frequent pawn in political games. There is no doubt that the Kraków events, as well as the pogrom in Kielce, were used to discredit political opponents. Similarly political in intent at this time was the appearance of posters depicting the wartime noncommunist Home Army as a stinking, reactionary dwarf alongside others that glorified the heroes of the Warsaw ghetto. The Polish writer Maria Dąbrowska noted in her diary: "I talked about the mistakes made in government spheres that alienated the nation. How was it possible to spit and trample on the memory of the Warsaw Uprising while simultaneously plastering all of Warsaw with posters saying 'Glory to the Ghetto Insurgents!' "[24]

At the same, we need to remember that among the communists and especially among the members of the prewar Communist Party of Poland (KPP) there were many Jews. August Grabski, in his analysis of the party's Jewish component, argues that the old KPP members "who decisively dominated the leadership of the KPP did not forget about Jewish communists, and their position in regard to the 'Jewish Question' must be recognized as one entirely of goodwill."[25]

In the activities of the Polskie Stronnictwo Ludowe (PSL, Polish People's Party), an opposition political organization that acted legally although it was repressed with impunity throughout the period of its postwar existence, Jewish issues were not of major concern. Its stance on the Jewish situation was represented primarily in the pages of its press, especially in *Gazeta Ludowa*. Yet in contrast to the communist press, where the Jewish theme was clearly linked with attacks on groups decisively opposed to the new regime, as well as on the Catholic Church, *Gazeta Ludowa* presented several aspects of the Jewish situation: the question of Palestine, Jewish emigration, the Holocaust, Polish aid to Jews during the occupation, antisemitism (particularly in articles related to the Kielce pogrom), and the life of the Jewish community in general in Poland after the war.[26]

It is important, however, to note the contexts in which *Gazeta Ludowa* addressed antisemitism. Those articles devoted to it were primarily in response to the way the issue had been formulated in the communist press. In those publications, there were clearly attempts to neutralize the problem of antisemitism, with more attention devoted to those activities of Polish society, or

23. See, for example, Gomułka's speech to a meeting of activists of the PPR and PPS, published in *Głos Ludu* 185, no. 573 (July 8, 1946): 5.

24. Maria Dąbrowska, *Dzienniki powojenne: 1945–1965* (Warsaw, 1996), 1:52.

25. August Grabski, "Kształtowanie się pierwotnego programu żydowskich komunistów w Polsce po Holokauście," in *Studia z historii Żydów w Polsce po 1945 roku*, ed. Grzegorz Berendt et al. (Warsaw, 2000), 69.

26. Dariusz Libionka, "Antysemityzm i zagłada na łamach prasy w Polsce w latach 1945–1946," in *Polska 1944/45–1989: Studia i materiały* (Warsaw, 1996), 2:165–68.

the Church, not discussed in the press organs of the PPR: statements of the Catholic hierarchy, information about the creation and activities of the Liga Walki z Rasizmem (League for the Struggle against Racism), materials related to the Kielce pogrom, statements from representatives of the Jewish community negating the assertion that "the Polish nation is antisemitic."[27] Such material naturally was also part of the political contest and not an objective look at the phenomenon of antisemitism.

In the case of opposition groups that acted illegally, one encounters a different view of Jewish issues. In her analysis of the underground press, Krystyna Kersten wrote, "It is noteworthy that Jews—as actually existing people or as an idea, a cliché—appear in underground publications exclusively as a threatening element."[28] Such a stance was connected with the extraordinarily complicated political situation in Poland during this period. Kersten notes elsewhere that "aggression was strengthened by a feeling of helplessness—a reaction to the postwar situation of the country—unable to find a way to deal openly with those actually responsible for Poland's catastrophe, they instead turned against a substituted enemy—Jews."[29] This statement about the entanglement of Jewish issues in the political situation points yet again to the abnormal conditions in which Polish-Jewish relations "played out" after the war.

Any discussion of the positions of leading political forces regarding the Jewish issue in postwar Poland would be incomplete without showing the position of the Roman Catholic Church. Jewish themes, as well as antisemitism, appear several times in the proclamations of some Polish bishops as well as those of the Primate, Cardinal Hlond. They were also the subject of a meeting between representatives of the Church and the Jewish community. It is difficult to make a singular assessment of the attitude of the Catholic Church in this regard. In the proclamations of the Church hierarchy, we find various statements. On the one hand, for example, there is the proclamation of Bishop Kubina of Częstochowa, which condemned all rumors of ritual murder: "Nothing, absolutely nothing, can justify the Kielce crime, which calls forth the wrath of God and of man, a crime whose background and causes must be sought in criminal fanaticism and cannot be justified by ignorance. . . . All assertions about the existence of ritual murders are lies."[30] On the other hand, in the statement of the suffragan bishop of Upper Silesia we find the formulation that "proof exists that the child whose alleged mistreatment by Jews provoked the Kielce pogrom actually was maltreated and that Jews took blood from his shoulder."[31] The commentary of the British ambassador, Victor

27. Ibid., 167.

28. Krystyna Kersten, *Między wyzwoleniem a zniewoleniem: Polska 1944–1956* (London, 1993), 37.

29. Krystyna Kersten, *Polacy, Żydzi, Komunizm: Antonomia półprawd* (Warsaw, 1992), 80.

30. *Antyżydowskie wydarzenia kieleckie 4 lipca 1946 r: Dokumenty i materiały* ed. Stanisław Meducki (Kielce, 1994), 2:113.

31. Aryeh Josef Kochavi, "The Catholic Church and Antisemitism in Poland following World War II as reflected in British Diplomatic Documents," *Gal-Ed* 11 (1989): 123.

Cavendish-Bentick, a witness to this statement, was as follows: "If a Bishop is prepared to believe this, it is hardly surprising that uneducated Poles would do so as well."[32]

In the statements of Cardinal Hlond, the most prominent figure in the Church at the time, one finds condemnations of antisemitism. In January 1946 at a meeting with the representative of the Jewish Religious Assemblies, Professor Michał Zylberg, to a question about "attacks on Jews immediately following Poland's liberation," the Primate answered: "They fill me with real sorrow. Without repeating arguments based on the principles of Christianity, there are no objective reasons in Poland today for the spread of antisemitism. It is the downright madness of those who forever conspire while remaining in the forests. They think they are acting politically, that by attacking Jews they are fighting the government. I condemn their activity as a Catholic and as a Pole."[33] After the Kielce pogrom, the cardinal's statement condemning the murders was, however, tempered by the remark that the responsibility for ruining Polish-Jewish relations belonged "in great measure . . . to the Jew who has occupied the leading positions in the life of the state and who is striving to impose structural forms that the vast majority of the nation doesn't want. This is a harmful game, because it gives rise to dangerous tensions."[34] As in the case of the secular political forces discussed previously, so too in several statements from the Church about Jewish issues one notes their inseparability from the contemporary political situation.

In contrast to the significantly greater amount of information contained in archival materials related to the Church hierarchy, the sources provide little indication of the Catholic clergy's attitude toward antisemitism. In the materials of the Jewish Press Agency we find information about a "special homily by the Rzeszów parish priest, in which he condemned racial hatred and called upon the population to oppose Nazi-like agitation."[35] This, however, is a single isolated account.

The political reality of postwar Poland influenced to a lesser degree the responses of Catholic intellectuals toward Jewish issues. The majority of articles or declarations that were published—especially in *Tygodnik Powszechny*—unequivocally condemned antisemitism, without any political qualification. After the Kielce pogrom, Polish intellectuals of various political affiliations denounced antisemitism itself, as well as the perpetrators of the events in Kielce.

The problem in postwar Poland, however, did not consist solely of outbursts of anti-Jewish violence. In accordance with the definition of antisemitism offered at the outset of this chapter, attitudes justifying such acts

32. Ibid.
33. "Ks. Kardynał Hlond o Żydach, Hitlerze i Palestynie," *Gazeta Ludowa* 13 (January 14, 1946): 3.
34. Archiwum Ministerstwa Spraw Wewnętznych, 750 (odezwy).
35. Archiwum Ministerstwa Spraw Zagraniczynych (AMSZ), Biuletyny Żydowskiej Agencji Prasowej, z. 6, w. 104, t. 1677:168.

should also be treated as antisemitic. In March 1946 the Jewish regional committee in Lublin submitted a letter to the provincial governor that stated: "Regardless . . . of the facts of murder and pillage, we are witnessing the illegal conduct of anti-Jewish agitation. The results of this agitation cannot be ignored, since it finds fertile ground and sympathetic ears among those portions of Polish society that under the influence of the German occupiers became depraved and lost any sense of ethical and civil morality."[36] As already mentioned, the Jewish population was portrayed in negative contexts in the press of some underground organizations and, to a certain extent, in opinions expressed by Poles more generally in regard to the political situation.

Postwar antisemitism was nourished in a soil characterized by the isolation of and distance between the Polish and Jewish communities, in conditions that were difficult and complicated for them both, and that were further encumbered by painful and tragic wartime experiences. The entanglement of Jewish issues and antisemitism with the political conflicts added one more obstacle that obviated the possibilities of dialogue. Given this background, it is therefore all the more important to consider those initiatives and responses that unconditionally condemned the murders committed against the Jewish population. In July 1945 the Central Committee of Jews in Poland appealed for statements condemning "the bestial murders committed against the remaining handful of the [Jewish] population." Stefan Jaracz, Aleksander Zelwerowicz, the writer Wacław Rogowski, and Karol Adwentowicz, among others, spoke out in response to this appeal. Some, like Jaracz, went beyond mere condemnation. "What you are doing," he declared, "is a disgrace to Poland and a disgrace to humanity." Another of those who responded to the committee's appeal was Father Stanisław Warchałowski, the general chaplain of the Polish army: "As a Pole, I am on the side of those who fought Hitler's brigands, . . . among them . . . the Jewish nation. . . . As a chaplain I hold the highest honor and respect for those victims felled by the hands of criminals."[37]

The activity of the Liga do Walki z Rasizmem (League for the Struggle against Racism) deserves separate consideration. The impetus for the league's founding arose among former activists of Żegota (the popular cryptonym for the wartime Rada Pomocy Żydom, the Council of Aid to the Jews). According to Władysław Bartoszewski, one of the founders of the league, the desire was "to take up in a public forum the problem of the danger and the moral and political harm to Poland and Poles of activities motivated by antisemitic attitudes and anti-Jewish prejudice, regardless of their source."[38] What is interesting about the league is that it brought together people of different political views in a common cause, Poles and Jews alike. The circumstances surrounding the end of this institution's existence are symptomatic and demonstrate

36. Blus-Węgrowska, 92.
37. AMSZ, Kabinet Ministra, z. 15, w. 9, t. 92:2.
38. Władysław Bartoszewski, "Powstanie Ligi do Walki z Rasizmem w 1946 r.," *Więź*, special number (1998): 239.

quite starkly how this sort of activity had no chance during this period. One of the league's activists (Bartoszewski) was arrested by the communist authorities under false pretenses; another (A. Berman) emigrated to Israel; a third (a Professor Górka) was appointed Polish consul in Jerusalem. That still others "resigned voluntarily from further social activities" was related to the character of the political transformation that Poland experienced during this period and when "the further activity of the league became directed against . . . 'the American and British imperialists' who were persecuting blacks and other people of color."[39]

The years 1945–48 are critical to understanding issues related to antisemitism in postwar Poland At this time old and new circumstances converged which significantly influenced Polish-Jewish relations. It is worth emphasizing that it was precisely in this form that they became preserved in the memory of both Poles and Jews and at a time when any depiction of social behaviors, other than that articulated by the authorities, would soon become impossible.

The year 1948 marked the beginning of a new period. In May of that year, Israel became a state, and Poland to an ever greater extent became a Soviet satellite. We know very little about Polish-Jewish relations during the Stalinist era, but the subordination of all organizational contacts to the state, as well as the state's control over society, made it impossible to close the impasse that had been created between Poles and Jews as a consequence of the war and immediate postwar period. The lack of any kind of independent discourse deepened the mutual isolation and intensified negative perceptions. The government's monopoly of propaganda and the press made consideration of Jewish issues dependent on the political line of the day. We have few source materials that would permit a reconstruction of Polish-Jewish relations during the apogee of Stalinism. The little that can be found in source materials includes information about continued outbursts of antisemitic violence. The last account comes from 1949. In that year there were antisemitic incidents in Częstochowa and Włocławek, as well as Kraków; they followed a similar course, although in Włocławek, rumors of the murder of a Pole by a Jew led to the formation of a large crowd. In the other instances, rumors of the kidnapping of Polish children served as a pretext for meetings of an antisemitic character; according to official reports, the meetings in Częstochowa and Kraków involved 150 people. None of these 1949 incidents resulted in casualties.[40] Nonetheless, the continued readiness of a part of Polish society to believe rumors of ritual murder is noteworthy.

In the following years, up to 1956, the Jewish theme in Polish society appears only in relation to unfavorable comments about the political situation, in oral utterances, in rumors and innuendo. Even here, the antisemitic

39. Ibid., 245–46.

40. Dariusz Jarosz, "Problem antysemityzmu w Polsce w latach 1948–1956 w świetle akt niektórych centralnych instytucji państwowych i partyjnych," *Biuletyn Żydowskiego Instytutu Historycznego* 2/97, no. 182 (April–June, 1997): 50–51.

component of recorded expressions of political dissatisfaction appears as a marginal element. During this period we do, however, find some examples of favorable attitudes toward Jews in Polish society. These positive images were connected, above all, to the struggle of the Jewish people to create and defend their own state. Independent of the pro-Israeli policy of the government in Warsaw, which had to accord with Moscow's current line regarding Israel, Poles demonstrated considerable sympathy for the cause of the Jewish state. Evidence of such sympathy was documented by the various Jewish committees still active in Poland. Moreover, in the official declarations of Polish delegates to the United Nations during debates over the future of Palestine, one can perceive genuine displays of emotional involvement in the issue. For example, the impassioned speech to the U.N. General Assembly in January 1948 of Ksawery Pruszyński on behalf of the Polish delegation in support of an Israeli state was positively received in Jewish circles.[41]

Nonetheless, there would be no genuine rapprochement of the Polish and Jewish communities between 1949 and 1956. The reality of totalitarianism prohibited normal relations, whether among individuals or between communities. Similarly, as in the previous period, both sides were occupied with their own fates, despite the fact that experience of Polish Stalinism affected them both. The monopolization of political life by the PPR and then the PZPR (United Polish Workers Party) resulted from the liquidation of the opposition and subordination of the PPS to the communists (the equivalent on the Jewish political scene was the liquidation of Zionist parties and the forced dissolution of the Bund, whose members entered the PZPR). This was accompanied by a new policy on organizations, which amounted to their subordination to the authorities. In the place of the Jewish committees and cultural associations, a new organization, the Towarzystwo Społeczno-Kulturalne Żydów (TSKŻ, Jewish Social-Cultural Society), emerged as "a transmission belt of our party to the Jewish community,"[42] while other independent Jewish institutions, organizations, as well as Zionist schools, were closed. The imposition of Soviet-style uniformity on culture and the press (the only permitted Jewish newspaper was an organ of the TSKŻ and therefore of the PZPR), as well as changes in economic policy (the subordination of Jewish cooperatives to the centralized Polish organization), completed the process.

The most characteristic feature of Stalinism, however, was terror. In the activities of the security organs, there also appeared a Jewish component, primarily in the realization of new directives from Moscow regarding the struggle against "Zionism." Its victims were Jewish activists as well as communists of Jewish ancestry (a Polish version of the 1952 Rudolf Slánský trial in Czechoslovakia was under preparation). The change in Soviet policy regarding Israel

41. *Opinia* 28 (January 25, 1948), 1.
42. Archiwum Państwowe we Wrocławiu, Komitet Wrocławski Polskiej Zjednoczonej Partii Robotniczej (PZPR), sygn. 74/V/2, 52.

meant that Israeli diplomatic posts in Poland became objects of interest to the security forces. In Poland, the repressive measures also affected individual members of the Israeli diplomatic corps. In December 1952 the Israeli ambassador and the deputy chief of mission were expelled from the country. Beginning in the fall of 1952 and into the winter of 1953, arrests—among others, of an Israeli embassy official in Warsaw and the former chair of the Jewish committee in Lower Silesia—were preceded by investigations of members of the Jewish community by the security police. The prepared purge was interrupted by Stalin's death in March 1953. Before that, an intensified propaganda campaign, not only in the controlled Polish-language press but also in Yiddish-language publications, complemented the regime's anti-Jewish and anti-Israeli activities.

The apogee of Stalinism in Poland, from 1948 to 1953, was significant to Polish-Jewish relations for several reasons. Prejudices of Poles and Jews toward each other not only persisted but to a certain extent became frozen. In the absence of contacts, further separation of the two communities ensued. Antisemitism during this period was present, above all, in the actions of the authorities. The image of Israel as an enemy of Poland among parts of the party apparatus and the security forces was the consequence of their policies. The context in which the Jewish people and the Israeli state were portrayed in propaganda was also important: Israel was deemed suspect and dangerous to Poland, while parts of the Jewish community were cast as disloyal to the Polish state.

Stalin's death was followed by the period known as the "Thaw." Subsequent changes in political, economic, and social life were not without influence on Polish-Jewish relations. They appeared, above all, in the context of antisemitism and the policy of the government toward national minorities. The political crisis in Poland of the mid-1950s brought with it a revival of antisemitic attitudes. In reference to the events of 1956, Paweł Machcewicz wrote: "In the period 1948–1955 any autonomous expression and unhindered articulation of actual social attitudes were very difficult, practically impossible. National resentments disappeared from the surface of public life, which doesn't mean that they ceased to exist. At the moment when increasingly wider crevices began to appear in the Stalinist corset, everything that had been hidden underneath it began to come out into the broad light of day."[43]

The problem of antisemitism in 1956 has been described in several contexts. On the one hand, it was a component of the political contest waged by part of the party apparatus. The "us" versus "them" formula was strengthened both by the anti-Jewish policies of the Kremlin and by the presence among the authorities in Poland of communists of Jewish descent. In the political reality of 1956 it became an instrument in the political struggle between the hard-line Natolin and reformist Puławy party factions. An indication of

43. Paweł Machcewicz, *Polski rok 1956* (Warsaw, 1993), 218.

antisemitic attitudes among certain communist party apparatchiks can be found in their statements at the sixth and seventh plenary sessions of the Central Committee.[44]

Antisemitic attitudes were also manifested within part of Polish society during the period of the Thaw. Although antisemitic slogans did not accompany the demonstrations in Poznań that would eventually bring about a change in party leadership in October, there were many anti-Jewish outbursts throughout Poland over the course of 1956. In the documents from this period we find information about the beating of Jews, persecutions, antisemitic slogans, and loss of employment. Frequently, in the background of these incidents, we see the Jewish community being held responsible for the repressions of the Stalinist era.

There were also, however, activities directed *against* the antisemitic sentiments and deeds during this period. The best-known text in this regard appeared in the May issue of *Po prostu*, the article of Leszek Kołakowski titled "Antisemitism—Five Old Theses and a Warning."[45] At the same time, a circular of the Central Committee secretariat devoted to the sources and manifestations of antisemitism was apparently designed to counter its spread within the party.[46]

In his work devoted to 1956, Paweł Machcewicz analyzed antisemitism "in terms of three dimensions. The first consisted of the manipulations of the Natolin faction that sought to maximize its influence, discredit and eliminate its opponents, and mobilize social support by using antisemitic slogans. The second dimension was the real antisemitism of a numerous part—and everything seems to indicate that this was so—of the apparatus and active party membership. It seems that it was precisely these groups that were the most determined—and most influential on a social scale—carriers of antisemitism. ... The third dimension was that of antisemitism from below, an elemental antisemitism flowing from the deepest recesses of social consciousness, irreducible to purely political categories. ... Between these three dimensions of antisemitism it is not always possible to draw clear lines of demarcation; it cannot always be known what was an expression from below, of spontaneous antisemitism, and what was politically inspired manipulation and instrumentalization. Finally, in certain contexts these three types of antisemitism were able to come together and to intensify and nourish one another."[47]

The political changes of 1956 were considered by the Jewish population, above all, in terms of the appearance of new opportunities for the Jewish Social-Cultural Society and the easing of restrictions on emigration, but also in terms of the antisemitism noted above. On the one hand, we can observe

44. Ibid., 217.
45. *"Po prostu" 1955–1956: Wybór artykułów* (Warsaw, 1956), 160–171.
46. AAN, Komitet Centralny PZPR, 295/VII-149:265.
47. Machcewicz, 229–30.

the involvement of new groups in the activity of an organization that had previously been shunned; young people began to make their appearance at meetings of the TSKŻ. On the other, many Jews now decided to leave Poland. Among them were those who had been unable to emigrate earlier, but they were joined by those disillusioned with the direction of political changes in Poland, as well as those who felt threatened by the resurgence of antisemitic sentiments.

In 1956 the Jewish theme once again became an element of the political contest. Undoubtedly, the mood of a part of Polish society that was not particularly favorable to the Jewish population became a point of departure for this sort of activity. Political reality, however, served as a backdrop, a constant element in the persistence of phobias and prejudice, whether anti-Jewish, anti-German, or any other.

In the 1960s, Poles and Jews again became pawns in a political contest played out between factions within the PZPR. One of these factions was led by Minister of Internal Affairs Mieczysław Moczar, also head of the Związek Bojowników o Wolność i Demokrację (ZBoWid, Union of Fighters for Freedom and Democracy). Anti-Jewish tendencies were particularly powerful in this group. Its slogan, "the nationalization of cadres," meant in practice purges of the Ministries of Internal and Foreign Affairs.

In the 1960s two phenomena within the Jewish community were occurring side by side: assimilation and the return to Judaism, the latter connected to the change in policy toward national minorities after 1956. The new policy of the authorities permitted the establishment of contacts, broken in the 1950s, with international Jewish organizations as well as with Israeli diplomatic representatives.

As earlier, the Polish and Jewish populations lived alongside each other in the 1960s, each little interested in the affairs of the other. It should be noted, however, that Jewish issues began to appear increasingly in those periodicals connected with the Catholic intelligentsia which managed to distance themselves from the authorities. Articles and reviews regarding different aspects of Polish-Jewish history (antisemitism, assistance to Jews during the occupation, the Holocaust) were published in *Tygodnik Powszechny* and *Więź*. In 1962 the Warsaw Club of the Catholic Intelligentsia devoted an evening observance to the nineteenth anniversary of the destruction of the Tłomackie Street synagogue. The publication in 1967 of *Ten jest z ojczyzny mojej* (He is from my country) by Zofia Lewinówna and Władysław Bartoszewski, about the rendering of aid to Jews by Poles during the Holocaust, was a potentially significant event. Such important initiatives were the beginning of an opening, if only among individuals, that was soon closed again by the events of 1967 and 1968, when Poles and Jews perceived each other, one more time, through images inspired and manipulated by the authorities.

Translated by Lisa Di Bartolomeo and Robert Blobaum

13

Fighting against the Shadows

The Anti-Zionist Campaign of 1968

DARIUSZ STOLA

In March 1968 the entire Polish media—from newspapers, radio, and television to posters, banners, and leaflets—focused on the threat that a Zionist conspiracy posed to the stability and security of Poland. The Zionists, allied with neo-Nazis, American imperialists, ex-Stalinists striving to return to power, German revanchists, and a few cosmopolitan intellectuals, had recently incited students in several Polish universities to attack the principles of the socialist regime and the national interest. Contrary to the instigators' expectations, the workers, peasants, and most of the intelligentsia showed their civic maturity, firm patriotism, and full support for the party leadership and particularly for First Secretary, Comrade Władysław Gomułka. To eradicate the anti-socialist and anti-national elements, the party organization at all levels, along with the trade unions and various associations, engaged in efforts to cleanse the workplaces, schools, and offices of those individuals corrupted by alien influences.

The foregoing paragraph summarizes official accounts of the infamous events of the spring of 1968 in Poland. This chapter discusses the anti-Jewish campaign of that time in terms of the images of the Jew that it construed, spread, and exploited. As one may suppose, in 1968 the terms "Zionism" and "Zionist" were not used to refer to a particular variety of nationalism or its proponents but were substitutes for "Jews" and "Jewish," including cases where the person referred to as a Zionist was not Jewish at all. Thus, these terms appear here in italics, together with other terms reminiscent of Orwellian newspeak, the peculiar language of the communist regime.

By 1967, there were approximately 25,000–30,000 Jews among Poland's more than 32 million inhabitants. This was only a miniscule fraction of the once great Polish Jewry, which the Holocaust had destroyed almost entirely. Two waves of postwar emigration (in the late 1940s and in 1956–58) had reduced the community of survivors to a statistically insignificant minority. In the 1960s, as this remnant group was aging, its younger strata were undergoing accelerated acculturation and integration into Polish society, a phenomenon that simultaneously implied the further erosion of Yiddish culture and the community's secularization. This relatively small minority, however, possessed impressively developed secular institutions which—unique in the Soviet bloc—were permitted to receive significant material support from the West. Yet at the same time the Jewish community did not have a single qualified rabbi, and in the entire country there were only a few functioning synagogues. Demographic and cultural processes led to an evolution of Polish-Jewish ethnic identity that in its dual nature was becoming increasingly Polish.[1]

The *anti-Zionist* campaign in Poland began in the summer of 1967, following the outbreak of the Six-Day Arab-Israeli war, but reached its main and most dramatic stage in the spring of 1968. In the summer of 1967 the Cold War and political subordination to Moscow caused the communist leaders of Poland to take the Arab side in the distant conflict in the Middle East. Two weeks later, the Polish communist party leader, Władysław Gomułka, introduced a domestic, anti-Jewish dimension into the ongoing anti-Israeli campaign by comparing Polish Jews sympathetic to Israel to a subversive "fifth column" and claiming that "one should have only one fatherland." In response, the brilliant writer Antoni Słonimski commented that certainly one should have only one fatherland, but he asked why this fatherland had to be Egypt.[2] As Gomułka's initiative met angry reactions, even among some members of the Politburo, the propaganda campaign regained its focus on

1. On Polish Jewry in the 1960s, see Michael Steinlauf, *Bondage to the Dead: Poland and the Memory of the Holocaust* (Syracuse, N.Y., 1997), 67–68; Alina Cała, "Mniejszość żydowska," in *Mniejszości narodowe w Polsce: Państwo i społeczeństwo polskie a mniejszości narodowe w okresach przełomów politycznych (1944–1989)*, ed. Piotr Madajczyk (Warsaw, 1998), 245–88; Andrzej Kwilecki, "Mniejszości narodowe w Polsce Ludowej, *Kultura i Społeczeństwo* 7, no. 4 (1963): 86–87; Jaff Schatz, *The Generation: The Rise and Fall of the Jewish Communists of Poland* (Berkeley, Calif., 1991); "Informacja o sytuacji politycznej, organizacyjnej i finansowej w Towarzystwie Społeczno-Kulturalnym Żydów w Polsce," July 1967, Central Archive of the Ministry of Interior (hereafter CA MSW), MSW.II.51:234–62; attachments to the protocol of the MSW Collegium of April 4–11, 1967, CA MSW, MSW.II.50:196–99.

2. The attribution of this comment to Słonimski has been confirmed by contemporaries, including professors Stefan Amsterdamski and Marcin Kula (in response to a question posed by this author in 2002).

Israel and the Western imperialism it supposedly served. But the Security Service (secret police) began a systematic screening of people of Jewish origin in search of alleged *Zionists*.

In March 1968, in reaction to a wave of student protests (which were completely unrelated to the Six-Day War) and the ferment among intellectuals, the authorities unleashed a large-scale hate campaign against alleged internal enemies, among whom the *Zionists* suddenly appeared in first place. Although its deceleration had begun earlier, this campaign was officially terminated in July 1968, but its most significant aftereffect, a wave of mass Jewish emigration from Poland, lasted for many months thereafter.[3]

The noisy campaign, combined with a political crisis and a wave of disturbances in this largest Soviet satellite, evoked considerable interest in the West, where it stimulated numerous commentaries, essays, and analyses. In Poland as well the goals and intrigues of the March campaign stimulated understandable interest, but with the mass media under communist control, the topic for many years remained the object of public lies or enforced silence on the one hand, and private guesses, rumors, and conjecture on the other. The situation changed somewhat only a decade later with the growth of the uncensored press, yet the independent publications devoted to the anti-Jewish campaign itself or to the events of March 1968 more generally, although sometimes highly interesting and testifying to their authors' investigative spirit, all suffered from a basic weakness: namely, they had very limited or no access to information from those institutions that initiated the campaign and carried it out. Only recently, especially since the termination of the thirty-year long freeze period that protects Polish archives from historians, have more primary sources become available for research and thus made possible the appearance of new publications based on them. My analysis is derived from research into these newly accessible materials,[4] mainly from the voluminous collection of the United Polish Workers Party (Polska Zjednoczona Partia Robotnicza—PZPR) and the archives of the Ministry of Internal Affairs (Ministerstwo Spraw Wewnętrznych—MSW) and has benefited as well from earlier publications.[5]

3. For an extensive discussion of the campaign, see Dariusz Stola, *Kampania antysyjonisty-czna w Polsce, 1967–1968* (Warsaw, 2000).

4. My research was made possible by a grant from the American Jewish Committee.

5. Major publications on the events of March 1968 are *Marzec 1968: Trzydzieści lat później*, ed. Marcin Kula, Piotr Osęka, and Marcin Zaremba, 2 vols. (Warsaw, 1998); Jerzy Eisler, *Marzec 1968: Geneza, przebieg, konsekwencje* (Warsaw, 1991); Krystyna Kersten, *Polacy, Żydzi, komunizm: Antonomia półprawd, 1939–1968* (Warsaw, 1992); Josef Banas, *The Scapegoats: The Exodus of the Remnants of Polish Jewry* (London, 1979); Michael Chęciński, *Poland: Communism, Nationalism, Anti-Semitism* (New York, 1982); *Krajobraz po szoku*, ed. Anna Mieszczanek (Warsaw, 1989); *Czystka w korpusie oficerskim: Wydarzenia 1967 roku w Wojsku Polskim w dokumentach*, ed. E. J. Nalepa (Warsaw, 1999); Piotr Osęka, *Syjoniści, inspiratorzy, wichrzyciele: Obraz wroga w propagandzie Marca 1968* (Warsaw, 1999); *Marzec '68: Między tragedią a*

While the social background, particularly the persistence of anti-Jewish prejudice in Poland many years after the Holocaust, may be well known, a few
words about the lesser known, intraparty aspects of the campaign are in order
here. The origins of the tensions within the communist elite that surfaced in
1967–68 could already be seen in the late 1940s, when Władysław Gomułka,
the leader of the party until that time, together with a group of other communist leaders who likewise had spent the war years in Poland, was accused of
right-wing nationalist deviation, removed from power and subsequently
arrested. The group of communists that consequently emerged triumphant was
dominated by those who had spent the war years in the Soviet Union and
included prominent Jewish party members. In 1956, Gomułka returned to
power and to a party leadership divided into two factions. The relatively
reformist group, called "Puławy," included leading Jewish communists; the
other faction, known as "Natolin," did not hestitate to exploit the ethnic argument against its rival. Gomułka initially formed a strategic pact with the first
group, but as time passed he put his own people in key positions, and under
the slogan of fighting against *revisionism* he was able to weaken the Puławy
faction's position. In the 1960s a new force appeared on the political scene, the
so-called Partisans, a rather loose group of party leaders and lower-level
activists united by similar political backgrounds, wartime experience, unap-
peased ambitions, and a worldview combining nationalism and communism,
under the unquestioned leadership of General Mieczysław Moczar.[6]

The campaign that began in March 1968 was neither the first nor the last
hate campaign organized by the communist regime in Poland, and not only
against the Jews. These Polish campaigns were local mutations of the Soviet
models developed during the great purges and show trials of the 1930s, when
the communist language of hate acquired its most distinctive forms. In Poland,
they were most frequent, intensive, and fatal in the years before 1956, yet the
regime returned to the tested patterns in later years as well. Barely two years
before the March events a wave of protests and condemnation was carefully
prepared and carried out in earnest against the Roman Catholic episcopate.
The *anti-Zionist* campaign itself had not yet concluded when the propaganda
machine was set in motion against the reform movement in Czechoslovakia
to justify intervention by the combined Warsaw Pact forces.[7]

---

podłością, ed. J. Sołtysiak and J. Stępień (Warsaw, 1998); Marek Tarniewski [Jakub Karpiński],
Krótkie spięcie (marzec 1968) (Paris, 1977); *Wydarzenia Marcowe*, Biblioteka "Kultury" (Paris,
1968); Włodzimierz Rozenbaum, "The Background of the Anti-Zionist Campaign of 1967–68 in
Poland," *Essays in History* 17 (1973): 71–95; Włodzimierz Rozenbaum, "The Anti-Zionist Campaign in Poland, June–December 1967," *Canadian Slavonic Papers* 20, no. 2 (1978): 218–36.

6. The relative power, reach, and character of the factions remain controversial, but their existence has been widely accepted in Polish historiography. See, for example, Eisler, *Marzec 1968*,
134.

7. On the 1968 campaign's affinity with Soviet campaigns, see Michał Głowiński, *Nowom-
owa po polsku* (Warsaw, 1990); and Jerzy Jedlicki, *Źle urodzeni czyli o doświadczeniu historycznym: Scripta i postscripta* (London, 1993), 56–70.

A distinctive feature of the March campaign in comparison with other communist hate campaigns was its targeting of a population that historically had been the object of attack by anticommunist groups, along with its borrowing part of the antisemitic legacy of those groups. Noisy and aggressive anti-Jewish communist propaganda, only now in the light camouflage of *anti-Zionism*, had no precedent in postwar Poland, where the stereotype of *Żydokomuna* (Jewish communism) was alive and well, where antisemitism as a rule combined with anticommunism, where Jewish communists occupied many important posts and did not fall victim to show trials such as the Rudolf Slánský trial of 1952 in Czechoslovakia, and where antisemitism clearly contradicted the officially worshiped precepts of Marxism.[8] Thus the party-sponsored witch hunt of Jews in 1968 came as a surprise, the more so as it also targeted and even focused on members of the communist establishment.[9] From the chauvinist antisemitism of the Polish radical right the 1968 campaign borrowed certain clichés and slogans—part and parcel of the Polish historical legacy of anti-Jewish prejudice and resentment. From the arsenal of previous communist purges and hate campaigns, it added even more slogans and stereotypes. From that arsenal it also took ready-made patterns for manipulating individual and group behavior, organizations well trained in the use of these patterns, and the appropriate newspeak to express aggression publicly in forms acceptable to the regime.

While pointing at such diverse roots of the 1968 campaign as pogroms and show trials, we also need to stress an important difference. The anti-Jewish campaign of 1968 was a campaign of symbolic aggression. During the student protests in March 1968, police and party activists eagerly resorted to violence, but the *anti-Zionist* stream of the March events was a verbal rather than physical pogrom. Real pogroms such as those incited by the antisemitic right in the 1930s had been acts of physical mob violence, and Stalin's purges had culminated not in dismissals but in executions.

The main features of the March events were the student rebellion and its pacification by the authorities. Three days after the outbreak of the university riots, the first article appeared in the press attributing the instigation of the disturbances to *Zionists* and "bankrupt politicians": that is, to ex-Stalinsts, also Jewish, now operating on the political sidetrack. Readers here learned of the threat posed by "Zionists in Poland [who] took their political orders from the FRG (Federal Republic of Germany)" and who in addition "bear responsibility for the errors and lawlessness of the Stalinist period." As an example of such *Zionists*, the article named Stefan Staszewski, a former communist

---

8. On Jews in communist Poland, see Kersten, *Polacy, Żydzi, komumizm*; Chęciński, *Poland*; Eisler, *Marzec 1968*; Schatz, *The Generation*.

9. See Lucjan Blit, "The Anti-Jewish Campaign in Contemporary Poland," a 1968 report for the Institute of Jewish Affairs in London, translation in the PRL (Polska Rzeczpospolita Ludowa) Archives in Warsaw (Archiwum Dokumentacji PRL—APRL), Starewicz file; K. Chylińska, "Emigracja polska po 1967 r.," *Kultura* 10 (1970): 22.

party Central Committee secretary but actually an ex-Stalinist and Jewish member of the Puławy faction who had drifted to revisionist Marxism yet had nothing to do with the student rebellion.[10]

From that point on, the quantity and intensity of attacks against *Zionism* snowballed in the media and in public speeches. In particular, within the course of a week, mass meetings were organized throughout the country. Regional and local party organizations mobilized their members and satellite organizations to express emotions and opinions congruent with examples coming from Warsaw. Resolutions and letters were sent to the party leadership by the hundreds and in an increasingly radical tone. "We swear in memory of those who died for power to the people that we will clean from Polish soil, with our workers' fists, all the instigators and leaders of the coup against the working-class and peasant government. We will not permit revisionist and Zionist rioters to accuse of us of antisemitism," declared the workers from the Polfer factories. Meanwhile, workers from the Baildon steel works demanded "a purge of Zionist elements from party ranks, removal from their positions, and the refusal to permit their children to continue further university studies."[11] Once the *working masses* had expressed the demands conveyed to them by the party apparatus, it was up to the authorities to respond to the *will of the people* and punish the alleged instigators and *alien elements*.

Although the general patterns of the campaign were quite typical of earlier hate campaigns, it also had some unusual features. The regular top-down procedure of preparing and launching campaigns was altered. In the early stage, there apparently were no specific instructions from the party's Central Committee departments as to who in particular was to be targeted and what the exact content of the slogans should be. Because of limited time for preparations and, more important, conflict inside the party leadership (Politburo) and intraparty struggle—which were essential aspects of and reasons for the campaign—its initiators employed other channels of communication with lower-level echelons. The mass media in particular provided models of behavior to be adopted. For example, the press, radio, and television publicized images and descriptions of the first mass rally in a Warsaw factory on March 11, where the Warsaw Committee secretary, Józef Kępa, made an appropriate speech that included attacks on *Zionists*. Other provincial secretaries followed suit—within a week all of them attended rallies and gave similar speeches. There were also telephone calls to trustworthy comrades in provincial committees and a good deal of imitation and "horizontal" consultation between midlevel apparatchiks on what to do. Of course, the patterns of behavior had been prepared and well-rehearsed during previous campaigns. For example, the structure of slogans and speeches was much the same as in the 1950s; one

10. "Do studentów Uniwersytetu Warszawskiego," *Słowo Powszechne* (March 11, 1968).
11. Quoted in Mieszczanek, *Krajobraz*, 43–46, and J. Nowicki [Jakub Karpiński], "Mowi Warszawa . . . ," *Kultura* 9–10 (1972): 116–17.

simply had to replace the old slogans against "right-nationalist deviation," "émigrés—lackeys of American imperialism," "kulaks," and so on, with "Zionism."

The campaign was not limited to verbal attacks; a purge began immediately the day after the first rally in Warsaw. Its primary target was the most prominent member of the former Puławy faction, Roman Zambrowski, a man who had been a devoted party member for forty years and was a former member of the Politburo. Having served as Central Committee secretary, speaker of Parliament, and government minister, Zambrowski lost his positions by an evidently inspired decision of the local party cell in his absence, following baseless accusations.[12] News of his dismissal sent a clear message: if such a prominent figure was defenseless, anybody could be attacked. Soon several other high-ranking Jewish officials lost their ministerial posts. In a few weeks a nationwide purge of Jews from their positions and the party had already gathered momentum and was descending from top government officials and editors-in-chief to university professors, bookkeepers in cooperatives, teachers, factory foremen, and workers.

The *Zionist* was not the only enemy targeted by the unfolding propaganda campaign, but it was the primary one. As Michał Głowiński, a distinguished analyst of the language of propaganda, wrote, "Behind everything evil in the world, enemies of every kind, emerges the face of the Jew called Zionist."[13] The Jewishness of the enemy usually did not appear explicitly but was conveyed through indirect signals. There is no single text that portrays the *March Jew* completely. Various texts contain a few traits, but fragments of articles, speeches, brochures, books, letters to the editor (regardless of who wrote them), and speeches—taken together—create a rich mosaic, a model of that Jew. Thanks to studies focusing on the 1968 propaganda we can now present a synthesis derived from a rich collection of texts written in the course of barely three months following the initial events of March 8.[14]

Besides his *Zionism* (that is, Jewishness), the enemy had three other features worth mentioning. The first was their politicized nature—they were conscious and determined enemies of socialist Poland. The word "political" and its derivatives were those most frequently used that March to depict the enemy: political instigators, political rabble-rousers, political imposters, political bankrupts, political delinquents, political degenerates, political provocateurs, political saboteurs, shrewd political players, and pseudopoliticians.

The second characteristic of the enemy was an elitist nature that alienated him or her from the masses. The enemy belonged to some kind of exclusive,

---

12. "Listy R. Zambrowskiego do władz partyjnych," *Krytyka* 6 (1980): 75.

13. Michał Głowiński, "Marcowe fabuły," in his *Pismak 1863 i inne szkice o różnych brzydkich rzeczach* (Warsaw, 1995), 63.

14. Osęka, *Syjoniści, inspiratorzy, wichrzyciele*; Nowicki, "Mowi Warszawa"; Głowiński, "Marcowe fabuły"; A. B. Jarosz, "Marzec w prasie," in Kula et al., *Marzec 1968*, vol. 1.

antiegalitarian political, financial, or cultural establishment. They were detached from the people and secretly or openly held the ordinary man in contempt.

The third feature of the image of the enemy was something that might be called the coherent variety of their repulsiveness: they possessed traits which in a rational mind cannot appear together but coexist in the propaganda image as complementary and not mutually exclusive. Thus "Jewish nationalists" could be simultaneously "rootless cosmopolitans," and "Stalinists" could act as "agents of American imperialism." The glue that enabled the linking of such contrary traits, as well as the combining into stories of facts that had nothing in common, was the radical rhetoric masking muddy thinking and the exploitation of certain deeply held conceptual structures—the myths about Jews and the conspiratorial nature of history. Despite the real difficulty of reconciling such mutually exclusive traits, in the propaganda imagery of 1968 their combination intensified the moral repugnance of the enemy.

Such self-contradictory representations are not unique in the rich demonology of antisemitism. To the contrary, as pointed out by Gavin Langmuir, such fantasies are at the core of the hostility that has enabled the mobilization of the majority of radical and fatal anti-Jewish actions since the Middle Ages. It was Langmuir who introduced the term *chimeria* to contrast routine ethnoreligious bias and "assertions presenting figments of imagination, monsters which . . . have never been seen and are projections of a mental process unconnected with real people."[15] The Chimera of Greek mythology was an impossible mixture, a winged beast part goat and part snake, with a lion's head. Lions, goats, and snakes are real but the composite of the three is an imaginary creature, similar to the Stalinist agents of American imperialism and cosmopolitan Zionists. Belief in or use of chimeras is more than prejudice, more powerful and persistent. Fed by hostile emotions and opinions, they are immune to ordinary criteria of proof and testing.

To be sure, 1968 was not the first time that *chimeria* appeared in communist propaganda, nor were the Zionists their first target. Patterns of chimerical accusations had developed in the USSR during the show trials of the 1930s, and Polish communists had used them at least since the late 1940s against a variety of "enemies of the people." Nonetheless, in the anti-Jewish current of the March propaganda we find old antisemitic clichés as well as new charges— or a combination of the old and the new, testifying to the creativity of their authors. The old accusations, which could have been copied from prewar antisemitic literature (and sometimes actually were), pointed mainly to the essen-

---

15. Gavin Langmuir, "Toward a Definition of Antisemitism," in *The Persisting Question: Sociological Perspectives and Social Contexts of Modern Antisemitism* (Berlin, 1987), 109; see also Langmuir, *Toward a Definition of Antisemitism* (Berkeley, Calif., 1990); and David Norman Smith, "The Social Construction of Enemies: Jews and the Representations of Evil," *Sociological Theory* 14, no. 3 (November 1996): 203–39.

tially alien nature of Jews and their perverse methods. The message: Jews are alien and an enemy; they attack Poland and Poles because of inborn hatred, egoist interests, or some Machiavellian plan in which they are joined with other enemies. The allegation that their preferred allies in the anti-Polish plot were the West (i.e., bad) Germans was to touch another sensitive nerve—the fear and hatred of Germans—which also emphasized the *Zionists'* perverse character: the *Zionists* in Poland exploit Poles, or at least undeservedly occupy positions rightfully belonging to Poles, to whom they refer with superiority and disdain; they achieve their goals through manipulation and conspiracy. *Zionist* plots in Poland were said to have some hidden connections with the Jewish conspiracy in the West, where the headquarters of a "World Zionist Mafia" was located. The Joint Distribution Committee, the World Jewish Congress, and Bnai B'rith were allegedly agents of the CIA, Israeli intelligence, or the most secret "Zionist Center." Sometimes it is unclear in the propaganda whether *Zionists* are evil because they serve American imperialism or vice versa; in any case, there is nothing worse than American *Zionists*.

In such a light Jews emerged not as a population or ethnic group but as an organization. To be a Jew implied membership in a secret organization. Various goals were attributed to Jews (everyone could find something he or she feared or despised), but they were invariably threatening and damaging. The goals were usually portrayed vaguely and obscurely, which nevertheless strengthened the impression that if the enemies were able to realize their intentions, Something Terrible would occur. The applications of the "Jewish explanation" to various events were as a rule unsophisticated adaptations of the conspiracy theories developed over the preceding century, of which *The Protocols of the Elders of Zion* is the classic model. They contained grains of truth with large portions of obvious falsehoods stuck together with convoluted or muddy reasoning and communist newspeak. They attempted no coherence (aside from the particular coherence of the chimerical image of the abhorrent enemy), but rather conveniently linked elements derived from recycled antisemitic claims and the regular propaganda schemes well known in all communist countries.

The newer accusations referred to certain behavior or thoughts that were considered crimes, or at least something suspect, in the specific environment of a communist country. Thus, Jews are Marxist revisionists, that is, carriers of a dangerous ideological disease; they have an inclination to oppose the party line in general and Comrade Gomułka in particular. Another crime is the Jews' disrespect for the Cold War division of the world, since they have families and friends in the West; they are open (or hidden and thus even more dangerous) sympathizers with Israel and, therefore, with Israel's American imperialist backers.

Paradoxically, probably the most powerful slogan of the communist propaganda that March was to accuse the Jews of being zealous communists. To be more precise, it blamed Jews for a major part, if not all, of the crimes and horrors of the Stalinist period. This accusation exploited the popular stereotype of Jewish communism and gave it a new twist: the Jews are the dark side of communism; what is wrong with communism is because of them. This charge both compromised the Jews and absolved other communists and the regime itself from the crimes and misdeeds of the recent past. The stereotype of Jewish communism in turn seemed to be rooted in an incomparably older myth known in Europe since the Middle Ages—of Jews spreading disease.

Similarly transformed was the stereotype of the treacherous Jew. The conviction that Jews were inclined to treason and cooperation with the enemies of Poland had been popular at least since the Polish-Soviet war of 1920. It thus had a symbiotic relationship with the myth of Judeo-communism, and it followed a tradition of similar stereotypes elsewhere (e.g., the Dreyfus affair in France). In 1968 it was reinterpreted: since they lost power in 1956, the Jews tend to betray socialist Poland, to betray the party and socialism; this "fact" is exemplified in the high security and army officers such as Józef Światło, Władysław Tykociński, and Paweł Monat, who had escaped to the West. "Poland never was their Fatherland. . . . Their Fatherland is the American dollar, . . ." reads a March article. Although the spies had no fatherland, they did have an ethnicity: the article unmasks their Jewish origin immediately by revealing their original names: for example, Józef Światło—Izaak Fleischfarb, Władysław Tykociński—Eliasz Tikothiner.[16] Once again we can uncover much older roots of the cliché of the Jewish traitor to the party: Colonel Józef Światło is painted with the features of Judas Iscariot. (Quite unintentionally, he also shares some of the characteristics of Emanuel Goldstein, the archetypal traitor of the Party and Big Brother in George Orwell's *1984*.)

A particular theme of the journalism initiated in March was the battle against "the campaign of mean invective against the Polish nation, intending to render it obnoxious in the eyes of world opinion." Poles learned that "Israel and international Zionism, in exchange for damages in the amount of 3 billion marks, agreed to the rehabilitation of Nazi criminals. On this basis . . . Zionists, seeking to absolve the Germans for their crimes committed against Jews, attempt to convince both Jews and the entire world that the real culprits of those crimes were . . . Poles."[17] As proof of this anti-Polish campaign, the press gathered citations from various publications in the West about Polish anti-semitism, drawn especially from articles and public speeches of Jewish politicians. These charges were in fact sometimes unjustified or exaggerated; in any case, they were incompatible with the self-perceptions and images of the war in the Polish collective memory, thus striking an extremely sensitive nerve in Polish identity. The heated debates on wartime Polish-Jewish relations inspired by the publication of *Neighbors* by Jan Tomasz Gross more than thirty years after the 1968 events, testify to the persistence of that sensitivity. In this way

16. "Co ich łączyło?" *Kurier Polski* (March 27, 1968).
17. "Syjonizm w służbie wojny psychologicznej," *Sztandar Młodych* (April 1, 1968).

the March propaganda fed on its own fruit: the persecution of Jews in Poland caused a wave of protests abroad, including irritating generalizations about Polish antisemitism, which were then exploited to spread the campaign further and allowed the communist authorities to present themselves as defenders of Polish national honor and to call for unity under their leadership.

Yet even the most creative combinations of old and new antisemitic slogans could not have created the required effect without the power of the communist party and its propaganda machine. Control over the mass media was a basic principle of party rule. The party had at its disposal the monopolized radio and television and almost all newspapers and magazines. In addition, it used such instruments as workplace radio broadcasts; wall newspapers, posters, banners, and signs placed on buildings; newsreels shown at movie screenings; books, brochures, and leaflets; and even deliberately spread rumors. Newspapers either belonged directly to the party and its satellites—the PZPR press published nearly 60 percent of the daily press run, which totaled almost 8 million copies—or were formally apolitical but actually under party control. The authorities based this control on various forms of dependency: the *nomenklatura* system of overseeing the posts of executive editors, the penetration of staffs by the Security Service, the watchful eye of party cells at workplaces, and state control of financial resources. "Soft" exceptions were a few censored Catholic publications with limited press runs. The only real alternative to the party's monopoly of information was the reception of foreign radio broadcasts, chiefly those of Radio Free Europe.

For many weeks after March 1968, that propaganda machine was a war machine. It produced a powerful noise which, even when its broadcast messages were not entirely persuasive, was able to block independent, contrary communication. From the party's point of view, the satisfactory effect of the campaign was not necessarily to make people think and feel as instructed but to control their behavior: that is, to make people behave as if they supported the campaign. This required preventing (or minimizing) undesirable, disobedient behavior, particularly if collective. The noise of intense verbal and symbolic aggression, as well as the incitement of hostile emotions, affected capacity for sending and receiving independent communication, which is the prerequisite for collective action. Under such conditions, people who think independently prefer to keep their opinions to themselves or to a narrow circle of trustworthy friends. Generally, the periods of hate campaigns were times to maintain a low profile except for people who wanted to distinguish themselves in obedience or zeal. Consequently, it is difficult to assess actual popular opinion and its extent. Certainly there were many people who, for various reasons—including sincere belief in the Jewish threat to Poland—welcomed the campaign or shared the prejudice and resentment it exploited. But how many belonged to this group, what its social structure may have been, and so on, seem to be questions that are impossible to answer. Even more difficult to assess is the possible scope of resistance and opposition to the campaign, since their expressions were—contrary to participation in the campaign—usually inconspicuous.[18]

The military connotations of the word "campaign" capture well the aggressive language as well as the scale of mobilization of forces against "the enemies of the Socialist Fatherland." There were not many publications that did not participate in the campaign, and they were conspicuous as exceptions—for example, the weekly *Polityka*, which itself came under fire in the intraparty factional struggle.[19] Such resistance meant not active rebuttal of lies and slander but withdrawal from or minimization of participation in the campaign, which also required courage. The remaining publications, out of either desire, the habit of obedience, or fear, joined in the witch hunt, although the depth of their involvement as well as the enthusiasm of their authors was not uniform.

As the head of the Central Committee's press bureau, Stefan Olszowski, noted with satisfaction, 250 relevant articles had appeared in the central and regional press during the first ten days of the campaign.[20] A significant portion of this propaganda barrage on Polish readers contained more or less openly antisemitic content. If we accept that at least half of the 250 articles attacked *Zionists*, and multiply the number of texts by the size of the print runs, we can estimate that in the first four days Poland was literally showered with millions—and in time, tens of millions—of antisemitic propaganda messages. Anti-Jewish accents could be found in a wide variety of newspaper departments—above all, in editorials, current information, and notes from PAP (Polish Press Agency, which received special praise from Olszowski) but also in the foreign, historical, legal, and economic news sections, in letters to the editor, and in articles reprinted from other sources. Propaganda messages were contained even in the illustrations. On front pages readers saw photographs of meetings displaying *anti-Zionist* banners, and on the back were satirical cartoons with caricatures of the *Zionist* enemy.

All this was guided by the press bureau, as its director proudly asserted: "[Having] read all the materials in the domestic press ... the employees of press bureau undertook a check, carried out consultations, and in specific circumstances formulated together with the editors appropriate sentences and paragraphs of articles, commentary, and information about the events." Olszowski praised most strongly "the radio and particularly television for playing the chief role in the widespread transmission of our political argu-

18. I distinguish resistance to the campaign (i.e., various forms of noncooperation) from opposition (i.e., conscious attempts to counteract it). Certainly opposition was more risky, requiring greater courage and determination, and was thus less frequent.

19. See the memoirs of the chief editor of *Polityka*, Mieczysław F. Rakowski, *Dzienniki polityczne*, vol. 3 (Warsaw, 1999).

20. Minutes of Olszowski's conference with editors of April 5, 1968, in Archiwum Akt Nowych (AAN), Central Committee collection (KC), 6137.

mentation."[21] The 1968 campaign was the first hate campaign in the Polish People's Republic to exploit the power of television, a new medium that became widespread in Poland in the 1960s: the number of set owners grew from 400,000 in 1960 to 2 million in 1965 and 3.4 million in 1968, mainly in the cities.[22]

Though using the power of modern media, the party did not forget the more traditional forms of communication. The scale and reach of public meetings, for example, were immense. Some meetings were huge undertakings, with crowds numbering more than 100,000 participants, but all together, more people participated in the tens of thousands of meetings on a smaller scale that were organized virtually everywhere. There were factory and department meetings; meetings in basic party (POP) units and in provincial, county, and district party organizations; conferences of the *aktiv* (professional party activists); sessions of party committees and executive committees at various levels; meetings of the party-controlled trade union, youth, and women's organizations and of the PAX association ("progressive" Catholics) and the ZBoWiD Veterans Union. The Warsaw party committee alone, and this in just the first two weeks of the campaign, organized more than 1,900 POP meetings, nearly 400 rallies, approximately 700 meetings of the *aktiv*, and 600 meetings of various party groups.[23] The number of different kinds of gatherings throughout the country in the course of the three-month duration of the campaign is difficult to specify, but 100,000 is a very conservative estimate. The army alone directed 25,125 officers and cadets to lead explanatory sessions and take part in 42,000 meetings (including 27,000 in the country, 4,000 at workplaces, and 10,500 in schools), which reportedly gathered a total of 3.7 million people.[24] The ministry most involved was the Ministry of Internal Affairs with its secret services. Its role in sowing antisemitism during the campaign is beyond doubt.

Local party secretaries, agitators and instructors, delegated officers, and other designated individuals were invited or volunteered to deliver speeches at these meetings. They were written according to instructions from propaganda departments, modeled on examples from the press, radio, and television, and supplemented with the speakers' own ideas under such titles as "The Battle with Contemporary Zionism and Its Influences on People's Poland," "Goals and Tasks of Contemporary Zionism," and "The Background of the Current Events at Home and the Goal of Party Organizations in Light of Comrade Wiesław's [Gomułka's] Speech."

Meetings, in particular the party meetings, were more than a propaganda channel. They served to educate, to transmit vocabulary, to prescribe forms of

21. Ibid.
22. The Main Statistical Office (Główny Urząd Statystyczny—GUS) Statistical Yearbook, 1969.
23. Information "A" of March 25, 1968, in Kula et al., *Marzec 1968*, 2:242.
24. J. Poksiński, "Wojsko Polskie wobec Marca," in Kula et al., *Marzec 1968*, 1:80.

behavior that were currently desired and approved and to warn against those that were inappropriate and condemned. This education was not limited to listening to speeches but required participation in rituals such as applause for the speakers, raising hands to vote, holding banners, participating in discussions using correct words and phrases, and responding with the appropriate shouts. Attendance in itself at meetings of many hours' duration and listening to extended speeches required patience and self-denial. The latter was at the core of these political liturgies, and one should not underestimate the psychological effects of repeated participation, even if routine. The meetings were also a tool of supervision and an evaluation of those convened—a test of the correct performance of rituals which permitted evaluation of group and individual obedience. The discussions usually did not differ much from this report of a meeting in Warsaw:

> Almost all the discussants condemned privileged individuals of Jewish background in various fields, demanded improvements in party information, the strengthening of the role of party organizations—particularly in the education of party cadres, denounced the excessive concentration of persons of Jewish origin in certain institutions, called attention to the damage caused by Zionist activity, ... criticized the political and moral attitudes of certain employees [of their institution], ... demanded that the process of purging enemy elements from the state and party apparatus be seen through to its conclusion, ... [and] protested against the slander of the Polish nation by international Zionism.[25]

Meetings were a particular place of symbolic aggression against *Zionists* and other specified enemies, who were accused of various offenses, condemned, stigmatized, and, if possible, punished through exclusion from the party or dismissal from their positions. Sometimes the accusation of *Zionism* fell on individuals who were not known to be Jewish: that is, on people who had concealed their origins or didn't possess any Jewish ancestry whatsoever. Amateur genealogical researchers appeared, spontaneously or encouraged by the MSW. An effective way to reveal the Jewish origin of "disguised Zionists" was simply to smear someone with the label of *Zionist*, leaving the burden on the accused to prove his or her innocence. Used freely to strike at anyone, this tactic greatly contributed to the witch-hunting atmosphere. One could be accused not only of active or verbal offense but also of inactivity or silence, of "displaying a passive attitude toward the current events." As was stated in one such case: "Since the Israeli aggression on the Arab lands until the last

25. Notes from the POP (basic party cell) meeting of April 1968, Warsaw University Museum collections, file 599d.

POP meeting, he has not taken a position, . . . and silence carries a message as well, from which we must draw conclusions."[26]

Sometimes the dynamics of the hate campaign spun out of control as discussion transgressed the boundaries of the permissible, and participants began to proclaim with increasing enthusiasm that "the Central Committee is full of Jews, the Voievodship Provincial Committee is full of Jews"; "Poles ought to rule Poland"; "A minority ethnic group shouldn't fill all the positions, while the ethnic majority works for them. The central administration should get to work, or otherwise we'll take action into our own hands . . . Let's get those sons-of-bitches out of here."[27] A variety of party documents contain recommendations to counteract antisemitic speeches or declarations, but these obviously were not acted on with a conviction equal to the encouragement of attacks against *Zionists*. Additionally, the definition of antisemitic behavior became quite narrow in March.

It was as a consequence of the campaign and the party leadership's decision to "let the Zionist go" that the last wave of Jewish emigration left Poland. In 1968–70 about 13,000 people departed, declaring Israel as their destination. Only a minority actually went to Israel, however; others settled mainly in the United States, Sweden, and France. As a joke circulating in Warsaw in 1969 put it, "How does a wise Jew talk to a stupid one? By telephone from the West."[28] One unexpected effect of the campaign was a return to stronger Jewish identities among many Jewish Poles and Poles of Jewish origin whom the campaign had alienated, forcibly "de-Polonized," or simply made aware of their family ancestry; this process was noted among both the emigrants and those who decided to stay. Similarly, the campaign ideologically compromised the regime. It led a number of young people to abandon their hopes for reform of the regime and set them on a track that led to open opposition. Several years later, these people made essential contributions to the development of the Solidarity movement and eventually to the dismantling of the communist regime in 1989.

Why did Gomułka unleash the campaign? Although its origins may be traced back to the Security Service of the Ministry of Internal Affairs, Gomułka as the party's First Secretary—that is, the most powerful person in the regime—contributed essentially to the development of the campaign through at least approving and not counteracting it. Politburo protocols leave no doubt that responsibility lay with this leading decision-making body and particularly with Gomułka, its chairman. Yet observers believe that personal anti-Jewish resentments or prejudice were not a key driving force for Gomułka's actions (or

---

26. These examples of witch-hunting are taken from AAN, KC 6092; and Starewicz to Gomułka, April 7, 1968, in APRL, Starewicz file.

27. Such statements may be found in AAN, KC 3015:15–16, 70–71, and AAN KC 6092.

28. For detailed data on the emigration, see Stola, *Kampania antysyjonistyczna*, 207–33.

inactions) in 1968; in fact, unleashing antisemitic emotions carried dangers for him, as his wife was Jewish. A closer look is needed to provide the reasons that most likely played a decisive role in bringing Gomułka and his close collaborators to approve the campaign.

First, the campaign was a handy instrument to fight the student rebellion by compromising its leaders and goals, painting them as alien and perverse. Second, it served to prevent the spread of the student revolt beyond the universities to broader groups, particularly to workers, a prospect that party leaders deeply feared. At least since the autumn of 1967, when a series of strikes and other workers' protests followed a rise in food prices, the leaders had been seriously concerned with a possible new eruption of popular unrest. The campaign aimed at alienating the masses from the dissident students and intellectuals precisely by portraying the latter as "the Alien"—that is, as Poland-hating Jews, Stalinists attempting to return to power, allies of the German expansionists (who still evoked widespread fear and hate), and arrogant and egoist members of the establishment. The campaign not only separated the masses from potential leaders but channeled a part of popular frustration with the grim realities of "real socialism" against the *Zionist* scapegoats.

The third main objective, which the decision-makers never revealed explicitly, was to change the political balance in the party leadership. Gomułka's main opponent, Edward Ochab, resigned from the Politburo and his state positions; another Politburo member, Adam Rapacki, simply ceased going to his job as Minister of Foreign Affairs and went on extended vacations. Also pratically neutralized was Marshal Marian Spychalski, Gomułka's former friend, who left the Ministry of Defense. Gomułka may also have been concerned with the political ambitions of General Moczar, who evidently was pushing for changes in the leadership. Following the campaign Gomułka made Moczar a member of the Politburo but at the same time deprived him of control over the MSW. Thus, though formally advancing upward (Poliburo membership was considered more important than being a minister), Moczar could no longer use (and abuse) the secret services, which had been vital to his career.

Gomułka's reconsolidation of the party leadership on his own terms was of great importance in the context of developments in Czechoslovakia. Brutal repression of students, the propaganda campaign, consolidation of party leadership, and the mobilization of the party combined to serve as a preventive strike against potential followers of the Czech path. Finally, the general attack on *Zionists* and dismissals of several high-ranking Jewish officials eliminated once and for all a group of once-powerful individuals and initiated a wider wave of changes in cadres, which allowed many frustrated meddle- and lower-level apparatchiks, especially those of the generation that joined the party in the early 1950s, to satisfy at last their personal ambitions.

What paradoxically links these goals is the lack of any essential connection between them and *Zionism* (whatever its meaning), and the incommensurably large scale and intensity of the *anti-Zionist* campaign. Resorting to *anti-Zionism* was not inevitable or even necessary, but it was useful. It was useful because it served well in reaching all the foregoing objectives. Playing the Jewish card was multifunctional. As a good politician, Gomułka adopted a strategy that promised the attainment of several objectives at the same time.

For each of these purposes, *anti-Zionism* was an instrument used in a more or less cynical way. It should be stressed, however, that for some people the attack on the Jews was the chief goal and their anti-Jewish prejudice and resentment were sufficient motives for action. MSW and Central Committee archival documents do not present such motives explicitly, but their implicit obsession with Jewish conspiracy and the *Zionist* threat leaves no doubt as to what kind of sentiments and opinions about Jews some of their authors had. One finds similar meaning in their deeds. Thus, the campaign originated both in the pursuit of rationally defined interests and in irrational impulses. Between these two extremes—cold cynicism in manipulating the antisemitic prejudices of others in order to achieve one's interests, and an antisemitic paranoia that is too sincere to be cynical—there is room for a spectrum of attitudes combining cynicism and prejudice in various proportions.

Let us combine this typology with the chimerical nature of the "March Jews," whom the campaign rhetorically targeted. As Jews have been the primary object of *chimeria* in Europe since the Middle Ages, the fact that the Polish communists resorted in March 1968 to chimerical images is not surprising. What is noteworthy was their skill in waking up the chimeras, and in riding them. Faced with student rebellion, the dissent of intellectuals, and dangerous developments in Czechoslovakia, and fearing a larger wave of social unrest, the communist leaders and their propagandists decided to unleash the chimeras and harness them to their cart. They put their hope no longer in historical determinism, class instinct, or workers' loyalty to the "People's Government" but in phantasmagoric monsters and sheer violence. Some of them could ride the chimeras as cynical detached masters, yet quite a number, it seems, entered an intimate relationship with the monsters and were unable to control the demons they aroused, even in their own minds.

14

Memory Contested

Jewish and Catholic Views of Auschwitz in Present-Day Poland

JANINE P. HOLC

The aims of imagination are not the aims of history.

Cynthia Ozick

The issues of contested memory surrounding Auschwitz, the group of concentration camps that now functions as a memorial site in southern Poland, are complex and wide-ranging and have been treated by scholars from a variety of perspectives.[1] The physical territory and buildings of Auschwitz have functioned as the collective symbol of the Holocaust itself for many different audiences; thus, there is much at stake in the particular materialized forms and geographies that find expression at the

I thank Robert Blobaum, Jill Ehnenn, Marek Kucia, John Markoff, Małgorzata Markoff, and Inez Pietrzak for their helpful comments and assistance.

1. For example, Sławomir Kapralski, "Oświęcim: Miejsce wielu pamięci," *Pro Memoria* 8 (January 1998): 17–24; James E. Young, *The Texture of Memory: Holocaust Memorials and Meaning* (New Haven, 1993); Teresa Świebocka, Jonathan Webber, and Connie Wilsack, *Auschwitz—A History in Photographs* (Oświęcim, 1995); Deborah Dwork and Robert Van Pelt, *Auschwitz: 1270 to the Present* (New York, 1997); Jonathan Huener, *Auschwitz, Poland, and the Politics of Commemoration, 1945–1979* (Athens, Ohio, 2003); and a scholarly journal consistently publishing on this topic, *Pro Memoria* (Oświęcim: Publishing House of the State Museum of Auschwitz-Birkenau).

site itself.[2] My analysis focuses on the emergence of a highly publicized and much-debated form of Auschwitz memorialization which took place from early 1998 through 1999: the "crosses at Auschwitz controversy." Although the illegal action involved does not fit into standard views of "memorialization," it did function as an enactment of previously unstated tensions over the place of Auschwitz in national histories. The controversy also generated new opportunities for revisiting and renarrating Jewish-Catholic relations in Poland, in directions that at times reinforced antisemitism and at other times allowed challenges to antisemitism to be voiced.

In brief, the "crosses controversy" was sparked in 1998 when a nationalist activist, Kazimierz Świtoń, asserted the right to install a cross, as a Christian religious symbol, on the territory of the Auschwitz Museum, which is located on the land that was the Auschwitz I concentration camp. For many people inside and outside of Poland, the unique nature of Jewish vulnerability and loss during World War II makes Auschwitz—as the historical site of a significant portion of this loss—a place where either no religious symbols at all or no Christian symbols should exist. However, 10 percent of those killed at the Auschwitz complex of camps were Polish Catholics. Świtoń and his supporters claimed that these deaths were insufficiently memorialized, in part because of what they termed "Jewish influences." When governmental authorities and nongovernmental groups attempted to prevent the establishment of a long-term Catholic monument, a number of individuals responded by illegally filling the space with several crosses, escalating the legal and symbolic stakes for both Catholics and Jews. The "crosses action" became an explicit countermemorial to the Holocaust as a uniquely Jewish experience.

The crosses controversy merits careful attention for several reasons. First, it created the opportunity for a number of antisemitic voices to gain at least partial legitimacy in public culture, when those voices attacked critics who wanted the crosses removed as "anti-Polish," "anti-Church," and part of a "Jewish conspiracy." The particular form of these protests highlighted the ambiguities of national identity that Auschwitz itself embodies. The building complex is located on the territory of the state of Poland. Yet it is at the same time subject to regulatory codes as a UNESCO cultural site; to the policies of the international commission vested with overseeing Auschwitz in particular; to the city, county, and regional authorities overseeing economic development and infrastructure in the area; and to the less institutionalized but nevertheless powerful claims of Jewish communities worldwide. Additionally, the location in Poland and the deaths of Catholics there opens Auschwitz to claims

---

2. These forms range from the signage on the preserved buildings, the sorts of literature available in the bookstore, the statements and actions of guides, the location and nature of boundary markers, and the relation of building locations to how the site is viewed by visitors. See Deborah Dwork and Robert Jan van Pelt, "The Politics of a Strategy for Auschwitz-Birkenau," *Cardozo Law Review* 20, no. 2 (December 1998): 687–93.

by Catholic authorities locally and internationally. These claimants were openly pitted against one another during the controversy.

Second, the controversy forced opponents of antisemitism to grapple more directly than in the past with the link between the Catholic Church and the experiences of Jews in the history of Poland, in part because these opponents had to articulate the reasons a cross might be an unwelcome symbol at Auschwitz. Thus, the action raised questions about a number of unresolved tensions in Catholic-Jewish relations. Modern forms of communication enabled the circulation of these questions. Polish television broadcast the protests and counterprotests throughout the country and created an atmosphere of urgency that was difficult to ignore. This kind of communication suggests something about the particularities of antisemitism in post-1989 Poland, when the publics it addresses incorporate radio, television, and print media in multiple ways. A single action can be communicated immediately and indeed—in contrast to earlier historical periods—with its immediacy privileged by the form of its representation.

Third, the controversy can be productively viewed as a cultural formation emerging as a reaction not only to an increasingly secularized Polish culture but to anxieties about national identity and its disruption by "Europeanization." Although it is tempting to locate the crosses action at the beginning of an apparently renewed antisemitic rhetoric, because the controversy was so vivid and the position of the activists so unambiguous, such a strategy of location would be reading unwarranted causality into a phenomenon that itself was a product of long-standing tensions between Catholic and Jewish interpretations of Polish national identity. The crosses controversy was one of a series of crises that have punctuated Catholic-Jewish relations since 1945; these crises have brought tacit and even taboo subjects out into the open, even while they opened up space for the expression of antisemitism. But why a crisis over crosses, and why particularly in 1998? As I argue below, both the content and the form of the controversy speak directly to identity issues at a time when the government was negotiating Poland's NATO membership and discussing eventual entry into the European Union, and when the multicultural character of Poland's history and present identity was taken up in earnest by local advocacy organizations.

Finally, the controversy revealed the essentially contested status of Jewish-Catholic relations in Poland itself. The debates over the crosses in 1998–99 exposed different interpretations of what "Auschwitz" refers to historically, who is covered by the term "Holocaust," what it means in the present day, and how Auschwitz functions in creating a bounded and containable "memory" for a global audience. The crosses action thereby made explicit the unsettled nature and multiplicity of meanings of Auschwitz. The temptation to respond to such multiplicity in a disciplinary mode—to resolve it "once and for all"—became immense, fueled in part by the compulsion to shut down the antisemitic speech suddenly so prevalent throughout the country, and in part by a defensiveness in light of the new scrutiny on Catholic motives, theology, and institutions.

Although the crosses controversy took place largely in 1998, it was fore-shadowed by events in 1996 (and the much earlier debate over a convent adjacent to Auschwitz, discussed below). After the end of communist rule in 1989, the Auschwitz Museum, like many institutions and organizations in Poland, began the process of revisiting its identity and mission. By 2000, the year of the fifty-fifth anniversary of the liberation of Auschwitz, the museum had reoriented its focus from Auschwitz as a place where Catholic and other non-Jewish Poles were imprisoned and killed by Nazis to one that highlighted to a greater degree the unique vulnerability and suffering of European Jews.[3]

The shift was complicated by the historical geography of what had been the Auschwitz camp complex. Auschwitz I was a concentration camp that imprisoned individuals of all nationalities, including 75,000 Polish Catholics, many of whom died by torture, disease, and execution. This camp is now mostly occupied by what is currently the Auschwitz Museum (sometimes called the Auschwitz-Birkenau Museum), although several buildings used by the Nazis are not included in the museum complex. Auschwitz II, or Birkenau, located two miles away, was the death camp at which most Jews were killed, the camp that contained the original gas chambers and crematoria that most people associate with the Shoah. Birkenau is not a museum but a preserved former death camp with a few museumlike elements such as a restored shower building, with a small exhibition of photographs, and a modest bookstore.

Auschwitz III comprises forty labor camps in the surrounding area which are not marked or memorialized; Jews and Gentiles both participated in forced labor at these sites. Even beyond Auschwitz III, additional places of forced labor, torture, and death were scattered throughout the towns surrounding Auschwitz and in the town of Oświęcim itself.

From the early 1990s the museum staff worked to alter the representations of the victims of World War II.[4] As noted above, Auschwitz I had previously been presented as a site of Polish national suffering, at which victims' Jewish identity was secondary to their state citizenship.[5] During the fifty years after

3. The communication of the message that it was Jews who were targeted above all by the "Final Solution" and who were most vulnerable once in the camp is still not a completed process at the Auschwitz Museum. Its main priority seems to be to reproduce Auschwitz I as a representation of a defunct concentration camp, and to preserve Birkenau and its character. Since Nazi and other camp authorities organized the people imprisoned there by state citizenship (in part because each train transport was often composed of citizens of a single state), such identities remain organizing categories at the museum exhibits.

4. Marek Kucia, "KL Auschwitz in the Social Consciousness of Poles, A.D. 2000," in *Remembering for the Future: The Holocaust in an Age of Genocide*, ed. Elisabeth Maxwell and John. K. Roth (London, 2001), 3:632–51.

5. For a good discussion, see Sławomir Kapralski, "Frontiers of Memory: The Jews in the Changing Landscapes of Poland," in *Mosaics of Change: The First Decade of Life in the New Eastern Europe*, ed. Susan C. Pearce and Eugenia Sojka (Gdańsk, 2000), 34–38.

the war, governmental authorities, educational institutions, and public culture supported a view of World War II that emphasized Polishness and Poland as a "nation" as the targets of Nazi exterminationist policies; Jewish deaths were blended into the category of "Polish." Access to the knowledge that Jews were uniquely victimized and that they constituted the vast majority of deaths (90 percent) at Auschwitz-Birkenau was available in schools but often overshadowed by a more urgent presentation of national victimization.

In part to change this viewpoint, the museum developed a more activist mission, holding conferences and seminars, developing educational outreach programs, and building its international contacts. Staff changed the wording of explanatory tablets, signs, maps, and brochures; the training given to guides; and the offerings of the bookstore. By 2000 they had developed a public relations initiative, focused on the fifty-fifth anniversary of liberation, to foster a deeper and more accurate understanding of the Shoah on the part of people living in Poland. Still, even after the concerted educational effort in 2000, 19 percent of Polish residents believed that "Poles"—not specifying whether Gentile or Jewish—constituted the greatest number of victims at Auschwitz-Birkenau.[6]

Even as Auschwitz I evolved to include a greater emphasis on the Jewish experience of the Shoah, aspects of its previous character as a monument to Polish national identity remained unproblematized; there seemed to be a tacit belief that Catholic and Jewish expressions of commemoration could coexist.[7] Visitors to the museum from the late 1990s through 2001 encountered in a waiting room inside the first building a showcase of some of the religious and social writings of the Polish Catholic priest and prisoner (and future saint) Maksymilian Kolbe. No other individuals were identified in this way, and Kolbe's writings for a prewar antisemitic newspaper were excluded from the display. During a visit to Auschwitz and Birkenau in 1995, a group of scouts left some small crosses in Birkenau as well as some similarly sized markers with stars of David attached to crosses; at this point, religious symbols were unpoliced by the museum staff. In addition, until 1989 a very tall cross, installed for a papal Mass in 1979, had been left standing on the Birkenau grounds. The museum's policies did not seem to attend much to the potential influence of religious symbols and other martyrological expressions on how the history of Auschwitz was received by visitors.

6. Kucia, 638. Kucia, conducting surveys both before and after the 2000 celebrations and media campaign, found that even among those who had never visited the museum or Birkenau, accurate knowledge about Auschwitz and its victims did increase. For example, "the perception of Auschwitz as a Jewish rather than Polish symbol has grown among Poles steadily from a mere 8 percent in 1995 (before the anniversary) to 32 percent in 2000 (after the anniversary)" (644).

7. The idea that from a Catholic perspective, Jewish symbols and spaces can coexist unproblematically alongside Catholic religious symbols was prevalent throughout Poland and elsewhere. For an example, see Dorota Gołębiewska, "Kilkaset metrów od żwirowiska," *Tygodnik Powszechny* (January 17, 1999): 10.

Jewish visitors from abroad noticed these symbols, however. In 1996, Elie Wiesel, a prominent visitor to ceremonies commemorating Gentile violence against Jews in the 1946 Kielce pogrom, asked publicly that the crosses be removed. He and other visitors argued that the immense number of Jewish deaths at Birkenau made the site a Jewish cemetery, a place at which Christian symbols in general, and the cross in particular, were violations.[8] Wiesel's statements took on particular meaning because of the moral authority that many audiences invest in him. Because of the public attention given to the Kielce ceremonies and to Wiesel as a visitor, his statements were widely available in the press and on radio and television.[9]

The new contextualization of the presence of the cross as a response to Poland's Jewish history, crystallized in the Auschwitz Museum's work and Wiesel's statements, was perceived as threatening by some Catholics in Poland. Prominent figures in the Catholic Church such as Bishop Tadeusz Pieronek initially defended the existence of crosses on the terrain of Auschwitz by arguing that "both sides of the issue have to be taken into account" and by stating that Wiesel ignored legitimate Catholic claims to memorialize the dead.[10] Other Catholic clergy previously associated with antisemitic discourse took Wiesel's statements as an opportunity to remobilize the connections between Jewish views on memorialization at Auschwitz and threats to Polish national identity. A very public figure in the Catholic Church because of his association with the Solidarity social movement, Father Henryk Jankowski, flatly articulated these concerns: "Jews want to take over Auschwitz-Birkenau."[11]

Jankowski's brief statement conflated the claims by Jewish individuals and groups to have a say in how the Shoah experience in Auschwitz is memorialized, on the one hand, with an antisemitic characterization of Jewish people as colonizing (often for financial gain), on the other. This particular shorthand is a powerful statement of antisemitism. It can easily invoke a larger logic of antisemitism in part because a stereotype of Jewish people as financially controlling outsiders is of such long standing in Europe. Any claims to Auschwitz memorialization that privileged Judaism or Jewish experience were vulnerable to this strategy, which attributed an ostensible threat to Poland on the part of "Jews" who were enemies, organized, conspiratorial (that is, who hid the main

8. Anna Wielopolska, "Kielce proszą o przebaczenie," *Rzeczpospolita* (July 8, 1996). For a follow-up analysis, see Anna Wielopolska, "Dysonans," *Rzeczpospolita* (July 9, 1996).

9. In addition, Wiesel's statements in 1996 were regarded as the spark initiating the crosses controversy and the wider discussion of antisemitism in Poland, both at the time and later. For example, see Stefan Bratkowski, "Tak, tak, nie, nie," *Rzeczpospolita* (August 14, 1998).

10. Adam Szostkiewicz, "Nie ma co gadać z ekstremistami," *Tygodnik Powszechny* (February 14, 1999). See also Anna Wielopolska and Marcin Dominik Zort, "Żal i zdziwienie," *Rzeczpospolita* (July 10, 1996).

11. "Czy prałat jest antysemitą," *Gazeta Wyborcza* (October 29, 1997). This particular statement has been cited by many observers as emblematic of Polish antisemitism. At the same time, Jankowski has been positioned as an atypical "extremist" member of the clergy. See Tadeusz Zachurski, "Zwłoka i niepełne potępienie," *Rzeczpospolita* (June 23, 1995).

aims of their actions), and colonizing. This set of characteristics invoked the equivalencies of a persistent Europe-based antisemitism found in past historical periods and, today, in a number of non-European contexts as well.

Pieronek's response to Wiesel did not invoke European antisemitic formulas, but the logic he used would repeat itself in future arguments about relations between Catholics and Jews and has in common with Jankowski's antisemitism the delegitimation of the Jewish voice. In a 1999 interview, Pieronek expanded on his earlier statements, saying that Wiesel had "relied exclusively on the Jewish point of view, that in Auschwitz there cannot be a single religious sign because for a number of Jews, God had not been present [at Auschwitz]. But this answer speaks to the fact that Elie Wiesel does not have the slightest idea about how Christianity expresses itself."[12] Pieronek here appeared to hear part of what Wiesel was asking for (although he simplified it and attributed it to a self-serving "exclusive point of view"), but he made a case for the presence of the crosses anyway. For Pieronek, the cross was a well-intentioned symbol of the universal good, and Jewish views of the cross as an insult to Jewish culture, history, or sacred space were simply unfounded.

Within Pieronek's statement, which was typical of responses by people identifying closely with Catholicism in Poland, are the kernels of two central themes that emerge in arguments about Catholic-Jewish relations and historical commemoration throughout this period: (1) that religious symbols can coexist in a single space without referring to each other, and in so doing reflect an equivalence (but not commonality) of experience; and (2) that Christianity encompasses Jewish suffering in its embrace of brotherhood and love. Of course, these themes are not exclusive to Polish public culture or Catholic thinking. But in Poland of the 1990s–2002, their articulation in the particular, materialized context of crosses at a concentration camp museum, in a culture in which the role of Judaism and Jewish life is under constant reevaluation, brings their implications for political power and voice into sharp relief. Specifically, does a Catholic standpoint pose inherent obstacles to a full recovery of a valid Jewish voice in Poland?

The crosses controversy as a discrete event was not sparked until two years after Wiesel's visit. Following his speech the government asked the Auschwitz Museum staff to remove the crosses *and* stars of David at Birkenau. At the same time, authorities considered what to do with the large papal cross that had remained in Birkenau for ten years before being moved to another Auschwitz location. The small crosses and stars of David were removed, despite some public protest, but not the large cross.

Visitors to Auschwitz I had noticed this large cross periodically. In 1989 a local priest had appropriated the tall Birkenau cross left over from the pope's 1979 visit and placed it in a small section of grass adjacent to the Auschwitz

12. Quoted in Szostkiewicz, "Nie ma co gadać."

I camp.[13] The choice of location and the timing constituted an intentional political statement.

As noted above, the Auschwitz Museum complex does not include every building in the area that was used by the Nazis as part of the Final Solution—these buildings are scattered throughout what is now the large town of Oświęcim. But one such building, so close to the wall of the camp that it appears visually to be part of the museum complex, was deeded to the Carmelite order by the Oświęcim town council in 1984. International and domestic groups, both Jewish and non-Jewish, protested the close location of a Catholic convent to Auschwitz I and, until 1993, struggled to force the convent to leave Auschwitz I and move to another building nearby.[14] This struggle had its dramatic moments as well, in part because both the government and the Church hierarchy vacillated in their commitment to moving the convent.

What was left after the convent did relocate was a building and small grassy area that symbolized for some Polish Catholics a Catholic surrender to illegitimate pressure—pressure that came from abroad, was Jewish in character, shamed Poland's national identity, and violated Poland's sovereignty. Activists seeking to revive a Catholic presence at Auschwitz thus found this space a powerful home for the other contested religious symbol from Birkenau, the large papal cross.[15]

The dispute over the location of the Carmelite convent prefigures the 1998 crosses controversy in the way that Jews were posed as external threats to a legitimate Catholic presence at Auschwitz. Perhaps more important, the dramatic enactment of the struggle over the location of the convent and the "story" of that enactment became key elements of the narrative constructing and rationalizing the view of Jews in the crosses controversy.[16] When international groups drew attention to the convent in 1985 and an international group of Catholics and Jews decided to relocate it, it became clear that the people living in the convent would not cooperate. They claimed that their

---

13. Exactly when this cross was moved, with whose cooperation, and by whose initiative are facts that many sources disagree on. There seem to be coexisting stories, one "official" and one "real." Informal interviews with local residents in the town of Oświęcim and the nearby city of Kraków yielded a variety of "real" stories.

14. The convent controversy was itself a crisis in Auschwitz memorialization. For details, see Emma Klein, *The Battle for Auschwitz: Catholic-Jewish Relations on the Line* (London, 2001); Władysław T. Bartoszewski, *The Convent at Auschwitz* (New York, 1990); and Lawrence Weinbaum, "The Struggle for Memory in Poland: Auschwitz, Jedwabne, and Beyond," Institute of the World Jewish Congress Policy Study No. 22 (Jerusalem, 2001).

15. The use of the term "papal" varies according to the political strategy of the speaker. Although this large cross was built and installed for a mass at Birkenau held by the pope, the pope did not bless the cross explicitly or render it "papal" in any theological sense, yet it stubbornly retains its association with the pope and an enhanced sacral status. See Stanisław Musiał, "Prawda o Oświęcimskim Krzyżu," *Gazeta Wyborcza* (April 22, 1998).

16. For example, see Wojciech Markiewicz, "Strażnicy krzyży," *Polityka* (August 22, 1998): 16–17.

stance was a principled one, in support of their mission as Carmelite nuns, and that their only activity was to pray for the dead. The individuals living in the convent used their culturally protected status as nuns, their vows of silence and withdrawal from public life, and their gender to insulate themselves from external pressures to relocate. Newspaper and radio reports frequently referred to the vulnerability and powerlessness of the pious "sisters," whose silence was not interpreted as a resistance to the negotiators from the Church and Jewish groups but rather as a desirable quality of womanhood, connected with humility, modesty, faith, and lack of worldliness. Those who would disturb such a silence seemed morally stained.

An earlier event at the convent served to frame subsequent perceptions of the Jewish presence at Auschwitz. In 1989 a Jewish group from the United States arrived in Oświęcim and went to the convent itself, intending to speak directly with the residents. When no Carmelite nun would answer their requests for a meeting, they entered the grounds of the convent and staged a protest, using a combination of sit-in tactics, shouts, and the playing of a shofar. Non-Jewish Polish workers arrived and confronted the protesters, who would not leave the premises. The workers forcibly expelled them. The confrontation attracted enormous media attention, and the group came to be identified by the name of its leader, Rabbi Avi Weiss.

Although the incident took place in the course of only a few hours, it quickly gained status as a defining moment in Polish-Jewish relations. The media offered a story of an aggressive group of Jewish males, disrespectful both of the boundaries of a religious site and of a place where women lived without men. The violence between the Gentiles and the Jews was portrayed as a masculinized showdown between defenders and invaders, with Jews in the role of trespassers invading sacred space. These elements came to shape the larger story of memorialization at Auschwitz, and throughout the 1990s individuals and groups commenting on the legitimacy of Jewish claims to limit religious symbols would frequently refer to "Weiss" or to "extremists," the latter a code word for the Jewish antagonists in the convent tale. Thus, when Wiesel made his comments at Kielce in 1996, his insistence that crosses be removed from Birkenau and Auschwitz was placed in the context of the preexisting dramatic framework established in 1989. Jankowski's response that "Jews were taking over" reminds us that this framework itself has dramatic precursors: the stories that make up European antisemitism.

In late 1997 it appeared that the Polish government was ready to take down the large papal cross at the Auschwitz wall. Kazimierz Świtoń, a right-wing activist with Solidarity credentials, responded by demonstrating at the site and calling for others to join him.[17] In early 1998 some men installed a second large cross and, later, several small crosses. Świtoń and others occupied the

17. Detailed overviews of the events are available in the Polish press throughout the second half of 1998. For example, see Zofia Stachura, "Wojna krzyżowa," *Wprost* (August 16, 1998).

grassy area, decorated the fence with banners announcing their intentions, built first an altar and then a small makeshift chapel, and invited clergy to hold Mass at the site. Photographers and video camera operators visited the site frequently to capture the changing tableau, and soon the demonstration became an ongoing story in the international media. Local authorities and police decided not to intervene by force, but the status of the large papal cross and of Catholic religious activity and symbols at Auschwitz gained enormous attention, and many public figures felt compelled to comment on it. In March 1998 a group of parliamentary deputies issued a declaration of support for the continued presence of all the crosses, and informal groups such as the Cross Defense Committee were established throughout the country. By May 1998, pressure from abroad to dismantle the crosses had increased tremendously, but the issue of "defending the papal cross" had mobilized supporters, and they began a series of street protests in the capital city, Warsaw. In June Świtoń began a forty-two-day hunger strike "in defense of the papal cross." He also asked for 152 crosses to represent the number of Gentile Poles who had been shot by the Nazis at that particular location. By August, supporters had installed more than 200 crosses.

A variety of interpretations of the crosses action at Auschwitz circulated throughout Poland during 1998 and after.[18] Świtoń's version of Auschwitz memorialization generated a number of opportunities for rhetoric on Catholic-Jewish relations, the Shoah, prewar Polish history, and the essential nature of "Jews." Both antisemitic arguments and arguments seeking to oppose antisemitism filled public space. The form of Świtoń's action influenced the pattern by which these arguments were played out in the crosses action, because textual elements were deemphasized in favor of the visual; in other words, the insistently visual nature of the crosses rendered their discursive power to reinforce ethnic and religious identity less vulnerable to counterarguments that lacked such visual components.[19]

The "defenders of the cross" frequently mobilized antisemitic discourse, but these narrative statements were so short and abrupt that they functioned less as isolated acts of speech than as soundings or chants of a familiar refrain. For example, Świtoń's banners had the words "Jews out of Poland," "No to NATO," and "Europeans out of Poland." But more immediate that any semantic structure of his written formulations was the visually discursive power of handmade banners hanging on the walls of Auschwitz—or, to be

18. For an analysis of responses outside of Poland, see Janusz Ryzner, "The Dispute over Auschwitz Crosses in the Foreign Press" (paper presented at the Association of Nationalities Studies Fifth Annual World Convention, April 13–15, 2000).

19. The intention here is not to separate and dichotomize "the visual" and "the textual/word" as two opposed modes of discursive reality; all articulations have a visual form and invoke visual images. The meaning created by words and that created by visual images, however, may have different effects; in fact, the visual at times can gesture toward that which is silent or unarticulated more effectively than textual narrative can.

precise, the walls next to the walls of Auschwitz. Both semantic and visual spectatorship are forms of discourse and may contribute to a single discursive reality; however, in the crosses action, the visual was privileged. The crosses themselves were clearly powerful visual statements that needed no textual elaboration to communicate meaning; the presence of numbers of people watching from outside the wall or entering the grassy area to support Świtoń made the space itself worthy of attention; the added visual elements of the altar, the small tent that served as a chapel, the wagon that Świtoń used to house himself all created a tableau that utterly transformed the previously empty space into a stage on which Catholic identity was asserted. Finally, Świtoń himself was a colorful figure who produced controversial statements that were easily consumed by spectators, and his hunger strike rendered his own body simultaneously a spectacle and an assertion of cultural power.

The crosses action thus differed from other crises in Catholic-Jewish relations in its fundamentally filmic quality. By "filmic," I mean composed of visual elements that are recognizable yet open to interpretation by an interested spectator, elements that mean more than what they are by virtue of their context, their positioning in relation to other elements, and their sense of realism. For example, the creation of an altar outdoors, in an area where religious activity is prohibited, denaturalizes both the altar and its location.[20] This denaturalization captures our attention and compels us to think about altars and lawns next to Auschwitz in new ways. The humble, simple crosses planted in the grass in an apparently haphazard fashion invoked for many Christians a certain vulnerability of the victims of Auschwitz by symbolizing the tale of Jesus Christ's suffering multiplied. Finally, film, like photography, appears hyperrealist in its ability to capture and preserve a moment in time; the objects in photos seem to be accurately portrayed with no manipulation on the part of the author and thus a transparent representation of reality. The tableau of elements created by Świtoń communicated, for some at least, this quality of a "something that is really happening," as opposed to a narrative text or story that reports on an event already past.

The filmic quality of the crosses action was also enhanced by the sense of an ongoing drama or plot.[21] Świtoń frequently altered his tactics in unpredictable ways, and one had to pay attention—to look again and again—to follow the story. As governmental authorities, diplomats from abroad, Church

---

20. Legally, the "protected" nature of this area was under dispute because the law was ambiguous. Recall that the town of Oświęcim had owned the deed to the land and building before giving it to the Carmelite order, which upon its relocation, transferred the deed not to the museum but to a nationalist organization. By 2000, the Polish government successfully passed a law creating a "protective zone" around the Auschwitz Museum. I use "prohibited" here to signify the intent of the government at this point; Świtoń's actions were subversive not of the letter of the law but of policy toward the museum.

21. For a sense of the drama, see Zbigniew Pendel and Mirosław Łukaszuk "Odzyskać żwirowisko," *Gazeta Wyborcza* (August 14–16, 1998).

officials, and public opinion leaders made statements either condemning
Świtoń's action, threatening to intervene in the drama, or halfheartedly supporting his intentions, they became actors fueling the story line.[22] Of course,
many public figures eagerly entered the narrative because of the enormous
visibility and potential public support they might acquire as a result of their
words. Furthermore, the action itself generated related stories and rumors,
such as the widely-spread rumor that the pope would visit the site during his
June 1999 visit to Poland and hold a mass there in gratitude for the perse-
verance of the papal cross's defenders.

In the fall of 1998 the grassy area had acquired not only the 152 crosses
that were to stand in for the 152 Poles killed there but many more. The action
then shifted from representing itself as memorializing victims who had been
ignored to an assertion of the cohesiveness and Catholic nature of Polish ethnic
identity. Świtoń made a public announcement asking for 1,032 crosses by the
following Constitution Day (May 3), an important national holiday; that
number referred to the years since 966, when Mieszko, the founder of the Piast
dynasty, began attempts to convert to Christianity the population living in
Polish territory.[23] As Sławomir Kapralski noted, "Instead of being a sign commemorating individual victims, the cross has turned into an emblem of nationhood and has been placed within the traditional context of defining Polish
national identity as first and foremost Catholic."[24] A banner at the site stated,
"Only under this cross, only under this symbol, Poland is Poland, and a Pole
is a Pole."

Thus, the crosses action repeatedly referred back to its own articulations
of Catholic and Polish identity and incorporated those references into new
forms of expression distinct from written arguments about Jews, Auschwitz,
and crosses. In addition, the self-citational nature of this memorialization converged with a cultural moment in Poland that enhanced that memorialization's
power. Whereas conditions of economic scarcity made the purchase of books,
journals, and even newspapers prohibitive for many residents of Poland,
almost everyone had access to a radio or television. Thus the images captured
on film or the urgency of a radio reporter on the scene allowed this particular cultural formation to penetrate many more private spaces than a written
argument would have done. In turn, these media could link or interpret their
presentations of the crosses action with other cultural expressions for specific
political purposes.

One important medium at this time was a specific radio station, Radio
Maryja. Broadcasting since 1990, Radio Maryja offers listeners a combina-

22. In March 1998, Cardinal Józef Glemp insisted that "the cross stands and will stand."
Adam Szostkiewicz, "Dolina krzyży," *Polityka* (August 15, 1998). The article also notes that some
figures, including members of the Catholic Church hierarchy, were conspicuously silent on the
issue.
23. Kapralski, p. 37.
24. Ibid.

tion of religious teachings, cultural commentary, news and reporting. The station allied itself with Świtoń's actions immediately in early 1998[25] and became an important transmitter of events at the Auschwitz Museum for those who could not see them personally. Radio Maryja also added new narrative to the drama of the crosses, connecting the standoff at the museum to other contested issues in Polish life, such as society's increasing secularization and perceived moral threats to the integrity of "the family."[26] In this way, Radio Maryja countered the tendency of Polish television and parts of the mainstream press to personalize the crosses action and attribute the drama at the museum to Świtoń's own character, vision, quirks, or mental illness. Radio Maryja defended Świtoń as a person but also highlighted the relevance of the action to ongoing concerns of people living in Poland.

The crosses action was simultaneously propelled forward by the drama of Świtoń's character and the ability of external voices to develop the themes of the drama beyond it. Many of his statements about the characteristics of Jewish people and the negative influence of Jews on Poland were direct appropriations of the antisemitism developed in Europe and Russia in the previous century and were viewed as so "outrageous" by many Poles that they could easily distance themselves and their communities from them.[27] That Świtoń was often excessive and politically clumsy in his statements and gestures reinforced the sense that he was an actor in the drama—or even an object among the other elements of the tableau—rather than the skillful author of a manipulated presentation of symbols and rhetoric. When at the end of May 1999 he finally claimed to have tear gas and explosives with him, police felt they had enough reason to arrest him and dismantle the site. Yet his refusal to participate in "rational argument" or politics-as-usual did not delegitimate the effects of the crosses action. When I asked people in Poland in 2000 what they thought of Świtoń, the most common response was "I don't agree with extremists of any sort, but I think the papal cross should stay."[28]

25. For an analysis of the crosses controversy as a part of the emergence of Radio Maryja, see (Jarosław) Makowski, "Niepokorni synowie Kościoła," *Tygodnik Powszechny* (August 30, 1998).

26. For textual examples of this broadcast strategy, see the newspaper allied with Radio Maryja, *Nasz Dziennik*. Radio Maryja has functioned to popularize a version of Catholicism throughout Poland while being consistently criticized by the secular press for antisemitism and conservatism and formally disavowed by moderate Catholic clergy such as Bishop Pieronek. For an overview of the controversies, see Luiza Zalewska and Marcin Dominik Zort, "Partia Maryja," *Rzeczpospolita* (October 7, 1999).

27. One example: "In parliament and in government 80% is decided by Jews . . . they want to degrade our nation." Quoted in Krzysztof Różycki, "Droga Krzyżowa," *Angora* (August 23, 1998).

28. In informal conversation. I asked approximately seventy-five people of differing occupations, backgrounds, and ages in Warsaw, Kraków, Oświęcim, and small towns near Suwałki.

The reference to "extremists" in the plural and the phrase "of any sort" reflect the context in which many people placed the crosses action.[29] In discussions of Świtoń, Rabbi Avi Weiss and the story of the showdown at the convent were mentioned frequently.[30] Świtoń's image as a defender of the collective entity "Poland" was enhanced not only by his concrete activities and his aggressive demeanor, but by his being positioned as an opposing twin to the "invader" that had first trespassed the exact same ground ten years before. In a way, the crosses action was Part Two of the convent tale, projecting meaning about the Polish national identity being at stake back into time and bringing actual Jewish people who did climb over a fence at Auschwitz into the 1998 controversy. "Jews taking over Auschwitz-Birkenau" was easily elided into "Jews attacking the sisters" and "Jews taking over Poland."

Naming Weiss and Świtoń as the two "extremists" who mark (supposedly) the limits of potential options in dealing with the papal cross lends credence to the perception that the actual outcome was a compromise.[31] What partly enabled authorities to dismantle the site was the passage by the parliament in early May 1999, after difficult and protracted internal discussions, of legislation creating a "protected area" of central governmental zoning power around the museum (and a handful of other sites in Poland). It had been clear that such legislation would be read by people living in Poland as a repudiation of Świtoń's action, and some legislators did not want to risk losing supporters over this issue, or they simply believed he was right. Świtoń's announcement of explosives allowed the police and military to find cause to intervene, and after his arrest they removed the many small crosses and other objects in a way that appeared part and parcel of the arrest, attempting to avoid a separate cultural "event" of cross removal.

Nevertheless, the media covered the removal of the crosses extensively and the government devised a plan to have them publicly carried to a nearby monastery. In the end, the papal cross remained in place. The removal of Świtoń and the many symbols surrounding his demonstration created the appearance that leaving the papal cross standing was a compromise. The prevailing view that Świtoń suffered from mental illness contributed to the idea that antisemitism was a pathology, frequently labeled "primitivism," shared by very few other people living in Poland.[32] Finally, there was a palpable sense

29. There were also views that placed the crosses action in the context of a history of Polish antisemitism, although these voices did not become dominant in the media. See, for example, Ewa K. Czaczkowska's interview with Israel Gutman, "Krzyż papieski punktem wyjścia," *Rzeczpospolita* (September 12–13, 1998).

30. See, for example, "Krzyże niezgody," *Życie Warszawy* (August 17, 1998).

31. Wiess's actions are often characterized as creating antisemitism. See, for example, Jan Nowak-Jeziorański's views in "Tzreba mówić prawdę," *Rzeczpospolita* (November 7–8, 1998).

32. For example, in a lengthy analysis Janusz A. Majcherek argues that antisemitism is a "specific type of banal, primitive . . . element of xenophobia, characteristic for societies that are traditionally closed." The solution for Majcherek is developmental and educational. "To nie tylko problem krzyża," *Rzeczpospolita* (August 12, 1998).

that the crosses action had negatively affected the public opinion of Poland abroad, and many Polish people were relieved that the drama itself had ended—even if they agreed that the cross should stay. The cross at Auschwitz *was* the end.

Throughout the 1990s and into 2002 the role of Jews in Polish history and in Polish political life in the present day was discussed publicly and privately to a much greater degree than during the communist period, with the exception of 1967–68. These discussions were bolstered in part by Pope John Paul II's giving priority to improving relations between Catholics and Jews. The Vatican recognized the state of Israel in 1994 and in 1998 issued "We Remember: A Reflection on the Shoah," calling on Catholics to remember the Holocaust. In 2000 the pope visited Israel and the Wailing Wall, in an act of atonement for past instances of Catholic antisemitism. During the same period, however, local cultural expressions of Catholic identity such as Radio Maryja tended to undercut the conciliatory impulse of the pope's official policies, in part because of their sense of immediacy and crisis, and in part because of their ability to embed antisemitism into local social issues.

Crises such as the convent issue and the crosses action became opportunities to revisit and revive discussion and, as noted above, much of this discussion constituted a repetition of standard antisemitic formulas and stereotypes, rooted in medieval Catholic Church teachings but reenergized in the nineteenth century as legitimate political rationalizations. The character of much commentary supporting Świtoń and Radio Maryja broadcasts did indeed have a ritualized, formulaic quality. Often shorthand phrases such as "cosmopolitan" or "Is he a real Pole?" stood in for a whole set of unstated assertions about Jewish and Polish history, politics, and culture. There is a quality to antisemitism, racism, and a few other ideological formations in which the unarticulated subject is anticipated discursively through indirect references, gestures, symbolic words or images—in other words, stand-ins for direct representations.

This is not to say that antisemitism is merely a semantic ritual. The attempt to set the ethnic or religious category of "Jew" as the main threat to Polish national identity had material consequences for both Jewish and Gentile Poles. One such consequence is the continued presence of the papal cross at the Auschwitz Museum. Another is the cost to a community of denying the multidimensionality of its own histories—national, regional, local, and family.

Antisemitism in its formulaic expression is difficult to refute through a presentation of "facts" or "history" because it is not itself concerned with history as such. Although individual attitudes may be altered through a reasoned discussion, for example, of the actual economic role of Jewish families and communities in eastern Poland before 1939, the self-citational quality of antisemitic formulas resists intervention by textual strategies that value precision, nuance, facticity, logic, and historical context. Many people in Poland who sought to oppose or counter the antisemitism raised by the crosses action found the effects of their voices limited in this way.

One prominent set of voices seeking to counter the images of Polish national identity "threatened by external Jewish forces" was that of the progressive Catholic clergy in Poland. Since the issue revolved around explicit Catholic imagery and the protest indeed was conducted in the name of the Church to some degree, clergy concerned to oppose antisemitism attempted to undermine Świtoń's project as soon as it was launched. Their arguments took the form of an authoritative refusal to condone the crosses action, explanations of the limited uses to which crosses should be put by Catholics, and an attempt to foster a deeper and more profound understanding of relations between Christians—particularly Catholics—and Jews. One of the most frequent contributors to the press in this vein was Stanisław Musiał, although many others such as Romuald Jakub Weksler-Waszkinel, Henryk Muszyński, and Stanisław Obirek spoke in meetings, wrote for the press, and participated in events supporting Catholic-Jewish dialogue and Jewish culture.

Musiał published pieces throughout 1998 and 1999 in *Tygodnik Powszechny*, an important weekly in Catholic intellectual circles; *Gazeta Wyborcza*, the most widely read daily newspaper in Poland; and other publications.[33] After condemning the explicitly antisemitic symbols and rhetoric of the activists, Musiał noted that the goal of some of the supporters of the crosses action was perhaps well-intentioned: to "endow that fragment of earth and former convent with sacral inviolability." The papal cross, however, does not itself carry the power to make such an endowment. The cross is so large, he continued, because it functioned as a "point of orientation" for the gathering of people at the pope's 1979 Mass in Birkenau, not because it has any theologically "monumental" character. After all, the pope has said Mass in a number of places in Poland and "none of the crosses [installed for those ceremonies] have remained in their original places"; they have been moved, and "no one has spoken about any profaning of the cross" in regard to them. Transferring this cross to the current building of the Carmelite convent (across the street from the museum) "would not in any way profane this religious symbol or show a lack of respect for Christ, whom the cross symbolizes."[34]

Musiał's argument sought to puncture the stated claims of the crosses activists to be "defenders of the papal cross" by questioning the theological capability of a human being to endow any symbol with transcendent meaning. To try to do so is to insult the cross, the Church, and the meaning of Christ's life. Similarly, to use the cross instrumentally, for political ends, is to usurp not only its real purpose but the right of the Catholic Church to determine the sacral status of religious symbols.[35] The cross as a symbol is not even

33. See *Tygodnik Powszechny* (January 11, 1998), a special issue devoted to the topic.
34. Musiał, "Prawda o Oświęcimskim Krzyżu."
35. Stanisław Musiał, "Zaciśnięte pięści przeciw," *Tygodnik Powszechny* (August 9, 1998).

central to the practice of being a good Catholic; all that is needed is to "love God and those close to you." Finally, "Christianity does not require monuments," and Christ's life had nothing to do with "monumentalization" but rather with humility.[36] "Christ's cross is not a clenched fist."[37]

As more clergy—who generally supported the idea of a cross at the museum—realized that they should distance themselves from the crosses action, they frequently invoked a representation of the action as an insult to the life of Christ and to the authority of the church.[38] Bishop Pieronek stated in *Gazeta Wyborcza*, "If someone says, 'I am the Church' and acts against the will of the [Church] hierarchy, he operates like many [fascistic] groups in Austria or France—he creates his own anti-Church."[39] According to Archbishop Muszyński, "Those who use the cross as a tool instrumentally in a battle against anybody in fact act as enemies of Christ's cross."[40]

Musiał also asked why the activists did not include Jewish victims in the deaths they were commemorating at the site. He reminded readers of the pain felt by Jews when reflecting on Auschwitz and the Shoah. For Musiał, "[Even] if only one Jew had been murdered at this site, one could not exclude Jews from consultations [about its memorialization]."[41] Muszyński also declared to his readers that "it is not permissible to forget that our brothers, Jews, non-Christians, see in the cross an entirely distinct content. They expect the same respect for their views as we Christians do. These contents cannot be reduced to a single denominator."[42]

The head of the Catholic hierarchy in Poland, Cardinal Józef Glemp, vacillated on the issue, although he had been involved in international negotiations in the convent controversy and was familiar with what was at stake for Jews. In August 1998 he appealed for a halt to the installation of new crosses at the demonstration site but also asserted that the papal cross should remain. His rationalization was that "non-Polish" voices should not influence how that particular space was used. "That earth is Polish, and any imposition of another's will there is taken as an interference of sovereignty." He added that the crosses action was a reaction to Jewish pressure: "One must in the name of truth say that [Świtoń's] group arose not out of a fantasy but due to the constant and increasing pestering on the part of the Jewish side on how to most quickly remove the cross." Indeed, he said, the "cross is not the prop-

36. Musiał, "Prawda o Oświęcimskim Krzyżu."
37. Musiał, "Zaciśnięte pieści przeciw."
38. For statements by a range of clergy throughout Poland, see "Co na to Kościół?" *Gazeta Wyborcza* (August 13, 1998); "Krzyże niezgody," *Polityka* (August 8, 1998), in the section summarizing the week's events, ". . . I w Polsce," as well as Henryk Muszyński, "Jak bronić krzyża," in *Tygodnik Powszechny* (August 16, 1998).
39. Tadeusz Pieronek, "To swoisty anty-Kościół," *Gazeta Wyborcza* (August 13, 1998).
40. Henryk Muszyński, "Co naprawdę znaczy krzyż," *Gazeta Wyborcza* (August 10, 1998).
41. Musiał, "Prawda o Oświęcimskim Krzyżu."
42. Muszyński, "Co naprawdę znaczy krzyż."

erty of the Catholic Church," and "the right to defend it" is open to all who accept the cross in their faith.[43]

Other important voices influencing the perception of what was at stake in the controversy were Polish Jewish intellectuals. Konstanty Gebert and Stanisław Krajewski were particularly vocal. Gebert, writing as "Dawid Warszawski," did not position Jews as victims of the Nazis whose pain required the compassion and understanding of the Catholic Church. After discussing the annual visits by Israeli youth to the Auschwitz-Birkenau complex, he argued: "The pain that we have experienced in thinking about Auschwitz, feeling Auschwitz in every tendon of our souls, walking on the road from Auschwitz to Birkenau over earth mixed with the ashes of our entire nation, is something so piercing that nothing will ever soothe it. . . . For Jews, Auschwitz as a place of their Holocaust is a symbol so formidable that there is no space there for any other sign, substance, or value. . . . This cross insults us—even though it was not erected for that purpose."[44] Gebert here did not even address the other crosses installed by Świtoń, or antisemitism per se. He was asserting the uniqueness of Auschwitz as a place and the inability of Catholic compassion to "soothe" the pain associated with it.

The contrast between the progressive Catholic view of the cross as a sign of humility and good intentions (even if Świtoń had contaminated its potential benefits) and the Jewish view of the cross as so irrelevant and powerless in the face of the Shoah that it is an insult reveals a general stance toward Catholic-Jewish relations on the part of many Catholics. Simply put, it is difficult for many Catholic believers to acknowledge the power implications embedded in the cross as a symbol. Many Jews experience the cross as the mark of supersessionism, or the notion that Christ's death signaled a new stage in revelation, relegating Judaism to a matter of purely historical interest.[45] In contrast, for many Catholics the idea that Jesus Christ would embrace any Jew who asks to enter the fold, and indeed would embrace her even if she did not ask, should be perceived by Jews as removing any menace or threat from Christianity. Since the Second Vatican Council of the 1960s, Jews are not offi-

---

43. Glemp's statement of August 6, 1998, was reprinted throughout the press: see "Krzyż nie jest własnością Episkopatu," *Tygodnik Powszechny* (August 16, 1998); and Ewa Czaczkowska and Kazimierz Groblewski, "Prymas za pozostawieniem papieskiego krzyża," *Rzeczpospolita* (August 7, 1998).

44. Dawid Warszawski [Konstanty Gebert], "Mieszkając na Ziemi Popiołów," *Gazeta Wyborcza* (April 21, 1998).

45. The theological discussion of supersessionism is quite complex, and many Christian theologians have struggled to reconcile the notion of God's covenant with the people of Israel with the nature of the Christian covenant. This discussion has taken place on a number of levels, in Protestant and Catholic faith contexts. The version of supersessionist tensions presented in this chapter capture the tensions that take place not within academic theology but in publications for a general audience. For treatments of the theological nuances, see Robert Davis Hughes III, "Christian Theology of Interfaith Dialogue: Defining the Emerging Fourth Option," *Sewanee Theological Review* 40 (1997): 383–408.

cially blamed for the death of Christ, and the Christian Bible is not intended
to displace or replace the Old Testament. However, both the Catholic Church
and other Christian traditions have not been able to transcend (nor would one
expect them to) the centrality of Christ as the ultimate savior of mankind; in
other words, Jews are expected to embrace Jesus eventually as the messiah—
on Judgment Day. Thus, even liberal Catholics and other Christians who seek
to include Judaism in the religious community of mankind cannot sustain the
integrity of the Jewish theological and historical experience in the face of the
more immediate urgency of the Crucifixion. And a possible (and frequently
voiced) Jewish response—that Christ was one prophet and great teacher
among many—seems to many to trivialize the essence of the Catholic faith
experience.

The particular form of a cross as the Auschwitz memorialization enacted
by Świtoń raised the issue of the role of "the cross" in Catholic-Jewish dialogue, in Poland and elsewhere. The ultimate response by the Catholic clergy
was to reassert the cross's symbolic power—representing the death of Christ—
but as a "pure" religious symbol not to be manipulated by political agendas.
This restoration of the cross, however, could not avoid reinforcing the cross's
role in signifying the displacement of Judaism by Christianity as the authoritative covenant with God. In an important sense, supersessionism ties together
the arguments of progressive Catholics such as Musiał, conservative Catholics
such as Glemp, and nationalists such as those who broadcast on Radio
Maryja. In the context of Poland's Jewish past and present, the conceptual displacement of Judaism seems to give antisemitism in a Catholic culture its sense
of certainty, purpose, and moral authority.

The theologian David Tracy offers an elaboration on this idea by criticiz-
ing the actions of the women living in the Carmelite convent, who had prayed
for the Jewish dead at Auschwitz: "A facile Christian inclusiveness of witness
and memory ('we Christians remember *all* the dead; we witness to *all* suffering') became, through the convent at Auschwitz, one more expression of
Christian supersessionism. To assume the Christian desire to pray for all so
thoughtlessly, to assume the cross as a symbol for Jewish suffering so care-
lessly, to misunderstand both Judaism and the history of Catholic antisemitism as recklessly as Cardinal Glemp did: these actions bear false witness
against the Jewish neighbor."[46] With this critique, Tracy appropriates a local
Polish Catholic problem and recontextualizes it as a larger problem for Christians and Christianity. He warns that the quickness to embrace all suffering
under the sign of the cross only appears to be an act of genuine inclusiveness; it is possible only when the Jewish voice is silenced, and thus it is an
extension of past Christian wrongs against Jews. Tracy challenges even well-
intentioned Christians to reconsider the implications of their prayers for Jews;

46. David Tracy, "Christian Witness and the Shoah," in *Holocaust Remembrance: The Shapes
of Memory*, ed. Geoffrey H. Hartman (Oxford, 1994), 82–83.

he hopes for the development of a Christianity that is capable of fully acknowledging the legitimacy of the Jewish covenant, in Poland and elsewhere.

Relevant here is the official statement of the Polish Episcopate on the crosses controversy, issued at the end of August 1998. The lengthy document confirms support for the continued presence of the papal cross at the site of the former convent, though condemning any other religious symbols there, and goes on to note that

> the dialogue between Jews and Christians has allowed for an understanding of what joins all of us as victims, as well as the ongoing view of the Shoah as the "greatest suffering" and "the most important experience in the history of our century." . . . We are open to dialogue on the form of this cemetery of our times, Auschwitz-Birkenau. We declare ourselves ready to seek a solution that could be accepted by all. . . . [A]t the same time, however, we are conscious of the fact that the concentration camp is located on the territory of the Third Republic [of Poland] and by this fact is subject to Polish law. For this reason it is understandable that the expectations of Poles are that Polish law is respected by all who visit the territory of the camp.

Finally the document cites Cardinal Stefan Wyszyński: "We have one fatherland and we are obliged to give it love, service, sacrifice, and even death, if God so demands. In order to be always ready, we need to be unified with Christ and with the Church. For this reason we ask everyone . . . not to denigrate this unity—because this would be a threat to the security of the fatherland and bring into being a divided nation, and thus many disagreements."[47]

This document is worth quoting at length because with it the Episcopate, led by Glemp, conditioned the continuation of negotiations over the papal cross with the cross's continued presence at the Auschwitz Museum. It also situated anyone who questioned the importance of the cross as a symbol of Christ with outsiders seeking to undermine the Polish state and nation. Although it did not explicitly articulate antisemitic formulas, they linger in the shadows of what is suggested. Jews have climbed fences, made their views known at sites of commemoration, protested the crosses at Auschwitz, pressured the Polish government; the Episcopal statement implies that what is at stake for Catholics is not just one religious symbol but the national unity of Poland itself.

Musiał and other clergy, as well as Catholic intellectuals, did not support the Episcopate's statement and continued to argue for greater space for Jewish voices on issues such as Auschwitz memorialization and, more recently, Jedwabne. Yet the limits of a specifically Catholic opposition to antisemitism have yet to be fully acknowledged. As David Tracy argues: "Christians often

---

47. The Episcopate's statement was published in *Gazeta Wyborcza* (26 August 1998).

tell themselves and their Jewish partners in dialogue how much both share: the covenant, the history of ancient Israel, the Hebrew bible—above all, the same covenanting God. This easy dialogical sharing is highly suspect. Arthur Cohen insisted that there was no historical reality behind the phrase the 'Judeo-Christian' tradition. That 'tradition' is a modern Christian invention designed to cover over 'Christian' history [of antisemitism] and relax the need to repent."[48] Tracy sees Jews and Judaism as frightening for Christians because they staunchly resist inclusion under the posited universality of Christ's embrace. In resisting, they remind Christians of the lack of universality that threatens the basis of Christianity; in engaging in dialogue, they allow Christians to "overcome" this fear and reassure themselves of their faith. "Judaism has served to solidify Christianity's fears for its own identity: hence Christian supersessionism . . . from the beginning . . . until now."[49]

Even if one is not ready to accept Tracy's view of Christian-Jewish relations, his insights invite new questions about the cross as a religious symbol and highlight what might be at stake not only for Jews but also for progressive Catholics in the controversy at Auschwitz. The cross as a symbol is easy to appropriate; one can construct a cross out of the simplest materials and transport it almost anywhere. Anyone can make and install a cross and thus instantly alter the environment.[50] It carries with it an overdetermined quality: it is nothing but the site and method of Christ's death, yet a cross also invokes a multitude of social and even personal histories. Some of these are negotiable by the spectator, and others are relatively fixed by shared history and dominant cultural ideologies. It seems that the cross is trouble for Catholic-Jewish relations, and not simply because Jews do not feel comfortable with it.[51]

If it is true that there is something about Christian or Catholic anxiety regarding Judaism and the potential Jewish disavowal of the cross that generates periodic crises in interfaith relations, what aspect of this dynamic was at work in the crosses controversy at Auschwitz? What might be revealed by viewing the crosses controversy as a reaction to the conditions of a specific historical moment in 1998 Poland?

One answer is suggested by the crosses action's fusion of the privileging of the cross itself at a place of primarily Jewish suffering and death with a sense of embattled national identity, evident in the nature of the banners, rhetoric, and symbols. The defensive tone threaded throughout the action and the dis-

48. Tracy, 83.

49. Ibid.

50. Jan Kubik demonstrated the manner in which crosses altered previously communist party–controlled environments during the Solidarity movement: see Kubik, *The Power of Symbols and the Symbols of Power: The Rise of Solidarity and the Fall of State Socialism in Poland* (University Park, Pa., 1994).

51. Mary C. Boys has proposed a theological reconsideration of Catholicism in which supersessionism is overcome as a problem by radically changing the role of the cross as a religious symbol; see Boys, *Has God Only One Blessing? Judaism as a Source of Christian Understanding* (New York, 2000).

course surrounding it points to an anxiety of Catholic identity and Polish identity, prompted by the increasing penetration of Polish culture by external cultural forms, the membership of Poland first in NATO and then in the European Union, economic uncertainty, and the rapid pluralization of political life. The papal cross as a threatened monument to Polishness and Catholicism was, then, an expedient materialization of anxieties that were otherwise difficult to articulate or resist. Also available was a ready-made antisemitic discourse which became, through Świtoń and Radio Maryja, a self-referential, repetitive expression of fear regarding unknown and unknowable forces named "Jews."

Polish observers have noted the importance of antisemitism to the expression of cultural anxiety at specific historical moments. One approach to contextualizing the general problem of the cross and antisemitism within a specifically Polish framework has been developed by Joanna Tokarska-Bakir in a number of articles.[52] Although she is not focused on the theological issues surrounding supersessionism, she is concerned with what is unique about Polish cultural formations in regard to antisemitism, Jewish history, and national consciousness. Tokarska-Bakir finds in Polish public culture a thread of an "obsession with innocence." As she responds to debates over Jedwabne, she means for the concept to apply to the postcommunist period and, in an article in *Res Publica Nowa*, finds it in earlier centuries as well.[53]

The "obsession with innocence" is a reflexive, reactive withdrawal to an assertion of Polish "innocence"—total and pure—when historical wrongs in relation to Jews, such as Jedwabne or Kielce, are opened for discussion. The obsession is perpetuated by a sense of cultural shame over antisemitism and violence toward Jews, which renders the acknowledgment of a measure of accountability for such acts very difficult. The obsession with innocence expresses itself in a defensive, polemical mode that disallows genuine engagement with historical fact, even while historical facts are corralled to support the case for innocence. Maria Janion finds fruitful connections between Tokarska-Bakir's notion and the "messianic myth" posing Poland as a Christ figure in national form.[54]

But although the notion of Poland as the Christ of nations has certainly been a frequent organizing trope for literature, essays, politics, and history writing in Poland, one cannot say that it is necessarily determinative of a collective consciousness or specific enough to explain the individual attitudes that make up antisemitism. The large number of voices that have accepted Jewish views of the cross at Auschwitz or Jan Tomasz Gross's representation of the

---

52. See particularly Joanna Tokarska-Bakir, "Obsesja niewinności," *Gazeta Wyborcza* (January 13–14, 2001).

53. Tokarska-Bakir, "Ganz Andere? Żyd jako czarownica i czarownica jako Żyd w polskich i obcych źródłach etnograficznych, czyli jak czytać protokoły przesłuchań," *Res Publica Nowa* 8 (August 2001): 3–31.

54. Maria Janion, "Trudna klasa w ciężkiej szkole," *Res Publica Nowa* (February 2002): 102–5.

events of Jedwabne demonstrated that the obsession with innocence is not common to everyone living in Poland.

It is possible, however, that the idea of such an obsession identifies a common mode taken by responses to accusations of complicity or blame in anti-Jewish violence. An alternative way of naming this mode, one more closely linked with social identity categories, is as a sense of "injury." As observers of the Polish political scene have noted, the use of the term "anti-semitic" to characterize Polish culture frequently evokes a response by non-Jewish Poles describing the usage itself as "anti-Polish." "Anti-Polishness" is represented as a systematic denigration of Polish ethnic identity, a discursive formula as ready-made as that of antisemitism. One element in the formula is the charge of antisemitism itself. According to this logic, any description of antisemitism in Poland is a stand-in for the repetition of a stereotype, the stereotype of the ethnic Pole as antisemite. The logic continues to identify a link between the calling up of "anti-Polish" stereotypes with the loss of status, prestige, resources, and voice in the eyes of an international audience.[55] The claim of "anti-Polishness" is a claim of harm done, of injury.

As the U.S. scholar Wendy Brown notes, an assertion of identity accompanied by a claim of injury to that identity has enormous consequences for the capacity to envision political possibilities.[56] The status of the injured beckons the dominant, uninjured party to compensate for or recover the loss that is the injury; but this loss can never be recovered, because it is itself the result of a type of anxiety over political accountability. In other words, it is a symptom of something else, posing as a genuine political vision.

Helpful here is a juxtaposition of two of the many possible stances on what the Shoah might mean for a Polish national identity heavily informed by Catholicism. On the one hand, Świtoń and those who supported him sought to recover a "lost" or damaged Catholic identity at Auschwitz I. Note that even after three hundred crosses had been planted in the lawn, this injury had not been fully addressed in the eyes of the activists. This shortcoming was due to the fact not that a few more crosses were needed but that the injury to identity was fundamentally unrecoverable. The crosses could be made to stand in for Catholic or Polish identity, but what felt threatened regarding these identities was not actually the absence of crosses.

In another stance, offered by Gebert in his commentary on the crosses issue, he too speaks about pain but not through an assertion of an injured identity. His "piercing" pain is inconsolable from the outset; nothing will ever "soothe" the effects of the Shoah.[57] The narrative Gebert offers doesn't seek consolation from any source and wants no relationship with any party that seeks to

---

55. For an example in a mainstream newspaper (the paper of record in Poland), see Małgorzata Dzieduszycka, "Z dala od żwirowiska," *Rzeczpospolita* (September 12–13, 1998).

56. See Wendy Brown, *Politics Out of History* (Princeton, 2001).

57. Warzawski, "Mieszkając na Ziemi Popiołów."

provide such consolation. The loss is ever present but grievable and part of his history, not his imagination. As a result, there can be no symbolic props that substitute for political alternatives on which to base the future.

This is not to say that Gebert's text is not asking for a specific response from the Catholic Church to a specific wrong: the installation of a cross at what for him is a Jewish cemetery. But it does suggest that the identificatory processes he notes in his writing on the crosses action is not a reaction to anxieties about a changing self stemming from causes best found elsewhere. As Stanisław Krajewski responded in a 1998 interview to the question, what do Jews expect from Poles, "I expect to be accepted as a Polish Jew, that Polish Jews are a part of Polish life. To be blunt, it is a fact that I—like many others similar to me—am fully a Jew and fully a Pole. If someone doesn't accept that, that's his problem."[58]

The purpose of juxtaposing the assertion of identity in an injured mode with the expression of an identity claim that incorporates pain in another way is not to crystallize only two options but to suggest the range of possibilities in renegotiating Polishness in light of the Shoah. Nor is it to say that Jewish identity never appears in an injured mode and that Catholic identity is always injured, or that Jewish people have no anxieties about identity. In fact, a case can be made that Rabbi Weiss's confrontation with the members of the Carmelite convent was an expression of injury. But in researching the crosses controversy, it was difficult to find Catholic or non-Jewish assertions of identity in public speech aimed at the typical Polish listener, reader, or viewer that did not have an aspect of injury.[59]

In conclusion, the prevalence of or even attachment to an injured identity has the potential to prevent a more honest engagement with antisemitism in Poland. Injury asks for a type of response that cannot be granted and that can always only be a partial representation of a more extensive trauma overlapping different religious and cultural communities. A detailed examination of the crosses controversy and responses to it reveal that when people speak the language of antisemitism, their speech functions not only to exclude and displace but to misrepresent their own experience in an injured mode.

The implications are that a recovery of ways to acknowledge cultural and personal losses—physical, generational, economic—seems crucial to supporting opponents of antisemitism, as well as Catholic-Jewish reconciliation. The Auschwitz Museum, Birkenau, and other physical sites of the Holocaust have

58. Quoted in Agnieszka Niezgoda, "Schematy: Z dr Stanisławem Krajewskim rozmawia Agnieszka Niezgoda," *Polis* 27 (April 1998): 9.

59. For an example, see Bratkowski, who incorporates into his analysis of the crosses controversy the "fact that contemporary Jews . . . don't even know . . . that hundreds of thousands of civilian Poles were shot, hung, tortured and gassed." It is interesting to revisit antisemitic speech through the framework of an injured mode. For an overview of such speech for a popular audience, see Alina Grabowska, "Porządek na własnym podwórku," *Rzeczpospolita* (October 12, 1996).

the potential to function as unique, materialized indications of a loss that is too vast to be fully represented and thus too vast to be fully integrated into identity, be it national, local, or personal. The challenge to opponents of anti-semitism in Poland is to create an Auschwitz that both memorializes and indicates the limits of memorialization. But it is also to create a re-visioning of Polish identity that incorporates the historical reality of Poland as a set of multicultural communities, each distinct in historical and social development but all linked by common experiences of citizenship, occupation, violence, and loss.

15

Works on Polish-Jewish Relations Published since 1990

A Selective Bibliography

STEPHEN D. CORRSIN

This bibliography represents a listing of significant new works on the topic of the history of Polish-Jewish relations from the middle of the nineteenth century to the start of the twenty-first. I have applied the following general selection criteria:

- Only books and articles published between 1990 and early 2003 are included.
- The items chosen are only in Polish, English, German, Hebrew, or French.
- All items are also, or will be, listed in the ongoing bibliographical work on the topic of the history of the Jews in Poland in the journal *Gal-Ed*.

That larger bibliographical project has appeared in four installments since 1995 in the journal *Gal-Ed: On the History of the Jews in Poland*, published by the Diaspora Research Institute of Tel Aviv University.[1]

1. Stephen D. Corrsin, "Works on Polish Jewry, 1990–1994: A Bibliography," *Gal-Ed: On the History of the Jews in Poland* 14 (1995):131–233; "Recent Works on Polish Jewry: A Bibliography," *Gal-Ed* 15–16 (1997): 143–259; "Recent Works on Polish Jewry: A Bibliography," *Gal-Ed* 17 (2000):105–203; and "Recent Works on Polish Jewry: A Bibliography," *Gal-Ed* 19 (2004): 99–302. I thank David Engel for his editorial direction and support, contributions, and encouragement for the duration of this project.

As concerns the present, quite brief listing, it is a *selective* bibliography, even within the terms noted above. It makes no claim to anything approaching a comprehensive level of coverage. In all, 171 items are listed here. Many hundreds more are relevant to the topic but have been left out because of space considerations. Moreover, it must be understood that the resulting sample is a skewed one. For reasons not only of space but of ready accessibility for a primarily North American audience, certain types of publications have been given preference: English-language versions of a piece over those in any other languages; Roman-alphabet versions (particularly English or Polish) over Hebrew-alphabet ones; more widely available journal articles over those in proceedings, *festschrifts*, or monographic collections, which tend to be harder to identify and locate; and monographs that have been formally published over the dissertations or theses on which they are based. When authors repeat themselves throughout a series of publications, I have chosen one or two items from the individual author's larger list. Further, it is especially regrettable that the constraints and complexities of not merely multilingual but multialphabet bibliographical entries led to the decision to limit sharply the number of entries representing items published in Hebrew and, even then, to translate the entries entirely into English. This is obviously a serious lacuna in any project that falls, even in part, within the area of Jewish studies; the small number of Hebrew-alphabet items in this bibliography by no means reflects the great level of interest and publication in the field in Israeli scholarship. Nonetheless, despite all these caveats, I can argue with cautious confidence that this bibliography presents an informative and useful summary of recent scholarly research in the field.

I must say a few more words about the larger bibliographical project from which this small selection has been drawn. In the early 1990s, Professor David Engel of Tel Aviv and New York Universities asked me to prepare an ongoing bibliography of new scholarly publications in the field of Polish-Jewish history. This bibliography has since appeared as a regular feature in *Gal-Ed: On the History of the Jews in Poland*, which prints both English- and Hebrew-language contributions and of which Dr. Engel has been an editor for many years. The bibliography has, so far, appeared in four installments. Only publications in English, Polish, Hebrew, German, French, and a few in Yiddish have been included in the bibliography, which now consists of a file of approximately 3,500 entries for items published between 1990 and the first months of 2003. Two long-term goals, the realization of which will presumably have to await appropriate funding, are to make the complete file available for searching on the Internet and to start working the collection and description of materials back through the decades to include items published in the 1980s, the 1970s, and so on.

The most striking fact to be seen in the field of Polish-Jewish studies is the greatly increased volume of publishing since the late 1980s. There has been an enormous upswing in quantity—even taking into account that it remains a very small field. Zachary M. Baker, a leading Judaica librarian, formerly of the Yivo Institute and now of Stanford University, stated in 1989: "One of the most striking developments in the Judaica publishing world during the past decade [the 1980s] has been the appearance in Poland of scores of books and journals devoted to Jews and Judaism. . . . [A]fter having been all but written out of Polish history since 1945, Poland's Jews are now finding themselves being reincorporated into the Polish literary, cultural, and historical consciousness." Baker links this reincorporation to wider trends in Polish society and politics, including the rejection of the communist state and system, which used antisemitism as a standard tool whenever unrest threatened (the most notable example in Poland coming in 1967–68). Baker concludes, "Given the obsession that so many Poles have with their country's fate, the present-day discovery of the Jewish skeletons in their nation's closet may mark only the beginning of a long voyage of [Polish] self-exploration."[2]

This point—that the increase in Polish interest in the country's Jewish heritage is a matter of "self-exploration"—is a very important one. Since 1989–90 the infrastructure of Poland's Jewish studies has developed rapidly. There are now a number of newly founded centers, societies, and university departments devoted to the field and two healthy scholarly periodicals: *Kwartalnik Historii Żydów* and *Studia Judaica*. It should be noted that these developments have all taken place within a general upsurge in interest in Jewish studies in many countries, again as can be seen in any survey of the Polish-Jewish studies infrastructure in North America, Israel, and western Europe. Matters of quantity aside, this wealth of recent work, represented in a small way in the present bibliography, has been at the highest scholarly level and covers a very wide range of periods and topics. There is no question that the field of "Polish-Jewish studies" has developed into a significant discipline in its own right.

I conclude this introduction with comments as a librarian and a bibliographer: the only valid purpose of any bibliographical project is its usefulness to the scholars and students of a given field. This is true as well for libraries and librarians in the academic world; their work—let me say *our* work—cannot be an end in itself. It gains significance and validity only in the support it provides for teaching and scholarship. It is my hope that this brief and selective bibliography will be of some significant use to students and scholars alike.

2. Zachary M. Baker, "The Chosen Book: Reinventing the Jew in Absentia; Recent Judaica Publishing Trends in Poland," *Judaica Librarianship* 5, No. 1 (1989–90): 62, 65. See also my "Bibliographical Projects on Polish-Jewish Studies since 1989," in *Slavic and East European Information Resources* 4, nos. 2–3 (2003):151–67, which tells more about the upswing in the area of Polish-Jewish bibliography in general in the last decade of the twentieth century and first years of the twenty-first.

General and Multiperiod

COLLECTIONS, FESTSCHRIFTS, BIBLIOGRAPHIES, ETC.

Barcz, Jan, ed. *Prawda i pojednanie: w 80. rocznicę urodzin Władysława Bartoszewskiego.* Warsaw: Rytm, 2002. 812 pp., ill., references. *Festschrift* for Bartoszewski. Includes articles on such topics as the Warsaw ghetto, Polish antisemitism, and Polish-Jewish relations.

Bartoszewski, Władysław, ed. *Pod wspólnym niebiem.* Warsaw: Więź, 1998. 349 pp., references. Special number of the journal *Więź*, with articles on Poles and Jews. Also published in English translation as *Under One Heaven: Poles and Jews.*

Błoński, Jan. *Biedni Polacy patrzą na getto.* Kraków: Wydawn. Literackie, 1994. 156 pp., references. Essays on Jews in Polish culture and on relations, beginning with Błoński's essay, which gives the book its title and focuses on Czesław Miłosz's poem on the destruction of the Warsaw ghetto, "Campo di Fiori."

Gutman, Israel. "Polish Antisemitism in the Nineteenth and Twentieth Centuries: Will Things Ever Change?" In *The Danger of Antisemitism in Central and Eastern Europe in the Wake of 1989–1990,* ed. Yehuda Bauer, 75–82. Jerusalem: Vidal Sassoon International Centre for the Study of Antisemitism, Hebrew University, 1991.

———. "The Popular Image of the Jew in Modern Poland." In *Demonizing the Other: Antisemitism, Racism, and Xenophobia,* ed. Robert S. Wistrich, pp. 257–66. Amsterdam: Harwood, 1999.

Polonsky, Antony. "Antisemitism in Poland: The Current State of Historical Research." In *Approaches to Antisemitism: Context and Curriculum,* ed. Michael Brown, 290–308. New York: American Jewish Committee, 1994.

Scharf, Rafael S. *Poland, What Have I to Do with Thee: Essays without Prejudice = Co mnie i tobie Polsko: eseje bez uprzedzeń.* Kraków: Fundacja Judaica, 1996. 342 pp. Bilingual, Polish and English, collection of the author's essays. Also published in English alone in 1998, and in a second bilingual edition in 1999.

Strauss, Herbert A., ed. *Bibliographie zum Antisemitismus: Die Bestände der Bibliothek des Zentrums für Antisemitismusforschung der Technischen Universität Berlin.* 4 vols. Munich: K. G. Sauer, 1989–93. Introduction in English and German. Includes significant amounts of Polish material.

———, ed. *Hostages of Modernization: Studies on Modern Antisemitism, 1870–1933/39.* 2 vols. Berlin: W. de Gruyter, 1993. References. The second volume, "Austria, Hungary, Poland, Russia," includes a number of important articles, chiefly reprints, on Poland.

Tomaszewski, Jerzy. "Polacy-Żydzi: tysiąc lat wspólnej historii." *Collectanea theologica* 66, no. 2 (1996): 9–25.

Wapiński, Roman, ed. *Polacy i sąsiedzi, dystanse i przenikanie kultur: Zbiór studiów.* 3 vols. Gdańsk: Stepan Design, 2000–2. References. Collection on relations between Poland and its minorities and neighbors in the nineteenth–twentieth centuries.

Żyndul, Jolanta, ed. *Rozdział wspólnej historii: Studia z dziejów Żydów w Polsce, Ofiarowane profesorowi Jerzemu Tomaszewskiemu w siedemdziesiątą rocznicę urodzin.* Warsaw: Cyklady, 2001. 418 pp., ill., references. *Festschrift,* with contributions chiefly concerning the twentieth century.

ART, LITERATURE, AND CULTURE

Frybes, Stanisław. "Literatura polska, literatura żydowska: Współistnienie i wzajemne przenikanie." *Collectanea theologica* 66, no. 2 (1996): 27–37.

Löw, Ryszard. *Rozpoznania: Szkice literackie*. Kraków: Księg. Akademicka, 1998. 129 pp., references. Polish-Jewish literary connections.

Nelken, Halina. *Images of a Lost World: Jewish Motifs in Polish Painting, 1770–1945*. London: I. B. Taurus in association with the Institute for Polish-Jewish Studies, 1991. 143 pp., ill., references.

Segel, Harold B., ed. *Stranger in Our Midst: Images of the Jew in Polish Literature*. Ithaca: Cornell University Press, 1996. Xiv, 402 pp., ill., references. Translations of stories and excerpts by Polish writers.

Shmeruk, Chone. *Legenda o Esterce w literaturze jidysz i polskiej: Studium z dziedziny wzajemnych stosunków dwóch kultur i tradycyj*. Warsaw: Ofic. Naukowa, 2000. 153 pp., ill., references. Previously published in Hebrew and English. See *The Esterke Story in Polish and Yiddish Literature* (1985).

Sitarz, Magdalena Joanna. *Yiddish and Polish Proverbs: Contrastive Analysis against Cultural Background*. Kraków: Polska Akademia Umiejętności, 2000. 161 pp., references.

Partitions Era and World War I

GENERAL WORKS

Himka, John-Paul. "Dimensions of a Triangle: Polish-Ukrainian-Jewish Relations in Austrian Galicia." *Polin* 12 (1999): 25–48.

Pachołkiw, Swiatosław. "GrenzNähe: Die Juden im Spannungsfeld interethnischer Beziehungen in Ostgalizien (1860–1939)." *Kwartalnik Historii Żydów* 199, no. 3 (2001): 327–55. Includes a sizable bibliography.

Żbikowski, Andrzej. *Ideologia antysemicka, 1848–1914: Wybór tekstów źródłowych*. Warsaw: Żydowski Instytut Historyczny, 1994. 140 pp., references. Sources drawn from the Polish press and other publications.

CATHOLIC AND OTHER CHRISTIAN CHURCHES

Lewalski, Krzysztof. *Kościoły chrześcijańskie w Królestwie Polskim wobec Żydów w latach 1855–1915*. Wrocław: Fundacja na Rzecz Nauki Polskiej, 2002. 348 pp., references.

Pollmann, Viktoria. " 'Ungebetene Gäste im christlichen Haus': Die Kirche und die Juden in Polen des 19. und frühen 20. Jahrhunderts." In *Katholischer Antisemitismus im 19. Jahrhundert: Ursachen und Traditionen im internationalen Vergleich*, ed. Olaf Blaschke and Aram Mattioli, 259–86. Zurich: Orell Fussli, 2000.

LITERATURE

Inglot, Mieczysław. *Postać Żyda w literaturze polskiej lat 1822–1864*. Wrocław: Wyd. Uniwersytetu Wrocławskiego, 1999. 295 pp., references.

Maurer, Jadwiga. *Z matki obcej: Szkice o powiązaniach Mickiewicza ze światem Żydów*. London: Polska Fundacja Kulturalna, 1990. 141 pp., references.

Opalski, Magdalena and Israel Bartal. *Poles and Jews: A Failed Brotherhood*. Hanover, N.H.: University Press of New England for Brandeis University, 1992.

Xi and 191 pp., references. "This study . . . examines Polish and Jewish perceptions of the short-lived Polish-Jewish rapprochement of the early 1860s and the
interpretations of interethnic relations in the January insurrection offered by both
literary traditions" (4).

Umińska, Bożena. *Postać z cieniem: Portrety Żydówek w polskiej literaturze od
końca XIX wieku do 1939*. Warsaw: Sic!, 2001. 173 pp.

Werses, Shmuel. "Polish-Jewish Relations in Two Stories by Mendele Mocher Sforim
(S. Y. Abramowicz)." *Gal-Ed: On the History of the Jews in Poland* 14 (1995):
Hebrew section.

POGROMS AND VIOLENCE

Ochs, Michael. "Tsarist Officialdom and Anti-Jewish Pogroms in Poland." In
Pogroms: Anti-Jewish Violence in Modern Russian History, ed. John D. Klier and
Shlomo Lambroza, 164–89. Cambridge, U.K.: Cambridge University Press, 1992.
Concentrates on the 1881 Warsaw pogrom, arguing against accusations of official
Russian instigation.

POLITICS AND PARTIES

Blobaum, Robert. "The Politics of Antisemitism in Fin-de-Siècle Warsaw." *Journal of
Modern History* 73, no. 2 (2001): 275–306.

Kraft, Claudia. "Die jüdische Frage im Spiegel der Presseorgane und Parteipro-
gramme der galizischen Bauernbewegung im letzten Viertel des 19. Jahrhunderts."
Zeitschrift für Ostmitteleuropa-Forschung 3 (1996): 381–409.

Mishkinsky, Moshe. "Polish Socialism and the Jewish Question on the Eve of the
Establishment of the Polish Socialist Party (PPS) and Social Democracy in the
Kingdom of Poland (SDKP)." *Polin* 5 (1990): 250–72. Focuses on the journal
Przedświt in the 1880s–1890s.

Oppenheim, Israel. "The Radicalization of the Endecja's Anti-Jewish Line during and
after the 1905 Revolution." *Shevut* 9, no. 25 (2000): 32–66.

Porter, Brian. *When Nationalism Began to Hate: Imagining Modern Politics in
Nineteenth-Century Poland*. New York: Oxford University Press, 2000. 307 pp.,
references. On Polish nationalism and National Democracy in particular,
including the rise of antisemitism in modern Polish politics.

Snyder, Timothy. "Kazimierz Kelles-Kraus, 1872–1905: A Polish Socialist for Jewish
Nationality." *Polin* 12 (1999): 257–70.

Struve, Kai. "Die Juden in der Sicht der polnischen Bauernparteien vom Ende des
19. Jahrhunderts bis 1939." *Zeitschrift für Ostmitteleuropa-Forschung* 47, no. 2
(1999): 184–225.

Śliwa, Michał. "The Jewish Problem in Polish Socialist Thought." *Polin* 9 (1996):
14–31.

Wapiński, Roman. "The Endecja and the Jewish Question." *Polin* 12 (1999):
271–83. From the movement's founding to the 1930s.

Weeks, Theodore R. "Poles, Jews, and Russians, 1863–1914: The Death of the Ideal
of Assimilation in the Kingdom of Poland." *Polin* 12 (1999): 242–56.

——. "Polish 'Progressive Antisemitism,' 1905–1914." *East European Jewish Affairs*
25, no. 2 (1995): 49–68.

Zimmerman, Joshua D. *Poles, Jews, and the Politics of Nationality: The Bund and
the Polish Socialist Party in Late Tsarist Russia, 1892–1914*. Madison: University
of Wisconsin Press, 2004. Xv, 360 pp., ill., maps, references.

WORLD WAR I

Black, Eugene C. "Squaring a Minorities Triangle: Lucien Wolf, Jewish Nationalists, and Polish Nationalists." In *The Reconstruction of Poland, 1914–23*, ed. Paul Latawski, 13–40. New York: St. Martin's, 1992.

Levene, Mark. "Britain, a British Jew, and Jewish Relations with the New Poland: The Making of the Polish Minorities Treaty of 1919." *Polin* 8 (1994): 14–41. On Lucien Wolf and Sir James Headlam-Morley.

Prusin, Alexander Victor. "War and Nationality Conflict in Eastern Galicia, 1914–1920: The Evolution of Modern Anti-Semitism." Ph.D. dissertation, University of Toronto, 2000. 303 pp., references.

Silber, Marcos. " 'May the New Poland be a Good Mother to All Her Children': Jews and Poles in Poland, 1916." *Zemanim* 65 (1998–99): 78–83 (in Hebrew).

Interwar Period

GENERAL WORKS

Bacon, Gershon C. "Polish Jews and the Minorities Treaties Obligations, 1925: The View from Geneva (Documents from the League of Nations Archives)." *Gal-Ed: On the History of the Jews in Poland* 18 (2002): 145–76. Includes French and English texts of documents on the use of Hebrew and Yiddish as languages of instruction in Jewish schools in Poland.

Bronsztejn, Szyja. "Polish-Jewish Relations as Reflected in Memoirs of the Interwar Period." *Polin* 8 (1994): 66–88.

Chodakiewicz, Marek J. *Żydzi i Polacy 1918–1955: Współistnienie, zagłada, komunizm*. Warsaw: Fronda, 2000. 731 pp., references.

Friedrich, Klaus-Peter. "Juden und jüdisch-polnische Beziehungen in der Zweiten Polnischen Republik (1918–1939): Neuere Literatur." *Zeitschrift für Ostmitteleuropa-Forschung* 46, no. 4 (1997): 535–60. Bibliographic survey of research literature in Polish and western European languages, chiefly since 1980.

Landau-Czajka, Anna. *W jednym stali domu: Koncepcje rozwiązania kwestii żydowskiej w publicystyce polskiej lat 1933–1939*. Warsaw: Wydawn. Neriton, IH PAN, 1998. 316 pp., references.

Natkowska, Monika. *Numerus clausus, getto ławkowe, numerus nullus, "paragraf aryjski": Antysemityzm na Uniwersytecie Warszawskim, 1936–1939*. Warsaw: Żydowski Instytut Historyczny, 1999. 188 pp., references.

Redlich, Shimon. *Together and Apart in Brzezany: Poles, Jews, and Ukrainians, 1919–1945*. Bloomington: Indiana University Press, 2002. Xi and 202 pp., ill., references. Scholarly study plus memoir focusing on interethnic relations in Berezhany (now in Ukraine).

Tazbir, Janusz. *Protokoły mędrców Syjonu: Autentyk czy falsyfikat*. Warsaw: Interlibro, 1992. 263 pp., references. Study of *The Protocols of the Elders of Zion*, its history and distribution, drawing on conspiracy theories in history. Includes a 1938 Polish translation of the *Protocols*. See also Tazbir, "Conspiracy Theories and the Reception of *The Protocols of the Elders of Zion* in Poland," *Polin* 11 (1998): 171–82.

Żbikowski, Andrzej. "Poles and Jews in the *Kresy wschodnie:* Interethnic Relations in the Borderlands, 1918–1939." *Jahrbuch des Simon-Dubnows Instituts* 1 (2002): 41–53.

CATHOLIC CHURCH

Libionka, Dariusz. "Obcy, wrodzy, niebezpieczni: Obraz Żydów i 'kwestii żydowskiej' w prasie inteligencji katolickiej lat trzydziestych w Polsce." *Kwartalnik Historii Żydów* 203, no. 3 (2002): 318–38.

Modras, Ronald E. *The Catholic Church and Antisemitism in Poland, 1933–1939.* Chur, Switz.: Harwood Academic, 1994. Xvi and 429 pp., references.

Napiorkowski, Stanisław C., ed. *A bliźniego swego: Materiały z sympozjum "Św. Maksymilian Maria Kolbe—Żydzi—Masoni."* Lublin: Wydawn. Katolickiego Uniwersytetu Lubelskiego, 1997. 175 pp. Proceedings of a conference on Kolbe and attitudes toward the Jews in interwar Poland.

Pollmann, Viktoria. "Der 'Ritter der Unbeflecken' und die 'Fahne Mariens': Marienkult und Judenfeindschaft in Polen auf der Grundlage ausgewählter katholischer Presse vor 1939." In *Maria, Tochter Sion? Mariologie, Marienfrommigkeit, und Judenfeindschaft,* ed. Johannes Heil and Rainer Kampling, pp. 211–39. Paderborn: Schöningh, 2001.

POGROMS AND VIOLENCE

Gontarczyk, Piotr. *Pogrom? Zajścia polsko-żydowskie w Przytyku 9 marcu 1936 r.: Mity, fakty, dokumenty.* Biała Podlaska: Ofic. Wyd. Rekonkwista, 2000. 385 pp., ill., references.

Liekis, Sarunas, Lidia Miliakova, and Antony Polonsky. "Three Documents on Anti-Jewish Violence in the Eastern *Kresy* during the Polish-Soviet Conflict." *Polin* 14 (2001): 116–49. Violence in Pinsk, Lida, and Wilno in March–April 1919, after Polish forces entered.

Michlic-Coren, Joanna. "Anti-Jewish Violence in Poland, 1918–1939 and 1945–1947." *Polin* 13 (2000): 34–61.

Żyndul, Jolanta. *Zajścia antyżydowskie w Polsce w latach 1935–1937.* Warsaw: Fundacja im. K. Kelles-Krauza, 1994. 96 pp., ill., references.

POLITICS AND PARTIES

Bergmann, Olaf. *Narodowa demokracja wobec problematyki żydowskiej w latach 1918–1929.* Poznań: Wydawn. Poznańskie, 1998. 399 pp., references.

Hagen, William W. "Before the 'Final Solution': Toward a Comparative Analysis of Political Anti-Semitism in Interwar Germany and Poland." *Journal of Modern History* 68, no. 2 (1996): 351–81.

Netzer, Shlomo. "The Role of the Jewish Representation in the Polish Sejm in the Fight against Economic Antisemitism." *Gal-Ed: On the History of the Jews in Poland* 14 (1995): Hebrew section.

Rudnicki, Szymon. "Ritual Slaughter as a Political Issue." *Polin* 7 (1992): 147–60.

——. "Walka o zmianę ustawy o adwokaturze w II Rzeczypospolitej." *Kwartalnik Historii Żydów* 201, no. 1 (2002): 49–61.

Weinbaum, Laurence. *A Marriage of Convenience: The New Zionist Organization and the Polish Government, 1936–1949.* Boulder, Colo.: East European Monographs, 1993. Xiii and 295 pp., ill., references.

World War II and Holocaust

GENERAL WORKS

Engel, David. *Facing a Holocaust: The Polish Government-in-Exile and the Jews, 1943–1945.* Chapel Hill: University of North Carolina Press, 1993. X and 317 pp., references. "This book is a sequel to an earlier work, *In the Shadow of Auschwitz: The Polish Government-in-Exile and the Jews, 1939–1942*, which appeared in 1987" (ix).

Gross, Jan Tomasz. "A Tangled Web: Confronting Stereotypes concerning Relations between Poles, Germans, Jews, and Communists." In *The Politics of Retribution in Europe: World War II and Its Aftermath,* ed. István Deák, Jan T. Gross, and Tony Judt, 74–129. Princeton: Princeton University Press, 2000. See also his *Upiorna dekada: Trzy eseje o stereotypach Żydów, Polaków, Niemców i komunistów, 1939–1948.* 2d ed. (Kraków: Universitas, 2001).

Grynberg, Henryk. *Prawda nieartystyczna.* Wołowiec: Czarne, 2002. 325 pp., references. Collection of essays on the Holocaust, Polish-Jewish relations, etc., originally published in 1984 in West Berlin. This is a third, much enlarged edition.

Hartman, John J., and Jacek Krochmal, eds. *I Remember Every Day: The Fates of the Jews of Przemyśl during World War II = Pamiętam każdy dzień: Losy Żydów przemyskich podczas II wojny światowej.* Przemyśl: Tow. Przyjaciół Nauk, 2002. 319 pp., ill., references. Collection of memories of Jews, Poles, and Ukrainians, with psychohistorical analysis of ethnic relations.

Kersten, Krystyna. *Polacy, Żydzi, komunizm: Anatomia półprawd, 1939–1968.* Warsaw: Niezależna Ofic. Wydawnicza, 1992. 185 pp., references. Contains two original research essays and three shorter pieces, previously published in whole or in part elsewhere, on Polish-Jewish relations during the Second World War and in Communist Poland.

Kozmińska-Frejlak, Ewa. "Świadkowie zagłady: Holocaust jako zbiorowe doświadczenie Polaków." *Przegląd Socjologiczny* 49, no. 2 (2000): 181–206.

Krakowski, Shmuel. "Podziemie polskie a Żydzi w latach drugiej wojny światowej." *Biuletyn Żydowskiego Instytutu Historycznego* 194, no. 2 (2000): 171–80. Surveys the broad range of the Polish underground's responses.

Kunert, Andrzej. *Polacy-Żydzi 1939–1945: Wybór źródeł.* Warsaw: Rada Ochrony Pamięci Walk i Męczeństwa, Instytut Dziedzictwa Narodowego, Ofic. Wydaw. Rytm, 2001. 528 pp., ill. Documents in Polish, German, and English.

Polonsky, Antony. "Beyond Condemnation, Apologetics, and Apologies: On the Complexity of Polish Behavior toward the Jews during the Second World War." *Studies in Contemporary Jewry* 13 (1997): 190–224.

Ringelblum, Emanuel. *Polish-Jewish Relations during the Second World War.* Ed. Joseph Kermish and Shmuel Krakowski. Evanston, Ill.: Northwestern University Press, 1992. Xlvi and 330 pp., references. Translated from Polish by Dafna Allon, Danuta Dąbrowska, and Dana Keren. Foreword by Yehuda Bauer. A new edition with added prefatory material and end matter.

Tych, Feliks. *Długi cień zagłady: Szkice historyczne.* Warsaw: Żydowski Instytut Historyczny, 1999. 166 pp., references. Collected essays chiefly on the Holocaust, historiography, and memory. Some essays have appeared in English translations: for example, "The Image of the Holocaust in Polish Historical Consciousness," *Polin* 14 (2001): 315–25; and "Witnesses of Shoah: The Extermination of the

Jews in Polish Diaries, Memoirs, and Reminiscences," *Biuletyn Żydowskiego Instytutu Historycznego* 192, no. 4 (1999): 3–18.

Wierzbicki, Marek. *Polacy i Żydzi w zaborze sowieckim: Stosunki polsko-żydowskie na ziemiach północno-wschodnich II RP pod okupacją sowiecką (1939–1941).* Warsaw: Biblioteka "Frondy," 2001. 360 pp., ill., references.

Zimmerman, Joshua D., ed. *Contested Memories: Poles and Jews during the Holocaust and Its Aftermath.* New Brunswick, N.J.: Rutgers University Press, 2003. Xx and 324 pp., references. Collection of essays.

Żbikowski, Andrzej. "Jewish Reaction to the Soviet Arrival in the *Kresy* in September 1939." *Polin* 13 (2000): 62–72.

———. "Local Anti-Jewish Pogroms in the Occupied Territories of Eastern Poland, June–July 1941." In *The Holocaust in the Soviet Union: Studies and Sources on the Destruction of the Jews in the Nazi-Occupied Territories of the USSR, 1941–1945,* ed. Lucjan Dobroszycki and Jeffrey Gurock, 173–79. New York: M. E. Sharpe, 1993.

CATHOLIC CHURCH

Bogner, Nahum. "The Convent Children: The Rescue of Jewish Children in Polish Convents during the Holocaust." *Yad Vashem Studies* 27 (1999): 235–85.

Kurek, Ewa. *Your Life is Worth Mine: How Polish Nuns in World War II Saved Hundreds of Jewish Lives in German-Occupied Poland, 1939–1945.* New York: Hippocrene, 1997. 255 pp., references. Introduction by Jan Karski. In Polish, see Kurek, *Gdy klasztor znaczył życie* (1992) and *Dzieci żydowskie w klasztorach* (2001).

Libionka, Dariusz. "Kościół w Polsce wobec zagłady w świetle polskiej publicystyki i historiografii." *Biuletyn Żydowskiego Instytutu Historycznego* 195, no. 3 (2000): 329–41.

HISTORIOGRAPHY AND BIBLIOGRAPHY

Aleksiun, Natalia. "Historical Studies on the Holocaust Published in Poland, 1945–1998." *Gal-Ed: On the History of the Jews in Poland* 17 (2000): Hebrew section.

Friedrich, Klaus-Peter. "Juden in Polen während der Schoa: Zu polnischen und deutschen Neuerscheinungen." *Zeitschrift für Ostmitteleuropa-Forschung* 47, no. 2 (1998): 231–74.

Krakowski, Shmuel. "Relations between Jews and Poles during the Holocaust: New and Old Approaches in Polish Historiography." In *Holocaust Literature: A Handbook of Critical, Historical, and Literary Writings,* ed. Saul S. Friedman, 203–15. Westport, Conn.: Greenwood Press, 1993.

Tomaszewski, Jerzy. "Historiografia polska o zagładzie." *Biuletyn Żydowskiego Instytutu Historycznego* 194, no. 2 (2000): 155–70.

LITERATURE

Brodzka-Wald, Alina, Dorota Krawczyńska, and Jacek Leociak, eds. *Literatura polska wobec zagłady: Praca zbiorowa.* Warsaw: Żydowski Instytut Historyczny, 2000. 291 pp., references. Proceedings from conference held in Warsaw in 1999.

Gross, Natan. *Poeci i szoah: Obraz zagłady Żydów w poezji polskiej.* Sosnowiec: OFFMAX, 1993. 191 pp.

Polonsky, Antony. "Polish Responses to the 'Final Solution' as Reflected in Some Recent Polish Literary Accounts." *British Journal of Holocaust Education* 2, no. 2 (1993): 166–88.

RESCUERS AND RIGHTEOUS GENTILES

Bartoszewski, Władysław. *Żegota: Juifs et Polonais dans la résistance, 1939–1945.* Paris: Criterion, 1992. 333 pp., 16 pp. of plates, maps, references.

Barzel, Neima. "Some Characteristics of Rescue Actions by Righteous Gentiles in Poland." *Dapim* 13 (1995/96): 101–27 (in Hebrew).

Bauminger, Arieh L. *The Righteous among the Nations.* Tel Aviv: Am Oved, 1990. 203 pp., ports, reference. Published originally in Hebrew and subsequently in Polish.

Czernianski, Irit. "Statistics on the Righteous Gentiles from Poland." *Dapim* 14 (1997/98): 339–65 (in Hebrew).

Grynberg, Michał. *Księga sprawiedliwych.* Warsaw: Państ. Wydawn. Naukowe, 1993. 766 pp., ill., references. Persons honored by Yad Vashem.

Grynberg, Michał, and Maria Kotowska, eds. *Życie i zagłada Żydów polskich, 1939–1945: Relacje świadków.* Warsaw: Ofic. Naukowa, 2003. 660 pp., ill., references.

Isakiewicz, Elżbieta. *Harmonica: Jews Relate How Poles Saved Them from the Holocaust.* Warsaw: Polska Agencja Informacyjna, 2000. 262 pp., ill. Published in Polish as *Ustna harmonijka.*

Kunert, Andrzej Krzysztof, ed. *Żegota: The Council for Aid to Jews, 1942–45.* Warsaw: Rada Ochrony Pamięci Walk i Męczeństwa, 2002. 162 pp., ill. "Selected documents preceded by an interview with Władysław Bartoszewski by Andrzej Friszke." Also published in Polish.

Paldiel, Mordechai. "Fear and Comfort: The Plight of Hidden Jewish Children in Wartime Poland." *Holocaust and Genocide Studies* 6, no. 4 (1991): 397–413.

Prekerowa, Teresa. "Who Helped Jews during the Holocaust?" *Acta Poloniae Historica* 76 (1997): 153–70.

Postwar Period (1945–1989)

GENERAL WORKS

Cała, Alina. *The Image of the Jew in Polish Folk Culture.* Jerusalem: Magnes Press, Hebrew University, 1995. 235 pp., ill., references. Appeared originally in Polish as *Wizerunek Żyda w polskiej kulturze ludowej* (1992), based on ethnographic research.

Chajn, Michał. "Stosunek rządów polskich do powstania żydowskiej siedziby narodowej w Palestynie w latach 1945–1948." *Biuletyn Żydowskiego Instytutu Historycznego* 195, 3 (2000): 356–73. Polish governmental support for Zionist aspirations in Palestine.

Coates, Paul. "Walls and Frontiers: Polish Cinema's Portrayal of Polish-Jewish Relations." *Polin* 10 (1997): 221–46. Discusses several major films made in the previous twenty years.

Engel, David. "Polen und Juden nach 1945: Historisches Bewusstsein und politischer Kontext als Faktoren polnisch-jüdischer Beziehungen in der Nachkriegszeit." *Babylon: Beiträge zur jüdischen Gegenwart* 15 (1995): 28–48.

Kapralski, Sławomir. "Battlefields of Memory: Landscape and Identity in Polish-Jewish Relations." *History and Memory* 13, no. 2 (2001): 35–58. "Landscape as a cultural construction of a group serves generally the purpose of creating and/or maintaining the group's identity. . . . This essay describes several manipulations of landscape in southeastern Poland" (35–37).

Kenney, Padraic. "Whose Nation, Whose State? Working-class Nationalism and Antisemitism in Poland, 1945–1947." *Polin* 13 (2000): 224–35.

Kersten, Krystyna. "Polish Stalinism and the So-called 'Jewish Question.'" In *Der Spätstalinismus und die "jüdische Frage": Zur antisemitischen Wendung des Kommunismus*, ed. Leonid Luks, 221–36. Cologne: Böhlau, 1998.

Mazierska, Ewa. "Non-Jewish Jews, Good Poles, and Historical Truth in the Films of Andrzej Wajda." *Historical Journal of Film, Radio, and Television* 20, no. 2 (2000): 213–26.

Zawadzki, Paul. "La Pologne." In *Histoire de l'antisemitisme, 1945–1993*, ed. Leon Poliakov, 221–55. Paris: Editions de Seuil, 1994.

LITERATURE

Adamczyk-Garbowska, Monika. *Polska Isaaca Bashevisa Singera: Rozstanie i powrót*. Lublin: Wydawn. Uniwersytetu Marii Curie-Skłodowskiej, 1994. 197 pp., ill., references. On Singer's literary and personal connections to Poland.

Pragier, Ruta. "Jews in Contemporary Polish Literature." *Polish Western Affairs* 34, no. 1 (1993): 3–23.

Shenfeld, Ruth. "The Image of Jews in Contemporary Polish Literature." *Gal-Ed: On the History of the Jews in Poland* 12 (1991): Hebrew section.

Werses, Shmuel. *Relations between Jews and Poles in S. Y. Agnon's Work*. Jerusalem: Magnes Press, 1994. 127 pp.

Wróbel, Józef. *Tematy żydowskie w prozie polskiej, 1939–1987*. Kraków: Universitas, 1991. 189 pp., index. Includes a list of works on Jewish themes, published since 1939.

POGROMS AND VIOLENCE

Cichopek, Anna. *Pogrom Żydów w Krakowie, 11 sierpnia 1945*. Warsaw: Żydowski Instytut Historyczny, 2000. 269 pp., ill., references.

Engel, David. "Patterns of Anti-Jewish Violence in Poland, 1944–1946." *Yad Vashem Studies* 26 (1998): 43–85.

Friedrich, Klaus-Peter. "Antijüdische Gewalt nach dem Holocaust: Zu einigen Aspekten des Judenpogroms von Kielce." *Jahrbuch für Antisemitismusforschung* 6 (1997): 115–47.

Gross, Jan Tomasz. "In the Aftermath of the Kielce Pogrom: The Special Commission of the Central Committee of Jews in Poland." *Gal-Ed: On the History of the Jews in Poland* 15–16 (1997): 119–36. Documents concerning organization of Jewish self-defense in 1946–47.

Kersten, Krystyna, et al. "O stanie badań nad pogromem w Kielcach: Dyskusja w Żydowskim Instytucie Historycznym (12 III 1996) z referatem wprowadzającym prof. Krystyny Kersten." *Biuletyn Żydowskiego Instytutu Historycznego* 180, no. 4 (1996): 3–17. Discussion by various scholars, following introduction by Kersten.

Kwiek, Julian. "Wydarzenia antyżydowskie 11 sierpnia 1945 r. w Krakowie: dokumenty." *Biuletyn Żydowskiego Instytutu Historycznego* 193, no. 1 (2000): 77–89.

Meducki, Stanisław. "The Pogrom in Kielce on 4 July 1946." *Polin* 9 (1996): 158–69.

Meducki, Stanisław, and Zenon Wrona, eds. *Antyżydowskie wydarzenia kieleckie, 4 lipca 1946: Dokumenty i materiały.* 2 vols. Kielce: Tow. Naukowe, Urząd Miasta, 1992–94. Ill., references.

Michlic-Coren, Joanna. "Polish Jews during and after the Kielce Pogrom: Reports from the Communist Archives." *Polin* 13 (2000): 253–67.

Szaynok, Bożena. *Pogrom Żydów w Kielcach, 4 lipca 1946 r.* Warsaw: Bellona, 1992. 127 pp., ill., references. Introduction by Krystyna Kersten. See also Szaynok, "The Pogrom of Jews in Kielce, July 4, 1946," *Yad Vashem Studies* 22 (1992): 199–235.

Wiącek, Tadeusz, ed. *Kulisy i tajemnice pogromu kieleckiego 1946.* Kraków: Temax, 1992. 146 pp. Documents, recollections, etc.

EVENTS OF 1967–68

Blatman, Daniel. "Polish Jewry, the Six-Day War, and the Crisis of 1968." In *The Six-Day War and World Jewry*, ed. Eli Lederhendler, 291–310. Bethesda, Md.: University Press, 2000.

Kosmala, Beate, ed. *Die Vertreibung der Juden aus Polen 1968: Antisemitismus und politisches Kalkül.* Berlin: Metropol, 2000. 191 pp., references. Collection of articles on 1968 and the "Jewish question" as a postwar political weapon in Poland.

Kula, Marcin, Piotr Osęka, and Marcin Zaremba, eds. *Marzec 1968: Trzydzieści lat później; Materiały konferencji.* 2 vols. Warsaw: Państ. Wydawn. Naukowe, 1998. References. Proceedings of a conference held in Warsaw in 1998: vol. 1 includes the papers, and vol. 2, "Dzień po dniu w raportach SB oraz Wydziału Organizacyjnego KC PZPR."

Osęka, Piotr. *Syjoniści, inspiratorzy, wichrzyciele: Obraz wroga w propagandzie marca 1968.* Warsaw: Żydowski Instytut Historyczny, 1999. 270 pp., ill., references.

Stola, Dariusz. *Kampania antysyjonistyczna w Polsce 1967–1968.* Warsaw: Instytut Studiów Politycznych PAN, 2000. 414 pp., references.

Postcommunist Period (1989–)

GENERAL WORKS

Brumberg, Abraham. "Poland, the Polish Intelligentsia and Antisemitism." *Soviet Jewish Affairs* 20, nos. 2–3 (1990): 5–25. Article appearing shortly after the end of communist rule in Poland, which set off a major controversy. Appeared in Polish in *Biuletyn Żydowskiego Instytutu Historycznego* 167–168, nos. 3–4 (1993), as "Polska inteligencja a antysemityzm." Discussion appeared in the same journal, 182, no. 2 (1997): 3–15, as "Dyskusja wokół tekstu Abrahama Brumberg 'Polska inteligencja a antysemityzm.'"

Cała, Alina, Dariusz Libionka, and Stefan Zgliczyński. "Monitoring Antisemitism in Poland, 1999–2001: Sponsored by Research Support Scheme of the Open Society Foundation." *Kwartalnik Historii Żydów* 204, no. 3 (2002): 501–14. See also (by

Cała alone) "Contemporary Antisemitism in Poland," *Polish Western Affairs* 32, no. 2 (1991): 161–71; and "Antisemitism in Poland Today," *Patterns of Prejudice* 27, no. 1 (1993): 121–27.

Kula, Marcin. "A Postcommunist Problem or a Historically Shaped Polish Problem? On Jews and Poles Once More." *Polish Sociological Bulletin*, no. 2 (1992): 95–114. Translation of article published originally as "Problem postkomunistyczny czy historycznie ukształtowany polski problem?" *Biuletyn Żydowskiego Instytutu Historycznego* 160, no. 4 (1991): 21–55.

Musiał, Stanisław, et al. "A Debate about Antisemitism in Poland Today." *Polin* 13 (2000): 303–28. Contributions by Musiał, Waldemar Chrostowski, Stanisław Krajewski, and Monika Adamczyk-Garbowska, focusing on Henryk Jankowski and antisemitism, previously published chiefly in Polish.

Polonsky, Antony. " 'Loving and Hating the Dead': Present-day Polish Attitudes to the Jews." *Religion, State, and Society* 20, no. 1 (1992): 69–79.

CATHOLIC CHURCH: CONTROVERSIES AND DIALOGUES

Bartoszewski, Władysław. *The Convent at Auschwitz.* London: Bowerdean, 1991. Vi and 169 pp., ill., references.

Chrostowski, Waldemar. *Rozmowy o dialogu.* Warsaw: Vocatio, 1996. 314 pp. Interviews with Polish figures conducted in 1990–95 on Christian-Jewish relations.

———. "The State and Prospects of the Catholic-Jewish Dialogue in Poland." *Occasional Papers on Religion in Eastern Europe* 10, no. 6 (1990): 14–27. Also appeared as "Stan i perspektywy dialogu katolicko-żydowskiego w Polsce," *Collectanea theologica* 61, no. 3 (1991): 55–70.

Gądecki, Stanisław. *Kto spotyka Jezusa, spotyka judaizm: Dialog chrześcijańsko-żydowski w Polsce.* Gniezno: Gaudentinum, 2002. 254 pp., references.

Ignatowski, Grzegorz. *Kościół i synagoga: O dialogu chrześcijańsko-żydowski z nadzieją.* Warsaw: Biblioteka Więzi, 2000. 159, [4] pp., references.

Krajewski, Stanisław. "10 lat dialogu katolicko-żydowskiego w Polsce: Perspektywa żydowska." *Collectanea theologica* 67, no. 2 (1997): 53–79.

Mikołajczyk, Mirosław. *Bibliografia dialogu chrześcijańsko-żydowskiego w Polsce za lata 1945–1995.* Ed. Waldemar Chrostowski. Warsaw: ATK, 1997. 431 pp., references.

Oppenheim, Bohdan W., ed. *Kościół katolicki w Polsce a walka z antysemityzmem: Wymiana doświadczeń amerykańskich i polskich. Materiały z konferencji w Centrum Kultury Żydowskiej, Kraków, 14 czerwca 2000 roku = The Polish Catholic Church and the Struggle against Anti-Semitism.* Kraków: Fundacja Judaica–Centrum Kultury Żydowskiej, 2000. 146 and 45 pp., [1] leaf of plates, ill., references.

———, ed. *Rachunek sumienia: Kościół polski wobec antysemityzmu 1989–1999. Konferencja, 20 stycznia 1999 r.: Materiały.* Kraków: Wyd-wo WAM Księży Jezuitów, [1999]. 244 pp., references. Proceedings of conference held at Loyola Marymount University.

Rittner, Carol Ann, and John K. Roth, eds. *Memory Offended: The Auschwitz Convent Controversy.* New York: Praeger, 1991. Xiv and 289 pp., ill., references. Collection of papers plus documents on the affair.

Turner, Charles. "Appropriating Auschwitz: The Zwirowisko Crosses." *Journal of Holocaust Education* 8, no. 2 (1999): 27–44.

HOLOCAUST EDUCATION AND SCHOOL TEXTBOOKS

Eden, Shevach. "The Work and Recommendations of the Polish-Israeli Textbooks Committee." *Polin* 14 (2001): 306–14. Joint committee to revise negative stereotypes in each country's textbooks.

"Tematyka żydowska w podręcznikach szkolnych." *Biuletyn Żydowskiego Instytutu Historycznego* 183–84, nos. 3–4 (1997): 13–116. Comments and reports concerning the presentation of Jews and Jewish topics in Polish school texts. The participants include Jerzy Tomaszewski, Feliks Tych, and Hanna Węgrzynek, among others.

Tomaszewski, Jerzy. "Holocaust Education in Poland." In *Holocaust and Education: Proceedings of the First International Conference*, prod. Lea Roshkovsky and Orna Elboim, 61–74. Jerusalem: Yad Vashem, International School for Holocaust Studies, 1999.

———. "Jewish Themes in Polish School History Textbooks and Popular Historical Literature, 1989–94." *East European Jewish Affairs* 24, no. 2 (1994): 89–101.

MEMORIALS AND MEMORIES: POLITICS AND HISTORICAL CONSCIOUSNESS

Blatman, Daniel. "Polish Antisemitism and 'Judeo-Communism': Historiography and Memory." *East European Jewish Affairs* 27, no. 1 (1997): 23–43.

Garstecki, Joachim, ed. *Auschwitz im Verständnis der Opfer: Das Gedächtnis der Toten aus jüdischer und aus polnischer Sicht, eine Dokumentation.* Bad Vilbel: Pax-Christi-Bewegung, 1992. 129 pp. Articles on Auschwitz in German-Polish-Jewish relations, the convent at the site, and Polish antisemitism.

Huener, Jonathan. *Auschwitz, Poland, and the Politics of Commemoration, 1945–1979.* Athens: Ohio University Press, 2003, Xxvi, 326 pp., ill., maps., references.

Michlic-Coren, Joanna. "The Troubling Past: The Polish Collective Memory of the Holocaust." *East European Jewish Affairs* 29, nos. 1–2 (1999): 75–84.

Steinlauf, Michael C. *Bondage to the Dead: Poland and the Memory of the Holocaust.* Syracuse, N.Y.: Syracuse University Press, 1997. Xiii and 189 pp., [22] pp. of plates, ill.

Wróbel, Piotr. "Double Memory: Poles and Jews after the Holocaust." *East European Politics and Societies* 11, no. 3 (1997): 560–74.

Young, James E. *The Texture of Memory: Holocaust Memorials and Meaning.* New Haven: Yale University Press, 1993. Xvii and 398 pp., ill., references. See part 2, "Poland: The Ruins of Memory."

Żebrowski, Leszek. *Paszkwil "Wyborczej:" Michnik i Tichy o powstaniu warszawskim.* Warsaw: Burchard, 1995. 149 pp., references. Controversy over 1994 articles about the Armia Krajowa and the Jews during the 1944 Warsaw uprising.

SOCIOLOGICAL STUDIES AND SURVEYS

Ambrosewicz-Jacobs, Jolanta. "Attitudes of Young Poles toward Jews in Post-1989 Poland." *East European Politics and Societies* 14, no. 3 (2000): 565–96.

Krzemiński, Ireneusz, ed. *Czy Polacy są antysemitami? Wyniki badania sondażowego.* Warsaw: Ofic. Naukowa, 1996. 305 pp., references. Collection of articles drawing on social science research.

THE JEDWABNE CASE

Brand, William, ed. *Thou Shalt Not Kill: Poles on Jedwabne.* Warsaw: Więź, 2001. 330 pp., references. Chiefly translated articles that appeared originally in Polish newspapers and periodicals in 2000–2001.

Gross, Jan Tomasz. *Neighbors: The Destruction of the Jewish Community in Jedwabne, Poland.* Princeton: Princeton University Press, 2001. 216 pp., ill., references. Has appeared in a number of languages and editions. The first Polish edition is *Sąsiedzi: Historia zagłady żydowskiego miasteczka* (Sejny: Pogranicze, 2000).

Henning, Ruth, ed. *Die Jedwabne-Debatte in polnischen Zeitungen und Zeitschriften.* Potsdam: Deutsch-polnisch Gesellschaft Brandenburg, 2002. Translations of previously published articles.

Jankowski, Robert, ed. *Jedwabne: Spór historyków wokół książki Jana T. Grossa "Sąsiedzi."* Warsaw: Fronda, 2002. 263 pp., references. Chiefly articles that had previously appeared in the Polish press.

Machcewicz, Pawel, and Krzysztof Persak, eds. *Wokół Jedwabnego.* 2 vols. Warsaw: Instytut Pamięci Narodowej, Komisja Ścigania Zbrodnia przeciwko Narodowi Polskiemu, 2002. References. Vol. 1, "Studia"; vol. 2, "Dokumenty."

Polak, Joseph A. "Exhuming Their Neighbors: A Halakhic Inquiry." *Tradition* 35, no. 4 (2001): 23–43. Halakhic inquiry, from an Orthodox Jewish perspective, into the question of exhumation and reinterment of the Jedwabne victims.

Polish Sociological Review 137, no. 1 (2002). "On Jedwabne, Gross' *Neighbors*, and Debate on Poles' National Identity." Contributions by Antoni Sułek, Dariusz Stola, Barbara Engelking, Kaja Kaźmierska, and Marta Kurkowska-Budzan, plus two "Trend Reports": "Poles' Opinions about the Crime in Jedwabne—Changes in Social Consciousness," and Janina Frentzel-Zagórska, "Leading Politicians on Jedwabne." An additional relevant piece in the same issue is Ireneusz Krzemiński, "Polish-Jewish Relations, Anti-Semitism, and National Identity."

Polonsky, Antony, and Joanna B. Michlic, eds. *The Neighbors Respond: The Controversy over the Jedwabne Massacre in Poland.* Princeton: Princeton University Press, 2004. Xiv and 489 pp., references. Chiefly translated articles from the Polish press and scholarly publications in response to the controversy following the appearance of Jan Gross's book *Sąsiedzi* (Neighbors), with an extended introduction and some contributions from non-Polish publications.

Slavic Review 61, no. 3 (2002). "Forum on Jan Gross's *Neighbors.*" Contributions by Janine P. Holc, Wojciech Roszkowski, William W. Hagen, and Norman M. Naimark, with a response by Jan T. Gross.

Yad Vashem Studies 30 (2002). "The Jedwabne Controversy." Contributions by Anna Bikont, Dariusz Stola, Daniel Blatman, Tomasz Strzembosz, and Israel Gutman.

A Note on the Contributors

Robert Blobaum is Eberly Family Distinguished Professor of History at West Virginia University.

Stephen D. Corrsin is associate chief of acquisitions at the New York Public Research Libraries.

William W. Hagen is professor of history at the University of California, Davis.

Janine P. Holc is associate professor of political science at Loyola College (Maryland).

Jerzy Jedlicki is professor at the Institute of History, Polish Academy of Sciences, Warsaw.

Katherine R. Jolluck is senior lecturer in history at Stanford University.

Dariusz Libionka holds dual appointments with the Institute of National Remembrance, Lublin, and the Institute of History of the Polish Academy of Sciences, Warsaw.

Antony Polonsky is Albert Abramson Chair of Holocaust Studies at Brandeis University and the United States Holocaust Memorial Museum.

Brian Porter is associate professor of history and director of Polish Studies at the University of Michigan.

Szymon Rudnicki is professor of history at Warsaw University and a former member of the Polish-Israeli Textbook Commission.

Konrad Sadkowski is associate professor of history at the University of Northern Iowa.

Keely Stauter-Halsted is associate professor of history and director of Jewish studies at Michigan State University.

Dariusz Stola is associate professor at the Institute of Political Studies, Polish Academy of Sciences, and dean of international programs at Collegium Civitas, Warsaw.

Bożena Szaynok is assistant professor of history at Wrocław University.

Theodore R. Weeks is associate professor of history and director of graduate studies at Southern Illinois University.

Index